Patti —
& thanks —
all the —
Pat Moate
1995

Gourmet's

MENU
COOKBOOK

A COLLECTION OF EPICUREAN MENUS AND RECIPES

Gourmet's

MENU
COOKBOOK

A COLLECTION OF EPICUREAN MENUS AND RECIPES

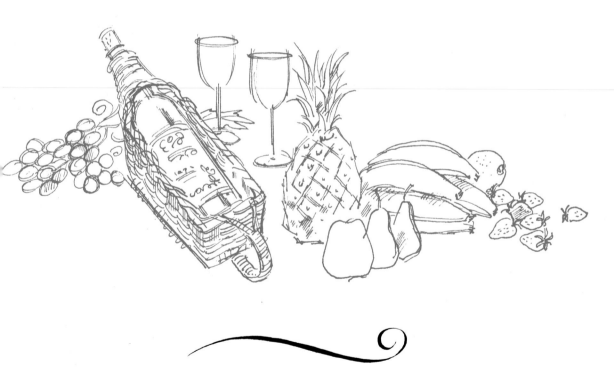

ALFRED A. KNOPF   New York   1984

THIS IS A BORZOI BOOK
PUBLISHED BY ALFRED A. KNOPF, INC.

Library of Congress Cataloging in Publication Data
Main entry under title:

Gourmet's Menu cookbook.

   Reprint. Originally published: New York: Gourmet Books,
1963.
   Includes index.
      1. Cookery, International. 2. Menus. I. Gourmet Books.
II. Title: Menu cookbook.
TX725.A1G59   1984   642   84-47896
ISBN 0-394-54032-8

Manufactured by Dai Nippon Printing Co., Ltd., Tokyo, Japan

FIRST ALFRED A. KNOPF EDITION
PUBLISHED SEPTEMBER 30, 1984
SECOND PRINTING, DECEMBER 1984

Contents

Color Photographs

7

Acknowledgments

We are grateful to many people for their assistance in the preparation of GOURMET'S MENU COOKBOOK, particularly to our editors, who performed their difficult tasks with enthusiasm and good humor. We also wish to express our deepest thanks to Inez M. Krech, for invaluable editorial assistance; Marilyn Miller, for the drawings; Jill Kingsbury and Willetta Bar-Illan, for styling the color illustrations; and Arthur Palmer, for taking the photographs. Detailed credits for the accessories used appear on page 649.

The Art of the Menu

I N AN ESSAY on gastronomy that he wrote for GOURMET several years ago, André Maurois observed that "Eating well depends upon two factors: the excellence of the cookery and the competence of those who eat it."

While granting M. Maurois' competence in the matter, we respectfully propose a third desideratum for eating well: a properly planned menu. However ingeniously devised and expertly prepared a dish is, its reception must be dependent on the meal of which it is a part. An entrée, for example, achieves its fullest measure of appreciation only when it is complemented by the dishes that precede it, by those that accompany it, and by those that follow.

The modern written menu probably had its origin during the reign of Henry VIII, at a banquet given by the Duke of Brunswick in 1541. One of the Duke's guests noticed His Grace consulting a piece of paper from time to time, and finally made bold to ask him its purpose. The Duke explained that it was a list of the dishes to be served, from which he could determine those that pleased him most and reserve his appetite for them. The idea gained wide popularity, and before long there was hardly a banquet at which menus, highly decorated and grown huge of size, were not in evidence. It is doubtful, however, that menus ever found their way to the tables of Henry VIII. There was no necessity for that trencherman to save his appetite for the dishes he liked best. Apparently he liked and ate everything.

Of course, written menus are uncommon on private tables today, but if a meal has achieved even a degree of perfection, one may be sure that it was as carefully planned as any sixteenth-century feast. Indeed, men of all civilizations have labored to devise well-planned meals. A clay tablet, dating from about 3,000 B.C. and inscribed with what has been determined to be a list of foods, has been unearthed in the lower Euphrates valley, once the home of the ancient Sumerians. It is believed that Sumerian priests used the tablet as a guide to the preparation of exalted meals which might properly be offered to the gods.

Such celestial banquets demanded prudent forethought. Today, menus for mortal epicures must be as carefully thought out.

In devising a perfect meal, several considerations must be borne in mind: the nature of the occasion, the number of guests, the season of the year, the time of day the food is to be served, and the way it is to be presented.

The occasion will, of course, decide the manner of entertaining. If it is a sufficiently important one, and one's facilities permit, a formal party may be the choice. If informality is to be the keynote, one must decide whether to serve the meal from a buffet or a table, or whether to entertain with a cocktail party. The number of guests expected and—most important—the facilities there are to accommodate them may provide the answers to these questions, just as they will probably determine the amount of food—and help, if any—that will be required.

The good host considers as well the hour and the season, and gauges the heartiness of the dishes accordingly. Summer invites an outdoor meal, but an August hot spell makes a luncheon in a cool dining room even more inviting. And, of course, no diner enjoys a heavy supper late in the evening.

In presenting the meal, let tasteful restraint be the rule. It is neither necessary nor proper to try to emulate the food service of a luxury liner. Even the most formal dinner is enhanced by floral arrangements and garnishes that are free from pretentiousness. Truffle cutouts and dice of aspic are most effective when they are kept to a minimum. On the other hand, informal meals do not demand starkness. Food at such repasts should be attractively arranged on serving platters, and garnished with sprigs of parsley or dustings of paprika. For dessert, a simple plate of *petits fours secs* is as pleasing to behold as the most elaborate ice carving.

Creating a menu is really a bit like painting a balanced, aesthetically satisfying picture. In selecting the food, one should choose the entrée first. The wise host serves his own specialties, if they have not worn out their welcome, but he must consider the tastes of the guests. If there is some doubt that all of them like seafood, for example, it is best to choose something else. Poultry and beef are usually considered "safest" as main courses.

Excessive repetition of ingredients and cooking methods should be avoided. A meal that begins with something garnished with pickled walnuts, and includes a roast chicken, nut dressing, and green beans amandine, before ending with a chilled pecan mousse, may prove something about the versatility of nuts, but it is certainly monotonous. So is a meal which presents a succession of dishes that are all sautéed, charcoal-grilled, or prepared in a chafing dish. Nor should any menu include more than one dish cooked with wine.

If the main course is to be a roast, it should be preceded by a clear soup. If the entrée is light, a hearty soup may begin the meal. Veal *scaloppine* may be followed by a rich dessert, but a hearty main dish such as a beef pot roast demands no more formidable a sweet than a simple fruit dessert.

Foods in season, or those which are correct for the season, should be used as much as possible. Shad roe and asparagus are delicious in the spring, but are not suitable for any other time of the year. The peach of January may be lovely to look at, but the enchantment can end there. And summer, special occasion or not, is a time to leave venison in the freezer—fall and winter are not far behind.

It is most important to include in each menu foods of different flavors, textures, and colors. The Chinese know the secret of this: their menus reflect the ancient philosophy of Ying and Yang, concerned with the mutual attraction of opposites. We could well adopt its principles, in the marrying of the bland with the spicy, the sweet with the pungent, the crisp with the smooth, and the colorless with the colorful, to achieve a beguiling harmony of contrast—exercising restraint in the process.

A further word of caution: it is not a good idea to wait until a party to serve a dish for the first time. However adept one may be at following a recipe, a special occasion is not a time to experiment. One may find too late that the dish is not what is was expected to be, and that it is not really suited to the menu.

Arrangements for serving the guests must also be considered. If the host or hostess is to do the cooking, the menu should not include dishes that will require much work in the kitchen after the guests have arrived. Many fine foods can be prepared quickly, or well in advance. And even if the meal is to be served buffet style, it is still necessary that the diners eat at tables. Forcing guests to eat from their laps can be a refined form of torture.

Whatever the occasion, the knowledgeable host provides small portions rather than large ones, and second helpings if they are desired.

The wines and spirits to be served should be integral to the plan of the menu. Wine, particularly red wine, should be in the house at least one day before it is to be served, to give it a chance to rest, and it should be opened at least an hour before it is poured. Wine, obviously, is not offered at morning meals, except at wedding breakfasts, and then only Champagne is served. Nor is wine generally served at brunch. Wine at an informal luncheon is optional; at a formal luncheon it is desirable. Informal dinners lend themselves well to the service of wine, and at formal dinners wine is imperative. Serve only one wine at an informal dinner, with the main course. Two wines are usually served at a formal dinner; three may be served, but never more. Wine is, after all, intended to complement a dinner, not to drown it.

Cognac and liqueurs always follow a formal dinner. At an informal dinner, they are frequently served.

GOURMET'S MENU COOKBOOK includes menus for all occasions and all seasons of the year. They are not, however, immutable, and may be altered to meet the requirements of a given occasion. It is hoped, too, that they may prove useful in suggesting new combinations of textures, colors, and flavors that will provide attractive and delectable meals. The possible variations are limited only by individual imagination and ingenuity.

Here, then, is a toast from GOURMET, with the wish that our readers will find, as they use these menus and plan their own, the true essence of good living.

Bon appétit!

EARLE R. MacAUSLAND

MENU
COOKBOOK

A COLLECTION OF EPICUREAN MENUS AND RECIPES

Breakfast and Brunch

The first meal of the day probably presents more possibilities for individual variation than does any other. Morning appetites vary enormously, but one can probably generalize to the extent of saying that breakfasts tend to grow larger the farther away one gets from the centers of our cities. This tends to be less true on weekends, when the city breakfast may suddenly become brunch—a vague sort of denominator that seems to mean simply a more substantial breakfast than one is used to.

In view of all this, the menus that follow cover a considerable range, from light to ample. Some include foods that are traditional morning favorites, with an additional item that is just a bit out of the ordinary—trout, for example. Others provide for a large buffet brunch, and offer a wide choice of dishes. All of them, however, can be accomplished with a maximum of ease and a minimum of flurry.

Whether one is entertaining weekend guests, or merely anticipating a quiet day with the Sunday newspapers, these menus may be easily modified to suit the dictates of the season and the region. For instance, one breakfast calls for ugli fruit. If this delicacy is not at hand, other citrus fruits are always available; grapefruit would serve as a suitable substitute.

No suggestions have been made for beverages to accompany brunch and breakfast. Almost invariably, the drink served with morning meals is coffee or tea.

Melon Filled with Raspberries
Codfish Kebabs
Tangerine Toast

Strawberries and Cream
White Burn Trout
Sherried Eggs
Honey Walnut Bread

Grapefruit and Cantaloupe Juice
Sausage with Sautéed Apples
Brioches or Croissants

Sliced Bananas with Cream
Chipped Beef Omelet
Corn Sticks with Honey

Honey Walnut Bread

Stewed Apples with Orange
Anchovy Roast
White Cheese Bread
Norwegian Cucumber Salad

Grilled Pineapple
Rice Griddlecakes
Scrapple

Melon and Citrus Frappé
Butter and Eggs
Virginia Ham Biscuits

Fresh Figs
Miniature Kulebyaka
Chicken Livers and Grapes
Brown Rice
Sautéed Corn with Cream

Sliced Pineapple
Fresh Peaches with Cream
Sour Cream Waffles
Broiled Ham Slices
Chafing Dish Eggs on English Muffins

Grapefruit Shells
Deviled Smelts
Stuffed Mushrooms with Bacon
Rice Muffins

Fresh Blueberries with Cream
Lamb Noisettes Brussels
Fried Parsley
Sliced Tomatoes with Brandy and Olive Oil
Cream Scones

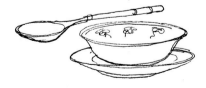

Ugli Fruit
Baked Egg Nests
Cheese Popovers

Eggs Baked in Tomato Shells

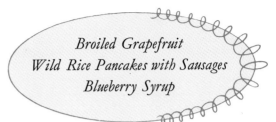

Broiled Grapefruit
Wild Rice Pancakes with Sausages
Blueberry Syrup

Strawberry Orange Juice
French Toast
Sautéed Canadian Bacon

Prunes and Cream
Eggs Baked in Tomato Shells
Bacon Strips

Minted Baked Apples
Kippered Herring
Scrambled Eggs
Toasted Swedish Rye Bread

Formal Luncheon

The formal luncheon, like all formal meals, is enhanced by simple, tasteful presentation, but the designation "formal" does demand that the fare reflect a certain amount of elegance. The menus which follow suit an "in honor of" occasion, or perhaps a special midday meal for a club, a sizable committee, or a board of directors. Attractive and delectable, the dishes meet formal requirements, yet their preparation is relatively easy. Some of them, however, must be prepared at the last moment and served immediately; these should be attempted on formal occasions only by those with help in the kitchen, and at table as well.

No wines are included in these menus. Such service is not requisite for the formal luncheon, but one wine, which will properly accompany the entrée, may be served. The beverage that concludes the meal will invariably be coffee in demitasse.

Cream of Crab Soup
Lamb Chops with Tarragon Butter
Purée of Green Peas
Bibb Lettuce with Caper Dressing
Glacéed Grapes

Shrimp and Oyster Bisque
Chicken à l' Angevine
Stuffed Tomatoes
Tossed Green Salad
Bombe Saigon

Artichokes Inez
Veal en Papillotes
Château Potatoes
Mimosa Salad
Edwardian Trifle

Cream of Cucumber Soup
Sole Paupiettes with Salmon Mousse
Romaine and Hearts of Palm Salad
Orange and Apple Tarts

Ham and Mushroom Pie
Jockey Club Salad
Crème de Cacao Chantilly
Sacristains

Beef in Anchovy Cream
Kasha and Onion Casserole
Asparagus Soufflé
Savarins with Strawberries

Smoked Salmon
Marinated Lamb Chops
Broiled Mushrooms
Baked Green Peas
Cantaloupe Frappé

Marinated Lamb Chops

Hors-d'Oeuvre Roll with Mushroom Filling
Scotch Grouse with Black Cherries
Wild Rice
Hearts of Lettuce with French Dressing
Fruit Compote Angleterre

Artichoke Bottoms with Smoked Salmon
Veal Birds
Spinach en Branche
Green Beans and Celery
Cream Beignets

German Wine Soup
Boned Breast of Chicken on Ham
Artichoke Hearts and Peas
Raspberries and Chocolate

Cold Casaba Soup
Quail with Braised Lettuce
Steamed Rice
Soufflé Rothschild

Consommé Cendrillon
Sautéed Soft-Shelled Crabs
New Potatoes with Chives
Celery Salad
Hazelnut Roll

Cream of Spinach Soup
Tournedos Henri IV
Brussels Sprouts Parmesan
Cantaloupes with Strawberries

White Bean and Lentil Salad
Sautéed Chicken with Parsley
Buttered Noodles
Spinach Caroline
Beignets Soufflés with Raspberry Sauce

Watercress and Apple Soup

Consommé Bruxelles
Scallops in Champagne with Mushroom Purée
Avocado and Litchi Salad
Pineapple Rice

Clear Celery Soup
Sautéed Chicken Breasts with Calvados
Baked Green Beans
Zucchini Salad
Macaroon Mousse

Watercress and Apple Soup
Broiled Squabs with Marjoram
Baloise Potatoes
Sautéed Cucumbers
Chestnut and Orange Compote

Informal Luncheon

T he informal luncheon is a versatile repast. It provides efficiently for everyday family meals, and can accommodate itself to entertaining small groups as well. It is unfortunate that so admirable an institution should have lost the ground it has over the years. Besieged on the right flank by the formal luncheon and—more seriously—on the left by the midday "snack," the informal luncheon has also been undermined from within as husbands and schoolchildren are increasingly absent from the midday board.

We hope that the menus following will serve to strengthen the informal luncheon situation. They take account of seasonal needs: some combat the chill of winter, others suit a balmy midsummer day. The meals are designed to cover the entire range of noontime appetites, from those of the lightest to the heartiest eaters. Many of these luncheons can be prepared entirely in advance, and others happily require only a minimum of quickly accomplished, last-minute cooking.

Vitello Tonnato
Rice and Green Pea Salad
Buttered Whole Wheat Toast
Strawberry Pernod Mousse

Chicken Hash
Popovers with Herb Butter
Green Salad with Radish Dressing
Apricots with Strawberry Purée

Crab Meat Mousse
Cheese Biscuits
Tomato and Onion Salad with Dill
Gooseberry Tart

Dilled Shrimp in Lettuce Cups
Cold Veal Loaf
Cucumbers with Caper Sauce
Pineapple Framboise Mousse

Gazpacho
Shrimp en Brochette
Lemon Pudding Cake

Watercress Soup
Rock Cornish Salad
Cheese Toasts
Peach Cream Mold

Cold Tomato and Cucumber Soup
Herbed Veal Chops
Cannelloni Filled with Cheese
Strawberries with Raspberry Whipped Cream Sauce

Chicken Cucumber Soup
Crab Meat with Almonds
Sliced Tomatoes with Herb French Dressing
Raspberry Fool

Lobster Omelet
Romaine and Pineapple Salad
Peach Compote
Lace Cookies

Carrot Soup with Rice
Sautéed Frogs' Legs
Italian Broccoli
Broiled Tomato Slices
Cold Lemon Soufflé

Cream of Almond Soup
Scallop and Potato Salad with Shallot Mayonnaise
Croissants
Brandied Tangerines and Cream Cheese

Steak Satés
California Sea Bass
Broiled Tomatoes
Dandelion Salad
Red Currant Sherbet

Tomato and Orange Consommé
Skate with Black Butter
New Potatoes with Parsley
Watercress and Scallion Salad
Greengage Plums in Port

Eggs Maison
Chicory and Orange Salad
Cheese Bread
Gingered Honeydew Melon

Mushroom Barquettes
Chicken Sautéed with Artichokes
Baked Carrots and Scallions
Highland Mist

Spiced Tomato Juice
Croûte de Münster
Orange and Olive Salad
Marsala Sponge

Lobster Crêpes with Mornay Sauce
Danish Cucumber Salad
Pineapple and Grapes in Kirsch

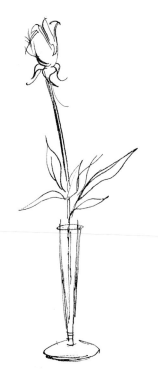

Chicken Pâté
Onion and Currant Hors-d'Oeuvre
Mushrooms à la Grecque
Saffron Mussels
Dandelion Eggs
Garbanzo Salad
French Bread with Sweet Butter
Fresh Fruit in Season

Buttermilk Tomato Soup
Baked Canadian Bacon
Broiled Corn on the Cob
Chive Biscuits
Fresh Pears and Bleu Cheese

Figs and Westphalian Ham
Sea Bass Baked with Mint
Baked Eggplant
Walnut Roll

Avocado Yoghurt Soup
Honey-Glazed Duckling
Saffron Rice
Skewered Peaches

Ham Steak with Camembert
Hazelnut and Leek Soufflés
Sesame Seed Crackers
Mocha Éclairs

Chafing Dish Jambalaya
Alexander Salad
Butter Flake Biscuits
Vanilla Ice Cream with Pecan Sauce

Chafing Dish Jambalaya

Mussel Soup
Poppy Seed Toast
Spinach and Watercress Salad
Mocha Cake

Garden Soup
Open Sandwiches
Cream Cheese and Apricots

Cold Beef Soup
Luncheon Sandwiches
Cantaloupe and Blackberries

Cold Watercress and Potato Soup
Butterfish Niçoise
Sautéed Zucchini
Spinach Salad
Port-Salut Cheese

Eggs Stuffed with Mushrooms
Poached Shad Roe
Asparagus Polonaise
Damson Kuchen

Cold Curried Lobster Bisque
Jellied Vegetable Salad
Green Curaçao Crown
Langues de Bœuf

Jellied Cucumber Soup
Veal Hash
Romaine with Curry French Dressing
Blackberry Compote

Grilled Lamb Chops with Kidneys
Broiled Mushrooms
Chiffonade Salad
Frozen Lemon Cream

Cold Poached Trout with Pink Mayonnaise

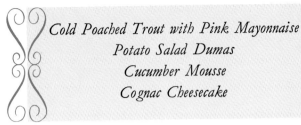

Cold Poached Trout with Pink Mayonnaise
Potato Salad Dumas
Cucumber Mousse
Cognac Cheesecake

Spring Greens Soup
Tongue in Swiss Fondue
Garlic French Bread
Coffee Ice

Cold Pea and Potato Soup
Roast Beef Salad
Whipped Cream Meringues

Formal Dinner

E legance and elaborateness are two different concepts, and they are further apart in this utilitarian age than they have frequently been in the past. For example, not so very long ago the formal dinner demanded no fewer than eight courses. Frequently, ten or twelve courses—with five or six wines—were served. Elegance and elaborateness virtually coincided.

Today, only five or six courses—with two or three wines—are called for. To go beyond this in elaborateness compromises contemporary elegance. Garnishes and flower arrangements also follow the trend to simple elegance today.

The formal dinner remains, as always, the classic occasion for enjoying the best of food and drink. Our menus include suggestions for wines to complement the dinners. If the number of guests is to be large, it will be necessary to have help for both the preparation and the service of the meal.

Consommé de Volaille à la Chiffonade
CHIFFONADE SOUP

SCHARZHOFBERGER
Moselle – White

Petits Soufflés de Homard
INDIVIDUAL LOBSTER SOUFFLÉS

POMMARD, LES ÉPENOTS
Red Burgundy

Filet de Bœuf en Croûte
TENDERLOIN OF BEEF IN PASTRY

Pommes de Terre Allumettes
MATCHSTICK POTATOES

Asperges aux Miettes Cirtonnées
ASPARAGUS WITH LEMON CRUMBS

Gâteau d'Amandes au Chocolat
ALMOND CHOCOLATE TORTE

Potage Crème de Brocoli
CREAM OF BROCCOLI SOUP

CHÂTEAU-MARGAUX
Red Bordeaux – Margaux

Chapon d'Or Parmentier
GOLDEN CAPON WITH POTATO MOUNDS

Céleris et Amandes au Gratin
CELERY AND ALMONDS AU GRATIN

Salade d'Épinards et de Doucette
SPINACH AND FIELD SALAD

Sauce Échalote au Citron
LEMON AND SHALLOT DRESSING

CHAMPAGNE, DEMI-SEC

Mille-Feuille

MUSCADET
White Loire

Croustades aux Huîtres
OYSTER CROUSTADES

Potage de Volaille et de Champignons
CHICKEN MUSHROOM SOUP

CLOS DE TART
Morey – Red Burgundy

Suprêmes de Pintade Sautés
SAUTÉED BREAST OF GUINEA HEN

Purée de Céleris Parmentier
CELERY AND POTATO PURÉE

Salade du Liban
LEBANESE SALAD

Triples Choux
TRIPLET CREAM PUFFS

Consommé au Vin
WINE CONSOMMÉ

NUITS–SAINT–GEORGES
Red Burgundy

Côtes de Bœuf Rôties
ROAST PRIME RIBS OF BEEF

YORKSHIRE PUDDING

Oignons et Céleris Amandines
ONIONS AND CELERY AMANDINE

Salade au Chapon
GREEN SALAD WITH GARLIC TOAST

CHAMPAGNE, DEMI-SEC

Mousse au Pralin de Noisettes
HAZELNUT PRALINE MOUSSE

Roast Prime Ribs of Beef with Yorkshire Pudding

CHÂTEAU DE SANCERRE
White Loire

Fonds d'Artichauts au Caviar
ARTICHOKE HEARTS WITH CAVIAR

Potage Crécy à la Tomate
CARROT AND TOMATO SOUP

FLEURIE
Beaujolais – Red

Filet de Veau Vézelay
FILET OF VEAL VÉZELAY

Pommes de Terre Macaire
MACAIRE POTATOES

Purée de Pissenlit et d'Oseille
DANDELION AND SORREL PURÉE

Salade d'Estrées
CELERY AND BLACK OLIVE SALAD

Mousse au Chocolat Caraïbe
CHOCOLATE MOUSSE WITH RUM

Langues de Chat
CATS' TONGUES

Potage Crème d'Artichauts
CREAM OF ARTICHOKE SOUP

CHÂTEAU HAUT-BRION
Red Bordeaux – Graves

Selle d'Agneau aux Pommes de Terre
ROAST SADDLE OF LAMB

Choux de Bruxelles et Petits Pois à la Menthe
BRUSSELS SPROUTS AND PEAS IN MINT SAUCE

Salade d'Endives Saucée au Vin Rouge
ENDIVE WITH RED-WINE DRESSING

CHAMPAGNE, DEMI-SEC

Omelette Norvégienne aux Cerises
CHERRY ALASKA

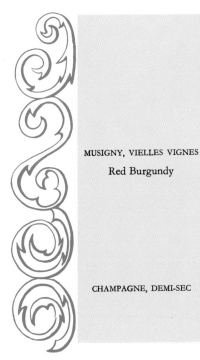

Champignons à la Bourguignonne
MUSHROOMS WITH GARLIC BUTTER

Consommé de Gibier
CLEAR GAME SOUP

MUSIGNY, VIELLES VIGNES
Red Burgundy

Filet de Bœuf Fervaal
FILET OF BEEF FERVAAL

Petits Pois à la Romaine
PEAS ROMAN STYLE

Salade Caroline

CHAMPAGNE, DEMI-SEC

Bombe Don Juan

CHAMPAGNE BRUT

Huîtres au Caviar
OYSTERS IMPERIAL

CHAMBERTIN – CLOS DE BÈZE
Red Burgundy

Rôti de Chevreuil Farci à la Canneberge
VENISON WITH CRANBERRY STUFFING

Pommes de Terre Nanette
POTATOES NANETTE

Turban de Carottes et d'Amandes
CARROT AND ALMOND RING

Salade de Laitue
BIBB LETTUCE WITH FRENCH DRESSING

Soufflé à la Mélasse, Sauce au Rhum
MOLASSES SOUFFLÉ WITH RUM SAUCE

Sole Walewska

Consommé Double
DOUBLE CONSOMMÉ

CLOS BLANC DE VOUGEOT
White Burgundy

Sole Walewska

CHÂTEAU PÉTRUS
Pomerol – Red Bordeaux

Cailles aux Raisins Noirs
QUAIL WITH BLACK GRAPES

Petits Pois au Four
BAKED PEAS

Zizanie
WILD RICE

Salade de Céleri-Rave et de Cœurs de Palmier
CELERIAC AND HEARTS OF PALM SALAD

Compote de Fruits au Champagne Frappé
FRUIT COMPOTE WITH ICED CHAMPAGNE

Goujons de Sole
SOLE GUDGEONS

MERSAULT, CLOS DES PERRIÈRES
White Burgundy

Poulet à la Crème Fouettée
CHICKEN IN WHIPPED CREAM

Nouilles Truffées
TRUFFLED EGG NOODLES

Haricots de Lima à la Marjolaine
BABY LIMAS WITH MARJORAM

CHAMPAGNE, BLANC DE BLANCS

Soufflé aux Pêches
CHAFING DISH PEACH SOUFFLÉ

POUILLY-FUMÉ
White Loire

Pâté de Saumon
SALMON PÂTÉ

Consommé Velouté
VELVET CONSOMMÉ

LE MONTRACHET
White Burgundy

Poussins au Vin Blanc
SQUAB CHICKEN IN WHITE WINE

Riz Brut en Pilaf
BROWN RICE PILAFF

Fonds d'Artichauts Choron
ARTICHOKE BOTTOMS CHORON

Salade de Chicorée et de Champignons
CHICORY AND MUSHROOM SALAD

Oranges à la Mandarine
ORANGES MANDARIN

Crevettes à la Russe
SHRIMP À LA RUSSE

FIXIN
Red Burgundy

Escalopes de Veau Truffées
TRUFFLED VEAL CUTLETS

Pommes de Terre Espagnole
PIMIENTO POTATOES

Épinards en Purée
SPINACH PURÉE

CHÂTEAU CLIMENS
Sauternes – White Bordeaux

Pouding aux Marrons
CHESTNUT PUDDING

Consommé aux Herbes
HERB CONSOMMÉ

ÜRZIGER WÜRZGARTEN
Moselle – White

Crevettes à la Marinière
SHRIMP IN MARINIÈRE SAUCE

CORTON, CLOS DU ROI
Red Burgundy

Tournedos, Sauce aux Champignons
TOURNEDOS WITH MUSHROOM SAUCE

Pommes de Terre Soufflées
SOUFFLÉED POTATOES IN POTATO NEST

Salade de Haricots Jaunes
WAX BEANS VINAIGRETTE

Glace à la Framboise
RASPBERRY ICE

DÔLE DE SION
Red Swiss

Quiche aux Poireaux
LEEK QUICHE

CHÂTEAU MOUTON ROTHSCHILD
Pauillac – Red Bordeaux

Suprêmes de Volaille Sautés Cintra
SAUTÉED CHICKEN BREASTS CINTRA

Pommes de Terre Nouvelles à la Vapeur
STEAMED NEW POTATOES IN THEIR JACKETS

Soufflé de Topinambours
JERUSALEM ARTICHOKE SOUFFLÉ

Fenouil à la Vinaigrette
FENNEL VINAIGRETTE

Crème au Limon avec des Fraises
LIME CREAM WITH STRAWBERRIES

Moules Farcies au Four
BAKED STUFFED MUSSELS

Soupe de Volaille au Xérès
CHICKEN SOUP WITH SHERRY

VOSNE-ROMANÉE, LES MALCONSORTS
Red Burgundy

Pintades à la Liégeoise
GUINEA HENS WITH JUNIPER BERRIES

Tranches d'Oranges Grillées
GRILLED ORANGE SLICES

Pommes de Terre Berrichonne
POTATOES BERRICHONNE

Croquettes de Panais
PARSNIP CROQUETTES

Salade de Concombres
CUCUMBER SALAD

CHAMPAGNE, DEMI-SEC

Manon

Cari de Moules
CURRIED MUSSELS

LA TACHE
Red Burgundy

Filet Mignon Lord Seymour

Pommes de Terre Noisette
NOISETTE POTATOES

Carottes à la Menthe
CARROTS AND MINT

CHAMPAGNE, DEMI-SEC

Crêpes à la Crème Chocolat
CRÊPES WITH CHOCOLATE CREAM

Jambon Cru et Melon
PROSCIUTTO AND MELON

Potage Purée de Marrons
CHESTNUT SOUP

CHÂTEAU CHEVAL BLANC
Red Bordeaux – St. Émilion

Baron d' Agneau Landaise
BARON OF LAMB WITH POTATO CAKE

Épinards aux Mandarines
SPINACH WITH TANGERINES

Oignons à la Crème
CREAMED ONIONS

Cœurs de Palmier en Salade
HEARTS OF PALM SALAD

VOUVRAY MOUSSEUX
Sparkling Vouvray – White Loire

Gâteau aux Fraises
STRAWBERRY MERINGUE CAKE

Champignons Farcis aux Moules
MUSHROOMS STUFFED WITH MUSSELS

MUSIGNY, VIELLES VIGNES
Red Burgundy

Canard Rôti aux Pommes
DUCK WITH APPLES

Pommes de Terre à la Parisienne
POTATOES PARISIENNE

Mousse de Choux de Bruxelles
BRUSSELS SPROUTS MOUSSE

CHÂTEAU D'YQUEM
Sauternes – White Bordeaux

Glace à l' Ananas
PINEAPPLE SHERBET

CHABLIS, LES PREUSES
White Burgundy

Huîtres Rôties
ROASTED OYSTERS

Consommé au Céleri-Rave
CELERIAC CONSOMMÉ

RICHEBOURG
Red Burgundy

Tournedos Sautés
SAUTÉED TOURNEDOS

RICHEBOURG

Faisans aux Champignons
ROAST PHEASANT WITH MUSHROOMS

Beignets de Groseilles et de Zizanie
WILD RICE AND CURRANT FRITTERS

Carottes et Raisins
CARROTS AND GRAPES

Salade de Cresson
WATERCRESS SALAD

Crème au Moka
MOCHA CREAM MOLD

Consommé à l'Estragon
CONSOMMÉ WITH TARRAGON

CÔTE RÔTIE, BRUNE ET BLONDE
Red Rhône

Quartier de Chevreuil Rôti
ROAST HAUNCH OF VENISON

Marrons et Pruneaux
CHESTNUTS AND PRUNES

Chiffonade de Laitue à la Béchamel
SHREDDED LETTUCE

CHAMPAGNE, DEMI-SEC

Crêpes Simon

Informal Dinner

The informal dinner is the convivial occasion *par excellence*. Though it is a meal prepared more often than any other, it still affords the greatest epicurean satisfactions in its planning, execution, and appreciation. The host is not restricted by the rigorous canon of courses that a formal dinner demands, and he need not concern himself with his guests' postprandial alertness, as he must at luncheon. He is free to structure his menu around some *spécialité de la maison* or other delight that he knows will please the friends he has invited. If he limits the number of courses to four, he may make the meal an occasion for serving a delicate dish such as sautéed *suprêmes de volaille* or *scaloppine*, which require split-second timing if they are to be cooked *à point*. He may conclude the repast with an airy dessert soufflé, which must be speeded to the table, and consumed promptly, or not at all.

It may be that the informal dinner is, as well, the one meal at which the family regularly gathers. Its menus must be varied constantly, for interest's sake. Dinners included here provide much of the needed change and variation, and the accompanying recipes will suggest still more.

No wines are indicated for these menus, but the meals lend themselves easily to the service of wine. Some merit accompaniment by the great château- and estate-bottled wines, but the majority will be overwhelmed by them. Any good wine merchant will be able to suggest less familiar wines that will handsomely complement the informal dinner.

Scallops in Ramekins
Veal Scallops with Green Noodles
Sautéed Cucumbers
Strawberry Cream

Pickled Shrimp and Onion
Italian Pot Roast
Risotto Milanese
Grated Apple Pie

Parsnip Soup
Stuffed Pork Chops
Shredded Beets
Rice and Oranges

Chicken Liver Ramekins
Veal Marengo
Potato Gnocchi
Caramel Pears

Veal Marengo

Eggplant Caviar
Lamb Stew
Celeriac and Watercress Salad
Baked Pears

Planked Steak with Duchess Potatoes,
Mushroom Caps, and Béarnaise Sauce
Cauliflower Salad
Grasshopper Pie

Vichyssoise with Watercress
Soft-Shelled Crabs with Brazil Nuts
Sautéed Fennel
Mango Chiffon Pie

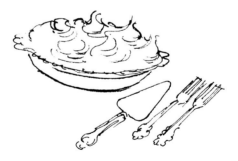

Cream of Tomato Soup
Chicken Croquettes with Butter Caper Sauce
Black Radish Coleslaw
Maple Custard

Buttermilk Shrimp Soup
Veal Birds Sophia
Braised Leeks
Cherry Compote

Marinated Mushrooms
Salmon Steaks with Spinach
Sautéed Cucumbers and Tomatoes
Orange Meringues

Mushroom Consommé
Sautéed Chicken Breasts with Kirsch
Orange Hubbard Squash
Crêpes with Chocolate Sauce

Tournedos with Tarragon
Bartholy Potatoes
Tomato and Mushroom Salad
Strawberries Isabelle

Summer Pudding

Orange Borsch
Ham Steak in Cider
Brabant Potatoes
Chinese Cabbage Salad
Summer Pudding

Cream of Snow Pea Soup
Broiled Turkey Rosemary
Vegetables with Aioli Sauce
Chicory Salad with Tomato French Dressing
Pumpkin Custard

Anchovy Fritters
Veal Scallops with Artichokes
Fettuccine alla Parmigiana
Green Bean and Cucumber Salad
Stuffed Pineapple

Cucumber Soup with Yoghurt
Marinated Boned Leg of Lamb
Spanakopita
Broiled Eggplant Slices
Melon Compote

Cream of Celery Soup
Braised Lamb Chops with Prunes
Orange-Stuffed Potatoes
Green Beans and Chestnuts
White-Wine Pudding

Munich Pot Roast
Mashed Potato Dumplings
Sliced Tomatoes with Horseradish Dressing
Apple Crisp

Chicken with Tangerines
Steamed Rice
Eggplant Fritters
Honey and Brazil Nut Turnovers

Seviche of Scallops with Avocado Dressing
Savory Chickens
Eggplant and Tomato Pie
Toasted French Bread
Cherries in Claret
Almond Refrigerator Cookies

Mushrooms Stuffed with Crab Meat
Sweetbreads with Almonds
Brussels Sprouts Salad
Danish Rice Fritters

Smoked Salmon and Capers
Broiled Ginger Duck
Orange Yams
Glazed Onions
Spiced Beet Salad
Country Cheesecake

Chestnut and Acorn Squash Soup
Breaded Pork Chops with Prune Sauce
Potatoes in Butter
Lemon Carrots
Jefferson Davis Pie

Apples with Roquefort
Chicken in Wine Sauce
Kasha with Noodles and Peas
Lebanese Cucumber Salad
Mango Mousse

Cream of Mushroom Soup with Sherry
Rib Steak with Shallot Sauce
Glazed Parsnips
Spinach and Anchovies
Rose Geranium Apples

Potage Germiny
Mustard Chicken
Mushroom Ragout
Poached Peaches
Chocolate Sablés

Cold Indian Lentil Soup
Toasted French Bread
Brandied Veal Kidneys
Watercress Salad
Raspberry Parfait

Cream of Lettuce Soup
Skewered Beef Birds
Carrots Julienne
Spring Peas
Hazelnut and Prune Soufflé

Eggs à la Tapinade
Chicken Livers in Red Wine
Celery and Almonds au Gratin
Ricotta Pie

Cold Shrimp and Tomato Bisque
Veal Scallops with Vermouth
Green Beans Italienne
Onions in White Wine
Pears Zingara

Coach House Black Bean Soup
Corn Sticks
Cheese Torte
Beet and Orange Salad
Peaches and Grapes with Sour Cream

Sorrel Roll
Chicken Stuffed with Grapes
Rice Pilaff
Salad Elizabeth
Prune Tart with Walnut Pastry

Baked Mushrooms
Trout in Wine Sauce
Continental Potatoes
Glazed Carrots
Apricot Tart

Vegetable Hors-d'Oeuvre
Lamb Kidneys and Mushrooms en Brochette
Valencian Rice
Field Salad Vinaigrette
Apple Macaroon Soufflé

Minestrone
Bread Sticks
Veal Scallops with Lemon
Stuffed Artichokes
Plum Milk Sherbet

Ginger Shrimp Toast
Stuffed Rib Steak
Stuffed Potatoes Palestine
Green Beans with Parsley
Apples and Camembert Cheese

Pot Roast in Ale
Spätzle
Garden Vegetable Salad
Pear and Ginger Compote

Cold Pea Soup
Sautéed Chicken Breasts in Butter
Deviled Tomatoes
Celeriac and Artichoke Salad
Honey Soufflé

Spiced Ham Steaks with Tangerines
Rice Croquettes
Green Bean Salad
Coffee Rum Pie

Carrot and Leek Soup
Tongue and Truffles Valenciennes
Saffron Rice
Honeycomb Pudding

Beef Birds in Red Wine
Toasted French Bread
Niçoise Vegetable Salad
Banana Cream Mold

Spinach Hors-d'Oeuvre
Roast Loin of Pork with Rhubarb
Barley Casserole
Braised Celery
Stuffed Cantaloupe

Crab Meat Soufflé
New Peas with Mint
Celery and Endive Salad
Lime Pie

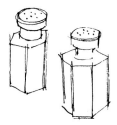

Sautéed Breast of Lamb
Deviled Parsnips
Creamed Spinach
Grapes Flambé

Roast Loin of Pork with Rhubarb

Anchovy Tongue
Noodles with Cottage Cheese
Asparagus Salad
Currant Purée

Cold Curried Watercress Soup
Salmon Steaks with Béarnaise Sauce
Potato Croquettes
Sautéed Artichoke Hearts
Mocha Chiffon Pie

Lamb Kebabs
Roast Chicken with Yoghurt
Persian Rice
Radish Salad
Apricots in Honey

Onion and Bacon Soup
Parsleyed Leg of Lamb
Zucchini in Sour Cream
Carrots with Sherry
Raspberry and Red Currant Tart

Cocktail Party

It is quite possible for the good host to manage a cocktail party for eight to ten guests by himself, without having to devote all his time to mixing drinks and serving hors-d'oeuvre. At a small party in a servantless house, guests can usually be counted on to offer assistance by helping themselves. For a sizable party, however, a bartender should be engaged, and probably a maid as well.

In the planning of a successful cocktail party, it is important to decide well in advance upon the liquors to be served, and the amount of each that will be needed. Once the number of guests is determined, and the duration of the party is set, the host may estimate the amount of liquor required by counting on an average of three or four drinks per guest, if the party begins at about six o'clock and ends at about eight-thirty. It is wise to purchase more spirits than seem strictly necessary.

Food that can be served from trays and eaten with the fingers is best for a small party. To attempt to manage a plate, a glass, and a cigarette all at once can prove most uncomfortable. Hors-d'oeuvre such as those that follow serve handsomely for a party in town. If the gathering is to be in the country or in a suburban area, and the guests must travel a good distance to attend, the food should be augmented by something a bit more substantial—perhaps a baked ham or a roast turkey, salad, and assorted breads, arranged on a buffet table. If the party is held outdoors, hibachi and barbecue dishes may be in order.

Assorted Hors-d'Oeuvre

Indonesian Satés (p. 160), Cheese and Ham Barquettes (p. 170), Salami
Cornucopias (p. 159), Miniature Pissaladière (p. 174).

Sautéed Almonds
Cheese Pot
Eggs Stuffed with Smoked Trout
Indonesian Satés
Raw Vegetables with Spinach Cream
Serves 8 to 10.

Miniature Crab Quiche
Duckling Saté
Mushrooms Stuffed with Anchovies
Cheddar and Olive Balls
Onion Sandwiches
Serves 8 to 10.

Stuffed Endive
Cheese and Ham Barquettes
Bagna Cauda
Brazilian Canapés
Serves 8 to 10.

Greek Meatballs
Creamed Crab Meat and Almonds
Eggs Stuffed with Chives
Chicken Liver and Onion Pâté
Radishes with Piquant Butter
Serves 8 to 10.

Potted Cheese Spread
Cold Shrimp with Curry Mayonnaise
Brochettes of Smoked Pork
Pickled Artichokes
Truffles in Pastry
Serves 8 to 10.

Veal Balls
Croque Demoiselle
Pickled Mushrooms with Tarama
Champagne Gorgonzola Spread
Serves 8 to 10.

Curried Almonds
Cherry Tomatoes Filled with Cheese
Skewered Scallops
Cheese Madeira
Serves 8 to 10.

Gingered Tuna Profiteroles
Cherry Tomatoes with Ham and Chicken Mousse
Mushrooms with Roquefort
Chicken Livers and Shrimp en Brochette
Fried Parmesan Balls
Pork Pâté
Eggs Stuffed with Anchovies
Steak Tartare Balls
Serves 20.

Foie Gras Pastries
Cucumbers Filled with Roquefort
Shrimp with Mustard Dip
Penthouse Onions
Pistachio Swiss Cheese Loaf
Tartare Spheres
Serves 20.

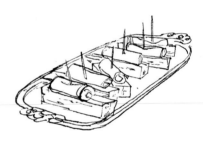

Potted Shrimp Pâté
Broiled Chutney Prunes
Vitello Tonnato Canapés
Jamaican Avocado Balls
Anchovy Cheese
Canapés Grecques
Dried Beef Rolls
Serves 20.

English Pork Cheese
Fennel with Dill Butter
Cheese Balls in Chipped Beef
Eggs Stuffed with Crab Meat
Kibbe Kebabs
Miniature Pissaladière
Shrimp Spread
Serves 20.

Toasted Brazil Nut Chips
Stuffed Grape Leaves
Anchovy Mousse
Celeriac Profiteroles
Spiced Edam Cheese
Eggs Stuffed with Chicken Livers
Pickled Shrimp
Brussels Sprouts with Tongue Mousse
Serves 20.

Spiced Brazil Nuts
Anchovy and Ham Turnovers
Cheese Soufflé Canapés
Eggs Stuffed with Oysters
Smoked Salmon Crescents
Pineapple with Shrimp and Dill
Blue Cheese Tartare Balls
Glazed Beef Tongue
Serves 50 or more.

French Fried Ravioli
Ribbon Cubes
Rollatini di Mortadella
Cucumber Cups
Stuffed Snow-Pea Pods
Kumquats with Smoked Tongue Mousse
Souffléed Crackers
Chicken and Ham Roll
Serves 50 or more.

Stuffed Olives
Cucumbers Filled with Anchovies
Bourekakia
Shrimp Balls
Swiss Cheese Mousse
Fig Roulades
Salami Cornucopias
Ham and Veal Pâté
Serves 50 or more.

Buffets

The menus for formal buffets presented here are designed to provide amply for an embassy reception, or for any large and elegant party in a well-staffed house. The informal menus meet a wider variety of entertaining needs: a summer gathering in the country, perhaps, or a gracious evening with friends in town.

Planning a buffet—formal or casual—demands much the same forethought as does any other successful meal. The good host makes sure there are places at table for those who do not enjoy balancing plates on their laps. If wine is to be served at an informal buffet, it should be poured at the table.

The choice of wine depends upon the main course. In the case of the formal buffet, which offers a number of main courses, it is best to serve only Champagne, which may accompany any dish.

Noisettes Sautées
TOASTED HAZELNUTS

Timbales de Saumon
SALMON TIMBALES

Pigeonneaux Froids
COLD ROAST SQUAB CHICKEN

Pâté de Bœuf en Roulade
BEEF PÂTÉ ROLL

Salade de Truffes Gambetta
TRUFFLE SALAD GAMBETTA

Œufs Durs au Cari
CURRIED STUFFED EGGS

Purée d' Avocat à la Coque
AVOCADO PURÉE SHELLS

Puits d' Amour
WELLS OF LOVE

Mousse de Fromage à la Crème
CREAM CHEESE MOLD WITH FIGS

Champagne Brut

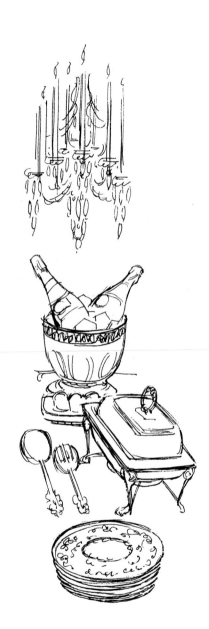

FORMAL BUFFET FOR 20

Œufs Durs au Caviar
EGGS STUFFED WITH CAVIAR

Petites Tartes au Crabe
CURRIED CRAB MEAT TARTS

Canapés aux Fonds d'Artichauts
ARTICHOKE ROUNDS

Salade de Riz
RICE SALAD

Ris de Veau à la Florentine
SWEETBREADS WITH SPINACH

Galantine de Veau
VEAL GALANTINE

Soufflé Froid au Parmesan
COLD PARMESAN SOUFFLÉ

Compote Rouge
COMPOTE OF RED FRUITS

Gâteau Rolla Amandine
ALMOND ROLLA CAKE

Champagne, Blanc de Blancs

Rice Salad

Broiled Shrimp in Beer
Roast Duck with Apples and Sauerkraut
Caraway Dumplings
Pumpernickel Bread
Sweet Butter
Green Onions
Almond Carrot Torte

Bœuf à la Mode en Gelée
Artichoke Bottoms Bouquetière
Romaine Lettuce with Green Goddess Dressing
Chocolate Cream Cake

Anchovy Crab
Turkey Filets in Sour Cream
Celeriac and Potato Purée
Spinach Salad
Kirsch Butter Spongecake

Roquefort Spread
Chili Peanuts
Spanish Lobster Stew
Barcelona Salad
Orange Brioche

Tarama Hors-d'Oeuvre
Braised Shoulder of Lamb
Flageolet Salad
Broiled Eggplant Wedges with Yoghurt Sauce
Spiced Oranges

Roast Loin of Pork with Sour Cream Sauce
Buttered Barley
Sautéed Lentils
Dried Peach and Raisin Pie

Mussels Vinaigrette
Squab Chicken Bonne Femme
Alsatian Potatoes
Avocado Mousse
Napoléons

Mushrooms Baked with Olives
Lobster Tetrazzini
Onion and Tomato Salad
Corn Meal Rolls
Chafing Dish Bananas

Beef Stew with Walnuts

Curried Veal
Beef and Ham Rolls in White Wine
Pissaladière
Melon in Sauterne Jelly

Mushroom Turnovers
Horseradish Olive Stars
Beef Stew with Walnuts
Tossed Green Salad
Bread Sticks
Chocolate Cheesecake

Lamb Pilaff
Sautéed Zucchini and Tomatoes
Rum Cheese Pie

Pork Chops Flambé
Stuffed Tomatoes Jardinière
French Fried Potatoes
Graham Pudding with Vanilla Ice Cream Sauce

Shrimp in Cucumber Boats
Ham in Cream
Stuffed Beets
Chafing Dish Apples

Sacher Cheese and Crackers
Onion Sandwiches
Cold Duckling in Aspic
Parmesan Asparagus
Andalusian Salad
Poppy Seed Toast Triangles
Currant Tarts

Eggs with Caviar Sauce
Braised Tarragon Chicken
Tomatoes à la Grecque
Avocado and Mushroom Salad
Macaroon Beignets

Curried Lamb with Walnuts
Steamed Rice
Mint Chutney
Cucumber Chutney
Golden Lemon Puffs with Red-Wine Sauce

Oriental Roast Pork
Noodles Charlotte
Asparagus Salad with Shrimp and Water Chestnuts
Peach Ice Cream
Almond Wafers

Limburger in Celery Stalks
Formosan Beets
Hash Tart
Kidney Bean Salad
Cold Chocolate Soufflé

Sardine Toast
Pastitsio
Vegetable Salad with Feta Cheese
Karidopita

Stuffed Clams
Spanish Duck
Cucumbers in Cream
Applesauce Tarts

Taramosalata
Lamb Filets with Artichokes and Potatoes
Sour Cream Coleslaw
Raspberry Trifle

Mushroom and Swiss Cheese Tart
Roast Chicken with Pistachio Stuffing
Bernoise Potatoes
Carrots with Yoghurt
Artichoke Bottoms with Grapes
Crêpes Flambées

Braised Shoulder of Pork with Lentils
Potatoes Boulangère
Sautéed Beets
Dried Fruit Compote
Orange Fruitcake

Mussels and Tomatoes
Stuffed Baked Tufoli
Sliced Tomatoes with Chilled Chili Sauce
Eggplant Chutney
Palermo Cheesecake

Poached Beef Marrow on Toast
Waterzooi
Pot Cheese Noodles
Endive Salad
Lemon Mousse

Shrimp with Green Sauce
Veal Birds with Pine Nuts
Artichoke Ring with Green Peas
Flaky Cheese Roll
Cointreau Apples

Sweetbread and Pear Salad
Potted Lobster
Camembert Shortbread
Sliced Westphalian Ham
Scotch Mist

Calf's Foot Jelly
Anchovy Cheese Crostini
Ham and Green Salad
Radishes
Black Olives
Raw Turnip Sticks
Nectarine Tarts

Supper

Many an evening's pleasure can be heightened by the prospect of an excellent supper. For the partygoer, a late meal is a calm restorative on the far side of gaiety. For the concertgoer, it provides a felicitous return to the physical world from the universe of pure sound. For the drama lover, it may afford the happy ending a script withheld.

There is a considerable variety in the menus that follow, not only in the dishes suggested but also in the composition of the meals. Only a few have a first course; two have no dessert. In planning a supper, the time and place, the season, and one's plans for the morrow should all be considered. Whether the hours before have been active or quiet, the meal that concludes the evening should be a lightly satisfying repast, a pleasant prelude to sleep.

Gougère
Tossed Green Salad
Pears in Red Wine

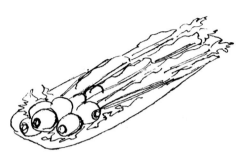

Scallops in Pastry Shells
Sautéed Peas with Mushrooms and Parmesan
Cordial Colettes

Clam Soufflé
Grapefruit and Water Chestnut Salad
Snapdragon

Baked Chicken Salad
Broiled Tomatoes with Chives
Mango Turnovers

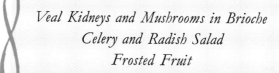

Veal Kidneys and Mushrooms in Brioche
Celery and Radish Salad
Frosted Fruit

Pipérade
Toasted Sourdough Bread
Raspberry Pudding

Mussels in White Wine
Cheese and Rice Casserole
Fruit and Tomato Salad

Crêpes Maison
Chicory and Fennel Salad
Pineapple with Crème de Menthe

Mussels in White Wine

Chilean Paella
Sourdough Bread
Rhubarb Sherbet

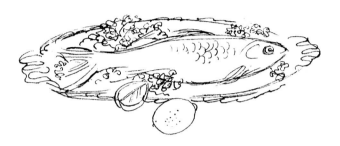

Velvet Chicken
Chinese Rice
Macaroon Trifle

Duck Liver Pâté
Cold Crab Curry
Blueberry Crêpes

Cioppino
Crusty Cuban Bread
Pear Cream Tart

Risotto with Mussels
Curried Vegetables
Italian Lemon Mousse

Salmi of Duck
Carrot Purée
Banana Gelée Catawba

Oysters à la King
Hot Buttered Toast
Caesar Salad

Calves' Brains Fritters
Anchovy and Cauliflower Soufflé
Danish Rum Cream with Clear Raspberry Sauce

Sweetbreads and Brains in Puff Paste Shell

Oyster Stew
Sliced Cold Turkey
Watercress and Orange Salad
Chafing Dish Pineapple

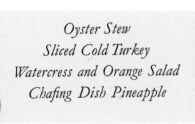

Mushroom Caps with Dilled Cheese
Brandade de Morue
Fennel Salad
Mocha Cream

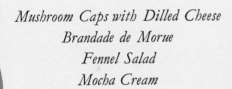

Lamb Liver Swiss Style
Mashed Potatoes and Carrots
Sautéed Tomatoes
Prune Cream

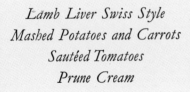

Clear Consommé with Lemon
Sweetbreads and Brains in Puff Paste Shell
Macédoine of Fruit Flambé

Caviar Omelets
Artichokes Vinaigrette
Melba Toast
Melon and Blackberry Compote

Curried Scallops in a Ring of Rice
Sliced Onions and Tomatoes with Cottage Cheese Dressing
Citron Pudding

Sausages in Ale and Wine
Mashed Potatoes
Stewed Tomatoes with Sour Cream
Apricots Cardinal

Veal and Ham Rolls with Hazelnut Sauce
Pasta with Broccoli
Crêpes with Currant Jelly

Swiss and Roquefort Ramekins
Fondue Bourguignonne
French Bread
Almond Pudding

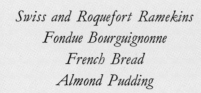

Crab Florentine
Endive with Aniseed Dressing
Brioches and Bar-le-Duc Jelly

Mushroom Fritters with Mustard Butter
Yellow and Red Tomato Salad
Apricot Mousse

Ham Rolls en Papillotes
Endive and Avocado Salad
Graham-Cracker Cheesecake

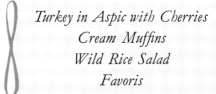

Turkey in Aspic with Cherries
Cream Muffins
Wild Rice Salad
Favoris

Tournedos Pompadour
Jerusalem Artichokes Avgolemono
Strawberry Cream Tart

Lobster and Shrimp Marinara
Artichoke Bottoms Saint Germain
Almond Macaroon Applesauce

Turkey Paprika
Baked Onions on Toast
Fresh Fruit Compote Chartreuse

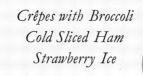

Crêpes with Broccoli
Cold Sliced Ham
Strawberry Ice

Eating Outdoors

Given the proper facilities and suitable weather, it is possible to serve almost any meal outdoors. Usually, however, it is desirable to capitalize on the outdoor situation, to some degree, in the menu.

This should not be taken to imply that an alfresco meal must necessarily be cooked outside. The implication is, rather, that the outdoors tends to deformalize any occasion slightly, and that some dishes seem more appropriate than others to the outdoor situation. Grilled meat or a fruit compote is more "at home" than an *escalope à la crème* or cherries Jubilee.

If the food is to be prepared on the terrace or the lawn, or in the patio, it is not desirable to serve only grilled dishes. Render unto the outdoor grill the food that is meant for it, and delegate to the kitchen that which can best be prepared there beforehand. The kitchen broiler will handily substitute for the open-air grill, in the event of an unexpected rainstorm.

The rainstorm is not so easily laughed off if the occasion is a picnic in some out-of-the-way place. Perhaps the suggestion still is to withdraw; the picnic menus in this section can be eaten at home, if need be.

Picnic

Lunch

Cherry Tomatoes
Eggs Stuffed with Chicken
French Bread with Olive Filling
Fruit Compote

Cold Curried Apple Soup
Skewered Sausage
Swiss Cheese Salad
Green Grape Tarts

Carrot Sticks
Celery Curls
Black and Green Olives
Terrine of Ham
Toasted Country White Bread
Melon Sherbet

Fisherman's Salad
Caraway Buns
Skewered Mixed Fruit

Sliced Ham, Tongue, and Turkey
Picnic Potato Salad
Watermelon with Rum

Mushroom Cream Cheese Spread
Sesame Crackers
Spit-Roasted Canadian Bacon
Sliced Yellow Tomatoes with Mustard French Dressing
Orange Butter Cream Roll

Savory Hamburgers
Sesame Coleslaw
Oatmeal Bread
Strawberries with Mock Devonshire Cream

Eggs Stuffed with Capers
Skewered Chicken with Peanut Dip
Red Onion Salad
Banana Ice Cream
Maple Syrup Cake

Duck and Orange Salad
Crackling Bread
Raspberries Romanoff

Terrace

Dinner

Cold Carrot and Orange Soup
Broiled Marinated Steak
Burgundy Onion Rings
Charcoal-Roasted Potatoes
Pineapple Ice Cream in Meringue Shells

Ham Steaks San Juan
Cheese-Stuffed Potatoes
Sliced Cucumbers with Avocado French Dressing
Skewered Caramel Apples

Duck and Orange Salad

Cream of Potato Soup with Saffron
Skewered Lamb
Ratatouille
Banana Tarts

Pâté Gourmet
Sweetbreads en Brochette
Mushrooms Stuffed with Pistachio Nuts
Avocado and Spinach Salad
Queen of Puddings

Barbecued Spareribs
Glazed Crab Apples
Grilled Sweet Potato Slices
Onion Bread
Green Salad with Chutney Dressing
Sour Cream Blackberry Pie

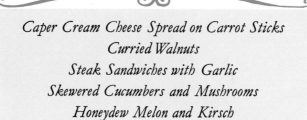

Caper Cream Cheese Spread on Carrot Sticks
Curried Walnuts
Steak Sandwiches with Garlic
Skewered Cucumbers and Mushrooms
Honeydew Melon and Kirsch

Radishes with Piquant Butter
Barbecued Duckling
Chinese Summer Squash
Black Currant Ice
Rolled Lace Cookies

Clear Beet Soup
Charcoal-Broiled Trout
Dilled Carrots
Gooseberry Custard
Honey Cookies

Baked Halibut with Maltaise Sauce

Fresh Vegetables with Sour Cream Dip
Sirloin Steak Gourmet
Potato Salad with Chestnuts
French Bread
Raspberry Ice Cream
Hazelnut Cookies

Bleu Cheese Profiteroles
Grilled Salmon
Charcoal-Broiled Mushrooms
Green Beans Vinaigrette
Mexican Cheesecake

Baked Halibut with Maltaise Sauce
Stuffed Potatoes Soubise
Red Radish Coleslaw
Poached Apples

Summer Buffet

Skewered Shrimp Armada
Cold Crown Roast of Smoked Pork with Fresh Fruit Salad
Scallions and Fennel
Toasted Portuguese Sweet Bread
Honey Cheesecake

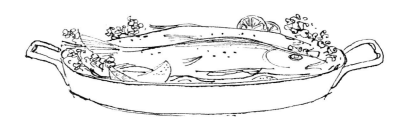

SUMMER BUFFET FOR 18

Canapés Grecques
Charcoal-Broiled Leg of Lamb
Tabbooli
Tian
Cobblestone Bread
Persian Oranges
Bichettes

Special Occasions

Holidays, and such occasions for celebration as weddings, are the subject of this chapter. The menus included are designed to meet a variety of entertaining needs that are somewhat out of the ordinary. Wedding receptions large and small, teas, an outdoor dinner for the Fourth of July, buffets and dinners for Thanksgiving and other holidays, a reception on New Year's Day—all find their places here.

Again, these menus are meant to be suggestive rather than prescriptive. If one Easter menu features Guinea hen as its main course we have no argument with those who are unshakable in their conviction that Easter Sunday dinner must include roast leg of spring lamb, new potatoes, and peas. Let the roast lamb be served, by all means. The Guinea hen will be just as delightful on Easter Monday's table!

A sufficient number of occasions has been covered so that these menus should be suggestive for many other special occasions. A wedding reception menu, for example, may very well serve for a silver anniversary. A birthday dinner, however, might better be found under formal or informal dinners.

SMALL WEDDING RECEPTION

Caviar
Hors-d'Oeuvre Roll with Chicken
Scallops and Shrimp in Patty Shells
Glazed Asparagus and Westphalian Ham
Ice Cream
Wedding Cake

Champagne

RECEPTION

Tongue and Olive Sandwiches
Chive Almond Profiteroles
Oyster Barquettes
Ham Bouchées
Chicken and Sweetbread Salad
Lobster Salad
Avocado Ring
Ice Cream
Wedding Cake

Champagne

LARGE WEDDING RECEPTION

Smoked Turkey Profiteroles
Beaten Biscuits with Ham
Fennel with Dill Butter
Cold Shrimp with Curry Mayonnaise
Pâté Sandwiches
Fresh Whole Strawberries

Lobster Salads with Caviar
Salmon Newburg
Chicken Breasts Jeannette
Sliced Beef Tongue Mayonnaise with
Ham Mousse

Mushroom and Artichoke Turnovers
Fresh Tomatoes with Spinach Purée
Asparagus Vinaigrette

Raspberries Chantilly with Chocolate Sauce
Wedding Cake

Champagne

Tea

Brazil Nut Tea Bread   Sweet Butter
Sandwiches
Palmiers
Petits Fours with Candied Fruit
Salted Almonds
Glacéed Tangerines

Cranberry Tea Bread   Marmalade Sandwiches
Hot Buttered Walnut Biscuits
Seed Cake
Stuffed Glacéed Prunes

Apricot Almond Bread   Cream Cheese
Sandwiches
Orange Madeira Cake
Chocolatines
Gitanes
Glacéed Strawberries

THANKSGIVING DINNER

FOLLE BLANCHE
American White

CABERNET SAUVIGNON
American Red

Oysters on the Half Shell
Pumpkin Soup
Roast Turkey
with Thanksgiving Stuffing
Cranberry and Kumquat Relish
Artichokes and Mushrooms in Cream
Braised Parsnips and Endive
Celeriac Salad
Crème Brûllée à l'Orange
Meringue Ladyfingers

THANKSGIVING BUFFET

CHENIN BLANC
American White

Shrimp Stuffed with Brazil Nuts
Parsnip Spread on Melba Rounds
Hot Baked Ham with Currant Jelly Sauce
Pumpkin Pancakes
Cranberry Apples
Stuffed Leeks
Musetta Salad
Banana Rum Mousse

CHRISTMAS DINNER

GAMAY
American Red

Clams on the Half Shell
Jellied Mushroom Soup
Truffled Capon
Tomatoes Stuffed with Potatoes
Sautéed Parsnips and Lettuce
Meringues Mont Blanc

CHRISTMAS DINNER

PINOT NOIR
American Red

Glacéed Nuts
Cream of Scallion Soup
Roast Goose Stuffed with Fruit
Sautéed Apples
Brussels Sprouts and Wild Rice
Pistachio Ice Cream
Christmas Spice Cookie Birds

CHRISTMAS BUFFET

Stuffed Rolled Breast of Turkey
Ham in Champagne
Scallops and Shrimp in White Wine
Rosemary Wild Rice
Chilled Green Beans Hollandaise
Buttered Finger Rolls
Mincemeat Flan
Marbled English Cream

Champagne

Truffled Capon

NEW YEAR DINNER

Oxtail Consommé
Foie Gras in Aspic
PULIGNY MONTRACHET   *Turkey with Oyster Sauce*
White Burgundy   *Lettuce Mousse*
Mushroom Tarts
Endive and Watercress Salad
Cold Chestnut Soufflé

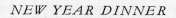

NEW YEAR'S DAY RECEPTION

Eggnog

Stuffed Virginia Ham
Corn Bread
Galletas
Salted Almonds
Toasted Hazelnuts
Pecan Cake
Pineapple Petits Fours

EASTER DINNER

CHÂTEANEUF-DU-PAPE
Red Rhône

Shad Pasties
Roast Guinea Hen
Parsley Fritters
Green Onions on Croûtes
Spinach Barquettes
Stuffed Tomatoes Idaho
Flaming Omelet Soufflé

EASTER BUFFET

GRENACHE ROSÉ
American Pink

Curried Smoked Salmon Spread
Cold Avocado Soup
Leg of Lamb in Aspic
Russian Salad
Egg Croquettes
Hot Asparagus Vinaigrette
The Queen's Custard
Swiss Bowknots

Swordfish Mirabeau

FOURTH OF JULY OUTDOOR DINNER

JOHANNESBERG RIESLING
American White

Bleu Cheese Mousse
Swordfish Mirabeau
Potato Balls
Vegetable and Sour Cream Salad
Raspberry and Peach Mousse
New England Poundcake

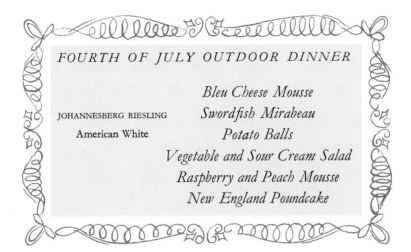

FOURTH OF JULY BUFFET

GAMAY ROSÉ
American Pink

Tartare Balls
Eggs Stuffed with Herbs
Hors-d'Oeuvre Roll with Red Caviar
Glazed Corned Brisket of Beef
Cold Curried Shrimp
Edwardian Chicken Salad
Blackberry Mousse

Hors-d'Oeuvre

Canapé Bases 🎗

CANAPÉ bases should be firm: certain breads, like the thinly sliced dark pumpernickel, will stand up under even a moist filling; others should be toasted. The shape of the canapé is a matter of taste—squares, ovals, diamonds, and triangles all lend interest.

CANAPÉS AU FONDS D'ARTICHAUTS

Artichoke Rounds 🎗

WHIP 12 ounces soft cream cheese with 2 tablespoons sour cream until the mixture is light and fluffy and season it with salt and cayenne to taste. Spread small rounds of pumpernickel bread with a thin layer of anchovy paste and put a small artichoke heart, preserved in oil and drained, in the center of each round. Using a pastry bag fitted with a small star tube, pipe the cheese mixture in a circle around each artichoke. Chill the rounds well before serving. Makes 40 canapés.

123

✺ Canapés Grecques   OLIVE AND EGG CANAPÉS

REMOVE the pits from 24 Greek olives, the type preserved in olive oil. Chop the olives finely and pound them to a paste or purée them in a blender. Put 6 hard-cooked eggs through a sieve and combine them with the olive paste, 1 tablespoon soft butter, and salt and pepper to taste. Spread the mixture on rounds of toast and garnish with flowers of hard-cooked egg. Makes 20 canapés.

✺ Horseradish Olive Stars

WITH a cookie cutter cut thin slices of dark rye into star shapes. Blend 3 ounces soft cream cheese with 2 teaspoons prepared horseradish and, using a pastry bag fitted with a plain tube, pipe the mixture into pitted ripe olives. Put a stuffed olive in the center of each star and pipe a line of the cheese mixture down each point of the star. Chill the stars well. Makes 12 canapés.

✺ Smoked Salmon Crescents

SPREAD thin slices of white bread with soft butter, sprinkle with freshly ground black pepper, and cover with thin slices of smoked salmon. Cut through the bread and salmon with a crescent cutter. Cover the canapés and chill them well.

✺ Sardine Toast

TRIM the crusts from slices of whole-wheat bread and cut them into thirds. Sauté the strips in melted butter until one side is a rich brown. Put a whole skinless, boneless sardine on the toasted side of each strip. Squeeze a little lemon juice over the sardines and brown the underside of the toast long enough to heat the fish through.

✺ Ginger Shrimp Toast

CHOP finely 1 pound cooked shrimp, shelled and deveined, and 1 onion, peeled. Grate enough fresh or dried gingerroot to make 3 teaspoons. Mix together the shrimp, onion, and gingerroot, season with salt and pepper to taste, and bind the mixture with 2 egg whites, beaten. Spread narrow strips of day-old bread on one side with the shrimp paste, coat the paste with fine bread crumbs, and fry the canapés in deep hot fat (375° F.) until they are golden brown. Drain on absorbent paper.

Pineapple with Shrimp and Dill 🦐

CUT fresh pineapple into slices 1/4 inch thick, remove the hard center core, and cut the slices into triangles. Spread the triangles with a thin layer of mayonnaise mixed with an equal amount of stiffly whipped cream. Arrange 2 or 3 tiny shrimp, cooked and shelled, on each triangle and pipe a rosette of dill butter at the top of the triangles. Chill the hors-d'oeuvre thoroughly.

Vitello Tonnato Canapés 🦐

TRIM the skin and fat from a 2-pound boneless loin of veal. Brush the meat with olive oil and roast it in a moderately slow oven (325° F.) for about 2 hours, or until it is tender. Cool the meat thoroughly and cut it into thin slices. Mash and pound 1/2 cup Italian-style tuna fish, packed in olive oil, with 2 anchovy filets, and add gradually a generous 1/2 cup olive oil, working the oil into the fish to make a light paste. Add a few drops of lemon juice and salt and pepper to taste. Cover thin slices of white bread with slices of the veal and cut through the meat and bread with an oval cutter. Top the meat with oval mounds of the tuna mixture, shaped with a teaspoon, and garnish the fish with a row of capers. Chill the canapés thoroughly. Makes about 40 canapés.

Beaten Biscuits with Ham 🦐

CAREFULLY split tiny beaten biscuits, butter them lightly with soft sweet butter, and sandwich them with paper-thin slices of Westphalian ham or *prosciutto.*

❧ Brazilian Canapés

COMBINE 1/2 pound lean round steak, ground twice, with 4 slices of cooked crumbled bacon, 1/4 teaspoon chili powder, and salt and pepper to taste. Form the meat into 20 bite-sized patties 1/4 inch thick. Broil the patties in a very hot broiler for 2 or 3 minutes, or until they are nicely browned on both sides. Cut firm-textured bread into thin slices and toast them lightly. Cut out 20 rounds of toast with a 1 1/2-inch cutter or a star cutter. Butter the rounds or stars lightly, cover each one with a meat patty, and top with a paper-thin slice of banana, soaked in lemon juice and drained. Serve immediately.

❧ Cheese Soufflé Canapés

IN a saucepan melt 1 tablespoon butter, remove the pan from the heat, and stir in 1 heaping teaspoon flour. Add gradually 1/3 cup hot milk and cook the sauce over low heat, stirring constantly, until it is thick and smooth. Add 1 teaspoon kirsch and 1/3 pound sharp Cheddar, grated, and cook the sauce, stirring, until the cheese is melted. Remove the pan from the heat, mix in well 1 beaten egg yolk, warmed with a little of the hot sauce, and cool the mixture. Fold in 1 egg white, stiffly beaten.

Toast 4 dozen 1 1/2-inch rounds of thinly sliced white bread. Mound 1 teaspoon of the cheese soufflé on each round. Put the rounds on a lightly buttered baking sheet, dust with paprika, and broil them until the cheese puffs up and is lightly browned. Serve immediately. Makes 48 canapés.

❧ Souffléed Crackers

SPLIT water crackers in half and soak them in ice water for about 3 minutes. Remove them with a perforated spatula and drain them on a towel. Transfer the crackers to baking sheets, dot them thickly with butter, and bake them in a very hot oven (450° F.) for about 30 minutes, until they are puffed, crisp, golden brown, and dry. Add more butter halfway through the baking, if desired.

Cheese Balls in Chipped Beef 𓆃

BLEND 1 pound cream cheese with 1/2 teaspoon each of ground sage, onion juice, and Worcestershire sauce, a few drops of lemon juice, and a dash of Tabasco. Chill the mixture for 1 hour. Shape the cheese into marble-sized balls (there should be about 24) and roll them in 5 ounces finely chopped chipped beef. Chill before serving.

Cheddar and Olive Balls 𓆃

COMBINE 1 pound grated sharp Cheddar with 1/2 cup chopped ripe olives, 4 tablespoons soft butter, 1 minced garlic clove, a few drops of Tabasco, and a dash of cayenne. Form the mixture into small balls (there should be about 24) and insert a cocktail pick in each ball.

Jamaican Avocado Balls 𓆃

CUT 2 large ripe firm avocados in half lengthwise and remove the pulp with a melon-ball cutter. Put the avocado balls in a glass or porcelain bowl and cover them with a marinade made by combining 1/2 cup olive oil with 3 tablespoons cider vinegar, 2 tablespoons heavy dark rum, and 1 large garlic clove, crushed. Chill the avocado balls in the marinade for 4 hours, drain them, and insert a cocktail pick in each. They are best with rum drinks.

Tartare Balls 𓆃

COMBINE 1 pound lean round steak, ground, with 1 beaten egg yolk and Worcestershire sauce and salt and pepper to taste. Form the meat into marble-sized balls and top each ball with a tiny cocktail onion or several capers. Makes about 20.

Bleu Cheese Tartare Balls 𓆃

COMBINE 2 pounds lean sirloin steak, ground, with 1 onion, grated, and 1 teaspoon each of salt and pepper. Cream together 1/2 pound each of cream cheese and bleu cheese. Form the cheese mixture into tiny balls. Enclose the cheese balls in balls of the ground meat. Dip the meat and cheese balls in lightly beaten egg and roll them in finely chopped parsley. Pierce each ball with a cocktail pick. Makes about 50.

Steak Tartare Balls

IN a mixing bowl combine 1 pound lean top round of beef, finely ground, with 1 tablespoon each of onion and parsley, both finely chopped, 1 tablespoon anchovy paste, 1 teaspoon Worcestershire sauce, 1/4 teaspoon prepared mustard, and salt and freshly ground pepper to taste. Form the meat into small balls and roll the balls in 1 cup coarsely chopped walnuts, coating them well. Chill the balls well. Makes about 40.

Tartare Spheres

SEASON 1 pound lean raw sirloin or tenderloin steak, ground, with salt and freshly ground pepper to taste. Form the meat into 40 flat rounds. Drain and press dry 1/2 pound fresh sauerkraut. Chop the sauerkraut very finely and mix it with 1 teaspoon crushed caraway seeds. Place 1/2 teaspoon of the mixture on each round of meat and shape the rounds into balls around the sauerkraut, enclosing it completely. Roll the balls in paprika, coating them well, and decorate each with 2 or 3 short blades of chive. Makes 20 servings.

Bleu Cheese Mousse

BEAT 6 egg yolks with 6 tablespoons cream in a saucepan over low heat until the mixture is creamy. Soften 1 1/2 tablespoons gelatin in 4 tablespoons cold water, dissolve the gelatin over hot water, and add it to the eggs. Force 3/4 pound bleu cheese through a sieve, add it to the gelatin mixture, and cool. Fold in 1 1/2 cups heavy cream, whipped, and 3 egg whites, stiffly beaten. Pour the mousse into an oiled mold and chill it for at least 2 hours. Unmold the mousse on a platter and garnish the top with watercress. Serve with rounds of toast.

Bleu Cheese Mousse

ℒ Swiss Cheese Mousse

MELT 1/4 cup butter, stir in 1/2 cup flour, and cook the *roux* over low heat, stirring constantly, for 3 minutes. Add gradually 1 1/4 cups milk and cook the sauce, stirring with a whisk, until it is smooth and thick. Soften 2 envelopes of gelatin in 1/2 cup chicken stock and dissolve it in the hot sauce, off the heat. Beat in 4 egg yolks, warmed with a little of the hot sauce, 2/3 cup grated Swiss cheese, 1/2 small onion, minced, 1 teaspoon dry mustard, and salt, pepper, and paprika to taste. Cool the mixture and fold in 4 egg whites, stiffly beaten, and 1/4 cup whipped cream. Sprinkle a lightly oiled 2-quart mold with 1/4 cup chopped chives. Pour in the cheese mixture carefully to keep the chives on the lining of the mold. Chill the mousse for 3 hours, unmold it on a platter, and surround it with a ring of parsley.

ℒ Anchovy Cheese

BLEND 1/2 pound grated Cheddar cheese with 1 pound cottage cheese, 1 onion, grated, 1 cup soft sweet butter, and 24 anchovy filets, finely chopped. Add enough beer to make a smooth mixture and season to taste with salt, dry mustard, and enough paprika to give a good color. Sprinkle the spread with 2 tablespoons caraway seeds and chill it. Serve with pumpernickel bread.

ℒ Cheese Madeira

MIX together 3 1/2 ounces Liederkranz, 3 ounces cream cheese, 4 tablespoons Madeira, 3 tablespoons heavy cream, and 1/4 teaspoon celery seeds. Whip the mixture until it is creamy. Rub the bottom and sides of an earthenware crock with a cut garlic clove and fill it with the cheese mixture. Cover the crock tightly and let the cheese ripen in the refrigerator for at least a week. Serve with squares of freshly made white toast.

ℒ Cheese Pot

IN a wooden bowl blend 1 pound grated sharp Cheddar with 3 ounces cream cheese and enough olive oil to give the paste a velvety consistency. Add 1 teaspoon dry mustard, a few caraway seeds, if desired, and 2 jiggers each of brandy and kirsch.

Pack the mixture in a stone crock, cover it, and let it ripen in the refrigerator for at least a week. Add any grated cheese, wine, or liqueur to the mixture as desired. Some of the original cheese mixture should be saved to act as the "mother" when the crock is renewed. A variety of cheeses may be used for the cheese pot. Remove the cheese from the refrigerator an hour before serving, and serve it from the crock with rye bread.

Potted Cheese Spread

SEASON 1 1/2 pounds grated Cheddar with 1/4 cup each of finely chopped parsley and onion, 3/4 teaspoon dry mustard, and 1/4 teaspoon salt. Work in 1/3 cup dry Sherry, 1/4 cup ketchup, 2 tablespoons soft butter, add a dash each of Tabasco and Worcestershire, and mix the cheese until it is smooth and creamy. Serve with squares of buttered rye bread. To store, pack the cheese in crocks and refrigerate.

Spiced Edam Cheese

SLICE the top from a 1-pound Edam and carefully scoop out the cheese, leaving the red shell intact. Put the cheese through a food chopper and blend the ground cheese with 1/2 cup each of soft butter and beer, 1/2 teaspoon each of caraway seeds, dry mustard, and powdered celery seed, and salt to taste. Beat the cheese mixture well and pile it into the shell. Serve with thin slices of pumpernickel.

Champagne Gorgonzola Spread

BLEND to a smooth paste 1/2 pound mellow Gorgonzola, 1/4 pound sweet butter, and cayenne pepper to taste. Moisten the spread with 3/4 cup Champagne and serve with crackers or any good bread.

Caper Cream Cheese Spread

CREAM together 3 ounces cream cheese, 1 tablespoon heavy cream, and 1 teaspoon juice from a bottle of capers. Stir in 1 tablespoon capers and salt and pepper to taste. Serve the spread on flat carrot sticks.

Assorted Hors-d'Oeuvre

Steak Tartare Balls (p. 128), Miniature Kulebyaka (p. 179), Radishes with
Piquant Butter (p. 148), Taramosalata (p. 135).

Mushroom Cream Cheese Spread ✑

CREAM together 3 ounces cream cheese and 1 teaspoon onion juice. Stir in 1/2 cup finely chopped raw mushrooms and season the spread with salt and white pepper to taste. Serve with crackers.

Roquefort Spread ✑

CREAM together 1/2 cup each of Roquefort cheese and soft butter. Add 2 tablespoons Calvados and blend the mixture well. Pack the cheese in crocks and store in the refrigerator. Serve the spread with Melba toast or pipe it into celery stalks.

Sacher Cheese ✑

PUT through a sieve 1 cup cottage cheese, 2 hard-cooked egg yolks, and 3 anchovies, chopped. Beat in thoroughly 1/4 cup soft butter and chill the paste. Serve with crackers.

Eggplant Caviar ✑

COOK a whole medium eggplant in simmering water to cover for about 30 minutes, or until it is tender. Or bake the eggplant on a pie plate in a hot oven (400° F.) for about 30 minutes. Cool and peel the eggplant, chop the pulp finely, and blend it thoroughly with 1 onion, finely minced, 1 garlic clove, mashed, 1 tomato, chopped and drained, 3 tablespoons olive oil, 2 tablespoons vinegar, 1 teaspoon sugar, and salt and pepper to taste. Chill the mixture well. Serve on a bed of crisp lettuce, or spread on thin buttered slices of rye bread or white toast rounds.

Parsnip Spread ✑

PEEL and grate 2 parsnips. Blend 8 ounces cream cheese with 1/4 cup white wine. Stir in the grated parsnips, 1 teaspoon each of chives and fresh dill, both minced, and salt and pepper to taste. Spread the mixture on rounds of Melba toast. To use as a dip instead of a spread, thin the mixture with a little more wine.

Anchovy Mousse

MASH the yolks of 6 hard-cooked eggs with 6 teaspoons anchovy paste, 2 tablespoons grated Parmesan, 1 teaspoon each of Worcestershire and soy sauce, and 1/4 teaspoon black pepper. Soften 1 tablespoon gelatin in 2 tablespoons cold water and dissolve it in 1 cup hot beef stock. Combine the gelatin with the egg mixture and cool the mixture until it is syrupy. Fold in 2 cups heavy cream, whipped, and 6 hard-cooked egg whites, finely chopped. Fill an oiled mold with the mousse and chill it for several hours, or until it is firm. Unmold the mousse on a chilled platter and surround it with quarters of hard-cooked egg and anchovy curls. Serve with narrow strips of buttered whole-wheat toast.

Caviar

SPREAD caviar on small thin rounds or squares of freshly made toast. Sprinkle the caviar with a few drops of lemon juice, finely chopped egg white and onion, and sieved egg yolk.

Potted Lobster

CRACK the claws and cut the tails of 5 pounds live lobsters. Remove the meat and cut it into thin slices. Reserve the rest of the lobster meat for another use. Put the slices in a saucepan with 1/2 cup butter, 12 boned anchovies, 9 peppercorns, and a little salt. Cook the lobster meat over low heat for 20 minutes, or until it is firm and not translucent. Pound the mixture to a paste in a mortar and pack it in a crock or jar. Cover the top with clarified butter and serve, well chilled, with rounds of white toast.

Curried Smoked Salmon Spread

PUT through the finest blade of a food chopper 1 pound smoked salmon and 1 medium onion. Blend in 1/4 cup sour cream, 1 tablespoon mayonnaise, and 1/2 teaspoon each of curry powder and grated orange rind. Pile the mixture into a bowl, cover the bowl, and chill the spread for 1 hour. Serve with triangles of buttered toast.

Shrimp Spread 🦐

FLAVOR 1 cup mayonnaise with 4 small shallots, minced. Combine the shallot mayonnaise with 1 pound cooked shrimp, shelled, deveined, and coarsely chopped, and stir in 2 tablespoons capers. Add salt and pepper to taste. Pile the shrimp spread in a bowl and sprinkle it with paprika. Serve with heated rounds of rye Melba toast.

Shrimp Butter Spread 🦐

PUT 2 pounds cooked shrimp, shelled and deveined, through the finest blade of a food chopper. Combine the shrimp with 1 pound soft butter and add mace, chili powder, salt, and pepper to taste. Pound the mixture to a smooth paste. Pack the spread in a crock and chill it. Serve with crackers.

Tarama Hors-d'Oeuvre 🦐

PUT *tarama* (cured red mullet roe) in a small bowl on a bed of crushed ice. Serve with strips of hot buttered toast.

RED MULLET ROE APPETIZER

Taramosalata 🦐

TRIM the crusts from five 1/2-inch slices of white bread and drench them in cold water. Squeeze out most of the water. The bread should be slightly soggy. Whip the bread with a rotary beater until it is fluffy, add 1 large onion, grated, and beat for 3 minutes. Still beating, add 1/2 pound *tarama* (cured red mullet roe, available at Greek specialty shops), a tablespoon at a time. After all the *tarama* has been incorporated beat the mixture for 5 minutes longer. Still beating, add alternately, both drop by drop, 1 cup olive oil and the juice of 2 lemons. Beat the mixture for 3 minutes longer, or until it is creamy. Stir in 2 tablespoons gelatin softened in 1/4 cup cold water and dissolved over hot water. Pour the *taramosalata* into a lightly oiled mold and chill it for 2 hours, or until it is set. Unmold it on a platter and garnish with a ring of finely chopped parsley. Serve with rounds of toasted white bread. If *tarama* is not available, red caviar may be substituted.

ᔥ Bagna Cauda

HEAT together in the blazer of a chafing dish 1/2 cup each of olive oil and butter, 4 garlic cloves, finely chopped, and 8 anchovy filets, pounded and chopped. Cook the mixture, stirring, until the anchovies melt into the fat. Add a little freshly ground pepper. Let the mixture mellow over hot water for 30 minutes. Serve in the chafing dish as a dip for celery, strips of green pepper, radishes, raw artichoke bottoms, or cauliflower flowerets.

ᔥ Mustard Dip

COMBINE 2 cups sour cream with 1/4 cup each of capers, chopped chives, and Dijon-type mustard, and 1/2 teaspoon dry mustard. Chill the mixture thoroughly. Serve as a dip for shrimp.

ᔥ Sour Cream Dip

COMBINE 1 cup sour cream with 1/4 pound bleu cheese, mashed, 1 onion, grated, and pepper to taste. Serve as a dip for carrot and turnip sticks, celery stalks, scallions, and radishes.

ᔥ Spinach Cream

COMBINE 2 cups sour cream with 1 cup raw spinach, finely chopped, 1/2 cup each of chives and parsley, both chopped, 1 teaspoon salt, and 1/2 teaspoon freshly ground black pepper. Serve as a dip for carrots, scallions, radishes, shreds of raw turnip, or stalks of celery.

ᔥ Stuffed Eggs

SIMMER the desired number of eggs gently for 15 minutes, turning them often during the cooking to help set the yolks in the middle. To prevent discoloration, cool the eggs quickly by plunging them into cold water. Remove the shells and cut each egg in half lengthwise. Or cut off the narrow ends, halve each egg crosswise, and cut a small slice from the round end so that both halves will stand upright. Carefully remove the yolks, leaving the whites intact.

The usual filling for stuffed eggs is composed of the mashed yolks blended with whatever seasonings and additives are indicated. For a lavish effect, pile the filling high in the whites. For decorative results, use a pastry tube. If possible, remove the stuffed eggs from the refrigerator half an hour before serving them; the flavor and texture improve at room temperature.

If stuffed eggs are to be served as a first course, allow 1 egg per person. If the eggs are to be served at a buffet or a cocktail party, where other foods are presented at the same time, 4 eggs will serve 6 persons.

Eggs Stuffed with Anchovies

FORCE the yolks of 6 hard-cooked eggs through a fine sieve and blend them well with 3 tablespoons finely chopped anchovies, 1 tablespoon finely chopped pickled onions, 1/2 teaspoon freshly ground pepper, and enough mayonnaise to make a paste. Fill the whites and sprinkle with paprika.

Eggs Stuffed with Capers

RICE the yolks of 6 hard-cooked eggs and mix them with 4 tablespoons soft butter, 4 teaspoons mayonnaise, 2 teaspoons minced onion, 1 teaspoon prepared mustard, and the grated rind of 1/2 lemon. Fill the whites and garnish with a circle of capers.

OEUFS DURS AU CAVIAR   ## Eggs Stuffed with Caviar

FORCE the yolks of hard-cooked eggs through a sieve. Fill the whites with caviar and garnish with sieved egg yolk.

For the formal buffet prepare 16 eggs.

OEUFS DURS AU CARI   ## Curried Stuffed Eggs

FORCE the yolks of 6 hard-cooked eggs through a fine sieve and add 1/4 cup finely chopped ham, 1 teaspoon grated onion, curry powder, salt and pepper to taste, and enough mayonnaise to bind the mixture. Fill the whites and arrange the eggs on a bed of watercress.

⟫ Eggs Stuffed with Chicken

MASH the yolk of 6 hard-cooked eggs and combine them with 1/4 cup cooked chicken, pounded to a paste. Add 2 teaspoons mayonnaise, curry powder to taste, and a dash of cayenne. Fill the whites, using a pastry tube or a spoon, and garnish each one with a sliver of toasted almond.

⟫ Eggs Stuffed with Chicken Livers

MASH the yolks of 6 hard-cooked eggs and force them through a sieve. Sauté 1/3 pound chicken livers in 2 teaspoons butter until they are just tender. Add 1/2 teaspoon grated onion to the pan and cook it for 2 minutes. Mash the onion and livers, force them through a sieve, and combine them with the yolks. Blend in 3 tablespoons butter and season with salt and pepper to taste. Fill the whites and garnish each with a tiny cocktail onion.

⟫ Eggs Stuffed with Chives

MASH the yolks of 6 hard-cooked eggs and combine them with 4 teaspoons chopped chives, 2 tablespoons mayonnaise, 1/2 teaspoon mustard, and salt and pepper to taste. Fill the whites and sprinkle lightly with paprika.

⟫ Eggs Stuffed with Smoked Trout

RICE the yolks of 6 hard-cooked eggs and mix them with about 3 tablespoons smoked trout paste, or to taste. Add 2 tablespoons each of mayonnaise and soft butter. Fill the whites and sprinkle with chopped almonds.

Dandelion Eggs 🦂

MASH the yolks of 6 hard-cooked eggs and combine them with 2 tablespoons butter, 1/4 cup young dandelion leaves, finely chopped, 1/2 teaspoon grated onion, 1/4 teaspoon dry mustard, and salt and pepper to taste. Using a pastry bag fitted with a small tube, pipe the mixture into the egg whites. Arrange the eggs on a bed of watercress.

Eggs Stuffed with Crab Meat 🦂

FORCE the yolks of 6 hard-cooked eggs through a fine sieve. Combine them with 1/2 cup mashed cooked crab meat, 3 tablespoons mayonnaise, 1 teaspoon each of prepared mustard and minced onion, a dash of Worcestershire sauce, and salt and pepper to taste. Fill the whites and garnish with strips of pimiento.

Eggs Stuffed with Herbs 🦂

FORCE the yolks of 6 hard-cooked eggs through a fine sieve and mix them with an equal amount of mayonnaise, some finely chopped chives and parsley, and salt to taste. Fill the whites, using a pastry tube, and arrange them in a serving dish. Garnish with mayonnaise and sprinkle with paprika.

Eggs Stuffed with Mushrooms 🦂

MASH the yolks of 6 hard-cooked eggs and combine them with 1/4 cup finely minced mushrooms sautéed in butter, 2 tablespoons grated onion, salt and pepper to taste, and enough mayonnaise to bind the mixture. Using a pastry bag fitted with a fluted tube, pipe the mixture into the egg whites.

Eggs Stuffed with Oysters 🦂

HALVE hard-cooked eggs lengthwise, remove the yolks, and reserve them for another use. Marinate raw oysters in French dressing. Put an oyster in each egg white, cover with mayonnaise, and sprinkle with finely chopped capers.

Eggs with Caviar Sauce

SPRINKLE 1/2 cup caviar with 4 tablespoons lemon juice. Mix in slowly 2 tablespoons chili sauce, 1 tablespoon oil, 2 teaspoons cider vinegar, 1/2 teaspoon salt,
1/4 teaspoon ground Nepal pepper, and a drop of Tabasco. Blend the mixture very
lightly with 2 cups mayonnaise.

Shell and halve lengthwise 6 hard-cooked eggs, arrange the eggs, cut side down,
on a serving platter and cover them with the sauce.

Eggs à la Tapinade

SHELL 6 hard-cooked eggs, halve them lengthwise, and remove the yolks. Mash the
yolks well.

In the container of a blender put 1 cup each of pitted ripe olives and capers,
1/3 cup each of anchovies, soaked in milk for 15 minutes, and tuna fish, and 2 tablespoons dry mustard. Cover the container and blend the mixture until it is very
smooth. Slowly stir in 1/2 cup olive oil, 1 1/2 tablespoons brandy, and 2 teaspoons
mixed white pepper, cloves, ginger, and nutmeg, all ground. Mix three fourths of
this mixture with the egg yolks and fill the whites. Arrange the eggs on a platter
and, using a pastry bag fitted with a small tube, pipe a border of the remaining
tapinade sauce around the eggs.

Apples with Roquefort

PREPARE the following spread: Blend 1/2 pound Roquefort cheese with 1/4 cup soft
butter and 1 tablespoon brandy. Core and slice as many unpeeled red apples as
needed and spread the slices with the cheese mixture.

Artichoke Bottoms with Smoked Salmon

COOK 24 artichoke bottoms and, with a cookie cutter, trim them to a diameter of
3/4 inch. Reserve the trimmings.

Put 1/4 pound smoked Nova Scotia salmon and the artichoke trimmings through
the finest blade of a food chopper and work the mixture to a paste. Blend together
2 tablespoons sour cream, 2 teaspoons mayonnaise, 1/4 teaspoon lemon juice, and

Assorted Hors-d'Oeuvre

Chicken and Ham Roll (p. 181), Bourekakia (p. 178), Miniature Crab Quiche (p. 174),
Onion Sandwiches (p. 180), Rollatini di Mortadella (p. 158).

1/8 teaspoon each of dry mustard and powdered coriander. Reserve 1 tablespoon of the mixture and beat the rest into the salmon. Fill the artichoke bottoms with the salmon paste and top each with a dot of the sour-cream mixture and a caper.

﴾﴿ Artichoke Bottoms with Caviar
FONDS D'ARTICHAUTS AU CAVIAR

FILL cooked artichoke bottoms with black caviar. Sprinkle the caviar with a drop of lemon juice and with hard-cooked egg yolk, finely chopped.

﴾﴿ Artichokes Inez

CLEAN 6 artichokes carefully, discarding the hard outer leaves, and cut the artichokes in quarters. Arrange them in a large pan so that they have plenty of space. Cover the artichokes with 1/4 pound each of mushrooms, sliced, and onions, coarsely chopped. Add 1/2 cup each of olive oil and dry white wine, the juice of 1 lemon, 1 garlic clove, peeled, a sprig of thyme, a bay leaf, 1/4 teaspoon coriander, and salt and pepper to taste. Cover the pan, bring the liquid to a boil, and boil it rapidly for about 1 minute. Transfer the pan to a moderate oven (350° F.) and bake the artichokes for about 30 minutes, or until they are tender. Let the artichokes cool slowly and serve them cold.

﴾﴿ Pickled Artichokes

REMOVE the leaves and chokes from as many small artichokes as desired. Trim the bottoms and drop them immediately into water acidulated with the juice of 1 lemon.

Bring to a boil 2 quarts cider vinegar seasoned with 1 tablespoon each of mixed pickling spices and whole cloves, 1 cinnamon stick, broken in pieces, 1/2 teaspoon thyme, and 1/8 teaspoon mace, all tied into a cheesecloth bag. Remove the vinegar from the heat and let the spices steep for 45 minutes. Stir in 2 cups sugar, return the vinegar to a boil, and let it simmer for 20 minutes. Add the artichoke bottoms, a few at a time, and boil them for 1 minute. Chill the bottoms in the vinegar and drain them. Serve as hors-d'oeuvre.

To keep the pickled artichokes for later use, remove them from the boiling vinegar with a perforated spoon and put them in hot sterilized jars. Discard the spice bag, fill the jars to the top with the hot vinegar, and seal them immediately.

Formosan Beets

WASH 2 dozen young beets, put them in a casserole, and bake them in a moderate oven (350° F.) for about 45 minutes, or until they are tender. Peel the beets and cool them. With the small end of a plain pastry tube core each beet almost through.

Cream 1/2 cup sweet butter and blend it with the yolks of 5 hard-cooked eggs, 1 teaspoon Chinese mustard dissolved in 2 teaspoons beer, and salt to taste. Chill the mixture until it is almost firm. Using a pastry bag fitted with a small tube, pipe the egg and butter mixture into the beets. Garnish each beet with a thin slice of green pepper.

Brussels Sprouts with Tongue Mousse

PUT 1 cup ground cooked smoked tongue through a food chopper with 2 tablespoons white raisins marinated in 1/4 cup warmed Madeira and drained. Stir in 2 tablespoons Madeira, 1 tablespoon tomato purée, and 1 teaspoon each of prepared mustard and finely chopped celery leaves. Pound the mixture in a mortar until it is very smooth or purée it in a blender.

Soak 2 teaspoons gelatin in 1/4 cup cold chicken stock for 5 minutes and dissolve it in 1/2 cup hot chicken stock. Add the gelatin stock to the tongue paste and heat the mixture thoroughly. Remove the pan from the heat, stir in 2 egg yolks, lightly beaten, and cool the mixture. Fold in 1/4 cup whipped cream and 2 egg whites, stiffly beaten. Chill the mousse for several hours, or until it is very firm.

Carefully separate the leaves of 24 small fresh Brussels sprouts, cut out the tightly closed hearts, and arrange the cored Brussels sprouts on a platter. Shape the mousse into 24 balls. Insert 1 ball into each cored Brussels sprout and reshape the outer leaves. Seal the platter tightly with plastic wrap (the sprouts turn brown quickly when exposed to air), and chill the Brussels sprouts thoroughly.

Limburger in Celery Stalks

CREAM together 3 ounces Limburger cheese and 1/2 cup butter. Blend in 2 tablespoons grated onion and 1/4 teaspoon salt. Chill the spread. Using a pastry bag fitted with a fluted tube, pipe the mixture into the center of cold trimmed celery stalks.

Assorted Hors-d'Oeuvre

Skewered Scallops (*p. 159*), Brussels Sprouts with Tongue Mousse (*p. 143*), Shrimp
with Green Tomato Sauce (*p. 154*), Cheese Soufflé Canapés (*p. 126*).

Cucumber Cups 🦪

PEEL cucumbers with a fluted vegetable knife and cut them into 1-inch slices. Remove enough of the seedy center from each slice to form tiny cups. Using a pastry bag fitted with a small tube, force fluted mounds of soft *pâté de foie gras*, horseradish and olive filling, or herb butter into the cucumber cups. Place the cups on pumpernickel rounds and chill well.

Cucumbers Filled with Anchovies 🦪

WITH an apple corer remove the centers from 6 cucumbers. Blend 1 pound soft cream cheese with 24 anchovy filets, finely chopped, and 2 tablespoons chopped fresh dill. Stuff the cucumber cavities with the anchovy-cheese mixture and chill for 2 or 3 hours. To serve, slice the stuffed cucumbers thinly and serve on rounds of Melba toast.

Cucumbers Stuffed with Roquefort 🦪

PEEL cucumbers with a fluted vegetable knive and cut them into 1-inch slices. Remove enough of the seedy center from each slice to form tiny cups. Cream together equal amounts of Roquefort cheese and soft butter and moisten the mixture with a little Cognac. Fill the cucumber cups with the cheese mixture and sprinkle them with chopped chives. Serve on rounds of white toast cut the same size.

Stuffed Endive 🦪

CHOP finely 12 anchovy filets and mix them with 1 tablespoon chopped chives and 8 ounces soft cream cheese. Using a pastry bag fitted with a plain tube, pipe the mixture into the centers of 12 cold trimmed endive stalks. Chill before serving.

Fennel with Dill Butter 🦪

IN a mixing bowl combine 3/4 pound each of soft cream cheese and sweet butter and 2 tablespoons heavy sweet cream. Add 3 tablespoons Cognac and 5 teaspoons minced fresh dill. Using a pastry bag fitted with a small fluted tube, pipe the mixture into the centers of 40 to 50 cold fennel stalks. Chill before serving.

Stuffed Grape Leaves

RINSE and drain 36 pickled grape leaves. Prepare the following stuffing: Sauté 3 large onions, finely chopped, in 1/2 cup olive oil until they are golden. Add 1 cup long-grain rice, mix well, and cook it over low heat, stirring occasionally, for 10 minutes. Add to the skillet 1 cup fresh dill, 1/2 cup parsley, and 8 green onions, all chopped, 1/2 cup water, 3 tablespoons pine nuts, the juice of 1 lemon, and salt and pepper to taste. Cook the mixture for about 10 minutes, or until all the liquid is absorbed. Remove the pan from the heat and cool the stuffing.

Lay the grape leaves on a board, shiny sides down, and put 1 teaspoon of the rice mixture in the center of each leaf. Fold the sides of the leaves to the center, then roll them up tightly, starting from the stem ends. Arrange the rolls in layers in a saucepan and cover them with 1 cup water, 1/2 cup olive oil, and the juice of 1 lemon. Place a plate over the rolls so they will not unroll. Bring the mixture to a boil over high heat and cook it for 5 minutes. Add 1/2 cup water, return to the boiling point, reduce the heat and simmer the rolls for about 45 minutes, or until the liquid is absorbed.

Cool and chill the grape leaves. Serve with wedges of lemon.

Mushrooms Stuffed with Anchovies

PEEL 1 1/2 pounds mushrooms, cut off the stems, and reserve them for another use. Mix 12 anchovy filets, chopped, with 8 ounces soft cream cheese and add 2 tablespoons chopped chives. Fill the raw mushroom caps with the cheese mixture.

Mushrooms with Roquefort

CREAM together well 1/2 pound each of Roquefort and sweet butter and blend in 4 tablespoons Cognac and 1/2 teaspoon Worcestershire sauce. Clean 20 large mushrooms with a brush and remove the stems. Using a pastry bag fitted with a star tube, pipe the cheese mixture into the raw mushroom caps. Garnish the centers with thin strips of green pepper. Chill the mushrooms thoroughly.

Pickled Mushrooms with Tarama 🍄

TRIM the crust from a 1/2-inch slice of white bread and soak the bread in cold water. Squeeze out most of the water and beat the bread with a rotary beater until it is fluffy. Add 1 tablespoon grated onion and beat 2 or 3 minutes more. Still beating, add 2 ounces *tarama* (cured red mullet roe, available at Greek specialty shops), a tablespoon at a time. Still beating, add alternately, drop by drop, 1/4 cup olive oil and 1 tablespoon lemon juice. Beat the mixture until it is creamy. Drain a large jar of small pickled mushrooms. Using a pastry bag fitted with a small tube, fill each mushroom with the *tarama* mixture. Chill well before serving. Fills 50 small mushrooms.

Marinated Mushrooms 🍄

PEEL 1 pound small mushrooms and remove the stems. Drop the caps in water acidulated with the juice of 1 lemon, bring the water to a boil, and simmer the mushrooms for 5 minutes, or until they are tender. Drain and rinse the caps under cold running water. Shake off any excess water and put the mushrooms in a bowl.

In a saucepan combine 3/4 cup vinegar with 1/3 cup olive oil, 1 crushed garlic clove, 1/2 bay leaf, 1 sprig of parsley, and 1/2 teaspoon each of salt and pepper. Boil the marinade for 5 minutes and pour it over the mushrooms. When the marinade has cooled, chill the mushrooms. Sprinkle with chopped dill just before serving.

Mushrooms à la Grecque 🍄

IN a saucepan combine 1 cup water with 1/2 cup olive oil and 1/4 cup lemon juice, and add a *bouquet garni* composed of 2 sprigs of parsley, 1 bay leaf, 1/2 teaspoon celery seed, and 12 peppercorns, all tied in a cheesecloth bag. Boil the mixture for 10 minutes, add 1 pound small uniform mushrooms, trimmed, and cook them for 10 minutes, or until they are tender. Cool the mushrooms in the liquid, drain them, and chill them. Serve the mushrooms garnished with thin slices of lemon and several small bunches of watercress.

﹩ Stuffed Olives

COMBINE equal amounts of whipped cream and horseradish and add salt to taste. Fill the cavities of large pitted ripe olives with the mixture. Chill the olives.

﹩ Penthouse Onions

COOK 24 small white onions in simmering water to cover for about 15 minutes, or until they are tender but still firm. Drain the onions, cool them, and scoop out the centers. Put enough lean cooked ham through the finest blade of a food chopper to make 1 cup. Work the ground ham to a paste with 1 teaspoon each of ketchup and A.1. Sauce and a dash of Tabasco. Stuff the onion cavities with the mixture and chill the onions thoroughly. Garnish each with a tiny sprig of fresh dill.

﹩ Onion and Currant Hors-d'Oeuvre

HEAT 1 1/2 pounds green grapes in 2 tablespoons water for a few minutes, or until they are tender. Mash the grapes and force them through a double layer of cheese-cloth. There should be about 2 cups juice. Cool the grape juice, pour it over 3 Spanish onions, thinly sliced, and 1 pound dried currants, and marinate the mixture in the refrigerator for 3 hours. Serve on chilled plates.

﹩ Radishes with Piquant Butter

WASH and trim 12 perfect radishes, leaving each with a 1/4-inch green stem. Dry the radishes and cut them in half lengthwise, making sure that each half retains a piece of stem.

Cream 1/4 pound lightly salted butter with 1 tablespoon cream cheese. Blend in 1/4 teaspoon each of dry mustard, lemon juice, and onion juice, and a dash of Tabasco. Chill the butter until it is firm enough to pipe through a pastry tube. Pipe a circle of butter onto the cut surface of each radish half, using about 1/2 teaspoon butter for each half. Chill the radishes. Serve sprinkled with nutmeg.

Stuffed Snow-Pea Pods 🐾

POUR boiling salted water over 50 small unopened snow-pea pods, no more than 1 1/2 inches long, and let them soak for 1 minute. Drain and dry the pods. While they are still warm make an incision 1/4 inch long across the width in the flat side of each pod. Using a sharp pointed knife, cut through just to the inside of the pod. The opposite side must not be cut. Cool the pods.

Blend 18 ounces softened cream cheese with 6 tablespoons fresh tomato purée, 6 teaspoons mayonnaise, 1/2 teaspoon dry mustard, 1/4 teaspoon powdered coriander, and salt and white pepper to taste. Using a metal cake decorator fitted with a small plain tube, pipe the cheese mixture into the pea pods through the incision. Chill the pods for at least 1 hour before serving.

Spinach Hors-d'Oeuvre 🐾

WASH 1/2 pound spinach and combine it with 1/2 cup parsley, loosely packed, 1 onion, coarsely chopped, and 2 tarragon leaves. Cook the mixture slowly in only the water that clings to the spinach leaves, for about 5 minutes. Drain the mixture, pressing out all the water, and combine it with 2 hard-cooked eggs, 3 sardines, and 2 anchovy filets, all chopped. Pound the mixture and force it through a sieve or purée it in a blender. Season it with salt and pepper to taste, spread it thickly on a baking sheet, and chill it. Cut the spinach hors-d'oeuvre into small pieces and arrange them on crushed ice in a silver dish. Serve with triangles of whole-wheat toast.

Cherry Tomatoes with Ham and Chicken Mousse 🐾

CUT a slice from the tops of 3 pints cherry tomatoes and scoop out the pulp.

Combine 1/2 cup each of finely ground ham and finely ground chicken breast, both cooked, with 2 tablespoons each of chicken stock and light cream, and 1 teaspoon each of parsley and celery leaves, both finely chopped. Force the mixture through a sieve or purée it in a blender.

Soak 1 envelope of gelatin in 1/2 cup cold chicken stock for 5 minutes and dissolve it in 1/2 cup hot chicken stock. In a saucepan lightly beat 1 egg yolk and gradually stir in the dissolved gelatin. Cook the mixture over low heat, stirring constantly, until it thickens. Do not let it boil. Remove the pan from the heat, add salt and freshly ground white pepper to taste, and cool the mixture thoroughly.

Combine the meat paste and cooled chicken jelly. Fold in 1/4 cup cream, whipped, and 1 egg white, stiffly beaten. Fill the tomato shells with the mousse and chill them until the mousse is set. Decorate each tomato with a circle of grated cucumber, thoroughly drained.

Cherry Tomatoes Filled with Cheese

MASH 1/4 pound bleu cheese and thin it with 1/2 cup sour cream. Add 1 small onion, grated, and black pepper to taste. Cut a slice from the tops of 1 pint cherry tomatoes and scoop out the pulp. Fill the shells with the cheese mixture.

Vegetable Hors-d'Oeuvre

ARRANGE in the center of an oval platter a mound of tiny cherry tomatoes. Around them arrange overlapping thin slices of cucumber and sprinkle the cucumbers with chopped chives. At either end of the platter arrange mounds of black olives and red radishes. Sprinkle French dressing lightly over all and chill the vegetables. Serve with thin slices of pumpernickel.

Blanching Almonds

REMOVE the shells from almonds, cover the nuts with boiling water, and let them stand for 1 minute. Drain the nuts, rinse them in cold water, and slip off the skins.

Spread the almonds in a single layer in a shallow pan and dry them, shaking the pan frequently, in a slow oven (300° F.) for about 15 minutes. Do not let them brown. The dry almonds can be slivered, grated, or ground, as the recipe indicates.

Sautéed Almonds

SAUTÉ 2 cups dried blanched almonds in 6 tablespoons butter, stirring with a wooden spoon, until the nuts are golden. Remove the skillet from the heat, add salt to taste, and stir for a few minutes more, or until the browning ceases.

Curried Almonds 𝕊

HEAT 1/4 cup olive oil in a chafing dish over direct heat. Add 2 cups dried blanched almonds and 1 tablespoon curry powder, and cook the nuts, stirring constantly, until they are golden. Sprinkle lightly with salt and serve hot.

Spiced Brazil Nuts 𝕊

IN a large heavy skillet sauté 2 cups Brazil nuts, shelled, in 6 tablespoons butter over low heat, stirring the nuts constantly with a wooden spoon. As the nuts brown, sprinkle them with 2 teaspoons ginger and 1 teaspoon dry mustard. Remove the nuts from the heat, continuing to stir until the browning ceases, and sprinkle them with 2 teaspoons coarse salt. For the large cocktail party, double the recipe, but sauté at one time only enough Brazil nuts to make a single layer in the skillet.

Toasted Brazil Nut Chips 𝕊

COVER 3 cups Brazil nuts, shelled, with cold water, slowly bring the water to a boil, and simmer the nuts for 2 or 3 minutes. Drain the nuts and cut them lengthwise into thin slices. Spread the nuts on a baking sheet, dot them with butter, and sprinkle them with salt. Bake the nuts in a moderate oven (350° F.) for 12 to 15 minutes, stirring them frequently. Serve with cocktails.

Toasted Hazelnuts 𝕊

NOISETTES SAUTÉES

IN a saucepan heat 1/2 cup butter or olive oil. Add 2 cups shelled hazelnuts and cook them, stirring with a wooden spoon, until they are golden brown. Remove the pan from the heat and continue to stir the nuts for a few minutes; they will turn a deeper brown. Sprinkle lightly with 1 to 2 tablespoons coarse salt.

Chili Peanuts 𝕊

TOAST shelled and peeled peanuts in a moderate oven (350° F.) until they are golden brown, shaking the pan occasionally to ensure even toasting. Sprinkle the

hot nuts with chili powder and salt. Cool the nuts and shake off the excess seasoning. Cashew nuts, almonds, or Brazil nuts, may also be toasted in this manner.

⸙ Curried Walnuts

HEAT 1/4 cup olive oil in a skillet and add 1 tablespoon each of curry powder and
Worcestershire sauce and a pinch of cayenne. Stir the mixture and, when it is very
hot, add 2 cups shelled walnuts. Stir the nuts until they are well coated. Spread the
nuts on a baking sheet lined with brown paper and bake them in a slow oven
(300° F.) for 10 minutes, or until they are crisp. Almonds or cashew nuts may
also be curried in this manner. Serve with cocktails.

⸙ Shrimp in Cucumber Boats

CUT a strip from the long side of 6 peeled cucumbers. Hollow out the cucumbers,
remove the seeds, and cut a thin slice from the bottom of each cucumber so that
they will balance evenly on the plates. Rub the insides with salt, pepper, oil,
and vinegar to taste. Fill the cucumber boats with well-seasoned chilled shrimp,
poached, shelled, and deveined. Decorate the shimp boats with mayonnaise and
sprinkle them with finely chopped dill. Garnish each plate with Italian parsley and
serve chilled.

⸙ Pickled Shrimp and Onion

BRING to a boil 6 cups water with 1/4 cup crab boil tied in cheesecloth. (Crab boil
is a mixture of spices and herbs especially prepared for seafood and available every-
where in the Louisiana area and at specialty shops elsewhere.) Boil the water and
crab boil for 5 minutes, add 2 1/2 pounds raw shrimp, and cook them for 5 minutes,
or until they turn pink. Drain the shrimp, shell and devein them, and arrange a few
in an earthenware bowl. Cover them with a layer of sliced raw onion and lay 3 bay
leaves on the onions. Fill the bowl with the alternating layers, finishing with a layer
of onion. Combine 1 cup olive oil with 3/4 cup white vinegar, 5 teaspoons celery
seed, and 3 teaspoons salt. Pour this dressing over the shrimp and onions, cover
the dish, and let the shrimp pickle for at least 24 hours in a cool place. Drain the
pickle to serve.

Shrimp in Cucumber Boats

Pickled Shrimp

SIMMER together for 15 minutes 2 cups each of white wine and water, 1 cup each of olive oil and white-wine vinegar, 2 leeks, diced, 2 hot red peppers, 1 bunch of parsley, 7 sprigs of celery leaves, 8 whole peppercorns, 3 whole cloves, a sprig each of tarragon and thyme, a 1-inch cinnamon stick and 1 tablespoon brown sugar. Add 4 pounds raw shrimp and simmer them for 5 minutes, or until they turn pink. Cool the shrimp in the broth, shell and devein them, and turn them into hot sterilized jars. Strain the broth and fill the jars to overflowing. Cover the jars and store pickled shrimp in the refrigerator. Drain them and serve with cocktails.

Shrimp with Curry Mayonnaise

SHELL and devein 2 pounds cooked shrimp and chill them thoroughly. Pierce the shrimp with cocktail picks and serve them in large bowls of crushed ice, with a bowl of curry mayonnaise in the center.

For the large wedding reception prepare 8 pounds shrimp.

Shrimp with Green Tomato Sauce

PUT 2 pounds raw shrimp in a saucepan with just enough beer to cover. Bring the beer to a boil, add a pinch of thyme and a bay leaf, and cover the pan. Simmer the shrimp for about 5 minutes, or until they turn bright pink. Cool the shrimp in the stock, shell and devein them, and chill them thoroughly. Arrange the shrimp on a chilled platter, pierce each with a cocktail skewer, and serve with green tomato sauce.

Clams on the Half Shell

FOR each serving, scrub and shuck 6 clams, being careful not to lose any of the juice, and discard the top shells. Arrange the clams on a bed of crushed ice and sprinkle them with lemon juice and finely grated horseradish.

Oysters on the Half Shell 𝕊𝕓

OPEN 36 oysters and leave the oysters loose in the deep bottom half of the shell. For each serving, arrange 6 opened oysters on a bed of finely chopped ice. Sprinkle with freshly ground black pepper and garnish with a wedge of lemon. If desired, put a small dish of horseradish or cocktail sauce in the middle of the plate.

HUÎTRES AU CAVIAR   ## Oysters Imperial 𝕊𝕓

FOR each serving, arrange 6 freshly shucked oysters on a bed of finely chopped ice. Spread each oyster with 1/2 teaspoon black caviar and sprinkle the caviar with minced chives and a few drops of lemon juice.

Mussels Vinaigrette 𝕊𝕓

PUT 24 mussels, cleaned and trimmed, in a kettle with 1/4 cup dry white wine, 1 bay leaf, and 1/2 stalk of celery. Cover the kettle and steam the mussels for 8 to 10 minutes, or until they open. Remove the mussels and cool and chill them. Reduce the liquor in the kettle to 1 cup, strain it, and combine it with 2 table-spoons olive oil, 1 tablespoon lemon juice, 1 teaspoon chopped fresh dill, 1/8 tea-spoon sugar, and salt and pepper to taste. Pour the sauce over the chilled mussels and marinate them in the refrigerator for several hours or overnight. Serve cold.

Smoked Salmon 𝕊𝕓

CUT 1/2 pound smoked salmon into paper-thin slices and arrange them on a chilled platter with sprigs of parsley, lemon wedges, and capers. Border the platter with thin slices of dark bread spread with sweet butter. Serve with a cruet of olive oil.

Foie Gras in Aspic 𝕊𝕓

LINE 1 1/2-inch molds with a layer of aspic flavored with Cognac. Pour more aspic into a shallow pan to set and reserve as garnish. In the bottom of each mold put a thin round of truffle, top with a 1-inch cube of *foie gras*, and cover with a slice of

Assorted Hors-d'Oeuvre

Jamaican Avocado Balls (p. 127), Cherry Tomatoes with Ham and Chicken
Mousse (p. 149), Truffles in Pastry (p. 177), Parsley Fritters (p. 444).

smoked tongue. Fill the molds with cool but still liquid aspic and chill them until the jelly sets. To serve, dip the molds in warm water and unmold them on a chilled platter. Spread the reserved aspic on wax paper and chop it with a large knife. Garnish the platter with the chopped aspic and with bouquets of watercress.

Calf's Foot Jelly

IN a kettle put 2 cleaned calf's feet, cut in pieces, in cold water to cover, bring the water to a boil, and cook the calf's feet for 10 minutes. Skim the broth, add 1 onion, 1 garlic clove, 3 bay leaves, and 1 teaspoon peppercorns, and simmer the calf's feet, covered, for 1 hour. Skim the broth again, and continue simmering the calf's feet, covered, for 3 hours more, or until the meat and gristle begin to fall from the bones. Strain the broth. Cut the usable meat into fine cubes, add them to the strained broth, and add 2 tablespoons lemon juice or 1/4 cup vinegar and salt to taste. Quickly bring the broth to a boil, cook it for 5 minutes more, and skim the surface.

Let the broth cool until it is partly jelled and remove any fat that rises to the surface. Slice 3 hard-cooked eggs, arrange some of the slices on the bottom of an oblong dish about 2 inches deep, and stand the remaining slices upright along the sides of the dish. Turn the partly jelled broth into the dish and chill the jelly for 3 hours, or until it is very firm. Unmold the jelly on a chilled platter and cut it into slices. Garnish with overlapping slices of lemon and cucumber.

Fig Roulades

CUT fresh figs into strips 3/4 inch long and 1/2 inch wide. Cut very thin slices of *prosciutto* into strips 3/4 inch wide and 2 inches long. Mash together an equal amount of Roquefort and cream cheese, enough heavy cream to make a mixture easy to spread, and a few drops of Cognac. Spread each strip of *prosciutto* with a thin layer of the cheese mixture. Put a strip of fig at one end and roll up the *prosciutto* jelly-roll fashion. Chill the *roulades* thoroughly.

Figs and Westphalian Ham

CUT 12 fresh figs into halves. For each serving place 4 halves on fig leaves or vine leaves on a plate with 2 very thin slices of Westphalian ham.

Kumquats with Smoked Tongue Mousse

PUT enough cooked smoked tongue through a food chopper to make 1 cup ground meat. Put the tongue again through the fine blade of the chopper with 2 tablespoons dried currants, plumped in warmed Madeira. Stir in 1 teaspoon each of chopped parsley and celery leaves. Work the mixture with a wooden spoon until it is smooth. Soften 2 teaspoons gelatin in 4 tablespoons cold chicken stock and dissolve it over low heat. Combine the puréed tongue and the gelatin and heat thoroughly. Remove the mixture from the heat, stir in 2 egg yolks, lightly beaten, and cool. Stir in 1/4 cup whipped cream and 2 egg whites, stiffly beaten, and chill the mixture for 2 hours, or until it is set. Halve 48 kumquats and set a mound of mousse on the cut side of each oval. Sprinkle with finely chopped parsley or mint and chill until serving time.

Prosciutto and Melon   JAMBON CRU ET MELON

CUT a chilled cantaloupe, honeydew, or Persian melon lengthwise in half and remove the seeds and rind. Cut the fruit into crescent-shaped slices and put 2 on each serving plate. Cover each melon slice with thin slices of *prosciutto* and garnish with a thin wedge of lime.

Dried Beef Rolls

BLEND 8 ounces soft cream cheese with 1/2 cup finely minced pickled mushrooms and 1 tablespoon minced chives. Spread the mixture on 20 thin slices of dried beef, roll them into cornucopias, and garnish the open end with a spray of watercress.

Rollatini di Mortadella   MORTADELLA SAUSAGE ROLLS

BLEND 8 ounces cream cheese with 1/2 cup heavy cream and spread it evenly on 8 very thin slices of large *mortadella* (Italian sausage). Blend 1/2 cup grated cucumber, well drained, with 2 teaspoons mayonnaise and spread it over the cheese. Roll up the *mortadella* like a jelly roll, wrap the rolls firmly in wax paper, and freeze them for at least 1 hour. Cut the rolls in 1/2-inch slices and serve them frozen. Makes about 50.

Salami Cornucopias 🐟

Cut Italian salami into 40 paper-thin slices and cut each slice in half. Twist the half slices into cornucopias and press the edges together to seal them. Place the cones upright in a wire rack and chill them for 30 minutes.

Blend 1 1/2 pounds soft cream cheese with 12 ounces bleu cheese and 4 tablespoons heavy cream. Add 4 teaspoons minced fresh dill and 4 tablespoons Cognac. Using a pastry bag fitted with a fluted tube, pipe the cheese mixture into the cornucopias. Chill them for at least 1 hour.

Chicken Livers and Shrimp en Brochette 🐟

Halve as many chicken livers as desired and wrap each half in a slice of bacon with a cooked shrimp, shelled and deveined. Skewer the liver and shrimp pairs and broil them, turning the skewers once, until the bacon is crisp.

Skewered Scallops 🐟

Wash and dry scallops and cover them with a mixture of equal parts of dry Sherry, soy sauce, and olive oil, 1 teaspoon finely chopped fresh gingerroot, and 1/2 teaspoon finely chopped garlic. Marinate the scallops for 30 minutes and drain them. Thread the scallops on skewers alternately with squares of Canadian bacon. Broil the scallops, turning the skewers frequently for even cooking, until they are cooked and lightly browned.

Duckling Saté 🐟

Cut the meat of a raw 4 1/2-pound duckling into 3/4-inch cubes, leaving some skin on each piece. Combine 1 cup soy sauce with 1/2 cup each of orange juice and peanut oil, 1/4 cup each of honey and lemon juice, 4 shallots, finely chopped, 1 teaspoon ground coriander, and 1/2 teaspoon freshly ground pepper. Marinate the duckling cubes in this mixture for 4 to 6 hours, drain them, and reserve the marinade. Thread the cubed duckling on skewers alternately with cubes of fresh pineapple and small pickled onions. Broil the duckling slowly over hot coals, or under the broiler, turning frequently, for 12 to 15 minutes, or until the meat is tender and the skin is crisp and browned. Strain the reserved marinade, heat it, and use as a dip.

Indonesian Satés

Cut 1 1/2 pounds very lean loin of pork into 3/4-inch cubes. Combine the juice of 2 lemons with 2 garlic cloves, finely chopped, 4 tablespoons *ketjap* (an Indonesian barbecue sauce), and 3/4 teaspoon salt. Marinate the cubes in this mixture, turning the pieces occasionally, for 2 to 4 hours. Drain the meat, reserving the marinade, and thread 4 or 5 cubes on each skewer. Broil the meat over hot coals or under medium heat for about 15 minutes, or until it is well done, and serve with the following sauce:

In a saucepan blend the reserved marinade with 2 tablespoons peanut butter, 1 tablespoon each of *ketjap*, butter, and lemon juice, and 1/2 teaspoon each of sugar and *sambal oelek* (dried red peppers, finely crushed). Cook the sauce over low heat, stirring constantly, until it is thick. Remove the pan from the heat and gradually stir in 1/4 cup light cream. If the sauce is too sweet, add lemon juice to taste. Reheat the sauce over low heat, but do not let it boil. Pour the sauce over the *satés* or serve as a dip. Makes about 20 *satés*.

Kibbe Kebabs

Rinse 1 1/2 cups bulgur, or cracked wheat, soak it in cold water for 1 hour, and drain it. Put 1 1/2 pounds lean raw lamb and 2 medium onions through a food chopper twice. Add to the ground mixture 1/2 cup pine nuts, the bulgur, and salt to taste. Shape the mixture into marble-sized balls and thread them on skewers alternately with pitted cherries. Brush the kebabs with melted butter and broil them over hot coals, or under the broiler, turning the skewers frequently, until the kebabs are browned. Makes about 30 kebabs.

Salmon Pâté   PÂTÉ DE SAUMON

Put 1 pound filets of sole or pike through the finest blade of a food chopper. Mix in well 1 cup soft butter. Moisten 1 cup fresh bread crumbs with 1/4 cup heavy cream and add 2 egg yolks, beaten, 1/4 cup each of parsley, shallots, and dill, all chopped, and salt and Nepal or cayenne pepper to taste. Combine the ground fish and bread-crumb mixtures and beat the forcemeat with a fork until it is light and fluffy. Line the bottom of a terrine or baking dish with a 1/2-inch layer of the forcemeat and cover it with a layer of thin salmon steaks, free of skin and bone. Season the steaks with salt and mace and continue to fill the dish with alternate layers of salmon and forcemeat. Dot the top with 1/4 cup butter, cover the terrine tightly, and seal it with adhesive tape. Bake the pâté in a slow oven (300° F.) for 2 1/2 hours. Let it cool before removing the cover. Unmold the pâté on a bed of lettuce or watercress and coat it with green mayonnaise.

Potted Shrimp Pâté 🦐

POACH 2 pounds shrimp in court bouillon for about 5 minutes, or until they turn bright pink. Shell and devein the shrimp and put them through the finest blade of a food chopper to obtain a smooth paste. Blend in well 3/4 cup lemon juice and powdered ginger, paprika, salt, and Nepal or cayenne pepper to taste. Beat in gradually 1 cup olive oil and continue whipping the mixture until it is creamy. Pack the pâté in a jar, cover the top with clarified butter, and seal the jar with a lid. Chill the pâté thoroughly. Serve with toasted crackers or buttered toast.

Chicken Pâté 🦐

POACH a 3 1/2- to 4-pound chicken, cool it, and remove the skin and the breast. Split the breast in half and cut each filet lengthwise into thick slices. Put the dark leg meat and 2 1/2 pounds fatty fresh pork through the finest blade of a food chopper and pound the meat until it is very smooth with a pinch each of orégano, thyme, savory, salt, and pepper. Mix in 1/2 cup Madeira. Line the bottom and sides of a terrine or baking dish with thin slices of salt pork and put a layer of the force-meat into the pan. Wrap each piece of chicken breast in a slice of salt pork and arrange the pieces lengthwise in the mold with 1/2 pound chicken livers. Fill the remaining spaces with the forcemeat and finish with 2 bay leaves and slices of salt pork. Cover the pâté with foil, put it in a pan half filled with water, and bake it in a hot oven (400° F.) for 2 hours. Chill the pâté. To serve, unmold the pâté on a chilled platter and garnish with small whole beets. Serve mayonnaise separately in a sauceboat.

ᔥ Pâté Gourmet

PUT 2 pounds chicken livers in a saucepan with water to cover and add several sprigs of parsley, a bay leaf, and a pinch of thyme. Simmer the livers, covered, for 20 minutes. Drain the livers, chop them coarsely, and put them through the finest blade of a food chopper. Mix the liver paste with 1 cup melted butter and stir in 1 1/2 teaspoons each of salt and mustard, 1/4 teaspoon ground cloves, a pinch each of cayenne and nutmeg, and 2 jiggers Cognac. Beat the mixture vigorously, pack the pâté in a crock, and chill it. Serve with toast rounds.

ᔥ Chicken Liver and Onion Pâté

SAUTÉ 2 large onions, thinly sliced, in 1/4 cup rendered chicken fat until they are golden. Add to the pan 1 pound chicken livers, diced, and 1 1/2 garlic cloves, chopped, and sauté the mixture until the livers are cooked but not browned. Season the mixture highly with coarsely ground pepper and salt and put it through a food chopper or mash it to a paste with a fork, gradually adding Port wine to taste. Pack the pâté in a jar, cover the top with clarified butter, and chill it thoroughly. Serve with buttered rye bread.

ᔥ Chicken Liver Ramekins

PUT 1 pound chicken livers through the finest blade of a food chopper. Add 2/3 cup finely chopped mushrooms, 4 egg yolks, well beaten, 4 tablespoons heavy cream, 3 tablespoons chopped parsley, 1 1/2 tablespoons melted butter, and salt and cayenne to taste. Butter 6 ramekins and pack them with the liver mixture. Cover the molds with buttered wax paper, put them in a pan of water, and bake them in a moderate oven (350° F.) for 30 to 40 minutes. Serve hot or cold.

ᔥ Duck Liver Pâté

PUT 1/2 pound duck livers in a saucepan, add water to cover, and cook the livers, covered, for about 15 minutes, or until they are tender. Drain the livers, cut them into pieces, and put them in the container of a blender. Add 1/3 cup soft butter, 2 tablespoons finely minced onion, 1/2 teaspoon each of salt and dry mustard, a pinch each of cloves, cayenne, and nutmeg, and 1 generous tablespoon of Bourbon. Cover the container and blend the mixture until it is smooth. Stir in 1 truffle, finely chopped. Pack the pâté in a crock and chill it thoroughly.

Ham and Veal Pâté

TRIM 1 pound veal cutlets and 1/2 pound thickly sliced ham, and cut the meat into equal-sized pieces. Lard the veal with ham fat and set aside the veal and sliced ham in layers. Chop the meat trimmings and blend them with 1 pound sausage meat and 1/2 cup bread crumbs. Moisten the mixture with 1/4 cup milk and season it with salt, pepper, and ground cloves to taste.

Line the bottom and sides of a terrine or long narrow baking dish with thin slices of bacon and add a bay leaf and a pinch of thyme. Spread a layer of the sausage mixture 1/4 inch thick on the bacon and top with a layer of ham and veal. Spread with another layer of the sausage mixture and arrange 3 hard-cooked eggs down the center of the dish, pressing them in firmly. Cover the eggs with a third layer of the sausage mixture and top with veal and ham slices. Fill the dish with the rest of the sausage mixture and top with 2 bay leaves and a pinch of thyme. Cover the dish, set it in a shallow pan in 1 inch of boiling water, and bake the pâté in a moderately hot oven (375° F.) for 1 1/2 hours. Cover the pan with wax paper and a 2-pound weight and chill the pâté thoroughly. Unmold it on a chilled platter and garnish with watercress.

Pork Pâté

PUT 1 pound each of pork fat and lean pork through the finest blade of a food chopper. Add 2 eggs, beaten, 1 teaspoon tarragon, 1/2 teaspoon cuminseed, and salt and pepper to taste. Ignite 1/4 cup heated Cognac, add it to the forcemeat, and put the mixture through a sieve. If necessary, pound the mixture in a mortar to obtain a smooth paste. Add 1 cup finely chopped truffles. Line the bottom and sides of a terrine or baking dish with thin sheets of larding pork and fill the terrine with the forcemeat. Bake the pâté in a moderate oven (350° F.) for 1 1/2 to 2 hours. Chill it, turn it out on a chilled platter, and serve in thin slices.

ᔍ English Pork Cheese

DICE finely 1 pound cold roast pork with some of the fat. Season the meat with 1/2 teaspoon grated lemon rind, 1/4 teaspoon freshly grated nutmeg, generous pinches of powdered sage and thyme, and salt and pepper to taste. Stir in 1 table-spoon finely chopped parsley. Pack the mixture into a loaf pan, pour over it 1/2 cup double-strength chicken stock, and bake the loaf in a moderate oven (350° F.) for about 1 1/4 hours. Chill the loaf, turn it out on a chilled platter, and serve as hors-d'oeuvre or as a sandwich spread.

ᔍ Broiled Chutney Prunes

SOAK large prunes overnight in Port wine to cover. Drain the prunes, remove the pits, and fill the cavities with chutney. Wrap each prune in a strip of bacon and secure the bacon with wooden picks. Cook the prunes in the blazer of a chafing dish over direct heat until the bacon is crisp. Drain on absorbent paper and serve hot.

ᔍ French Fried Ravioli

To make a meat filling, combine 1/2 cup minced cooked lamb or pork, 1/2 cup finely chopped cooked spinach, 2 teaspoons grated Parmesan, 1 egg yolk, 1 slice each of *prosciutto* and Italian salami, finely chopped, and salt, pepper, and nutmeg to taste.

To make a cheese filling, mix together 1/2 pound *ricotta* cheese, 1 egg, 1 table-spoon Parmesan, and salt and pepper to taste.

Sift 1 1/2 cups flour and a dash of salt into a bowl. Stir in 1 egg, lightly beaten, and enough lukewarm water to make a stiff dough. Knead the dough until it is smooth, cover it with a warm bowl, and let it rest for 30 minutes. Roll out the dough on a lightly floured board into 2 thin identical sheets. Drop the prepared meat or cheese filling by quarter teaspoons less than an inch apart on one sheet, cover with the second sheet, and press firmly around each mound to form small filled squares. With a pastry cutter, cut the dough between the mounds. Let the ravioli rest for 15 minutes.

Plunge the ravioli into deep hot fat (370° F.) and fry them until they are a rich golden brown. Drain them on absorbent paper, sprinkle with salt, and serve hot.

Fried Parmesan Balls 🝛

MIX together 1 1/2 cups fresh bread crumbs, 1/2 pound grated Parmesan, 1/4 teaspoon each of salt and pepper, and a dash of nutmeg. Blend in 3 eggs, lightly beaten, and 1/2 tablespoon chopped parsley. Shape the batter into small balls, roll the balls in flour, dip them in beaten egg, and fry them in deep hot fat (375° F.) until they are golden. Drain on absorbent paper and serve hot. Makes 30 to 40 cheese balls.

Greek Meatballs 🝛

BLEND 3/4 pound ground round steak with 1 egg, slightly beaten. Add 1 onion, finely chopped, 2 slices toast, soaked in water and squeezed dry, 1 tablespoon each of olive oil and lemon juice, 2 tablespoons chopped parsley, 1 tablespoon chopped fresh mint, 1/4 teaspoon cinnamon, and salt and pepper to taste. Let the mixture stand for 30 minutes. Shape it into 20 walnut-sized balls, roll the balls very lightly in flour, and brown them on all sides in hot butter.

Veal Balls 🝛

BLEND 2 cups ground cooked veal with 2 eggs, well beaten, 4 anchovy filets, chopped, 1/2 teaspoon finely chopped parsley, and pepper to taste. Form the mixture into small balls and roll them in cornstarch. Brown the veal balls in 6 tablespoons butter in the blazer of a chafing dish over direct heat. Pierce the balls with cocktail picks, and serve with a bowl of sour cream for dipping. Makes about 25.

Poached Beef Marrow 🝛

REMOVE the marrow from a split beef bone and cut it into small dice. Poach it in boiling salted water for 1 or 2 minutes and drain it. Serve on hot buttered toast.

Anchovy Cheese Crostini 🝛

CUT French bread into rounds 1/4 inch thick and on each put a slice of provolone or Bel Paese cheese. Arrange the rounds in an overlapping row in a baking dish and bake them in a hot oven (400° F.) until the cheese is melted. In a saucepan heat to-gether 10 anchovy filets, mashed, and 1/2 cup butter. Pour the sauce over the *crostini*.

ᔑ Anchovy Fritters

WASH 24 anchovy filets carefully in lukewarm water and dry them. Put the an-chovies in a bowl with 4 tablespoons lemon juice and 2 teaspoons finely chopped shallot or scallion, cover the bowl, and marinate them for 1 hour. Drain the an-chovies, dip them in the beer batter I, and fry them in deep hot fat (375° F.) until they are crisp and golden brown. Drain the anchovies on absorbent paper, sprinkle them with chopped parsley, and serve at once.

Beer Batter I

SIFT 1/2 cup sifted flour and 1/4 teaspoon salt into a bowl. Stir in 1 beaten egg and 1 tablespoon melted butter. Gradually add 1/2 cup flat beer and stir the batter until it is smooth. Let the batter stand at room temperature for 1 to 2 hours, and fold in 1 egg white, stiffly beaten.

ᔑ Stuffed Clams

SCRUB 24 clams and put them in a large kettle with 1/2 inch of salted water. Cover the kettle tightly and steam the clams for 6 to 10 minutes, or until they open. Discard any clams that do not open.

Remove the clams from the shells, reserving the bottom shells. Chop them finely and combine them with 1 tablespoon each of onion, parsley, and tarragon, all chopped, 1/2 cup buttered bread crumbs, and just enough béchamel sauce to bind the mixture. Add 1 tablespoon Sherry, salt and pepper to taste, and a few grains of cayenne. Fill the clam shells with this mixture, dot with butter and bread crumbs, and brown the surface very quickly under the broiler.

ᔑ Creamed Crab Meat and Almonds

IN the blazer of a chafing dish melt 4 tablespoons butter, add 1 pound cooked crab meat, and cook the crab, stirring, for 5 minutes, or until it is delicately browned.

Add 2/3 cup almonds, blanched, halved, and sautéed, 1/3 cup heavy cream, 3 tablespoons finely chopped parsley, and salt and pepper to taste, and cook all together for 2 minutes. Arrange the crab meat and almond mixture on rounds of toast.

HUÎTRES RÔTIES   Roasted Oysters 🦪

SCRUB and rinse under running cold water 36 oysters. Roast the unshucked oysters on a baking sheet in a very hot oven (450° F.) for about 15 minutes, or until the shells begin to open. Sprinkle the oysters with finely chopped fennel leaves. Serve in the shell, with hot melted butter and wedges of lemon.

CROUSTADES AUX HUÎTRES   Oyster Croustades 🦪

MELT 1/2 cup butter in the top of a double boiler over hot water. Add 1 1/2 teaspoons dry mustard and salt and pepper to taste and stir the mixture until it is thoroughly blended. Add slowly 2 cups heavy cream and cook the mixture, stirring, until it comes to a boil. Add 24 shucked oysters and cook them for 2 minutes, or until they just begin to curl. Add 2 tablespoons Sherry. Serve in croustades.

Shrimp Balls 🦪

MIX 4 cups ground cooked shrimp with 12 chopped water chestnuts and add 4 eggs and salt, pepper, and ground gingerroot to taste. Form the mixture into small balls, roll the balls in cornstarch, and brown them in 6 tablespoons butter in the blazer of a chafing dish over direct heat. Pierce the balls with cocktail picks. Makes about 50.

Shrimp Stuffed with Brazil Nuts 🦪

MAKE a paste of 1 1/2 teaspoons soy sauce and 3/4 teaspoon cornstarch, and combine it with 1/2 cup chopped Brazil nuts. Shell and devein 1 pound raw jumbo shrimp and split them down the backs without cutting them through. Stuff the shrimp with the Brazil-nut mixture, press the sides together, and chill the shrimp well.

Dip the shrimp in beer batter I and fry them in deep hot fat (380° F.) until they are puffed and golden. Drain on absorbent paper and serve with mustard butter.

Sole Gudgeons

CUT 6 filets of sole in small julienne and sauté them in butter for about 10 minutes, or until they are golden brown on both sides and flake easily at the touch of a fork. Sprinkle the strips with salt and arrange them in a mound on a platter. Garnish the mound with a ring of parsley and serve the filets with tartare sauce.

Baked Mushrooms

TRIM the stems of 1 1/2 pounds large mushrooms. Combine 1 tablespoon lemon juice and 3 tablespoons water in a bowl and add the mushroom caps. Chop the stems finely, combine them with 1/2 cup minced parsley, 1 teaspoon minced chives, and 1/2 teaspoon salt, and sauté the mixture in 3 tablespoons butter for 5 minutes.

Drain the mushroom caps, reserving the liquid, and arrange them in a buttered baking dish. Combine the reserved lemon water with the sautéed stems and put 1 teaspoon of the mixture in each mushroom cap. Bake the mushrooms in a moderate oven (350° F.) for 20 minutes.

Mushrooms with Garlic Butter

TRIM the stems of 1 1/2 pounds large mushrooms and reserve them for another use. Sprinkle the caps with lemon juice. Rub a skillet with a cut garlic clove, add 2 tablespoons oil, and sauté the mushroom caps until they are tender. Knead together 4 tablespoons each of butter and finely minced parsley and 2 garlic cloves, crushed. Spread the butter on large croûtes and arrange the mushrooms on the croûtes. Dot each mushroom with the seasoned butter and sprinkle liberally with minced parsley and paprika to taste. Broil the mushrooms under a hot broiler for 1 minute.

Mushrooms Baked with Olives

TRIM the stems of 1 1/2 pounds large mushrooms. Chop finely the stems and 12 pitted green olives and cook this mixture in 1/2 cup highly seasoned beef stock for

5 minutes. Add 2 tablespoons butter and, when the butter has melted, 1 cup bread crumbs. Fill the mushroom caps with the stuffing, arrange them in a baking dish, and pour 1/2 cup beef stock around them. Dot each cap with butter and bake the mushrooms in a moderate oven (350° F.) for about 20 minutes.

Mushrooms Stuffed with Crab Meat 🦀

COMBINE 1 cup cooked crab meat with 1 tablespoon dry bread crumbs, 1 tablespoon each of onion, parsley, and chives, all finely chopped, and 1 teaspoon salt. Stir in 1 egg, lightly beaten. Trim the stems of 1 1/2 pounds large mushrooms and reserve them for another use. Fill the caps with the crab-meat mixture. Sprinkle the mushrooms with buttered bread crumbs and freshly grated Parmesan and bake them in a moderate oven (350° F.) for 20 minutes.

Mushrooms Stuffed with Mussels 🦀

CHAMPIGNONS FARCIS AUX MOULES

STEAM 3 dozen mussels in 1/2 cup Sherry for 5 minutes, or until the shells open. Shell the mussels and set them aside.

Trim the stems of 1 1/2 pounds large mushrooms and chop them finely. Melt 2 tablespoons butter in a skillet and add the chopped stems, 1 teaspoon each of parsley and shallot, both minced, and salt, black pepper, and cayenne to taste. Sauté the mixture for 1 minute. Dip the mushroom caps in olive oil, seasoned with salt and pepper to taste, and broil them, 3 inches from the heat, for 5 minutes, or until they are tender. Spread the stem mixture on the caps, arrange a mussel on each cap, and sprinkle with buttered bread crumbs. Dot the crumbs with anchovy butter and brown the mushrooms quickly under the broiler. Serve on a heated platter, garnished with lemon wedges and watercress.

Mushrooms Stuffed with Pistachio Nuts 🦀

TRIM the stems of 1 1/2 pounds large mushrooms and chop them finely. In 2 tablespoons melted butter sauté the chopped stems, 1 cup ground pistachio nuts, and 2 teaspoons finely chopped onion for 5 minutes, stirring frequently. Remove the pan from the heat and add 1 cup soft bread crumbs, 1 tablespoon lemon juice, and salt and pepper to taste. Stuff the mushroom caps with this mixture. Melt 2 tablespoons butter in a skillet and sauté the mushrooms slowly for about 10 minutes, or until they are tender.

Cheese and Ham Barquettes

LINE 24 *barquette* molds with flaky pastry and chill them thoroughly.

Stir 3/4 cup scalded milk into 2 lightly beaten eggs. Add 1 1/2 cups ground cooked ham and 1/2 cup grated Swiss cheese and season with 1/4 teaspoon salt, a dash of pepper, and 1/8 teaspoon nutmeg. Fill the chilled *barquettes* to the brim with the mixture and bake them in a hot oven (400° F.) for 15 minutes, or until the crust browns and the custard is firm. Sprinkle the tarts with paprika, carefully remove them from the molds, and serve hot.

Mushroom Barquettes

LINE tiny *barquette* molds with unsweetened tart pastry, bake them, and remove the shells from the molds. Arrange them on a large baking sheet.

Melt 4 tablespoons butter in a saucepan and add 1 garlic clove, minced, 1 pound mushrooms, sliced, 2 tablespoons finely chopped parsley, and salt and pepper to taste. Cook the mixture, stirring frequently, until the mushrooms are tender. Fold in 1 cup hot sour cream and divide the mixture among the baked *barquettes*. Brown them quickly under the broiler and serve hot.

Oyster Barquettes

MAKE tiny boat-shaped shells of puff paste and bake them. Arrange the shells on a baking sheet. Put a cooked oyster in each baked *barquette* and mask the oysters with poulette sauce. Sprinkle the *barquettes* with fine dry bread crumbs, dot them with butter, and brown them quickly under the broiler. Serve hot.

Ham Bouchées

MAKE 30 *bouchées* and bake them.

Combine 2 cups cooked ham and 1/2 cup truffles, all finely chopped, with enough béchamel sauce to bind the mixture. Fill the shells with the ham mixture and top each *bouchée* with a thin slice of truffle.

Turkey Bouchées

MAKE 15 *bouchées* and bake them.

Put 1 cup cooked white meat of turkey through a food chopper and add enough mayonnaise, flavored with curry powder to taste, to bind the mixture. Fill the shells with the turkey mixture, and top each *bouchée* with a watercress leaf.

Bleu Cheese Profiteroles

MAKE 24 *profiteroles*, bake them, and cool thoroughly.

Blend 1/4 pound bleu cheese with 3 ounces cream cheese and 1/4 cup beer until the mixture is light and fluffy. Add 1/2 cup chopped toasted filberts or hazelnuts and soy sauce to taste. Split the *profiteroles* horizontally, fill them with the cheese mixture, and replace the tops.

Celeriac Profiteroles

MAKE 20 *profiteroles*, bake them, and cool thoroughly.

Simmer 2 celeriacs (also called celery knob or celery root) in salted water until they are tender. Cool the celeriacs, peel them, and dice them finely. Blend the dice with 1 teaspoon each of chopped chives and capers, a pinch of dry mustard, and enough mayonnaise to bind the mixture. Season with a dash of cayenne and salt and pepper to taste. Split the *profiteroles*, fill them with the celeriac mixture, and replace the tops.

Chive Almond Profiteroles

MAKE *profiteroles*, bake them, and cool thoroughly.

Whip cream cheese with enough heavy cream to make a fluffy paste. Add finely chopped almonds and chives to taste and blend the mixture well. Split the *profiteroles*, fill them with the cheese mixture, and replace the tops.

℘ Gingered Tuna Profiteroles

MAKE 40 *profiteroles*, bake them, and cool thoroughly.

Split the *profiteroles* and fill them with a mixture of 1 cup tuna fish mashed and blended with 3 tablespoons mayonnaise, 2 ounces cream cheese, 1 tablespoon grated fresh gingerroot, and salt and pepper to taste. Replace the tops to serve.

℘ Smoked Turkey Profiteroles

MAKE 75 *profiteroles*, bake them, and cool thoroughly.

Split the *profiteroles*, fill them with 2 cups very finely minced smoked turkey mixed with 1/2 cup finely chopped watercress and bound with mayonnaise, and replace the tops.

℘ Leek Quiche QUICHE AUX POIREAUX

ROLL chilled unsweetened tart pastry 1/8 inch thick. Line an 8-inch flan ring set on a baking sheet with the dough, prick it with a fork, and chill it for 30 minutes. Cover the inside of the shell with wax paper and fill it with dry rice or beans. Bake the tart in a hot oven (400° F.) for 10 minutes, or until the pastry is set but not browned. Remove the paper and rice and cool the shell. Put the shell on a platter and remove the flan ring.

In a heavy saucepan melt 3 tablespoons butter and add 1/2 cup water and 1 teaspoon salt. Add to the pan 3 cups sliced leeks, using the white parts only, cover the pan, and cook the mixture over moderate heat for 10 to 12 minutes, or until the pan juices have almost evaporated. Lower the heat, cook the leeks until they are soft, and drain them.

Beat together 3 eggs, 1 1/2 cups heavy cream, a generous grating of nutmeg, and 1/8 teaspoon pepper. Add the leeks and 1/4 cup grated Swiss cheese. Pour the mixture into the partially baked pastry shell, sprinkle the top with 1/4 cup grated Swiss cheese, and arrange thinly sliced triangles of Swiss or Gruyère cheese in a wheel-shaped pattern on the filling.

Dot the top of the *quiche* with 1 tablespoon butter and bake it in a moderately hot oven (375° F.) for 25 to 30 minutes, or until the pie is puffed and browned.

Assorted Hors-d'Oeuvre

Fig Roulades (p. 157), Penthouse Onions (p. 148), Canapés Grecques (p. 124),
Artichoke Bottoms with Smoked Salmon (p. 140).

ʃ♭ Miniature Crab Quiche

LINE 24 tiny fluted tart pans with unsweetened tart pastry and brush the dough with lightly beaten egg white. Bake the shells in a hot oven (400° F.) for 5 minutes, or until the pastry is just set. Cover the bottom of each shell with 1/4 to 1/2 teaspoon grated Parmesan, and add 1 teaspoon each of flaked cooked crab meat and grated Swiss cheese. Beat 1 egg and 1 egg yolk with 3/4 cup hot light cream, and add salt and pepper to taste and a pinch of ground coriander. Fill the tart shells nearly to the top with the mixture and bake the tarts in a moderately slow oven (325° F.) for about 15 minutes, or until the custard is set. Carefully remove the filled tarts from the pans. Serve hot.

ʃ♭ Miniature Pissaladière

LINE 24 tart pans, or gem pans, to half their depth with unsweetened tart pastry. Chill the tart shells on a baking sheet.

Sauté 2 Spanish onions, finely chopped, in 6 tablespoons butter until they are golden. In a saucepan heat 4 tablespoons olive oil, add 6 large ripe tomatoes, peeled, seeded, and chopped, and cook the tomatoes, mashing and stirring with a fork, until they form a thick paste and all the excess moisture is cooked away. Cover the bottom of the tart shells with freshly grated Parmesan and fill them with layers of the cooked onions, a pinch of rosemary, and the tomato paste. Top each tart with crossed anchovies and a slice of pitted ripe olive, and brush the surface with olive oil. Bake the tarts in a moderate oven (350° F.) for about 25 minutes, or until the shells are golden. Brush them again with olive oil. Carefully remove the tarts from the pans. Serve hot.

ʃ♭ Curried Crab Meat Tarts   PETITES TARTES AU CRABE

LINE 40 tiny tart pans with unsweetened tart pastry, bake them, and remove the shells from the pans.

Heat 2 cups flaked crab meat in 3 tablespoons melted butter. Add 1 cup hot rich cream sauce, 1 tablespoon grated onion, and 1 1/2 teaspoons curry powder, and heat the mixture just to the boiling point, stirring constantly. Divide the curried crab meat among the tart shells. Sprinkle the tarts with toasted chopped blanched almonds. Serve hot.

Mushroom and Swiss Cheese Tart 🦪

SAUTÉ 1 cup thinly sliced mushrooms in 1 1/2 tablespoons butter for 3 minutes. In another pan sauté 2 slices bacon, diced, until it is crisp and drain it on absorbent paper. Combine the mushrooms and bacon and add 1 cup cubed Swiss cheese and 1 onion, minced. Turn the mixture into a pie plate lined with flaky pastry.

Beat 4 eggs until they are light, stir in 2 cups heavy cream and 1/2 teaspoon each of nutmeg and pepper, and pour the mixture over the mushroom and cheese filling. Bake the tart in a hot oven (400° F.) for 10 minutes, reduce the heat to slow (300° F.), and bake the tart for 20 minutes longer.

Anchovy and Ham Turnovers 🦪

POUND to a paste 10 drained anchovy filets, 3 shallots, and 1 garlic clove. Add 2 tablespoons minced parsley, 2 tablespoons brandy, and 2 teaspoons each of oil from the anchovy tin, olive oil, and chopped chives. Let the mixture stand for 15 minutes and blend in thoroughly 2 cups chopped cooked ham, 4 tablespoons creamed butter, and 2 egg yolks.

Roll out chilled flaky pastry and cut out 50 small rounds. Put about 1 teaspoon of the paste in the center of each round, moisten the edges of the dough, and fold the rounds in half, pinching the edges together. Bake the turnovers in a moderate oven (350° F.) for about 15 minutes, or until they are golden brown.

Mushroom Turnovers 🦪

TRIM the stems from 1/2 pound mushrooms and chop and reserve the caps. Simmer the stems in 1 cup water with 1/4 teaspoon salt for 30 minutes. Strain and reserve the broth. Discard the stems.

Sauté 3 scallions and 2 tablespoons parsley, all finely chopped, in 2 tablespoons butter, until they are well coated. Add 1 teaspoon lemon juice, 1/2 teaspoon salt, and 1/4 teaspoon Tabasco and cook the mixture until the scallions are transparent. Add the mushroom caps and continue cooking the vegetables for 3 minutes, stirring occasionally.

In another pan blend together 2 tablespoons each of flour and melted butter. Gradually stir in 1/2 cup of the reserved mushroom broth and cook the sauce until it is smooth and thick. Blend in 1/2 cup sour cream. Add the sauce to the sautéed

Assorted Hors-d'Oeuvre

*Mushroom Turnovers (p. 175), Carrots and Mint (p. 412), Stuffed
Snow-Pea Pods (p. 149), Formosan Beets (p. 143).*

mushrooms and blend thoroughly. Remove the pan from the heat and cool the mixture. Roll out chilled unsweetened tart pastry and cut out 20 small rounds. Put 1 heaping teaspoon of the mushroom filling in the center of each round. Moisten the edges of the dough, fold the rounds in half, and pinch the edges together. Brush the tops of the turnovers lightly with *dorure* and bake them in a hot oven (400° F.) for 15 minutes, or until they are golden brown.

Mushroom and Artichoke Turnovers

CUT 3 pounds mushrooms into thin slices and sauté them gently with 5 tablespoons minced shallots or scallions in 4 tablespoons butter for 5 minutes. Add 4 tablespoons flour and cook the mixture, stirring, for 2 minutes. Add gradually 1 cup hot chicken stock and cook the sauce, stirring, until it is thick and smooth. Stir in 1 1/2 cups heavy cream and 4 tablespoons Madeira. Add salt and pepper and 1 1/2 cups finely diced cooked artichoke bottoms and cool the mixture.

Roll out chilled puff paste 1/8 inch thick and cut out 28 four-inch rounds. Put 1 teaspoon of the mushroom and artichoke mixture on half of each round and sprinkle it with a little finely chopped fresh dill. Fold the rounds in half, brush the edges with water, and crimp them to seal. Arrange them on a moistened baking sheet and chill for 20 minutes. Brush the turnovers with *dorure* and bake them in a very hot oven (450° F.) for 15 to 20 minutes, or until they are golden. Serve hot.

Truffles in Pastry

SIFT 2 cups sifted flour and 1/4 teaspoon salt in a mound on a pastry board. Make a well in the center of the mound and in it put 2 egg yolks, 1/2 cup soft butter, and 3/4 tablespoon olive oil. With the fingers, mix the center ingredients to a smooth paste, then quickly work in the flour, adding 1/2 to 3/4 cup cold water to make a firm dough that will not stick to the board. Cover the dough lightly with a cloth and let it rest for 1 hour. Roll out the dough 1/8 inch thick and cut it into 20 two-inch rounds.

Sauté 1 pound chicken livers in 3 tablespoons butter until they color slightly. Ignite 1 tablespoon heated Cognac and, when the flame subsides, pour the brandy over the livers. Continue cooking the livers until they are tender, mash them to a paste, and blend in all the liquid and fat remaining in the pan. Put 1/2 teaspoon liver paste in the center of each pastry round and 1 whole small peeled truffle on the paste. Fold the pastry around the filling and seal with a little cold water. Put the pastries on a lightly buttered baking sheet, brush them with beaten egg yolk, and bake them in a moderate oven (350° F.) for 15 minutes, or until they are well browned. Cool the pastries slightly before serving.

Foie Gras Pastries

ROLL out chilled flaky pastry or puff paste 1/8 inch thick and, with a fluted cutter, cut out 2-inch rounds. In the center of half the rounds put 1 teaspoon *purée de foie gras* blended with a little chopped truffle. Moisten the edges of the filled rounds, cover them with the remaining rounds, and press the edges firmly together. Arrange the pastries on a moistened baking sheet and chill for 20 minutes. Brush the tops of the pastries with *dorure* and bake them in a very hot oven (450° F.) for 15 minutes.

Purée de Foie Gras

WHIP 1 cup *pâté de foie gras* until it is light and fluffy, and stir in 1 tablespoon each of Cognac and chopped truffles.

Shad Pasties

CUT into tiny dice 2 medium potatoes, 2 carrots, and 2 onions, all cooked until barely tender. Combine the vegetables with 1 pound cooked shad, boned and flaked, and add 1 tablespoon finely chopped parsley and salt, pepper, and paprika to taste. Roll out chilled flaky pastry and cut out 6 circles 5 inches in diameter. Spoon the filling onto one half of each circle. Dot the filling with butter, fold over the other half, and crimp the edges together. Cut slits in the top to allow steam to escape and bake the pasties in a very hot oven (450° F.) for 10 minutes. Reduce the heat to moderately slow (325° F.) and bake the pasties for about 30 minutes, or until they are golden brown.

Bourekakia

GRATE 1/2 pound Feta cheese into a mixing bowl. Gradually work in 4 ounces cream cheese, 2 eggs, and a pinch of nutmeg, or purée the mixture in a blender.

Cut 8 commercial strudel leaves into 8 strips each, 8 by 1 1/2 inches. Keep the unused leaves covered tightly to prevent them from drying out. Lay 1 strip on a damp cloth and brush it lightly with melted sweet butter. Place 1/4 teaspoon of the cheese mixture on a corner of the strip and fold the corner over to cover the cheese and make a triangle. Continue to fold the strip of pastry in triangles along the full length of the strip. Repeat the procedure with the remaining strips. Chill the pastries on a buttered cookie sheet for 20 minutes, and bake them in a moderate oven (350° F.) for 15 minutes. Serve warm. Makes 64.

Miniature Kulebyaka

DISSOLVE 1 package of yeast in 1/4 cup lukewarm water. Sift 1 3/4 cups sifted flour, 2 teaspoons sugar, and 1/2 teaspoon salt onto a pastry board. Make a well in the center and in it put 3 eggs, lightly beaten. With the fingers work the flour into the eggs to make a soft dough and knead the dough for about 5 minutes. Scoop the dough up with the hands and crash it against the board at least 50 times. Cream 1/2 cup plus 2 tablespoons sweet butter and work it into the dough. Work in the dissolved yeast, knead in thoroughly an additional 1/2 cup sifted flour, and form the dough into a ball. Put the dough in a buttered and floured bowl, cover it with a damp towel, and let it rise in a warm place until it more than doubles in bulk. Punch down the dough, knead it for 2 minutes, and return it to the bowl. Cover the bowl and chill the dough in the freezer unit of the refrigerator for 1 hour, or overnight on a refrigerator shelf.

Roll out the dough 1/4 inch thick and cut out 2-inch squares. There should be about 48 squares. Brush the squares with 2 tablespoons melted butter. Sprinkle them evenly with 1/2 cup soft bread crumbs browned in butter, then with 2 hard-cooked eggs, finely chopped. Dot each square with 1/2 teaspoon sour cream. Put a 1 1/4-inch square of smoked salmon on each square and divide 8 large cooked shrimp, finely chopped, among the squares. Cover the shrimp with another 1/2 teaspoon sour cream, and sprinkle all with chopped dill, using about 2 tablespoons in all. Season lightly with salt and pepper. Roll up each square jelly-roll fashion, press the ends to seal them, and brush the rolls with beaten egg yolk. Arrange the *kulebyaka* on a buttered baking sheet and let them rise in a warm place for 15 minutes. Bake the rolls in a hot oven (400° F.) for about 20 minutes, or until they are nicely browned. Serve warm or at room temperature.

⤷ Croque Demoiselle

CUT very thin slices of white bread into 1-inch rounds and spread the rounds with a thin paste made by mixing grated Emmenthal cheese with a mixture of 3 parts heavy cream to 1 part Cognac. Cut cooked chicken breast into thin slices and cut the slices into 1-inch rounds. Put the chicken rounds on half the bread rounds and cover the chicken with thin slices of white truffle. Top the filled rounds with the remaining bread rounds. Dip the sandwiches in beaten egg and brown them on both sides in hot butter. Drain on absorbent paper and sprinkle lightly with paprika.

⤷ Onion Sandwiches

CUT thin slices of white bread into 1 1/2-inch rounds. Spread the rounds with butter and make sandwiches with thinly sliced sweet onion. Season with salt and pepper. Roll the edges of the sandwiches in mayonnaise and in chopped parsley. Chill for 2 hours before serving.

⤷ Pâté Sandwiches

SPLIT tiny finger rolls, butter them, and fill them with duck-liver pâté or with chicken-liver and onion pâté.

⤷ Tongue and Olive Sandwiches

MIX together 2 cups ground cooked tongue and 1 cup each of ground Brazil nuts and chopped black olives. Bind the mixture with mayonnaise and season it to taste with salt. Trim crusts from thin slices of white bread, butter the bread lightly, and spread each slice with the tongue and olive mixture. Roll up the slices, wrap them in wax paper, and chill them. Serve the rolls in thin slices. Makes about 50.

⤷ Ribbon Cubes

TRIM the crusts from 12 thin slices each of dark pumpernickel and light rye bread and trim the slices to uniform size and shape. It is convenient to spread 3 of the 6 sandwiches simultaneously. Assemble the sandwiches as follows: rye bread, smoked oyster butter, pumpernickel, seasoned cream cheese and mayonnaise, cooked breast of turkey, sliced 1/8 inch thick, seasoned cheese, pumpernickel, oyster butter, rye bread. Wrap the sandwiches in foil and chill them for at least 1 hour. Cut each sandwich into 16 cubes and arrange on a chilled platter.

Seasoned Cream Cheese and Mayonnaise

BLEND 6 ounces soft cream cheese with 3 tablespoons mayonnaise, 1 1/2 teaspoons prepared mustard, and 3/4 teaspoon sugar.

Smoked Oyster Butter

DRAIN a 3- to 4-ounce tin of smoked oysters and dry the oysters on absorbent paper. Force the oysters through a fine sieve. Cream 4 tablespoons sweet butter with the sieved oysters, 1/2 teaspoon lemon juice, and 1/4 teaspoon finely grated lemon rind. Chill the butter for 1 hour. Before using it, allow it to soften at room temperature until it can be spread easily.

Chicken and Ham Roll

PUT 1 1/2 pounds raw white chicken meat and 1/2 pound cooked ham through the finest blade of a food chopper. Sauté 1/4 pound chopped chicken livers in 1 tablespoon butter for 5 minutes and put them through the chopper. Combine the livers with the chicken and ham and blend in 3 eggs, beaten, 1 teaspoon grated onion, 3/4 teaspoon salt, and 1/4 teaspoon each of nutmeg and black pepper. Add 3 tablespoons crushed cracker crumbs and blend thoroughly. Turn the mixture out on wax paper, shape it into a roll about 2 1/2 inches thick and 12 inches long, and turn it out on a tea towel. Coat the roll with cracker crumbs, brush it with lightly beaten egg, and coat again with crumbs. Wrap the roll in the towel and tie the ends securely. Poach the roll gently in simmering salted water to cover for 1 hour, turning it after the first 30 minutes. Lift the roll from the liquid, cool it, and remove the cloth. Chill the roll for 12 hours and roll it in paprika to coat it thickly. Serve in very thin slices, on rounds of toast. Makes about 50 slices.

ᔥ Open Sandwiches

USE firm-textured bread for open sandwiches. Assemble the sandwiches at the last possible moment and cover them with plastic wrap until serving time.

Smoked Salmon

ARRANGE slices of smoked salmon on a thin slice of buttered pumpernickel bread. Place 3 little mounds of capers diagonally across the salmon and sprinkle all with finely chopped dill.

Roast Beef

LAY a slice of rare roast beef on a thin slice of buttered brown bread. Grind black pepper over the meat and garnish with curls of fresh horseradish.

Chicken

COVER a thin slice of buttered white bread with chopped watercress. Arrange on top a slice of cooked white chicken meat. Coat lightly with mayonnaise and decorate with 3 sprigs of fresh tarragon.

Goose Liver Pâté

SPREAD goose liver pâté on a thin slice of buttered white bread and sprinkle the pâté with chopped truffles.

ᔥ Luncheon Sandwiches

To serve luncheon sandwiches, arrange thin overlapping slices of pumpernickel, white, and whole-wheat bread around a large round platter. Fill the center with a circle of overlapping slices of French bread. Surround the platter of bread with bowls containing the following fillings.

Shrimp Filling

FLAVOR 1/2 cup mayonnaise with 2 small shallots, minced. Combine the shallot mayonnaise with 1/2 pound cooked shrimp, shelled, deveined, and coarsely chopped, and stir in 1 tablespoon capers. Add salt and pepper to taste. Pile the shrimp filling in a serving bowl and sprinkle it with paprika.

Tomato and Cream Cheese Filling

PEEL and halve 2 large ripe tomatoes, press the pulp through a fine sieve, and discard the seeds. Combine the purée with 8 ounces cream cheese, 2 garlic cloves, minced, and salt and pepper to taste. Pile the filling in a serving bowl and sprinkle it with chopped parsley.

Vegetable Filling

COMBINE 2 hard-cooked eggs, 1 bunch of radishes, 4 scallions, and 1/2 cup watercress leaves, all chopped, with 1/2 cucumber, peeled, seeded, and chopped. Season 1/2 cup mayonnaise with 1 teaspoon prepared mustard and stir it into the vegetables. Add salt and pepper to taste and put the filling in a serving bowl. Sprinkle with chopped dill.

Sorrel Roll

MELT 2 tablespoons butter, stir in 4 tablespoons flour, and cool the *roux* for a minute or two. Gradually add 1 cup milk and cook the sauce, stirring, until it is thick. Beat in 3 egg yolks, 1/2 teaspoon nutmeg, and salt and pepper to taste. Stir in 1 cup tightly packed chopped sorrel and fold in 3 egg whites, stiffly beaten. Line a jelly-roll pan, 12 by 15 inches, with buttered wax paper and sprinkle the paper thickly with bread crumbs. Spread the sorrel mixture evenly over the paper. Bake the roll in a moderately hot oven (375° F.) for 15 minutes, or until it starts to shrink from the sides of the pan. Heat together 1 cup each of sour cream and ground cooked ham and 1/4 cup chopped pistachio nuts, and spread the mixture on the baked roll. Roll it up and arrange it on a heated platter. Pour over it 1/3 cup melted butter mixed with 2 tablespoons lemon juice.

ꙮ Hors-d'Oeuvre Roll

OIL a jelly-roll pan, 10 by 15 inches, line it with wax paper, and oil the paper. Dust the paper lightly with flour.

In a saucepan melt 4 tablespoons butter. Add 1/2 cup flour and a pinch of salt and stir the *roux* over medium heat for about 1 minute. Gradually add 2 cups milk and cook the sauce, stirring constantly, for about 4 minutes. Remove the pan from the heat and blend in 4 egg yolks and 1 teaspoon sugar. Fold in 4 egg whites, stiffly beaten. Spread the batter evenly in the prepared pan and bake the roll in a moderately slow oven (325° F.) for 40 to 45 minutes, or until it is golden. Turn the pan over onto two overlapping sheets of wax paper, lift off the pan, and peel the paper from the bottom. Spread the roll with one of the fillings below and roll it up with the aid of the wax paper, lifting and rolling it gently onto itself. Serve the roll hot or cold, with lightly salted sour cream. This hors-d'oeuvre freezes well and may be reheated gently.

Red Caviar Filling

BLEND 4 ounces cream cheese with 2 tablespoons sour cream. Fold in 6 ounces red caviar. Force the mixture through a fine sieve, or purée it in a blender. Gently fold in 2 more ounces red caviar.

Chicken Filling

CHOP finely 1/4 pound mushrooms and sauté them lightly in 1 tablespoon butter until they are tender. Add 1 cup finely diced cooked chicken, 3 hard-cooked eggs, finely chopped, 4 tablespoons sour cream, 1 tablespoon chopped fresh dill, and salt and pepper to taste. Mix the ingredients well and heat the mixture in the top of a double boiler over hot water. Serve hot with sour cream seasoned with 1 teaspoon finely grated onion.

Mushroom Filling

SAUTÉ 2 large onions, chopped, in 4 tablespoons olive oil until they are soft and golden. Add 3/4 pound mushrooms, finely chopped, and cook them over low heat until they are tender. Add 4 tablespoons each of sour cream and finely chopped green onions, 2 tablespoons lemon juice, and salt and pepper to taste. Serve the roll hot when using this filling.

Hors-d'Oeuvre Roll with Red Caviar Filling

Ham Filling

MIX 1 1/2 cups cooked ham, finely chopped, with 1/2 cup chopped chives or green onions, 1 teaspoon grated horseradish, and 1/2 teaspoon Dijon-type mustard. Fold in 1 cup heavy cream, stiffly whipped.

Curried Shrimp Filling

COOK, shell, and devein 1 pound shrimp. Chop the shrimp finely with 3 tablespoons each of chutney and chopped preserved ginger and 2 teaspoons curry powder. Beat together 3 ounces cream cheese and 4 tablespoons sour cream and combine with the shrimp mixture.

❧ Stuffed Loaf

TRIM the ends from a long loaf of French or Italian bread and scoop out the crumbs to make a long hollow tube with a 1/4-inch crust. Fill the loaf with any of the following stuffings, wrap it in foil, and chill it for several hours or overnight. Cut the loaf in 1/4-inch slices.

Olive Stuffing

COMBINE the crumbs of the hollowed-out loaf of bread with 1 cup each of ripe olives and green olives stuffed with pimiento, all chopped, 4 tomatoes, peeled, seeded, and chopped, a little grated Parmesan, and chopped fresh herbs to taste. Mix in well about 2 tablespoons olive oil, or enough to moisten the mixture, a few drops of tarragon vinegar, and salt and pepper to taste.

Pistachio Swiss Cheese Stuffing

BLEND 1/2 pound grated Swiss cheese with 1/4 pound soft sweet butter and 1/2 teaspoon Dijon-type mustard. Mix in well 1/2 cup each of chopped roasted pistachio nuts and diced Swiss cheese.

Deviled Stuffing

CHOP finely enough cooked chicken to make 2 cups. Soften 1 cup deviled ham and 1/2 cup sweet butter and beat the mixture with a fork until it is light and fluffy. Season with 1 tablespoon Dijon-type mustard and add the chicken. If desired, add a little finely chopped fresh dill or 4 teaspoons finely chopped gherkins.

Liver Stuffing

MASH together 8 slices of liverwurst, 2 hard-cooked eggs, and 4 tablespoons each of grated Swiss cheese and mayonnaise. Season with 1 teaspoon Worcestershire sauce and prepared mustard and grated onion to taste.

Hunter's Stuffing

MASH 6 anchovies with 3 tablespoons sweet butter and blend them with 1 cup each of diced cooked ham and Edam cheese and 1/2 cup diced cooked tongue. Mix in lightly 3 small pickles, sliced, and 2 tablespoons caviar.

Beef Stock Preparation

Soups *and* Stocks

Beef Stock 🐚

PUT into a soup kettle 2 pounds veal knuckle, 3 pounds lean brisket of beef, 1 beef knuckle, 6 cleaned chicken feet, 4 leeks, 1 large onion stuck with 2 cloves, 1 stalk of celery with leaves, and 3 sprigs of parsley. Add 5 quarts water and bring it slowly to a boil, removing the scum as it accumulates on the surface. Cover the kettle and simmer the stock gently for 1 hour. Add 1 tablespoon salt and simmer the stock for three hours. Strain the stock through several layers of cheesecloth and let it cool, uncovered. Chill the stock and remove the layer of fat before using. Makes about 3 quarts.

Clear Celery Soup 🐚

CHOP a bunch of celery into coarse pieces. Bring 5 cups beef stock to a boil and add the celery. Simmer the soup gently for about 15 to 20 minutes, or until the celery flavor has sufficiently penetrated the broth. Correct the seasoning, strain the soup, and garnish the soup cups with tiny croutons.

℘ Beef Consommé

COMBINE 3 quarts beef stock with 1 1/2 pounds very lean beef, coarsely chopped, and the whites and shells of 2 eggs. Bring the stock slowly to a boil, stirring constantly, lower the heat, and simmer the soup slowly for 1 hour. The solid matter will settle on the bottom of the kettle. Strain the consommé through several thicknesses of cheesecloth. Makes about 2 quarts.

℘ Clear Consommé with Lemon

BRING to a boil 5 cups beef consommé and add the juice and rind of 1 lemon. Simmer the consommé for 15 minutes, correct the seasoning, and strain it. Garnish each serving with a thin slice of lemon.

℘ Wine Consommé   CONSOMMÉ AU VIN

BRING to a boil 4 cups beef consommé and stir in 1 cup dry red wine, 1 teaspoon sugar, salt and pepper to taste, and a dash of lemon juice. Serve the soup hot or cold, garnished with a thin slice of lemon and finely chopped chives.

℘ Oxtail Consommé

PUT in a soup kettle 2 pounds oxtail, 1 pound veal knuckle, 6 carrots, 3 white turnips, 2 leeks, 1 onion stuck with 3 cloves, 1 onion sautéed in butter until browned, and 1 teaspoon salt. Add 3 quarts cold water, bring it slowly to a boil, and skim the surface. Simmer the stock gently for 4 to 5 hours and strain it. Dice the oxtail meat and reserve it.

Brown 1 pound chopped beef lightly in 2 tablespoons butter, sprinkle it with 1 tablespoon potato starch, and brown the meat for 4 minutes more. Add the oxtail stock and simmer the soup slowly for 1 hour. Correct the seasoning, strain the soup through a fine sieve, and skim off the fat. Heat the soup before serving and garnish it with the reserved oxtail meat.

Veal Stock ༼

PUT a large knuckle of veal weighing about 3 1/2 pounds in a soup kettle with
1 pound veal, cut into cubes. Cover with 3 quarts cold water, add 1 tablespoon salt
and 12 peppercorns, and bring the mixture slowly to a boil. Remove the scum on
the surface and add 2 large white onions, each stuck with 1 clove, and a *bouquet
garni* composed of 2 sprigs of parsley, 1 stalk of celery with the leaves, 1 carrot, and
a sprig of thyme. Cover the kettle and simmer the stock slowly for at least 3 hours.
Strain the stock through a fine sieve lined with cheesecloth and let it cool, uncovered.
Chill the stock and remove the layer of fat before using. Makes about 1 quart.

Bouquet Garni

AN assortment of fresh herbs—usually including celery, parsley, thyme, and bay
leaf, and sometimes fennel, leek, marjoram, tarragon, and carrot—may be firmly
tied together with string or tied in a cheesecloth bag. The *bouquet garni* is then easy
to remove and discard.

CONSOMMÉ DE GIBIER

Clear Game Soup ༼

IN a large kettle combine the bones, skin, and leftover meat of 2 grouse or pheasant
with 1 onion and 1 carrot, both sliced, 2 whole cloves, 8 peppercorns, a *bouquet
garni* composed of 1 sprig each of parsley and thyme, 1 blade of mace, and 1 bay
leaf, 1 teaspoon sugar, and 10 cups veal stock. Bring the liquid to a boil, reduce
the heat, and simmer the soup for 3 hours, skimming it occasionally. Strain the soup,
cool it, and remove the fat from the surface. Pour the soup into a saucepan and add
1/2 cup Sherry, 2 eggshells, crushed, 2 egg whites, lightly beaten, and 2 ounces
lean raw ham. Heat the soup, stirring constantly, until it reaches a boil, reduce the
heat, and simmer it for 4 minutes. Let the soup rest for 20 minutes and strain it
through a sieve lined with cheesecloth. Reheat the soup and garnish it with finely
chopped chervil.

Chicken Stock ༼

PUT into a soup kettle a 4-pound fowl, 1 veal knuckle, 6 chicken feet, cleaned and
skinned, 2 tablespoons salt, 4 peppercorns, and 5 quarts of water. Bring the water

slowly to a boil, removing the scum as it accumulates on the surface. Cover the kettle and simmer the stock slowly for 1 hour, skimming it frequently. Add 6 small leeks, 4 large carrots, and 2 stalks of celery, all cut in pieces, 1 onion stuck with 3 cloves, 1/2 bay leaf, and a pinch of thyme. Cook the stock for 1 1/2 hours, or until the meat falls from the bones. Skim off the fat, correct the seasoning, and strain the stock through a fine sieve lined with cheesecloth. Cool the stock, uncovered, and chill it. Remove the layer of fat before using. Makes about 3 quarts.

Chicken Cucumber Soup

SAUTÉ 2 large cucumbers, peeled, seeded, and chopped, in 2 tablespoons butter for 1 minute. Combine them with 5 cups chicken stock, 2 thin slices of gingerroot, finely chopped, 1 scallion, chopped, and salt to taste. Simmer the soup, covered, for 15 minutes.

Chicken Mushroom Soup
POTAGE DE VOLAILLE ET DE CHAMPIGNONS

To 6 cups hot chicken stock add 1/2 cup finely diced celery and 2 tablespoons minced onion and simmer the soup for 1 minute. Add 1 cup sliced raw mushrooms and 2 ounces fine egg noodles and cook the soup for about 8 minutes, or until the mushrooms and noodles are tender.

Chicken Soup with Sherry   SOUPE DE VOLAILLE AU XÉRÈS

IN the container of a blender combine 4 eggs, 4 tablespoons Sherry, and 2 tablespoons lemon juice. Cover the container and blend the mixture for 15 seconds. Remove the cover and, with the motor running, slowly pour in 4 cups hot chicken stock. Season with salt and pepper to taste. Serve the soup garnished with chopped chives.

Chicken Consommé

To clarify chicken stock for consommé, beat 1 egg white lightly with 2 teaspoons cold water, and add it to the chicken stock with 1 eggshell, broken in pieces. Bring the stock to a boil over low heat and boil it for 2 minutes. Let it stand in a warm place for 20 minutes and strain it through several thicknesses of wet cheesecloth.

Consommé Bruxelles 🥄

WASH 24 tiny Brussels sprouts and remove and reserve the outer leaves. Cook the sprouts in boiling salted water barely to cover for about 10 minutes, or until they are tender. Heat 4 cups chicken consommé with the outer leaves of the sprouts. Strain out the leaves and add to the hot consommé about 1/2 cup of the water in which the sprouts were cooked. Put 4 sprouts in each soup plate and pour the hot consommé over them. Sprinkle the soup with grated Parmesan.

CONSOMMÉ AU CÉLERI-RAVE ## Celeriac Consommé 🥄

BRING to a boil 6 cups chicken consommé. Serve the soup in heated soup plates garnished with thin slices of cooked celeriac. Sprinkle each serving with 1 teaspoon finely chopped parsley.

CONSOMMÉ AUX HERBES ## Herb Consommé 🥄

To 4 cups hot chicken consommé add 3 tablespoons each of chervil and parsley, both finely chopped, 2 tablespoons chopped chives, and 1 tablespoon chopped tarragon. Let the herbs steep in the hot soup for 2 minutes. Strain the soup and heat it. Serve with a thin slice of lemon in each cup.

CONSOMMÉ DE VOLAILLE À LA CHIFFONADE ## Chiffonade Soup 🥄

COMBINE in a saucepan 1 head of lettuce, finely shredded, 4 green onions, finely chopped, 1 cup raw Frenched green beans, 1 tablespoon finely chopped chervil, and 2 leaves of fresh mint. Add 2 cups chicken consommé and salt and freshly ground black pepper to taste. Simmer the soup, covered, for about 10 minutes.

⬥ Consommé Cendrillon

BRING 6 cups chicken consommé to a boil and add 1/2 cup cooked rice and 1 truffle, poached in Marsala wine and cut into fine julienne. Serve very hot.

⬥ Consommé with Tarragon   CONSOMMÉ À L'ESTRAGON

ADD 2 whole sprigs of fresh tarragon to 4 cups chicken consommé. Bring the consommé slowly to a boil, keep it hot for 20 minutes without letting it boil, and strain it. Garnish each serving with a single blanched tarragon leaf.

⬥ Double Consommé   CONSOMMÉ DOUBLE

COMBINE in a soup kettle 3 quarts strained chicken stock, 1 small carrot, 2 leeks, and 2 stalks of celery, all chopped, some chicken necks and the carcass of a roast chicken, if available, and 6 prepared chicken feet. Stir in 2 egg whites, lightly beaten. Heat the soup, stirring briskly, until it reaches the boiling point. Stop stirring at once, cover the kettle, and boil the soup rapidly for 5 minutes. Reduce the heat and simmer the stock for 1 hour. Carefully put the clarified soup through a strainer lined with several thicknesses of cheesecloth and discard the solid ingredients. Reduce the consommé over high heat by half, stir in 2 teaspoons Cognac, and correct the seasoning.

⬥ Velvet Consommé   CONSOMMÉ VELOUTÉ

BRING to a boil 4 cups chicken consommé, add gradually 1/3 cup minute tapioca, and cook the soup over medium heat for 10 minutes. Stir in very gradually 1 egg yolk beaten with 1/2 cup heavy cream and 1/4 cup dry Sherry. Stir the soup constantly until it is slightly thickened. Add salt and cayenne to taste.

⬥ Mushroom Consommé

SIMMER 1 1/2 pounds raw mushrooms, chopped, in 6 cups chicken stock for 30 minutes. Strain them through a fine muslin cloth, pressing out as much of the liquid as possible. Stir into the strained stock 2 egg whites, lightly beaten, and boil the soup for 2 minutes. Put the clarified soup through a strainer lined with several thicknesses of cheesecloth. Reheat the soup and season it with 2 tablespoons Madeira and salt and pepper to taste. Serve hot, with a spoonful of salted whipped cream.

Duck Stock

Put into a soup kettle the carcasses of 2 roast ducks with 3 stalks of celery, diced, 2 large onions, quartered, 2 large carrots, diced, 2 tablespoons coarsely chopped parsley, 1 garlic clove, 1 bay leaf, and salt and pepper to taste. Add 3 quarts boiling water, cover the kettle, and simmer the carcasses for about 2 hours. Strain the stock through several layers of cheesecloth and let it cool, uncovered. Chill the stock and remove the layer of fat before using. Makes about 1 1/2 quarts.

Duck Soup

To 4 cups duck stock add 2 cups watercress leaves and 1 cup sliced raw mushrooms, and season the soup with salt, pepper, and monosodium glutamate to taste. Serve in hot soup plates, with 1 tablespoon Sherry in each serving.

Turkey Stock

To make turkey stock from the carcass of the bird, follow the recipe for duck stock.

Carrot Soup with Rice

Wash, peel, and shred 6 carrots. Put them in a large saucepan with 6 cups chicken stock, bring the stock to a boil, and simmer it for about 15 minutes, or until the carrots are very tender. Put the soup through a fine sieve, or purée it in a blender. Return the soup to the pan and bring it to a boil. Add 4 tablespoons raw rice and simmer the soup for 20 minutes, or until the rice is tender. Beat the 2 egg yolks with 1/2 cup of the hot soup, stir the mixture into the soup, and cook, stirring constantly, for 3 minutes longer, without letting the soup boil. Serve hot or cold, with a dollop of chilled sour cream on each portion.

ℬ Carrot and Tomato Soup   POTAGE CRÉCY À LA TOMATE

SAUTÉ 1 pound carrots, chopped, in 3 tablespoons butter for 3 minutes, add 1 cup chicken stock, and simmer the carrots gently for about 15 minutes, or until they are tender. Put the carrots through a sieve or purée them in a blender. Stir in 3 table-spoons tomato purée, 3 cups chicken stock, and 1/4 cup grated raw potatoes. Simmer the soup for 15 minutes. Beat 1 egg yolk with 1 tablespoon milk. Gradually pour some of the hot soup over the egg and return the mixture to the soup. Do not let the soup boil after the egg is added. Serve sprinkled generously with chopped chives.

ℬ Carrot and Leek Soup

COMBINE in a saucepan 5 carrots, 4 leeks, trimmed and sliced, 4 cups chicken stock, and salt and pepper to taste. Cook the vegetables for about 25 minutes, or until they are very soft. In the container of a blender put a handful of parsley. Add the vegetables and their broth, cover the container, and blend the soup until it is thick and smooth. If a thinner soup is desired, add a little more chicken stock. Heat the soup and serve with croutons.

ℬ Pumpkin Soup

MELT 2 tablespoons butter in a large saucepan, add 4 scallions, chopped, and 1 small onion, sliced, and cook them gently until they are almost soft but not brown. Add 1 1/2 pounds pumpkin, peeled and diced, 4 cups chicken stock, and 1/2 teaspoon salt. Simmer the pumpkin until it is soft. Stir in 2 tablespoons flour kneaded with 1 tablespoon butter and bring the soup to a boil. Rub the soup through a fine sieve or purée it in a blender. Correct the seasoning and add 3/4 cup hot light cream and 1 tablespoon butter. Heat the soup just to the boiling point and serve it garnished with tiny toasted croutons and lightly salted whipped cream.

ℬ Chestnut Soup   POTAGE PURÉE DE MARRONS

SHELL and peel 1 pound chestnuts. In a large saucepan brown 2 carrots, 2 leeks, 2 celery stalks, and 1 onion, all coarsely chopped, in 1 tablespoon olive oil for 5 minutes. Add the chestnuts and 6 cups chicken stock, 8 sprigs of parsley, and

Pumpkin Soup

3 whole cloves. Simmer the soup for at least 1 hour, or until the vegetables are very soft. Reserve enough chestnuts to garnish the soup plates and put the soup through a fine sieve or purée it in a blender. Return the purée to the pan and add 1/2 cup light cream and 2 tablespoons brandy. Adjust the seasoning and heat the soup to the boiling point. Garnish the soup plates with the reserved whole chestnuts.

ꮭ Chestnut and Acorn Squash Soup

SAUTÉ 1 small onion and 1 stalk of celery, both thinly sliced, in 2 tablespoons each of butter and oil for 3 minutes. Add 2 acorn squash, peeled, seeded, and diced, 2 cups chestnuts, shelled and peeled, and 4 cups chicken stock. Simmer the soup for about 40 minutes, or until the chestnuts are quite soft, and add salt and pepper to taste. Pour the soup into the container of a blender, cover the container, and blend it until it is smooth. Stir in 3 tablespoons light cream and heat the soup in the top of a double boiler over hot water. Sprinkle each serving with chopped parsley.

ꮭ Potage Germiny

IN a saucepan bring to a rapid boil 4 cups strong chicken stock. Add 1/2 cup finely shredded sorrel and simmer it for 5 minutes. Remove the soup from the heat and keep it hot. In another saucepan beat 4 egg yolks until they are light. Gradually pour 1 cup of the soup over the eggs, beating briskly to prevent them from curdling, and, still beating, slowly add the rest of the soup. Heat the soup but do not let it boil. Just before serving, add 2 tablespoons Sherry or Madeira.

ꮭ Dandelion Soup

WASH and chop finely 1/2 pound very young dandelion leaves. Put them in a large saucepan with 4 medium potatoes, peeled and sliced, 6 cups water, and a little salt. Simmer the soup, covered, for 1 hour. Force the soup through a fine sieve or purée it in a blender. Blend 2 egg yolks with 1 tablespoon melted butter and gradually stir in the soup. Heat the soup and serve in flat soup plates, garnished with sautéed croutons.

Spring Greens Soup 🍂

COOK 1 pound washed spinach or orach in 1/4 cup salted water until it is tender. Strain the greens, reserving the water, and put them through a sieve or purée them in a blender. Sauté 1/2 pound each of sorrel and scallions and 1 cup each of celery, parsley, and watercress, all chopped, in 4 tablespoons butter until all the greens are coated. Combine these vegetables with the spinach, the reserved spinach water, and enough stock to make 4 cups liquid. Simmer the soup until the vegetables are tender. Stir 1 tablespoon flour into 1 1/2 cups sour cream. Add the cream to the soup, season with salt and pepper to taste, and heat the soup without letting it boil. Place half a hard-cooked egg in each soup plate, and pour the soup over it.

Watercress Soup 🍂

REMOVE the stems from enough washed watercress to make 2 cups, tightly packed. Dice finely 1/2 pound lean beef, season it with 1 tablespoon soy sauce and 1 teaspoon each of oil and salt, and let the mixture stand for 30 minutes. Bring 3 cups each of chicken stock and water to a boil, add the watercress, and bring the soup to a boil again. Add a drop of sesame oil and the seasoned beef. Stir well and serve very hot.

Garden Soup 🍂

COMBINE in a saucepan 2 bunches of watercress, 1 head of lettuce, shredded, 1 cup dandelion leaves, 1 small bunch of parsley, 1/2 cup salted water, and 1/8 teaspoon chervil. Cook the greens for about 5 minutes, or until they are just tender. In a separate saucepan cook 1 large potato and 1 onion, both chopped, in 3 1/2 cups chicken stock, for about 15 minutes, or until the potato is tender. Add the greens and their liquid. Purée the soup in a blender or put it through a food mill. Add 3/4 cup light cream, season to taste with salt and pepper, and heat the soup without letting it boil. Garnish each serving with finely chopped chives.

Onion and Bacon Soup 🍂

SAUTÉ 8 slices of bacon, diced, until they are crisp. Remove the bacon and reserve it. In the fat remaining in the pan sauté 8 onions, thinly sliced, until they are tender.

Coach House Black Bean Soup

Remove the onions with a perforated spoon and discard the fat from the pan. Return the onions to the pan with 5 cups water and salt and pepper to taste, and simmer the soup for 30 minutes. Line the bottom of a casserole or an ovenproof tureen with thin slices of stale French bread and cover the bread with a layer of grated Parmesan. Sprinkle two tablespoons heavy cream over the cheese and add a layer of the diced bacon. Repeat this procedure. Add the hot onion soup and heat the tureen in a hot oven (400° F.) for 5 to 10 minutes.

Minestrone 🦪

HEAT 1/4 cup oil or lard in a large saucepan. Add 1 cup chopped onions, 1/4 cup each of chopped parsley and sweet basil, 2 small chili peppers, crushed, and 1/2 garlic clove, finely chopped. Brown the vegetables over low heat, stirring frequently. Add 1 pound pork neck bones and brown the meat on all sides. Add water to cover and a little salt and pepper. Simmer the soup for about 30 minutes, or until the meat is almost tender. Add 3 potatoes, cubed, and 2 cups each of spinach and Swiss chard, coarsely chopped, and cook the soup for 20 minutes, or until the meat and potatoes are tender. Adjust the seasoning with salt and pepper. Serve with grated Parmesan and Italian bread sticks.

Coach House Black Bean Soup 🦪

PICK over and wash 4 cups black beans, soak them overnight in cold water to cover, and drain them. Add 5 quarts cold water and cook the beans over low heat for 1 1/2 hours.

In a soup kettle sauté slowly 3 stalks of celery and 3 large onions, finely chopped, in 1/2 cup butter for about 8 minutes, or until they are tender. Blend in 2 1/2 tablespoons flour and 1/2 cup finely chopped parsley and cook the mixture, stirring, for 1 minute. Gradually stir in the beans and their liquid. Add the rind and bone of a cooked smoked ham, 3 leeks, thinly sliced, 4 bay leaves, 1 tablespoon salt, and 1/2 teaspoon freshly ground black pepper. Simmer the soup over very low heat for 4 hours.

Remove and discard the hambone, rind, and bay leaves and force the beans through a sieve. Combine the puréed beans with their broth and add 1 cup dry Madeira. Bring the soup to a boil, remove it from the heat, and stir in 2 finely chopped hard-cooked eggs. Float a thin slice of lemon on each serving.

Court Bouillon

PUT 2 quarts water in a large kettle and add 1 onion, 1 carrot, and 3 stalks of celery, all chopped, 2 sprigs of parsley, 1 bay leaf, 2 cloves, 6 peppercorns, and 1 tablespoon salt. Bring the water to a boil, add 2 tablespoons white vinegar, and simmer the court bouillon, covered, for 30 minutes.

White-Wine Court Bouillon

PUT 1 quart each of dry white wine and water in a large kettle and add 2 small carrots and 2 onions, sliced, a *bouquet garni* composed of 6 sprigs of parsley, 4 green celery tops, 2 large bay leaves, and 1 sprig of thyme, the juice of 1 lemon, 2 whole cloves, 12 bruised peppercorns, and 1 tablespoon salt. Bring the liquid to a boil and simmer the court bouillon, covered, for 30 minutes.

Fish Court Bouillon

PUT 2 quarts water in a large kettle and add some fish bones and trimmings, 1 onion, 1 carrot, and 1 stalk of celery, all chopped, 1 sprig each of parsley and chervil, 1 bay leaf, 4 peppercorns, and 1 1/2 teaspoons salt. Bring the mixture to a boil and simmer it, covered, for about 1 hour. Strain the court bouillon before using.

Fish Stock

MELT 4 tablespoons butter in a kettle and add 2 pounds chopped raw fish bones and trimmings, 1 onion, minced, and a few sprigs of parsley. Cover the kettle and cook the mixture slowly for 15 minutes. Do not let it brown. Add 2 quarts court bouillon or white-wine court bouillon and simmer the stock for 30 minutes. Strain the stock through a sieve lined with cheesecloth and let it cool, uncovered. Chill the stock and remove the layer of fat before using. Makes about 1 1/2 quarts.

Clam Broth

SCRUB thoroughly under running cold water 36 hard-shelled clams and rinse them in several waters. Put the clams in a large kettle and add 1 quart boiling water and 3 tablespoons lemon juice. Cover the kettle and steam the clams for about 10 minutes, or until the shells begin to open. Lift out the clams, remove them from the shells, and chop them, reserving any juice. Strain the liquid in the kettle, measure it, and add enough water to make 1 1/2 quarts liquid. Return the liquid to the kettle with the chopped clams and their juice and add 2 stalks of celery. Simmer the broth for 20 minutes, strain it through several thicknesses of cheesecloth, and add salt to taste.

Mussel Soup

CLEAN 36 mussels and put them in a kettle with 1 cup white wine, 1 onion and 1/4 cup celery leaves, both chopped, and 6 sprigs of parsley. Steam the mussels until they open. Remove them from the shells and reserve 6. Put the remaining mussels in the container of a blender and strain the broth through several layers of cheesecloth over the mussels. Cover the container and blend the soup until it is smooth. Pour the soup into a saucepan and add a dash of cayenne and salt and pepper to taste. Bring the soup to a boil, stir in 2 cups scalded light cream, and simmer the soup for 10 minutes. Serve in heated soup cups and garnish with a whole mussel in each cup.

Shrimp and Oyster Bisque

CHOP finely 2 cups each of freshly shucked oysters and shelled, deveined raw shrimp, reserving the oyster liquor. Put the oysters, shrimp, and liquor in the top of a double boiler and add 5 cups milk, 1/2 cup chopped celery, 3 tablespoons finely minced onion, 2 sprigs of parsley, minced, a pinch of mace, and salt and pepper to taste. Put the pan over boiling water and cook the bisque for 30 minutes. Strain it through a fine sieve.

In a saucepan melt 3 tablespoons butter, stir in 3 tablespoons flour, and gradually stir in the strained bisque. Heat the bisque, stirring constantly, but do not let it boil. Serve in soup plates, garnish each plate with 1 whole shrimp, and sprinkle with paprika.

❧ Cream of Almond Soup

POUND 2 cups almonds, blanched and thoroughly dried, to a paste in a mortar. The nuts may first be put through a food chopper but a blender should not be used. Stir the almond paste into 4 cups chicken stock, add 1 small onion, and simmer the mixture for 30 minutes. Discard the onion. Add to the soup 1 cup heavy cream and 1/2 teaspoon ground coriander. Beat 4 egg yolks lightly and warm them with a little hot soup. Stir the eggs slowly into the soup and cook it over low heat, stirring constantly, until it begins to thicken. Strain the soup through several thicknesses of cheesecloth. Serve hot or cold, garnished with minced chives and finely grated orange zest.

❧ Cream of Artichoke Soup   POTAGE CRÈME D'ARTICHAUTS

IN a saucepan heat 4 cups chicken stock with 4 thin onion slices, 1 whole clove, a pinch of nutmeg, and 1/4 teaspoon freshly ground pepper. Add to the stock 3 cooked artichoke bottoms, drained and forced through a sieve, and simmer the soup for 25 minutes. Add 2 tablespoons cooked rice and 1 1/2 cups scalded milk and bring the soup to a boil. Strain the soup into another saucepan. Season it with salt to taste, bring it again to the boiling point, and gradually stir in 1/2 cup light cream mixed with 1 beaten egg yolk. Just before serving, stir in 1 tablespoon Sherry.

❧ Cream of Broccoli Soup   POTAGE CRÈME DE BROCOLI

COMBINE in a saucepan 1 bunch of broccoli, washed and trimmed, and 1 stalk of celery and 1 small onion, both finely sliced. Add 3 cups chicken stock, bring it to a boil, and simmer the broccoli for 15 minutes, until it is just tender. Pour the soup into a blender. Add a pinch of dry mustard and salt to taste. Cover, and blend until the mixture is smooth. Stir in 1 cup light cream. Serve the soup hot, with a thin slice of lemon in each cup, or serve it cold, sprinkled with finely chopped chives.

❧ Cream of Celery Soup

SAUTÉ 1/4 cup coarsely chopped onion in 1/3 cup butter until the onions are soft. Add 2 cups celery, finely diced, 2 potatoes, diced, 1 cup water, 1/2 bay leaf, and salt and pepper to taste. Cover the pan and cook the vegetables slowly for 30 minutes, or until they are soft. Stir in 2 cups milk and pour the mixture into the container of a blender. Cover the container and blend the soup until it is smooth. Return the soup to the pan, correct the seasoning, and add 4 tablespoons chopped parsley and 1/2 cup heavy cream. Bring the soup just to a boil.

Cream of Crab Soup

MASH to a paste 2 tablespoons butter, the grated rind of 1 lemon, 1 tablespoon flour, 1 teaspoon Worcestershire sauce, a pinch of mace, and 2 chopped hard-cooked eggs. Mix the paste with 2 cups cooked crab meat.

In a skillet sauté 3 mushrooms, 3 stalks of celery, and 1 small scallion, all minced, in 1 tablespoon butter.

In the top of a double boiler combine 4 cups scalded milk, 1 cup scalded heavy cream, the crab-meat paste, and the sautéed vegetables. Season the soup with salt and pepper to taste and put the pan over hot water until the soup thickens. Add 1 cup dry Sherry and heat it slowly.

Cream of Cucumber Soup

IN the container of a blender combine 2 cups coarsely chopped cucumber, 1 cup each of chicken stock and light cream, 1/4 cup each of chopped chives and celery leaves, 3 sprigs of parsley, and 2 tablespoons each of soft butter and flour. Cover the container and blend the mixture until it is smooth. Heat the soup slowly until it reaches a boil and season it with salt and pepper to taste. Serve it hot, garnished with finely chopped dill, or serve it cold, garnished with finely chopped cucumber and grated lemon rind.

Cream of Lettuce Soup

WASH 2 heads of lettuce in several changes of cold water. In a saucepan sauté 6 scallions, finely chopped, in 4 tablespoons butter until they are transparent and add 1 garlic clove, minced, 1 tablespoon chopped parsley, 1 teaspoon salt, 1/4 teaspoon black pepper, the lettuce leaves, and 2 cups water. Cover the saucepan and simmer the lettuce for 20 minutes. Force the mixture through a fine sieve, or purée it in a blender. Add 4 cups chicken stock to the lettuce purée and bring the soup to a boil. Correct the seasoning and stir in gradually 2 egg yolks beaten with 1/2 cup hot heavy cream. Garnish with chopped parsley.

ℰ Cream of Mushroom Soup with Sherry

SLICE the caps of 3/4 pound mushrooms and chop the stems. Sauté the mushrooms in 3 tablespoons butter until they are lightly browned, sprinkle them with 3 table-spoons flour, and cook over low heat for 4 minutes. Add 4 cups scalded milk and simmer the soup, stirring, for 10 minutes. Mix 1 egg yolk, lightly beaten, with 1/2 cup Sherry and add the mixture to the soup. Add salt and pepper to taste and cook the soup for 2 minutes longer.

ℰ Parsnip Soup

IN the top of a double boiler combine 4 parsnips, peeled and diced, with 2 leeks, cut into 1/4-inch slices. Cover the pan and cook the vegetables over boiling water for about 20 minutes, or until they are tender. Purée the vegetables in a blender or force them through a fine sieve. Combine the purée with 2 1/2 cups chicken stock, 1 1/2 cups light cream, 3 tablespoons white wine, a pinch of allspice, and salt and pepper to taste. Heat the soup just to the boiling point and stir in 1/2 cup chopped watercress leaves. Garnish with croutons.

ℰ Cream of Potato Soup with Saffron

COOK 1 1/2 cups diced potatoes and 1 cup diced celery in 2 cups milk for about 10 minutes, or until the vegetables are tender. Pour the mixture into the container of a blender and add 1/4 teaspoon saffron and salt and pepper to taste. Cover the container and blend the soup until it is smooth. Pour the soup into a bowl, add 1 1/2 cups light cream, and chill the soup. Pour the soup into chilled soup cups and put a spoonful of black caviar in the center of each portion.

Cream of Scallion Soup ﷽

TRIM 24 scallions, leaving 1/2 inch of the green stem on each. Simmer the scallions in chicken stock to cover for about 6 minutes, or until they are tender. Pour the mixture into the container of a blender, adding a little hot milk if there is not enough liquid to cover the blades. Cover the container and blend the mixture until it is smooth. Scald 4 cups milk with 6 sprigs of parsley, 1 bay leaf, and salt and pepper to taste. Strain the milk into the scallion purée and cook the soup, stirring, until it is thoroughly blended. Beat 2 egg yolks with 1 cup light cream, warm the mixture with a little soup, and stir it in slowly. Serve sprinkled with finely chopped chervil.

Cream of Snow Pea Soup ﷽

COMBINE in a soup kettle 2 quarts snow peas, washed and stemmed, several lettuce leaves, 1 onion, 6 sprigs of parsley, 1 tablespoon butter, and 1 teaspoon salt. Add 3 cups water, bring it to a boil, and simmer the soup for 30 minutes. Force the soup through a fine sieve or purée it in a blender. Thicken the purée with a mixture of 1 tablespoon butter and 2 tablespoons flour. Bring the soup to a boil, add 1 cup light cream, and heat the soup without letting it boil.

Summer Squash Soup ﷽

SAUTÉ 8 scallions, chopped, in 2 tablespoons butter until they are golden. Add 6 summer squash, cut in pieces, and 3 cups chicken stock, and cook the mixture for about 15 minutes, or until the squash is tender. Put the soup through a sieve or purée it in a blender. Season it to taste with salt, pepper, and a pinch of nutmeg and add 2 cups heavy cream. Serve hot or cold, garnished with parsley.

Cream of Spinach Soup ﷽

MELT 4 tablespoons butter in a saucepan, stir in 4 tablespoons flour, and cook the *roux*, stirring constantly, until it starts to turn golden. Add 2 quarts hot chicken stock and simmer the soup, stirring, until it is smooth. Add 2 leeks, 1 onion, and 1 stalk of celery, all chopped, 2 sprigs of parsley, and a little salt, if necessary. Simmer the soup for 30 minutes, skimming it occasionally, and strain it through a fine sieve.

Cook 1 pound spinach in the water that clings to the leaves, drain it well, and rub it through a fine sieve. Add the purée to the soup, bring the soup to a boil, and cook it for a few minutes. Beat 2 egg yolks with 1 cup heavy cream, warm the mixture with a little soup, and gently stir it into the balance of the soup. Cook the soup, stirring, for 3 minutes without letting it boil. Correct the seasoning and strain the soup through a fine sieve.

ᑫ Cream of Tomato Soup

SAUTÉ 1/4 cup bacon, finely chopped, in 1 tablespoon olive oil until it is crisp. Add 3 onions, coarsely grated, and 1 split garlic clove. Cook the vegetables over low heat until they are lightly browned. Discard the garlic and add to the pan 4 cups tomato purée, 3 cups chicken stock, 3 stalks of celery, finely chopped, and 2 tablespoons chopped parsley. Blend 4 tablespoons hot mashed potato with 1/4 cup chicken stock, add it to the soup, and simmer the soup for 20 minutes. Lightly beat 3 egg yolks with 1/4 cup light cream, warm the mixture with a little soup, and stir it in slowly. Add 1 tablespoon white wine to each portion.

ᑫ German Wine Soup

BRING to a boil 4 1/2 cups white wine, preferably Moselle. Blend 1 tablespoon cornstarch with 1/2 cup white wine and stir this into the boiling wine alternately with 4 tablespoons sugar. Add the grated rind and the juice of 1 lemon and a 1-inch cinnamon stick. Simmer the soup for 3 or 4 minutes, stirring constantly. Remove the pan from the heat, cover it tightly, and let it stand for 10 minutes.

Strain the soup and, with a whisk, beat in 4 egg yolks, one at a time, beating well after each addition. Serve the soup in heated glass cups, garnished with finely grated lemon rind.

ᑫ Clear Beet Soup

IN a large soup kettle combine 7 cups cold strong beef stock, 10 medium beets, peeled and grated, 1/2 cup red wine, 1 tablespoon each of Sherry and tomato paste,

Clear Beet Soup

and 2 teaspoons lemon juice. Beat 4 egg whites until they are stiff and turn them out of the bowl onto the stock. Do not fold them in. Bring the mixture to a boil, whisking constantly back and forth across the center of the pan. When the mixture reaches a full boil, remove the pan from the heat and let it stand for 10 minutes.

Wring cheesecloth in cold water and use it to line a large fine-meshed sieve. Put the sieve over a deep bowl and slowly pour in the contents of the pan. Let the mixture stand until it has completely dripped through, and discard the egg whites. Chill the soup thoroughly.

Cut 6 cooked beets into julienne, divide the shreds among 6 chilled soup plates, and add the soup. Serve with a sauceboat of sour cream seasoned with grated lemon rind and salt and cayenne to taste.

ʃ◔ Orange Borsch

GRATE enough unpeeled beets to make 3 cups. Put the grated beets in a stainless steel or enamel saucepan, add 4 1/2 cups beef stock, and simmer the mixture for 20 minutes. Strain out the beets and add to the liquid 1 1/2 cups tomato juice, 1 teaspoon salt, and 1/2 teaspoon each of thyme and pepper. Bring the soup to a boil and add 1 cup orange juice, strained. Serve garnished with sour cream and chopped chives.

ʃ◔ Cold Curried Apple Soup

IN a kettle combine 3 cups strong chicken stock with 1 cup each of beef stock and heavy cream. Heat the soup but do not let it boil. Stir in 4 teaspoons curry powder mixed with 1/4 cup apple juice. Cool the soup, flavor it with 1 tablespoon Sherry, and chill it. Peel and chop finely 2 large apples, sprinkle the fruit with a few drops of lemon juice, and add it to the soup. Garnish each serving with thin strips of unpeeled apple.

ʃ◔ Cold Avocado Soup

MASH the flesh of 2 avocados with a silver fork and press it through a fine sieve into a saucepan. Add 2 1/2 cups chicken stock and heat the soup, stirring occasionally, until it reaches the boiling point. Stir in 1 1/2 cups heavy cream, season the soup with a dash of chili powder and 2 teaspoons grated onion, and chill it. Before serving, season the soup with salt and white pepper to taste, and stir in the pulp of 1 avocado, cut into 1/2-inch cubes. Garnish each portion with a dab of lightly salted whipped cream.

Avocado Yoghurt Soup

WITH a silver fork, mash enough avocado pulp to make 2 cups and force it through a sieve. Mix the purée well with 2 cups yoghurt, 1 1/2 cups beef stock, 3 teaspoons lime juice, 2 teaspoons onion juice, and 1 teaspoon chili powder. Chill the soup thoroughly.

Cold Beef Soup

COMBINE 3 cups beef consommé with 1 cup dry white wine and chill the soup. Garnish each serving with a thin slice of lemon and sprinkle it with finely chopped parsley.

Cold Carrot and Orange Soup

SAUTÉ 1 onion, minced, in 3 tablespoons butter for 2 to 3 minutes, or until it is golden. Add 8 carrots, sliced, 3 cups water, salt and pepper to taste, and 1/2 teaspoon cloves. Cover the pan and simmer the soup over low heat for 10 minutes, or until the carrots are tender. Blend 1 1/2 tablespoons potato starch with a little of the soup stock, return it to the pan, and simmer the soup for 2 minutes longer. Pour the soup into the container of a blender, cover it, and blend the soup until it is smooth. Add the juice of 1 lemon and 2 cups orange juice to the puréed soup and chill it thoroughly. Serve in chilled soup cups, garnished with finely chopped mint.

Cucumber Soup with Yoghurt

MIX 2 garlic cloves, minced, with 1 teaspoon salt and 2 tablespoons olive oil. Beat the mixture into 2 cups yoghurt and continue beating the mixture until it is smooth.

Cold Pea Soup

Blend in 1 cucumber, peeled, seeded, and chopped, the juice and grated rind of 1/2 lemon, and 2 cups cold water. Add 1/3 cup currants, 1/4 cup chopped mint, and salt and pepper to taste. Chill the soup thoroughly.

Gazpacho

COMBINE in the container of a blender 1 garlic clove, mashed, and 1 onion, peeled and chopped, and blend the mixture until it is smooth. Add 5 ripe tomatoes, peeled and chopped, 1 cup beef stock, 3 tablespoons olive oil, 2 tablespoons each of vinegar and chopped parsley, and a dash of paprika. Cover the container and blend the mixture until it is smooth. Chill the soup thoroughly. With the soup serve, in separate dishes, cucumber, green pepper, tomato, and onion, all finely chopped, and croutons.

Cold Indian Lentil Soup

SOAK 2 cups lentils in water to cover for 2 hours and drain them. Cover them with fresh cold water, bring the water slowly to a boil, and simmer the lentils for 10 minutes. Drain them again and put them in a kettle with 4 cups beef stock, 1 ham bone, 2 stalks of celery, 3 bruised garlic cloves, and 1/2 teaspoon cuminseed. Bring the soup to a boil and simmer it over low heat for 2 1/2 hours. Discard the bone and force the soup through a fine sieve. Mix 4 tablespoons curry powder with 1/2 cup sour cream and stir it into the soup. Cool the soup and chill it. Garnish each serving with a dollop of sour cream.

Cold Pea Soup

IN a saucepan combine 6 cups shelled young green peas, 6 scallions, chopped, 6 sprigs of chervil or 1 teaspoon dry chervil, and 1/2 teaspoon sugar. Add 1 cup shredded lettuce and 4 cups boiling beef stock. Add salt to taste and simmer the vegetables, covered, for about 15 minutes, or until the peas are soft. Force the mixture through a sieve, or purée it in a blender. Chill the purée thoroughly. Stir in

1/2 cup each of Sherry and heavy cream, blending well. Serve the soup in cups and garnish each serving with carrots cut into decorative shapes.

ꙮ Cold Pea and Potato Soup

COOK 3/4 cup minced scallions and 2 thinly sliced leeks in 2 tablespoons butter until the vegetables start to take on color. Add 3 cups chicken stock, 2 cups each of shelled green peas and peeled and diced potatoes, 1/2 teaspoon salt, and 1/4 teaspoon celery seed. Cook the vegetables for about 15 minutes, or until they are tender. Purée the mixture in a blender or force it through a fine sieve. Cool the soup, stir in 2 cups light cream, and chill thoroughly.

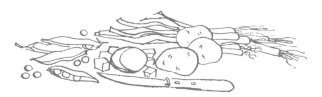

ꙮ Cold Tomato and Cucumber Soup

IN a saucepan combine 3 small tomatoes, peeled, seeded, and coarsely chopped, with 2 cups cold chicken stock. Bring the liquid to a boil, lower the heat, and simmer it gently for 25 minutes. Strain the stock, force the tomatoes through a sieve into another pan, and reserve the purée. Add 2 more cups chicken stock to the strained stock and season the soup with 1 teaspoon sugar, a dash of nutmeg, and salt and pepper to taste. Bring the soup to a boil and gradually add 1 tablespoon butter kneaded with 1 tablespoon flour. Simmer it for 15 minutes, stirring occasionally. Remove the pan from the heat, and stir in 1 cup diced peeled cucumber, the puréed tomatoes, 2 teaspoons each of parsley and dill, both finely chopped, and 3/4 cup sour cream. Chill the soup well, and sprinkle each portion with a little finely chopped dill.

ꙮ Tomato and Orange Consommé

BLEND together 2 cups each of tomato juice and strained orange juice and add lemon juice and celery salt to taste. Serve the soup hot or cold, sprinkled with chopped chives or mint.

Buttermilk Tomato Soup 🐾

CUT 2 pounds ripe tomatoes into sections, add 1 cup water, and simmer them for 15 minutes. Force the tomatoes through a sieve, and combine the purée with 4 cups buttermilk and salt to taste. Chill the soup thoroughly and serve garnished with tiny croutons.

Vichyssoise with Watercress 🐾

SAUTÉ the white parts of 4 leeks and 1 medium onion, all thinly sliced, in 2 tablespoons butter until the vegetables just start to turn golden. Add 4 medium potatoes, peeled and sliced, 3 cups chicken stock, and 1 teaspoon salt. Bring the liquid to a boil and cook the mixture for about 35 minutes, or until the potatoes are very soft. Rub the soup through a fine sieve, return it to the heat, and add 1 1/2 cups each of milk and light cream. Bring the soup to a boil, let it cool, and correct the seasoning. Rub the soup through a fine sieve and chill it. Serve in bouillon cups, sprinkling each serving with finely chopped watercress leaves. For a more pronounced watercress flavor, blend 1/2 cup leaves with a little of the soup and proceed as above.

Cold Curried Watercress Soup 🐾

IN a kettle bring to a boil 4 cups beef stock and add 4 medium potatoes, peeled and thinly sliced, and 8 scallions, sliced. Cook the mixture for about 45 minutes, stirring and mashing the potatoes in the stock until they completely disintegrate. Force the soup through a fine sieve. Clean 1 large bunch of watercress and discard the heavy stems. Chop the leaves finely and sauté them in 4 tablespoons butter for 4 minutes. Add the watercress and butter to the potato stock and simmer the soup over low heat for 10 minutes. Remove the pan from the heat and stir in 1 egg yolk beaten with 1 cup light cream and 3 teaspoons curry powder. Cool the soup and chill it. Garnish each serving with sprigs of watercress.

Watercress and Apple Soup 🐾

IN a saucepan sauté 3 leeks and 1 onion, all sliced, in 2 tablespoons butter until they are golden. Add 3 potatoes, peeled and sliced, and 3 cups chicken stock and simmer the mixture for about 35 minutes, or until the potatoes are very soft. Press the mixture through a fine sieve or purée it in a blender. Stir in 1 cup each of milk and heavy cream and add salt to taste.

Cook 1 bunch of watercress in boiling water for a few minutes, drain it well, and force it through a fine sieve. Stir the watercress purée into the soup and chill the soup well. Just before serving stir in 1 grated apple. Garnish each portion with a sprig of watercress and slices of apple sprinkled with lemon juice.

Cold Watercress and Potato Soup

COOK 3 potatoes, sliced, and 4 onions, chopped, in 4 cups salted water for about 25 minutes, or until the vegetables are soft. Press the vegetables through a sieve, return the purée to the pan, and bring it to a boil. Add 2 bunches of watercress, chopped, and cook the soup for 15 minutes longer. Press the soup through a sieve and cool and chill it. Stir in light cream to taste and chill again. Serve in chilled soup cups and garnish each serving with a sprinkling of chopped watercress.

Cold Curried Lobster Bisque

CUT 4 pounds live lobsters into serving pieces, reserving any juice. Put the lobster pieces in a kettle with 2 quarts fish stock, the lobster juice, 4 tablespoons chopped celery, 4 peppercorns, and 1 bay leaf. Bring the soup to a boil and simmer it for 20 minutes. Remove the lobster meat from the shells, dice it, and reserve it. Strain the stock and return it to the kettle. Add 2 tablespoons rice and simmer it over low heat until it is tender. Sauté 1/4 cup each of onion, parsley, celery, and green pepper, all finely chopped, in 4 tablespoons peanut oil until the vegetables are soft. Add them to the stock and cook them over low heat until they are very soft. Force the soup through a fine sieve or purée it in a blender and cool the purée. Add 1/2 cup light cream mixed with 1 teaspoon curry powder and chill the soup. Garnish each serving with the reserved lobster meat.

Buttermilk Shrimp Soup

IN the container of a blender combine 1 1/2 cups cooked shrimp, shelled and deveined, 2 small cucumbers, peeled and chopped, 1 tablespoon each of parsley and chives, both chopped, 2 teaspoons prepared mustard, 1 teaspoon sugar, and a dash of nutmeg. Add 1 1/2 cups buttermilk, cover the container, and blend the soup until it is smooth. Chill the soup thoroughly. At serving time, thin the soup with 2 to 2 1/2 cups buttermilk, depending on the consistency desired, and pour it into chilled soup bowls. Garnish with tiny whole cooked shrimp and sprinkle with paprika.

Cold Shrimp and Tomato Bisque

IN a kettle melt 3 tablespoons butter, stir in 4 tablespoons flour, and add gradually 3 1/2 cups fish stock. Bring the stock to a boil, stirring constantly, and simmer it for 15 minutes. Cook 2 pounds shrimp, shelled and deveined, in boiling salted water for 5 minutes. Drain the shrimp and crush them to a paste in a mortar or purée them in a blender, using a little of the stock to moisten them. Add 1 tablespoon tomato paste to the shrimp purée and combine it with the fish stock, blending well. Stir in 2 teaspoons curry powder and 1 cup light cream. Cool the soup and chill it. Garnish each serving with thin pimiento strips, tomato slices, and halved cooked shrimp.

Cold Casaba Soup

REMOVE the pulp from a casaba melon, cut enough of it into small dice to make 1 cup and reserve the dice. Coarsely chop the remaining pulp. In a saucepan melt 1/3 cup butter and add the chopped melon, 1 tablespoon sugar, the grated rind of 1 lemon, and a pinch of salt. Cook the mixture for a few minutes and add 4 cups milk. Bring the soup to a boil and simmer it for 10 minutes. Put the soup through a sieve or purée it in a blender and chill it. Garnish each serving with a few of the reserved melon dice.

Jellied Chicken Consommé

CHICKEN consommé made from rich stock will jell naturally when it is cold, but, if necessary, it can be stiffened with unflavored gelatin. Chill the consommé thoroughly. If it does not thicken, add 1 tablespoon gelatin for each 2 cups liquid. Soften the gelatin in 1/4 cup cold consommé and dissolve it in boiling consommé. Chill the consommé for several hours or overnight. Stir the jellied consommé with a fork before serving.

ʃ❧ Citrus Soup Frappé

SOFTEN 1 1/2 tablespoons gelatin in 1/4 cup red wine and dissolve it over hot water. Stir in 1 cup orange juice, 3/4 cup raspberry juice, and 1/4 cup lemon juice, all strained. Add 1 cup sauterne, 2 tablespoons kirsch, a pinch of salt, and nutmeg to taste. Add 1 cup orange sections, free of seeds and membranes. Chill the soup, and freeze it for at least 2 hours. At serving time, break up the jelly with a fork and serve the soup in chilled cups. Garnish with thin slices of orange, dipped in sugar.

ʃ❧ Jellied Cucumber Soup

PEEL 1 large cucumber, halve it lengthwise, and remove the seeds. Grate the cucumber and 1/4 onion and add 1/4 cup chopped mint and the juice of 1/2 lemon. Stir the mixture into 4 cups jellied chicken consommé melted to the syrupy stage. Season the soup with salt and pepper, pour it into soup cups, and chill thoroughly.

ʃ❧ Jellied Grapefruit and Avocado Bisque

PEEL 2 avocados, remove the pits, and put the pulp through a fine sieve. Beat 1/4 cup each of heavy cream and grapefruit juice into the avocado purée until it is thick and smooth, and season with salt and chili powder to taste. Combine the purée with 4 cups jellied chicken consommé and beat it well with a fork. Serve the soup in chilled cups, garnished with whipped cream and grapefruit sections.

ʃ❧ Jellied Mushroom Consommé

SIMMER 1 pound mushrooms, chopped, in 3 1/2 cups chicken stock for 30 minutes. Strain the mixture through cheesecloth into a bowl, pressing the pulp to extract all the liquid. Measure the soup and, if necessary, add enough more stock to make 3 3/4 cups liquid. Add 2 tablespoons Sherry and salt and pepper to taste. Bring the soup to a boil. Soften 1 tablespoon gelatin in 1/4 cup cold water and dissolve it in the hot soup. Chill the soup until it jells and serve in chilled soup cups with a spoonful of sour cream.

Breads

White Bread

IN a large warm bowl dissolve 1 package of yeast in 1 cup lukewarm water. Scald 1 cup milk and stir in 6 tablespoons butter, warmed to room temperature, until it is melted. Put 2 1/2 teaspoons salt in a measuring cup, add enough sugar to make 1/4 cup, and dissolve it, stirring, in the milk. Cool the milk mixture to lukewarm and stir it into the yeast. Stir in 3 cups sifted flour, a cup at a time, beating the batter well with a wooden spoon until it is smooth. Beat in 3 more cups sifted flour, one by one, to obtain a rather sticky dough. As it becomes more difficult to stir with the spoon, use a beating motion. Or the dough may be mixed with the cupped hand until all the flour is absorbed.

Turn out the dough on a lightly floured board. Work it with the cupped hands, drawing it toward you and pushing it back. As soon as the dough can be handled easily, knead it by drawing it toward you and pressing it down and away from you with the heels of the hands. Bread dough may be roughly treated. The dough should be kneaded for about 7 to 9 minutes, or until it is glossy and bubbles appear under the surface.

Put 1 teaspoon soft butter in the warm mixing bowl and add the dough, rolling it around to coat it thoroughly. Cover the bowl with a damp towel and let the dough stand in a warm place until it doubles in bulk, about 1 to 1 1/2 hours. (Ideally, the temperature should be 82° F., and the dough free from drafts or changes of tem-

219

perature. The warmer the place, the more rapidly it will rise, but if the place is too warm and the dough rises too rapidly, the quality of the bread will suffer.)

Turn out the dough again on the lightly floured board and punch it down to its original bulk to push out the air. Cover the dough with the damp towel and let it rest for 15 minutes. Butter 2 bread pans, 9 by 5 by 3 inches. Cut the dough in half, work the halves until they are smooth, and form the dough into 2 loaves a little shorter than the pans. Place the loaves in the pans, seam side down.

Cover the loaves with a damp towel and let them rise again until the centers are higher than the edges of the pans, about 1 hour. Put the loaves on the center rack of a hot oven (400° F.) and bake them for 15 minutes. Reduce the heat to moderate (350° F.) and bake the loaves for 35 to 40 minutes longer, or until they shrink a little from the sides of the pans and sound hollow when tapped.

Remove the loaves from the oven. Brush the tops with 1 tablespoon melted butter and lay the loaves on their sides across the pans to cool, covering them with a towel. If a harder, crisper crust is desired, cool the loaves without covering them. These loaves are at their best for slicing and eating on the following day.

℈ Country White Bread

IN a large bowl combine 1/3 to 1/2 cup sugar, 1 heaping tablespoon coarse salt or 1 level tablespoon ordinary salt, 1/3 cup shortening, and 2 cups boiling water. Let the mixture cool to lukewarm.

Into a 1-cup measure put 1/4 cup lukewarm water, 1 teaspoon sugar, and 2 packages of yeast, and let the yeast bubble until it reaches the top of the cup. Add the yeast to the mixture in the bowl, and stir in 2 eggs, well beaten. Add 4 cups unsifted flour and stir the dough until it is smooth. Add another 4 cups flour and work the dough until the flour is incorporated. Cover the bowl lightly and chill the dough for 3 hours.

Cut the dough into three parts. Rub the hands with vegetable shortening and work each piece of dough in the hands, squeezing out the air. Shape the pieces of dough into 3 loaves and put them, smooth side up, in 3 seasoned, unbuttered bread pans. Cover the loaves and let them stand in a warm place or until the centers of the loaves rise above the edges of the pans, about 1 1/2 hours.

Put the loaves in a moderate oven (350° F.) and immediately reduce the heat to moderately slow (325° F.). Bake the loaves for about 25 minutes, or until they come out of the pans easily. Cover a wire rack with a towel, remove the loaves from the pans, and lay them on their sides on the towel. Cover them and let them cool.

French Bread

IN a warm bowl dissolve 1 package of yeast in 1 1/4 cups lukewarm water. With a wooden spoon stir in 1 1/2 teaspoons salt, 3 tablespoons soft butter, and 2 cups sifted flour. Add 2 more cups sifted flour and turn the dough out on a lightly floured board. Knead the dough for about 6 to 8 minutes, until it is smooth. Put the dough in a buttered bowl and turn it until the whole surface is coated. Cover the dough with a damp towel and let it rise in a warm place until it doubles in bulk, about 1 1/2 to 2 hours.

Punch down the dough, cover it with a damp towel, and let it rise again for 45 minutes. Punch down the dough, cover it again, and let it rest for 15 minutes. Shape the dough into a rectangle, 10 by 15 inches, roll it up the narrow way, and seal the edges well. Roll it gently to elongate it into an even narrow roll with tapered ends.

Butter a baking sheet, sprinkle it with corn meal, and arrange the loaf on it. Brush the top with cold water. Cut diagonal slashes 1/4 inch deep along the top, spacing them 3 inches apart. Let the dough stand, uncovered, for 1 1/2 hours. Brush the top again with cold water and bake the bread in a moderately hot oven (375° F.) for 20 minutes. Brush the top with *dorure* and bake the bread for 25 minutes longer.

Dorure

BEAT 1 egg yolk with 1 tablespoon milk or water. For glazing breads and pastries.

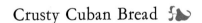

Crusty Cuban Bread

DISSOLVE 1 package of yeast in 2 cups lukewarm water and stir in 1 1/4 tablespoons salt and 1 tablespoon sugar. With a wooden spoon stir in a cup of the sifted flour at a time, beating well after each addition, using 6 to 7 cups in all, or enough to make a smooth and rather stiff dough. Shape the dough into a ball and put it in a buttered bowl. Cover it with a damp towel and let it rise in a warm place until it doubles in bulk. Punch the dough down and knead it on a lightly floured board for several minutes. Divide the dough in half and shape each half into a long cylindrical loaf. Put the loaves on a baking sheet liberally sprinkled with corn meal and let them rise for 5 minutes. Cut small diagonal slits 1/4 inch deep along the top of the loaves and brush the surface with cold water. Put the loaves in a cold oven. Turn on the heat, set the thermostat at hot (400° F.), and bake the loaves for about 45 minutes, or until they are golden brown. For crustier bread, put a large flat pan filled with boiling water on the rack below the loaves during the baking period.

Sourdough Bread

INTO a warm bowl measure 1 cup sourdough starter. Scald 1/2 cup milk, stir in 1 1/2 tablespoons each of sugar and melted butter, and let the mixture cool. Add the milk mixture to the starter. Sift 3 1/2 cups sifted flour over the starter and mix all together. Turn the dough out on a lightly floured board and knead it for 2 minutes. Put the dough in a buttered bowl, cover it with a damp towel, and let it rise in a warm place until it doubles in bulk, about 1 1/2 hours. Punch down the dough, cover it with a damp towel, and let it rise for about 30 minutes. Punch down the dough again, shape it into a ball, and let it rest for 10 minutes.

Pat the ball into a loaf shape and turn it into a buttered bread pan. Cover the loaf lightly with a damp towel and let it rise again until it doubles in bulk. Bake the loaf in a hot oven (400° F.) for 45 minutes, or until it is brown. Lay the loaf on its side across the pan to cool, covering it with a warm towel.

Sourdough Starter Without Yeast

IN a glass jar or an enamel or earthenware container mix 2 cups each of white flour and warm water, preferably water in which potatoes have been cooked. Let the mixture stand in the sun or in a warm place for 2 to 4 days, or until the mixture is sour and bubbly. The sourer the smell, the better.

Sourdough Starter With Yeast

IN a glass jar or an enamel or earthenware container dissolve 1 package of yeast in 1/4 cup lukewarm water. Add 2 cups warm water, preferably water in which potatoes have been cooked, 2 cups white flour, and 1 tablespoon each of salt and sugar. Cover the mixture lightly with a warm towel and let it stand until it is sour and bubbly, about 2 to 4 days.

Whole-Wheat Bread 🐖

IN a large warm bowl combine 1 3/4 cups scalded milk, 1/4 cup each of soft butter and honey or molasses, and 1 tablespoon salt, and let the mixture cool to lukewarm. Dissolve 1 package of yeast in 1/4 cup lukewarm water and add it to the milk mixture. Add 3 cups sifted whole-wheat flour and stir the mixture well with a wooden spoon. Add 3 more cups sifted whole-wheat flour, working it in 1/2 cup at a time. Turn the dough out on a floured board and let it rest for 10 minutes.

Knead the dough for 10 minutes. Put it in a buttered bowl, cover it with a damp towel, and let it rise until it doubles in bulk, about 1 1/4 hours. Punch down the dough, cover it, and let it rise again for 1 hour. Divide the dough in half, cover it again with a warm towel, and let it rest for 10 minutes. Shape the dough into 2 loaves and put them in 2 buttered bread pans. Cover them with a damp towel and let them rise again until the centers are higher than the edges of the pans. Bake the loaves in a hot oven (400° F.) for about 35 minutes, or until they shrink from the sides of the pans. Lay the loaves on their sides across the pans to cool, covering them with a warm towel.

Swedish Rye Bread 🐖

IN a large bowl cream 4 tablespoons shortening with 1 cup brown sugar. Stir in thoroughly 1/2 cup corn syrup and add 1 heaping teaspoon salt and 1 teaspoon anise, fennel, or caraway seeds. Gradually add 1 quart lukewarm water, stirring constantly. Put the mixture in a saucepan and boil it for a few minutes. Cool the liquid to lukewarm and add 2 packages of yeast dissolved in 1/2 cup lukewarm water. Return the mixture to the bowl and stir in 3 cups sifted rye flour and about 5 cups sifted white flour, to make a firm dough. Knead the dough thoroughly and put it in a buttered bowl. Cover it with a damp towel and let it rise in a warm place until it doubles in bulk. Knead the dough lightly and shape it into 2 loaves. Put them in bread pans to rise again to double volume. Bake the bread in a moderate oven (350° F.) for 1 hour, or until the loaves are well browned and test done.

Pumpernickel Bread 🐖

IN a warm bowl dissolve 3 packages of yeast in 1 1/2 cups lukewarm water, and stir in 1/2 cup molasses, 3 tablespoons caraway seeds, and 1 tablespoon salt. With a wooden spoon mix in 2 tablespoons soft butter and 3 cups sifted rye flour. Add 3 cups sifted white flour and turn the dough out on a lightly floured board. Knead the dough for about 8 to 10 minutes, or until it is smooth. Put the dough in a buttered bowl and turn it until it is thoroughly coated. Cover the dough with a damp towel and let it rise in a warm place until it doubles in bulk, about 2 hours.

Punch down the dough, divide it in half, and shape each half into a ball. Put the balls of dough on a baking sheet sprinkled with corn meal, cover them with a damp towel, and let them rise for 45 minutes. Brush the tops of the loaves with water and bake them in a very hot oven (450° F.) for 10 minutes. Reduce the heat to moderate (350° F.) and bake them for 30 minutes longer. Cool before slicing.

Cheese Bread

In a large bowl dissolve 1/4 cup sugar and 2 teaspoons salt in 1 cup boiling water, and let the liquid cool to lukewarm. Stir in 1 package of yeast dissolved in 2 tablespoons lukewarm water. Add 1 egg, beaten, 1/2 cup wheat germ, and 6 ounces grated aged light Cheddar (about 1/2 cup) and gradually beat in 3 1/2 cups sifted flour. Turn the dough out on a lightly floured board and knead it until it is smooth and elastic. Shape the dough into a ball and put it into a buttered bowl. Brush the dough with melted butter, cover it lightly with a damp towel, and let it rise in a warm place until it doubles in bulk, about 1 hour. Turn the dough out on the board, punch it down, and shape it into a loaf. Put the loaf in a buttered bread pan and let it double in bulk again, about 40 minutes. Bake the bread in a moderate oven (350° F.) for about 40 minutes. Remove it from the pan to a wire rack and brush the crust with melted butter. Cool before slicing.

White Cheese Bread

In a large warm bowl combine 2 1/2 cups scalded milk, 2 tablespoons sugar, 4 teaspoons soft butter, and 3 teaspoons salt, and let the mixture cool to lukewarm. Stir in 2 packages of yeast dissolved in 1/2 cup lukewarm water. Stir 4 cups sifted flour into the milk mixture and add 3 cups grated Swiss Gruyère. Mix in another 1 1/2 cups sifted flour, mixing with the hands when the dough becomes too stiff to stir. Turn the dough out on a floured board and knead it for 6 to 8 minutes, working in another 1/2 cup sifted flour.

Put the dough in a buttered bowl, cover it with a damp towel, and let it rise in a warm place until it doubles in bulk, about 1 hour. Punch down the dough, knead it briefly, and divide it in half. Shape the halves into loaves a little smaller than the pans. Lay the loaves in 2 buttered bread pans, cover them with a damp towel, and let them rise again until they double in bulk, about 1/2 hour. Bake the loaves in a moderate oven (350° F.) for 35 to 40 minutes, or until they shrink from the sides of the pans. Lay the loaves on their sides across the pans to cool, covering them with a warm towel.

Onion Bread 🐦

IN a skillet sauté 5 onions, diced, in 3 tablespoons butter until they are golden. In another skillet sauté 4 slices bacon, diced, until it is crisp. Drain the bacon and onion dice on absorbent paper and let them cool.

Combine 2 eggs, well beaten, with 1 cup sour cream, 1 teaspoon caraway seeds, the onions and bacon, and salt and pepper to taste. Line a square 9-inch baking dish with 1/3 the recipe for white bread and spread the onion mixture over the dough. Let the dough rise in a warm place until it doubles in bulk. Bake the bread in a moderately hot oven (375° F.) for 35 minutes, or until the bread tests done.

Bread Sticks 🐦

IN a large bowl dissolve 1 package of yeast in 1/2 cup lukewarm water. Melt 3 tablespoons lard in 1/2 cup hot water, cool it slightly, and add it to the yeast. Add 1 cup sifted flour and beat the dough until it is smooth. Fold in 2 stiffly beaten egg whites. Add about 2 cups sifted flour and knead the dough for about 5 minutes until it is smooth and elastic. Put the dough in a buttered bowl, brush it with soft butter or lard, and cover it lightly with a damp towel. Let it rise in a warm place until it doubles in bulk. Punch the dough down and let it rise again until it doubles in bulk. Punch it down again and let it rest for 15 minutes.

Divide the dough in half and roll out each half on a floured board into a rectangle 1/3 inch thick. Cut the dough into 2-inch squares and roll the squares with the palm of the hand into narrow rolls the length and thickness of a pencil. Put the rolls on a buttered baking sheet, cover them lightly with a damp towel, and let them rise for 30 minutes. Bake the bread sticks in a moderate oven (350° F.) for 12 to 15 minutes, or until they are golden brown.

℘ English Muffins

DISSOLVE 1 package of yeast in 1/4 cup lukewarm water. Scald 1 cup milk and add to it 2 tablespoons sugar, 1 teaspoon salt, and 3 tablespoons butter. Cool the milk to lukewarm and stir in well 2 cups sifted flour. Stir in the yeast and 1 egg, slightly beaten, and beat the mixture thoroughly. Add about 2 more cups sifted flour, or enough to make a moderately soft dough. Turn the dough out on a lightly floured board and knead it until it is smooth and satiny.

Put the dough in a buttered bowl, butter the surface lightly, and cover it with a damp towel. Let the dough rise in a warm place until it doubles in bulk, about 1 hour. Punch the dough down and let it rest for 10 minutes. Roll it out 1/4 inch thick on a board lightly covered with corn meal and cut it into 3-inch rounds. Sprinkle the top of the rounds with corn meal, cover them with a dry towel, and let them rise on the board until they double in bulk, about 45 minutes. Bake the muffins slowly on an ungreased heavy griddle. For each batch of muffins have the griddle hot at first, then reduce the heat to brown them slowly. Bake them for 5 or 6 minutes on each side. Cool the muffins, pull them apart—do not use a knife—and toast them. (These muffins freeze well. Defrost them before toasting.) Makes 24 to 30 muffins.

℘ Finger Rolls

SCALD 3/4 cup milk, stir in 1/4 cup sugar, 1 1/4 teaspoons salt, and 4 1/2 tablespoons butter, and cool the mixture to lukewarm. Dissolve 2 envelopes of yeast in 3/4 cup lukewarm water and add it to the milk. Add 2 1/4 cups sifted flour and beat the dough with a wooden spoon until it is smooth. Beat in another 2 1/4 cups sifted flour, to make a rather rough and sticky dough. Turn the dough out on a lightly floured board and knead it for about 8 minutes, or until it is smooth and shiny. Put the dough into a buttered bowl, brush it lightly with melted butter, and cover it with a damp towel. Let the dough rise in a warm place until it doubles in bulk, about 1 hour. Punch the dough down and pat it out on a lightly floured board into a rectangle about 1/2 inch thick. Break off small pieces of dough and form them into cylindrical shapes, about 3 inches long, with tapered ends. Put the rolls 1 inch apart on buttered baking sheets. Cover them with a damp towel and let them rise in a warm place until they double in bulk, about 45 minutes. Bake the rolls in a hot oven (425° F.) for about 15 minutes, or until they are golden brown.

Brioches 🐀

DISSOLVE 1 package of yeast in 1/4 cup lukewarm water. With the fingertips mix in 1/2 cup sifted flour, adding, if necessary, a little more lukewarm water to make a soft sponge. Roll the sponge into a ball, cut a cross on top, and drop it into a deep bowl of warm water. It will rise to the surface of the water.

Sift 1 1/2 cups sifted flour onto a pastry board and make a well in the center. Break in 2 eggs and begin to knead the paste, adding, little by little, a third egg to make a soft dough. A good brioche dough is very elastic. Scoop up the dough in the hand, raise it, and crash it violently against the table or board. Repeat this crashing action about 100 times, or until the dough becomes very elastic and detaches itself cleanly from the fingers and the board.

Knead into the beaten dough 1/2 teaspoon salt and 1 tablespoon sugar. Knead 3/4 cup butter until it is soft and mix it in thoroughly but gently. Overworking at this point will cause the dough to lose its elasticity.

Remove the ball of sponge from the surface of the water to a towel to drain, and add it to the dough. Mix the dough, form it into a ball, and put it in a floured bowl. Cover it with a damp towel and let it rise in a warm place until it doubles in bulk, about 3 hours. Turn the dough out on a lightly floured board and punch it down to its original size. Return it to the bowl and chill it, covered, for 6 hours or overnight. It will rise a little. In the morning punch it down, and it will be ready to shape and bake.

For individual brioches, use small fluted molds or large muffin pans. Shape the dough into balls just large enough to half fill the molds. Cut a cross in each ball and insert a small ball of dough, to make the head or crown of the brioche. Cover the brioches and let them rise in a warm place for about 30 minutes. Brush them with *dorure* and bake them in a hot oven (425° F.) for about 15 minutes, or until they are brown.

For a large brioche, follow the procedure for making little brioches, only fill a large mold half full with the dough. Bake the brioche in a hot oven (425° F.) for 30 minutes, or until it is brown.

Croissants 🐀

DISSOLVE 2 packages of yeast in 1/2 cup lukewarm water, add 1 cup sifted flour, and form the sponge into a ball. Cut a cross in the top and drop the ball into a deep bowl of warm water, leaving it to rise.

Sift 3 cups sifted flour, 1/2 teaspoon salt, and 1 tablespoon sugar onto a pastry board. Make a well in the center and gradually stir in 1 1/2 cups lukewarm milk. Work the mixture until it becomes elastic. The dough for croissants should not be as soft as brioche dough. Remove the ball of sponge from the surface of the water to a towel to drain, and add it to the dough, cutting and folding it in. Working the dough at this point destroys its elasticity. Cover the dough with a damp towel and let it stand for 30 minutes.

Knead 1 cup butter until it is soft and free of water. Roll out the dough into a rectangle about 1/2 inch thick. Form the butter into a flat cake and place it in the center of the dough. Fold one third of the dough over the butter in the center and fold the other third of the dough on top to make 3 layers. Turn the folded dough so that an open end faces you. Roll it out again into a long rectangle, fold it over as before, and turn it. Each series of rolling, folding, and turning is called a turn. Make another turn, wrap the dough in wax paper, and chill it for several hours.

Roll out the dough, fold it, and turn. Repeat this procedure, making 2 more turns. Chill the dough for 1 hour.

Cut the dough into 4 equal parts and roll out each part into a circle 1/8 inch thick and about 12 to 14 inches in diameter. Cut the circle into 8 pie-shaped triangles. Starting at the base, roll each triangle of dough loosely to form a cylinder thicker at the center than at the ends. Shape the rolls into crescents and put them on a lightly floured baking sheet. Cover the croissants with a towel and let them rise in a warm place for 30 minutes. Brush them with *dorure* and bake them in a hot oven (400° F.) for 5 minutes. Reduce the temperature to moderate (350° F.) and bake the croissants for 15 to 20 minutes longer, or until they are well browned.

Caraway Buns

DISSOLVE 2 packages of yeast in a generous 1/2 cup lukewarm water. Scald 1 3/4 cups heavy cream, add 1/2 cup each of sugar and butter, and cool the mixture to lukewarm. Stir in the yeast and 2 teaspoons caraway seeds. Gradually work in 8 cups sifted flour sifted with 2 teaspoons salt, 1 teaspoon nutmeg, and 1/8 teaspoon each of cloves and mace, adding more flour, if necessary, to make a soft but not sticky dough. Turn the dough out on a lightly floured board and knead it for about 5 minutes until it is smooth and satiny. Put the dough in a buttered bowl, cover it lightly with a damp towel, and let it rise in a warm place until it doubles in bulk, about 2 hours. Punch the dough down and let it rest for about

Brioches, Croissants, and Café au Lait

10 minutes. Break off pieces of dough and shape them into large, flat, round buns. Arrange the buns on a buttered baking sheet and brush them with *dorure*. With a knife, cut a deep cross on each bun so that when baked the buns can be broken easily into triangular pieces. Cover the buns with a damp towel and let them rise in a warm place until they double in bulk, about 45 minutes. Bake the buns in a hot oven (400° F.) for 10 minutes, reduce the heat to moderately hot (375° F.), and bake them for 10 to 15 minutes longer, or until they are golden brown.

✺ Corn Meal Rolls

SCALD 1 cup milk and stir in 1/4 cup shortening, 1 cup corn meal, 2 eggs, well beaten, and 2 cups sifted flour sifted with 1 teaspoon salt. Dissolve 1 package of yeast in 1/4 cup water and work it into the dough. Knead the dough on a lightly floured board, adding a little flour, if necessary, to make it easy to handle. Put the dough in a buttered bowl, cover it with a damp towel, and let it rise until it doubles in bulk. Punch the dough down, knead it again, and roll it out 1 inch thick. Cut the dough with a biscuit cutter into any desired shape, and space the rolls well apart on a buttered baking sheet. Let them rise again until they double in bulk. Bake the rolls in a hot oven (400° F.) for 15 to 20 minutes, or until they are nicely browned.

✺ Melba Toast

SLICE a loaf of stale bread as thinly as possible and trim the crusts. Leave the slices whole or halve them. Arrange the bread slices on a baking sheet and toast them in a very slow oven (250° F.), turning the pieces frequently, until they are crisp and evenly browned. Melba toast may be made in quantity and stored in a dry airtight tin.

✺ Toast Sticks

CUT a loaf of stale bread into slices 3/4 inch thick, trim the crusts, and cut each slice into 3 or 4 narrow strips. Dip the strips of bread in melted butter and arrange them on a baking sheet. Bake the strips in a hot oven (400° F.) for 6 to 8 minutes, or until they are lightly browned.

Croûtes 🐾

CUT slices 1/2 inch thick from a two-day-old loaf of French bread. Cut the slices with a cutter into rounds, ovals, or any other desired shapes. Dry them in a slow oven (300° F.). Or brush them with melted butter and bake them on baking sheets in a hot oven (400° F.) until they are golden brown. Or sauté them on both sides in butter until they are golden brown.

Croutons 🐾

Cut slices of bread into small or large cubes, or into 1/2-inch squares 1/8 inch thick, and dry or brown them as for croûtes. A little sliced garlic or onion may be added to the melted butter and removed before the butter is used. Or add celery salt, one of the herbal salts, or any dried herb to the butter. Or, when the cubes are browned, sprinkle them with grated cheese.

Croustades 🐾

CUT a loaf of firm white bread lengthwise into slices 1 inch thick. With a cookie cutter cut out rounds 1 1/2 inches in diameter. Hollow out each round, leaving a shell about 1/8 inch thick. Spread the rims and cups of the shells with soft butter and arrange them on a baking sheet. Bake the croustades in a hot oven (400° F.) for about 12 minutes, or until they are crisp and golden brown. Larger croustades may be made in the same fashion. Croustades may also be made from flaky pastry baked in shallow molds of the appropriate sizes.

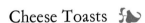

Cheese Toasts 🐾

SAUTÉ narrow strips of bread in butter until they are golden brown. While the bread strips are still hot, roll them in grated Parmesan and sprinkle them with paprika.

Gougère

Poppy Seed Toast ❦

TRIM the crusts from 12 thin slices of white bread and flatten each slice with a rolling pin. Spread the slices with butter and sprinkle them with poppy seeds. Roll up the slices, secure them with picks, and arrange them on a buttered baking sheet. Bake the toast in a hot oven (425° F.) for 10 minutes, or until they are golden, and remove the picks. Serve hot.

Poppy Seed Toast Triangles ❦

TRIM the crusts from slices of white bread, butter the slices and cut them into triangles. Arrange the triangles on a buttered baking sheet and sprinkle them liberally with poppy seeds. Bake the toast triangles in a slow oven (300° F.) for about 15 minutes, or until they are golden.

THICK WAFERS

Galletas ❦

SIFT together 4 cups sifted flour, 2 teaspoons salt, and 1 teaspoon baking powder, and blend in 1 1/4 cups milk or light cream and 2 eggs, beaten. Roll out the dough thinly on a lightly floured board and cut into small rounds. Bake the wafers on a buttered baking sheet in a hot oven (400° F.) for 5 to 8 minutes, or until they are brown.

Gougère ❦

SCALD 2 cups milk and cool it. Strain the milk into a large saucepan and add 1/2 cup butter, cut up, 2 teaspoons salt, and a dash of freshly ground black pepper. Bring the mixture to a rolling boil and add all at once 2 cups sifted flour. Cook the paste over low heat, beating it briskly with a wooden spoon, until the mixture forms a ball and leaves the sides of the pan clean. Remove the pan from the heat and beat in 8 eggs, one at a time, incorporating each egg thoroughly before adding the next. When the paste is shiny and smooth mix in 6 ounces natural Gruyère or Swiss cheese, cut into very fine cubes. Let the dough cool.

Divide the dough in half. With an oval soup spoon scoop out from one half of the dough pieces the size of an egg. With a rubber spatula push them off the spoon onto a buttered baking sheet in a ring, leaving a space in the middle about 2 1/2 inches in diameter. Use a teaspoon to make smaller ovals on top of the first layer. Repeat the procedure with the remaining dough, to make 2 rings. Brush the *gougères* with milk and sprinkle each one with 2 tablespoons finely diced cheese. Bake the *gougères* in a moderately hot oven (375° F.) for about 45 minutes, or until they are well puffed and golden brown. *Gougère* is traditionally served with red Burgundy.

ﾟ꙳ Beaten Biscuits

SIFT together 6 cups sifted flour, 1 1/2 tablespoons sugar, and 1/2 teaspoon salt. With the fingers cut in 1 cup shortening. Make a well in the center, add 1 3/4 cups ice water, and quickly work the flour mixture into the water. Beat the dough with a wooden mallet for 25 to 30 minutes, adding as much additional flour as the dough will hold. It must be shiny and blistered. Roll out the dough very thinly on a floured board. Dust it with flour, fold it in half, and roll it out again 1/3 inch thick. Cut out the biscuits with a small round cookie cutter (for hors-d'oeuvre biscuits, use the round cutter of a truffle set). Prick the tops well with a fork and bake the biscuits in a hot oven (400° F.) for 25 to 30 minutes. Do not let them brown or they will become very hard. The biscuits are easily split with just the touch of a sharp knife point.

ﾟ꙳ Butter Flake Biscuits

SIFT 2 cups sifted flour with 3 teaspoons baking powder and 3/4 teaspoon salt. With 2 knives or a pastry blender quickly cut in 5/8 cup cold sweet butter until the mixture resembles coarse meal mixed with some lumps the size of peas. Make a well in the center and in it put 2 eggs, well beaten, and 1/2 cup cold milk. Combine the ingredients quickly and lightly with a fork.

Turn the dough out on a lightly floured board and roll it very lightly into an oblong about 1/2 inch thick. Fold the dough in three and roll it again into an oblong. Repeat the folding and rolling once more, using as little flour as possible and handling the dough very lightly. Roll out the dough 1/2 inch thick and cut it into 2-inch rounds with a floured biscuit cutter. Put the biscuits on a dry baking sheet and bake them in a very hot oven (475° F.) for about 5 minutes, or until they are puffed and golden.

Cheese Biscuits

SIFT 2 cups sifted flour with 2 teaspoons baking powder and 1/2 teaspoon salt, and add 1 cup grated Parmesan. With 2 knives or a pastry blender cut in 1/4 cup butter until the mixture resembles coarse meal. With a fork stir in 3/4 cup milk, or enough to make a soft dough. Turn the dough out on a lightly floured board and knead it for about 30 seconds. Roll it out 1/2 inch thick and cut it in 2-inch rounds. Put the biscuits on a buttered baking sheet and bake them in a very hot oven (450° F.) for 12 to 15 minutes, or until they are golden brown.

Chive Biscuits

SIFT 2 cups sifted flour with 2 teaspoons baking powder and 1/2 teaspoon salt. With 2 knives or a pastry blender cut in 4 tablespoons butter and add 1/2 cup finely chopped chives. With a fork stir in about 3/4 cup milk, or enough to make a soft dough. Turn the dough out on a lightly floured board and knead it briefly. Roll it out 1/2 inch thick and cut it into small rounds. Put the biscuits on a buttered baking sheet, brush the tops with melted butter, and bake them in a very hot oven (450° F.) for 12 to 15 minutes, or until they are golden brown.

Popovers

IN a large bowl combine 1 cup sifted flour sifted with 1/2 teaspoon salt, 3 eggs, lightly beaten, 1 cup milk, and 2 tablespoons melted butter. Beat the batter with a rotary beater until it is smooth. Butter iron popover pans and heat them until they are sizzling hot. Fill the cups half full with the batter and bake the popovers in a very hot oven (450° F.) for 20 minutes. Reduce the temperature to moderate (350° F.) and bake the popovers for about 20 minutes more, or until they are brown and crisp.

Cheese Popovers

IN a large bowl combine 2 cups sifted flour sifted with 1 teaspoon salt and 1/4 teaspoon paprika, and 2 large eggs, well beaten, 2 cups milk, and 1/2 cup grated Cheddar. Beat the batter until it is as thick as heavy cream. Butter iron popover pans and heat them until they are sizzling hot. Fill the cups half full with the batter and bake the popovers in a very hot oven (450° F.) for 30 minutes. Reduce the heat to moderate (350° F.) and bake the popovers for about 10 minutes longer, or until they are brown and crisp.

꩜ Cream Scones

IN a large bowl combine 1 cup sour milk with 6 tablespoons sugar and 1 egg, beaten. Sift into the mixture 4 cups sifted flour, 2 heaping teaspoons cream of tartar, and 1 heaping teaspoon baking soda. Beat the mixture well and gradually add 1/2 cup melted butter. Turn the dough out onto a floured board and roll it out 1/4 inch thick. Cut the dough into rounds and cut the rounds into 8 pie-shaped wedges. Dust the wedges with flour and cook the scones on a hot griddle, turning once, for 10 to 15 minutes, or until both sides are golden.

꩜ Virginia Ham Biscuits

SIFT 2 cups sifted flour with 4 teaspoons baking powder and stir in 1/2 pound ground Smithfield ham and a pinch of salt. With 2 knives or a pastry blender cut in 2 tablespoons shortening. With a fork stir in 3/4 cup milk, or enough to make a soft dough. Pat out the dough on a lightly floured board, handling it as little as possible, and cut it into small rounds. Put the biscuits on a buttered baking sheet and bake them in a very hot oven (450° F.) for about 15 minutes, or until they are golden brown.

꩜ Corn Bread

COMBINE 1 1/2 cups yellow corn meal, 1/2 cup sifted flour, 1 tablespoon baking powder, and 1 teaspoon each of salt and sugar. Add 3 eggs, lightly beaten with 1 cup milk, and beat the batter until it is thoroughly blended. Stir in 1/3 cup melted butter and 1/4 cup heavy cream. Butter a large shallow baking pan and heat it. Pour in the batter and bake the corn bread in a hot oven (400° F.) for about 15 to 20 minutes, or until it is well browned.

Corn Sticks 🐿

SCALD 1 cup milk, add 2 tablespoons butter and 1 tablespoon sugar, and stir the mixture until the butter is melted. Stir in 1 egg, beaten, 2 cups yellow corn meal mixed with 2 teaspoons baking powder, and 1/2 teaspoon salt. Butter corn-stick pans and heat them until they are sizzling hot. Pour in the batter and bake the corn sticks in a very hot oven (450° F.) for 12 to 15 minutes. Serve hot, with butter and honey.

Rice Muffins 🐿

SIFT 2 cups sifted flour with 4 teaspoons baking powder and 1/2 teaspoon salt, and stir in 1 cup cold cooked rice. Combine 2 eggs, well beaten, with 1 cup milk and pour the liquid into the dry ingredients, stirring only until the flour is moistened. Stir in 3 tablespoons melted butter. Pour the batter into buttered muffin tins and bake the muffins in a hot oven (425° F.) for about 25 minutes, or until they test done.

Cream Muffins 🐿

SIFT 2 cups sifted flour with 2 tablespoons sugar, 2 teaspoons baking powder and 1/2 teaspoon salt. Combine 1 egg, well beaten, with 1 cup heavy cream and pour the liquid into the dry ingredients, stirring only until the flour is moistened. The batter will be lumpy. Gently stir in 2 tablespoons melted butter and pour the batter into buttered muffin tins. Bake the muffins in a hot oven (400° F.) for about 25 minutes, or until they test done.

Tangerine Toast 🐿

TRIM the crusts from 6 slices of day-old white bread. Butter the slices generously and arrange them on a buttered baking sheet. Peel 6 small tangerines, separate them into sections, and remove the membranes. Top each slice of bread with tangerine sections, spacing them evenly, and sprinkle heavily with sugar, filling in the spaces between the fruit. Sprinkle each portion with a little almond or vanilla extract and bake the toast in a moderate oven (350° F.) for about 30 minutes, or until the bread is crisp and the fruit is caramelized. Serve hot.

ꙅꙬ French Toast

Cut slightly stale French or Italian bread, egg twist, or brioche into 8 to 12 slices 1/2 inch thick. Trim the crusts, if desired. Combine 2 eggs, slightly beaten, with 2 cups milk, 4 tablespoons sugar, and 1/4 teaspoon salt. Dip the bread into the egg mixture and sauté the slices on both sides in hot butter. Serve the toast hot, with honey or cinnamon sugar.

ꙅꙬ Rice Griddlecakes

Sift 1 cup sifted flour with 3/4 teaspoon baking soda. Add 1 cup cooked rice, 1 beaten egg, 1 1/2 cups sour cream, 2 tablespoons melted butter, and 1 teaspoon salt, and stir the mixture vigorously until it is well blended. Brown the cakes on both sides on a hot griddle. Serve with honey or maple syrup.

ꙅꙬ Wild Rice Pancakes

Beat 2 eggs until they are light and fluffy and stir in 2 cups buttermilk and 1 teaspoon soda. Sift together 2 cups sifted flour, 2 teaspoons baking powder, and 1 teaspoon salt. Gradually add the flour to the liquid, beating after each addition to make a smooth and rather thin batter. Stir in 1/4 cup melted butter and 3/4 cup cooked wild rice. Bake the pancakes on a hot buttered griddle, turning them once. Roll each pancake around a small sautéed sausage link. Serve hot, with blueberry syrup.

ꙅꙬ Sour Cream Waffles

Beat 2 egg yolks until they are thick and light and stir in 2 cups sour cream. Sift together 2 cups sifted flour, 1 tablespoon corn meal, and 1 teaspoon each of baking soda and salt. Stir the dry ingredients into the sour-cream mixture and fold in 2 egg whites, stiffly beaten. Bake the waffles on a hot buttered waffle iron. Serve with warm maple syrup and melted butter.

Entrée Crêpes

SIFT 1 cup sifted flour with 1/2 teaspoon salt. Beat together 2 eggs and 2 egg yolks, and add gradually the dry ingredients. Add 1 3/4 cups milk and stir the batter until it is smooth. Strain it through a fine sieve and let it stand for 2 hours.

Butter lightly a hot 5- to 5 1/2-inch skillet or iron crêpe pan. Pour in a generous tablespoon of batter and quickly tilt and rotate the pan so that the batter runs to the edges and covers the bottom with a thin layer. The crêpe should set and the bottom brown in 1 or 2 minutes. Turn the crêpe over carefully and cook the other side for about 30 seconds, or until it is golden brown. Slide the crêpe onto a wire rack. Cook the remaining crêpes and stack them. To keep the crêpes warm, cover them with a bowl and set them in a slow oven (250° F.). Makes 24 to 30 crêpes.

Oatmeal Bread

SOAK 1 1/3 cups rolled oats in 1 1/2 cups buttermilk for 2 hours. Sift 2 cups sifted flour with 1 teaspoon each of salt, baking soda, and cream of tartar, and stir the dry ingredients into the oatmeal and milk mixture. Knead the dough lightly on a floured board, form it into a loaf, and put it in a buttered bread pan. Bake the bread in a hot oven (400° F.) for 30 to 40 minutes, or until it tests done.

Crackling Bread

MIX well 1 1/2 cups corn meal, 2 tablespoons flour, 3 teaspoons baking powder, 1/2 teaspoon salt, 1 egg, well beaten, and 1 1/4 cups milk. Stir in 1 1/2 cups cracklings and beat all together well. Butter generously a shallow baking dish, heat it, and pour in the batter. Bake the bread in a very hot oven (450° F.) for about 20 minutes.

Cracklings

CUT fatback or salt pork into 1/4-inch cubes and sauté them slowly in a heavy skillet until all the lard has been extracted. Pour off the lard to save for shortening, if desired. Drain the cracklings on absorbent paper and reserve them.

Camembert Shortbread

CREAM 1/4 cup butter and blend in 3 ounces ripe Camembert cheese. Add 3 eggs, one at a time, beating well after each addition. Stir in 2 cups sifted flour sifted with 1 teaspoon salt, and mix the dough until it is soft. Pat out the dough lightly on a floured board until it forms a 10-inch circle. Put the circle on a buttered baking sheet and cut it into 16 wedges. Bake the shortbread in a hot oven (400° F.) for 25 minutes, or until it is brown.

Apricot Almond Bread

COOK 1 1/2 cups dried apricots in simmering water to cover for 5 minutes. Drain the fruit and reserve the juice. Chop the apricots, or cut them into small pieces with scissors. Cream 3 tablespoons soft butter with 1 1/2 cups sugar and stir in 1/2 cup reserved apricot juice. Sift 2 cups sifted flour with 2 teaspoons baking powder and 1/2 teaspoon each of salt and soda. Stir the dry ingredients into the creamed mixture alternately with 1/3 cup milk, stirring the batter only until it is blended. Fold in the apricots and 1/2 cup coarsely chopped blanched almonds. Pour the batter into a buttered bread pan and bake the bread in a moderate oven (350° F.) for about 1 hour, or until it tests done. This bread slices more easily if allowed to stand overnight.

Brazil Nut Tea Bread

SIFT together 2 cups each of whole-wheat flour and sifted white flour, 1/2 cup sugar, and 1 teaspoon each of salt and baking soda. Stir in thoroughly 2 cups buttermilk and 1/2 cup molasses, and fold in 1 cup each of chopped Brazil nuts and plumped seedless raisins. Turn the batter into 2 small buttered bread pans, and bake the loaves in a moderate oven (350° F.) for 1 hour, or until they test done. Turn the loaves out on wire racks to cool.

Assorted Cheese Breads

Cheese Bread (p. 224), White Cheese Bread (p. 224), Cheese Biscuits (p. 235),
Camembert Shortbread (p. 240).

୬ Cranberry Tea Bread

Sift 3 cups sifted flour with 1/4 cup sugar, 4 teaspoons baking powder, and 1 tea-spoon salt. Combine 1 egg, well beaten, with 1 cup milk and 2 tablespoons melted butter, and blend the liquid with the dry ingredients. Put 1 cup cranberries, washed, through a food chopper, add to them 1/4 cup sugar, and stir the cranberries into the batter. Fold in 1/2 cup chopped pecans and 1 teaspoon vanilla extract. Pour the batter into a buttered bread pan and bake the bread in a moderate oven (350° F.) for about 1 hour, or until it tests done.

୬ Honey Walnut Bread

Scald 1 cup milk, add 1 cup honey and 1/2 cup sugar, and stir over medium heat until the sugar is dissolved. Cool the mixture. Beat in 1/4 cup soft butter and 2 egg yolks. Sift together 2 1/2 cups sifted flour and 1 teaspoon each of salt and bak-ing soda. Stir the flour into the batter and blend it thoroughly. Fold in 1/2 cup walnuts, coarsely chopped. Pour the batter into a buttered and floured bread pan and bake the bread in a moderately slow oven (325° F.) for about 1 hour, or until it tests done. Leave the bread in the pan for 15 minutes and turn it out on a wire rack to cool. Serve thinly sliced, with sweet butter and honey or with cream cheese and preserves.

୬ Cobblestone Bread

Dissolve 1 1/2 packages of yeast in 1 cup lukewarm scalded milk. Stir in 4 table-spoons sugar, 1 teaspoon salt, 1/2 cup melted butter, and 3 1/2 cups sifted flour. Beat the dough thoroughly with a wooden spoon and knead it briefly. Put it in a buttered bowl, turning it to coat it evenly, and cover it with a damp towel. Let the dough rise in a warm place until it doubles in bulk, about 1 1/2 hours. Punch the dough down and pat it out on a lightly floured board into a rectangle about 1/2 inch thick. Cut the dough into diamond-shaped pieces about 2 1/2 inches long and roll each one in melted butter. Arrange the diamonds in layers in a 9-inch ring mold. The mold will be about half full. Cover the dough with a damp towel and let it rise until it fills the mold. Bake the bread in a hot oven (400° F.) for about 25 minutes, or until it is golden brown. Turn the bread out on a wire rack to cool, handling it gently so that the pieces do not separate.

Portuguese Sweet Bread 🦤

DISSOLVE 2 packages of yeast in 1/4 cup warm water. In a large bowl mix together 1 cup each of sugar and hot scalded milk, 1/4 cup butter, and 1 teaspoon salt. Stir the mixture until the butter melts. Cool the mixture until it is lukewarm and beat in 3 eggs, well beaten, and the yeast mixture. Gradually beat in 7 1/2 cups sifted flour, blending well until the dough is smooth. Turn the dough out on a well-floured board and sprinkle the dough with more flour. Knead the dough for 15 to 20 minutes, or until it is very smooth and small blisters appear on the surface. Add more flour to the board if necessary. Put the dough in a buttered bowl, cover it with a damp towel, and let it rise in a warm place for about 2 hours, or until it doubles in bulk. Punch the dough down and shape it into 2 small round loaves. Flatten the loaves and put them in buttered pie plates. Let the loaves rise in a warm place for about 1 hour, or until they are almost double in bulk. Bake them in a moderate oven (350° F.) for about 20 minutes, or until they are golden brown and test done. Turn the loaves out on their sides on a wire rack and let them cool.

Walnut Biscuits 🦤

SIFT 2 cups sifted flour with 2 teaspoons baking powder and 1 teaspoon salt. With 2 knives or a pastry blender cut in 4 to 6 tablespoons butter. Stir in 3/4 cup milk, or enough to make a soft but not sticky dough. Knead the dough on a lightly floured board for 30 seconds, roll it out into a sheet 1/4 inch thick, and spread it with soft butter. Spread the butter thickly with brown sugar and 1 cup chopped walnuts, and roll up the dough lengthwise as for a jelly roll. Cut the roll into 1-inch slices, lay the slices on a buttered baking sheet, and bake them in a hot oven (400° F.) for 15 minutes, or until they are lightly browned.

BATTER DUMPLINGS   ## Spätzle 🦤

SIFT 3 cups flour into a bowl, make a well in the center, and into it break 3 eggs. Add 3/4 teaspoon salt, 1/4 teaspoon each of black pepper and nutmeg, and 1 cup water, or enough to make a moderately heavy batter. Blend the batter only until it is smooth. Pour the batter into a colander with holes sufficiently large to let the dumplings fall through into a large saucepan of boiling salted water. Stir gently so

Munich Pot Roast with Mashed Potato Dumplings

that the dumplings do not stick together. When they rise to the surface, they are cooked. Drain the dumplings well and sprinkle them liberally with grated Parmesan. Sauté 1 onion, finely chopped, in 4 tablespoons butter until it is transparent and sprinkle it over the *Spätzle*.

Mashed Potato Dumplings

MASH 4 boiled potatoes and combine them with 2 eggs, lightly beaten, 2 slices of toast, finely crushed, 1 teaspoon each of potato flour and chopped parsley, a pinch of nutmeg, and salt and pepper to taste. Shape the mixture into balls the size of walnuts. Drop the dumplings, one at a time, into rapidly boiling salted water. Lift them out as they rise to the top and drain them. Brown the dumplings in butter. Serve with roasts or with hot soup.

Caraway Dumplings

SIFT into a mixing bowl 2 cups sifted flour, 2 teaspoons baking powder, and 1/2 teaspoon salt. Cut in 1 tablespoon butter and add 3 tablespoons caraway seed. Mix in 3 egg yolks, beaten, with 3/4 cup milk, stirring the batter only until the flour is moistened. Drop the dumplings by tablespoons into boiling chicken stock and cook them, covered, for 15 minutes. Remove them with a slotted spoon and drain on absorbent paper.

Eggs and Cheese

Hard-Cooked Eggs

LOWER eggs into boiling water and reduce the heat to simmering at once. Simmer the eggs for 10 to 12 minutes, turning them several times to center the yolks.

Cheese Tomato Eggs

SAUTÉ 1 onion, finely chopped, in 3 tablespoons butter until it is golden. Add 5 cups cooked tomatoes, 1 teaspoon chervil, 1/2 teaspoon basil, and 1/4 teaspoon salt and cook the mixture over low heat until it is reduced to 2 cups. Combine 4 ounces cream cheese with 1/2 cup of the hot sauce and blend the mixture into the sauce, stirring until the cheese is melted. Add 12 hard-cooked eggs, sliced.

Chutney Eggs

COMBINE in a saucepan 4 tablespoons each of gooseberry jam and chutney, 3 tablespoons chopped parsley, 2 tablespoons each of lemon and orange juice, and the grated rind of 1 orange. Season the sauce with salt and cayenne to taste and simmer it for 10 minutes. Combine the sauce gently with 12 hard-cooked eggs, sliced. Serve with fluffy rice.

Eggs Maison 🪶

MELT 6 tablespoons butter in a saucepan and add 4 tablespoons each of Escoffier Sauce Robert and Harvey Sauce or A.1. Sauce, and 1 tablespoon Dijon-type mustard. Stir the mixture well and add gradually 2 cups heavy cream. Add 12 hard-cooked eggs, sliced, and cook the mixture over low heat for 15 minutes. Stir in 1 tablespoon lemon juice.

Olive Eggs 🪶

MELT 4 tablespoons butter and stir in 3 tablespoons grated onion and 2 tablespoons flour. Add gradually 2 cups beef stock and cook the sauce over low heat, stirring constantly, until it is thick. Warm 2 beaten egg yolks with 2 tablespoons of the hot sauce and gradually add them to the pan. Add 12 hard-cooked eggs, quartered, 1/2 cup black olives, sliced, 1 tomato, peeled and diced, 2 tablespoons each of capers and lemon juice, and 1 teaspoon salt. Heat the mixture, but do not let it boil.

Eggs with Onion Sauce 🪶

SAUTÉ 12 small white onions, chopped, in 4 tablespoons butter until they are golden. Sprinkle the onions with 2 tablespoons flour and cook the *roux*, stirring, for 1 minute. Gradually stir in 3 cups heavy cream and cook the sauce, stirring constantly, until it is smooth and thick. Season with salt and pepper to taste and a dash of nutmeg. Cut 12 hot hard-cooked eggs in quarters, arrange them in a serving dish, and cover them with the hot sauce.

Sherried Eggs 🪶

SAUTÉ 1 cup cooked cubed ham and 1/2 cup shredded green pepper in 4 tablespoons butter for 10 minutes, stirring frequently. Add 1 cup sliced mushrooms and cook the mixture over low heat for 5 minutes. Add 1 cup heavy cream, 1/2 cup dry Sherry, and 12 hard-cooked eggs, halved. Heat the mixture but do not let it boil and season with salt and pepper to taste.

ꙮ Vineyard Eggs

MELT 6 tablespoons butter in a shallow pan and add 2 tablespoons chopped shallots and 8 mushrooms, coarsely chopped. Cook the mixture over low heat for 4 to 5 minutes, add 1 cup white Port, and simmer the sauce until it is reduced to 1/4 cup. Add to the pan 1 1/2 cups heavy cream, 1/4 teaspoon salt, and enough paprika to color the sauce well. Add 12 hard-cooked eggs, sliced, and heat the eggs slowly. Serve with triangles of buttered toast.

ꙮ Baked Egg Nests

SEPARATE 6 eggs, keeping the yolks whole in half an eggshell. Prop the eggshells against the side of a dish to keep them from falling. Beat the whites until they are stiff but not dry and fold in 2 tablespoons minced ham, and salt and pepper to taste. Pile the whites into individual baking dishes. Make a well in the center of each mound of egg white and drop in the yolks. Bake the eggs in a moderate oven (350° F.) for about 15 minutes, or until they are set. Carefully spoon a little Mornay sauce around each yolk.

ꙮ Eggs with Creamed Chicken

MAKE 6 large croustades from a loaf of unsliced sandwich bread. Fill the croustades with creamed chicken and break an egg on top of each. Dot the eggs with butter and bake them in a moderate oven (350° F.) for about 12 minutes, or until the whites are set. Dust with paprika.

ꙮ Eggs Baked in Green Peppers

HALVE lengthwise 3 green peppers, remove the ribs and seeds, and blanch the peppers in boiling water for 10 minutes. Half fill them with buttered bread crumbs, seasoned with salt and pepper. Break an egg into each pepper half, sprinkle with grated Parmesan, and bake the peppers in a moderate oven (350° F.) for about 15 minutes, or until the eggs are set.

Eggs Baked in Tomato Shells 🌿

CUT a thin slice from the tops of 6 firm ripe tomatoes. Scoop out the pulp and turn the shells upside down to drain. Arrange the shells in a buttered flameproof baking dish. Break an egg into each tomato, sprinkle with salt and pepper, and dot with butter. Bake the stuffed tomatoes in a moderate oven (350° F.) for about 15 minutes, or until the whites are just set. Sprinkle the eggs generously with grated Parmesan and brown the tops quickly under the broiler. Serve the eggs on hot croûtes garnished with chopped parsley.

Shirred Eggs in Tomato Juice 🌿

BUTTER generously a flameproof casserole large enough to hold 6 eggs in a single layer. Fill half the dish with well-seasoned tomato juice and bring the juice to the boiling point. Carefully break the eggs into the juice and leave the casserole over low heat for a few minutes until the juice returns to the boiling point. Season the eggs with salt and pepper and dot them with slivers of butter. Finish cooking the eggs in a moderate oven (350° F.). The whites should be opaque and firm, the yolks soft.

Molded Eggs Polignac 🌿

MELT 1 1/2 teaspoons butter in each of 6 small molds or ramekins and lay a large slice of truffle in the bottom of each mold. Break an egg into each mold and set the molds in a pan of hot water. Bake the eggs in a moderate oven (350° F.) for 8 to 10 minutes, or until they are just set. Remove the molds from the hot water and let the eggs set for a few minutes. Unmold each egg on a small round of toast and garnish with melted maître d'hôtel butter.

🦢 Eggs Royal

USING a pestle and mortar, pound 1 cup diced cooked chicken meat to a smooth paste. Gradually beat in 1/4 cup heavy cream, or enough to make a soft mixture that will hold its shape. Season the filling with salt and cayenne to taste and rub it through a fine sieve.

Line 6 tart pans with unsweetened tart pastry, prick the shells well, and bake them in a very hot oven (450° F.) until they are golden. Put a little of the chicken purée in each shell. Lightly poach 6 eggs and trim them neatly. Put an egg in each tart and cover the eggs with more of the purée, mounding it in the center. Sprinkle each tart with fresh bread crumbs mixed with a little grated cheese, decorate with a star-shaped truffle slice, and dot with butter. Bake the tarts in a moderate oven (350° F.) for 5 minutes, or until the topping browns slightly.

🦢 Egg Croquettes

SAUTÉ 1/4 cup chopped cooked ham in 2 tablespoons butter for 5 minutes. Chop 6 cooled hard-cooked eggs, mix them gently with 1 cup white sauce, and add the ham. Chill the mixture for 2 hours and shape it into croquettes. Roll the croquettes in bread crumbs, fry them in deep hot fat (390° F.) until they are golden, and drain them well on absorbent paper.

🦢 Poached Eggs

FILL a large skillet with 1 or 2 inches of water, add 1 tablespoon vinegar and 1 teaspoon salt, and bring the water to a boil. Reduce the heat so that the water is simmering. Break 1 egg at a time and slip it gently onto the surface of the water. (Sometimes it is helpful to stir the water with a long-handled spoon, swirling it rapidly in one direction to form a hollow whirlpool in the center. When the egg is slipped into this whirlpool, the motion of the water helps to keep its shape intact.) Simmer the eggs over low heat for about 3 minutes, or until the whites are barely firm. The water should not come to a boil again. Remove the eggs from the water with a perforated spoon and trim the whites. If necessary, the eggs may be kept hot for a few minutes in warm salted water.

Eggs may also be poached in milk, meat stock, tomato juice, or wine.

Poached Eggs with Yoghurt 🐦

BEAT 3 cups yoghurt until it is smooth and fluffy and stir in 1 garlic clove, mashed to a paste with 1 tablespoon vinegar and salt to taste. Pour the mixture into a serving dish. Poach 6 eggs and carefully arrange them in the serving dish.

Melt 2 tablespoons butter and stir in 1 teaspoon paprika and salt and pepper to taste. Cook the butter over low heat, stirring, until it turns a deep red, and pour the sauce over the eggs and the yoghurt.

Eggs Benedict Gourmet 🐦

SAUTÉ 6 tomato slices in 2 tablespoons butter for 1 minute on each side. Sauté 6 slices Canadian bacon in 1 tablespoon butter for about 2 minutes on each side. Poach 6 eggs. With the fingers split 3 English muffins and place on each half a slice of Canadian bacon, a slice of sautéed tomato, and a poached egg. Cover the eggs with hollandaise sauce.

Basic Omelet 🐦

FOR each serving, mix 2 eggs lightly with a fork and add 1/2 teaspoon salt. Heat a 7- to 8-inch omelet pan over high heat and in it melt 1 teaspoon butter. The pan should be so hot that the butter sizzles at once, but not so hot that the butter browns. Immediately pour in the eggs and stir them briskly with a fork, shaking the pan constantly. When the fork makes a visible track through the eggs, the omelet is set. The omelet will set in a minute or less. Remove the pan from the heat.

If the omelet is to be served with a filling, put the filling in the center of the omelet at this point.

Gently raise the handle of the pan and let the omelet slide toward the opposite edge of the pan. Fold the edge nearest the handle over the center (or over the filling) with the aid of the fork. Hold the pan over a heated oval platter and turn it upside down to deposit the omelet on the dish. The omelet will be an oval with three folds. The whole procedure should take less time than it takes to describe. As each omelet is cooked, keep it warm in a very slow oven (200° F.) until the others are finished.

Barante Omelet

SAUTÉ 3/4 pound mushrooms, thinly sliced, in 3 tablespoons butter until they are pale golden. Add 3/4 cup Port, cover the pan, and simmer the mixture until the liquid is reduced by one half. Add 6 tablespoons heavy cream and 6 slices cooked lobster meat. Cover the pan and keep the filling hot.

Make a 2-egg omelet for each serving, and fill the omelets with the lobster mixture.

Caviar Omelets

FOR each serving make a 2-egg omelet, blending the eggs with 1 teaspoon water and seasoning them with a pinch of salt and a dash of cayenne. Fill each omelet with a little caviar and serve with sour cream.

Chipped Beef Omelets

SAUTÉ 1/2 cup chipped beef in 2 teaspoons butter for 1 minute. Stir in 1 1/2 teaspoons heavy cream. Make a 2-egg omelet for each serving. Fill the omelets with the chipped-beef mixture.

Lobster Omelet

IN the top of a double boiler brown lightly 1 green onion and 2 tablespoons green pepper, both minced, in 3 tablespoons butter. Put the pan over hot water, blend in 2 tablespoons flour, and slowly add 1/2 cup milk and 2/3 cup heavy cream. Season the sauce with a dash of nutmeg and salt and pepper to taste. Cook the sauce, stirring, until it begins to thicken and add 1 1/2 cups cooked lobster meat. Heat the lobster thoroughly and stir in 2 tablespoons Sherry.

Make a 2-egg omelet for each serving. Fill the omelets with half the lobster sauce.

Caviar Omelets

Garnish the omelets with the rest of the sauce and sprinkle each one with 1 table-spoon each of melted butter and grated Parmesan.

❧ Scallop Omelet Lucullus

COOK 3/4 cup scallops, washed and drained, in enough dry white wine to cover for 10 minutes, or until they are firm. Drain and dry them. In a large skillet melt 1 tablespoon butter and add the scallops, 1 tablespoon each of shredded ham and mushrooms, and 1 teaspoon grated Parmesan. Cook the mixture for 2 minutes. Add 1 tomato, peeled, seeded, and chopped, and salt and pepper to taste. Simmer the mixture until the tomato is soft.

Make a 2-egg omelet for each serving and fill the omelets with the scallop mixture. Serve with tomato sauce.

❧ Omelet Agnès Sorel

SAUTÉ 1/2 onion, finely chopped, in 1 tablespoon butter until it is soft. Add 3 mush-rooms, sliced, and salt and pepper to taste and cook for 1 minute. Melt 1/4 tea-spoon *glace de viande,* or meat extract, in 1/4 cup hot chicken stock and stir in 1/2 teaspoon potato flour. Simmer the mixture until it is thick, add the mushrooms and onions and 1/2 cup finely minced cooked chicken, and cook for 1 minute.

Make a 2-egg omelet for each serving. Fill the omelets with the chicken mixture. Sprinkle each omelet with 2 tablespoons finely shredded cooked ham or tongue, and pour over it 3 tablespoons hot chicken stock, 1 teaspoon butter, and 1/2 teaspoon *glace de viande,* all heated together.

❧ Truffle Omelet

PUT 2/3 cup sauterne, 6 tablespoons brandy, 6 small truffles, finely diced, and 2 tablespoons butter in a saucepan and simmer the mixture covered, until the liquid is evaporated. For each serving mix 2 large eggs lightly with a fork, add 1/2 tea-spoon salt, and stir in some of the truffle mixture. Cook the omelets and turn them out on a heated platter.

Cottage Cheese Omelet 🐦

BEAT together 6 egg yolks, 1 cup cottage cheese, 3/4 cup light cream, 3 tablespoons finely chopped parsley, and salt and pepper to taste. Fold in 6 eggs whites, stiffly beaten. Heat 1 1/2 tablespoons butter in a skillet, add the mixture, and cook the omelet over low heat until the bottom is golden brown. Transfer the skillet to a moderate oven (350° F.) and bake the omelet for 15 or 20 minutes, or until the top is golden brown.

Scrambled Eggs 🐦

BREAK 12 eggs into a bowl and beat them until the whites and yolks are well mixed but not frothy. Heat 3 tablespoons butter in a heavy skillet, add the eggs, and cook them, stirring constantly, over low heat. Or cook the eggs in the top of a double boiler over hot water. As the eggs begin to set, add 2 tablespoons butter and 1/4 cup heavy cream. Season with salt and white pepper to taste.

Scrambled Eggs with Smoked Salmon 🐦

SCRAMBLE 12 eggs and season them with salt and white pepper to taste. Arrange the eggs on a heated platter and surround them with thin slices of smoked salmon.

Butter and Eggs 🐦

BREAK 12 eggs into a bowl and beat them until the whites and yolks are well mixed but not frothy. Heat 1 1/2 tablespoons butter in a skillet and add the eggs. Cook them, stirring constantly, over very low heat (or in the top of a double boiler over hot water), and add 1/2 pound butter, bit by bit. When the eggs are set and creamy, sprinkle them lightly with salt and cayenne. Serve the eggs in heated croustades.

Eggs Buckingham 🐦

SPREAD 6 slices of toast lightly with anchovy paste mixed with a little English mustard. Beat 12 eggs lightly with 1/2 cup diced cooked ham, 3 tablespoons sweet

Pipérade

vermouth, 1 1/2 tablespoons scraped onion, and salt and pepper to taste. Heat 3/4 cup butter in a heavy skillet, add the eggs, and cook them over moderate heat, stirring constantly, until they are thick but still soft and creamy. Heap the scrambled eggs on the toast, cover them with grated Cheddar, and sprinkle with a few drops of Worcestershire sauce and with paprika. Brown the topping under the broiler.

Pipérade 🍃

SLICE thinly 6 green peppers and 2 large onions and sauté the vegetables slowly in 4 tablespoons olive oil until they are soft. Add 5 tomatoes, peeled, a crushed garlic clove, and salt and pepper to taste. Simmer the vegetables until they are very soft, crushing them occasionally with a fork.

Beat 10 eggs lightly with 1/2 cup heavy cream. In a large skillet heat 4 tablespoons butter. Add the eggs and cook them, stirring constantly, over low heat, until they are just set. Arrange the scrambled eggs on a heated platter, surround them with the *pipérade,* and garnish with diamonds of sautéed white bread.

Chafing Dish Eggs on English Muffins 🍃

SAUTÉ 1/4 pound chipped beef, cut in thin strips, in 2 tablespoons butter in the top pan of a chafing dish over low heat, stirring constantly, until the beef starts to brown. Remove the pan from the heat and set it over the hot-water pan. Blend 1/2 cup cottage cheese with 6 eggs, well beaten. Beat the mixture until it is very smooth and stir in 3 tablespoons minced chives. Pour the eggs over the beef and cook the mixture over hot water, stirring frequently, until the eggs are thick but still soft. Serve on toasted English muffins, sprinkle lightly with paprika, and garnish each serving with watercress.

Cold Parmesan Soufflé 🍃

SOFTEN 1 tablespoon gelatin in 1/4 cup cold water, dissolve it in 1/2 cup hot milk, and combine it with 1 teaspoon each of onion juice and lemon juice, a pinch each of salt, curry powder, and dry mustard, and a dash of Tabasco. Stir the mixture well and blend it thoroughly with 2 cups grated Parmesan. Fold in 1 cup heavy cream, whipped. Pour the mixture into a mold rinsed with cold water and chill the soufflé for 3 hours, or until it is firmly set. Unmold the soufflé on a platter, sprinkle it with grated Parmesan, and garnish it with watercress.

To make 12 servings, double the ingredients and make 2 soufflés.

ᔟ Croûte de Münster

FOR each serving cut 1 slice of bread into small dice. Pour 1/4 cup beer over the bread and combine with 3 eggs, well beaten. Heat 2 tablespoons butter in a skillet, pour in the egg mixture, and add 1/2 cup Münster cheese, diced. Cook the mixture over low heat until the bottom is just set. Brown the top lightly under the broiler and transfer the croûte to a heated plate.

ᔟ Swiss and Roquefort Ramekins

MELT together over low heat 1/2 pound butter and 1/4 pound each of Swiss and Roquefort cheeses. Soak 1 cup soft bread crumbs in 1/2 cup hot heavy cream, add them to the cheese, and blend them well. Remove the pan from the heat and stir in 8 egg yolks, well beaten. Fold in 8 egg whites, stiffly beaten. Fill 6 individual ramekins about two thirds full with the batter, and bake them in a very slow oven (250° F.) for about 20 minutes, or until the puddings are puffed and browned.

ᔟ Cheese Torte

LINE a 9-inch pie plate with flaky pastry, fluting the edges to make a very high rim. Blend together 2 cups *ricotta* or cottage cheese, 3 tablespoons cream cheese, 2 eggs, beaten, 1 garlic clove, crushed, and a generous pinch each of salt and cracked black peppercorns. Fill the pastry shell with the mixture and bake the pie in a moderately hot oven (375° F.) for about 45 minutes, or until the filling is firm and the crust browned. Serve hot.

Fish and Shellfish

Anchovy Roast 🐟

WASH and drain 40 to 50 anchovy filets and soak them in milk for 1 hour. Mix together 1 cup cracker crumbs and 1/2 cup each of bread crumbs and melted butter. Spread half this mixture in a thin layer in the bottom of a buttered shallow baking dish. Add the anchovy filets and cover them with the remaining buttered crumbs. Sprinkle with 1/4 cup brandy or whiskey and dot with bits of butter. Bake the anchovies in a hot oven (400° F.) for 15 to 20 minutes, or until they are very hot.

California Sea Bass 🐟

COMBINE 1/2 cup melted butter with 3 ounces Cognac, 3 tablespoons soy sauce, the juice of 1 1/2 lemons, and 1 large garlic clove, crushed. Brush 6 sea-bass steaks, each weighing about 1/2 pound, with this sauce and arrange the steaks in a well-oiled hinged broiler. Cook the steaks over moderately hot coals for about 5 minutes, basting and turning them frequently. Sprinkle both sides of the fish generously with seasame seeds, and cook the fish for 2 minutes longer, or until the seeds are toasted and the fish is brown. Serve with melted butter and wedges of lemon or lime

ᔰ Sea Bass Baked with Mint

SPLIT and bone 2 sea bass, each weighing about 3 pounds, and wipe the fish with a damp cloth.

Combine 1 cup bread crumbs with 2 sprigs of parsley, chopped, 2 crushed leaves of basil, and salt and pepper to taste. Add 4 tablespoons olive oil and 1 garlic clove, minced.

Lay one half of each bass in a buttered baking dish and spread the fish with the bread-crumb mixture. Pour 1/2 cup dry white wine over the halves and arrange 3 sprigs of mint on each. Lay the other half of each fish on top and skewer the re-formed fish at each end. Pour 1/2 cup olive oil over the fish.

Combine 6 sprigs of mint, chopped, with 1/2 cup dry white wine, 1 garlic clove, minced, and salt and pepper to taste. Bake the fish in a moderate oven (350° F.), basting them with half the mint mixture, for about 25 minutes, or until the flesh flakes easily at the touch of a fork. Arrange the fish on a heated platter and pour the remaining mint sauce over them, or serve the sauce separately.

ᔰ Skillet Bass in Butter

MELT 1/2 cup butter in a large skillet and arrange in the pan 6 crosswise slices of bass, each about 2 inches thick. Cover each piece of fish with a slice of tomato and sprinkle all with the juice of 2 lemons and salt and pepper to taste. Cover the skillet and simmer the fish over low heat, basting frequently with the butter sauce, for about 25 minutes, or until the flesh flakes at the touch of a fork.

ᔰ Butterfish Niçoise

WIPE 6 butterfish with a damp cloth. Dip the fish in milk, roll them in flour, and brown them on both sides in 3 tablespoons olive oil. In another pan sauté 2 tomatoes, cut into wedges, with 1/2 garlic clove, minced, and a pinch of tarragon in 1 tablespoon olive oil for 5 minutes.

Arrange the fish on a heated platter, tails to the center, like the spokes of a wheel. Decorate each fish with 2 anchovy filets and fill in the spaces between the fish with alternating mounds of cooked carrots, sautéed potato balls, and the sautéed tomato wedges. Garnish the platter with pitted ripe olives and sprinkle the vegetables with finely chopped parsley.

Butterfish Niçoise

🐟 Grilled Salmon

SPLIT an 8- to 10-pound whole salmon, rub it on both sides with salt and olive oil, and lay it in a well-oiled hinged broiler. Cook the salmon, flesh side down, over moderately hot coals until it is lightly browned. Turn the salmon, rub the flesh with a mixture of 1/2 cup butter, the juice of 1 lemon, and 4 tablespoons minced parsley, and broil it slowly, skin side down, for about 35 minutes, or until the flesh flakes easily at the touch of a fork. Do not overcook it. Serve with melted butter and lemon wedges.

🐟 Poached Salmon

CLEAN and scale a 10-pound salmon, lay it on a thin wooden board that will fit on the rack of a fish kettle, wrap the fish and board in cheesecloth, and tie the fish to the board with string.

Prepare a white-wine court bouillon in the fish kettle and cool it. Lower the salmon onto the rack in the kettle, bring the court bouillon to a boil, and simmer the salmon, covered, for 30 minutes to 1 hour, depending upon the thickness of the fish, until it flakes readily at the touch of a fork. Turn off the heat and leave the salmon in the stock, covered, for half an hour. Lift out the fish, drain it well, and carefully remove the string and cheesecloth. Serve with hollandaise sauce.

🐟 Poached Salmon Steaks

IN a large skillet arrange 6 salmon steaks, each 1 inch thick, and add 2 cups white-wine court bouillon. Poach the steaks, covered, for about 8 minutes, or until the flesh flakes readily at the touch of a fork. Arrange the steaks on a heated platter and serve with béarnaise sauce.

🐟 Salmon Steaks with Spinach

SPRINKLE 6 salmon steaks, each 3/4 inch thick, with flour and sauté them in 6 tablespoons butter until they are browned on both sides and flake easily at the touch of a fork. Season with salt and pepper to taste. Arrange the steaks on a bed of cooked chopped spinach seasoned with lemon juice and chopped tarragon.

Salmon Newburg 🦐

MELT 8 tablespoons butter in the top of a double boiler, stir in 6 tablespoons flour, and cook the *roux*, stirring, for a minute or two without letting it brown. Gradually add 4 cups hot heavy cream and cook the sauce, stirring constantly, until it is thick and smooth. Add 5 tablespoons grated Parmesan, 3 tablespoons paprika, 1 teaspoon dry mustard, and salt and cayenne to taste. Pour the sauce slowly over 6 egg yolks, well beaten, stirring constantly. Put the pan over boiling water and cook the sauce, stirring, for 3 minutes. Flavor with 4 tablespoons each of brandy and dry Sherry and stir in 6 cups flaked poached salmon. To serve, heat the mixture in 2 chafing dishes and sprinkle it lightly with paprika. Makes 12 servings.

TIMBALES DE SAUMON

Salmon Timbales 🦐

IN a saucepan melt 3 tablespoons butter and stir in 1/3 cup bread crumbs. Gradually add 1 cup light cream, a pinch of cayenne, and salt and pepper to taste. Add 1 teaspoon lemon juice and cook the mixture, stirring constantly, until it is smooth. Remove the pan from the heat and beat in 2 egg yolks, beaten with a little of the hot sauce. Cook the sauce, stirring it briskly from the bottom of the pan, for 2 or 3 minutes more. Remove the pan from the heat, stir in 1 1/2 cups flaked poached salmon, and mix thoroughly. Fold in 2 egg whites, stiffly beaten.

Divide the mixture among 6 individual buttered molds, set the molds in a pan of hot water, and bake the timbales in a moderate oven (350° F.) for about 25 minutes, or until the mixture is set. Turn out the timbales on heated plates and mask them with hollandaise sauce.

Baked Halibut with Maltaise Sauce 🦐

CLEAN a 4- to 5-pound chicken halibut, wipe it with a damp cloth, and sprinkle it with paprika, salt, and pepper. Oil a sheet of aluminum foil and set it in a shallow baking pan. Lay the fish on the foil, cover it with 4 or 5 bay leaves, and bake it in a moderate oven (350° F.), basting frequently with a mixture of 1/2 cup each of melted butter and white wine, for about 45 minutes, or until the flesh flakes easily at the touch of a fork. Transfer the fish to a heated platter and garnish it with the bay leaves and sprigs of fresh dill. Serve with maltaise sauce flavored with finely chopped dill.

Brandade de Morue

Halibut with Almonds and Yoghurt 🐟

IN a large skillet sauté 4 onions, sliced, in 4 tablespoons butter with a 1-inch cinnamon stick until the onions are golden. Arrange on them 6 halibut steaks, each weighing about 1/2 pound. Sprinkle the fish with 1 1/2 teaspoons turmeric and 1 teaspoon pepper. Add 1 1/2 cups milk, cover the pan, and simmer the mixture, shaking the pan frequently, for about 10 minutes, or until the fish is almost cooked through. Discard the cinnamon stick. Pour off the liquid, add 2 tablespoons butter, and sauté the fish for 5 minutes more, or until it is tender.

Pound 2 cups blanched almonds in a mortar and stir them into 1 cup each of yoghurt and light cream. Simmer the sauce over low heat until it is reduced by half and pour it over the fish. Cover the pan and let the fish rest for 10 minutes before serving.

SALT COD WITH GARLIC, OIL, AND CREAM ## Brandade de Morue 🐟

SOAK 2 pounds salt codfish in cold water for 12 hours or overnight, changing the water occasionally. Drain the cod and rinse it well. Put the cod in a saucepan, cover it with fresh cold water, and bring the water slowly to a boil. Remove the pan from the heat, drain the cod, and bone and flake the fish. Put the warm fish in a saucepan and add 1 or 2 garlic cloves, crushed. Over low heat beat in alternately 1 cup each of heavy cream and olive oil, adding only a spoonful at a time and beating the mixture constantly until it has the consistency of thick cream. Or purée the mixture in a blender. Serve the *brandade* warm, garnished with triangles of sautéed bread and pitted ripe olives.

Codfish Kebabs 🐟

SOAK 1 pound salt codfish in cold water for 6 hours, drain the fish well, and flake it into a bowl. Add 1 egg, well beaten, and 1 cup mashed potatoes and beat the mixture thoroughly with a fork. Season with 1 teaspoon finely chopped parsley and pepper to taste. Form the mixture into walnut-sized balls and dip them in melted butter. Thread the balls on skewers alternately with partially cooked squares of bacon and broil the codfish kebabs, turning frequently, for 4 to 6 minutes.

ʃ🐦 Kippered Herring

ARRANGE kippers, skin side up, in a baking dish. Dot them with butter and heat them thoroughly in a moderate oven (350° F.). Sprinkle them with lemon juice and finely chopped chives.

ʃ🐦 Mackerel with Orange Mustard Sauce

CLEAN and scale 3 mackerel and remove the heads. Split the fish, brush them generously with melted butter, and sprinkle with salt and paprika. Put the fish, skin side down, on an oiled broiling pan and broil them 4 or 5 inches from the heat for 15 or 20 minutes, or until the flesh is golden brown and flakes readily at the touch of a fork. Arrange the mackerel on a heated platter. Pour orange mustard sauce over the fish and garnish with the peeled sections of 3 oranges.

Orange Mustard Sauce

IN a saucepan melt 6 tablespoons butter and add 1/2 cup orange juice, 2 tablespoons finely chopped parsley, 1 tablespoon chervil, and 1 teaspoon each of dry mustard and grated orange rind. Simmer the sauce over low heat until it thickens slightly.

ʃ🐦 Poached Shad Roe

FOR each shad roe, melt 6 tablespoons butter in a skillet. Dip the roe lightly in flour and turn it in the melted butter to coat both sides. Cover the skillet and poach the roe for 10 minutes. Turn the roe, sprinkle it generously with finely chopped parsley, and poach it for 10 minutes longer. Season the roe with salt, freshly ground pepper, and lemon juice. Serve with the pan juices. Allow 3 shad roe for 6 servings.

ʃ🐦 Skate with Black Butter

POACH 3 pounds skate wings, cut into serving pieces, in a mixture of 3 quarts water, 1 quart vinegar, and 1 tablespoon salt for about 15 minutes, or until the flesh flakes easily at the touch of a fork. Drain the wings well and arrange them on a heated platter. Melt 1/2 pound butter and cook it slowly until it is a very dark brown. Add 2 tablespoons vinegar, pour the sauce over the skate, and sprinkle liberally with capers.

Deviled Smelts 𝔰𝔩

SPLIT 24 smelts along the backs and remove the large bones. Spread the fish lightly with prepared mustard, dip them in crumbs, and sprinkle them with salt and cayenne to taste. Brown the smelts on both sides in 3 tablespoons butter over high heat. Arrange the smelts on a heated platter and serve with *sauce diable*.

Sole with Anchovy Oyster Sauce 𝔰𝔩

POACH 6 filets of sole or whitefish in milk to cover for 6 to 8 minutes. Drain them, reserving the milk. Transfer the fish to a heated dish and keep them warm.

Cook 2 tablespoons minced shallots in 3 tablespoons butter for 2 minutes. Add 2 tablespoons flour, 1 tablespoon anchovy paste, and a pinch of cayenne. Slowly stir in 1 cup of the reserved milk and stir the sauce over moderate heat until it is thickened. Add 12 freshly shucked oysters and 1/2 cup of their liquor and poach the oysters gently for 2 minutes. Pour the hot anchovy oyster sauce over the filets and garnish with a latticework of 12 to 14 anchovy filets. Sprinkle with the riced yolks of 3 hard-cooked eggs.

Filets of Sole Messalina 𝔰𝔩

ARRANGE 3/4 pound sliced mushrooms on the bottom of a buttered baking dish. Fold 6 filets of sole in half and arrange them on the mushrooms. Sprinkle the filets with salt and pepper to taste, pour over them 1 cup dry white wine, and bake them in a moderately hot oven (375° F.) for about 25 minutes, or until the flesh flakes easily at the touch of a fork. Drain the liquid into a saucepan without disturbing the fish. Stir in 1 1/2 tablespoons tomato paste and cook the sauce over high heat until it is reduced by half. Add 3/4 pound very ripe Italian plum tomatoes, peeled, seeded, and chopped, and cook the sauce for 20 minutes, or until it is thick. Finish with 6 tablespoons melted butter and salt and pepper to taste. Arrange the filets on a heated platter, place the mushrooms on the fish, and pour the sauce over all.

༄ Sole Paupiettes with Salmon Mousse

PUT 1/2 pound fresh salmon, free of skin and bones, through a food chopper and beat in 2 eggs and 1/2 cup finely chopped parsley. Put the mixture through the chopper twice more and pound it until it is smooth. Add salt and pepper to taste. Spread this mousse preparation evenly on 6 uniform filets of sole, roll the filets, and secure them with wooden picks. Lay them side by side in a saucepan and add 1 1/2 cups white wine. Cover the pan and simmer the fish, basting frequently, for 8 to 10 minutes, or until the flesh flakes at the touch of a fork. Transfer the filets to a heated platter and keep them warm.

In a small saucepan melt 2 tablespoons butter. Stir in 1 1/2 tablespoons flour and cook the *roux* for a minute or two. Do not let it brown. Stir in the wine in which the fish was poached and cook the sauce, stirring, until it is smooth and thick. Sauté 12 raw mushroom caps and 6 cooked artichoke hearts lightly in butter. Pour the sauce over the fish rolls, surround them with the artichoke hearts, and arrange the mushroom caps on the fish. Serve very hot.

༄ Sole Walewska

SPRINKLE 1 shallot, finely chopped, in a buttered flameproof dish. Add 6 filets of sole, folded in half, dot them with butter, and cover them with 1/2 cup each of white wine and water. Bring the liquid to the simmering point over low heat. Cover the dish with buttered paper, transfer it to a moderate oven (350° F.), and bake the fish for 8 to 10 minutes, or until it flakes readily at the touch of a fork. Carefully remove the fish to a heated platter, reserving the wine broth. On the filets arrange slices of cooked lobster alternately with thin slices of truffle. Garnish both sides of the platter with half a lobster shell.

Strain and reheat the wine broth. Melt 3 tablespoons butter, blend in 4 tablespoons flour, and gradually add the hot broth, stirring constantly. Add 3/4 cup milk and continue to cook the sauce, stirring, for 1 minute. Blend together 2 egg yolks and 1/2 cup heavy cream and gradually stir the hot sauce into the egg mixture. Return the pan to the heat but do not let the sauce boil. Gradually beat in 4 to 6 tablespoons lobster butter. Spoon the hot sauce around the fish and lobster shells.

Swordfish Mirabeau

WASH and dry a 1 1/2- to 2-pound swordfish steak, cut 1 inch thick, and sprinkle it on both sides with a little freshly ground pepper. Put the steak on a broiling rack and brush the top with oil flavored with anchovy paste to taste. Broil the steak about 2 inches from the heat for 6 to 7 minutes. Turn it over, brush the uncooked side with the anchovy oil, and broil it for 4 minutes longer. Transfer the swordfish to a heated platter and keep it warm while assembling the garnish. Cover the top with a latticework of anchovy filets and fill the spaces in-between with slices of green stuffed olives. Surround the steak with a border of finely chopped parsley. If necessary, heat the steak in a slow oven (300° F.) before serving.

Sautéed Brook Trout

DIP 6 cleaned brook trout in milk, then in flour seasoned with salt and pepper, and sauté them in 1/4 inch hot oil until they are golden brown on both sides. Remove the fish to a serving dish and sprinkle them with a few drops of lemon juice. Brown lightly 6 tablespoons butter and pour the butter over the fish. Sprinkle the fish with chopped parsley and garnish them with lemon slices.

Trout in Wine Sauce

POACH 6 brook trout in fish court bouillon for about 8 minutes, or until the flesh flakes easily at the touch of a fork. Remove the fish, lay them on a dry cloth, and remove the skins.

Blend 1 tablespoon cornstarch with the juice of 2 lemons and the grated rind of 1 lemon, and 4 egg yolks, well beaten. In the top of a double boiler heat 1 cup white wine and 1/2 cup butter. Put the pan over hot water and gradually add the egg-yolk mixture. Cook the sauce, stirring constantly, until it is thick. Add salt to taste, a pinch of cayenne, and 1 cup peeled seedless grapes. Arrange the fish on a heated platter and cover them with the sauce. Sprinkle the trout with 1/4 cup slivered toasted almonds.

🐟 White Burn Trout

CLEAN, split, and bone 6 fresh trout and drain and dry them thoroughly. Sprinkle the fish with salt and pepper and coat them lightly with oatmeal. Sauté the trout in 1/3 cup butter until the fish is crisp and cooked through. Serve with wedges of lemon.

🐟 Cold Poached Trout

POACH 6 whole cleaned brook trout in white-wine court bouillon for 5 minutes, or until they are just cooked through. Drain the fish, arrange them on a cold platter, and chill them. Remove part of the skin from the top of the trout, leaving the heads and tails intact. Garnish the fish with cucumber wedges, tarragon leaves, and slices of lemon and hard-cooked egg. Serve on a bed of pink mayonnaise.

🐟 Charcoal-Broiled Trout

ARRANGE each cleaned brook trout in a ring by running skewers through the head and tail. Dip the fish in seasoned flour, then in melted butter. Broil them over hot coals, brushing them frequently with melted butter, for about 10 minutes, or until they are cooked through. Serve with wedges of lemon or lime and more melted butter.

🐟 Clam Soufflé

MAKE a *roux* of 2 tablespoons each of melted butter and flour, and stir in gradually 1/2 cup each of strained hot clam broth and heavy cream, 4 thin slices of onion, 1 teaspoon finely chopped parsley, 1/2 bay leaf, and a dash of cayenne. Cook the sauce, stirring, until it thickens, strain it, and return it to the pan. Add 3/4 cup minced raw clams, heat them thoroughly, and remove the pan from the heat. Warm 3 egg yolks, well beaten, with a little of the hot sauce, and blend them into the sauce. Cool the sauce slightly and fold in 4 egg whites, stiffly beaten, and a pinch each of salt and nutmeg. Turn the soufflé into a buttered soufflé dish and bake it in a hot oven (400° F.) for 25 minutes, or until it is well puffed and lightly browned. Serve at once.

Cooking Hard-Shelled Crabs 🦀

WASH live hard-shelled crabs in several waters and put them in a kettle filled with salted water or court bouillon. Bring the water very slowly to a boil and simmer the crabs for about 15 minutes, or until the shells turn red. Drain the crabs, plunge them into cold water, and drain them again. Let the crabs cool.

Crack the claws and legs and remove the meat. Break off the apron, the segment that folds under the body from the rear, force a strong knife into the opening, and force the shells apart. Discard the gills and sand bag, washing the crab under running water. Remove the body meat. Six average-sized crabs will yield about 1 cup meat.

Anchovy Crab 🦀

WITH a fork crush 6 anchovy filets in 1 1/2 cups white wine. Heat the wine in a saucepan and add 1 1/2 cups soft bread crumbs and a pinch of nutmeg. Mix 2 cups cooked crab meat with 1/2 cup melted butter and add it to the hot wine mixture. Cook all together for 5 minutes and serve in patty shells on heated plates.

Curried Crab Meat with Almonds 🦀

IN a skillet sauté 3 cups flaked cooked crab meat in 1/3 cup butter until the crab is hot and well coated with butter. Season 1 cup hot white sauce with 1 1/2 tablespoons grated onion and 2 teaspoons curry powder and cook the sauce, stirring, until the ingredients are blended. Add the sauce to the crab meat, mix well, and stir in 1/3 cup slivered toasted almonds. Serve over fluffy rice.

Crab Florentine 🦀

IN a large skillet, in 6 tablespoons butter, sauté 3 cups cooked crab meat with 2 tablespoons finely chopped parsley, 1/2 cup shredded blanched almonds, and salt and freshly ground pepper to taste for 2 to 3 minutes, or until the meat is heated through. Combine the crab meat with 2 cups Mornay sauce. Serve in a casserole over cooked, chopped, well-seasoned spinach.

ৡ Cold Crab Curry

SAUTÉ 1 apple, peeled, cored, and sliced, and 4 shallots, chopped, in 1/4 cup butter until they are soft and add 1 tablespoon curry powder and 1 teaspoon each of crushed coriander seed and flour. Add just enough milk or coconut milk to make a thick paste. Cool the paste and stir it into 2 cups mayonnaise. Add a little lemon juice to taste and adjust the seasoning. On a bed of cold cooked rice place 3 cups cold cooked crab meat and mask it with the curry sauce.

ৡ Crab Meat Mousse

SOFTEN 1 tablespoon gelatin in 3 tablespoons cold water and dissolve it over hot water. Mix the gelatin with 1/4 cup mayonnaise, 2 tablespoons each of lime and lemon juice, 1 tablespoon each of parsley and chives, both chopped, 1 tablespoon prepared mustard, and salt and pepper to taste. Fold in 2 cups flaked cooked crab meat and 3/4 cup heavy cream, whipped. Pour the mixture into a buttered ring mold and chill it until it is set. Unmold the mousse on a chilled platter and garnish with thin slices of lime. Fill the center with avocado mashed with lime juice and sprinkled with chopped chives.

ৡ Crab Meat Soufflé

SEASON 1 cup hot white sauce with 1/2 teaspoon dry mustard and salt and pepper to taste. Stir in 2 cups flaked cooked crab meat, 1/4 cup shredded almonds, and 4 egg yolks, lightly beaten. Fold the mixture into 6 egg whites, stiffly beaten. Pour the batter into a buttered soufflé dish and bake it in a moderately hot oven (375° F.) for 35 minutes, or until the soufflé is puffed and golden. Serve with clarified butter sauce.

Crab Meat Mousse

⌇ Cleaning Soft-Shelled Crabs

RINSE 12 soft-shelled crabs in salted water. Using scissors, cut off the heads about one-fourth inch behind the eyes and discard the green bubble. Lift the soft shell where it comes to a point at each side and cut off the white gills. Peel back the apron and cut it off. Rinse the crabs in salted water and dry them.

⌇ Sautéed Soft-Shelled Crabs

IN a large skillet melt 1/2 cup butter. Sprinkle 12 soft-shelled crabs with salt and pepper, coat them with flour, and sauté them, back side down, in the hot butter for 5 minutes. Turn the crabs over and sauté them for 3 minutes longer. Transfer the crabs to a heated platter, sprinkle them with lemon juice, and pour the pan juices over them.

⌇ Soft-Shelled Crabs with Brazil Nuts

CLEAN, wash, and dry 18 soft-shelled crabs. In a large skillet melt 3/4 cup butter. Sprinkle the crabs with salt and pepper and sauté them in the hot butter, back side down, for 5 minutes. Turn the crabs over and cook them 3 minutes longer. Transfer the crabs to a heated platter. Add 1 cup sliced Brazil nuts to the pan juices and sauté them until they are golden. Pour the nuts and the pan juices over the crabs. Serve garnished with lemon quarters and clusters of parsley.

⌇ Crayfish Mousse with Champagne

MELT 2 tablespoons butter in a saucepan and add 2 carrots, 2 onions, 2 stalks of celery, and a strip of lean bacon, all finely chopped, 1 bay leaf, crushed, a pinch of thyme, and a generous amount of salt and pepper. Simmer this *mirepoix* for about 20 minutes, or until the vegetables are soft. Add 1 pint Champagne.

Wash well 3 dozen crayfish, add them to the pan, and cook them over high heat for about 6 minutes. Strain the stock and reserve it. Drain and shell the crayfish and discard the green intestinal veins under the tails.

Pound the crayfish shells as finely as possible in a mortar with 1/2 cup butter and combine the purée with 1 cup of hot fish *velouté* and 2 1/2 envelopes of gelatin softened in 1/2 cup cool crayfish stock, dissolved over hot water. Add the remaining stock and simmer all together for 10 minutes. Strain the mixture through a fine sieve lined with cheesecloth into a bowl and stir it over cracked ice until it begins to thicken. Fold in 2 cups heavy cream, lightly whipped, and pour the mixture into a large mold.

Chill the mousse until it is firm and turn it out on a chilled platter. Garnish the top with a few of the shelled crayfish and with thin slices of truffle and chervil leaves. Brush the garnish with a thin coating of cool but still liquid white-wine aspic. Arrange the rest of the crayfish around the mousse.

Frogs' Legs

DUST 2 pounds frogs' legs with flour and sauté them in a generous amount of butter until they are golden brown. Sprinkle the frogs' legs liberally with finely chopped parsley and serve them on toast with wedges of lemon.

Preparing and Cooking Lobster

IF the lobster is to be served plain, with butter, or the meat is to be used in sauces, omelets, salads, and the like, cook it by boiling. Put the lobsters in a large kettle filled with salted water or court bouillon. Bring the water very slowly to a boil and simmer the lobsters for 15 to 25 minutes, depending on their size, until they turn bright red. Let the lobsters cool in the liquid if they are to be served cold. Otherwise, remove them from the kettle and, when they are cool enough to handle, but still hot, twist off the claws. Crack each claw and remove the meat. Separate the tail from the body by arching the back until it cracks. Bend back and break off the flippers at the end of the tail and remove the tail meat. Unhinge the body from the shell, discarding the head sac, the dark intestinal vein, and the spongy lungs. Reserve the green tomalley, or liver, and the coral, if any. Split the body apart and remove the meat.

Lobster Crêpes

MELT 1 tablespoon butter in a skillet and add 2 cups sliced boiled lobster, 1 truffle, chopped, a pinch of cayenne, and salt and pepper to taste. Heat the lobster

Lobster Tetrazzini

thoroughly and stir in 1 cup heavy cream and 1 tablespoon lobster roe butter.

Make entrée crêpes and put a mound of the lobster filling in the center of each. Roll up the crêpes and arrange them side by side in a buttered shallow baking dish. Cover them with hot Mornay sauce and put them in a moderately hot oven (375° F.) until they are heated through.

Lobster Tetrazzini

CUT the meat from 4 pounds boiled lobster into strips or dice, reserving any coral. Simmer the water the lobster was cooked in until it is reduced to 2 cups and reserve it. Sauté 1/2 pound mushrooms, thinly sliced, in 3 tablespoons butter until they are soft and slightly browned and reserve them.

In a saucepan melt 3 tablespoons butter, stir in 2 tablespoons flour and cook the *roux*, stirring, for a few minutes. Add the lobster coral and stir in gradually the reserved cooking liquid. Cook the sauce, stirring, until it is smooth and thick and stir in 1 cup heavy cream and 3 tablespoons Sherry. Add a little nutmeg and salt and pepper to taste and simmer the sauce slowly for 10 minutes. Add the lobster meat, the mushrooms, and 1/2 cup diced truffles.

Arrange 1/2 pound hot cooked spaghetti in coils on a heated platter. Make a weil in the center of the spaghetti and pour in the lobster sauce. Sprinkle all with 2 truffles, finely chopped.

PETITS SOUFFLÉS DE HOMARD ## Individual Lobster Soufflés

CHOP finely the meat from 2 pounds boiled lobster. Reserve any coral.

Melt 3 tablespoons butter, stir in 3 tablespoons flour, and cook the *roux*, stirring constantly, until it starts to turn golden. Gradually add 1 cup warm milk and simmer the sauce, stirring, for 10 minutes. Add the lobster coral and 1/2 teaspoon minced shallot, a pinch of cayenne, and salt and pepper to taste. Remove the sauce from the heat, cool it slightly, and beat in 3 egg yolks. Add the chopped lobster meat, 3 truffles, peeled, chopped, and poached in Madeira, and 2 ounces brandy. Beat 5 egg whites until they are stiff and add 3 tablespoons whipped cream. Fold this into the lobster and sauce. Divide the mixture among 6 individual buttered soufflé molds and set them in a shallow pan of water. Bake the soufflés in a moderately hot oven (375° F.) for about 15 to 20 minutes, or until they are puffed and golden. Serve at once.

ᔑᑉ Spanish Lobster Stew

BOIL 3 pounds live lobsters in 4 cups white wine. Strain the wine and reserve it. Keep the lobsters in their shells and cut them into serving portions.

In a heavy skillet heat 2 tablespoons olive oil to the smoking point and add 2 tomatoes, peeled and chopped, 1 onion, 2 garlic cloves, and 1 carrot, all minced, a sprig of parsley, and 1 bay leaf. Cook the vegetables for about 10 minutes, or until they are soft. Add the reserved wine and cook the mixture over high heat for 10 minutes to reduce the liquid. Add the cooked lobster pieces, heat the stew, and serve in deep plates.

ᔑᑉ Lobster and Shrimp Marinara

CUT 2 pounds live lobster into serving pieces. Sauté the pieces on all sides in 3 table-spoons olive oil until the shells are bright red. Add 1 pound raw shrimp, shelled and deveined, 2 garlic cloves, chopped, and 2 teaspoons chopped parsley. Cook the mixture, stirring frequently, for 3 minutes, or until the vegetables begin to soften. Add 2 cups dry white wine and a little salt, bring the wine to a boil, and simmer the stew over low heat for 5 minutes. If desired, thicken the sauce slightly with 1 teaspoon potato starch mixed with 2 teaspoons water. Simmer the stew for a minute or two, until the sauce is clear and thickened.

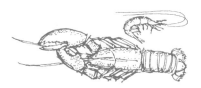

ᔑᑉ Cleaning and Opening Mussels

PICK over 72 mussels, discarding any that feel too heavy or have open or broken shells. Soak the mussels in a solution of 1/2 cup dry mustard and 2 quarts water for about 30 minutes. Scrub the mussels with a stiff brush under running water and scrape off the beards. Wash the mussels in several waters until they are free from sand and grit.

To open mussels by steaming, put them in a large kettle, add 1/2 to 1 cup white wine or other liquid, or a small amount of olive oil, and steam them, covered, for 5 to 8 minutes, depending on the thickness of the shells, until they open. Discard any mussels that do not open. Strain the mussel liquor through a fine sieve or a double thickness of cheesecloth.

Mussels in White Wine 🐟

COVER the bottom of a deep kettle with a thin layer of olive oil. Heat the oil and add 72 cleaned mussels. Steam them until they open.

Strain the mussel liquor into a small saucepan and add 1 cup white wine, 2 garlic cloves, minced, and 1/2 cup finely chopped parsley. Bring the mixture to a boil, reduce the heat, and simmer it until it is thick and the liquid reduces by half. Pile the mussels into soup plates and pour a little sauce over each serving.

Saffron Mussels 🐟

IN a saucepan sauté 1 small onion and the white part of 1 leek, chopped, in 3 tablespoons olive oil for 3 minutes. Add 1 tomato, peeled, seeded, and chopped, 2 garlic cloves, 1 sprig of thyme, 1/2 bay leaf, 1 teaspoon powdered saffron, and 1 cup white wine, and cook the mixture slowly until almost all the liquid has evaporated. Add to the pan 72 cleaned mussels and steam them until they open. Remove the meat from the shells, discard the shells, and arrange the mussels in a serving dish. Strain the sauce through a fine sieve and spoon it over the mussels. Chill the mussels thoroughly.

Mussels and Tomatoes 🐟

STEAM 72 cleaned mussels in 1/2 cup dry white wine until they open. Discard one shell from each mussel, leaving the meat attached to the other shell. Strain the liquor and reserve it.

In a skillet sauté 2 shallots, chopped, in 2 tablespoons butter until they are golden and add 1 pound tomatoes, peeled, seeded, and chopped, 1 garlic clove, 1/2 cup chopped parsley, and 1/2 cup bread crumbs previously soaked in milk and squeezed dry. Cook the mixture, stirring, for a few minutes, or until the tomatoes are soft, and discard the garlic. Stir in 1/4 cup of the reserved liquor and 1 teaspoon grated lemon rind. Arrange the mussels in a deep flameproof casserole, cover them with the sauce, and simmer the mixture until the mussels are heated through.

ᔰ Baked Stuffed Mussels   MOULES FARCIES AU FOUR

STEAM 72 cleaned mussels in 3/4 cup white wine until they open. Remove the meat from the shells, reserve the shells, and chop the mussels. Strain the liquor and reserve it.

Sauté 3 tablespoons chopped onion, 2 tablespoons chopped celery, and 1 tablespoon chopped green pepper in 4 tablespoons butter until the onion is golden. Stir in 3 tablespoons chopped parsley, 3/4 cup toasted bread crumbs, 3/4 teaspoon each of salt and dry mustard, a pinch of cayenne, the chopped mussels, and enough reserved liquor to bind the mixture. Divide the filling among the shells and dot each with butter. Bake the mussels in a very hot oven (450° F.) for a few minutes, or until the stuffing is lightly browned.

ᔰ Curried Mussels   CARI DE MOULES

PUT 72 cleaned mussels in a kettle with 3/4 cup white wine, 1/2 cup mushrooms, 1/3 cup onions, and 1/4 cup each of parsley and celery, all chopped, 2 teaspoons curry powder, and 1 bay leaf. Steam the mussels until they open, remove the meat from the shells, and discard the shells. Strain the liquor, reduce it over high heat by half, and reserve it.

Beat 2 egg yolks with 2 tablespoons heavy cream and gradually add it to the reserved liquor, stirring constantly. Add to the sauce the mussels and salt and pepper to taste. Divide the mixture among 6 scallop shells and sprinkle each shell with bread crumbs and 2 teaspoons melted butter. Bake the shells in a moderate oven (350° F.) for about 10 minutes, or until the crumbs are browned.

ᔰ Cioppino

CUT 2 pounds live lobster into serving pieces and a 3-pound sea bass into slices 2 inches thick. Shell and devein 3/4 pound raw shrimp, leaving the tails intact.

Clean 18 mussels and 18 clams and steam them in 1 cup white wine with a bay leaf until they open. Strain the broth and reserve it. Soak 1/2 cup dried mushrooms in cold water for 1 hour. Drain them and cut into small pieces.

Heat 1/2 cup olive oil in a large iron kettle and add 3/4 cup chopped parsley, 1/2 cup shredded green onions, 6 shallots and 2 garlic cloves, all finely chopped, 1/2 small dried red pepper, and the mushrooms. Cook the mixture over low heat

Cioppino

for 4 minutes and add 4 tomatoes, peeled, seeded, and coarsely chopped, 1/4 cup tomato purée, and the reserved clam and mussel broth. Cover the kettle and simmer the mixture for 3 minutes. Season with salt, if necessary. Add the lobster, unshelled, the bass, and the shrimp, cover the kettle, and cook the *cioppino* slowly for 20 minutes. Just before serving, add the clams and mussels.

Shucking Oysters

HOLD the oyster firmly, cup side down. Insert the blunt-tipped blade of an oyster knife near the pointed edge of the oyster. Twist the knife to force the shells apart. Cut the large muscle close to the flat upper shell, and cut the lower muscle attached to the deep half of the shell. If the oyster is to be served in the shell, leave it loose in the deep half.

Oyster Stew

POACH 18 freshly shucked oysters in their own liquor for about 2 minutes, until they plump and the edges curl. Add 2 cups each of scalded light cream and milk, 2 tablespoons butter, and salt, pepper, and paprika or cayenne to taste. Serve the stew as soon as the butter has melted.

Oysters à la King

POACH 36 freshly shucked oysters in their own liquor for about 2 minutes, or until the edges curl. Drain and reserve them. Strain the liquor and add enough milk to make 3 cups liquid. Sauté 1/2 cup each of finely chopped celery and green pepper in 6 tablespoons butter until the vegetables are tender. Stir in 6 tablespoons flour, gradually add the milk mixture, and cook the sauce, stirring, until it is thickened. Add the oysters and salt and pepper to taste. Warm the sauce gently until the oysters are heated through. Serve on hot buttered toast and garnish with chopped parsley.

Oyster and Chicken Hash 🦪

POACH 18 oysters in their own liquor for about 2 minutes, or until the edges curl. Drain the oysters and, if necessary, add enough water to make 1 cup liquid. Melt 3 tablespoons butter, add 3 tablespoons flour, and add gradually the oyster liquid. Cook the sauce, stirring, until it bubbles. Slowly stir in 1 cup light cream and cook the sauce until it is thick and smooth. Coarsely chop the oysters, add them to the sauce with 2 cups diced cooked chicken, and add a dash of cayenne and salt and pepper to taste. Turn the hash into a flameproof serving dish, spread it with 1/2 cup Mornay sauce mixed with 1 tablespoon whipped cream, and glaze it under the broiler.

Chafing Dish Jambalaya 🦪

IN the blazer of a chafing dish over direct heat sauté 1 cup shredded cooked ham and 1/4 cup each of chopped green pepper and onion in 3 tablespoons butter. Add a dash of Tabasco, 2 cups cooked fresh tomatoes, 18 freshly shucked oysters, and 18 poached shrimp, shelled and deveined. Cook the mixture for 2 minutes, or until the oysters are plump. Set the pan over hot water, add 3 cups hot cooked rice, and cook the mixture, stirring, until it is heated through. Serve sprinkled with parsley.

Scallops Broiled in Butter 🦪

MELT 1/2 pound butter in a shallow flameproof baking dish, add 2 pounds scallops, washed and dried, and season them with 1 1/2 teaspoons salt and a dash of cayenne. Broil the scallops, 3 inches from the heat, for 3 to 5 minutes, turning occasionally, until they are lightly browned. Sprinkle the scallops with paprika and serve with wedges of lemon.

Scallops in Champagne 🦪

WASH and drain 2 pounds scallops and put them in a saucepan with 3 cups water, a little salt, 6 peppercorns, and a *bouquet garni* composed of 4 sprigs of parsley tied with 2 sprigs of fresh thyme and 1 bay leaf. Bring the water to a boil and reduce the heat. Simmer the scallops for 5 minutes and drain them.

Curried Scallops in a Ring of Rice

Melt 6 tablespoons butter in a saucepan, add 1 onion and 3 shallots, both finely chopped, and sauté the vegetables until they are soft but not brown. Add 1 tablespoon flour and stir in 3 egg yolks, one at a time, 1/2 cup heavy cream, and 1/2 teaspoon salt.

Bring to a boil 2 cups Champagne, reduce the heat, and gradually add the cream and egg mixture, stirring constantly with a wooden spoon. Add the cooked scallops and heat the sauce without letting it boil. Keep the mixture hot over simmering water. Serve in 6 heated patty shells, lined with mushroom purée.

Curried Scallops in a Ring of Rice

WASH and dry 2 pounds scallops and dust them lightly with seasoned flour. Heat 8 tablespoons butter in a skillet and in it sauté 6 shallots, finely chopped, for 3 minutes. Add the scallops and cook them quickly, turning frequently to brown all sides, for about 3 minutes. Sprinkle the scallops with 1 1/2 tablespoons curry powder and add 1/3 cup dry white wine. Serve in a ring of rice and garnish with watercress.

Scallops in Pastry Shells

LINE 6 coquilles, or scallop shells, with flaky pastry and bake them.

In a saucepan combine 2 pounds scallops, washed and drained, with 2 shallots, finely chopped, 2 cups dry white wine, 2 tablespoons butter, and the juice of 1 lemon. Cook the scallops for 5 minutes, drain them, and divide them among the pastry shells. Reduce the sauce over high heat to about 1 1/2 cups and add 2 egg yolks beaten with 6 tablespoons heavy cream and 1/2 teaspoon thyme. Heat the sauce but do not let it boil. Pour it over the scallops in the shells. Dot each shell with butter and brown lightly under the broiler.

Scallops in Ramekins

WASH and drain 2 pounds scallops and put them in a saucepan with 3/4 cup clam broth, 1/4 cup melted butter, 2 teaspoons paprika, 1 teaspoon Worcestershire sauce, and 3/4 teaspoon each of celery salt, dry mustard, and salt. Bring the liquid to a boil and cook the scallops gently for 5 minutes. Stir in 1 cup tomato purée and bring the sauce slowly to a boil. Add 3 tablespoons heavy cream and serve in ramekins.

❧ Seviche of Scallops

WASH and drain 2 pounds scallops and put them in an enamel saucepan with 1 large onion, thinly sliced, 4 bay leaves, 1 tablespoon white-wine vinegar, and generous pinches of dried red pepper, crushed peppercorns, tarragon, and chopped garlic. Add 1 cup lime or lemon juice and 1/2 cup orange juice and bring the mixture to the boiling point. Remove it from the heat, cool it, and add 1 tomato, peeled and sliced. Chill the *seviche* for at least 6 hours. Serve on chilled plates, sprinkled with chopped parsley and celery leaves.

❧ Scallops Bordeaux Style

HEAT 4 tablespoons butter in a skillet and add 1 small carrot, 1 onion, 2 shallots, and 2 stalks of parsley, all finely chopped. Sauté the vegetables until they are lightly browned, add a pinch of powdered thyme and 1 bay leaf, and cook the mixture over low heat for 15 minutes. Add 2 pounds scallops, washed and dried, and brown them lightly. Add 1 cup white wine and 3 tomatoes, peeled, seeded, and chopped, and simmer the mixture for 5 minutes. Pour into the pan 1/4 cup heated brandy and set it aflame. Remove the scallops and keep them warm. Reduce the pan juices over high heat to 1 1/2 cups. Add 4 tablespoons butter, cook the sauce for 2 minutes, and return the scallops. Serve hot, garnished with triangles of toast.

❧ Scallops and Shrimp in White-Wine Sauce

COMBINE in a saucepan 1/4 cup each of bottled clam juice and white wine, 3 shallots, minced, and 1 bay leaf. Bring the liquid to a boil and add 1 1/2 pounds each of raw scallops, washed and drained, and raw shrimp, shelled and deveined. Simmer the seafood for 5 minutes and drain it, reserving the broth.

Melt 3 tablespoons butter in a saucepan, stir in 3 1/2 tablespoons flour, and gradually add the reserved broth. There should be 1 1/4 cups. Cook the sauce, stirring, until it is smooth and thickened, and add salt and cayenne to taste and the juice of 1/4 lemon. Stir in slowly 2 egg yolks beaten with 1/2 cup light cream. Heat the sauce without letting it boil.

Slice the sea scallops into thin rounds and the shrimp in half lengthwise. Put them in the blazer of a chafing dish, cover with the sauce, and sprinkle with chopped parsley. Makes 8 servings.

Scallops and Shrimp in Patty Shells 𝕊

SIMMER together 1 pound raw scallops and 1 pound raw shrimp, shelled and deveined, in 2 cups white wine for 5 minutes. Drain the scallops and shrimp and strain the wine.

In a saucepan sauté 3 shallots, finely chopped, and 12 mushrooms, sliced, in 3 tablespoons butter. Add 2 tablespoons parsley, finely chopped, and salt and pepper to taste, blend in 2 tablespoons flour, and stir in the strained wine. Cook the sauce, stirring constantly, until it thickens and stir in 2 tablespoons heavy cream. Add the shrimp and scallops to the sauce, pour the mixture into 8 individual patty shells, and sprinkle the tops with finely chopped parsley. Makes 8 servings.

Poaching Shrimp 𝕊

IN a kettle combine 2 quarts water, 1 tablespoon each of white-wine vinegar and salt, 4 peppercorns, 1 garlic clove, crushed, and 1 bay leaf. Bring the liquid to a boil, add 2 pounds raw shrimp, and simmer them, covered, for 5 minutes. Do not over-cook the shrimp as they will toughen and lose a considerable amount of flavor. Remove the pan from the heat and let the shrimp cool in the court bouillon for 20 minutes. Drain the shrimp and shell and devein them. (Or, if desired, shell and devein them before poaching. Cook the shrimp for 3 to 4 minutes, cool them in the court bouillon, and drain them.) Chill them, tightly covered, until serving time. This amount of shrimp will serve 6 as main course or 8 as a first course.

When poaching larger amounts of the shellfish, increase the ingredients of the court bouillon in proportion.

CREVETTES À LA MARINIÈRE   ## Shrimp in Marinière Sauce 𝕊

POACH 2 pounds raw shrimp, shelled and deveined, in white-wine court bouillon for 5 minutes. Drain the shrimp and split them. Strain the court bouillon. In a saucepan melt 2 tablespoons butter and blend in 1 tablespoon flour. Gradually add 3/4 cup of the court bouillon and cook the sauce, stirring constantly, until it is thick and smooth. Add 2 tablespoons lemon juice and a pinch of cayenne. Pour the sauce slowly over 2 egg yolks, well beaten. Put the mixture in the top of a double boiler over boiling water, add 1/2 cup heavy cream, and cook for 3 minutes. Add the shrimp and heat all together without boiling. Serve in patty shells.

⬩ Shrimp à la Russe　　　　　　　　CREVETTES À LA RUSSE

BRING to a boil 2 cups sour cream, 1 cup white wine, 1 teaspoon thyme, and 1/2 teaspoon salt. Add 2 pounds raw shrimp, shelled and deveined, and simmer them for 5 minutes, or until they turn pink. Serve the shrimp and their sauce on triangles of toast.

⬩ Shrimp Umberto

SAUTÉ 1 garlic clove, minced, in 1/2 cup melted butter until it is golden. Add 2 tablespoons parsley, 1 teaspoon savory, 1/2 teaspoon grated lemon peel, and salt and paprika to taste. Cook the mixture for 5 minutes and mix in 1 cup dry bread crumbs and 2 tablespoons grated Parmesan.

Arrange 2 pounds poached shrimp, shelled and deveined, in a buttered baking dish, add the bread-crumb mixture, and sprinkle 2 ounces dry Sherry over the top. Bake the casserole in a moderately slow oven (325° F.) for 20 minutes, or until the crumbs and cheese are golden.

⬩ Broiled Shrimp in Beer

BLEND 1 1/2 cups beer with 1 tablespoon each of chopped chives and parsley, 2 teaspoons dry mustard, 1 garlic clove, finely chopped, 1 teaspoon salt, and 1/2 teaspoon black pepper. Cover 2 pounds raw shrimp, shelled and deveined, with this mixture and marinate them for 10 hours or overnight, stirring from time to time to ensure even seasoning. Drain the shrimp and broil them 3 inches from the heat for about 2 minutes on each side, or until they turn pink.

⬩ Shrimp en Brochette

PUT 2 pounds raw shrimp, shelled and deveined, in a bowl and cover them with a mixture of 1/3 cup each of soy sauce and white wine, 1 teaspoon ground pepper, and 1/2 teaspoon ground ginger. Marinate them, covered, for several hours. Drain the shrimp, reserving the marinade, and roll them in sesame seeds. Thread the shrimp on skewers and broil them over hot coals, or under the broiler, for 4 or 5 minutes, turning the skewers and basting once or twice with the marinade.

Skewered Shrimp Armada 𝔰

SHELL and devein 36 large raw shrimp and split them lengthwise almost through. Poach the shrimp for about 4 minutes, or until they turn pink, and drain them. In the pocket of each shrimp put an anchovy filet, press the shrimp together firmly, and wrap each one in a half slice of bacon. Thread the shrimp on skewers and cook them over moderately hot coals, turning frequently, until the bacon is crisp.

Cold Curried Shrimp 𝔰

SAUTÉ 1 garlic clove, crushed, and 1/4 cup each of onion and apple, both minced, in 4 tablespoons melted butter until the onion is golden. Discard the garlic. Stir in 2 tablespoons flour and add 1 cup stewed tomatoes, 2 teaspoons curry powder, and salt and pepper to taste. Bring the sauce to a boil, strain it through a fine sieve, and cool it. Measure the sauce and add an equal amount of mayonnaise and 1 tablespoon lemon juice. Fold in 2 pounds poached shrimp, shelled and deveined, and chill the curry for 3 hours. Serve on a glass plate, garnished with a ring of thinly sliced cucumbers and sprinkle with slivered toasted almonds.

Roast Prime Ribs of Beef

RUB a rib roast of beef with salt and spread it generously with butter or fat. Put it on a rack in a roasting pan, resting on the bone ends. If it lacks a thick layer of natural fat, lay a slice of beef suet on top. Sear the beef in a very hot oven (450° F.) for about 20 minutes, reduce the heat to moderate (350° F.), and continue to roast the meat, basting frequently, until it is done. Allow about 16 minutes per pound for rare beef, 20 minutes for medium, and 23 minutes for well done. If the roast is very large, add a few tablespoons of water to the pan to prevent the fat from burning. Remove the meat to a large platter and let it stand for about 10 minutes before carving. Serve with Yorkshire pudding.

Yorkshire Pudding

SIFT 1 cup sifted flour with 1/2 teaspoon salt into a bowl. Break in 2 eggs and add 1 cup milk. Mix the ingredients together just enough to moisten them. There should be some lumps in the batter. Pour the batter into well-buttered fluted muffin tins, filling them two thirds full, and put the tins in a cold oven. Turn on the oven to hot (400° F.) and bake the puddings for 30 to 40 minutes, or until they are puffed and lightly browned.

FILET DE BOEUF FERVAAL ## Filet of Beef Fervaal

HAVE the butcher trim a large filet of beef, tie the thin end back toward the center to make a shorter and thicker roast, and lard the meat at 3/4-inch intervals with strips of larding pork. Lay the filet in a deep earthenware dish and cover it with 2 carrots, 1 large onion, and 1 peeled lemon, all thinly sliced. Add 3 sprigs of parsley, 1 crumbled bay leaf, 1/2 teaspoon dried thyme, a dash of white pepper and 1/2 cup oil. Cover the dish with a cloth and marinate the filet for 3 hours, turning it six times.

Reduce 4 cups beef stock over high heat until it is thick and syrupy. Set this glaze aside.

Remove the meat from the marinade, lay it on a rack in a buttered roasting pan, and roast it in a very hot oven (450° F.), basting it occasionally with 1/2 cup melted butter, to the rare stage. Allow about 12 minutes per pound. During the last 5 or 6 minutes of roasting, brush the meat three times with most of the prepared glaze, reserving the rest for the sauce. Turn off the oven heat and open the door for 3 minutes. Close the door and let the meat rest in the oven for 12 minutes. Arrange the filet on a flameproof platter in a ring of duchess potatoes and ham, and put the platter under the broiler long enough to brown the potatoes lightly. Garnish the platter with cooked artichoke bottoms sprinkled with chopped herbs.

Add the remaining glaze to the roasting pan with 1/2 cup Madeira and cook the sauce over moderate heat, stirring in all the brown bits that cling to the pan, for a few minutes. Strain the sauce and add 1 truffle, finely minced and heated for 5 minutes in 1/4 cup Madeira. If the sauce is too salty, add a little more Madeira. Pour the sauce into a heated sauceboat and serve separately.

FILET DE BOEUF EN CROÛTE ## Tenderloin of Beef in Pastry

BROWN a whole filet of beef on all sides over high heat and let it cool.

Prepare the following filling: Combine 3/4 pound veal, 1/2 pound ham, and 1/4 pound larding pork, all cut in pieces, and 1 onion, finely chopped. In a large heavy skillet brown the meat and onion in 1/2 cup butter and add 4 tablespoons Sherry, 2 tablespoons beef stock, 6 spinach leaves, 2 bay leaves, and salt and pepper to taste. Cook the mixture over low heat until the meat is tender and put it through a food chopper. Stir in 2 egg yolks and 1/3 cup grated Parmesan.

Roll out chilled flaky pastry into a rectangle large enough to enclose the filet of beef. Spread the dough with a thin layer of filling, and wrap it around the filet, turning in the ends securely. Lay the filet on a rack in a roasting pan and roast it in a moderate oven (350° F.) for about 20 minutes. Remove the pan from the oven and let the filet stand for 10 minutes. With a large spatula, carefully transfer the filet to a platter, taking care not to break the pastry, and serve it with périgourdine sauce.

ᏕᎲ Planked Steak

Rub a 3- to 4 1/2-pound porterhouse steak with a cut garlic clove and brush it with 2 tablespoons melted butter. For a rare steak, broil it on one side for about 5 minutes. Sprinkle the steak with salt and pepper and lay it, cooked side down, on a wooden plank rubbed with oil. Surround the meat with alternate mounds of duchess potatoes and mushroom caps, and brush the mushrooms with butter. Put the plank under the broiler, 3 to 4 inches from the heat, for about 10 minutes, or until the steak is done to the rare stage. Fill the mushroom caps with béarnaise sauce and serve the steak on the plank.

ᏕᎲ Sirloin Steak Gourmet

Trim a 5-pound sirloin steak, cut 2 inches thick, and marinate the steak in 1 cup Cognac for 30 minutes, turning it once. Drain the steak and score the edges at 1/2-inch intervals to prevent them from curling. Broil the steak over hot coals until it is cooked to the desired degree of doneness. Season the steak with salt and freshly ground pepper to taste.

For very rare steak of 2-inch thickness, broil the steak for 14 to 20 minutes; for rare, 20 to 30 minutes; for medium, 30 to 35 minutes; for well done, 45 minutes.

ᏕᎲ Broiled Marinated Steak

Combine 2 cups red wine, 1 onion, minced, 1 garlic clove, crushed, and 1/2 teaspoon freshly ground black pepper. Marinate a sirloin or porterhouse steak in this mixture for at least 2 hours, turning it from time to time. Remove the steak, reserving the marinade, pat it dry, and rub it with butter. Broil the steak over hot coals to the desired degree of doneness. Boil the marinade until it is reduced by two thirds. Discard the garlic clove and pour the sauce over the steak.

Planked Steak

❧ Broiled Steak Orientale

COMBINE 1/2 cup each of pineapple juice and soy sauce, 1/4 cup Sherry, 2 table-spoons chopped preserved ginger, 1 tablespoon olive oil, 1 teaspoon dry mustard, 1/2 teaspoon curry powder, and 1 garlic clove, crushed. Marinate a 4- to 5-pound sirloin steak in the mixture for 3 hours, turning it once. Drain and dry the steak and reserve the marinade. Broil the steak over hot coals to the desired degree of doneness. Heat the marinade and serve it as a sauce.

❧ Rib Steak with Shallot Sauce

COOK 2 teaspoons finely chopped shallots in 1/2 cup white wine until the wine is reduced by one half, and let the mixture cool. Cream 4 tablespoons butter with 2 teaspoons finely chopped parsley, and add the butter to the wine mixture with salt and pepper to taste. Broil 2 large rib steaks to the desired degree of doneness. Turn the steaks in the sauce, coating them well. Remove them to a heated platter and top with a lump of butter and a sprinkling of chopped parsley. Serve the sauce separately.

❧ Stuffed Rib Steak

HAVE the butcher cut 6 small boneless rib steaks 1/2 inch thick and split them to make a pocket. Mix together 1 pound ground sirloin, 4 shallots and 1/4 cup parsley, both chopped, 3/4 teaspoon salt, and 1/2 teaspoon freshly ground black pepper. Fill the pockets with a 1/4-inch-thick layer of this forcemeat, pressing firmly to hold in the filling. Sauté the steaks quickly in a small amount of butter, turning them frequently. Remove the meat to a heated platter. To the pan add 1/4 cup red wine, 1 teaspoon *glace de viande*, or meat extract, 1/2 teaspoon dry mustard, and 2 table-spoons Cognac. Deglaze the pan, stirring in all the brown bits that cling to the bottom, and pour the sauce over the steaks. Serve immediately.

❧ Sautéed Tournedos   TOURNEDOS SAUTÉS

TOURNEDOS are small, uniform slices cut from the heart of the filet of beef. They may be broiled, but they are most often sautéed in butter or olive oil.

Season 6 tournedos with salt and pepper. Coat a hot heavy skillet with butter and a few drops of olive oil and in it sauté the tournedos quickly on both sides. They should be rare. Arrange them on round croûtes. Add a little red wine to the butter remaining in the pan and cook the sauce for a few minutes, stirring in all the brown bits that cling to the pan. Strain the sauce over the tournedos. Garnish each serving with sprigs of parsley.

Tournedos Henri IV

SEASON 6 tournedos with salt and pepper and cook them as for *tournedos sautés*. Remove them from the pan and keep them warm. In the same pan sauté 6 rounds of bread, cut to the size of the tournedos, until they are golden brown, adding more butter as needed. On a platter arrange the tournedos on the croûtes. Put a large cooked artichoke heart on each tournedos and fill the heart with béarnaise sauce.

Tournedos with Mushroom Sauce

TOURNEDOS, SAUCE AUX CHAMPIGNONS

COOK 6 tournedos as for *tournedos sautés* and arrange them around a heated platter. Add 1/4 cup chicken stock to the pan and cook the sauce over high heat, stirring in the brown bits that cling to the pan. Stir in 1 1/2 cups mushroom sauce and heat the sauce but do not let it boil. Pour the mushroom sauce into the center of the platter.

Tournedos Pompadour

SEASON 6 tournedos with salt and pepper and cook them as for *tournedos sautés*. Arrange them on a heated platter and spread each with tomato purée. Arrange a sautéed slice of ham cut the size of the tournedos on the purée and a slice of truffle on the ham. Serve with the pan juices.

Tournedos with Tarragon

TRIM 6 slices of bread to the size of tournedos, sauté them in butter until they are browned, and arrange them on a heated platter. Cook 6 tournedos as for *tournedos sautés* and top each croûte with a steak. Add to the pan 1/2 cup each of white wine

Bœuf à la Mode en Gelée

and veal stock in which 4 or 5 tarragon leaves have soaked for at least 30 minutes. Cook the sauce over high heat, stirring in the brown bits that cling to the pan, until it is reduced by one half. Swirl 1 tablespoon butter into the sauce and pour it over the meat. Decorate each tournedos with 2 crossed tarragon leaves.

Filet Mignon Lord Seymour

COOK 6 filet mignons as for *tournedos sautés* and arrange them around a heated platter. Top each steak with a small cooked artichoke bottom filled with béarnaise sauce and chopped truffles. To the pan add 1 cup brown sauce and 1 tablespoon *glace de viande*, or meat extract, and bring the sauce to a boil. Simmer the sauce for 10 minutes, stirring occasionally, and add 2 tablespoons Madeira and 1/2 cup sliced green olives stuffed with pimientos. Pour the sauce around the meat.

Bœuf à la Mode en Gelée

LARD a 4- to 5-pound eye round of beef with 6 or 7 strips of salt pork and sprinkle the meat with salt, pepper, and nutmeg. Marinate the meat in 1/2 cup brandy for 2 hours, turning it several times. Drain the meat, reserving the marinade, and dry it well.

Heat 3 tablespoons bacon fat in a heavy Dutch oven and sear the meat on all sides. Remove it from the pan and keep it warm.

Parboil 2 split calf's feet for 10 minutes, drain them, and chop coarsely. Brown the pieces on all sides in the fat remaining in the kettle. Add the reserved marinade and cook it, scraping in all the brown bits on the bottom of the pan, for a few minutes. Add 3 cups red wine, 1 cup cooked tomatoes, 12 small onions, 2 shallots, halved, 6 carrots, sliced, 1 onion stuck with cloves, 1 garlic clove, and a *bouquet garni* composed of a bay leaf, a few green celery tops, and a few sprigs of parsley and thyme. Return the meat to the kettle and cook it, covered, over low heat for 4 to 5 hours, turning occasionally.

Remove the meat from the kettle, cool it, and cut it into slices. Remove the bones from the calf's feet and shred the meat. Skim the fat from the liquid in the kettle and strain the liquid through a fine sieve into a bowl set in cracked ice. Chill 6 small molds and 1 medium mold and coat them with the cooking aspic when it is cool but still liquid. Chill the molds well.

Cook separately 2 carrots and 1 cup shelled peas in boiling salted water until the vegetables are tender. Drain the vegetables and chill them well. Slice the carrots and arrange 6 slices in a flower pattern on the bottom of the larger mold. Use a small slice for the center of the flower. Arrange the peas in a ring around the bottom of the 6 small molds and add a few carrot slices to each. Fill all the molds with alternating layers of the sliced beef and shredded calf's feet and cool but still liquid aspic, ending with the aspic. Chill them thoroughly, until they are set. At serving time, unmold the aspics on a chilled platter.

Dill Pot Roast

SEASON a 3- to 4-pound top or bottom round of beef with salt, pepper, and nutmeg, and put the meat in a deep earthenware bowl. Cover it with a marinade made of 2 cups red-wine vinegar, 2 onions and 2 carrots, both sliced, 1 bay leaf, 4 cloves, 4 peppercorns, 1 lemon, thinly sliced, 1 tablespoon salt, and a dash of nutmeg. Marinate the meat in the refrigerator for 3 or 4 days, turning it occasionally.

Drain and dry the meat. Strain the marinade and reserve it. In a Dutch oven brown the meat on all sides in butter. Add the marinade, bring it to a boil, and simmer the meat, covered, for about 3 hours, or until it is tender. If necessary, replenish the liquid with beef stock. Remove the meat to a heated platter.

Strain the pan juices and stir in 1 cup sour cream and a generous handful of chopped fresh dill. Heat the gravy and pour it over the pot roast.

Pot Roast in Ale

PUT a 3- to 4-pound top or bottom round of beef in a deep earthenware crock or bowl. Pour over it 3 bottles dark ale and 1/2 cup red wine. Add cold water, if necessary, to cover the meat, and salt and pepper to taste. Marinate the meat in the refrigerator for at least 12 hours.

Drain and dry the meat. Strain the marinade and reserve it.

In a Dutch oven brown the meat on all sides in butter. Add half the marinade, 1 teaspoon caraway seeds, and a *bouquet garni* composed of a sprig each of thyme and rosemary and 3 sprigs of parsley. Cover the pot and cook the meat slowly for about 3 hours, or until it is tender, adding more marinade as needed. Remove the meat to a heated platter. Discard the *bouquet garni* and thicken the sauce with a *beurre manié* made by kneading together 1 tablespoon each of flour and butter. Correct the seasoning and strain the sauce into a sauceboat. Serve with *Spätzle*.

Italian Pot Roast 🐖

WITH a sharp pointed knife, make small incisions in a 3- to 4-pound top or bottom round of beef and fill the slits with 3 or 4 garlic cloves cut in slivers. Rub the meat with salt, pepper, thyme, and rosemary. Bard it with sheets of pork fat, tying the fat in place with string. Brown the meat in butter on all sides in a deep flameproof casserole. Add 2 large turnips and 2 onions, both sliced, 4 large carrots, diced, a generous strip of orange peel and one of lemon peel, 1 1/2 cups tomato purée, and 1 cup Burgundy. Cover the casserole, put it on an asbestos pad over very low heat, and simmer the meat very slowly for about 7 hours. The meat should be tender enough to cut with a spoon and the sauce very thick. Serve sprinkled with a little chopped lemon and orange peel, if desired.

Munich Pot Roast 🐖

LARD a 3-pound top or bottom round of beef with strips of salt pork and with 3 or 4 pickles cut in strips. In a Dutch oven melt 1/2 cup butter and in it brown lightly 1 celery root, 1 onion, and 1 carrot, all sliced. Brown the meat well on all sides and add 1/2 cup beef stock, 1 bay leaf, and a dash each of nutmeg and thyme. Cover the pot and cook the meat over low heat for 2 to 3 hours, or until it is tender. Remove the meat to a heated platter. Skim the fat from the pan and add to the juices 1/2 cup red wine and 2 tablespoons cornstarch mixed to a paste with a little water. Cook the sauce until it thickens and strain it, and stir in 1/2 cup sour cream. Heat the sauce but do not let it boil. Garnish the platter with mashed potato dumplings and serve the sauce separately.

Beef in Anchovy Cream 🐖

HAVE the butcher cut 2 pounds center cut of sirloin into 18 slices about 1/8 inch thick. Heat 4 tablespoons butter in a skillet and brown the slices on both sides. Remove them from the pan, reserving the pan juices.

Chop finely 12 anchovies, 2/3 cup parsley, 6 shallots, 2 small stalks of celery, and 2 small carrots. Lay 1 slice of sirloin on the bottom of a flameproof casserole. Sprinkle it with a little of the anchovy, 1/2 teaspoon each of the parsley, shallot, celery, and carrot, and a dash each of freshly ground pepper and coriander. Stack 5 more slices of beef on the first in the same manner, sprinkling each slice with anchovy, chopped vegetables, and spices. Repeat the procedure with the remaining 12 slices of sirloin, to make 3 separate stacks of meat.

To the juices in the skillet add 1/4 cup dry Madeira and 1/2 cup beef stock and cook the sauce over high heat for 2 minutes. Pour it over the meat and add 1 cup hot heavy cream. Cover the casserole, put it on an asbestos pad, and cook the meat over very low heat for about 1 hour, or until it is tender. Add cream and stock as needed, to keep the meat almost covered with liquid during the cooking. Transfer the meat in one piece to a heated platter. Heat 2 tablespoons Cognac, ignite it, and pour it flaming over the meat. Strain the sauce in the casserole and simmer it until it is slightly thickened. Stir in 1 tablespoon paprika and cook the sauce for 1 minute. Pour it over the meat and garnish with chopped parsley.

৸ Beef Pâté Roll   PÂTÉ DE BOEUF EN ROULADE

PUT 1 pound lean beef, 1/2 pound bacon, and 1 onion through the medium blade of a food chopper. Blend in 1/2 cup each of beef stock and bread crumbs, 2 eggs, beaten, 1/4 teaspoon nutmeg, and salt and pepper to taste. Shape the mixture into a long loaf on a cloth. Wrap it in the cloth and tie it securely at both ends. Lower the roll into simmering beef stock and cook it very slowly for 2 to 2 1/2 hours. Drain the pâté, cool it under a weight, and chill it. Carefully remove the cloth, brush the roll with *glace de viande,* or meat glaze, and serve on lettuce.

৸ Beef Birds in Red Wine

PLACE twelve 1/4-inch slices of sirloin steak, about 5 by 3 inches, between wax paper and pound them very thin. Sauté 1 small onion, chopped, and 1 stalk of celery, diced, in 1 teaspoon butter until they are transparent. Combine them with 1 1/2 cups toasted bread crumbs, a pinch of marjoram, and salt and pepper to taste. Divide the filling among the slices, roll them up, and tie them with string. Dredge the beef birds with flour and brown them on all sides in 2 tablespoons butter. Add to the pan 1 1/2 cups dry red wine and cook the beef birds, covered, over low heat for 30 minutes, or until the meat is tender. Carefully remove the strings.

Beef and Ham Birds in White Wine 🐦

PLACE twelve 1/4-inch slices of sirloin steak, about 5 by 3 inches, between wax paper and pound them very thin. Lay a thin slice of lean ham on each slice of beef. Make a filling of 1 cup finely chopped parsley, 1/4 cup each of pine nuts and raisins, and 3 tablespoons grated Parmesan and divide the filling among the beef slices. Roll up the slices and tie them with string. Brown the birds on all sides in 2 tablespoons olive oil. Add to the pan 3/4 cup white wine and cook the birds, covered, for about 30 minutes, or until the meat is tender. Carefully remove the strings.

Skewered Beef Birds 🐦

PLACE 18 small thin beef slices, cut from the filet, between wax paper and pound them very thin. Put a thin slice of mozzarella on each beef slice and cover it with several slices of hot Italian pork sausage. Roll up the slices and thread 3 birds on each skewer alternately with small cubes of stale bread. Dip the skewers in olive oil and broil the beef birds for about 8 minutes, turning them once, until they are brown on all sides.

Steak Satés 🐦

CUT 3 pounds sirloin steak into 1-inch cubes. Put the meat in an earthenware bowl and add 1 cup soy sauce, 3/4 cup peanut oil, 3 onions, finely chopped, 2 garlic cloves, minced, and 3 tablespoons toasted sesame seeds. Marinate the meat for three hours, and drain it, reserving the marinade. Thread the steak cubes on small wooden skewers and brush them with a mixture of 1 tablespoon ground cuminseed and 1 1/2 teaspoons lemon juice. Broil the meat over hot coals, or under the broiler, basting it with the marinade and turning the skewers from time to time, until it is tender. Sprinkle with salt and pepper to taste.

Steak Sandwiches with Garlic 🐦

BROIL a large sirloin or porterhouse steak, cut at least 1 1/2 inches thick, over hot coals to the desired degree of doneness. Remove the steak to a heated platter and cut it in thin diagonal slices.

Split loaves of French bread lengthwise and toast them. Spread them with soft butter mixed with 1/2 cup chopped parsley and 1 garlic clove, crushed, for each 1/2 cup butter. Arrange the slices of steak on the bottom slices of bread and top them with the upper halves. Slice the long loaves and serve the sandwiches with slices of sweet onions.

Beef and Oyster Kebabs

Cut 2 pounds sirloin steak into 1 1/2-inch cubes. Thread the cubes on skewers alternately with oysters wrapped in strips of bacon. Broil the kebabs over hot coals until the meat is tender. Serve with béarnaise sauce.

Beef Stew with Walnuts

In a Dutch oven brown 2 pounds lean chuck beef, cut into large cubes, in 1 1/2 tablespoons each of olive oil and butter. Remove the meat from the pot and in the fat remaining brown 12 small white onions. Remove the pot from the heat and stir in 1 tablespoon flour. Return the pot to the heat and add the beef, 3/4 cup dry red wine, a *bouquet garni* composed of 1 bay leaf and a sprig each of parsley and thyme, 1 crushed garlic clove, salt and pepper to taste, and enough beef stock to cover the meat. Bring the liquid slowly to a boil, cover the pot, and simmer the stew for about 1 1/2 hours, or until the meat is tender.

Twenty minutes before the end of the cooking, add 1 bunch of celery, cut in crosswise slices and browned in butter. Add 1 more tablespoon butter to the skillet in which the celery was browned and, when it foams, add 3/4 cup walnuts. Sprinkle the nuts with salt and sauté them, shaking the pan occasionally, until they are crisp. Add them to the stew. Serve sprinkled with 1 tablespoon shredded blanched orange rind.

Fondue Bourguignonne

Cut 1 1/2 pounds tender filet of beef into 3/4-inch cubes. Melt 1/2 pound butter over direct heat in a fondue pan or in the blazer of a chafing dish. Add 2/3 cup olive oil and bring the mixture to a boil. Adjust the heat to keep the oil and butter bubbling hot all during the cooking process.

Supply each guest with a fork with heatproof handle. Or provide two forks, so that one can cool off while the other is being used. Each guest should also have several small dishes of sauce into which he dips the meat: rémoulade, tomato, béarnaise, curry, and sweet and sour sauces are the customary choices. Capers, hard-cooked eggs, chopped onion, and various relishes and preserved fruits are compatible extras.

Each guest spears a cube of meat with his fork, cooks it in the boiling oil and butter until it is done to his taste, and embellishes it with sauces and garnishes. Warm crusty French bread is an essential adjunct to the *fondue bourguignonne.*

Hash Tart

COMBINE 3 cups chopped cooked roast beef with 1 onion, chopped, 1 green pepper, seeded and chopped, 1/2 cup seedless raisins, 1 teaspoon Worcestershire sauce, and salt and pepper to taste. Moisten the hash with 2 tablespoons whiskey and a little roast-beef gravy. Cover the hash with 2 cups mashed potatoes combined with 1/2 cup grated Cheddar and 1/4 cup finely chopped chives, and sprinkle the potatoes with 1/2 cup more grated cheese. Bake the hash in a very hot oven (450° F.) until it is thoroughly heated and the potato crust is nicely browned.

Savory Hamburgers

IN a saucepan combine 2 cups red wine, 1 onion, chopped, and 2 garlic cloves, finely minced. Cook the sauce until the wine reduces to 1 cup and add 3 tablespoons butter, 2 tablespoons lemon juice, and 1 tablespoon minced parsley. Let the sauce cool and blend it with 3 pounds seasoned ground sirloin. The mixture will be moist. Divide the meat into 12 portions and shape them into patties.

Broil each hamburger over hot coals to the desired degree of doneness (with the sauce in the mixture, the meat will remain moist and the center rare). Serve on buttered buns, 2 to each person.

Glazed Corned Brisket of Beef

IN a large kettle combine 4 quarts water, 1 1/2 cups salt, 2 tablespoons pickling spices, 1 tablespoon sugar, 1/2 ounce saltpeter, and 8 bay leaves. Bring the brine to a boil, simmer it for 5 minutes, and let it cool.

Put a 5-pound brisket of beef in a stone crock or large glass dish. Add 8 garlic cloves and the cooled brine and spices. Put a weight on the meat to keep it submerged and cover the crock with several thicknesses of cheesecloth and then a lid. Put the crock in a cool place for 12 days, to pickle the meat.

Remove the meat from the brine and rinse it in water. Put the meat in a kettle, add water to cover, and bring it to a boil. Skim the surface as necessary. Simmer the meat for about 3 hours, or until it is tender. Let the meat cool in the broth for 12 hours. Drain the meat and dry it well.

Put the brisket on a platter. Brush the top with apricot jam to form a glaze. Decorate the top with blanched almond halves, green grapes, shredded and blanched orange rind, and tarragon leaves. Surround the meat with lettuce cups filled with pitted whole grapes and preserved kumquats in mustard sauce. Cut in thin slices and serve hot or cold.

Cooking Beef Tongue

WASH thoroughly a 4- to 5-pound fresh beef tongue and put it in a large kettle. Add 3 celery stalks, 1 onion stuck with 3 cloves, 6 sprigs of parsley, 1 red pepper pod, 1 tablespoon salt, and 6 peppercorns. Add enough cold water just to cover the meat and bring the liquid slowly to a boil, skimming the surface frequently. Simmer the tongue, covered, over low heat for about 3 1/2 hours, or until it is tender. Let the tongue cool in the stock. Drain the tongue, peel off the skin, and trim away the root and gristle. Serve hot or cold.

To cook a smoked beef tongue, soak it overnight in cold water to cover. Eliminate the salt and the red pepper pod, and add 1 carrot and 1 bay leaf to the cooking liquid. Simmer as for fresh beef tongue. It may require a little less cooking.

Anchovy Tongue

CUT into slices a cooked fresh beef tongue, weighing about 5 pounds.

Cream together 1/2 cup butter and 1/4 cup each of anchovy paste and chopped parsley. Spread each slice of tongue with the anchovy butter, reshape the tongue, and lay it on an ovenproof platter. Pour 1/2 cup melted butter over the meat and bake it in a moderately hot oven (375° F.) for 20 minutes.

Glazed Corned Brisket of Beef

ᵹ Glazed Beef Tongue

PUT a cooked fresh beef tongue, weighing about 5 pounds, in a heavy saucepan and add 1 cup water, 1/2 cup vinegar, 1/4 cup sugar, and 1/2 teaspoon cloves. Simmer the mixture, turning the tongue frequently, until the liquid is evaporated and the tongue is glazed.

Cool and chill the tongue and cut it into slices. Overlap the slices on a platter. Serve with buttered whole-wheat bread.

ᵹ Beef Tongue with Ham Mousse

CHILL thoroughly 2 cooked smoked beef tongues, each weighing 4 to 5 pounds. Cut the meat into thin slices, spread the slices with a thin layer of ham mousse, and reshape the tongues. Coat the tongues with 2 cups *mayonnaise collée* and arrange them on chilled platters. Garnish with sprigs of watercress. Makes 15 servings.

ᵹ Tongue and Truffles Valenciennes

SAUTÉ 4 chicken livers, chopped, in 2 tablespoons butter over high heat until they are browned but still pink inside. Remove them from the pan and keep them warm. Stir 1 1/2 tablespoons flour into the pan juices and cook the *roux*, stirring, over low heat until it is blended and browned. Add gradually 1 1/2 cups strong beef stock, bring the sauce to a boil, and cook it for 5 minutes, stirring constantly. Skim off the fat and strain the sauce through a fine sieve. Return the livers to the sauce, add 2 cups cooked fresh beef tongue and 1/2 cup truffles, cut into julienne, and cook the mixture for about 10 minutes, or until the sauce is slightly thickened. Add 1/3 cup Madeira, bring the mixture just to a boil, and remove it from the heat. Serve in a border of saffron rice mixed with grated Parmesan.

ᵹ Tongue in Swiss Fondue

CUT into cubes enough cooked smoked beef tongue to make 2 cups. Divide the cubes among 6 small serving dishes.

In the blazer of a chafing dish over hot water (or in a fondue casserole), melt 6 ounces Swiss cheese in 1 1/2 cups Chablis. Season the cheese with salt, pepper, and 4 drops of Tabasco sauce. Each guest spears a cube of tongue on a long fondue fork or a wooden skewer and dips it in the cheese mixture. Serve with hot garlic French bread.

Roast Veal with Cherries

RUB a boned 4-pound leg of veal with salt and let it stand for 1 hour. Remove the pits from 1 pound ripe cherries. With a very sharp knife cut incisions at 1-inch intervals in the meat and insert 1 cherry in each slit. To the remaining cherries add 1/2 cup water and sugar to taste. Simmer the fruit for 10 minutes, or until it is tender, and drain it. There should be about 1/2 cup syrup. Reserve it and the cherries.

Put the veal on a rack in a buttered roasting pan and brush it with melted butter. Sprinkle the meat with 1/2 teaspoon cinnamon and 2 teaspoons crushed cardamom seeds. Sear the meat in a hot oven (400° F.) for about 20 minutes. Brush it again with melted butter, sprinkle it with flour, and cover the pan. Reduce the heat to moderate (350° F.) and cook the meat for 45 minutes longer. Add 1/2 cup Madeira, the cherry syrup, 1 cup veal stock, and 1 tablespoon melted butter. Continue to cook the veal, covered, for 1 hour, basting it every 15 minutes.

Remove the roast to a heated platter and skim the fat from the pan juices. Stir in 1 1/2 tablespoons flour mixed to a paste with 1/4 cup water and simmer the sauce for a few minutes, or until it thickens slightly. Add the cooked cherries to the sauce and serve it separately.

FILET DE VEAU VÉZELAY ## Filet of Veal Vézelay

LAY a 3-pound filet of veal on a rack in a roasting pan and roast it in a moderate oven (350° F.), basting it frequently with 1 cup veal stock, for about 1 1/4 hours, or until it is tender and well done. Cool the veal, reserving the pan juices, and cut the meat into thin slices.

Melt 2 tablespoons butter, blend in 2 tablespoons flour, and gradually add 1 1/4 cups veal stock and 1/2 cup grated Parmesan. Cook the sauce, stirring, until it is thick and smooth. Spread the veal slices with half the sauce and press the slices together to reshape the filet. Cover the filet with the remaining sauce and sprinkle the top and sides with bread crumbs. Arrange the filet on an ovenproof platter. Heat

Vitello Tonnato

the reserved pan juices and deglaze the pan with 2 tablespoons Madeira. Pour the juices around the meat and bake it in a very hot oven (450° F.) for about 10 minutes, or until the crumbs are nicely browned.

VEAL WITH TUNA FISH SAUCE ## Vitello Tonnato 🐖

REMOVE the skin and fat from a 2-pound boned leg of veal. Make several incisions in the meat and insert 2 anchovy filets, cut into small pieces. Roll up the meat and tie it with string. Put the meat in a kettle and cover it with boiling water. Add 1 onion stuck with 2 cloves, 1 bay leaf, 1 stalk of celery with the leaves, 1 carrot, cut into quarters, a few sprigs of parsley, and a little salt and pepper. Cover the kettle and simmer the meat for 1 1/2 hours. Remove the meat from the broth and let it cool thoroughly.

Pound 1 cup tuna fish packed in oil with 4 anchovy filets and add gradually 1 generous cup olive oil, working the oil into the fish to make a light paste. Thin the sauce with the juice of 2 lemons and add 1/4 cup drained capers. The sauce should be very smooth and quite thick.

Slice the cold meat thinly, arrange the slices in a shallow terrine, and pour the sauce around them. Marinate the meat overnight in the refrigerator. Serve in the terrine, garnished with rolled anchovies stuffed with capers.

Herbed Veal Chops 🐖

SEASON 6 thick veal chops with salt and pepper and dredge them lightly with flour. Sauté the chops slowly in 4 tablespoons melted butter for 12 to 15 minutes on each side. Arrange them on a platter and keep them warm.

To the butter remaining in the pan add 2/3 cup dry white wine and cook the mixture over high heat until the wine is reduced by one half. Add 1 teaspoon each of chives, tarragon, and parsley, all chopped, swirl in 2 tablespoons butter, and pour the sauce over the meat.

Veal en Papillotes 🐖

COMBINE 1/2 pound each of tomatoes, peeled and chopped, and mushrooms, thinly sliced, 1/2 cup white wine, 3 tablespoons minced ham, and 1 tablespoon minced capers. Cook the mixture over low heat, stirring, until the vegetables are soft and most of the liquid has been absorbed.

Sprinkle 6 veal chops with salt and pepper and sauté them in 1 tablespoon oil for about 10 minutes on each side. Cut aluminum foil into 6 large heart shapes and brush the foil with oil. Lay a chop on half of each foil heart and cover it with the sauce. Fold the other half of the heart over the chop and fold the edges together to seal the packets. Bake the chops in a moderately hot oven (375° F.) for 10 minutes. Serve in the foil *papillotes*.

🐦 Veal Birds

PLACE 12 veal scallops, about 5 by 3 inches, between wax paper and pound them very thin. Sauté 1 onion, finely chopped, in 1 tablespoon butter until it is golden and combine it with 4 hard-cooked eggs, finely chopped, 4 tablespoons chopped chives, and salt and pepper to taste. Spread the veal slices with the filling, roll up the slices, and tie them with string. Brown the veal birds on all sides in 4 tablespoons butter. Flame the meat with 3 tablespoons heated brandy and remove it from the pan. Stir in 2 tablespoons flour and add 2 cups veal stock, 1/2 cup white wine, 1 teaspoon tomato paste, and 1/2 teaspoon *glace de viande*, or meat extract. Cook the sauce, stirring, until it comes to a boil. Return the birds to the pan, reduce the heat, and cook them, covered, for 15 minutes, or until the meat is tender. Carefully remove the strings, arrange the veal birds on a bed of rice, and spoon the sauce over them.

🐦 Veal Birds with Pine Nuts

PLACE 12 veal scallops, about 5 by 3 inches, between wax paper and pound them very thin. Lay a slice of boiled ham or uncooked bacon on top of each scallop. Mix together 1/2 cup pine nuts, 6 or 7 sprigs of parsley, chopped, 2 tablespoons grated Parmesan, and 2 tablespoons sultana raisins, and put a generous tablespoon of stuffing on each ham slice. Roll up the meat and secure the stuffing with wooden picks. Brown the birds on all sides in 3 tablespoons hot olive oil, add 3/4 cup white wine, and cook them, covered, for about 15 minutes, or until the meat is tender. Arrange the birds on a heated platter, cover with the sauce, and garnish with parsley.

Veal Birds Sophia 🐦

PLACE 12 veal scallops, about 5 by 3 inches, between wax paper and pound them very thin. Sprinkle each slice with salt, pepper, and a few drops of lemon juice. Lay a thin slice of ham on each veal slice and 1/2 hard-cooked egg on the ham. Roll up the slices and tie them with string. Brown the veal birds slowly on all sides in 4 tablespoons butter and stir in 1 1/2 cups light cream. Slowly simmer the birds, covered, for about 15 minutes, or until the meat is tender, and carefully remove the strings. Arrange the meat on a heated platter and cover it with the sauce.

Veal Scallops with Artichokes 🐦

TRIM 3 large artichokes and rub the cut surfaces with lemon juice to prevent discoloration. With a sharp knife cut off the leaves about 1/2 inch from the base. Draw the knife through a cut lemon and cut each artichoke in half. Remove and discard the prickly chokes. Squeeze more lemon juice over the artichokes and cut each half into thin slices. Melt 3 tablespoons butter in a large skillet and in it sauté the artichoke slices slowly for about 5 minutes. Add 2 pounds veal scallops, pounded very thin, seasoned with salt, pepper, and lemon juice, and lightly floured. Brown the scallops over high heat for 3 or 4 minutes on each side. Add to the pan 3/4 cup white wine and simmer the mixture for 2 minutes.

Veal Scallops with Lemon 🐦

SEASON 2 pounds veal scallops, pounded very thin, with salt and pepper and flour them lightly. Brown the scallops on both sides in 6 tablespoons butter. Add to the pan 1/4 cup each of white wine and chopped parsley and the juice of 1 lemon. Cover the skillet and cook the meat over low heat for about 6 minutes, or until it is tender. Arrange the scallops on a heated platter. Add 1 egg yolk to the pan juices, stirring it in rapidly with a fork. Pour the sauce over the meat.

Veal Scallops with Green Noodles 🐦

TOSS 3/4 pound green noodles, cooked *al dente*, with 1/2 cup browned butter, put them in a heated serving dish, and keep them warm.

Season 2 pounds veal scallops, pounded very thin, with salt and pepper and flour them lightly. Brown the scallops in 4 tablespoons butter and 1 tablespoon oil over high heat for 3 or 4 minutes on each side. Put each scallop on a slice of ham, lightly sautéed in butter, and arrange the meat on the noodles. Add to the pan 4 tomatoes, peeled, seeded, and chopped, and cook them over high heat until they are reduced almost to a purée. Put a tablespoon of the stewed tomatoes on each slice of veal and ham and top with a pitted ripe olive. Pour more browned butter over the meat.

ᔅᐤ Veal Scallops with Vermouth

SEASON 2 pounds veal scallops, pounded very thin, with salt and pepper and flour them lightly. Brown the scallops with 1 onion, finely chopped, in 4 tablespoons each of butter and oil for 3 or 4 minutes on each side. Remove the meat from the pan. Add to the pan 2/3 cup sweet Italian vermouth and simmer it over high heat until it is reduced by one half. Stir in 1 teaspoon tomato paste and 1/4 teaspoon mace, return the veal to the pan, and heat well. Garnish with sliced Brazil nuts and flowerets of cooked cauliflower.

ᔅᐤ Truffled Veal Cutlets   ESCALOPES DE VEAU TRUFFÉES

MIX together well 1/2 pound ground veal, 1 tablespoon finely chopped shallots, 1/2 tablespoon chopped parsley, and 1 egg. Season the mixture with salt, pepper, and nutmeg to taste and gradually add 1 1/2 tablespoons heavy cream. With a mallet flatten 6 uniform veal cutlets until they are 1/8 inch thick and cut each one in half. Spread half of each cutlet thinly with the veal forcemeat. Spread the other half with 2 slices of mushroom, sautéed in butter, and 2 slices of truffle, and sprinkle with a little parsley and shallot, both minced. Put one half on the other and pinch the edges together. Dredge each cutlet lightly in 1/2 cup seasoned flour, then in 2 beaten eggs, and finally in 1 cup fine bread crumbs. In a large skillet melt 4 tablespoons butter and sauté the prepared cutlets over moderate heat for about 15 minutes, turning them several times, until they are golden brown on both sides. Arrange the cutlets on a heated platter, garnish them with sliced truffles, and sprinkle with 4 tablespoons melted butter.

Veal Scallops with Vermouth

❧ Veal and Ham Rolls with Hazelnut Sauce

HAVE the butcher cut 1 pound each of veal and ham into thin slices. Sprinkle each slice with finely chopped parsley and a little crushed garlic. Lay a slice of veal on a slice of ham, roll up the meat, and secure the rolls with string. Brown on all sides in 4 tablespoons butter until the ham has changed color. Remove the rolls and arrange them side by side in a baking dish.

In the butter remaining in the pan sauté 1/2 cup chopped hazelnuts and 2 onions, chopped, until the onion is golden. Stir in 1/2 cup white wine, a pinch of cinnamon, and pepper to taste. Pour the sauce over the rolls and cover the dish. Bake the rolls in a moderate oven (350° F.) for about 20 minutes, or until the meat is tender.

❧ Veal Galantine   GALANTINE DE VEAU

HAVE the butcher bone a 3-pound breast of veal. Spread the meat out flat and season it with salt and pepper and 1 tablespoon mixed chopped herbs—thyme, marjoram, and rosemary. Combine 1 1/2 pounds ground pork sausage and 1/4 cup Sherry. If the sausage is very mild add more seasoning. Spread the sausage over the veal, leaving a 1-inch border all around. Cut 1/2 pound lean ham into even strips and arrange the strips in rows down the length of the meat. Put 2 whole hard-cooked eggs in the center of the meat and sprinkle with 2 tablespoons chopped pistachio nuts. Roll up the meat tightly and sew it with thread. Wrap the roll in cheesecloth and tie the ends securely. Put the galantine in boiling veal or chicken stock, reduce the heat, and simmer it for 2 hours. Remove the galantine and unwrap it. Clarify the stock and pour it into a shallow pan. Chill the aspic until it is firm.

Wrap the galantine in a dry cloth. Weight it with a board and a 5-pound weight and chill it overnight. Unwrap the galantine and remove the thread. Chop the aspic, spread it on a chilled platter, and arrange the chilled galantine on top. Surround the galantine with watercress. Makes 12 servings.

❧ Cold Veal Loaf

HAVE the butcher crack the bone of a meaty 4- to 6-pound veal knuckle. Put the knuckle in a large kettle in cold water to cover, bring the water slowly to a boil, and skim the surface. Cover the kettle and simmer the stock for 1 hour. Add 1 onion, 1 large carrot, and 2 stalks of celery, all sliced, 1 tablespoon salt, pepper to taste, and 1 bay leaf. Cover the kettle and simmer the stock for 2 hours. Remove the meat from the bones and chop it finely. Strain the stock and pour 1 quart of it into a saucepan. Add the chopped meat and simmer it, covered, for 1 hour.

Line a loaf pan with 2 hard-cooked eggs, sliced, and arrange slices of stuffed olives between the eggs. Carefully add the veal and its stock, and chill the loaf for 3 hours or until it is firm.

Curried Veal 🦩

CUT 3 pounds boneless shoulder of veal into slices and brown them lightly in 1 tablespoon bacon fat. Add 3 apples and 2 onions, all finely chopped, and cook them until they are soft. Add 2 tablespoons curry powder, 1 tablespoon chutney, and enough veal stock to cover the meat, and cook the mixture over very low heat for 4 to 5 hours. Pour the mixture into a mold rinsed in cold water and chill it until it is set. Turn the veal out onto a platter and cut it in slices.

Veal Marengo 🦩

IN a heavy kettle brown 3 pounds lean shoulder of veal, cut in cubes, in 3 table-spoons oil. Add 1 onion, finely chopped, and 1/2 cup tomato purée, and cook the mixture for 2 minutes. Stir in 1 tablespoon potato flour and add gradually 2 cups veal or chicken stock and 1 cup white wine. Add 1 garlic clove, 2 bay leaves, 1/4 teaspoon thyme, and salt and pepper to taste. Cover the kettle and simmer the meat slowly for 1 hour. Sauté 12 small white onions in 4 tablespoons butter, sprinkle them with 1 tablespoon sugar, and cook them until they are browned and glazed. Sauté 12 mushrooms in 2 tablespoons butter for 3 or 4 minutes. Peel and seed 3 tomatoes and cut them into sections. Add the onions, mushrooms, and tomatoes to the kettle and cook the stew for about 30 minutes, or until the meat is tender. Serve sprinkled with chopped parsley.

Veal Hash 🦩

SAUTÉ 2 scallions, minced, in 2 tablespoons butter until they are transparent. Stir in 2 1/2 tablespoons flour and gradually add 1 cup each of milk and light cream. Add the finely chopped white and mashed yolk of 1 hard-cooked egg, 2 tablespoons

Veal Kidneys and Mushrooms in Brioche

chopped celery, 2 teaspoons chopped parsley, and salt and pepper to taste. Add 3 cups diced cooked veal, heat the hash, and turn it into a serving dish. Garnish with sprigs of parsley and thin lemon slices.

Terrine of Veal

MARINATE 1 1/2 pounds calf's liver and 3/4 pound lean veal in 4 cups milk for 24 hours. Drain the meats, discarding the milk, and put them through the finest blade of a food chopper. Combine them with 8 tablespoons soft sweet butter and pack the mixture into a buttered loaf pan. Set the pan in a larger pan of hot water and bake the pâté in a slow oven (300° F.) for 3 hours. Cool the meat and put it through a fine sieve. Season it with salt and pepper to taste and mix in 1/4 cup bourbon. Fill a rectangular terrine with alternate layers of the pâté and whole truffles and chill thoroughly.

Liver with Basil in Wine

DIP 2 pounds sliced calf's liver in milk and then in seasoned flour. Brown the slices slowly in 5 tablespoons olive oil and remove them from the pan. Brown 2 slashed garlic cloves slowly and remove from the pan. Sauté 2 shallots, minced, in the oil until they are soft. Add 4 large basil leaves, chopped, return the liver slices to the pan, and add 1 cup white wine and salt and pepper to taste. Simmer the liver, covered, over low heat for 30 minutes, turning it as it cooks.

Veal Kidneys and Mushrooms in Brioche

MAKE a large brioche in an 8-inch fluted brioche mold.

Remove the skin, membranes, and tubes from 4 veal kidneys. Cut the meat into 1-inch dice and season them with salt and pepper to taste. Melt 2 tablespoons butter in a heavy saucepan, add the diced kidneys, and sauté them over high heat for 5 minutes. Remove the kidneys from the pan. Add to the pan 6 mushrooms, quartered, and sauté them for 5 minutes, stirring constantly. Return the kidneys to the pan. Heat 2 tablespoons Cognac, ignite the spirit, and pour it flaming over the meat and mushrooms. Blend 3 teaspoons potato flour into the pan juices, stir in 1 1/2 cups chicken stock, and cook the sauce until it is thickened and clear.

Remove the top of the brioche and scoop out the crumbs. Fill the case with the kidney and mushroom mixture. Replace the top of the brioche, allowing the filling to show. Heat the filled brioche in a moderate oven (350° F.) before serving.

ᔧ᠉ Brandied Veal Kidneys

REMOVE the skin, membranes, and tubes from 4 veal kidneys, and sprinkle the kidneys with salt and pepper. Heat 4 tablespoons butter in a casserole and in it brown the kidneys over high heat. Cover the casserole and put it in a moderate oven (350° F.) for 15 minutes. Remove the kidneys to a hot plate and cover them.

Add 1/2 cup brandy to the juices in the casserole and cook the sauce over high heat until it is reduced by one half. Add 1 tablespoon butter and 1 teaspoon dry mustard. Slice the kidneys, return them to the casserole, and heat them thoroughly. Arrange the kidneys on a heated platter. Add to the sauce 1/4 cup chopped chives and the juice of 1/2 lemon and pour it over the kidneys.

ᔧ᠉ Preparation of Sweetbreads

SOAK as many pairs of sweetbreads as desired in ice water for several hours and drain them. Cover the sweetbreads with fresh cold salted water, acidulated with the juice of 1 lemon. Bring the water slowly to a boil and blanch the sweetbreads for 5 minutes. Drain them and plunge them into cold water. Remove and discard the tubes and membranes. Spread the sweetbreads on a platter and weight them with a plate to flatten and firm them as they cool. They are now ready to use in sweetbread recipes.

ᔧ᠉ Sweetbreads en Brochette

PREPARE 3 pairs of sweetbreads. Cut each sweetbread into 4 pieces and dip the pieces first in a mixture of 2 eggs beaten with 2 tablespoons white wine, and then in bread crumbs. Thread the sweetbreads on skewers alternately with mushroom caps and squares of bacon. Broil them slowly over hot coals, basting frequently with melted butter. Serve with tarragon white-wine sauce.

Tarragon White-Wine Sauce

SIMMER 1 cup dry white wine with 2 shallots, finely chopped, until the wine is slightly reduced. Add 2 tablespoons *glace de viande*, or meat extract, and, when the glaze has melted, add 2 tablespoons butter, 2 teaspoons finely chopped fresh tarragon, 1 teaspoon lemon juice, a pinch of cayenne and salt and freshly ground pepper to taste.

RIS DE VEAU À LA FLORENTINE ## Sweetbreads with Spinach 🦢

PREPARE 6 pairs of sweetbreads. Split the sweetbreads in half lengthwise and dust them lightly with flour. Sauté them quickly in 6 tablespoons butter and add 6 table-spoons heated Sherry. Remove the sweetbreads from the pan and keep them warm. Add to the pan 12 mushrooms, sliced, and a little more butter, if necessary. Cook the mushrooms for 3 minutes, sprinkle them with salt and pepper to taste, and stir in, off the heat, 2 teaspoons tomato paste and 2 tablespoons potato flour. Stir in 5 cups chicken stock and cook the sauce, stirring, until it comes to a boil. Lower the heat and add the sweetbreads and a bay leaf. Cover the pan and cook all together slowly for 10 minutes. Remove the bay leaf.

Chop finely 6 pounds spinach. Heat the spinach in a heavy pan over moderate heat, add salt and pepper to taste, and stir in 2/3 cup sour cream. Spread the spinach on 2 platters, arrange the sweetbreads on top, and pour the sauce over all. Makes 24 servings.

Sweetbreads with Almonds 🦢

PREPARE 3 pairs of sweetbreads. Cut the sweetbreads into slices 1/4 inch thick and dice them.

Heat 1 1/2 cups heavy cream and add 1/2 cup sliced blanched almonds, 4 egg yolks, well beaten, 1/4 cup Sherry, 2 tablespoons brandy, 1/2 teaspoon salt, and a pinch of cayenne. Cook the sauce, stirring constantly, until it thickens. Add the sweetbreads and heat the mixture. Serve on toast points.

ꕤ Sweetbreads and Brains in Puff-Paste Shell

WASH 3 lambs' brains in cold water, remove the membranes, and soak the brains in cold water for 1 hour. Cook the lambs' brains in boiling salted water acidulated with 2 tablespoons vinegar for 10 to 15 minutes. Prepare 1 pair sweetbreads.

Cook 1/4 pound button mushrooms in simmering salted water acidulated with 1 tablespoon vinegar for 5 minutes.

Poach 6 slices of truffle in Madeira to cover for 5 minutes, and add the Madeira to 2 cups hot *sauce suprême.*

Dice the sweetbreads and the brains and combine them with 1 cup diced cooked ham. Combine the meats with the sauce and add the mushrooms and truffles. Bring the mixture just to a boil and turn it into a square puff-paste shell. Leave the lid of the shell half off to display the filling.

ꕤ Calves' Brains Fritters

TRIM 3 calves' brains by removing the black veins and membranes and soak the brains in cold water to cover for several hours, changing the water frequently. Drain the brains and combine them with 3 cups chicken stock, 2 tablespoons vinegar, 3 sprigs parsley, 3 cloves, 1 garlic clove, 1/8 teaspoon thyme, 1 bay leaf, and salt and pepper to taste. Bring the stock to a boil, reduce the heat, and poach the brains, covered, for 25 to 30 minutes. Let the brains cool in the stock. Remove the brains, drain them on absorbent paper, and dice them.

Blend together thoroughly 3/4 cup sifted flour, 1/2 cup dry white wine, 1 table-spoon salad oil, and 1/8 teaspoon salt. Dip the diced brains in the batter and fry them in deep hot fat (390° F.) until they are brown. Serve on a mound of white rice with *sauce diable.*

ꕤ Marinated Lamb Chops

HAVE the butcher trim short the bones of 6 thick French lamb chops. Season the chops with salt and pepper and marinate them for 3 hours in 1/2 cup each of olive oil and dry white wine, 1 crushed garlic clove, and 1 bay leaf. Drain and dry the chops, reserving the marinade.

Melt 2 tablespoons butter in a heavy skillet and brown the chops over very low heat, turning them frequently and resting the fat edges of the chops in the pan to

brown them evenly. The chops should be pink in the center. Lay the chops on a
heated platter, cover the end bones with gold cutlet frills, and garnish the platter
with crescents of puff paste. Add the marinade to the juices in the skillet and simmer
the liquid until it is reduced by one half. Add the juice of 1 lemon and serve the
sauce in a heated sauceboat.

Lamb Chops with Tarragon Butter

HAVE the butcher cut 6 pairs of loin or rib lamb chops 1 1/2 inches thick across the
saddle or rack without separating the bone, so that the chops are joined side by side.
Trim the excess fat from the paired chops, brush the meat with olive oil and broil
it under low heat, turning often, until the outside is browned and crisp and the inside is slightly pink. Mix 1/2 pound soft sweet butter with 1 cup finely chopped
tarragon and spread 6 pieces of toast with some of the mixture. Put a chop on each
piece of toast and pipe or spread the remaining tarragon butter on the surface of
the meat.

Lamb Noisettes Brussels

HAVE the butcher cut 6 loin lamb chops 2 inches thick, remove the bone and any
gristle and fat, and flatten the filets lightly with the broad side of a cleaver.
Spread each filet with a 1/4-inch-thick layer of sausage meat and with finely chopped
truffles, pressing the truffles firmly into the sausage and against the lamb. Broil
the *noisettes* until the sausage is thoroughly cooked and the lamb is browned but
still pink inside.

Braised Lamb Chops with Prunes

IN a heavy skillet brown 6 shoulder lamb chops, cut 3/4 inch thick, on both sides
in 3 tablespoons butter. Sprinkle the chops with salt and pepper and cover them
with thin slices of onion. Add to the pan 18 large dried prunes, 3/4 cup each of
dry red wine and water, 4 whole cloves, and a 1-inch cinnamon stick. Cover the
skillet and cook the chops slowly for about 40 minutes, or until they are tender,
adding a little more wine if necessary. Remove the chops and prunes to a heated
platter and keep them warm.

Skim the fat from the pan and stir 1 tablespoon cornstarch blended with 1/4 cup water into the pan juices. Cook the sauce, stirring, until it has thickened slightly. Adjust the seasoning and strain the sauce over the chops and prunes.

﹌ Grilled Lamb Chops with Kidneys

HAVE the butcher bone and tie 6 English lamb chops with the kidney. Put the chops on a broiler rack and sear them on both sides under high heat. Lower the heat and continue to broil the chops, turning once, until they are browned and crisp but still pink inside.

﹌ Baron of Lamb with Potato Cake   BARON D'AGNEAU LANDAISE

RUB a baron of lamb (both legs and both loins of a baby lamb) with butter and sprinkle it with salt and pepper. Put the baron on a rack in a roasting pan and roast it in a hot oven (400° F.), allowing about 15 minutes per pound. The lamb should be medium rare. Baste the meat frequently with the pan juices.

Peel 10 medium potatoes and slice them into even rounds. Sauté the slices on both sides in rendered chicken fat until they are brown and crisp, and season them with salt and pepper to taste. Form the potatoes into a large flat cake in the center of a platter and sprinkle them with minced parsley and a little finely chopped garlic. Arrange the baron of lamb on the bed of potatoes and pour the pan juices over it. Garnish the platter with watercress.

﹌ Parsleyed Leg of Lamb

REMOVE most of the fat from a 6- to 7-pound leg of lamb and lay the leg on a rack in a roasting pan. Arrange 3 or 4 slices of bacon on top and add 6 or 7 unpeeled garlic cloves to the pan. Roast the meat in a moderately slow oven (325° F.), basting frequently with white wine, for about 2 1/2 hours, or until the meat is tender but still pink inside. Remove the meat from the oven and coat it with a mixture of fresh bread crumbs and parsley. Return the pan to the oven and continue to roast the lamb until the coating is golden brown. Remove the meat to a heated platter and add to the pan 2 or 3 tablespoons heavy cream and 2 teaspoons anchovy paste. Cook the sauce until it thickens slightly and strain it. Serve in a heated sauceboat.

Marinated Boned Leg of Lamb 🐑

HAVE the butcher bone a 6- to 7-pound leg of lamb and shape it so that it lies flat. Make a marinade of 2/3 cup chopped onions, 3/4 cup olive oil, 1/4 cup vinegar, 1 teaspoon each of peppercorns and salt, 1/4 teaspoon orégano, and 1 bay leaf and 1 garlic clove, both crushed. Marinate the lamb overnight in the refrigerator, and drain it, reserving the marinade. Put the leg, fat side up, on a rack in a shallow pan. Brush the meat with the marinade and broil it for about 10 minutes on each side, or until it is golden brown, basting it occasionally. Transfer the lamb to a moderately slow oven (325° F.) and roast it, fat side up, basting occasionally, for about 2 1/2 hours, or until the meat is tender but still pink inside.

Charcoal-Broiled Leg of Lamb 🐑

HAVE the butcher bone 2 six-pound legs of lamb and split each leg apart at the heaviest section. The meat should be as uniformly thick as possible. Put the meat in a wide container and cover it with a mixture of 3 cups red wine, 1 cup chopped parsley, and 3 onions, thinly sliced. Marinate the meat for 12 hours, turning it occasionally, and drain and dry it.

Arrange the split legs in 2 basket grills, or hinged broilers, laying them as flat as possible. Brush the meat with olive oil and broil them over hot coals, 3 or 4 inches from the heat, for 10 to 15 minutes on each side. The lamb should be slightly pink in the center. Lay the meat on a heated platter and put several tablespoons butter on the surface. The butter will blend with the juices when the lamb is sliced. Cut the meat against the grain in thin diagonal slices.

Lamb Filets with Artichokes and Potatoes 🐑

PEEL 4 or 5 potatoes and slice them into thin rounds. Chop enough trimmed raw artichokes to make 2 cups. Butter a large deep baking dish and fill it with alternating layers of the sliced potatoes and chopped artichokes. Sprinkle each layer with salt and spread it with 2 tablespoons butter. Press the mixture down firmly, leaving 2 inches at the top of the dish, and bake the vegetables in a hot oven (400° F.) for about 30 minutes, or until they are almost tender.

Have the butcher bone both loins from a saddle of lamb and roll and tie the filets securely. Melt 2 tablespoons butter in a roasting pan and brown the filets on all sides over high heat. Lay the meat on the vegetables in the casserole, return the dish to the oven, and continue to bake the mixture, basting frequently with butter, for about 20 minutes, or until the meat is tender but still pink inside.

Roast Saddle of Lamb SELLE D'AGNEAU AUX POMMES DE TERRE

HAVE the butcher tie a saddle of lamb with soft string. Put the lamb on a rack in a roasting pan and roast it in a hot oven (400° F.), basting frequently with white wine, for about 1 hour, or until the meat is tender but still pink inside. Transfer the meat to a heated platter. Discard the fat from the pan juices.

Prepare the following garnish: Peel 6 medium potatoes, cut them in the shape of large olives, and sprinkle them with salt and pepper. Cook the potatoes slowly in clarified butter, shaking the pan frequently, until they are golden and tender. Peel 4 firm tomatoes of uniform size and heat them briefly in a little oil or clarified butter. Sprinkle 1 pound cooked asparagus stalks with melted butter. Garnish the saddle of lamb with watercress and the platter with mounds of the potatoes, the whole tomatoes, and the cooked asparagus. Serve the pan gravy separately.

Braised Shoulder of Lamb

HAVE the butcher bone and roll a 5-pound shoulder of lamb. Stud the meat with slivers of garlic. In a Dutch oven brown the roll on all sides in 5 tablespoons olive oil. Add to the pot 12 small white onions, 6 tomatoes, peeled and seeded, 2 teaspoons salt, and 3/4 teaspoon each thyme and pepper. Cover the pot and simmer the meat slowly for 1 1/2 hours. Transfer the lamb to a heated platter and arrange the vegetables around it. Bring the sauce in the pot to a boil, reduce it over high heat for 4 or 5 minutes, and pour it over the lamb and vegetables. Sprinkle all lavishly with chopped parsley and lemon juice.

Sautéed Breast of Lamb

IN a kettle put 2 trimmed breasts of lamb, weighing 3 pounds each, 2 onions, 1 large bay leaf, 1 tablespoon salt, and water to cover. Bring the water to a boil, cover the kettle, and simmer the meat for 30 minutes, or until it is almost tender. Remove the lamb breasts to a large platter. Cover them with heavy aluminium foil, flatten them

Roast Saddle of Lamb

with heavy weights, and let them cool. Carefully remove and discard as many bones as possible, leaving the meat in longish pieces. Dip the pieces in beaten egg and in fine bread crumbs and sauté them on both sides in butter until they are brown and crisp. Sprinkle with lemon juice and capers.

𝄢 Curried Lamb with Walnuts

IN a Dutch oven sauté 2 garlic cloves, minced, and 4 onions, sliced, in 3/4 cup butter until the onions are golden. Dredge 3 pounds boned shoulder of lamb, cut in 2-inch cubes, with flour, and sauté the meat for 10 minutes, stirring frequently. Add to the pot 3 tablespoons curry powder and 3 apples, peeled, cored, and chopped. Simmer the mixture for 5 minutes, stirring occasionally. Add 1 cup chopped walnuts, 2 lemons, sliced, 4 tablespoons each of raisins, shredded coconut, and brown sugar, 1 tablespoon salt, and 1/2 teaspoon grated lime peel. Add 3 cups water and bring it to a boil. Reduce the heat, cover the pan, and simmer the mixture for about 1 hour, or until the lamb is tender.

𝄢 Lamb Stew

PUT 3 pounds boned shoulder of lamb, cut into serving pieces, in a kettle and cover with boiling salted water. Add a *bouquet garni* composed of 8 sprigs of parsley, 1 bay leaf, and 1 sprig of thyme, and simmer the meat gently for 25 minutes. Add 24 small carrot balls, 12 small white onions, 6 potatoes, quartered, 3/4 cup chopped celery, 2 garlic cloves, minced, 1 whole clove, and salt and pepper to taste. Cover the pot and simmer the stew for about 40 minutes, or until the meat is tender. Discard the *bouquet garni*.

Thicken the stock with 1 tablespoon flour kneaded with 1 tablespoon butter. Add 18 mushrooms, peeled and thinly sliced. Cover the pot and simmer the stew for 15 minutes. Correct the seasoning and stir in 1 tablespoon each of lemon juice and chopped parsley.

𝄢 Lamb Pilaff

IN a saucepan sauté 1 pound boned shoulder of lamb, cut in 1-inch cubes, and 2 onions, chopped, in 1/2 cup butter until the meat is brown and the onions are golden.

Add 1 cup rice and cook, stirring, until it is coated with butter. Add 2 cups beef stock, 1 teaspoon orégano, and salt and pepper to taste. Cover the pan and cook the mixture slowly for about 40 minutes, or until the meat is tender and the rice fluffy. Combine 1 teaspoon tomato paste with 1 tablespoon melted butter, add it to the pan, and stir in 1/2 cup plumped seedless raisins.

Skewered Lamb

CUT 2 pounds loin of lamb into 1-inch cubes. Season the cubes with salt and pepper and thread them on skewers alternately with 1-inch squares of bacon. Dip the skewers in melted butter and in fine bread crumbs, and sprinkle them with more melted butter. Broil the skewered meat over hot coals, turning often to brown the meat evenly. Garnish the brochettes with watercress and with thin slices of lemon.

Lamb Kebabs

CUT 2 pounds loin of lamb into rounds about 1/2 inch thick and 1 1/4 inches in diameter. Drain a jar of preserved unpeeled quartered oranges and combine the syrup with 3 tablespoons soy sauce and 1 crushed garlic clove. Marinate the lamb in this mixture for 2 hours and drain it, reserving the marinade. Trim the quartered oranges and 2 seeded green peppers into rounds to match the lamb. Arrange the rounds of lamb, orange, and pepper alternately on skewers. Brush the kebabs with the marinade and broil them over hot coals, turning frequently, until the meat is browned but still rare.

Crêpes Maison

MAKE 5-inch entrée crêpes and put a generous tablespoon of lamb hash on each one. Roll up the crêpes and arrange them side by side in a shallow flameproof dish. Sprinkle them with grated Parmesan and melted butter. Put the dish under the broiler until the cheese is browned.

Lamb Hash

SAUTÉ 3/4 cup minced onion in 1/4 cup butter until it is transparent. Blend in

Leg of Lamb in Aspic

3 tablespoons flour, stir the *roux* for a few minutes, and add gradually 3/4 cup each of veal stock and red wine. Cook the sauce, stirring constantly, until it is smooth. Add to it 2 1/2 cups coarsely chopped cooked lamb and 2 tablespoons minced parsley. Season the hash with salt and pepper to taste.

Lamb Liver Swiss Style

CUT 2 pounds lamb liver into strips 1 1/2 inches long and 1 inch wide. Roll the strips in flour seasoned with salt, pepper, and paprika, and spread them in a shallow dish to dry. Sauté the liver strips in 1/2 cup butter over high heat, shaking the pan constantly, until they are browned. Transfer the liver to a heated platter, deglaze the pan with 3/4 cup dry white wine, and pour the sauce over the liver.

Lamb Kidneys and Mushrooms en Brochette

HALVE 12 lamb kidneys and trim 24 large mushrooms. Thread 6 skewers alternately with the mushrooms and the kidney halves and brush them lavishly with melted butter. Broil the kidneys and mushrooms under high heat, turning them frequently to cook all sides, and season them with salt, pepper, and finely chopped chives to taste. Serve on a bed of fluffy white rice.

Leg of Lamb in Aspic

HAVE the butcher remove the bone from a 5- to 6-pound leg of lamb and reshape the leg as nearly as possible with twine. Put the meat on a rack in a roasting pan and add 4 or 5 garlic cloves, unpeeled, and 1 cup white wine. Roast the lamb in a moderately slow oven (325° F.) for about 2 hours, or until the meat is tender but still pink inside. Transfer the lamb to a rack to cool and chill it thoroughly.

Set the lamb on a rack over a jelly-roll pan. Spread the leg thickly with *purée de foie gras*, making a smooth rounded surface. Spoon or pour cool but still liquid *mayonnaise collée* over the leg, coating it thoroughly. The *mayonnaise collée* will jell almost at once. Decorate the meat with hard-cooked egg white and vegetables cut in flower shapes, and with the blanched leaves of tarragon, chervil, and dill. Spoon cool but still liquid clear aspic over the lamb and decorations. Chill the leg until the aspic is set.

Transfer the lamb to a chilled platter. Surround it with a ring of chopped aspic and garnish the platter with small molds of clear aspic.

Roast Loin of Pork in Sour Cream Sauce

WIPE a 4- to 5-pound loin of pork with a damp cloth, rub it with the juice of 1/2 lemon and garlic, salt, and rosemary. Add a few leaves of rosemary to the roasting pan and roast the pork in a moderate oven (350° F.), allowing about 35 minutes per pound, until it is well done. Arrange the loin on a heated platter. Skim the excess fat from the pan and add to the pan 1/2 cup sour cream and 1/4 cup white wine. Heat the sauce but do not let it boil, and season it with salt and pepper. Serve the sauce separately.

Oriental Roast Pork

PUT a 5-pound boned loin of pork in a deep bowl and cover it with a mixture of 1 cup each of Sherry and soy sauce, 2 tablespoons fresh or dried grated gingerroot, and 3 garlic cloves, minced. Marinate the meat for several hours. Drain and dry the meat, reserving the marinade. Arrange the pork on a spit and roast it for 1 hour at high heat (425° F.). Reduce the heat to moderate (350° F.) and roast for 1 hour longer. During the cooking brush the meat with a mixture of honey and the marinade. Use the mixture twice during the last half hour of cooking.

Roast Loin of Pork with Rhubarb

HAVE the butcher bone and tie a 4- to 5-pound loin of pork. Brush the roast with olive oil and sprinkle it lightly with salt and pepper. Put the meat, fat side up, on a rack in a roasting pan and add 1 small onion, sliced, 1 cup white wine, and a little rosemary. Roast the meat in a moderate oven (350° F.), allowing about 35 minutes per pound, basting occasionally with the pan juices, until it is well done. Carve the roast into 3/4-inch slices and overlap them on a bed of baked rhubarb. Skim the excess fat from the pan and strain the juices into a sauceboat. If desired, thicken the sauce with a little potato flour or arrowroot mixed to a paste with orange juice or cold water.

Baked Rhubarb

WASH 3 pounds rhubarb (do not peel the stalks or the rosy color will be lost) and cut the stalks into 1/2-inch slices. Put the rhubarb in a buttered baking dish with the juice of 1 orange and 3/4 cup sugar. Bake the rhubarb in a slow oven (300° F.) for about 30 minutes, or until it is tender. If necessary, sweeten it with a little more sugar.

Braised Shoulder of Pork with Lentils 🐖

IN a kettle put 1 pound lentils with cold water to cover, 1 onion stuck with 2 cloves, 1 bay leaf, and salt to taste. Bring the liquid to a boil, cover the kettle, and simmer the lentils for 2 hours, or until they are tender. Drain the lentils, discarding the onion and bay leaf.

Have the butcher skin, bone, and roll a 5-pound shoulder of pork. Brown the meat quickly in 3 tablespoons butter. Add 1 cup beef stock and 2 garlic cloves, chopped, cover the pot, and simmer the pork for 30 minutes. Add the drained lentils and a little of their liquid, if necessary, and cook the pork for about 2 1/2 hours, or until it is well done. Stir in 1 tablespoon tomato purée and 1/4 cup parsley, finely chopped, and correct the seasoning.

Pork Chops Flambé 🐖

RUB 6 large pork chops with a mixture of 1 1/2 teaspoons salt, 3/4 teaspoon dry mustard, and 1/4 teaspoon black pepper. Brown the chops on both sides in 1 1/2 tablespoons butter. Remove the chops from the pan, add 3 tablespoons butter, and in it sauté 1 large onion, thinly sliced, until it is golden. Stir in 1 1/2 teaspoons tomato paste and add 3/4 cup white wine. Return the chops to the pan and simmer them, covered, for about 45 minutes, or until they are well done. Arrange the chops and the sauce on a heated platter. Heat 1/3 cup brandy, ignite it, and pour it flaming over the chops.

ᔕ Stuffed Pork Chops

HAVE the butcher cut 6 loin pork chops about 1 1/2 inches thick and slit them to make a pocket for stuffing.

Sauté 1 large onion, finely chopped, in 3 tablespoons butter until it is soft but not brown. Stir in 3/4 cup soft bread crumbs, 2 tablespoons chopped parsley, a pinch of nutmeg, and salt and pepper to taste. Remove the mixture from the heat and bind it with 1 egg, lightly beaten. Fill the chops with this stuffing and close the pockets with wood or metal skewers. Put the stuffed chops in a shallow baking dish and bake them in a moderate oven (350° F.) for about 1 hour or until they are well cooked and browned.

ᔕ Breaded Pork Chops with Prune Sauce

SIMMER 6 well-trimmed pork chops in boiling salted water to cover for 15 minutes. Drain the chops and cool them. Dip the chops first in a mixture of 1 egg beaten with 1 tablespoon each of oil and water, and then in bread crumbs. Sauté the chops in 2 tablespoons butter for 5 minutes on each side, reduce the heat, and continue to cook them for 20 minutes, turning them to brown both sides evenly. Arrange the chops on a heated platter and cover them with hot prune sauce.

Prune Sauce

RUB through a sieve enough cooked prunes to make 1 cup purée. Add to the purée 1 tablespoon sugar, 1 teaspoon grated lemon rind, and 1/4 teaspoon each of cinnamon and cloves, and cook the mixture for 10 minutes, adding a little water if it seems too thick. Stir in 1/2 cup Port and bring the sauce to a boil.

ᔕ Cold Crown Roast of Smoked Pork

HAVE the butcher form a loin of smoked pork into a crown. Have the ends of the bones trimmed evenly; they should not be too long. Put the crown roast on a rack in a roasting pan and roast it in a moderate oven (350° F.) for 1 hour. Remove the meat from the oven and let it cool. Arrange the roast on a chilled platter and surround it with lemon leaves. Line the center of the roast with lettuce leaves and fill it with a pineapple fresh fruit salad tossed with French dressing. Set the leafy

Cold Crown Roast of Smoked Pork.

top of a fresh pineapple on the salad and garnish the crown roast with wedges of fresh lime.

ʃ❧ Brochettes of Smoked Pork

CUT 2 pounds smoked pork tenderloin into 3/4-inch cubes. Arrange the cubes on skewers alternately with white seedless grapes. Broil the pork over hot coals, turning frequently, until it is lightly browned. Smoked pork chops, which also need only minimum cooking, may be substituted for the tenderloin, if desired.

ʃ❧ Barbecued Spareribs

CUT 6 pounds lean spareribs into serving portions. Lay the ribs in a shallow enamel or glass dish and sprinkle them with salt, pepper, and paprika to taste. Add 3 garlic cloves, finely chopped, and the juice of 1 lemon. Marinate the meat for 3 hours.

Sauté 3 medium onions and 1/2 cup celery, both chopped, in 2 tablespoons bacon fat until the vegetables are golden. Add 1 cup vinegar, 1/2 cup each of tomato paste and chili sauce, 2 tablespoons each of Worcestershire sauce, chili powder, and sugar, 1 tablespoon each of dry mustard and thyme, and 2 red pepper pods. Brush both sides of the ribs with the sauce and broil them over hot coals, turning and basting often, until the meat is well done.

ʃ❧ Chinese Spareribs

PUT 6 pounds spareribs in a wide enamel pan and cover them with a mixture of 1 1/2 cups chicken stock, a scant 1/2 cup each of honey, soy sauce and tomato purée, 6 garlic cloves, finely chopped, and 3 tablespoons salt. Marinate the spareribs for several hours, turning them occasionally. Drain and dry the meat, reserving the marinade.

Roast the ribs in a very hot oven (450° F.) for 10 minutes, reduce the heat to moderate (350° F.) and continue to cook them, basting frequently with the marinade, for 1 hour, or until they are well done. Separate the ribs into serving pieces. Add enough water to the pan drippings to make 1 1/2 cups sauce. Thicken the sauce with 1 1/2 tablespoons cornstarch mixed to a paste with a little water, cook it for a few minutes, and serve it with the spareribs.

Sautéed Sausage Links 🐖

PRICK link sausages with a fork and put them in a large skillet. Cover them with boiling water and simmer them, covered, for 5 minutes. Drain off the water and continue to cook the sausages until they are brown on all sides, turning them frequently.

Skewered Sausage 🐖

PRICK 1 pound link sausages with a fork and simmer them, covered, in boiling water for 2 minutes. Drain and cool the links and cut them into 3/4-inch pieces. Arrange the sausage on skewers alternately with slices of tomato and water chestnut. Broil the sausage over hot coals, turning frequently, until it is well browned.

Sausage Patties with Sautéed Apples 🐖

PEEL, core, and slice thinly 6 green apples. Sauté the slices on both sides in 4 tablespoons butter until the edges are lightly browned. Sprinkle the apples with 2 teaspoons sugar while they are cooking.

Shape 1 1/2 pounds sausage meat into patties and cook them in a lightly buttered skillet over low heat, turning them to brown evenly, until they are cooked through. Arrange the patties on a platter and surround them with the apple slices.

Sausages in Ale and Wine 🐖

ARRANGE 6 smoked pork sausages in a saucepan and cover them with 1/2 cup ale. Cover the pan tightly and simmer the sausages over low heat for 30 minutes. Remove the sausages to a plate. Skim the fat from the pan juices and add 1 cup each of beef stock and brown bread crumbs, 1/2 cup claret, 1/4 cup vinegar, 1 teaspoon each of caraway seeds, salt, pepper, and sugar, and the grated rind of 1/2 lemon. Cook the sauce, stirring constantly, until it is thick and smooth. Return the sausages to the pan and heat them thoroughly.

Terrine of Ham

Scrapple

HAVE a hog's head cut in half and the eyes and brain removed. Wash the head, put it in a large kettle, and cover it with cold water. The liver, heart, and sweetbreads of the hog may be added to the kettle, or the 4 feet, thoroughly scraped. Bring the liquid to a boil and skim the surface. Cover the kettle and simmer the mixture gently for 2 to 3 hours, or until the head meat falls easily from the bones. Remove all the meat from the kettle, chop it, and discard the bones. Skim the broth and season it with a generous 1/2 teaspoon sage and salt and pepper to taste. Weigh the meat. For every 3 pounds set aside 2 pounds meal: either all yellow corn meal, or 2 parts corn meal and 1 part buckwheat flour.

Return the meat to the broth, bring the broth to a boil, and sift in the meal, stirring constantly, to make a soft mush. Cook the mixture over low heat for 1 hour, stirring it frequently to prevent scorching. Adjust the seasonings and pour the mixture into bread pans rinsed with cold water. Set the pans in a cool place until the scrapple is firm. Cut the scrapple in thin slices and fry the slices in hot butter or drippings until they are crisp and brown.

Terrine of Ham

LINE a deep earthenware dish or terrine with about 1/2 pound thin slices of bacon. Spread a thin layer of sausage meat (about 1/4 pound) on the bacon. On the sausage arrange 3 or 4 large strips of cooked ham, 1/2 inch thick and 1/2 inch wide. Cover the ham with a thin layer of 1 cup ground cooked ham and pack it firmly between the ham strips. Sprinkle the mixture with a few tablespoons whole pistachio nuts, shelled, and a few drops of Madeira. Add 3 or 4 half-inch-square strips of cooked tongue and cover them with another layer of sausage meat (about 1/4 pound), packing it down firmly. Continue in this manner with the strips of ham, ground ham, pistachio nuts, tongue, and sausage meat until the terrine is filled level with the top. If the ends of the bacon slices hang over the edge, fold them onto the meat. Put 2 bay leaves on top. Cover the dish, set it in a pan of hot water, and bake it in a moderate oven (350° F.) for about 2 hours, or until the melted fat surrounding the meat is very clear. If it is cloudy, return the terrine to the oven and bake it a little longer. Remove the lid and cover the pâté with aluminum foil. Set a heavy weight on the foil and let the pâté cool. Serve in the terrine.

ᘓ Ham Mousse

MEASURE 4 cups ground cooked ham and put it through the finest blade of a food chopper 4 or 5 times with 5 tablespoons white raisins and 2 tablespoons Madeira and 2 teaspoons each of horseradish and prepared mustard. Soften 2 tablespoons gelatin in 2 tablespoons cold water for 5 minutes, and dissolve it in 1 cup boiling chicken stock. Add the dissolved gelatin to the ham, mix well, and rub the mixture through a fine sieve. Cool the mousse, stirring it occasionally, and fold in 1 cup heavy cream, whipped. Makes 12 servings.

ᘓ Ham in Champagne

MARINATE a boned ham in 3 cups Champagne for 8 hours, turning it frequently. Bake the ham in a slow oven (300° F.) for about 2 hours, basting it often with the marinade. Remove most of the skin and trim it at the shank end in a scalloped pattern. Score the exposed fat with a knife and brush the ham well with white corn syrup. Bake the ham for 1 hour longer and let it cool. Slice it as thinly as possible, from the butt end, leaving one third of the ham uncut. Reshape the ham on a board or platter and fill the bone cavity with sprigs of holly.

ᘓ Stuffed Virginia Ham

SCRUB a well-aged Virginia ham thoroughly and soak it in cold water for 24 hours. Drain the ham, put it in a Dutch oven, and cover it with fresh cold water. Bring the water to a boil and simmer the ham, covered, until it is tender and the bone can be readily removed. Allow about 18 minutes per pound. Drain the ham and remove the bone.

Make the following stuffing: Mix 3 cups soft bread crumbs with 8 hard-cooked egg yolks, mashed, 1/2 cup minced sweet pickles, 1/4 cup each of stuffed olives and finely minced celery, 2 tablespoons brown sugar, and salt and pepper to taste. Moisten the stuffing with 3 tablespoons melted butter and with a little of the ham liquor if the mixture seems dry. Stuff the bone cavity with part of this dressing, and spread the rest over the ham. Lay the ham on a rack in a roasting pan and bake it in a moderate oven (350° F.), basting it from time to time with a mixture of ham liquor, brown sugar, and the vinegar drained from the sweet pickles, until the ham is golden brown. Serve it cold, in thin slices.

Ham Stuffed with Fruit 🙚

COOK an 8- to 10-pound ham according to its type in simmering water to cover until it is tender.

Soak 1/2 cup each of prunes, dried apricots, and raisins in 1 cup Madeira or Sherry for 3 hours. Drain the fruit and reserve the wine. Pit the prunes and put all the fruit and 1 cup almonds through the finest blade of a food chopper. Mix the fruit thoroughly with 1 teaspoon dry mustard and 1/2 teaspoon each of cloves, nutmeg, and ginger. Moisten the stuffing with enough of the reserved wine to make a thick paste. Cut deep slashes to the bone of the ham and pack in the stuffing. Tie the ham securely, score the fat, and rub the surface with a mixture of brown sugar, ground cloves, and dry mustard. Bake the ham in a moderate oven (350° F.) for 1 to 1 1/2 hours, or until it is well glazed.

Ham in Cream 🙚

SCRUB a country ham thoroughly and soak it in cold water for 24 hours. Drain the ham, put it in a Dutch oven, and cover it with fresh cold water. Add 1 carrot and 1 onion, sliced, a generous *bouquet garni* composed of several sprigs each of parsley, thyme, and celery tops, all tied together, 1 cup white wine, and a few peppercorns, and bring the liquid to a boil. Lower the heat and simmer the ham, covered, until it is tender and the bone can be readily removed. Allow about 18 minutes per pound. Lay the ham in a roasting pan on a bed of thinly sliced carrots and onions. Cover the pan and braise the ham in a moderate oven (350° F.) for 1 hour, basting it frequently with the pan juices. Remove the ham to a carving board and keep it hot. Strain the pan juices and stir in 1 cup heavy cream and 1/2 cup each of Sherry and white stock. Reduce the sauce over high heat by one third and season it with paprika and freshly ground black pepper to taste. Carve the ham in thin slices, arrange the slices on a platter, and pour the sauce over the meat. Serve at once.

Broiled Ham Slices 🙚

BROIL thin slices of ham under medium heat, turning them once, until the edges are crisp and curled.

Ham Steak with Camembert

IN a skillet melt 2 tablespoons butter and in it sauté a large ham steak, cut about 1 1/2 inches thick, until it is nicely browned on both sides. Spread the ham thickly with creamed ripe Camembert cheese and serve as soon as the cheese has melted.

Ham Steak in Cider

WIPE a large ham steak, cut about 1 1/2 inches thick, with a damp cloth and press 1 heaping tablespoon brown sugar onto each side. Put the ham steak in a buttered baking dish and stud the fat on the side with cloves. Surround the ham steak with 18 white onions and add enough cider to cover the ham. Bake the ham in a hot oven (400° F.) for 30 minutes, basting it frequently. Peel, core, and quarter 6 apples. Turn the ham over and add the apples to the baking dish. Bake the ham for 30 minutes more, adding cider as needed and basting frequently. The ham, apples, and onions should have a rich brown glaze.

Ham Steaks San Juan

TRIM·2 ham steaks, each cut about 1 inch thick, and score the edges at 1/2-inch intervals to prevent their curling. Parboil the steaks for 5 minutes and drain them. Put the steaks in a bowl and cover them with a mixture of 1 cup light rum, 2 tablespoons honey, 1 tablespoon dry mustard, and 3 whole cloves, crushed. Marinate the meat for at least 30 minutes and drain it, reserving the marinade. Broil the ham steaks over moderately hot coals, turning them frequently and basting them each time with the reserved marinade, for about 30 minutes, or until they are well browned.

Spiced Ham Steaks with Tangerines

IN a saucepan combine 1/2 cup each of Marsala and gooseberry preserves, 4 tablespoons each of vinegar and grated tangerine rind, 2 tablespoons red wine, 2 tablespoons arrowroot mixed to a paste with 2 tablespoons water, and 1/2 teaspoon each of allspice and dry mustard. Cook the sauce over high heat, stirring constantly, until it is reduced by one half.

Peel 3 tangerines, separate them into sections, and remove the membranes. Make a syrup by boiling together for 5 minutes 1 cup water, 1/2 cup sugar, and 4 tablespoons Sherry. Add the tangerine sections, simmer for 5 minutes, and drain them.

Arrange 2 ham steaks, each cut about 1 inch thick, in a lightly buttered baking dish and add the tangerines. Pour the sauce over the meat and bake it in a moderate oven (350° F.), basting frequently, for about 30 minutes.

Ham Rolls en Papillotes

SAUTÉ 1/4 pound mushrooms and 1 garlic clove, both chopped, in 2 tablespoons butter. Stir in 1 cup cooked wild rice and season with salt and pepper to taste. If the mixture is too dry, add a little melted butter. Spread the stuffing on 12 thin slices of boiled ham, fold or roll the slices, and wrap them in aluminum foil or in buttered parchment. Bake the ham rolls in a moderate oven (350° F.) for 15 to 20 minutes. Serve in the cases.

Ham and Spinach Soufflé

To 1 cup thick béchamel sauce add 3/4 cup each of ground cooked spinach and ground cooked ham and salt, pepper, and nutmeg to taste. Stir in 4 egg yolks, well beaten, fold in 4 egg whites, stiffly beaten, and blend the ingredients well. Pile the mixture into a buttered soufflé dish, sprinkle the surface with grated Parmesan, and bake the soufflé in a moderately hot oven (375° F.) for about 40 to 45 minutes, or until it is nicely puffed.

Ham and Mushroom Pie

TRIM 2 pounds mushrooms and reserve the stems for another use. In a large skillet heat 4 tablespoons butter, add the mushroom caps, and sprinkle them with salt, pepper, and the juice of 1/2 lemon. Cover the skillet and cook the mushrooms for 10 minutes, shaking the pan frequently. Arrange the mushrooms in a buttered 1-quart baking dish, piling them high in the center, and cover them with 2 cups diced cooked ham. To the juices remaining in the pan add 2 tablespoons butter and stir in 3 tablespoons flour. Gradually add 1 1/2 cups chicken stock, and cook the sauce, stirring constantly, until it is smooth and thick. Stir in 1/2 cup

Madeira and 1/2 cup hot heavy cream and season the sauce with salt and freshly ground pepper to taste. Pour the sauce over the mushrooms and cover the pie with flaky pastry. Brush the crust with beaten egg, make a few slits near the center, and bake the pie in a very hot oven (450° F.) for 15 minutes. Reduce the heat to moderate (350° F.) and bake the pie for 10 to 15 minutes longer, or until the crust is golden.

Sautéed Canadian Bacon

SAUTÉ thin slices of Canadian bacon in a well-buttered skillet over low heat until the lean meat is reddish-brown and the fat golden. Turn the slices frequently. Drain on absorbent paper.

Baked Canadian Bacon

PUT a 2-pound piece of Canadian bacon, fat side up, on a rack in a roasting pan. Pour over it 1/2 cup beer and bake the meat in a moderate oven (350° F.) for 15 minutes, basting it occasionally with the beer in the pan.

Combine 3/4 cup sugar with 1/2 teaspoon dry mustard and enough beer to make a smooth paste. Spread the glaze over the bacon and bake it for 1 hour longer, basting it frequently.

Spit-Roasted Canadian Bacon

ARRANGE a 2-pound piece of Canadian bacon on a spit. Cook the bacon, basting it frequently with a mixture of 1 cup cider, 1 cup brown sugar, 1 teaspoon mustard, and 1/2 teaspoon ground cloves, for about 40 minutes, or until it is tender.

Poultry and Game

Roast Chicken 🐓

WASH and dry a plump young roasting chicken weighing about 5 pounds. Season the chicken inside and out with salt and pepper and stuff it or not, as desired. Truss the bird and rub about 2 tablespoons butter into the skin. Roast the chicken in a moderate oven (350° F.), allowing 15 to 20 minutes per pound. Baste it frequently with chicken stock, white wine, or a combination of both.

Pistachio Stuffing

CRUMBLE enough white bread, free of crusts, to make 4 cups coarse crumbs. Combine the bread with 1 1/2 cups shelled pistachio nuts and sauté the mixture in 1/3 cup melted butter, stirring, until each piece is coated with butter. Add about 1 cup chicken stock to moisten the mixture, and adjust the seasoning with salt and pepper. Makes enough stuffing for a 5-pound chicken.

ꙮ Chicken Stuffed with Grapes

WASH and dry a 5-pound roasting chicken and stuff it loosely with the following mixture: Combine 7 slices of dry crumbled bread with 2 onions, chopped, 1 cup white seedless grapes, 6 tablespoons melted butter, 1 teaspoon finely chopped parsley, 1/4 teaspoon thyme, and salt and pepper to taste. Skewer the vent, truss the chicken, and rub it with butter, salt, pepper, and paprika. Roast the bird in a moderate oven (350° F.), basting it occasionally with 1/2 cup white wine, for about 1 1/2 hours, or until it is tender.

ꙮ Chicken with Olives

WASH and dry a 5-pound roasting chicken, rub it with butter, salt, and pepper, and truss it. Roast the bird in a hot oven (400° F.) for 30 minutes, or until it is well browned. Remove the chicken from the pan. To the pan juices add 1 tablespoon flour and cook until the flour is golden brown. Add gradually 3/4 cup chicken stock and 1/2 cup white wine and cook the sauce, stirring briskly, until it is smooth and thickened. Season with salt and pepper and return the chicken to the pan. Cover the pan and cook the chicken in a moderate oven (350° F.) for 30 to 45 minutes, or until it is tender. Carefully transfer the whole chicken to a heated platter and keep it warm.

Parboil 24 pitted green olives in a little water for about 5 minutes to remove the excess salt. (If black olives are used, no parboiling is necessary.) Add the olives to the sauce in the roasting pan and pour it over the chicken.

ꙮ Roast Chicken with Yoghurt

WASH and dry a 6-pound roasting chicken. Prick the skin with a fork and rub it well with a mixture of 2 teaspoons pepper and 1 1/2 teaspoons ground ginger. Truss the bird and roast it in a moderate oven (350° F.) for 10 minutes.

Combine 1 cup each of yoghurt and heavy cream with 3 onions, chopped, 3 cardamom seeds, pounded, 1 tablespoon turmeric, and salt to taste. Add the yoghurt mixture to the roasting pan and roast the chicken, basting it frequently with the sauce, for about 1 1/2 hours, or until it is tender. Arrange the chicken on a heated platter, surround it with rice pilaff, and pour some of the sauce over the bird. Serve the remaining sauce in a sauceboat.

Roast Chicken with Yoghurt

꩜ Velvet Chicken

REMOVE the skin of a 4- to 5-pound roasting chicken, cut the meat from the bones, and cut the meat into thin slices. Pound the slices with the flat edge of a knife to flatten them.

Beat 2 egg whites with 1/2 teaspoon each of monosodium glutamate and salt and a dash of pepper, and coat the chicken slices with this mixture. In a skillet heat 2 tablespoons vegetable oil with 2 slices of fresh gingerroot, or 1/4 teaspoon ground ginger. Stir in the chicken slices and cook them, stirring, over high heat for 2 or 3 minutes. Remove the chicken to a heated platter. To the juices remaining in the pan add 1 tablespoon more oil, if necessary, 3/4 cup snow peas, 1/2 cup each of sliced mushrooms, diced celery, and diced green beans, and 1/3 cup slivered blanched almonds. Cook the vegetables for about 8 minutes or until they are just tender. Return the chicken to the skillet, mix the slices lightly with the vegetables, and cook for 1 minute longer.

꩜ Braised Tarragon Chicken

WASH and dry 2 roasting chickens, each weighing about 4 1/2 pounds, and sprinkle the cavities with salt. Into the cavity of each chicken put 1/4 cup butter and 2 sprigs of fresh tarragon, or 2 teaspoons of the dried herb. Truss the chickens, brown them on all sides in a skillet in 1/2 cup butter, and transfer them to a Dutch oven. Add 1 1/2 cups chicken stock to the skillet and simmer it over high heat, stirring and scraping in all the brown bits, for a minute or two. Pour 3/4 cup of this broth over the chickens, cover the pan, and simmer the chickens over low heat, basting them occasionally with the remaining chicken broth, for about 1 hour, or until they are tender. During the last 10 minutes of braising, pour 2 cups warm heavy cream over the birds and sprinkle 2 tablespoons chopped fresh tarragon, or 2 teaspoons dried tarragon, into the pan. Baste the chickens constantly until the cream reaches the boiling point. Arrange the chickens on a heated platter and pour the sauce into a heated sauceboat.

꩜ Poached Chicken

CLEAN and singe a 4- to 5-pound fowl and truss the wings and legs close to the body. Put the chicken in a deep kettle, cover it with water, and bring the water to a boil. Boil the fowl for 4 to 5 minutes. Remove the fowl, pour off the water, and wash the kettle. Return the chicken to the kettle, cover it with fresh cold water, and bring to a boil again. Skim it well. Add 2 carrots, 2 onions, a *bouquet garni* composed of 2 stalks of celery, 4 sprigs of parsley, 1 bay leaf, and a sprig of thyme, and 1 tablespoon salt. Reduce the heat, cover the kettle, and simmer the chicken slowly for about 2 hours, or until it is tender.

To poach tender young chickens, eliminate the initial boiling and cook the birds for 30 to 35 minutes, or until the juice runs clear when pierced with a fork. Test them after 25 minutes to avoid overcooking.

To poach chicken breasts, for use in salads and other cooked dishes, cook them for about 30 minutes, or until they are tender. If the poached breasts are used in a recipe which calls for further cooking, cook them for about 20 minutes, or until they are barely tender.

Poached Duck or Turkey

DUCK, turkey, or other poultry, may be poached following the recipe for poached chicken. Duck or turkey will take a little longer per pound to cook and smaller birds less time per pound. Poaching is the preferred cooking method for duck or turkey which is afterward to be used in cold dishes such as salads, or in hashes or other preparations which call for further cooking, as the meat will be more tender and moist. Allow the poultry to cool in the cooking liquid.

Mustard Chicken

REMOVE the meat in large pieces from a poached 4-pound chicken. Arrange the pieces in a shallow baking dish and spread them thinly with prepared mustard. In a saucepan, melt 2 tablespoons butter and stir in 2 tablespoons flour. Add 1 cup heavy cream and cook the sauce, stirring constantly, for a few minutes, until it is smooth and thick. Add salt to taste and pour the sauce over the chicken. Bake the chicken in a moderate oven (350° F.) for 15 minutes.

Chicken Hash

CHOP enough white meat from a poached chicken to make 3 cups. Combine the chicken with 1 cup light cream and cook the mixture until the cream is reduced

Chicken Breasts Jeannette

by half. Make a *roux* of 1 1/2 tablespoons each of melted butter and flour and add gradually 1 cup milk. Cook the sauce, stirring constantly, until it is smooth and thick, and stir in 1/2 cup light cream. Add 1 cup of the sauce to the chicken mixture and add salt and pepper to taste. To the remaining sauce add 1 beaten egg yolk and 2 tablespoons whipped cream. Arrange the hash in a serving dish, spread the sauce over it, and brown it quickly under the broiler.

Chicken Croquettes

COMBINE 2 cups each of diced poached chicken and cooked rice, 1 egg beaten with 4 tablespoons lemon juice, the grated rind of 1 lemon, and 3/4 teaspoon salt. Spread the mixture on a platter and chill it. Form it into pear-shaped croquettes and dip them in beaten egg and in fine cracker crumbs. Fry the croquettes in deep hot fat (375° F.) for 4 minutes, or until they are nicely browned, and drain them on absorbent paper. Sprinkle with chopped parsley and serve with butter caper sauce.

Chicken Breasts Jeannette

POACH 25 half-breasts of chicken in simmering water until they are tender. Remove the skins and trim the meat into uniform ovals. Cover each oval with 1 tablespoon *pâté de foie gras*, rounding the surface, and chill the meat thoroughly. Put the breasts on a rack over a shallow pan and coat them evenly with cool but still liquid *chaud-froid blanc*. Leave the chicken breasts on the rack, chill them again, and top them with truffles cut in decorative shapes, fixing the decorations with a little clear aspic. Spoon cool but still liquid aspic over the chicken and chill thoroughly. Arrange the breasts on chilled platters and surround them with chopped aspic. Garnish the breasts with truffle cutouts. Makes 25 servings.

Sautéed Chicken

CUT two 3-pound chickens into serving pieces, splitting the breasts in half so that each retains a large bone, and separating the thighs from the legs just above the cartilage that joins them. There is so little meat on the wing that this part is usually reserved for making stock. Wash and dry the chickens, sprinkle them with salt and pepper, and dredge them lightly with flour.

To sauté the chickens, use 2 *sauteuses*, heavy-bottomed pans with straight sides that help keep in the steam and prevent the meat from overbrowning. Melt 1/4 cup clarified butter in each of the 2 *sauteuses*, or skillets, and add the pieces of chicken, skin side down. Cook the chicken over moderately low heat until it is golden brown. Turn the pieces and cook them, partly covered, for about 25 minutes. Transfer the chicken breasts to a heated platter and cook the remaining chicken pieces for 5 to 10 minutes, or until they are tender. The breasts always cook faster than the legs. If the recipe calls for a liquid to be added to the skillet with the chicken, do not let it boil or the meat will become tough. Remove the chicken legs to the platter and keep the chicken warm. Deglaze the pan with wine, water, or stock, according to the recipe, and pour the sauce over the chicken. Double the following recipes, using 2 chickens, to make 6 servings.

ꙮ Chicken à l'Angevine

FOLLOW the recipe for sautéed chicken, browning the chicken with 12 tiny white onions. Pour over the meat 1/4 cup heated Cognac and ignite it. Add 1 cup dry white wine and salt and pepper to taste. Cook the chicken, covered, over low heat for about 25 minutes. Remove the breast, add 1/2 pound mushrooms, and cook the chicken legs for 5 minutes more. Transfer the chicken, onions, and mushrooms to a heated platter with the breast and keep the mixture warm.

Reduce the sauce slightly over high heat, correct the seasoning, and stir in 1 cup warm heavy cream. Pour the sauce over the chicken and garnish the platter with small bunches of parsley.

ꙮ Chicken Sautéed with Artichokes

FOLLOW the recipe for sautéed chicken. During the last 15 minutes of cooking, add to the pan 12 raw artichoke bottoms and 1 shallot, chopped. Pour 1/4 cup heated apple brandy or Calvados over the chicken and ignite the spirit. Stir in 1/2 cup white wine and 1/2 cup cream, correct the seasoning, and simmer the mixture for 2 minutes. Arrange the chicken on a heated platter, pour the sauce over it, and garnish the platter with buttered croutons.

Sautéed Chicken with Parsley 🔊

FOLLOW the recipe for sautéed chicken, rubbing the skin of the raw chicken with a lemon slice. Transfer the cooked chicken to a heated platter and keep it warm.

To the juices remaining in the pan add 1/2 cup white wine and 2 heaping tablespoons chopped parsley. Stir the sauce well, scraping all the brown bits from the bottom, and pour it over the chicken.

Chicken with Tangerines 🔊

IN a mixing bowl combine 1 cup flour, 3/4 cup tangerine juice, 1/2 cup dry vermouth, 1 teaspoon salt, and 1/4 teaspoon pepper. Follow the recipe for sautéed chicken, dipping the chicken into the batter before sautéing. Transfer the cooked chicken to a heated platter and keep it warm.

Add to the juices in the skillet 3 tangerines, peeled and separated into sections. Cook the fruit for 3 minutes, until it is lightly glazed. Pour the pan juices and fruit around the chicken.

POULET À LA CRÈME FOUETTÉE Chicken in Whipped Cream 🔊

FOLLOW the recipe for sautéed chicken. Heat 1/4 cup brandy, ignite it, and pour it over the browned chicken. Cover the pan, reduce the heat, and cook the chicken slowly for about 25 minutes, or until it is tender. Remove the breast and cook the chicken legs for about 5 minutes longer.

Lightly brown 1 pound mushrooms, thinly sliced, in 3 tablespoons butter, stirring them frequently. Combine the chicken and mushrooms in a serving dish. Blend the pan juices from the chicken and mushrooms with 1 cup white wine. Bring the mixture to a boil, reduce the heat, and carefully fold in 1 1/2 cups heavy cream, whipped. Add salt and pepper to taste and pour the sauce over the chicken.

Chicken in Wine Sauce 🔊

FOLLOW the recipe for sautéed chicken. Cook the browned chicken with 1/2 pound mushrooms, sliced, 4 tomatoes, peeled, seeded, and quartered, and a pinch each of marjoram and rosemary for a few minutes, and add 1 cup each of white wine and chicken stock. Reduce the heat and cook the chicken, covered, for about 25 minutes. Remove the breast and cook the chicken legs for about 5 minutes more. Transfer the pieces to a heated platter with the breast and keep them warm.

To the mixture remaining in the pan add 4 tablespoons minced onion and 2 tablespoons minced parsley and cook the sauce very slowly for about 5 minutes. Add 1 ounce brandy, stir the sauce well, and pour it over the chicken.

Singapore Chicken

SAUTÉ 2 small onions and 2 garlic cloves, all chopped, in 4 tablespoons butter until they are golden. Follow the recipe for sautéed chicken, adding 4 tablespoons butter to the onions in the skillet. Brown the chicken pieces and sprinkle them with a pinch of ginger and salt to taste. Cover the pan and cook the chicken over low heat for 5 minutes. Combine the juice of 2 lemons with 1 cup water and pour the mixture over the chicken. Add 4 green peppers, finely diced, and a pinch of turmeric, and cover the pan. Cook the chicken for about 15 minutes, remove the breast, and cook the chicken legs for about 5 minutes. Serve with fluffy rice.

Sautéed Chicken Breasts

REMOVE the breasts with the wings attached from three 2 1/2-pound chickens and split them. Reserve the rest of the birds for another use. With a cleaver or heavy shears, cut off the first 2 wing joints, leaving the main wing bones attached to the breasts. Remove the tiny breast bones but leave the main bone that runs the length of the filet: it will help the breast hold its shape while it cooks. The procedure for sautéing chicken breasts is almost the same as for sautéed chicken.

Melt 6 tablespoons clarified butter in a *sauteuse*, or skillet, and sauté the breasts over moderate heat, turning them occasionally, for about 25 minutes, or until they are golden brown and tender. If the recipe calls for a liquid to be added to the pan with the sautéed breasts, do not let it boil. Remove the chicken to a heated platter and keep it hot.

Deglaze the pan with wine, water, or stock, according to the recipe, and pour the sauce over the chicken. Always serve sautéed chicken breasts as soon as possible; they harden on standing.

Sautéed Chicken Breasts in Butter 🐦

FOLLOW the recipe for sautéed chicken breasts. Transfer the cooked breasts to a heated platter and keep them hot. To the hot pan juices add 4 tablespoons butter and 2 tablespoons *glace de viande*, or meat extract. Stir the sauce well, incorporating the brown particles on the bottom of the pan, and pour it around the chicken. Serve at once.

Sautéed Chicken Breasts Bordelaise 🐦

FOLLOW the recipe for sautéed chicken breasts, sautéing the breasts in 3 tablespoons each of butter and olive oil. Arrange the chicken in the center of a heated oval platter and garnish it with cooked and buttered artichoke hearts, sliced sautéed potatoes, and French fried onion rings.

To the pan juices add 1 garlic clove, crushed, and cook for 2 minutes. Add 1/2 cup each of chicken stock and dry white wine and 1 teaspoon *glace de viande*, or meat extract. Stir the sauce well, add 1 teaspoon tomato paste, and reheat without boiling. Strain the sauce over the chicken and vegetables. Serve at once.

Sautéed Chicken Breasts with Brandy 🐦

FOLLOW the recipe for sautéed chicken breasts. Pour 1/4 cup heated brandy over the cooked breasts and ignite it. Cook the chicken, covered, over low heat for 5 minutes and transfer it to a heated platter. Deglaze the hot pan with 1/2 cup white wine or Madeira and add 3/4 cup chicken stock. Reduce the sauce a little over high heat and strain it over the chicken. Serve at once.

Sautéed Chicken Breasts with Calvados 🐦

FOLLOW the recipe for sautéed chicken breasts, sautéing the breasts very slowly with 6 shallots, finely chopped, 12 mushroom caps, quartered, and 2 teaspoons tarragon for about 10 minutes. Do not let the meat brown. Heat 1/4 cup Calvados, ignite it, and pour it flaming over the chicken. Add to the pan 1/2 cup white wine, 1 leek, a few sprigs of parsley, and a green celery top. Cook the chicken, covered, for 15 to 20 minutes, or until it is tender, and arrange it on a bed of buttered noodles on a platter. Discard the herbs and greens. Stir into the sauce 1/2 teaspoon potato starch mixed to a paste with 1 tablespoon water and simmer the sauce until it is clear and thickened. Pour the sauce over the chicken and noodles and serve at once.

Sautéed Chicken Breasts Cintra

SUPRÊMES DE VOLAILLE SAUTÉS CINTRA

FOLLOW the recipe for sautéed chicken breasts, sautéing the breasts with 1 shallot and 1 garlic clove, both peeled and chopped. Add to the pan 1/2 cup each of light Port and dry white wine and 1/4 cup each of brandy and cherry brandy. Bring the spirits just to the boiling point, ignite them, and baste the chicken breasts until the flames die. Transfer the breasts to a heated platter.

Reduce the sauce by one half and stir in 1 cup heavy cream mixed with 2 egg yolks. Simmer the sauce, without letting it boil, until it thickens, and strain it over the chicken. Serve at once.

Sautéed Chicken Breasts in Cream

FOLLOW the recipe for sautéed chicken breasts, sautéing the breasts in 3 tablespoons each of oil and butter with 6 shallots and 1/2 onion, all finely chopped. Transfer the cooked chicken to a heated platter and keep it hot.

Add to the pan juices 1/2 cup each of armagnac and chicken stock, 1/2 cup heavy cream mixed with 3 egg yolks, 1 teaspoon lemon juice, and salt and cayenne to taste. Simmer the sauce, stirring constantly, for about 3 minutes, or until it is thick. Do not let it boil. Mask the chicken with some of the sauce and serve the remainder in a heated sauceboat.

Sautéed Chicken Breasts Dijon

FOLLOW the recipe for sautéed chicken breasts. Transfer the cooked breasts to a heated platter and keep them hot. Add to the pan 1 1/2 cups white wine, 1/2 teaspoon dried tarragon, 1 small bay leaf, and salt and pepper to taste. Reduce the liquid over high heat to 1 cup and discard the bay leaf. Blend together 2 egg yolks, 3 tablespoons sour cream, 2 tablespoons Dijon-type mustard, and a pinch of cayenne. With a whisk, stir the mixture into the sauce and cook it, still stirring, until it thickens. Do not let it boil. Pour the sauce around the chicken and serve at once.

Sautéed Chicken Breasts with Kirsch 🦆

FOLLOW the recipe for sautéed chicken breasts. Transfer the cooked breasts to a heated platter and keep them hot. Add to the pan 1/4 cup each of brandy and kirsch and ignite the spirits. Stir in slowly 2 egg yolks mixed with 1 cup hot heavy cream, and cook the sauce, stirring, until it thickens. Do not let it boil. Pour the sauce over the chicken and serve at once.

Sautéed Chicken Breasts Lyonnaise 🦆

FOLLOW the recipe for sautéed chicken breasts. Transfer the cooked breasts to a heated platter and keep them hot. Deglaze the pan with 2 tablespoons tarragon vinegar, and add 1/2 cup each of dry white wine and heavy cream and 1 cup tomato purée. Mix the ingredients well and simmer the sauce, covered, for 10 minutes. Pour the sauce over the chicken and serve it at once, with buttered rice.

Sautéed Chicken Breasts with Oranges 🦆

FOLLOW the recipe for sautéed chicken breasts, removing the skin from the breasts before cooking. Sauté the chicken very slowly for about 10 minutes, or until it is lightly browned. Add to the pan 1/2 cup each of chicken stock and Port, 2 teaspoons salt, the grated rind of 1 orange, and a pinch of cayenne. Cook the mixture gently, without letting it boil, basting it occasionally, for about 15 minutes, or until the chicken is tender. Remove the chicken to a heated platter and keep it hot.

Strain the sauce and gradually add 2/3 cup heavy cream, shaking and swirling it in. Pour the sauce over the chicken and garnish with sautéed orange sections. Serve at once.

Sautéed Chicken Breasts Talleyrand 🦆

TOSS 1 pound hot cooked macaroni with 2 tablespoons butter and 4 small truffles, finely chopped. Arrange it on a heated platter and keep it warm.

Follow the recipe for sautéed chicken breasts, removing the skin from the breasts before cooking. Sauté the chicken very slowly in 1/2 cup butter until it is cooked through. Do not let the meat brown. Arrange the chicken on the bed of macaroni.

Add to the pan juices 1 1/2 cups heavy cream and bring it just to a boil. Mix 6 ounces *pâté de foie gras* with 1/2 cup hot heavy cream and stir it into the sauce. Season with salt to taste and pour the sauce over the chicken and macaroni. If necessary, heat the mixture in a moderate oven (350° F.) for a few minutes. Serve at once.

Boned Breast of Chicken on Ham

HAVE the butcher bone 3 chicken breasts, split them in half, and remove the first 2 wing bones, leaving the main wing bone. Put the breasts between 2 sheets of wax paper and pound them with the flat side of a cleaver. Cut 6 thin slices of baked ham the same shape as the pounded breasts. Beat 3 eggs with 1 teaspoon water, dip the ham slices into the mixture, and press the slices on the 6 halved breasts. Dip the paired ham and chicken in the egg and roll them in fine bread crumbs, patting off the excess crumbs. Using 2 large skillets, sauté the chicken breasts very carefully in 1 cup clarified butter over low heat until they are lightly browned on both sides. Transfer the chicken and ham to a baking dish, reserving the butter in the skillet. Bake the chicken breasts in a slow oven, basting frequently with the butter, for 10 to 20 minutes. Arrange the chicken breasts on heated individual serving dishes, or overlap them on a large platter. Melt 1/2 cup butter, stir in 2 tablespoons *glace de viande*, or meat extract, and pour the mixture around the breasts. Garnish with slices of lime and sprigs of watercress.

Southern Fried Chicken

COAT a 2 1/2- to 3 1/2-pound chicken, cut into serving pieces, with a mixture of equal parts of white corn meal and seasoned flour. Heat 1/2 inch of shortening in a heavy skillet. When the shortening sizzles add the chicken pieces, putting the largest on the bottom, and brown them on all sides over moderate heat. Add 1/4 cup water, lower the heat, and cook the chicken, covered, for 30 to 40 minutes, or until it is tender. Remove the chicken to a heated platter and keep it warm.

Pour off all but 1 tablespoon of the fat remaining in the skillet. Blend in 2 teaspoons flour, stirring in all the brown bits on the bottom of the pan, gradually add 1 cup light cream, and cook the sauce, stirring, until it thickens. Season the sauce with a pinch of mace and salt and pepper to taste. Makes 3 servings. For 6 servings, double the ingredients and cook the chickens in 2 skillets.

Boned Breast of Chicken on Ham

🐦 Waterzooi

BROWN two 2 1/2- to 3 1/2-pound chickens, cut into serving pieces, in 1/2 cup butter. Add 6 stalks of celery, 4 sprigs of parsley, 4 leeks, 1 onion, 1 bay leaf, a pinch of mace, a few peppercorns, and salt to taste. Add 5 cups chicken stock, or enough to cover the chicken, bring the broth to a boil, and skim the surface. Lower the heat and simmer the chicken for about 30 minutes, or until it is tender. Remove the chicken and keep it warm.

Strain the broth and add 1 lemon, thinly sliced, and 4 egg yolks beaten with 1/4 cup heavy cream. Cook the sauce over low heat, stirring constantly, until it thickens slightly. Do not let it boil. Return the chicken to the sauce. Serve the *waterzooi* from a tureen and garnish each bowl with a slice of lemon.

🐦 Savory Chickens

BLEND thoroughly 1/2 cup sesame oil, 3 tablespoons each of lime juice and white-wine vinegar, 1 1/2 tablespoons Worcestershire sauce, 1 teaspoon each of tarragon, brown sugar, and salt, 3/4 teaspoon paprika, 1/4 teaspoon each of Tabasco sauce and freshly ground pepper, and 1 garlic clove, minced.

Wash and dry 3 halved 1 1/2-pound chickens, and marinate them in this mixture, turning occasionally, for at least 2 hours. Cook the chickens, skin side up first, over moderately hot coals, or under a broiler, turning them occasionally and basting them frequently with marinade, for 25 to 35 minutes, or until they are brown.

🐦 Skewered Chicken

CUT 3 pounds boned chicken into 1 1/2-inch cubes and thread them on skewers. Dip the skewers in a mixture of 1 cup chicken stock, 1 teaspoon lemon juice, 3/4 tea-spoon each of minced garlic and cuminseed, and 1/3 teaspoon salt. Cook the chicken over hot coals or under the broiler for about 15 minutes. Serve with peanut dip.

🐦 Chicken Livers and Grapes

BROWN 2 pounds chicken livers in 6 tablespoons melted butter over high heat. Add 1/2 pound seedless green grapes and cook the livers over low heat for about 4 minutes, or until they are cooked through. Remove the grapes and the livers to a heated platter and surround them with a ring of brown rice. Deglaze the pan with 1/2 cup Port, carefully scraping in the bits on the bottom. Pour the sauce over the livers and grapes and garnish the platter with a small bunch of green grapes.

Chicken Livers in Red Wine 🐓

SAUTÉ 1/2 pound whole raw mushrooms and 2 sweet peppers, chopped, in 3 tablespoons melted butter for 3 minutes. In another pan sauté 2 pounds chicken livers in 6 tablespoons butter for 2 minutes. Combine the mushroom and liver mixtures, add 1/2 cup red wine, 1 bay leaf, and salt and pepper to taste, and simmer the mixture for 10 minutes. Serve on hot buttered toast.

CHAPON D'OR PARMENTIER   ## Golden Capon 🐓

TRUSS a 6-pound capon, rub it with salt and pepper, and brown it on all sides in a heavy kettle in 5 tablespoons butter. Add 2 cups boiling water, 2 carrots, 1 large onion, 1 leek, and a *bouquet garni* composed of parsley, tarragon, and 1 bay leaf. Cover the kettle and poach the capon for about 1 1/2 hours, or until it is tender. Remove the capon to a heated platter and surround it with potato mounds. Reduce the broth over high heat to 3 cups. Strain the broth, return it to the pan, and add 1 1/2 pounds mushrooms, trimmed. Cook the sauce for 5 minutes. Stir in 1 cup butter, bit by bit, and 1 cup light cream. Pour the butter and mushroom sauce over the capon and around the potato mounds.

Potato Mounds

MASH 2 pounds cooked potatoes and beat in 1/2 cup melted butter and 6 egg yolks. Using 2 tablespoons, form the potatoes into egg shapes and coat them with melted butter. Heat the potato ovals in 6 tablespoons butter but do not let them brown.

Truffled Capon 🐓

SPRINKLE 10 large slices of truffle with salt, pepper, and Cognac. Carefully loosen the skin from the breast of a 10- to 11-pound capon by slipping the fingers under

Squab Chicken Bonne Femme

the skin, and lay 4 of the truffle slices over each breast on each side. Loosen the skin from the legs in the same way and insert 1 truffle slice over the leg meat on each side. Sprinkle the bird with a little flour, wrap it in buttered paper, and tie it securely. Chill the capon overnight to let the truffle flavor permeate the bird.

Put twice through the finest blade of a food chopper 3/4 pound each of fresh lean pork and fresh pork leaf fat. Add 1 1/2 teaspoons salt mixed with 1/4 teaspoon poultry seasoning, 2 truffles, finely chopped, 1/3 cup each of Cognac and Sherry, 3 tablespoons juice from the truffle can, and 2 beaten eggs.

Stuff the neck and body cavities of the capon with the pork and truffle mixture, sew the vent, and truss the bird. Tie a thin slice of pork fat over the breast, rub the exposed skin of the bird with pork fat, and season it with a little salt. Lay the bird on its side in a deep roasting pan, sear it in a hot oven (400° F.) for 15 minutes, and roast it for 1 hour, turning it from side to side every 15 minutes and basting it frequently with the fat. Reduce the heat to moderately hot (375° F.) and continue roasting the bird, turning it every 15 minutes and basting it, for about 2 hours, or until it is tender. Transfer the capon to a heated platter.

Skim the fat from the pan juices, add 1/2 cup water, and cook the sauce, stirring in all the brown bits that cling to the pan, for a few minutes. Serve the bird with the pan juices and garnish the platter with sautéed mushroom caps and whole truffles, heated in butter.

Squab Chicken Bonne Femme

TRUSS 6 squab chickens and sprinkle them with salt and pepper. Brown the birds on all sides in 1/2 cup butter in 2 heavy flameproof casseroles. Mix together 1 cup each of hot chicken stock and white wine and divide the mixture between the casseroles. Add 1 bay leaf and 1 sprig of fresh thyme to each casserole. Roast the chickens in a moderate oven (350° F.), basting and turning them frequently, for about 25 minutes, or until they are tender. Combine the broth from the casseroles in a saucepan and thicken it with 2 teaspoons potato starch mixed to a paste with 3 tablespoons water. Adjust the seasoning.

Cook 1 pound small white onions in 1/3 cup butter until they are tender. Add 1 cup fluted button mushrooms and cook them 2 or 3 minutes. Cook separately 24 small young carrots and 2 cups peas. Arrange the chickens in individual casseroles and divide the onions, mushrooms, carrots, and peas among the casseroles. Add the sauce, heat the casseroles, and sprinkle the chickens with chopped parsley before serving.

ꙮ Broiled Squab Chicken with Marjoram

RUB 6 split squab chickens well with butter, salt, pepper, and minced marjoram leaves, and let them stand for about 2 hours. Lay the birds, breast side up, on a broiling rack and lay slices of bacon across the breasts. Broil the chickens under moderately high heat, turning them once during the cooking and basting them with the hot juices and with butter, for 15 to 20 minutes, or until they are tender. Pour 2 teaspoons Cognac over each bird during the last 5 minutes of broiling.

ꙮ Squab Chicken in White Wine POUSSINS AU VIN BLANC

TRUSS 6 squab chickens. In a large heavy skillet heat 3 tablespoons each of olive oil and butter and in it brown the birds lightly on both sides. Add 2 cups dry white wine and salt and pepper to taste, cover the pan loosely, and cook the birds for 15 minutes. Add the birds' livers, 2 chicken livers, 8 shallots, finely chopped, 3 whole cloves, and 2 cups raw button mushrooms, and cook the mixture, covered, for 15 minutes longer, or until the birds are tender. Transfer the birds to a heated platter, pour the pan juices over them, and sprinkle with chopped parsley.

ꙮ Squab Chicken with Wild Rice

IN a large heavy skillet brown 6 split squab chickens in 3/4 cup butter. Season the chickens with salt and pepper, partially cover the pan, and cook the birds over low heat for about 30 minutes, or until they are tender. Transfer the chickens to a heated platter and keep them warm.

Pour off the excess butter in the pan, add 6 tablespoons brandy and 3/4 cup orange juice, strained, and cook the sauce, stirring, until it comes to a boil.

Toss 3 cups hot cooked wild rice in butter with 1/2 cup slivered blanched almonds and pile it in a mound on a platter. Arrange the chicken halves on the rice. Garnish the platter with sections of orange and spoon the sauce over and around the chickens.

ꙮ Cold Roast Squab Chicken PIGEONNEAUX FROIDS

WIPE as many squab chickens as desired inside and out with a damp cloth. Rub the cavities with salt. Put a lump of butter and a sprig of rosemary in each cavity and rub the skin of the chickens with butter, salt, and pepper. Truss the chickens and roast them in a moderate oven (350° F.) for about 45 minutes, or until they are tender, basting them frequently with melted butter. Chill the chickens and serve garnished with watercress.

Roast Guinea Hen 🐦

SAUTÉ 4 shallots, finely chopped, and 1/2 cup chopped mushrooms in 1/4 cup butter until the shallots are golden. Add 1 cup smoked ham, cut in tiny dice, 1/4 cup chopped parsley, 1/2 teaspoon each of tarragon and freshly ground black pepper, and salt to taste. Add 1 cup toasted bread crumbs and 1 beaten egg and blend well. Use the mixture to stuff three 2-pound guinea hens and sew or skewer the vents. Truss the birds, spread them with butter, and roast them in a hot oven (400° F.) for 10 minutes. Reduce the heat to moderate (350° F.) and continue roasting the birds, basting frequently with melted butter, for about 45 minutes, or until they are tender. Arrange the birds on a heated platter and pour over them a mixture of the juice of 1 lemon and 1/2 cup each of browned butter and toasted bread crumbs.

PINTADES À LA LIÉGEOISE   ## Guinea Hen with Juniper Berries 🐦

CLEAN three 2-pound guinea hens, truss the wings and legs close to the bodies, and spread with 1 cup soft butter. Roast the hens in a hot oven (400° F.), basting them frequently, for 15 minutes. Add 3 tablespoons crushed juniper berries and roast the birds, basting frequently with the pan juices and adding more butter as needed, for about 40 minutes longer, or until they are tender. Pour off the fat from the pan and flame the birds with 1/2 cup heated brandy, tipping the pan to prolong the flaming, and stirring in the brown bits that cling to the bottom of the pan. Add 1/2 cup chicken stock and salt and pepper to taste and cook the sauce, stirring constantly, over low heat for a few minutes. Carve the birds for serving, arrange them on a heated platter, and strain the sauce over them.

Guinea Hen en Casserole 🐦

IN a Dutch oven brown 1 split garlic clove in 1/3 cup olive oil, add 2 tablespoons each of finely chopped onion and green pepper, and sauté the vegetables until they are translucent. Discard the garlic. In the same pan brown three 2-pound guinea hens, cut into serving pieces, over low heat. Pour over the birds 1/4 cup heated brandy and ignite it. Add white wine almost to cover, 24 ripe olives, pitted and sliced, 3/4 cup sliced mushrooms, 2 bay leaves, 1 teaspoon tarragon, and a dash of nutmeg. Cover the pan and cook the birds over very low heat for about 30 minutes, or until they are tender. Arrange the birds on a heated platter and keep them hot.

Simmer the liquid in the pan over high heat until it is reduced by half, beat in 2 tablespoons heavy cream, add salt and pepper to taste, and stir the sauce until it is very smooth. Pour the sauce over the hens.

Guinea Hen with Rice

IN a Dutch oven melt 3 tablespoons each of oil and butter and in it brown three 2-pound guinea hens, quartered. Add 2 cups raw rice, 2 onions, chopped, 1 cup ground cooked ham, and salt and pepper to taste. Stir the rice until each grain is coated and add 8 cups chicken stock and a piece of fresh gingerroot, thinly sliced. Bring the liquid to a boil, cover the pan, reduce the heat to the lowest possible point, and simmer the birds for about 30 minutes, or until the meat is tender and the liquid has been absorbed. Sprinkle the rice lavishly with parsley and the juice of 1 lemon.

Sautéed Breast of Guinea Hen   SUPRÊMES DE PINTADE SAUTÉS

REMOVE the breasts with the wings attached from three 2-pound guinea hens and split them. Reserve the rest of the birds for another use. With a cleaver or heavy shears cut off the first 2 wing joints, leaving the main wing bones attached to the breasts. Remove the skin and tiny breastbone but leave the main bone that runs the length of the filet; it will help the breast to hold its shape while it cooks.

Sprinkle the suprêmes with salt, paprika, and a pinch of ginger, dip them in heavy cream, and dredge them with flour. Melt 6 tablespoons clarified butter in a pan and gently brown the breasts on both sides over moderate heat. Arrange the breasts in a flameproof baking dish and pour the pan juices over them. Bake the suprêmes in a hot oven (400° F.), basting frequently, for about 30 minutes, or until they are tender. Arrange each breast on a sautéed slice of Virginia ham.

Skim all but 3 tablespoons fat from the baking dish, stir in 3 tablespoons flour, and cook the *roux*, stirring constantly, for a few minutes. Add gradually 2 1/2 cups heavy cream and 1/4 cup Sherry. Season the sauce and strain it over the suprêmes.

Breast of Guinea Hen Sautéed with Grapes 🦃

PREPARE 3 breasts of guinea hen as for sautéed breast of guinea hen. Season the suprêmes with 1/2 teaspoon ground cuminseed and salt and pepper to taste. In a large skillet melt 5 tablespoons clarified butter and in it gently brown the breasts on both sides. Add a little water, cover the pan, and cook the breasts slowly for about 20 minutes, or until they are tender. Heat 1/2 cup Cognac, ignite it, and pour it over the suprêmes. Add 1/2 cup each of Madeira and white wine, bring the sauce to a boil, and simmer it for 10 minutes. On a heated platter arrange the breasts on buttered croûtes lightly spread with *pâté de foie gras*. Strain the sauce over the birds and garnish the platter with 2 cups seedless white grapes, soaked in brandy and drained.

Roast Turkey 🦃

FILL the body and neck cavities of a 12- to 15-pound turkey loosely with Thanksgiving stuffing and close the vents with skewers and twine. Truss the legs and wings close to the body. Put the turkey, breast side up, on a rack in a roasting pan and spread it thickly with butter. Enclose the bird loosely with aluminum foil and roast it, allowing about 18 minutes per pound, in a moderately slow oven (325° F.) until it is tender. (Insert a fork in the meatiest part of the leg: the juices should show no pink.) Transfer the bird to a heated platter.

Giblet Stock

PUT the neck, gizzard, and heart of a 12- to 15-pound turkey in a large saucepan with 2 stalks of celery, 1 onion stuck with 2 cloves, 1 bay leaf, 1 teaspoon salt, and a few peppercorns. Add cold water to cover, bring it to a boil, and simmer the stock for about 1 1/2 hours. Add the liver of the bird and cook it for 5 minutes. Remove the giblets and reserve them for Thanksgiving stuffing. Reserve the liver for the gravy. Strain the stock to use for gravy.

Thanksgiving Stuffing

COOK 3 cups rice in 5 quarts boiling salted water for 14 minutes and drain it. Rinse the rice thoroughly under running cold water and set the colander over simmering water to steam the rice dry. Sauté 2 cups chopped onions in 3/4 cup butter until they

are golden. Using 2 forks, toss the onions with the rice. In the same way mix in
the cooked giblets, 1/2 cup each of heavy cream and dry Sherry, 2 teaspoons each
of tarragon and thyme, 1 teaspoon allspice, and the juice of 1 lemon.

Crumble coarsely 1 pound chestnuts, shelled and cooked, and add them to the
stuffing. Season the stuffing with salt and pepper to taste and chill it before using.

Roast Turkey Gravy

SKIM off all but 1/4 cup fat from the juices in the roasting pan. Stir 1/4 cup flour
into the pan juices and cook the *roux*, stirring constantly to dissolve the brown bits
that cling to the pan. Gradually stir in about 3 cups giblet stock and cook the gravy
for 5 minutes, stirring constantly. Mash the cooked turkey liver and add it to the
gravy. Add 2 teaspoons onion juice and salt and pepper to taste. Serve in a heated
sauceboat.

﷽ Turkey with Oyster Sauce

HAVE the butcher remove the breastbone of a 10- to 14-pound turkey. Brush the
cavity with brandy and sprinkle it lightly with salt.

To make the stuffing, sauté the turkey liver, finely chopped, in 1 tablespoon
butter until it is browned and combine it with 2 pounds veal, finely chopped, 1 cup
fresh bread crumbs, 1/2 cup ground ham, 2 truffles, finely chopped, 1 teaspoon salt,
and 1/4 teaspoon each of white pepper and nutmeg. Toss this forcemeat well to
mix it, stuff the turkey loosely, and sew up the vent, reshaping the breast.

Truss the bird as for roasting and lay it in an oval braising kettle with 3 carrots,
3 onions, 2 stalks of celery, and 4 sprigs of parsley. Add chicken or veal stock barely
to cover the turkey and poach it, covered, over very low heat for 3 hours, or until it
is tender. Transfer the bird carefully to a heated platter.

In a saucepan heat 36 freshly shucked oysters with their liquor and 1/4 cup butter
for 3 minutes. Do not let the mixture boil. Strain the oysters, reserving the meat and
the liquor. Melt 1/2 cup butter in a saucepan and stir in 8 tablespoons flour, 1/2 teaspoon salt, and a pinch of cayenne. Gradually add the reserved oyster liquor and
about 1/2 cup light cream to make 2 cups liquid. Stir the sauce over low heat for
8 to 10 minutes and strain it. Just before serving mix 2 egg yolks with a little cream
and add them to the sauce with the reserved oysters and 1 teaspoon lemon juice.
Blend the sauce well and heat it gently without letting it boil. Mask the turkey with
some of the sauce and serve the rest in a heated sauceboat.

Stuffed Rolled Breast of Turkey 🦃

HAVE the butcher remove the breast meat from a 10- to 12-pound hen turkey and detach the skin as far beyond each breast as possible. Cover the breast filets and skin with 1/2 cup each of Madeira and white wine, flavored with 3 shallots, 1 teaspoon dried tarragon, 1/4 teaspoon thyme, and salt and pepper. Marinate the meat in the refrigerator for 36 hours.

Combine 1/4 pound each of mushrooms and chicken livers, both sautéed and chopped, and 2 truffles, finely chopped, to make a stuffing.

Drain the turkey skin and meat, reserving 1/2 cup marinade. Dry the turkey breasts with a cloth, lay them, smooth side down, on wax paper on a board, and cover them with a sheet of wax paper. Flatten the breast filets slightly with a cleaver. Lay each breast on a piece of skin, spread it with stuffing, and roll it up. Encircle the rolls at intervals with strips of bacon and secure the strips, not too tightly, with string. Arrange the rolls in a baking dish, add 1/2 cup turkey stock, and braise the turkey, covered, in a moderately slow oven (325° F.) for about 1 hour, basting often, until the meat is tender. Remove the bacon and string. Slice the rolls 1/4 inch thick and arrange the slices in overlapping layers on a heated platter.

Skim some of the fat from the pan juices, add the reserved marinade, and bring the mixture to a boil. Add 1 tablespoon Bénédictine and strain the sauce into a saucepan. Thicken it with 2 egg yolks beaten with 1/4 cup heavy cream and heat it without letting it boil. Add 3 truffles, finely chopped, and pour some of the sauce over the sliced turkey. Serve the rest in a heated sauceboat.

Turkey Filets in Sour Cream 🦃

HAVE the butcher remove the breast meat from a 12-pound hen turkey, skin each filet, and cut it into 8 uniform pieces. Dip the pieces in seasoned fine bread crumbs, in 2 eggs beaten with 2 tablespoons water and a little salt, and again in crumbs. In a heavy skillet brown the filets on both sides in 1/2 cup butter and transfer them to a baking dish. Sprinkle the turkey with 1 tablespoon each of finely minced onion and parsley and add 1/4 cup water. Pour 2 cups sour cream over the filets, cover the dish, and bake them in a moderate oven (350° F.) for 15 minutes. Reduce the heat to very slow (250° F.) and bake the filets for 45 minutes, or until they are tender. Remove the cover and increase the heat for the last few minutes of cooking to achieve a crisp crust. Transfer the turkey to a heated platter. Stir 1 tablespoon flour into the sauce in the baking dish, cook it for a few minutes, and strain it over the turkey.

Broiled Turkey Rosemary

SPLIT and remove the backbone from a 5- to 6-pound turkey. Put the halved bird in a shallow pan, sprinkle it with salt, add 1 cup each of white wine and olive oil, and sprinkle generously with minced rosemary. Marinate the turkey in the refrigerator overnight. Broil the turkey 5 to 6 inches from the heat, turning the bird frequently and basting it with the marinade occasionally, for about 1 1/4 hours, or until the turkey is tender.

Turkey and Chestnuts

IN the blazer of a chafing dish over direct heat sauté 1/4 cup finely chopped onions in 1/4 cup butter until they are golden. Add 1 teaspoon minced parsley, a pinch of rosemary, and 3 tablespoons flour. Cook the mixture, stirring, for 2 to 3 minutes, and stir in 1/2 cup turkey stock and 1/4 cup red wine. Add 2 cups diced cooked turkey meat and 1/2 pound chestnuts, shelled, cooked, and crumbled. Add 1 cup sour cream, correct the seasoning, and heat the mixture without letting it boil.

Curried Turkey

IN the blazer of a chafing dish over direct heat melt 3 tablespoons butter and add 1/2 cup each of chopped apple and onion, 1 garlic clove, crushed, and 1 tablespoon curry powder. Cook the mixture until the onion is transparent, add 1 tablespoon flour, and continue to cook it, stirring, for 2 minutes. Add 1 cup turkey stock and cook the sauce, still stirring, until it is smooth and thickened. Add 2 cups diced cooked turkey meat and cook the mixture slowly until the meat is heated through.

Turkey Paprika

IN the blazer of a chafing dish over direct heat sauté 1 onion, sliced, in 1/4 cup butter until it is transparent. Add 1 tablespoon paprika, 1/4 teaspoon thyme, and

Broiled Turkey Rosemary

2 tablespoons flour. Cook the *roux* for 3 minutes, stirring, and add 2 cups sour cream and 2 cups diced cooked turkey meat. Put the pan over hot water and cook the mixture until the sauce is thickened.

Turkey in Aspic with Cherries

CUT cooked breast of turkey into thin slices. Large thin slices of dark meat may also be used. Cover the bottom of a deep platter with a 1/4-inch layer of cool but still liquid aspic and chill it until it is set. Arrange overlapping slices of turkey in neat rows on the aspic, and garnish the platter with pitted sweet red cherries. Coat the platter to the inside of the rim with aspic, covering turkey and fruit. Chill until the aspic is very firm.

Duck Stuffed with Apples   CANARD RÔTI AUX POMMES

WASH and dry two 4- to 5-pound ducklings and sprinkle the cavities with salt and pepper. Stuff each duck loosely with stewed apples, skewer the vents, and truss the birds. Lay the birds on a rack in a roasting pan. Sprinkle the skin with 1 tablespoon sugar and pour 1/4 cup Calvados into the pan. Roast the ducks in a very hot oven (450° F.) for 20 minutes, reduce the temperature to moderate (350° F.), and pour off the fat from the pan. Roast the ducks, basting them with the pan juices every 10 minutes, for about 1 1/2 hours, or until they are tender. Transfer the ducks to a heated platter.

Skim the fat from the roasting pan and stir 2 tablespoons currant jelly into the pan juices. Bring the sauce to a boil and pour it over the ducks.

Roast Duck with Apples and Sauerkraut

WASH and dry a 4- to 5-pound duckling and sprinkle it inside and out with salt and pepper. Stuff the cavity with a quartered onion stuck with cloves and as many apples, peeled and quartered, as it will hold. The apples may be rolled in a mixture of sugar and cinnamon. Roast the bird in a moderate oven (350° F.), basting frequently with white wine, for about 1 1/2 hours. Increase the temperature to hot (400° F.) and roast the duck for about 15 minutes, or until it is tender. Transfer the duck to a heated platter.

Skim off most of the fat from the juices in the pan and thicken the juices with 1 teaspoon cornstarch mixed to a paste with a little water. Reserve the gravy.

Rinse 2 pounds fresh sauerkraut, cover it with water, and simmer the kraut for 1 hour. Drain the kraut and arrange it around the duck on the platter. Sprinkle the kraut with a little of the gravy and serve the rest with caraway dumplings.

Chinese Duck 🦆

SELECT a 5- to 6-pound duck that is not too fat. Scald it in boiling water three or four times and dry it thoroughly.

Mix together 1 tablespoon each of soy sauce, brown sugar, and finely chopped leek or chives, 2 teaspoons Sherry, 1 teaspoon each of cinnamon, monosodium glutamate, and salt, 1/8 teaspoon freshly ground black pepper, a pinch each of ground cloves and ground aniseed, and 3 garlic cloves, crushed. Cook the mixture over low heat for 2 to 3 minutes and spread it in the cavity of the duck. Sew up the vents securely and truss the bird. Lay the duck on a rack in a roasting pan.

Mix together 2 tablespoons each of soy sauce and honey and 1 tablespoon white wine, rum, or Sherry, and rub the mixture over the skin of the duck. Roast the duck, uncovered, in a very hot oven (500° F.) for 2 to 3 minutes and baste it with the soy sauce and honey mixture. Reduce the temperature to hot (425° F.), cover the pan tightly, and roast the duck for about 45 minutes. Uncover the pan, baste the duck, and roast it, turning and basting it frequently, for about 15 minutes.

Transfer the duck to a heated platter and, using poultry shears, cut it into bits, not just joints and slices. Serve very hot.

Broiled Ginger Duck 🦆

HAVE the butcher quarter two 5- to 6-pound ducks and remove the wing tips and backbones. Cut off the excess fat. Sprinkle the pieces with 4 tablespoons lemon juice, 2 teaspoons salt, and 1 1/2 teaspoons ground ginger, and let them stand for 1 hour. Arrange pieces of the duck, skin side down, on a rack and broil them 5 inches from the heat for about 25 minutes on each side. Arrange the duck on a heated platter and brush the pieces with lemon juice.

Cold Duckling in Aspic

Honey-Glazed Duckling 𝕾𝕭

CUT two 5-pound ducklings into quarters and brush them with a mixture of 2/3 cup honey, 1/2 cup orange-flavored liqueur, and 2 teaspoons dry mustard. Arrange the pieces of duck, skin side down, on a rack and broil them, turning the pieces occasionally and basting them frequently, under low heat for about 50 minutes, or until the duck is tender. Toward the end of the cooking time, broil the ducklings closer to the heat to make a crisp skin.

Barbecued Duckling 𝕾𝕭

SAUTÉ 1/2 cup chopped onion and 1 garlic clove, minced, in 2 tablespoons butter until the onions are golden. Add 1/2 cup each of red-wine vinegar and honey, 2 tablespoons Worcestershire sauce, 1 1/2 teaspoons each of dry mustard and salt, 1 teaspoon soy sauce, 1/4 teaspoon each of marjoram and freshly ground pepper, and a pinch of rosemary. Bring the mixture quickly to a boil, stirring it constantly, reduce the heat, and simmer the marinade for 5 minutes.

Wash and dry two 4-pound ducklings and halve them with poultry shears. Brush each piece generously with the marinade. Cook the ducks, skin side up first, over moderately hot coals for about 40 minutes, or until they are brown and tender. Turn the pieces once during the cooking and baste them frequently with the marinade.

Cold Duckling in Aspic 𝕾𝕭

WASH and dry two 5-pound ducklings. Rub the cavities with lemon juice and in each cavity put 2 oranges, sliced, and 2 whole cloves. Put the ducks, breast side up, on a rack in a shallow pan. Roast the birds in a moderately slow oven (325° F.) for 30 minutes. Drain the fat from the pan, add 1 1/2 cups dry white wine, and roast the ducks, basting them with the pan juices every 20 minutes, for about 1 1/2 hours, or until they are tender. Cool the birds and chill them.

In a large pan combine 7 cups rich beef or chicken stock, free of fat, with 5 tablespoons gelatin, 1/4 cup each of red wine and Grand Marnier, and 1 tablespoon tomato paste. Beat 4 egg whites until they are stiff and add them to the stock. With a wire whisk beat the mixture over moderate heat until it comes to a full boil. Remove the pan from the heat and let it stand for 10 minutes. Gently pour the aspic through a fine strainer lined with a damp cloth into a chilled bowl.

Set the bowl in a pan of ice and stir the aspic until it thickens and is on the point of setting. Spoon it carefully over the ducks. Return the birds to the refrigerator. Chill the remaining aspic in shallow flat tins and, when it is set, chop it with a knife on wax paper. Arrange the aspic-coated ducks on a chilled platter, surround them with the chopped aspic, and garnish with watercress.

Salmi of Duck

CUT enough cooked duck meat in medium-sized pieces to make 2 1/2 cups. In a sauce-pan or in the blazer of a chafing dish melt 4 tablespoons butter. Add 4 tablespoons *pâté de foie gras*, 1/2 cup Madeira, 1/4 cup chicken or duck stock, 3 tablespoons each of chopped chervil and chives, and 2 teaspoons lemon juice. Add the duck meat to the sauce and heat the mixture thoroughly.

Spanish Duck

CUT into quarters 6 ripe tomatoes, cook them in 2 tablespoons butter until they are just soft, and season them with salt and pepper. Keep the tomatoes warm. In another saucepan brown 1 pound mushrooms, quartered, in 2 tablespoons butter. Add 2 cups shredded cooked duck meat, 2 teaspoons grated orange rind, and salt and pepper to taste. Heat the mixture thoroughly. Serve the duck in the center of a ring of cooked buttered rice and surround the rice with the sautéed tomatoes.

Duck Soufflé

PUT enough meat from a cooked duck through the finest blade of a food chopper to make 1 3/4 cups. Melt 3 tablespoons butter and stir in 3 tablespoons flour. Add 1 cup each of light cream and chicken or duck stock and cook the sauce, stir-ring constantly, until it is smooth and thick. Season highly with salt, pepper, dry mustard, and nutmeg. Add 3 tablespoons Madeira and 1 tablespoon each of chopped parsley and chives. Add the ground duck meat, mixed with 1 tablespoon finely chopped shallots, and 3 beaten egg yolks. Cool the batter slightly, fold in 3 egg whites, stiffly beaten, and pour the mixture into a buttered 1-quart soufflé dish. Bake the soufflé in a moderately hot oven (375° F.) for 35 minutes, or until it is well puffed and golden brown, and serve it immediately.

Roast Goose Stuffed with Fruit 🦢

WIPE a 10- to 12-pound goose with a damp cloth and stuff it loosely with 8 large dried prunes, halved, 8 dried apricots, halved, and 4 tart apples, peeled, cored, and quartered, and sew up the vent. Rub the bird with 1 tablespoon salt, turn the skin of the neck backward, and secure it with a small skewer. Twist the wings back and skewer the thighs. Prick the bird well with a fork, lay it on a rack in a roasting pan, and roast it in a moderately hot oven (375° F.), allowing 20 to 25 minutes per pound, until it is tender. During the roasting, prick it with a fork from time to time. Arrange the goose on a heated platter and garnish it with sautéed apples.

Roast Goose with Haricot Beans 🦢

WIPE a 10- to 12-pound goose with a damp cloth and rub the cavity and the skin with salt. Turn the skin of the neck backward and secure it with a small skewer. Twist the wings back and skewer the thighs. Prick the bird well with a fork, lay it on a rack in a roasting pan, and roast it in a moderately hot oven (375° F.), allowing 20 to 25 minutes per pound, until it is tender. During the roasting, prick it with a fork from time to time.

Combine 2 cups white beans, soaked in water overnight and drained, with 2 quarts rich white stock, the liver of the goose, 1 garlic clove, and salt and pepper to taste. Cook the beans until the liver is tender, about 30 minutes. Remove the liver, chop it, and reserve. Continue cooking the beans for about 1 hour, or until they are tender but not broken. Drain the beans, discard the garlic, and put them in a large buttered baking dish. Sprinkle the beans with the juice of a lemon and the chopped liver and bake them in a moderate oven (350° F.) for 15 minutes. Arrange the beans on a heated platter, lay the goose on top, and garnish the platter with a ring of finely chopped parsley.

Roast Deviled Goose 🦢

WIPE a 10- to 12-pound goose with a damp cloth, rub the cavity and the skin with salt and pepper, and stuff the bird loosely with potato stuffing. Sew up the vent. Turn the skin of the neck backward and secure it with a small skewer. Twist the wings back and skewer the thighs. Prick the bird well with a fork and lay it on a rack in a roasting pan. Pour over the goose a mixture of 4 tablespoons vinegar, 2 tablespoons prepared mustard, and 1 tablespoon white pepper. Roast the goose in a moderately hot oven (375° F.), allowing 20 to 25 minutes per pound, until it is tender. During the cooking, baste it frequently and prick it with a fork from time to time.

Potato Stuffing

SAUTÉ 1 large onion, chopped, in 1 tablespoon goose fat until the onion is golden. Add 2 cups mashed potatoes, 1 cup sausage meat, 1 tablespoon chopped parsley, 1/2 teaspoon poultry seasoning, and salt and pepper to taste.

Foie Gras with Grapes

IN a heavy saucepan sauté a 1 1/2-pound goose liver in 1 tablespoon goose fat over low heat for 30 minutes. Pour off any excess fat and season the liver with salt and pepper. Add 1/2 cup white wine and continue cooking the liver for 2 minutes longer. Add 24 each of white and black grapes and cook the mixture very slowly for 10 minutes, or until the grapes are plump but not broken.

Scotch Grouse with Black Cherries

CLEAN 6 small plump grouse and sprinkle the cavities with salt and pepper. Rub the birds with 4 tablespoons soft butter and sprinkle them with salt and pepper. Put the birds in a casserole and brown them well in a hot oven (400° F.) for 10 minutes. Soak 1 pound black cherries, drained and pitted, in 1/2 cup Cognac for 30 minutes. Add the cherries and Cognac to the casserole, reduce the temperature to moderate (350° F.), and cook the birds, covered, for about 20 minutes, or until they are tender. Transfer them to a heated platter. Add to the pan 1/2 cup rich chicken stock and cook the sauce, stirring, for 5 minutes. Add 1/4 cup kirsch and bring the sauce to a boil. Spoon the cherries around the birds and pour the sauce over all.

Salmi of Grouse with Red Wine

CLEAN 3 large grouse and split them in half. Sprinkle the grouse lightly with salt and pepper, and sauté them in 4 tablespoons butter for about 15 minutes. Remove the birds, cut them into serving pieces, and return them to the pan. Add 2 cups red wine, 2 truffles, peeled and sliced, 2 or 3 anchovy filets, and about 1 teaspoon washed and dried capers, and cook the meat for about 15 minutes, or until it is tender. Remove the meat. Add to the pan 1/2 cup rich beef stock and boil the sauce for a moment or two. Return the meat to the pan and heat it. Just before serving, add the juice of 1 orange.

FAISANS AUX CHAMPIGNONS **Roast Pheasant with Mushrooms**

TRIM the stems of 3 pounds small mushrooms, reserve them for another use, and sauté the caps in 1/2 cup butter for a few minutes. Add 3 shallots, chopped. Stuff 3 pheasants with this mixture and skewer the vents. Truss the birds and sprinkle them with salt. Cover the birds with buttered paper and roast them in a moderately hot oven (375° F.) for 45 minutes, basting frequently with butter. Remove the paper and continue roasting the birds, basting every 5 minutes with the pan juices, for about 25 minutes, or until they are tender. Remove the pheasant to a heated platter and strain and reserve the pan juices.

Simmer the wing tips, necks, and giblets of the birds in 3 cups salted water with 1/2 bay leaf and 1 stalk of celery for 45 minutes. Strain the stock. Sauté 4 shallots, finely chopped, in 2 tablespoons butter until they are golden. Add the pheasant livers and 3 chicken livers and sauté them for 3 minutes. Stir in 2 tablespoons flour and crush the livers with a fork. Gradually stir in the strained stock and the reserved roasting pan juices. Serve the sauce separately.

Roast Pheasant on Chestnut Purée

CLEAN and truss 3 small pheasants, rub them with soft sweet butter, and roast them in a moderately hot oven (375° F.) for 15 minutes. Add 6 tablespoons Madeira to the pan and continue to roast the birds, basting them often with the pan juices, for 45 minutes, or until they are tender. Arrange the birds on a heated platter and surround them with a ring of chestnut purée.

༄ Braised Pheasant with Endive

WIPE 3 small pheasants with a cloth soaked in brandy and rub them inside and out with salt and pepper. Let the birds stand at room temperature for 20 minutes. Truss the birds and cover the breast of each with strips of bacon. In a deep heavy pot melt 1/2 cup butter and brown the pheasants on all sides over moderate heat. Add 2 small onions, quartered, and 2 small carrots, cover the pan, and cook the birds over low heat for 30 minutes, or until they are tender.

Cut 12 heads of endive into 1-inch strips. In a saucepan melt 1/4 cup butter, add the endive, about 3/4 cup water, the juice of 1 lemon, and salt and pepper to taste. Slowly cook the endive, covered, for about 45 minutes, or until it is tender and most of the liquid has evaporated.

Remove the pheasants from the pot, discard the strings and bacon, and arrange them on a heated platter. Add a little water or stock to the pot and cook the sauce over high heat, stirring in the brown bits, until it is slightly reduced. Strain the sauce and pour it over and around the pheasants. Surround them with the endive.

༄ Quail with Cherries

CLEAN and truss 6 quail and sprinkle them lightly with salt and pepper. Cook the quail gently in 4 tablespoons butter in a flameproof casserole, turning them to brown all sides, for about 25 minutes, or until they are tender. Transfer the quail to a heated platter and keep them warm.

Drain a medium can of pitted sour cherries and put 3 or 4 tablespoons of the syrup in a saucepan with 3/4 cup Port, a large strip of orange peel, and a pinch of cinnamon. Simmer the sauce for a few minutes. Add 1/2 cup veal stock and cook the sauce until it is reduced by one half. Add 1 tablespoon currant jelly and cook the sauce until the jelly melts. Remove the orange peel, add the cherries, and simmer the sauce for 3 minutes. Pour it over the quail on the platter.

༄ Quail with Black Grapes   CAILLES AUX RAISINS NOIRS

CLEAN and truss 6 quail and sprinkle them with salt. Brown the quail slowly in a Dutch oven in 1/3 cup butter, turning them carefully and basting constantly, for 15 minutes. Cover the pot and cook the birds in a moderate oven (350° F.) for about 10 minutes, or until they are tender. Remove the birds and keep them hot.

Add to the pan 1/2 cup heated brandy, ignite it, and deglaze the pan juices, scraping in all the brown bits from the sides and bottom. Add 1 scant cup black grapes, peeled and seeded, the sections and juice of 1 orange, and 3/4 cup Port. Return the quail to the pan and cook them for about 10 minutes, or until they are tender. Transfer the quail to a heated platter and remove the trussing strings. Correct the seasoning of the sauce and pour it over and around the birds.

Quail with Braised Lettuce

BROWN lightly 2 carrots and 2 onions, both grated, in 4 tablespoons butter in a large heavy skillet. Add a *bouquet garni* composed of parsley, thyme, and 1 bay leaf, and 6 quail, trussed and sprinkled with salt. Cover the pan and simmer the quail for about 20 minutes, or until they are tender. Transfer the birds to a heated platter and keep them warm.

Simmer the pan juices until almost all the moisture is evaporated. Add 3/4 cup each of white wine and rich brown stock, reduce the sauce a little, and strain it. Add 4 tablespoons peeled and sliced truffles, lightly sautéed in 4 tablespoons butter. Simmer the sauce for a few minutes and pour it over the quail. Garnish the quail with 3 small heads of lettuce, cut in halves and braised in 2 tablespoons butter. Serve with steamed rice.

Quail with Truffles and Foie Gras

CLEAN and truss 6 quail, sprinkle them lightly with salt, and brush the cavities with 2 teaspoons *fine champagne*. Cover the breast of each quail with 2 strips of bacon.

In a deep kettle make a *mirepoix* of 1 onion and 1 carrot, both chopped, 1 sprig each of parsley and thyme, 1 bay leaf, 6 ounces of lean veal, diced, the peelings from 3 medium truffles, and 1/2 cup butter. Lay the birds on the *mirepoix* and cook them, covered, turning occasionally, for about 25 minutes, or until they are tender. Discard the bacon and transfer the quail to a heated terrine. Cover the birds with 3 truffles, thickly sliced, and season with salt and freshly ground pepper. Sauté 3 ounces *foie gras*, thinly sliced, in butter and spread it on the truffle slices. Keep the terrine warm.

Add to the *mirepoix* 1/4 cup *fine champagne* and 1/2 cup each of Madeira and white wine. Cook the mixture over high heat until it is reduced by two thirds, and strain it over the quail in the terrine.

⟊ Roast Haunch of Venison   QUARTIER DE CHEVREUIL RÔTI

PUT a 6- to 7-pound haunch of venison in a large crock and add 2 carrots and 2 onions, all chopped and sautéed in butter, 5 whole cloves, 1/2 teaspoon each of marjoram, thyme, basil, and tarragon, and enough red wine to cover the meat. Marinate the venison for 8 hours and drain and dry it. Lard it with strips of salt pork and season it with salt. Put the meat on a rack in a roasting pan, add a generous amount of the marinade, and roast the venison in a very hot oven (450° F.) for 30 minutes. Reduce the temperature to moderate (350° F.) and roast the meat for about 1 1/2 hours, or until it is tender. Transfer the meat to a heated platter.

Strain the pan juices and add 1 cup each of red wine and currant jelly and 1/4 teaspoon each of ground ginger and cloves. Simmer the sauce until it is reduced by one half and serve it in a heated sauceboat.

⟊ Venison with Cranberry Stuffing
RÔTI DE CHEVREUIL FARCI À LA CANNEBERGE

HAVE the butcher bone a 7- to 8-pound rib roast of venison. Spread the meat flat and wipe it with a damp cloth. Sprinkle the roast with salt and pepper and spread it with cranberry stuffing. Roll it up, tie it securely with string, and sprinkle the meat with salt, pepper, and a little flour. Lay the roast on a rack in a roasting pan and sear it in a very hot oven (500° F.) for 20 minutes. Reduce the heat to moderate (350° F.) and cook the meat for about 2 hours, or until it is tender.

Cranberry Stuffing

IN a skillet sauté 1/4 cup finely chopped suet until it is crisp. Add 4 cups cranberries, finely chopped, sprinkle them with 1 1/2 cups sugar, and cook them, stirring, until they are transparent. Add 2 cups dry bread crumbs, 1 tablespoon grated orange rind, 1 1/2 teaspoons salt, and 1/4 teaspoon pepper, and blend well.

⟊ Venison Cutlets with Spätzle

MARINATE six 1-inch slices of loin of venison in 1/2 cup olive oil, the juice of 1 lemon, and salt and pepper to taste for 1 hour. Drain and dry the meat and broil the cutlets for 10 minutes on each side, or until they are well browned and tender. Serve the cutlets with *Spätzle* and spiced cranberry sauce.

Pasta and Grains

Cooking Pasta

PACKAGED pasta usually comes with directions for cooking. As a general rule, however, allow about 4 quarts water and 4 teaspoons salt for each pound of pasta. Bring the water to a boil in a large kettle and add the pasta gradually so that the water maintains a brisk boil. Cook the pasta according to taste, 8 to 10 minutes for *al dente*, until it is still firm to the teeth, or 10 to 15 minutes for tenderer pasta. If the shapes are large, as lasagne, cook only a few at a time, to prevent them from sticking together. Drain the pasta in a colander, pouring boiling water over them to remove any excess starch and to keep the shapes separated.

Pasta with Broccoli

DISCARD the hard outer leaves of a large head of broccoli. Separate the rest of the leaves from the flowers and cut the threads out of the stalks. Make several incisions in the central stem, but do not cut through it. Cook the stems and leaves in 1 1/2 quarts boiling salted water for 5 minutes, or until they are half done. Add the broccoli flowerets and cook the broccoli for a few minutes more. Remove the broccoli to a colander to drain and reserve the water.

In the same water cook 1 pound small pasta shapes—shells, snails, elbows, or the like—for a few minutes until they are almost tender, and drain them.

Sauté 2 garlic cloves, crushed, in 3 tablespoons each of olive oil and lard until they are golden brown and discard them. Add the broccoli to the pan and cook it for a few minutes.

Spread a baking dish with 1 1/2 tablespoons lard and fill it with alternate layers of pasta, broccoli, and grated Parmesan. Spread the last layer of cheese with 1 1/2 tablespoons lard, cut up, and bake the mixture in a hot oven (400° F.) for 10 minutes, or until the cheese is brown.

ᔒ Fettuccine alla Parmigiana

PUT 1 pound cooked *fettuccine*, or fine noodles, in a large bowl. Add 1 pound each of grated Parmesan and thinly sliced butter. Toss the pasta with a fork and spoon until the butter melts. Serve on heated plates.

ᔒ Linguine with Ricotta

COMBINE 1/2 pound *ricotta* cheese and 1/2 cup butter in a skillet and cook the mixture, stirring constantly, over low heat for about 8 minutes. Combine it gently with 1 pound cooked *linguine*, and sprinkle it generously with grated Parmesan and salt and pepper to taste.

ᔒ Sicilian Spaghetti

SAUTÉ 1 onion, chopped, in 2 tablespoons butter, until it is golden. Add 1 1/2 pounds tomatoes, peeled and chopped, and cook them over high heat, stirring occasionally, for about 5 minutes. Add to the sauce 10 anchovy filets, chopped, and 1/4 cup each of raisins, pine nuts, and chopped fennel and simmer the sauce a few minutes longer. Pour it over 1 pound cooked pasta.

Stuffed Baked Tufoli 🌶

COOK 1 pound *tufoli*—large elbow-shaped macaroni—in boiling salted water for 5 minutes. Rinse the *tufoli* in cold water and drain them. They should be just flexible enough to handle.

Sauté 1 onion, chopped, in 1/4 cup olive oil until it is golden brown. Add 1 teaspoon each of chopped parsley and salt and a pinch of pepper. Stir in 1 six-ounce can tomato paste and pour in slowly 4 cups boiling water. Cover the pan and simmer the sauce for 20 minutes. Pour half the sauce into a shallow baking dish.

Combine and mix thoroughly 1/2 pound each of beef and veal, ground, 2 beaten eggs, 2 tablespoons each of olive oil and grated Parmesan, 1 tablespoon chopped parsley, 1 teaspoon salt, and pepper to taste. Stuff the *tufoli* with this mixture and lay them side by side in the sauce. Cover the *tufoli* with the remaining sauce and bake them in a moderate oven (350° F.) for about 45 minutes, or until they are well done.

GREEK MACARONI CASSEROLE

Pastitsio 🌶

MELT 1/2 cup butter and in it brown 2 pounds ground lean beef and 2 onions, chopped, stirring constantly. Add 1/4 cup dry white wine mixed with 4 tablespoons tomato paste and 1/2 teaspoon cinnamon. Simmer the mixture over low heat until the meat is cooked. Add salt and pepper to taste and beat in 2 eggs, well beaten, and 3 tablespoons bread crumbs.

Cook 1 pound macaroni in boiling salted water until it is just tender and drain it well. Put half the macaroni into a large buttered baking dish, sprinkle it with 1/3 cup grated Parmesan, and spread it with the meat mixture. Add the remaining macaroni and sprinkle it with another 1/3 cup grated Parmesan. Pour 3 cups thin white sauce over all, sprinkle with another 1/3 cup grated cheese, and dot generously with butter. Bake the *pastitsio* in a hot oven (400° F.) for about 30 minutes, or until the topping melts and browns.

Fagottini 🌶

DISSOLVE 1 package of yeast in 1/2 cup lukewarm water. Sift 2 cups sifted flour onto a pastry board, make a well in the center, and pour in the dissolved yeast and 1 cup lukewarm water. Blend the dough with the hands and knead it until it is smooth and elastic. Turn the dough into a buttered bowl, cover it with a damp towel, and let it rise in a warm place for 2 hours. Roll out the dough on the lightly floured board into a very thin sheet, and cut it into 2 1/2-inch circles.

Mix together 1/2 pound mozzarella, diced, 10 anchovy filets, drained and cut into pieces, 1 tablespoon chopped parsley, and 1/4 teaspoon each of salt and pepper. Place a generous teaspoon of the filling in the center of each circle of dough and fold the circles in half, gathering the edges together tightly to form a little bundle. Fry the bundles in deep hot fat (370° F.) until they are crisp and golden and drain them on absorbent paper.

Dough for Pasta

SIFT 2 cups sifted flour onto a large pastry board and make a well in the center. In the well drop 2 eggs, 4 eggshell halves of water, 4 tablespoons olive oil, and 1/4 teaspoon salt, and blend the dough thoroughly with the fingers. Knead and stretch and beat the dough against the board, adding a little flour as necessary, for 20 minutes. When the dough is blistered and smooth as silk, divide it in half. Roll out one half into a round. Hang half the dough over the edge of the board. Roll the rest of the dough away from you twice (lift the pin to bring it back; don't roll it back across the dough). Then stretch the dough and roll it twice from side to side, keeping it tightly under the pin. Reverse the dough and roll the part that hung over the board in the same manner, flouring it very lightly as you go. Continue rolling the dough until it is 1/16 inch thick. Dust it lightly with flour, roll it up, and cut it to the desired width. Repeat the rolling procedure for the remaining dough. Shake out the pasta, or lay it flat, and let it dry for at least 1 hour before cooking. Cook the pasta in 2 quarts boiling salted water until it is *al dente* and drain it. Makes about 3/4 pound pasta, or about 4 servings.

Trenette

MAKE dough for pasta and follow the procedure for rolling, only roll out each piece as thinly as possible. Each sheet should be quite translucent and large enough almost to cover a big breadboard. Dust the dough very lightly with flour, roll it up lengthwise, and, with a very sharp knife, cut it into pieces less than 1/8 inch thick. Gently shake out each length and hang it up on a chair back to dry, or spread the lengths on a cloth. Let the *trenette* dry for 1 hour or more. Cook the pasta in 4 quarts boiling salted water, stirring occasionally, for 5 minutes, and drain it. Serve with *pesto*. Makes about 4 servings.

Baked Lasagne 𝕊◗

MAKE dough for pasta and divide the dough into 4 parts. Roll out each piece 1/16 inch thick as for pasta and cut each sheet into strips 1 1/2 inches wide. Add 4 drops of olive oil to a kettle filled with boiling salted water. Drop in the strips and cook the pasta for 2 or 3 minutes. Drain the pasta and immediately plunge it into cold water. Drain it again and spread it on a pastry board to dry.

To make the filling, melt 2 tablespoons butter in a saucepan, stir in 2 teaspoons flour, and add gradually 1 1/4 cups milk. Cook the sauce, stirring, until it is thickened. Beat 2 egg yolks and warm them with a little of the hot sauce. Add the egg yolks to the sauce very gradually, stirring constantly with a wire whisk, and heat it slowly. Do not let the sauce boil. Blend the cream sauce thoroughly into the filling for ravioli.

Prepare 2 3/4 cups Bolognese meat sauce. Fill a large baking dish with alternate layers of meat sauce, lasagne, and filling, finishing with a layer of sauce and 1/4 pound mozzarella, thinly sliced. Bake the lasagne in a hot oven (400° F.) for about 30 minutes, or until the cheese is bubbly.

Filling for Ravioli

CUT into small dice 1 chicken breast, boned, 6 ounces each of lean pork (or *mortadella* sausage) and lean beef, 2 ounces veal, and 1 pair of sweetbreads, soaked, blanched, and trimmed. Melt 2 tablespoons butter in a heavy skillet, add the diced meats, 1 branch of fresh rosemary or a small handful of dried rosemary, and salt and pepper to taste, and sauté the mixture until the meat is tender. Put the mixture through the coarsest blade of a food chopper, or chop it finely. Wash 2 pounds spinach thoroughly and cook it in the water that clings to its leaves for about 5 minutes. Drain the spinach, pressing out any remaining moisture, and chop it finely. Add salt and pepper to taste. Combine the chopped meat and spinach lightly but thoroughly with 3 teaspoons grated Parmesan, a pinch each of nutmeg and cinnamon, a little salt, and 2 eggs, slightly beaten.

✺ Lasagne and Spinach Casserole

HEAT 4 tablespoons olive oil in a saucepan and add 1/4 pound each of Italian fresh "sweet" pork sausage and Italian fresh "hot" pork sausage, both peeled and chopped, 2 teaspoons fresh chopped basil, 2 garlic cloves, chopped, and a pinch each of salt and pepper. Sauté the mixture for 3 or 4 minutes and add 1 six-ounce can tomato paste and 4 cups canned Italian-style tomatoes, well mashed or sieved. Simmer the sauce until it is fairly thick.

Cook 1 pound lasagne and fill an oiled baking dish with alternate layers of the lasagne, spinach and *ricotta* filling, and sausage and tomato sauce, finishing with the sauce and grated Romano or Parmesan cheese. Bake the dish in a hot oven (425° F.) for 15 minutes, or until the cheese is browned.

Spinach and Ricotta Filling

MIX lightly but thoroughly with a fork 1 pound *ricotta* cheese, 1/2 cup grated Parmesan, 1/2 pound spinach, cooked, well drained, and finely chopped, 3 eggs, beaten, 2 or 3 tablespoons lukewarm water, and salt, pepper, and a good dash of nutmeg.

✺ Lasagne with Pesto

FILL a heated baking dish with alternate layers of *pesto* (basil sauce) and cooked lasagne, finishing with a layer of sauce and grated Parmesan. Bake the lasagne in a hot oven (400° F.) for about 20 minutes, or until the topping is browned.

✺ Dough for Egg Pasta

SIFT 4 cups sifted flour onto a large pastry board, make a well in the center, and put in 3 eggs, lightly beaten. Add 2 teaspoons salt and mix the flour into the eggs, a little at a time. Add, a few drops at a time, 1/4 to 1/2 cup lukewarm water, or just enough to make the dough soft enough to knead. Flour the board lightly and knead the dough with the heel of the hand for 10 to 12 minutes, or until it is smooth and elastic. Use as the recipe indicates.

Cappelletti in Broth 🐟

MIX together 3 slices *prosciutto*, thinly sliced Italian ham, 1/4 pound cooked chicken, and 1/8 pound roast pork, all chopped, 1 egg, 2 teaspoons grated Parmesan, 1/4 teaspoon salt, and 1/8 teaspoon each of black pepper and nutmeg.

Roll out the dough for egg pasta thinly and cut it into 2 1/2-inch circles. Put 1 teaspoon filling in the center of each circle, fold the circles in half, enclosing the filling, and pull the edges together to give each the shape of a little dunce cap. Bring 2 quarts chicken stock to a boil and add the *cappelletti*. Cook them for 8 to 10 minutes, or until they are tender, and drain them carefully. Or serve them in hot beef or chicken consommé for a hearty soup.

Manicotti 🐟

CREAM 1 pound *ricotta* cheese and blend in 1/4 pound chopped cooked ham, 2 eggs, and salt and pepper to taste. Roll out the dough for egg pasta thinly, cut it into 3-inch squares, and let it dry for 1 hour. Put 1 1/2 tablespoons filling on each square, roll up the squares, and press the edges together. Cook the *manicotti* in 3 to 4 quarts boiling salted water for about 10 minutes, or until they are tender. Remove the *manicotti* with a perforated spoon and drain them carefully. Put them in individual baking dishes and cover with tomato sauce. Bake the *manicotti* in a hot oven (400° F.) for 10 minutes.

Dough for Green Noodles 🐟

COOK 1/2 pound spinach in the water clinging to the leaves until it is just soft and put it through a fine-meshed sieve. If the spinach is very wet, heat it in a saucepan for 1 minute to evaporate the moisture, and cool it.

Sift 4 cups sifted flour and 1 teaspoon salt onto a large pastry board, make a well in the center, and in it put 2 eggs, well beaten, and the puréed spinach. Using the fingers, mix the paste gradually until it is well blended. If all the flour is not incorporated, add a few drops of water; if the paste is too soft, add more flour. Knead the dough thoroughly for at least 12 minutes, or until it is smooth and elastic. Divide the dough into 4 pieces and, with a rolling pin, roll out each piece 1/16 inch thick. Roll up the sheets, cut the rolls crosswise into strips of the desired width, and let them dry for 30 minutes. Use as the recipe indicates.

✒ Cannelloni Filled with Cheese

COOK 1 pound wide green noodles until they are almost tender and drain them on damp towels. Cut the noodles into 4-inch squares or into rectangles and transfer them to dry towels liberally sprinkled with grated Parmesan.

Combine and blend thoroughly 1 pound *ricotta* cheese, 1 cup each of grated Parmesan and ground cooked ham, 1/4 cup minced parsley, 1 garlic clove, minced, 2 eggs, and salt and pepper to taste. Put 1 tablespoon of the stuffing in the center of each square or rectangle, and roll up the noodles. Lay them side by side in the center of a large rectangular buttered baking dish and sprinkle them lavishly with grated Parmesan. On one side of the noodles pour in a layer of tomato meat sauce, and on the other a layer of béchamel sauce seasoned with nutmeg. Cover the dish with foil and bake the *cannelloni* in a slow oven (325° F.) for about 20 minutes, or until they are heated through.

✒ Buttered Noodles

TOSS 3/4 pound cooked noodles with 4 tablespoons each of butter and toasted bread crumbs.

✒ Noodles with Cottage Cheese

COMBINE 1 pound cottage cheese with 3/4 cup hot water, 3 tablespoons melted butter, and 2 tablespoons olive oil. Beat the mixture until it is smooth and add salt and pepper to taste. Heat the sauce in the top of a double boiler over hot water and stir it into 1 pound cooked noodles.

✒ Pot Cheese Noodles

CREAM 1/4 cup butter until it is light and fluffy and beat in 1/2 cup pot cheese and 1 egg. Add 1 1/4 cups or more sifted flour, to make a soft dough, and 1/2 teaspoon salt. Mix the dough well and roll it out on a floured board into a very thin rectangle. Roll the sheet up tightly and cut the roll into strips 1/4 inch wide. Spread the noodles on the board to dry for several hours. Cook the noodles in boiling salted water for 8 minutes and drain them. Serve with melted butter and poppy seeds.

Cannelloni Filled with Cheese

ᘯ Truffled Egg Noodles NOUILLES TRUFFÉES

MAKE dough for egg pasta and divide the dough into 4 parts. Roll out each part, one at a time, as thinly as possible on a lightly floured board. Flour the sheets lightly, roll them up, and cut the rolls into strips about 1/4 inch wide. Spread the strips on towels to dry for at least 20 minutes.

Drop the noodles into 4 quarts boiling salted water and cook them for 5 minutes, or until they are just tender. Drain the noodles, toss them with 1/2 cup soft butter, and season with salt and coarsely ground pepper to taste. Stir in 1/2 cup finely chopped truffles and 1/4 cup hot heavy cream. Serve on heated plates.

ᘯ Noodles Charlotte

MASH 2 pounds farmer cheese with 2 cups sour cream, 3/4 cup sugar, 2 eggs, beaten, and 1 small can crushed pineapple, drained, and combine with 1/2 pound cooked wide egg noodles. Brown 1 tablespoon butter in a 12-inch square baking dish in a very hot oven (450° F.). Pour in the noodle mixture and bake it for 30 minutes.

ᘯ Potato Gnocchi

MASH 2 pounds hot cooked potatoes or put them through a ricer. Beat in 2 tablespoons butter, 2 eggs, lightly beaten, and salt and white pepper to taste. Sift in 2 cups sifted flour, to make a stiff dough, and mix and knead the dough until it is smooth. Shape the dough into long rolls the thickness of a finger and cut the rolls into 3/4-inch pieces. Press each piece with a thumb to make a rough crescent shape. Cook the *gnocchi*, a few at a time, in a large kettle of boiling salted water for about 10 minutes, or until they rise to the surface. Remove the *gnocchi* with a perforated spoon and arrange them in a heated baking dish. Sprinkle them generously with melted butter and grated Parmesan and set the dish in a moderate oven (350° F.) for a few minutes until the cheese melts. Serve in the baking dish.

ᘯ Ricotta Gnocchi with Mushroom Sauce

PUT 1 pound *ricotta* cheese through a medium-fine sieve and stir in 1/2 cup each of grated Parmesan and melted butter, 4 eggs, 6 tablespoons flour, and salt, pepper, and nutmeg to taste. Form the mixture into small balls and drop them, a few at a time, into simmering water. (If a test dumpling does not hold together, add a little more flour.) Cook the *gnocchi* for 4 to 5 minutes, or until they rise to the top and seem springy. Drain them and put them in a serving dish. Cover them generously with mushroom sauce and sprinkle with grated Parmesan and melted butter. Bake the *gnocchi* in a moderate oven (350° F.) for about 10 minutes.

Corn Meal with Cheese 🦃

IN the top of a double boiler bring to a boil 6 cups water with 1 teaspoon salt. Stir in very gradually 2 cups corn meal and cook it for about 5 minutes, stirring constantly, until the mixture is thick and smooth. Put the pan over boiling water and cook the mush for 30 minutes, stirring occasionally and adding more boiling water if necessary. Butter a shallow casserole and spread half the corn-meal mush in the bottom. Sprinkle it thickly with 1 1/2 cups shredded Cheddar cheese, add the remaining mush, and cover with 2 1/2 cups thick sour cream. Bake the mixture in a moderately hot oven (375° F.) for 10 minutes.

Bulgur 🦃

SAUTÉ 3 onions, chopped, in 1/3 cup oil until they are golden. Add 3 cups bulgur, or cracked wheat, and cook it, stirring, until it is well coated with the oil. Add 7 cups boiling chicken or beef stock and salt and pepper to taste, cover the pan, and cook the bulgur slowly until the grains are tender.

Kasha and Onion Casserole 🦃

HEAT 1 tablespoon butter or rendered chicken fat in a heavy skillet. Add 1 1/2 cups *kasha*, or coarse buckwheat groats, and cook them over moderate heat, stirring constantly, for 10 minutes. Add 1/3 cup finely chopped onion, 3 tablespoons butter, salt and pepper to taste, and 4 cups chicken stock. Cover the pan and cook the *kasha* over low heat, stirring occasionally, for 25 minutes. If it becomes too dry, add a little

Kasha with Noodles and Peas

boiling water. Stir in 1 cup cooked small white onions, browned in 2 tablespoons butter or rendered chicken fat, and turn the *kasha* into a baking dish. Cover the dish and bake the *kasha* in a moderate oven (350° F.) for 30 minutes. It should be tender but moist.

Kasha with Noodles and Peas ❧

IN a heavy skillet heat 1 1/2 cups *kasha*, or coarse buckwheat groats, for 1 minute, stir in 1 egg, and cook the mixture, stirring, over low heat until it is dry and the grains are well coated with the egg. Add 4 cups chicken stock and salt to taste, cover the skillet, and simmer the *kasha* over low heat for 30 minutes, or until the groats are tender and the stock is absorbed. If it becomes too dry, add a little boiling water. Toss the *kasha* lightly with 6 tablespoons butter, using a fork to keep the grains separated. Add 1/2 pound hot cooked noodle shells, 1 cup hot cooked peas, and a little melted butter.

Boiled Rice ❧

WASH 1 cup raw long-grained rice in warm water and drain it. In a large kettle bring to a rolling boil 2 quarts water with 2 teaspoons salt. Add the rice very slowly, reduce the heat, and boil the rice gently, uncovered, for 12 to 15 minutes, or until the grains are tender and have no hard center when pinched. Drain the rice at once in a colander or a sieve and pour boiling water through it to remove any loose starch and to separate the grains. Cover the colander with a cloth and set it over hot water on the back of the stove or in a warm oven for a short time. Just before serving, stir in a large nugget of sweet butter.

Steamed Rice ❧

IN a large saucepan combine 1 cup raw rice with 2 1/2 cups water, 1 tablespoon butter, 2 teaspoons lemon juice, and 1 teaspoon salt. Bring the liquid to a boil, stir the rice once with a fork, and cover the pan. Simmer the rice over very low heat for about 20 minutes, or until it is tender and the liquid is absorbed. Minced herbs or other seasonings may be added about 5 minutes before the cooking is finished.

Baked Rice

WASH 1 cup raw rice in several waters and drain it. Melt 2 tablespoons oil or butter in a flameproof baking dish, add the rice, and cook, stirring constantly, until the rice is golden brown. Add 1 teaspoon salt and 2 cups chicken stock and bake in a moderate oven (350° F.) for about 30 minutes, or until the rice is tender and the liquid absorbed. Add more chicken stock during the baking if needed.

Rice Ring

WHITE or brown rice may be pressed into a ring to serve as a border for other cooked and sauced foods. Season hot cooked rice with salt and pepper to taste and stir in 2 tablespoons butter. With the back of a fork press the rice into a well-oiled mold, let it stand for 8 to 10 minutes in a warm place, and turn it out on a heated platter.

Rice Pilaff

BREAK up 1 twist of vermicelli until the pieces are about the size of grains of rice. Brown the vermicelli in 1/4 cup butter with 1/2 onion, minced. Add 1 cup raw long-grained rice and cook it, stirring, until it is well coated with the butter. Add 2 cups boiling beef stock and salt and pepper to taste, cover the pan, and simmer the rice for 15 to 20 minutes, or until it is tender and the liquid is absorbed.

Rice Pilaff with Chicken Livers

IN 2 tablespoons melted butter quickly brown 1/2 pound chicken livers. Remove them from the pan with a slotted spoon and slice them. Add 4 tablespoons butter to the pan in which the livers were browned, and in it sauté 1 onion, chopped, until it is golden. Add 1 1/2 cups raw rice and 1/2 cup pine nuts, and sauté them until the rice is translucent. Soak 3/4 cup raisins in orange juice to cover for 30 minutes, and add the raisins and liquid to the mixture in the pan with 2 cups chicken stock and the livers. Cover the pan, bring the mixture to a boil, and cook the rice mixture for 10 minutes, or until the liquid is absorbed. Add another cup of chicken stock and continue cooking until the rice is tender and all the liquid is absorbed. Turn the pilaff onto a serving dish, and sprinkle it with finely chopped parsley.

Brown Rice Pilaff

RIZ BRUT EN PILAF

IN a large saucepan combine 3 cups chicken stock with 1 1/2 cups raw brown rice and 1 teaspoon turmeric. Cover the pan, bring the mixture to a boil, stir it once with a fork, and reduce the heat to the lowest possible point. Cook the rice for 45 minutes. Remove the pan from the heat and let the rice stand, covered, for 10 minutes.

Soak 1/4 cup currants in 1/4 cup Madeira for 30 minutes. Drain the currants and combine them with 1/2 cup minced scallions, 1/3 cup pine nuts, and 1 tablespoon minced preserved ginger. Stir the mixture into the rice.

Chinese Rice

WASH 1 cup raw rice first in cold water and then 6 times in warm water. Soak the rice in water to cover for 15 minutes and drain it. Put the rice in a heavy saucepan with 1 1/2 cups cold water, bring the liquid to a boil, and stir it once with a fork. Cover the pan and simmer the rice over the lowest possible heat for 25 minutes. Do not remove the cover during the cooking. If the liquid is not completely absorbed and the rice is not dry and soft, steam the rice, covered, for 3 to 5 minutes more. Remove the rice from the heat and let it stand, covered, for 5 minutes.

Mexican Rice

WASH, drain, and dry thoroughly 1 cup raw rice. Heat 3 tablespoons lard in a wide-bottomed saucepan, add the rice, and cook it, stirring constantly, until the grains begin to brown. Push the rice to one side and brown in the fat 2 or 3 garlic cloves, crushed or put through a press. Stir the garlic into the rice. Repeat this procedure with 1 onion, minced, and with 2 tomatoes, peeled and cut into pieces. Add 2 cups beef stock, cover the pan, and cook the rice slowly for about 20 minutes, or until it is tender and the liquid is absorbed. If necessary, add a little more stock.

ᔭ Nicaraguan Rice

SAUTÉ 1 small garlic clove and 3 tablespoons chopped onion in 2 tablespoons olive oil until the onion is golden. Add 1/2 cup drained cooked tomatoes, 1 small green pepper, seeded and chopped, 1 cup raw rice, 3/4 teaspoon salt, and 3 cups boiling water. Stir the mixture once with a fork and cover the pan. Simmer the rice for about 30 minutes, or until the liquid is absorbed and the rice is tender. Remove the cover during the last 5 minutes of cooking to let the rice dry.

ᔭ Persian Rice

SOAK 1 cup raw rice with a piece of rock salt tied in a cheesecloth in water to cover. Next day, drain the rice but do not rinse it. Slowly pour the rice into 2 quarts boiling salted water and boil it, uncovered, for 10 minutes. Drain the rice in a colander, pour lukewarm water over it 3 times, and shake the colander to allow air to pass through the rice.

Combine 1/4 cup melted butter with 1/2 cup water and pour half the mixture into a flameproof casserole. Shake the rice into the casserole so that it forms a cone-shaped mound. Sprinkle over the rice 1 small onion, finely minced, 1/4 cup seedless raisins, 2 tablespoons chopped dried dates, 1 1/2 tablespoons chopped dried apricots, and 1 tablespoon chopped blanched almonds. Pour the remaining butter and water mixture over the rice and simmer the mixture, covered, over very low heat for 30 minutes. A crisp, golden-brown crust will form on the bottom of the casserole. Serve this crisp portion separately.

Saffron Rice

STEEP 1/2 teaspoon saffron shreds in 1/2 cup warm chicken stock for 30 minutes. Drain the saffron and discard it, reserving the liquid. Put the saffron liquid in a large saucepan with 2 cups chicken stock, 1 cup raw rice, and salt to taste. Bring the liquid to a boil, cover the pan, and simmer the rice over low heat for about 25 minutes, or until it is tender and the liquid is absorbed.

South African Rice

IN a heavy saucepan combine 1 cup raw rice, 1 1/4 cups water, 1 teaspoon grated lemon rind, a 1-inch cinnamon stick, and a scant 1/2 teaspoon each of salt and turmeric. Cover the pan, bring the liquid to a boil, and simmer the rice for 15 minutes. Stir the rice once with a fork, add 3/4 cup seedless raisins, and cook the rice, covered, for about 20 minutes, or until it is tender and the liquid is absorbed. Combine 2 tablespoons melted butter with 3 tablespoons sugar and carefully stir the mixture into the rice. Arrange the rice in a buttered baking dish, dot it with butter, and put it in the broiler under low heat for 3 minutes.

Valencian Rice

SAUTÉ 2 onions, finely chopped, and 3 garlic cloves, minced, in 2 1/2 tablespoons olive oil, until the vegetables are golden. Add 1 1/4 cups raw rice and cook the mixture, stirring, until the grains are coated with oil. Stir in 4 peeled tomatoes and 3 pimientos, all chopped, 3 1/2 cups chicken stock, 1/4 teaspoon powdered saffron, a dash of cayenne, and salt to taste. Cook the rice, uncovered, over high heat for 10 to 15 minutes. Cover the pan, reduce the heat, and cook the rice for 5 to 10 minutes, or until it is tender and the liquid is absorbed.

Rice Croquettes

IN the top of a double boiler over hot water combine 2 1/2 cups cooked rice with 3 tablespoons hot milk, 2 1/2 tablespoons butter, 2 eggs, well beaten, 1 tablespoon each of parsley and chives, both finely chopped, and salt and pepper to taste. Cook the mixture, stirring, until it thickens. Spread the rice on a platter to cool and chill it thoroughly. Mold the cold rice into 12 croquettes. Roll them in seasoned dry bread crumbs, dip them in 1 egg beaten with 2 tablespoons milk, and roll them again in the bread crumbs. Fry the croquettes in deep hot fat (390° F.) until they are golden brown and drain them on absorbent paper.

Risotto Milanese

In a heavy saucepan sauté 1 small onion, finely chopped, in 4 tablespoons butter until it is golden. Add 2 tablespoons beef marrow and 1 cup raw rice and stir the mixture until the grains are well coated with butter. Add 2/3 cup dry white wine, cover the pan, and simmer the rice for about 8 minutes, or until the wine is absorbed. Add 1/2 teaspoon powdered saffron and 2 3/4 cups chicken stock, stir the rice once with a fork, and simmer it, covered, for about 30 minutes, or until the liquid is absorbed and the rice is fluffy. Add 2 tablespoons butter and 1/4 cup grated Parmesan and stir the rice lightly.

Risotto with Mussels

Clean 6 dozen mussels. In a deep saucepan heat 2 tablespoons olive oil with 2 tablespoons butter, 1 garlic clove, chopped, and 1/2 cup chopped parsley. Add the mussels and steam them, covered, for about 3 minutes, or until they open. Remove the meat from the shells and discard the shells. Strain the liquor and reserve it.

In a flameproof earthenware casserole, in 4 tablespoons butter, sauté 1 onion, finely chopped, until it is golden. Add 2 cups raw rice and cook it, stirring constantly, until it takes on color. Add 3 cups boiling chicken stock, 4 tablespoons white wine, the reserved mussel liquor, and salt and pepper to taste. Cook the mixture, stirring occasionally, for about 20 minutes, or until the rice is almost tender. Add the mussels, 2 tablespoons butter, and 1/4 cup grated Parmesan, and cook for about 5 minutes, or until the mussels are heated through and the grains of rice are tender. If necessary, add more stock, but the mixture should be dry.

Risotto alla Finanziera 🐾

SAUTÉ 2 tablespoons finely chopped onion in 4 tablespoons each of beef marrow and butter for 5 minutes. Add 8 chicken livers, diced, and 1 slice of lemon peel, 1 by 2 inches, and sauté them for 3 minutes. Add 1/4 cup dry Marsala and salt and pepper to taste and simmer the sauce for 10 minutes. Discard the lemon peel.

In another pan, in 4 tablespoons butter, sauté 2 tablespoons finely chopped onion until it is golden. Stir in 2 cups raw rice, cover the pan, and cook the rice for 2 to 3 minutes. Add 1 cup beef stock and simmer the rice, uncovered, until the liquid is absorbed. Repeat this procedure, using 4 to 5 cups beef stock in all, until the rice is cooked, 15 to 18 minutes. Correct the seasoning, add the sauce to the rice, and stir in 1/4 cup grated Parmesan. Transfer the *risotto* to a warm serving dish, sprinkle it with another 1/4 cup grated Parmesan, and dot it with butter.

Cheese and Rice Casserole 🐾

COOK 1 scant cup raw rice in boiling salted water for 13 minutes and drain it. The grains should be very firm. Combine 1/3 cup each of Provolone, Bel Paese, and Gruyère cheeses, all cut into cubes, with 1/2 cup each of diced cooked shrimp and grated Parmesan.

Butter generously a timbale or baking dish and spread the bottom with half the rice. Add the mixed cheeses and shrimp, dot with butter, and cover with the remaining rice. Sprinkle with 1/2 cup grated Parmesan and 3 tablespoons melted butter and set the casserole in a pan of water. Bake the casserole in a hot oven (400° F.) for about 35 minutes, or until the topping is a rich golden brown.

Chilean Paella 🐾

SAUTÉ 2 onions and 1 green pepper, both chopped, and 1 crushed garlic clove in 1/2 cup olive oil until the onion is golden. Stir in 2 cups raw rice and cook it, stirring, until the grains are coated with oil. Stir in 1 pimiento, sliced, and a pinch each of orégano and cuminseed. Add 5 cups chicken stock, 1 cup each of green beans and peas, 1 Italian sausage, cut in pieces, 1/2 pound Canadian bacon, diced, 1 small bottle of capers, drained, 1 teaspoon powdered saffron, a few peppercorns, and salt to taste. Cook the mixture, covered, for 25 minutes, or until the rice is tender and the liquid is absorbed.

Sauté 2 chicken breasts in 2 tablespoons each of oil and butter for about 20 minutes, or until they are tender. Do not overcook. Remove the skin and bones.

Split 2 lobsters in half and remove and discard the sac from behind the eyes. Heat 2 tablespoons each of oil and butter and in it sauté the lobsters, split side down, for 5 minutes. Cover the pan and continue to cook them until the shells turn bright red. Remove the meat from the shells and cut it into chunks.

Stir the lobster, chicken, and 1 pimiento, sliced, into the rice mixture. Arrange the *paella* on a large serving dish and surround it with a ring of artichoke hearts and cooked peeled shrimp. Put a sautéed mushroom on each artichoke.

ᔐ Cooking Wild Rice

WASH 1 cup raw wild rice in several waters until it is clean. Drain the rice, put it in a saucepan, and pour in 3 cups boiling water. Cover the pan and let the rice stand for 20 minutes. Drain the rice and repeat the procedure three times, adding 3 teaspoons salt with the final 3 cups boiling water. Season the rice with salt and pepper to taste, and stir in 3 tablespoons butter. Cover the pan of rice and set it over hot water or in a warm oven for 10 to 15 minutes before serving.

Or put the rice, well washed and drained, in a saucepan with 3 cups water and 1 teaspoon salt. Cover the pan, bring the liquid to a boil, and remove the cover. Boil the rice, without stirring, for about 30 minutes, or until it is tender and the liquid is absorbed. Keep it warm as above.

ᔐ Rosemary Wild Rice

SOAK 2 cups wild rice for 12 hours in cold water to cover. Wash the rice in several changes of water and put it in a flameproof casserole with 5 cups chicken stock, 1 teaspoon salt, and a little freshly ground pepper. Slowly bring the rice to a boil and add 3 tablespoons chopped parsley and 1/2 teaspoon dried rosemary. Cover the casserole, transfer it to a moderate oven (350° F.), and bake the rice for 35 to 40 minutes, or until it is tender and the liquid is absorbed. Stir in 3 tablespoons grated Parmesan. Lift the rice into a heated dish and sprinkle it with finely chopped chives.

Chilean Paella

Wild Rice and Currant Beignets

BRING to a boil 1/2 cup water, 1/4 cup butter, and a dash of salt. Remove the pan from the heat and add all at once 1/2 cup sifted flour. Return the pan to the heat and cook the mixture, stirring, until it forms a ball and cleanly leaves the sides of the pan. Remove the pan from the heat and add 2 eggs, one at a time, beating well after each addition. Add 3/4 cup cooked wild rice mixed with 1 tablespoon currants plumped in boiling water. Drop the batter by spoonfuls into deep hot fat (375° F.) and brown the *beignets* on both sides. Drain on absorbent paper.

Buttered Barley

IN a saucepan combine 3 cups water and 1 cup barley. Bring the liquid to a boil, add salt to taste, and simmer the barley, stirring from time to time, until all the water has been absorbed. Stir in 3 tablespoons butter and cook the barley very slowly until it is tender.

Barley Casserole

SAUTÉ 1 cup barley in 2 tablespoons butter, stirring, until it turns golden, and put in a buttered baking dish. Sauté 1 onion, diced, in 2 tablespoons butter and add it to the barley. In the same skillet sauté 3/4 cup sliced mushrooms in 1 tablespoon butter and add them to the dish. Add 1 cup chicken stock, cover the dish, and bake the barley in a moderate oven (350° F.) for 40 minutes. Add 1 more cup chicken stock, stir the barley, and cook it for another 40 minutes. Add another 1/2 cup chicken stock and cook the barley for 25 minutes more.

Vegetables

Cooking Whole Artichokes 🍃

WASH artichokes under cold running water, remove the tough or discolored outer leaves and, using a knife or scissors, cut off about 1/2 inch of the top leaves. Trim the base and stem of each with a sharp knife and put lemon slices on the bases to prevent discoloration. Tie the artichokes with kitchen thread to secure the leaves and lemon during cooking and cook them in a large quantity of boiling salted water acidulated with a little lemon juice for 40 to 50 minutes, or until they are tender. When a leaf pulls out easily, the artichokes are done.

Remove the strings and invert the artichokes to drain. Pull out and discard the yellow prickly leaves in the center and scrape out the hairy section, or choke, that covers the heart. Serve the artichokes hot with melted butter or hollandaise sauce or cold with vinaigrette sauce.

Artichokes Vinaigrette 🍃

TRIM 6 artichokes and cook them in boiling salted water with the juice of half a lemon, a few peppercorns, and 1 garlic clove. Simmer the artichokes for about 40 minutes, or until they are tender, and drain and cool them. Serve with vinaigrette sauce.

Artichoke Ring with Green Peas

Stuffed Artichokes 🌶

LOOSEN the leaves and remove the chokes from 6 firm artichokes and sprinkle the bottoms with lemon juice. Trim the leaves and cut off the stems flush with the base. Combine 1 1/2 cups bread crumbs, 1 1/2 tablespoons minced mint leaves, and 3 garlic cloves, finely chopped, with 3/4 cup olive oil and salt and pepper to taste. Stuff the artichokes with the mixture and stand them side by side in a roasting pan in 1 inch of water. Add a slice of lemon and 1 teaspoon salt to the water. Cover the pan and bake the artichokes in a moderate oven (350° F.) for about 1 hour, or until they are tender.

Cooking Artichoke Bottoms 🌶

REMOVE the stems of artichokes and pull off all the leaves level with the base. Peel the bottoms with a sharp paring knife, as you would a potato. Rub all the cut surfaces with lemon juice to prevent discoloration.

Bring to a boil 6 cups water, 1 tablespoon flour, 2 teaspoons salt, and the juice of 1 lemon, add the artichoke bottoms, and simmer them for about 30 minutes, or until the spiny chokes can be easily removed. Cool the bottoms and pull out the chokes, leaving a rim.

The artichoke bottoms, or *fonds*, are now ready for use in other preparations, or for stuffing.

Artichoke Ring with Green Peas 🌶

MAKE a thick white sauce by stirring 2 tablespoons flour into 2 tablespoons melted butter, slowly adding 1/2 cup warm light cream, and cooking the sauce until it is thick. Remove the sauce from the heat, add 1 teaspoon grated onion and 1/2 teaspoon salt, and let the sauce cool slightly. Stir in 4 egg yolks, lightly beaten, add 1/2 cup fine cracker crumbs, and fold in 2 cups mashed artichoke bottoms and lemon juice to taste.

Beat 4 egg whites until they are stiff and fold them into the artichoke mixture. Pour the mixture into a buttered ring mold, set the mold in a pan of warm water, and bake it in a moderate oven (350° F.) for about 45 minutes, or until it is set. Remove the ring from the oven and let it stand for a few minutes. Unmold it on a heated platter and fill the center with buttered green peas.

❧ Artichoke Bottoms and Peas

ARRANGE in a buttered baking dish 18 cooked artichoke hearts, 6 small white onions, and 2 cups green peas. Add 1 cup chicken stock, 1/4 cup olive oil, and salt and pepper to taste. Cover the dish and bake the vegetables in a hot oven (425° F.) for about 30 minutes, or until they are tender.

❧ Artichokes and Mushrooms in Cream

CHOP finely 2 pounds mushrooms and put them in a buttered baking dish. Bake the mushrooms in a moderately slow oven (325° F.) for about 10 minutes.

Chop finely 3 or 4 large cooked artichoke bottoms, sprinkling them in the process with lemon juice to prevent discoloration. Add the artichokes to the mushrooms with 3/4 cup béchamel sauce and blend the mixture well. Season to taste with freshly grated nutmeg. Increase the oven temperature to hot (400° F.) and bake the artichokes and mushrooms for 8 minutes. Combine 1/4 cup heavy cream, whipped, with 5 tablespoons hot melted butter and stir the sauce into the vegetables.

❧ Sautéed Artichoke Bottoms

SAUTÉ small cooked artichoke bottoms in butter until they are heated through. Turn them into a serving dish and sprinkle them with a little lemon juice and salt and pepper to taste.

❧ Artichoke Bottoms Bouquetière

FILL cooled cooked artichoke bottoms with a mélange of carrot and turnip balls, diced string beans, and green peas, all cooked and cooled. Sprinkle with vinaigrette sauce and finely chopped parsley.

❧ Artichoke Bottoms Choron   FONDS D'ARTICHAUTS CHORON

FILL cooked artichoke bottoms with fresh peas cooked *à la française* with lettuce, chopped onion, and a pinch of thyme.

Artichoke Bottoms Saint Germain ❧

FILL cooked artichoke bottoms with a thick purée of peas. Use a pastry tube to shape the purée into a large rosette.

Artichoke Bottoms Véronique ❧

FILL cooked artichoke bottoms with white grapes, peeled, seeded, and soaked in brandy. Sprinkle with melted butter and finely chopped parsley.

Cooking Green Beans ❧

TRIM the ends of green beans. If they are small, leave them whole. Cut large beans into 1-inch lengths or French them by slitting the beans and slicing them on the diagonal. Put the beans in a saucepan and add salted water barely to cover. Cover the pan tightly, simmer the beans over low heat for 10 to 15 minutes, or until they are tender but crisp, and drain them.

Baked Green Beans ❧

STIR 2 beaten egg yolks into 1 1/2 cups béchamel sauce, and pour 1/4 cup sauce into a buttered baking dish generously sprinkled with grated Swiss cheese. Arrange 1 1/2 pounds cooked green beans in the baking dish and cover them with the remaining sauce. Sprinkle 1/3 cup grated Swiss cheese over the beans and sauce and dot with 3 tablespoons butter. Bake the beans in a very hot oven (450° F.) for 15 minutes, or until the cheese is nicely browned.

Green Beans Italienne ❧

CUT in halves 1 1/2 pounds green beans, cook them with 1 small onion, sliced, and drain them. In another saucepan sauté 1 garlic clove, minced, in 4 tablespoons olive oil for 2 minutes. Add the beans and cook them, stirring, until they are lightly coated with the oil. Turn the beans into a serving dish and sprinkle them with toasted bread crumbs and grated Parmesan.

꒱ Green Beans with Parsley

CUT 1 1/2 pounds green beans into 1-inch lengths, cook them in chicken stock, and drain them. Toss the beans with 1/3 cup each of melted butter and minced parsley and 3 tablespoons lemon juice.

꒱ Green Beans Vinaigrette

COOK 1 1/2 pounds young green beans, drain them at once in a colander, and rinse them under cold running water to cool them quickly. Sprinkle the beans with salt and chill them. Arrange the beans on a platter, cover them with vinaigrette sauce, and sprinkle with chopped chervil or parsley.

꒱ Chilled Green Beans Hollandaise

COOK 1 1/2 pounds young green beans in 1/3 cup water, 1 tablespoon vegetable oil, and 1/8 teaspoon celery salt. Drain the beans and let them cool.

Chop and pound in a mortar 1 cup each of raw spinach and watercress leaves, a few sprigs of parsley and tarragon, and 2 tablespoons tarragon vinegar. Strain the mixture and add the essence to 1 cup hot hollandaise made with tarragon vinegar. Arrange the green beans in bundles on a chilled platter and decorate the bundles with ribbons of hollandaise.

꒱ Green Beans and Celery

SAUTÉ 1 cup celery, cut in thin crosswise slices, in 2 tablespoons butter for 8 minutes. Combine the celery with 1 1/2 pounds cooked Frenched green beans, season the vegetables with salt, and sprinkle them with paprika.

꒱ Green Beans and Chestnuts

COOK 1 1/2 pounds Frenched green beans, and chop coarsely 1 pound cooked chestnuts. Fill a buttered baking dish with alternating layers of the beans and chestnuts.

Dot each layer of chestnuts with butter and sprinkle with salt and pepper to taste. Bake the beans and chestnuts in a moderate oven (350° F.) for 20 minutes.

Baby Limas with Marjoram 🙜

HARICOTS DE LIMA À LA MARJOLAINE

MELT 6 tablespoons butter in a heavy skillet and stir in 2 teaspoons parsley, 1 teaspoon marjoram, and 1 small onion, all minced. Add 3 cups baby lima beans (about 1 1/2 pounds, shelled), and cook them, covered, over very low heat for about 20 minutes, or until they are barely tender.

SALADE DE HARICOTS JAUNES

Wax Beans Vinaigrette 🙜

ARRANGE 2 pounds cooked wax beans in a serving dish and chill them. Combine thoroughly 3/4 cup olive oil, 1/4 cup red-wine vinegar, 1 tablespoon each of capers and chopped green olives, 2 teaspoons finely chopped shallot, 1 teaspoon salt, and 1/2 teaspoon each of freshly ground black pepper and finely chopped fresh thyme. Pour the marinade over the wax beans and chill them for at least 24 hours.

Sautéed Beets 🙜

WASH, peel, and dice 12 beets. In a heavy saucepan melt 6 tablespoons butter, add the diced beets and a little salt and coarsely ground pepper, and sauté the beets over low heat, stirring constantly, for 1 minute. Cover the pan and cook the beets for about 15 minutes, stirring them frequently, until they are tender. Sprinkle the beets with finely chopped Italian parsley.

Shredded Beets 🙜

WASH, peel, and shred 12 large beets, and put them in a heavy saucepan with 3/4 cup butter, cut into small pieces. Season the beets with salt and freshly ground black pepper to taste and cook them over low heat, stirring constantly, until the butter has melted. Add 4 tablespoons water and cover the pan. Cook the beets for about 15 minutes, stirring occasionally. Sprinkle the beets with 2 teaspoons each of parsley and chives, minced, a pinch of dried tarragon, and the juice of 1/2 lemon.

ᔍ Stuffed Beets

SCRUB 12 large beets and cook them, covered, in simmering water for about 40 minutes, or until they are tender. Slip off the skins and trim the roots and stems. Scoop out the center pulp, leaving shells 1/4 inch thick. Combine 1 cup cooked rice with 1/2 cup chopped blanched almonds, 1/4 cup melted butter, 2 tablespoons minced chives, and salt and pepper to taste. Stuff the beets with the mixture and bake them in a moderate oven (350° F.) until they are heated through.

ᔍ Beets with Orange Sauce

IN the top of a double boiler, over hot but not boiling water, melt 1 tablespoon butter and blend in 4 tablespoons brown sugar mixed with 2 teaspoons flour. Stir in 3/4 cup orange juice and cook the mixture, stirring, until it is thickened. Add 1/8 teaspoon each of salt and pepper and 2 1/2 cups diced cooked beets. Cook the mixture, stirring, until the beets are heated through.

ᔍ Beet Greens

WASH 3 pounds tender young beet greens in several changes of water. Remove any wilted leaves but do not discard any tiny beets. Put the greens (and any beets) in a saucepan with 1/2 cup water, cook them, covered, for about 12 minutes, or until they are tender, and drain them. Chop finely, return them to the pan, and cook them, stirring, until all the moisture has evaporated. Stir in 1/4 cup butter, the juice of 1 lemon, and salt and pepper to taste.

ᔍ Beet Greens with Orange Sauce

SAUTÉ 1 onion, chopped, in 3 tablespoons bacon fat. Stir in 3 pounds tender young beet greens, washed and coarsely chopped. Cover the pan and cook the greens over low heat for about 15 minutes, or until they are tender. Drain the liquid from the pan into a small saucepan. Transfer the greens to a serving dish and keep them hot. Combine 1/4 cup orange juice and the juice of 1 lemon. Add 1 teaspoon cornstarch, dissolved in a little of the fruit juice. Stir this mixture into the pan juices and cook the sauce, stirring, until it is thick. Pour it over the beet greens and serve.

Carrot Purée ʃ♪

SLICE 2 pounds scraped young carrots, cover them with water, and add 1/2 teaspoon each of sugar and salt. Cook the carrots, covered, over low heat for about 15 minutes, or until all the water has been absorbed and the carrots are tender. Add 1/3 cup butter, mash the carrots, and season them with freshly ground black pepper and a dash of lemon juice. Pile the purée into a serving dish and sprinkle liberally with finely chopped parsley.

Carrots Julienne ʃ♪

CUT 2 pounds young carrots in julienne. (If the carrots are very tiny, leave them whole.) Put the carrots in a saucepan with 3 tablespoons each of butter and water and cook them, covered, for about 6 or 7 minutes, or until they are tender. Drain off any remaining water. Add salt and freshly ground pepper to taste and 6 or 7 mint leaves, finely shredded. Cook the carrots over low heat for a minute or two, shaking the pan gently.

Dilled Carrots ʃ♪

SCRAPE 2 pounds young carrots and cut them into quarters lengthwise. Simmer the carrots, covered, in 1 1/2 cups dill-pickle juice for 10 to 15 minutes, or until they are tender but still firm. Let the carrots cool and chill them overnight in the pickle juice.

Drain the carrots and sprinkle them with 3 tablespoons fresh dill and 1 1/2 tablespoons chives, both minced. Garnish the carrots with 1 1/2 cups sour cream.

Glazed Carrots ʃ♪

CUT 2 pounds scraped young carrots into balls with a vegetable cutter. Simmer the carrots in salted water to cover for 10 to 15 minutes, or until they are tender, and drain them. In a skillet melt 1/3 cup butter, add the carrots, and sprinkle them with

2 teaspoons each of minced parsley and sugar and 1/2 teaspoon paprika. Cook the carrots over moderate heat, shaking the pan constantly, until each carrot ball is well coated with the sauce.

𝕾 Lemon-Glazed Carrots

CUT 2 pounds scraped young carrots into small balls with a vegetable cutter. Simmer the carrot balls in salted water to cover for 10 to 15 minutes, or until they are tender, and drain them. In a skillet melt 1/2 cup butter and 2 tablespoons sugar, 2 teaspoons minced parsley, and the juice of 1 lemon. Sauté the carrots for 5 minutes, shaking the pan to coat each carrot ball with the sauce.

𝕾 Carrots and Grapes   CAROTTES ET RAISINS

SAUTÉ 2 pounds carrots, cut in thick diagonal slices, in butter for a few minutes. Sprinkle the carrots with 1/8 teaspoon sugar and cook, stirring, for a minute or two. Add 1 tablespoon vodka and 1/2 cup water. When the carrots are almost tender, add 1 cup Malaga grapes, seeded. Cover the pan and continue to cook the carrots until they are very tender. Season with salt and pepper to taste.

𝕾 Carrots and Mint   CAROTTES À LA MENTHE

SCRAPE 2 pounds young carrots and put them in a baking dish with 1 cup orange juice, 1/2 cup olive oil, 1 small piece of gingerroot, grated, and 1/2 teaspoon each of salt and sugar. Cover the dish and bake the carrots in a moderate oven for about 45 minutes, or until they are tender. Chill the carrots, drain them well, and serve on a bed of chopped fresh mint.

𝕾 Baked Carrots and Scallions

ARRANGE alternate rows of scraped young carrots and trimmed scallions in a buttered baking dish. Put 1 whole clove in each carrot. Sprinkle all with salt and sugar to taste and brush with melted butter. Cover the dish and bake the vegetables in a moderate oven (350° F.) for about 45 minutes, or until they are tender.

Carrots and Grapes

℘ Carrots with Sherry

CUT 2 pounds scraped young carrots in halves and cut the halves lengthwise. Sauté the carrots in 3 tablespoons butter, turning them until they are well coated. Sprinkle them with salt, pepper, and sugar to taste, add 1/2 cup Sherry, and simmer them gently for 5 minutes. Add water just to cover and slowly cook the carrots, covered, for about 14 minutes, or until they are tender. Cook the carrots, uncovered, over high heat until only a little sauce remains in the pan. Sprinkle with minced parsley.

℘ Carrots with Yoghurt

COOK 2 pounds scraped young carrots in salted water to cover for about 5 minutes. Drain the carrots, cool them, and cut them into 1/2-inch slices. Sprinkle the slices with seasoned flour and sauté them in 1/2 cup oil, turning frequently, until they are cooked through. Beat 2 cups yoghurt until it is smooth, pour it over the carrots, and add salt and pepper to taste.

℘ Carrot and Almond Ring   TURBAN DE CAROTTES ET D'AMANDES

IN a saucepan melt 2 tablespoons butter, add 2 tablespoons flour, and stir the *roux* until it is smooth. Add gradually 1/2 cup warm milk, bring the sauce to a boil, stirring constantly, and simmer it for 5 minutes. Remove the pan from the heat and add 2 cups mashed cooked carrots (about 1 pound), 1/2 cup finely grated blanched almonds, and 1/2 teaspoon salt. Blend in 4 egg yolks, lightly beaten, cook the mixture over very low heat for 4 to 5 minutes, and cool it.

Beat 4 egg whites until they are stiff and fold them into the carrot mixture. Pour the mixture into a buttered 9-inch ring mold, set the mold in a pan of hot water, and bake the carrot ring in a moderate oven (350° F.) for 50 to 60 minutes, or until it is firm. Let it stand for a minute or two and turn it out on a platter. Fill the center with buttered green peas and garnish the platter with parsley.

℘ Cooking Asparagus

WASH the asparagus, snap off the tough ends, trim the stalks evenly, and peel the stalks a few inches below the tips to remove the scales. Tie the asparagus into bundles and stand the bundles, tips up, in the bottom of a double boiler half full of boiling water. Cover the pan with the inverted top of the double boiler and cook the asparagus stalks briskly for about 10 minutes, or until they are just tender. The stalks cook in the boiling water and the tips cook in the steam. Later in the season asparagus may need to be cooked an extra minute or two, but do not overcook. Put the drained bundles on a serving dish and remove the strings. Allow 3 pounds asparagus for 6 to 8 servings.

Hot Asparagus Vinaigrette

COOK 3 pounds asparagus, arrange the drained bundles on a serving dish, and remove the strings. Pour vinaigrette sauce over the asparagus and sprinkle with chopped parsley.

Asparagus Vinaigrette

COOK 10 pounds asparagus, tied into 25 bundles, drain them, and let them cool. Arrange the bundles on platters and remove the strings. Sprinkle each bundle with 1 teaspoon vinaigrette sauce and with a little chopped parsley, and serve without chilling. Makes 25 servings.

Asparagus Polonaise

COOK 3 pounds asparagus, arrange the drained bundles on a platter, and remove the strings. Pour a little polonaise sauce over each bundle of stalks and sprinkle with chopped hard-cooked egg.

Asparagus with Lemon Crumbs

ASPERGES AUX MIETTES CITRONNÉES

COOK 3 pounds asparagus, arrange the drained bundles on a serving dish, and remove the strings. Brown 1/2 cup bread crumbs lightly in 1/2 cup melted butter.

Glazed Asparagus and Westphalian Ham

Add the grated rind of 2 lemons and salt and pepper to taste. Sprinkle the lemon crumbs over the hot asparagus and the browned butter over all.

Parmesan Asparagus

COOK 3 pounds asparagus, arrange the drained bundles in a wide shallow baking dish, and remove the strings. Pour 6 tablespoons melted butter over the stalks, sprinkle 1/2 cup grated Parmesan over the tips, and bake the asparagus in a hot oven (400° F.) for about 10 minutes, or until the cheese is lightly browned.

Glazed Asparagus and Westphalian Ham

COOK 4 pounds asparagus, tied into 8 bundles, drain them, and let them cool. Remove the strings and put the stalks on a wire rack set over a baking sheet. Spoon cool but still liquid aspic over the stalks, chill them well, and serve on a bed of overlapping slices of Westphalian ham. Garnish with a lettuce leaf filled with sieved hard-cooked eggs and capers. Makes 8 servings.

Asparagus Soufflé

COOK 3 pounds asparagus, drain the bundles, reserving the cooking water, and remove the strings. Force the asparagus through a sieve or purée it in a blender to make 1 1/2 cups purée. Melt a generous 1/4 cup butter in a heavy saucepan, stir in 6 tablespoons flour, and add gradually 3/4 cup milk and 1/4 cup of the reserved water. Cook the sauce over low heat, stirring constantly, until it thickens. Add the asparagus purée and cool the sauce slightly. Beat in 4 egg yolks, season with salt and pepper to taste, and fold in 6 egg whites, stiffly beaten. Pour the mixture into a buttered soufflé dish, set the dish in a pan of water only slightly larger than the dish, and bake the soufflé in a moderately hot oven (375° F.) for about 45 minutes, or until it is puffed and brown. Brown 3/4 cup bread crumbs in 1 cup butter and add 1 teaspoon grated orange rind and salt to taste. Serve the soufflé at once, with the brown butter sauce in a sauceboat.

Potatoes in Butter

CUT potatoes into various shapes and parboil them in salted water for 5 minutes. Drain the potatoes and sauté them quickly in clarified butter until they are golden and soft.

Or sauté raw potatoes, cut in various shapes, in clarified butter until they are cooked through and golden, and season them with salt and pepper.

Alsatian Potatoes

CUT potatoes in the shape of large almonds, parboil them in salted water for 5 minutes, and drain them. Sauté the potatoes in clarified butter until they are golden and soft, and serve them with chopped sautéed onions and a generous sprinkling of minced parsley.

Baloise Potatoes

CUT potatoes into slices and sauté them in clarified butter, turning frequently but carefully to avoid breaking, until they are golden and soft. Season the potatoes with salt and pepper and arrange them in a deep serving dish.

Bartholy Potatoes

PARBOIL small new potatoes in salted water for 5 minutes, drain them, and sauté them in clarified butter until they are golden and soft. Just before the potatoes are cooked, stir in a small amount of *glace de viande*, or meat extract.

Bernoise Potatoes

CUT potatoes into 1/2-inch cubes, parboil them in salted water for 5 minutes, and drain them. Sauté the potatoes in clarified butter until they are golden and soft, season them with salt, and sprinkle with mixed chopped herbs.

Potatoes Berrichonne

CUT potatoes into ball shapes, parboil them in salted water for 5 minutes, and drain them. Sauté the potatoes in clarified butter until they are golden and soft, and serve them with chopped sautéed onions, a sprinkling of *fines herbes*, and crisp bacon dice.

Brabant Potatoes

CUT potatoes into tiny dice, parboil them in salted water for 5 minutes, and drain them. Sauté the potatoes in clarified butter with finely chopped shallots, allowing 1 shallot for 2 large potatoes, until they are golden and soft, and sprinkle them with chopped parsley.

Château Potatoes

CUT potatoes into large olive shapes, season them with salt and pepper, and sauté them in clarified butter until they are golden and soft. Sprinkle with chopped parsley.

Continental Potatoes

CUT potatoes into semicircular slices, sauté them slowly in clarified butter until they are golden and soft, and blend them with finely chopped truffles.

Potatoes Nanette

CUT potatoes into slices and sauté them in clarified butter until they are golden and almost soft. Arrange the potatoes in a baking dish, sprinkle them with chives and parsley, both finely chopped, and moisten them with a little veal stock. Finish the cooking in a moderate oven (350° F.).

ᶘᶕ Noisette Potatoes   POMMES DE TERRE NOISETTE

WITH a ball cutter scoop out rounds of potatoes the size of hazelnuts. Sauté the potatoes in clarified butter until they are golden and soft, and season them with salt and pepper.

ᶘᶕ Potatoes Parisienne   POMMES DE TERRE À LA PARISIENNE

WITH a ball cutter scoop out potatoes in rounds smaller than hazelnuts. Sauté the potatoes in clarified butter until they are golden and soft, and serve them with a sprinkling of chopped parsley.

ᶘᶕ Pimiento Potatoes   POMMES DE TERRE ESPAGNOLE

CUT potatoes into large olive shapes, parboil them in salted water for 5 minutes, and drain them. Sauté the potatoes in clarified butter until they are golden and soft. Stir in strips of pimiento and sprinkle the potatoes with a mixture of parsley, chervil, and chives, all finely chopped.

ᶘᶕ Steamed New Potatoes in Their Jackets
POMMES DE TERRE NOUVELLES À LA VAPEUR

SCRUB 18 small new potatoes, without removing the skin, or remove a small strip of skin from around the middle. Put the potatoes on a rack in a steamer, cover the pot, and steam the potatoes for 20 to 30 minutes, or until they are tender but not too soft. Dry the potatoes on absorbent paper. Heat 6 tablespoons clarified butter in a large skillet and roll the potatoes in the butter until they are completely coated. Sprinkle with 1 teaspoon ground mace.

ᶘᶕ New Potatoes with Parsley

COOK 18 unpeeled new potatoes, covered, in simmering salted water for 20 to 25 minutes, or until they are just tender. Drain them and slip off the skins. Heat 1/2 cup butter in a skillet and roll the potatoes in the butter until they are well coated. Sprinkle them generously with finely chopped parsley and lightly with salt.

New Potatoes with Chives

FOLLOW the procedure for new potatoes with parsley, but sprinkle the buttered potatoes with 2 tablespoons finely minced chives and salt to taste.

Baking Potatoes

SELECT large mealy potatoes, such as the Idaho variety, and scrub them thoroughly. Wipe the potatoes dry and spread them lightly with butter. Put the potatoes on a rack in a hot oven (400° F.) and bake them for 30 minutes. Pull out the rack, prick the potatoes in several places with a fork, and bake them for about 30 minutes more, or until they are tender when pierced with a fork.

Charcoal-Roasted Potatoes

WRAP 6 baking potatoes in aluminum foil and bury them in hot coals for about 45 minutes, or until they feel soft when pierced with a fork. Serve the potatoes with plenty of butter, salt and pepper, and grated Cheddar.

Macaire Potatoes

POMMES DE TERRE MACAIRE

BAKE 6 large baking potatoes, halve them lengthwise, and scoop out and mash the pulp. Add 6 tablespoons butter to the purée, beat well, and season with salt and pepper to taste. Form the mixture into 6 thick patties and brown the patties on both sides in butter.

Cheese-Stuffed Potatoes

BAKE 6 medium baking potatoes, cut lengthwise slices from the tops, and scoop out the pulp. Mash the pulp with 6 tablespoons milk or heavy cream, 4 tablespoons butter, 1/2 cup grated Cheddar, and celery salt and pepper to taste. Beat the purée

well and fill the potato shells. Ridge the stuffing with a knife, sprinkle it with more
grated Cheddar, and bake the stuffed potatoes in a hot oven (400° F.) until they
are browned.

❧ Orange-Stuffed Potatoes

BAKE 4 large baking potatoes, halve them lengthwise, and scoop out the pulp. Mash
the pulp with 4 tablespoons butter, 3 tablespoons heavy cream, 2 egg yolks, the
grated rind of 2 oranges, and salt to taste. Add enough orange juice to make a soft
purée. With a pastry tube pipe the purée into 6 of the potato shells and decorate
them with rosettes. Bake the potatoes in a hot oven (400° F.) until they are golden
brown.

❧ Stuffed Potatoes Palestine

BAKE 3 large baking potatoes, halve them crosswise, and scoop out the pulp. Mash
the pulp with 1/2 cup butter, 1/4 cup sour cream, 2 cups puréed Jerusalem artichokes, and salt and pepper to taste. Pile the stuffing into the potato shells. Set
the shells upright and pipe a border of the remaining stuffing around the edges.
Bake the stuffed potatoes in a hot oven (400° F.) until they are golden brown.

❧ Stuffed Potatoes Soubise

BAKE 6 medium baking potatoes, cut lenghtwise slices from the tops, and scoop out
the pulp. Mash the pulp with 4 tablespoons hot milk, 2 tablespoons butter, 2 egg
yolks, and salt, cayenne, and freshly grated nutmeg to taste. Fill the potato shells
with the stuffing, mounding the tops high. Make a depression in the center of each
and fill it with thick soubise sauce. Sprinkle the potatoes with grated Parmesan and
brown them lightly under the broiler.

❧ French Fried Potatoes

PEEL potatoes and cut them into pieces about as long and thick as the little finger.
Wash the pieces in cold water and dry them well. Cook them in deep hot fat or

oil (375° F.) for 7 to 8 minutes, or until they are soft but just beginning to brown. Remove the potatoes from the fat and drain them on absorbent paper. Heat the fat until the thermometer registers 390° F. to 400° F. and return the potatoes. Cook them for 1 or 2 minutes more, or until they are golden brown and crisp. Drain the potatoes, sprinkle them with salt, and serve at once. Do not cover the potatoes after they are cooked.

POMMES DE TERRE ALLUMETTES   Matchstick Potatoes

PEEL potatoes, cut them into thin matchlike pieces, and dry them thoroughly on a towel. Fry them in deep hot fat (375° F.) for 4 to 5 minutes, or until they are golden brown. Drain them well on absorbent paper and sprinkle them with salt.

NIDS DE POMMES DE TERRE   Potato Nests

PEEL 2 pounds potatoes and put them in cold water, to prevent discoloration. Shred the potatoes finely, keeping the shreds in cold water until all the potatoes are used. Drain the potatoes and dry them thoroughly.

Dip the larger half of a 5 1/2-inch bird's nest fryer into hot fat and line the bottom and sides with shredded potatoes. Dip the smaller wire basket into hot fat and press it into the bottom of the potato nest, clamping the handles together. Trim off any pieces of potato that extend above the rims of the baskets. Plunge the potato nest into deep hot fat or rendered beef suet (375° F.) and fry it until it is crisp and golden brown. Carefully remove the small top basket and unmold the potato nest on a platter. Fill with souffléed potatoes and serve hot.

POMMES DE TERRE SOUFFLÉES   Souffléed Potatoes

PEEL uniform baking potatoes and trim them so that all the surfaces are regular. Cut the potatoes lengthwise into long, narrow, and even slices a scant 1/8 inch thick or into pointed ovals uniformly thick. Use a mechanical slicer if possible, for much of the success of *pommes de terre soufflées* depends on the evenness of the slices. Wash the slices in cold water and dry them thoroughly on a towel.

Half fill a kettle, equipped with a handle and a deep-fat thermometer, with rendered beef suet. Heat the fat until the thermometer registers 275° F. and drop the potato slices, one at a time, into the fat. With a perforated spoon or strainer raise the slices, one at a time, from the hot fat for a few seconds and return them to the kettle for about 8 minutes, or until they begin to swell. Drain the potatoes on absorbent paper and cool them for at least 5 minutes before the final frying. Chill them for a longer time, if possible.

For the final frying, heat the fat to 400° F. and lower the potatoes, a few at a time, into the fat. The extreme heat will cause them to puff into small balloons. Turn the puffs until they are well browned on both sides. Remove them from the fat and drain them on absorbent paper. Sprinkle them with salt and serve at once.

The first part of the process may be done in advance. After the first frying, remove the potatoes from the kettle of hot fat when they are well puffed and lightly golden. Drain them well on absorbent paper and leave them between towels for several hours or even overnight. They will deflate but will puff again during the second frying in fat heated to 400° F.

Mashed Potatoes

PEEL 2 pounds potatoes, cut them into quarters, and cook them, covered, in simmering salted water for 15 to 20 minutes, or until they are soft but not mushy. Drain the potatoes and dry them by shaking the pan over the heat. Rub the potatoes through a fine sieve or purée them in a blender, and return them to the pan. Add salt and pepper to taste, a little nutmeg, and 4 tablespoons butter. Gradually stir in enough hot cream or milk to obtain the desired consistency. Beat the potatoes over low heat until they are fluffy.

Mashed Potatoes and Carrots

COOK separately in boiling salted water 1 1/2 pounds potatoes, peeled, and 1 pound young carrots until the vegetables are tender. Drain the vegetables and put them through a fine sieve or purée them in a blender. Combine the purées and beat in 1 cup light cream, 1 egg yolk, and 1/4 pound butter. Season with 1 teaspoon prepared mustard and salt and pepper to taste. Heat the potatoes very gently, beating well.

Souffléed Potatoes in Potato Nest

⬮ Duchess Potatoes

PEEL 2 pounds potatoes, cut them into quarters, and cook them, covered, in simmering salted water to cover for 15 to 20 minutes, or until they are soft but not mushy. Drain the potatoes and dry them by shaking the pan over the heat. Rub the potatoes through a sieve or put them through a ricer. Beat the mixture with a wooden spoon until it is very smooth and add 2 tablespoons butter, 1 teaspoon salt, pepper and freshly grated nutmeg to taste, and 2 whole eggs lightly beaten with 2 egg yolks. Beat the mixture briskly until it is very fluffy. (These potatoes may be made up ahead of time. A little butter brushed over the top will prevent a crust from forming.) Heat the potatoes slowly, stirring constantly.

If the potatoes are to be used as a garnish, they may be piped through a pastry tube to make a border for any meat or fish dish. Or they may be shaped decoratively with a pastry tube into individual servings and browned under the broiler.

⬮ Potato Balls

MASH 1 1/2 pounds hot boiled potatoes until they are very smooth, add 1/2 cup hot milk, 1/3 cup grated Cheddar, and 3 tablespoons melted butter, and beat the mixture until it is light and fluffy. Form the mixture into little balls and roll the balls in beaten egg and then in bread crumbs. Arrange the potato balls on a buttered baking sheet and bake them in a very hot oven (450° F.) for 10 minutes, or until they are well browned.

⬮ Potato Croquettes

PEEL 1 pound potatoes, cut them into quarters, and cook them, covered, in simmering salted water for 15 to 20 minutes, or until they are soft. Drain the potatoes and dry them by shaking the pan over the heat. Rub them through a sieve into a heated bowl, or purée them in a blender. Work the purée with a wooden spoon until it is very smooth and beat in 1 tablespoon butter, 1/2 teaspoon salt, a little white pepper, a dash of ground nutmeg, 1 egg, and 1 egg yolk. Cool the mixture and shape it into croquettes. Roll the croquettes in flour, dip them into 1 egg beaten with 2 tablespoons milk, 1 tablespoon salad oil, and 1/2 teaspoon salt, and coat them with fine bread crumbs. Fry the croquettes in deep hot fat (370° F.) until they are golden brown and drain them on absorbent paper.

Potatoes Boulangère 🦶

PEEL and slice 2 pounds potatoes and combine them with 2 onions, very thinly sliced. Add 1 teaspoon chopped parsley, 1/2 teaspoon salt, and a little pepper. Spread the mixture in a shallow baking dish, dot with 3 tablespoons butter, and add 1 cup boiling water. Bake the potatoes in a hot oven (400° F.) for 30 to 40 minutes, or until they are brown and crusty on top and the water is absorbed.

Grilled Sweet Potato Slices 🦶

COOK 6 unpeeled sweet potatoes in simmering salted water for 15 to 20 minutes, or until they are barely tender. Peel the potatoes, cut them into thick slices, and thread them on skewers. Dip the slices in melted butter and cook them over hot coals, turning frequently, until they are golden brown.

Orange Yams 🦶

COOK 2 pounds unpeeled yams in simmering salted water for 25 to 30 minutes, or until they are tender. Peel the yams, cut them into thick slices, and arrange them in a glass baking dish. Cream together 1/2 cup butter, 2 tablespoons each of sugar and orange juice, and 2 teaspoons grated orange rind. Cover the yams with the sauce and bake them in a moderately hot oven (375° F.) until they are nicely glazed.

Cooking Broccoli 🦶

WASH 1 bunch (about 2 pounds) broccoli in cold water and discard the large coarse leaves and the tough lower parts of the stalks. Split the stalks and soak them in cold salted water for 30 minutes. Drain the broccoli, and stand it in a deep saucepan half full of boiling water. The flowerets should be out of the water. Cover the pan and steam the broccoli for about 10 minutes, or until it is just tender.

Crêpes with Broccoli

Italian Broccoli

COOK 3 pounds broccoli for about 8 minutes, or until it is barely tender, and drain it. Sauté 2 garlic cloves, chopped, in 1/2 cup olive oil for a minute or two. Add the broccoli and sauté it, turning it frequently, for 3 minutes. Season it with salt and pepper.

Crêpes with Broccoli

COOK 2 pounds broccoli for about 7 minutes, or until it is barely tender, and remove all the tiny flowerets.

Make 5-inch entrée crêpes and put a mound of the broccoli flowerets on each one. Fold the crêpes in quarters and arrange them side by side in a shallow baking dish. Cover the crêpes with hollandaise sauce and heat them in a moderately hot oven (375° F.).

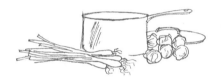

Brussels Sprouts in Butter

MELT 1/2 cup butter in a heavy saucepan and in it sauté 6 scallions, chopped, for 2 or 3 minutes, or until they are soft but not brown. Add 2 pints washed and trimmed Brussels sprouts and 2 tablespoons water. Cover the pan tightly and steam the sprouts over low heat for 10 to 12 minutes, or until they are tender.

Brussels Sprouts Parmesan

WASH and trim 2 pints Brussels sprouts and halve them lengthwise. Melt 1/2 cup butter in a large skillet and in it brown lightly 1 garlic clove, chopped. Add the sprouts and 2 tablespoons chicken stock, cover the pan, and steam the sprouts over low heat for 10 to 12 minutes, or until they are tender. Sprinkle the mixture with salt, pepper, and 1/2 cup grated Parmesan, stir it, and cook until the cheese blends with the butter. Put the sprouts in a heated serving dish, pour the cheese sauce over them, and sprinkle lightly with browned butter.

✺ Brussels Sprouts and Peas in Mint Sauce

CHOUX DE BRUXELLES ET PETITS POIS À LA MENTHE

COOK 2 pints washed and trimmed Brussels sprouts in boiling salted water to cover for about 15 minutes, or until they are tender. Drain the sprouts and sauté them in butter for a few minutes. Steam 1 cup fresh green peas in a little boiling water until they are tender and carefully mix them with the sprouts. Put the vegetables in a heated serving dish and sprinkle them with mint sauce.

✺ Brussels Sprouts Mousse ⎯ MOUSSE DE CHOUX DE BRUXELLES

COOK 2 pints washed and trimmed Brussels sprouts in boiling salted water or beef stock to cover for about 15 minutes, or until they are tender. Drain the sprouts, pressing them to remove as much moisture as possible, and force them through a sieve or purée them in a blender. Soak 1/2 cup dry bread crumbs in 1/2 cup hot milk and beat this into the purée with a wooden spoon. Beat in 6 tablespoons soft butter and 2 egg yolks, and add salt, pepper, and nutmeg to taste. Pour the mixture into a buttered 3/4-quart soufflé dish or mold and put the mold in a pan of hot water. Bake the mousse in a moderate oven (350° F.) for 1 hour. To serve, turn the mousse out on a heated platter and serve with béchamel sauce.

✺ Brussels Sprouts and Wild Rice

SIMMER 1 cup wild rice in boiling water to cover for 2 minutes and drain it. Cover the rice again with boiling water and repeat the procedure twice more. Bring 2 1/2 cups water to a boil with 1 teaspoon salt, add the rice, and cook it for about 30 minutes, or until it is tender and the water is absorbed. Keep the rice hot in a slow oven (300° F.).

Melt 1/4 cup butter in a heavy saucepan and in it sauté 3 shallots, finely chopped, and 1 garlic clove, finely minced, for 2 minutes, or until the shallots are soft. Cook 1 pint washed and trimmed Brussels sprouts in boiling salted water to cover for about 15 minutes, or until they are tender. Drain the sprouts and chop them coarsely. Toss them gently with the wild rice and shallots and season the mixture with salt and pepper to taste.

Anchovy and Cauliflower Soufflé 🦅

STEAM a medium head of cauliflower in a little boiling water for about 25 minutes, or until it is very tender. Rub the cauliflower through a sieve or purée it in a blender. Season the purée with salt, pepper, and a little onion juice to taste, and add 2 tablespoons grated Parmesan and 8 anchovy filets, chopped.

In a saucepan melt 2 1/2 tablespoons butter, add 3 tablespoons flour, and cook the *roux* until it starts to turn golden. Stir in 1 1/4 cups hot milk and cook the sauce for 8 to 10 minutes, stirring constantly, until it is very thick. Beat 6 egg yolks and warm them with a little of the sauce. Combine the two mixtures and stir in the cauliflower purée. Beat 6 egg whites until they are stiff but not dry. Carefully fold one fourth of the egg whites into the mixture and lightly and quickly fold in the remaining whites. Fill a buttered 1-quart soufflé dish with the mixture, crisscross the top with anchovy filets, and bake the soufflé in a moderate oven (350° F.) for about 30 minutes, or until it is well puffed and brown.

Cheese and Cauliflower Casserole 🦅

BLANCH 2 small heads of cauliflower in boiling salted water for 3 minutes. Drain the heads, cut them into small dice, and arrange them in a buttered baking dish. Cream 1 pound *ricotta* cheese with 3 ounces cream cheese, 4 eggs, beaten, 1 cup grated Parmesan or Romano cheese, and mace, salt, and pepper to taste. Cover the cauliflower dice with the cheese mixture and bake the casserole in a moderate oven (350° F.) for 35 to 40 minutes. Serve hot in the casserole; or cool the mixture, turn it out of the casserole, and slice to serve.

Braised Celery 🦅

TRIM off the tops of 8 to 10 stalks of celery, halve them lengthwise, and clean them well. Blanch the celery in a little boiling salted water for 5 minutes and rinse it in cold water to remove any remaining sand. Put a few slices each of onion and carrot in a baking dish, arrange the celery on top, with the stalks parallel to each other, and add enough chicken stock or water to cover. Dot with 1 tablespoon butter and sprinkle with salt to taste. Over the vegetables lay a piece of wax paper, cut the size of the baking dish, and braise the celery in a moderately hot oven (375° F.) for about 1 hour, or until it is tender. Remove the celery to a serving dish. Cook the remaining liquid until it is reduced to about 1/2 cup and thicken it with *beurre manié*, made by creaming together 1 tablespoon butter and 1/2 tablespoon flour. Strain the sauce and pour it over the celery.

Celery and Almonds au Gratin

CÉLERIS ET AMANDES AU GRATIN

CUT enough celery into 1-inch dice to make 4 cups. Cook the diced celery in a little boiling salted water for 5 minutes and drain it. Put it in a baking dish with 1/2 cup slivered blanched almonds and cover it with 2 cups white sauce made with 1 1/2 cups chicken stock and 1/2 cup heavy cream. Sprinkle the mixture with bread crumbs and dot with butter. Bake the celery in a moderate oven (350° F.) until the sauce bubbles and the topping browns.

Celery and Potato Purée   PURÉE DE CÉLERIS PARMENTIER

STRIP and discard the leaves from a large bunch of celery. Dice the stalks and cook them in a little boiling salted water until they are tender. Drain the celery dice and sauté them in 1 to 2 tablespoons butter until most of the moisture has evaporated. Force the celery through a fine sieve, or purée it in a blender, and combine the purée with three times as much hot mashed potatoes. Season with salt and pepper to taste and serve the purée hot.

Celeriac and Potato Purée

PEEL and quarter 2 celeriacs (also called celery root or celery knob), and cook them, covered, in boiling water to cover acidulated with 2 tablespoons lemon juice, for 20 or 30 minutes, or until they are tender. Drain the celeriac, force it through a sieve, and combine it with an equal amount of mashed or riced potatoes. Add 4 tablespoons butter and gradually stir in enough heavy cream to make a thick purée.

Sautéed Fennel

WASH, peel, and cut into 1/4-inch slices 2 medium bulbs of fennel. Dry the slices and sprinkle them lightly with seasoned flour. Sauté 1 teaspoon chopped onion in

3 tablespoons butter for 2 minutes. Add the fennel and sauté the slices, turning once, for 5 minutes, or until they are golden brown. Sprinkle with finely chopped parsley. Serve at once.

Jerusalem Artichokes Avgolemono

PEEL 2 pounds Jerusalem artichokes and cut them into uniform rounded shapes, dropping them into cold water so they will not darken. Drain them and pat dry before cooking. In a saucepan melt 3 tablespoons butter and sauté the artichokes over low heat until they are lightly browned on all sides. Add 1 cup water, cover the pan, and cook the artichokes for 15 minutes. Drain the artichokes and reserve 2 tablespoons of the stock. Beat 3 egg yolks until they are light and gradually beat in 3 tablespoons lemon juice and the reserved stock. Combine the sauce and the artichokes in a saucepan and cook the mixture over very low heat, stirring constantly, until the sauce is thickened.

Purée of Jerusalem Artichokes

COOK 2 pounds Jerusalem artichokes in boiling salted water for 20 to 30 minutes, or until they are just tender. Drain the tubers, peel them, and force them through a fine sieve. Beat in enough butter and light cream to make a smooth purée and season with salt and pepper to taste. Pile the purée into a serving dish and serve hot.

SOUFFLÉ DE TOPINAMBOURS   Jerusalem Artichoke Soufflé

PUT 1 cup purée of Jerusalem artichokes in a saucepan, add 2 tablespoons butter and salt, pepper, and grated nutmeg to taste, and cook the purée slowly until it thickens.

In another pan melt 2 1/2 tablespoons butter, add 3 tablespoons flour and cook the *roux*, stirring, until it is golden. Stir in slowly 1 1/2 cups hot milk and cook the sauce for 8 minutes, or until it is thick, stirring it constantly with a whisk. Beat 6 egg yolks, warm them with a little of the hot sauce, and combine the two mixtures. Bring the sauce just to a boil, stirring constantly, but do not let it boil. Add the artichoke purée and fold in, little by little, 6 egg whites, stiffly beaten. Turn the mixture into a buttered 1 1/2-quart soufflé dish and bake the soufflé in a moderate oven (350° F.) for about 25 minutes, or until it is puffed and brown.

❧ Broiled Mushrooms

TRIM 1 1/2 pounds large mushrooms and soak them in cold water acidulated with a little lemon juice for 5 minutes. Drain and dry the mushrooms, season them with salt and pepper, and brush them with olive oil. Broil the mushrooms very slowly, at some distance from the heat, until they are tender. Top each with 1/4 teaspoon maître d'hôtel butter.

❧ Charcoal-Broiled Mushrooms

ARRANGE large mushrooms, open side up, on a hinged broiler. Cream a little butter with finely chopped chives and put a dot of the mixture inside each cap. Broil the mushrooms over hot coals until they are tender.

❧ Mushroom Purée

TRIM 1 1/2 pounds mushrooms and blanch them in water acidulated with a little lemon juice for 5 minutes. Drain and dry the mushrooms and force them through a sieve. Combine the purée with 1 cup white sauce or béchamel sauce, and season with salt, pepper, and nutmeg to taste.

❧ Sautéed Mushrooms with Marjoram

TRIM the stems of 1 1/2 pounds large mushrooms. In a skillet heat 4 tablespoons butter and 1 tablespoon olive oil. Add the mushrooms, cap side down, sprinkle them with salt and pepper and 1 teaspoon minced marjoram leaves, and sauté them until they are golden. Turn the caps, sprinkle each with a drop of lemon juice, and continue to cook them until they are tender.

❧ Mushroom Caps with Dilled Cheese

TRIM the stems of 1 1/2 pounds large mushrooms. Sprinkle the caps with lemon juice. Chop the stems finely and add them to 8 ounces soft cream cheese. Blend in 2 tablespoons finely chopped dill and salt and pepper to taste. Pipe the mixture into the mushroom caps through a pastry tube, sprinkle with paprika or cayenne, and chill the caps thoroughly.

Stuffed Mushrooms with Bacon 🐖

TRIM the stems of 24 large mushrooms. Sprinkle the caps with lemon juice. Chop the stems finely and sauté them with 3 shallots, chopped, in 4 tablespoons butter until the shallots are golden. Add 2 cups soft bread crumbs, a dash of Worcestershire sauce, and salt and pepper to taste. Fill the mushroom caps with the mixture. Put a small square of bacon on each filled cap, and arrange them in a buttered baking dish. Bake the mushrooms in a moderate oven (350° F.) for about 20 minutes.

Mushroom Tarts 🐖

LINE individual tart pans with unsweetened tart pastry and prick the paste well. Line the pans with wax paper and fill them with uncooked rice or beans. Bake the shells in a hot oven (400° F.) for 20 minutes, or until the crust is golden brown. Discard the rice and paper and cool the shells.

Trim the stems of 1 1/2 pounds mushrooms and slice the caps. In a skillet heat 2 tablespoons each of olive oil and butter. Add the mushroom caps and cook them, stirring, until they are tender. Sprinkle the mushrooms with salt, pepper, and a little lemon juice. Fill the tart shells with the mixture and sprinkle each tart with a mixture of chopped parsley and chives.

Mushroom Fritters 🐖

TRIM the stems, a quarter inch below the caps, of 2 pounds mushrooms. Reserve the stems for use in sauces or soups. Wipe the caps clean with a damp cloth, arrange them on a platter, stems up, and sprinkle them with 1/2 teaspoon salt. Let them stand for 1 hour. Turn the mushrooms upside down, sprinkle them with 1/2 teaspoon salt and the juice of 1/2 lemon, and let them stand for 1 hour more.

Dip the caps in beer batter II and fry them, a few at a time, in deep hot fat

(375° F.) for about 4 minutes, or until they are golden. Drain the fritters on absorbent paper, sprinkle them with chopped parsley, and serve with mustard butter.

Beer Batter II

POUR 1 1/2 cups very light beer into a mixing bowl. Blend in about 1 cup flour, to make a fritter batter the consistency of heavy cream.

Mushroom Ragout

TRIM the stems of 1 1/2 pounds mushrooms. Chop the stems finely and sauté them in 2 tablespoons butter for 4 minutes. Add 1/2 cup each of celery, string beans, carrots, and cabbage, all diced, 1/2 cup peas, and the mushroom caps, quartered. Season the vegetables with salt, pepper, and nutmeg to taste, and cook them, covered, over very low heat for 30 minutes. Stir in 3 tablespoons whole blanched almonds and serve with crisp buttered croutons.

Baked Eggplant

PEEL 2 small eggplants, cut them into 1/2-inch slices, and drain the slices under a weight. Spread both sides of each slice generously with soft butter, and sprinkle them with salt and paprika to taste. Arrange the eggplant slices on a baking sheet and bake them in a hot oven (400° F.), turning them once, for about 15 minutes, or until they are tender. Sprinkle the slices with finely chopped parsley and chives.

Eggplant and Tomato Pie

LINE a fluted pie plate or dish with unsweetened tart pastry, and roll the pin firmly over the rim to cut off the excess dough. Sprinkle the bottom of the shell with 2 tablespoons grated Parmesan and fill it with alternate layers of sautéed eggplant, tomato and onion slices, and raw pepper rings. Sprinkle the top of the pie with 1/2 teaspoon crushed garlic, 1/4 cup olive oil, salt and pepper to taste, and more grated Parmesan. Bake the pie in a moderate oven (350° F.) for 40 to 45 minutes, or until the vegetables are tender and the crust is golden brown. Serve the pie in wedges, with a bowl of grated Parmesan.

Eggplant and Tomato Pie

❧ Broiled Eggplant Slices

PEEL a large eggplant and cut it into 1/2-inch slices. Put them in a glass dish and add garlic olive oil almost to cover. Marinate the eggplant for at least 1 hour. Drain the slices and arrange them in a hinged double broiler. Broil them over hot coals or under the broiler until they are golden brown.

❧ Broiled Eggplant Wedges

PEEL a medium eggplant and cut it lengthwise into 6 sections. Crush a garlic clove with 2 teaspoons salt, a pinch of orégano, and 1/4 cup olive oil, and mix in 1 table-spoon wine vinegar. Brush the wedges of eggplant with this mixture and broil them over hot coals or under the broiler, turning occasionally, until they are nicely browned.

❧ Eggplant Fritters

PEEL a small eggplant and cut it into cubes. Steam the cubes, covered, in a little boiling water for 15 minutes and drain them. Mash the eggplant, beat it until it is smooth, and stir in 1 beaten egg, 3 tablespoons flour, and 1/2 teaspoon each of salt and baking powder. Drop the mixture by spoonfuls into deep hot fat (350° F.), fry the fritters until they are brown, and drain them on absorbent paper.

❧ Cooking Chestnuts

WITH a sharp knife cut a slit on the convex sides of the shells of chestnuts. Bake them in an oiled baking pan in a very hot oven (450° F.) for 5 or 6 minutes; or cook them, covered, in boiling water for about 10 minutes. When the chestnuts are cool enough to handle remove the shells and skins with a sharp knife. Cook the chestnuts in boiling white stock for 20 to 30 minutes, or until they are tender.

Chestnut Purée

COOK chestnuts, drain them, and, while they are still warm, force them through a sieve or purée them in a blender. Season the purée with salt and pepper to taste, and beat in 1 tablespoon butter for each pound of chestnuts. If a thinner purée is desired, beat in some of the white stock in which the nuts were cooked.

MARRONS ET PRUNEAUX ## Chestnuts and Prunes

SOAK 1/2 pound prunes in water to cover for 2 hours. Add to the water 2 bay leaves and a 1-inch cinnamon stick and cook the prunes for 30 minutes. Drain them and remove the pits. Combine the prunes with 1 pound cooked chestnuts, 1 cup dry white wine, 2 tablespoons sugar, 1 tablespoon butter, and 1/2 teaspoon salt. Simmer the mixture for 10 minutes.

Sautéed Corn with Cream

HUSK 12 ears of corn and cut off the kernels. Sauté 1 small onion, minced, in 6 tablespoons butter until it is transparent, add the corn, and cook the mixture, stirring, for 5 minutes, or until the corn is tender. Add salt and pepper to taste and stir in 1/2 cup hot heavy cream.

Broiled Corn on the Cob

PUT ears of corn, free of silk but wrapped in their own husks, on a grill and broil them over hot coals or under a broiler for about 12 minutes. Remove the husks and serve the ears with butter, salt, and freshly ground pepper.

Braised Leeks

TRIM the roots of 18 leeks and cut off the tops, leaving an inch or two of leaves. Halve the leeks lengthwise and wash them thoroughly under cold running water. Sauté 1 onion, minced, in 3 tablespoons butter until it is translucent. Add the leeks, 2 cups chicken stock, and salt and pepper to taste. Cover the pan and cook the leeks

Hazelnut and Leek Soufflés

over low heat for about 15 minutes, or until they are tender. Serve on toast with a little of the pan juices spooned over each portion.

Stuffed Leeks 🦃

TRIM 12 large leeks and scald them in boiling salted water for a minute or two. Remove the inside layers to form hollow tubes.

Sauté 2 medium onions, finely chopped, in 2 tablespoons olive oil until they are golden. Add 1/2 cup rice and stir until the grains are well coated and lightly gilded. Add enough beef stock to cover the rice generously, a pinch of thyme, and a little salt. Cover the pan and cook the rice slowly until it is just tender and the stock is absorbed. Add a little more stock, if necessary. Stuff the leek tubes with the rice, handling them very carefully. Dust the leeks lightly with flour and sauté them in a little butter until they are nicely browned. Arrange the stuffed leeks in a buttered baking dish sprinkled with bread crumbs and cover them with 3/4 cup tomato sauce mixed with the juice of 1/2 lemon. Heat the leeks in a moderate oven (350° F.) for about 10 minutes.

Hazelnut and Leek Soufflés 🦃

CHOP finely 10 trimmed leeks and 1 onion, and cook the vegetables in 1 cup milk for 15 minutes. Stir the mixture into 1 cup hot white sauce and add 1/2 cup chopped hazelnuts, 1/4 cup grated Parmesan, 4 beaten egg yolks, 1 tablespoon finely chopped parsley, and salt and white pepper to taste. Fold in 5 egg whites, stiffly beaten. Pour the mixture into 6 individual buttered soufflé dishes and bake the soufflés in a moderate oven (350° F.) for about 45 minutes, or until they are well puffed and golden brown.

Sautéed Cucumbers 🦃

PEEL and slice 3 large or 5 small cucumbers, enough to make 5 cups. Melt 1/2 cup butter in a heavy skillet and cook the slices, turning, until all are coated with butter. Sprinkle them with a little salt and white pepper. Continue to cook the cucumbers, stirring occasionally, for 5 to 7 minutes longer, or until they are tender but still a little crisp. Sprinkle them with finely chopped parsley or chives.

ॐ Sautéed Cucumbers and Tomatoes

SAUTÉ 12 scallions, chopped, in 1/4 cup butter until they are golden. Add 2 cucumbers, peeled, seeded, and cut into 1/4-inch slices, and sauté the mixture for 2 minutes. Add 4 tomatoes, peeled and cut in wedges, and cook, stirring, for about 5 minutes, or until the tomatoes are soft. Season the vegetables with salt and pepper and stir in 2 teaspoons chopped fresh mint.

ॐ Cucumbers with Caper Sauce

SLICE 3 large cucumbers, plunge the slices into boiling salted water, and cook them for 10 minutes, or until they are tender. Drain the cucumbers and arrange them in a serving dish. Melt 4 tablespoons butter, stir in 2 1/2 tablespoons lemon juice, and add 1 heaping tablespoon each of finely minced parsley and capers. Pour the sauce over the cucumbers.

ॐ Cucumbers in Cream

PEEL 3 cucumbers, cut them lengthwise into quarters, and cut each quarter into 1-inch pieces. Simmer the pieces in a little boiling salted water for 3 minutes and drain them. Melt 4 tablespoons butter in a baking dish, add the cucumbers, and sprinkle them with salt and pepper to taste. Bake the cucumbers, covered, in a moderately slow oven (325° F.) for 15 minutes. Cover them with 1/2 cup heavy cream and bake them for 5 minutes more. Serve sprinkled with lemon juice.

ॐ Skewered Cucumbers and Mushrooms

PEEL large firm cucumbers and cut them into 1-inch slices. Thread the slices on skewers alternately with large mushroom caps. Dip the vegetables in melted butter, and broil them over hot coals for 8 to 10 minutes. Brush the vegetables with more melted butter and sprinkle them with freshly ground pepper.

PURÉE DE PISSENLIT ET D'OSEILLE Dandelion and Sorrel Purée 🍃

WASH thoroughly and drain 1 1/2 pounds each of young dandelion leaves and sorrel. Cook the greens in the water that clings to the leaves over high heat for about 15 minutes, or until they are very soft. Drain the greens, pressing out as much water as possible, and rub them through a sieve. Add to the purée 2 tablespoons butter and salt and pepper to taste. Makes 2 cups.

CHIFFONADE DE LAITUE À LA BÉCHAMEL Shredded Lettuce 🍃

MELT 6 tablespoons butter in a saucepan and add 6 cups shredded lettuce, stirring until the shreds are well coated. Sprinkle the lettuce with salt to taste and cook it, covered, over low heat for 5 to 10 minutes, or until it is tender and all the liquid has been absorbed. Stir in 2 cups béchamel sauce and 1 1/2 teaspoons lemon juice. Arrange the lettuce on a serving dish and surround it with croutons cut in triangles.

Lettuce Mousse 🍃

WASH thoroughly 4 heads of lettuce and steam them, covered, in the water that clings to the leaves for 5 minutes. Drain the lettuce, pressing out as much water as possible, and chop it very finely. Purée it in a blender or force it through a coarse sieve. Season 4 cups hot mashed potatoes with salt and pepper and beat in 1/4 cup butter. Add the lettuce purée and 4 egg yolks, one at a time, beating well after each addition. Fold in 4 egg whites, stiffly beaten, and pile the mixture lightly in a well-buttered 1 1/2-quart soufflé dish. Bake the mousse in a moderately hot oven (375° F.) for about 35 minutes, or until it is puffed and golden brown.

Sautéed Lentils 🍃

SOAK 1 pound lentils in water to cover overnight and drain them. Cover them with fresh water and simmer them, covered, over low heat for about 1 hour, or until they are tender. Drain the beans well and sauté them lightly, stirring occasionally, with 1 onion, coarsely chopped, in 2 tablespoons bacon fat. Transfer the lentils to a heated serving dish and sprinkle them with 2 tablespoons chopped parsley and 4 slices crisp diced bacon.

❧ Fried Parsley

WASH sprigs of parsley and dry them well. Fry them in deep hot fat (375° F.) for a few seconds, or until they rise to the surface. Drain the parsley on absorbent paper and sprinkle with salt.

❧ Parsley Fritters

IN a bowl combine 1/2 cup sifted flour, 1 egg, and 1 egg yolk. Stir in 3 tablespoons milk, 1 tablespoon melted butter, and 1/4 teaspoon salt. Beat the mixture with a rotary beater until it is smooth. Add 3 tablespoons milk and 1 teaspoon baking powder and mix thoroughly. Fold in 1 egg white, stiffly beaten, and chill the batter for 30 minutes. Beat the batter before using.

Wash and dry thoroughly 24 sprigs of curly parsley with long stems. Hold each sprig by the stem, dredge it with flour, then dip it in the batter. Shake off any excess batter, as the sprigs should be thinly coated. Dip the sprigs, one or two at a time, in deep hot fat (370° F.). Drain the fritters on absorbent paper and salt them.

❧ Glazed Parsnips

PEEL 9 medium parsnips and halve them lengthwise. Put the parsnips in a pan in 1 inch boiling water and cover the pan. Cook the parsnips for about 20 minutes, or until they are tender, and drain them. Arrange the halves in a baking dish and dot them with 3 tablespoons brown sugar, 1/2 teaspoon dry mustard, and salt and white pepper to taste. Bake the parsnips in a hot oven (400° F.) for about 20 minutes, or until they are well glazed.

❧ Deviled Parsnips

PEEL and slice 9 medium parsnips. Brown the slices on both sides in 1/3 cup melted butter over moderate heat, turning them occasionally. Stir in 2 tablespoons each of brown sugar and wine vinegar, 1 teaspoon each of dry mustard, minced chives, and chopped fresh basil, and salt and pepper to taste. Cover the pan and cook the parsnips over moderate heat for about 20 minutes, or until they are tender. Serve sprinkled with paprika.

Parsnips with Rosemary 𝔰𝔟

PEEL 6 parsnips, cook them in boiling salted water for 10 minutes, and drain them. Cut the parsnips into slices 1/2 inch thick. Dip the slices into 2 well-beaten eggs and roll them in a mixture of 1/4 cup dry bread crumbs, 1/2 teaspoon dried rosemary, and salt and pepper to taste. Brown the slices on both sides in 1/4 cup butter over moderate heat.

CROQUETTES DE PANAIS
Parsnip Croquettes 𝔰𝔟

PEEL 8 parsnips and halve them lengthwise. Put them in a pan in 1 inch boiling water and cover the pan. Cook the parsnips for about 20 minutes, or until they are tender, and drain them. Purée the parsnips in a blender or force them through a fine sieve. Stir into the purée 1/2 cup grated Brazil nuts, 1/3 cup fine dry bread crumbs, 2 tablespoons finely chopped parsley, 1 teaspoon sugar, and salt and pepper to taste. Blend 2 beaten egg yolks and 1 beaten egg white into the parsnip mixture, shape it into croquettes, and chill them.

Combine 1/4 cup each of fine dry bread crumbs and grated Brazil nuts and 1/2 teaspoon grated lemon rind. Dip the croquettes into 1 egg white, lightly beaten, and roll them in the bread-crumb and nut mixture, coating each croquette well. Fry the croquettes in deep hot fat (365° F.) until they are brown and crisp and drain them on absorbent paper.

Braised Parsnips and Endive 𝔰𝔟

PEEL 4 parsnips and cut them lengthwise into thin strips. Halve lengthwise 4 heads of endive. Sauté the vegetables in 1/4 cup melted butter over high heat for 2 minutes, turning them frequently. Add to the pan 1/2 cup water or chicken stock, 3 tablespoons lemon juice, 1 teaspoon brown sugar, and salt and pepper to taste. Cover the pan and cook the vegetables over low heat for about 10 minutes, or until the parsnips are tender. Remove the lid, increase the heat slightly, and continue cooking the vegetables, stirring occasionally, until they start to brown and the liquid is absorbed. Arrange the vegetables in a serving dish and sprinkle them with 2 tablespoons toasted slivered almonds.

ʃ♪ Sautéed Parsnips and Lettuce

PEEL 6 parsnips and cut them lengthwise into thin strips. Put them in a pan with 3 tablespoons melted butter, 2/3 cup boiling water, 1 tablespoon sugar, a dash of ginger, and salt and pepper to taste. Cover the pan and cook the parsnips over moderate heat for about 15 minutes, or until they are tender. Stir in 2 cups finely shredded lettuce and continue cooking the vegetables, stirring constantly, until they are lightly browned and all the liquid has evaporated. Correct the seasoning.

ʃ♪ Spring Peas

SHELL 3 pounds new peas and put them in a saucepan with 3 tablespoons melted butter. Sprinkle the peas with salt and shake the pan until they are coated with the butter. Add 3 tablespoons hot water and cook the peas, covered, for 10 minutes, or until they are tender. Just before serving add 1 1/2 teaspoons minced orégano.

ʃ♪ Baked New Peas   PETITS POIS AU FOUR

SHELL 3 pounds new peas and put them on a large lettuce leaf in a baking dish. Add 3 tablespoons water, cover the casserole tightly, and bake the peas in a moderate oven (350° F.) for 10 minutes. Add 4 tablespoons sweet butter and salt and freshly ground pepper to taste. Cover the casserole and bake the peas for 20 minutes longer, or until they are tender.

ʃ♪ Peas à la Française

PUT 2 tablespoons butter in a saucepan and add 6 tiny white onions, 5 or 6 leaves of lettuce, shredded, 3 sprigs of parsley tied with 3 sprigs of chervil, 1 tablespoon sugar, and 1/2 teaspoon salt. Mix in 3 pounds freshly shelled green peas and add 1/2 cup water. Bring the liquid to a boil, cover the pan, and simmer the vegetables for 15 minutes, or until the peas are almost tender. There should be only 2 or 3 table-spoons water left in the pan. Discard the herbs. Cream 1 tablespoon butter with 1/2 teaspoon flour and add to the peas. Shake the pan over low heat until the *beurre manié* has combined with the liquid. As soon as the sauce comes to a boil, remove the pan from the heat and serve the peas.

Purée of Green Peas

SHELL 3 pounds green peas and cook them, covered, in a little boiling salted water for 10 to 15 minutes, or until they are tender. Drain the peas and force them through a sieve into a saucepan. Cook the purée over low heat until it is quite dry. Stir in 1 tablespoon butter and slowly add about 1/2 cup heavy cream, or enough to moisten the purée.

New Peas with Mint

SHELL 3 pounds new peas and cook them with 1/4 cup fresh mint leaves, covered, in a little slightly salted boiling water for about 10 minutes, or until the peas are just tender. Drain the peas and add 1 or 2 tablespoons butter.

PETITS POIS À LA ROMAINE ## Peas Roman Style

MELT 2 to 4 tablespoons butter in a saucepan and in it sauté 1 or 2 tablespoons raw ham and 1 small onion, both finely chopped, until the onion starts to take on color. Add 3 pounds freshly shelled green peas, 1 cup beef stock, and salt and pepper to taste. Cook the peas over high heat for no more than 8 minutes. Just before they are done sprinkle them with a little sugar.

Sautéed Peas with Mushrooms and Parmesan

IN a large skillet sauté 1 1/2 pounds mushrooms, halved or quartered, in 3 tablespoons olive oil until they are tender. Season them with salt and pepper and add 4 tablespoons grated Parmesan and 1 1/2 cups cooked peas. Cook the mixture, stirring constantly, for 5 minutes, and stir in 2 tablespoons Madeira.

Sautéed Tomatoes

CUT 6 firm tomatoes into thick slices, season the slices with salt, and roll them in flour. Heat enough butter or olive oil to cover the bottom of a skillet and gently brown the tomato slices on both sides.

Broiled Tomatoes

CUT 6 firm tomatoes into halves, brush the halves with butter, and sprinkle them with finely chopped basil and with bread crumbs. Arrange the tomatoes in a hinged broiler and broil them over hot coals until they are lightly browned.

Broiled Tomato Slices

CUT large firm tomatoes into 12 slices 1 inch thick and sprinkle the slices with salt and pepper. Combine 1 cup dry bread crumbs with 2 tablespoons chopped chives. Dip the tomato slices in the mixture and arrange them on a buttered baking sheet. Dot the tomatoes with butter and broil them 3 inches below the heat for about 2 minutes on each side. Sprinkle them with 1 tablespoon chopped chives.

Deviled Tomatoes

SLICE thickly 6 large firm tomatoes, sprinkle them with salt and pepper, and dredge them with flour. Brown the tomatoes on both sides in 3 tablespoons butter over moderate heat.

Cream 6 tablespoons butter and add 3 tablespoons vinegar, 1 1/2 teaspoons dry mustard, 1 egg, lightly beaten, the sieved yolks of 2 hard-cooked eggs, and 1/2 teaspoon salt. Cook the sauce in the top of a double boiler over hot water, stirring constantly, until it thickens. Arrange the tomatoes on a serving dish and cover them with the sauce.

Preparing Tomatoes for Stuffing

CUT thin slices from the tops of tomatoes and carefully scoop out the seeds and pulp. Discard the pulp or reserve it for the stuffing, according to the recipe. Sprinkle the insides of the tomato shells lightly with salt and turn them upside down on a rack. Let them drain for about 15 minutes. If the filled tomatoes are to be baked, lay them side by side in a shallow pan or baking dish. A little hot water added to the dish prevents the tomatoes from sticking to the bottom.

Tomatoes à la Grecque ⁋

PREPARE 6 tomatoes for stuffing. Combine the tomato pulp with 2 cups cooked rice, 2 tablespoons each of chopped onions and currants, 2 garlic cloves, minced, and salt and pepper to taste. Fill the tomato shells with this mixture and sprinkle them with a little olive oil. Arrange the tomatoes in a well-oiled baking dish, cover the dish, and bake them in a moderate oven (350° F.) for about 20 minutes.

Stuffed Tomatoes Jardinière ⁋

PREPARE 6 tomatoes for stuffing. Put through a food chopper 3 stalks of celery, 3 sprigs of parsley, 2 small carrots, 1 1/2 cups raw spinach, 1 small green pepper, and 1 large onion. Sauté the chopped vegetables in 2 tablespoons melted butter until the onion is golden, and stir in 3/4 cup bread crumbs, 1/3 cup milk, 1 egg, beaten, and salt and pepper to taste. Fill the tomato shells with the stuffing and sprinkle them with grated Parmesan. Put the tomatoes in a buttered baking dish with 1/2 cup hot water. Bake them in a hot oven (400° F.) for 20 minutes.

Tomatoes Stuffed with Potatoes ⁋

PREPARE 6 tomatoes for stuffing and arrange the drained shells in a shallow pan with 1/4 cup hot water. Bake the shells in a moderate oven (350° F.) for 10 minutes. Fill the baked shells with mashed potatoes and sprinkle them with slivered blanched almonds and a dash of paprika. Return the stuffed tomatoes to the oven and bake them for 5 minutes more.

Stuffed Tomatoes with Saffron Rice ⁋

SAUTÉ 1 onion, chopped, in 2 tablespoons butter until it is golden and blend it with 1 cup cooked saffron rice.

Prepare 6 large tomatoes for stuffing. Add the tomato pulp to the rice with 1 teaspoon finely minced basil and a pinch of sweet marjoram. Fill the tomato shells with the rice mixture and put them side by side in a baking dish. Sprinkle the tomatoes with grated Parmesan, dot them with butter, and bake them in a moderately hot oven (375° F.) for 20 minutes.

℘ Stewed Tomatoes with Sour Cream

SAUTÉ 1 large onion, finely chopped, in 2 tablespoons butter until it is soft. Add 6 large tomatoes, peeled, seeded, and cut into sections, and cook them, stirring occasionally, for 10 minutes. Pour off a little of the tomato juice and add gradually 3 tablespoons flour, stirring until the mixture is well blended. Return the mixture to the pan and simmer the tomatoes until the sauce thickens. Add 1 1/2 cups sour cream and salt and pepper to taste and cook the tomatoes for 1 minute longer.

℘ Fresh Tomatoes with Spinach Purée

PEEL 25 firm tomatoes of uniform size and shape. Slice off the tops and reserve them. Carefully scoop out the center seeds and turn the tomatoes upside down on a rack to drain. Sprinkle the tomatoes with salt and pepper and chill them.

Rub twice through a fine sieve 4 cups hot cooked spinach and season the purée with salt, pepper, and freshly grated nutmeg to taste. Fill the chilled tomatoes with the hot purée and replace the reserved tomato tops. Arrange the tomatoes on platters and garnish with watercress. Serve the tomatoes while the purée is still hot. Makes 25 servings.

℘ Watercress Fritters

WASH sprigs of watercress and dry them thoroughly. Holding them by the stems, dip the sprigs in beer batter II, drop them into deep hot fat (390° F.), and fry them for a few seconds, or until they rise to the surface of the fat and begin to crisp. Drain the watercress on absorbent paper and sprinkle lightly with salt. Serve as a garnish for poultry, meat, or fish.

℘ Spinach en Branche

WASH thoroughly 3 pounds spinach, drain it, and sprinkle it lightly with salt. Cook the spinach in the water that clings to the leaves for 4 to 5 minutes. Turn the spinach into a colander or sieve, and shake it to remove as much water as possible. Serve the spinach with melted butter and a dash of lemon juice.

Spinach Purée 🦋

RUB twice through a fine sieve 3 cups hot cooked spinach and beat 1 cup rich white sauce into the purée. Season it with salt, pepper, and freshly grated nutmeg to taste, and, if desired, 1/4 cup chopped chives. Heat the purée in the top of a double boiler over hot water.

Creamed Spinach 🦋

COOK 3 pounds spinach, drain it, and chop it finely. Sauté 2 tablespoons grated onion in 3 tablespoons butter over low heat, stirring, until the onion just begins to take on color. Blend in 3 tablespoons flour. Add gradually 1 1/2 cups scalded milk and cook the sauce, stirring, until it is smooth and slightly thickened. Strain it through a fine sieve into another saucepan, add the chopped spinach, and season with salt and pepper to taste. Simmer the mixture gently for 2 to 3 minutes. Beat 2 egg yolks with 3/4 cup heavy cream and gradually add the mixture to the spinach, stirring constantly. Stir in 1 tablespoon finely minced parsley.

Spinach and Anchovies 🦋

COOK 3 pounds spinach and drain it well. Melt 3 tablespoons butter in a saucepan, add the spinach, and cook it for 3 minutes. Season with salt and pepper to taste and stir in 1 teaspoon lemon juice and 6 anchovy filets, finely chopped. Serve in a heated vegetable dish, garnished with slices of hard-cooked egg and curled anchovy filets.

Spinach Caroline 🦋

COOK 3 pounds spinach and drain it. Melt 4 tablespoons bacon drippings in a saucepan, add the spinach, and cook it for 5 minutes, stirring occasionally. Sprinkle the spinach with salt and pepper and a pinch of nutmeg, and stir in 1 tablespoon raisins.

⤷ Spinach with Tangerines   ÉPINARDS AUX MANDARINES

COOK 3 pounds spinach and drain it, pressing out as much water as possible. In a skillet heat 4 tablespoons olive oil with a split garlic clove and discard the garlic. Toss the spinach well with the oil, add salt and nutmeg to taste, and stir it over low heat until the water has entirely evaporated.

Halve 3 large firm tangerines, remove the sections, and reserve the shells. Remove the membranes and cut the flesh coarsely. Combine the tangerines with the cooked spinach. Fill the tangerine shells with the mixture, sprinkle with grated Parmesan, and dot with butter. Heat the filled shells in a moderate oven (350° F.) and serve immediately.

⤷ Spinach Barquettes

LINE *barquette* molds with unsweetened tart pastry, prick the shells with a fork, and bake them in a very hot oven (450° F.) for about 10 minutes, or until they are golden. Fill the *barquettes* with hot creamed spinach.

⤷ Spanakopita   SPINACH PIE

WASH thoroughly 3 pounds spinach and drain it. Chop the spinach finely, sprinkle it with salt and pepper, and let it stand for an hour. Press the spinach to draw out the bitter liquid. In a large skillet sauté 1 cup finely chopped onion in 1/2 cup olive oil until it is golden. Add the drained spinach and cook it, stirring, until it wilts. Combine the spinach and onions and oil with 3/4 pound Feta cheese, crumbled, 1/2 cup pine nuts, 3 tablespoons each of chopped parsley and dill, and salt and pepper to taste.

Brush a shallow baking pan with melted butter and line it with 1 sheet of *phyllo* pastry (paper-thin pastry, similar to strudel, used in Middle Eastern cuisine, and sometimes available frozen). Brush the sheet lightly with melted sweet butter and cover with 4 more *phyllo* leaves, brushing each with melted butter. Fill the dish with the spinach mixture and cover the top with 4 more buttered sheets of *phyllo*. Trim the edges of the top sheets to fit the dish, brush the edges with water, and fold over the bottom sheets to seal the pie. Bake the pie in a moderate oven (350° F.) for about 40 minutes, or until the top is golden. Cool it slightly before cutting and serve warm or cold.

Spanakopita

⤷ Baked Onions on Toast

PEEL 12 onions and cut them in half crosswise. Arrange the halves in a buttered baking dish, sprinkle them with 2 teaspoons brown sugar, a dash of paprika, and salt and pepper to taste, and dot them with 3 tablespoons butter. Bake the onions in a moderate oven (350° F.) for about 1 hour, or until they are tender. Arrange the baked onions on rounds of buttered toast, and sprinkle them with finely chopped parsley and a dash of lemon juice.

⤷ Creamed Onions   OIGNONS À LA CRÈME

PEEL 24 small uniform white onions, blanch them in boiling salted water for 5 minutes, and drain them. Put the onions in a skillet with 4 tablespoons melted butter, sprinkle them with 1 teaspoon sugar, and brown them slowly, turning them carefully to avoid breaking them. Remove the onions to a flat baking dish. To the butter and sugar mixture remaining in the pan add 1/4 cup cold water. Cook the mixture, stirring, until the liquid is brown and syrupy. Pour the syrup over the onions and add 1 cup thin white sauce. Bake the onions in a moderate oven (350° F.) for 20 minutes.

⤷ Glazed Onions

MELT 3 tablespoons butter in a skillet and add 2 tablespoons sugar. Peel 24 small white onions and sauté them in the butter until they are golden brown, turning them frequently. Add 1/2 cup chicken stock and cook the onions quickly over high heat, basting them frequently, until they are tender and the liquid is reduced to a syrup.

⤷ French Fried Onions

PEEL Bermuda onions and cut them into 1/4-inch slices. Soak the slices in cold milk to cover for 30 minutes, drain and dry the slices, and separate them into rings. Dredge the rings with flour and fry them, a few at a time, in a frying basket in deep hot fat (360° F.) until they are golden brown. Drain the rings on absorbent paper and keep them in a warm oven with the door open until all the rings are fried. Sprinkle with salt and serve immediately.

Onions in White Wine 🐄

PEEL 24 small white onions, blanch them in boiling salted water for 5 minutes, and drain them. Put them in a saucepan and add white wine to cover, 1 tablespoon butter, and salt to taste. Cook the onions over low heat for about 20 minutes, or until they are tender. Drain them and sprinkle with paprika.

Onion and Apple Casserole 🐄

CUT 3 large Bermuda onions into 1/4-inch slices and simmer the slices in 1 cup water for 10 minutes. Drain the onions, reserving the liquid. Peel, core, and slice 4 or 5 tart cooking apples. Arrange the apples and onions in alternate layers in a baking dish. Sprinkle the apple layers with cinnamon and sugar and dot them with butter. Sprinkle the onion layers with salt and pepper and dot them with butter. Add 1/3 cup of the reserved onion liquid and bake the onions and apples in a moderately hot oven (375° F.), basting with more of the liquid when necessary, for about 45 minutes, or until they are tender.

OIGNONS ET CÉLERIS AMANDINES **Onions and Celery Amandine** 🐄

PEEL 24 small white onions and cook them with 1 bay leaf in boiling salted water for about 20 minutes, or until they are tender. Drain them, reserving 1/2 cup stock. Cut 3 celery hearts in half and cut the halves into 2-inch lengths. Put them in a saucepan with equal parts of light beef stock and white wine to cover. Adjust the lid and cook the celery for about 15 minutes, or until it is just tender. Drain it, reserving 1/2 cup stock.

Melt 3 tablespoons butter in a saucepan and stir in 3 tablespoons flour and a pinch of cayenne. Gradually add 1/2 cup of each of the reserved vegetable stocks and cook the sauce until it is thick and smooth. Add enough light cream to make a medium-thick sauce, bring the sauce to a boil, and simmer it for 5 minutes. Combine the celery, onions, and cream sauce in a baking dish and sprinkle generously with toasted shredded almonds. Bake the onions and celery in a moderate oven (350° F.) for 20 minutes.

Burgundy Onion Rings and Broiled Marinated Steak

Sautéed Onion Rings 𝕤𝕓

Cut 6 large yellow onions into 1/4-inch slices and separate them into rings. Heat 1 tablespoon each of butter and olive oil in a skillet, add the onions, and cook them, stirring, until they are well coated. Stir in 1 teaspoon sweet marjoram and salt, pepper, and cayenne to taste. Cover the skillet and cook the onions over low heat for about 15 minutes, or until they are tender but not mushy. If too much moisture has collected in the pan, cook the onions, uncovered, over high heat for a few minutes more.

Burgundy Onion Rings 𝕤𝕓

Cut 6 large yellow onions into 1/4-inch slices and separate them into rings. Heat 3 tablespoons hot butter in a skillet, add the onions, and cook them, stirring, until they are well coated. Add 2 whole cloves and salt and pepper to taste and sauté the onions until they are golden. Put the onions into a flameproof casserole. Add 1 cup Burgundy, cover the dish, and simmer the onions for about 15 minutes, or until they are tender. Discard the cloves. Remove the cover and cook the onions until the wine is reduced almost to a glaze. Serve in the casserole.

Green Onions on Croûtes 𝕤𝕓

Wash 3 bunches of green onions, or scallions, cut off the fibrous ends of the roots, and trim the stalks to a length of 4 inches. Divide the onions into 6 bundles, tie them with string, and lay them in a large skillet in 1/4 inch of water. Cover the pan tightly and steam the onions over high heat for about 6 minutes, or until they are just tender. Arrange each bundle on a buttered croûte and remove the strings. Sprinkle the onions with 2 teaspoons chopped parsley, the juice of 1 lemon, and the sieved yolks of 2 hard-cooked eggs. Brown 1/2 cup soft bread crumbs in 4 tablespoons butter and pour the sauce over the eggs.

ONION TART   ## Pissaladière

Peel and slice 6 large onions and separate them into rings. In a skillet, in 1/2 cup hot olive oil, cook the onions, covered, over very low heat until they are transparent but not browned. Season with salt and pepper to taste. Drain off the oil, reserving 2 tablespoons.

Sift 2 cups sifted flour with 1/2 teaspoon salt onto a pastry board and make a well in the center. Dissolve 1/2 package of yeast in 1/2 cup lukewarm water and pour it into the well. Work the flour gradually into the liquid, knead the mixture for several minutes, and work in the reserved olive oil. Knead the dough for 15 minutes, until it is smooth, and shape it into a ball. Cover it with a damp cloth and let it rise in a warm place for 1 hour. Punch the dough down and roll it out (or stretch it over the back of the hands) to form a large circle, slightly thicker at the edges than in the middle. Lay the dough in a lightly oiled 10-inch pie plate and spread it thickly with the cooked onions. Arrange 12 anchovies in the shape of a star on top and cover the spaces between the anchovies with pitted black olives. Sprinkle the tart with 2 garlic cloves, finely chopped, and with 1/2 cup olive oil. Bake the *pissaladière* in a moderate oven (350° F.) for 30 to 40 minutes, or until the crust is golden. Cut it in wedges and serve very hot.

𝔰 Buttered Summer Squash

WASH and dice 2 pounds small summer squash and cook it, covered, in a little boiling salted water for 10 to 12 minutes, or until it is tender. Drain the squash, mash it, and add 4 tablespoons butter, 1/2 teaspoon salt, and a generous sprinkling of freshly ground black pepper.

𝔰 Chinese Summer Squash

WASH 2 pounds uniform summer squash and cut them into slices 1/8 inch thick but do not peel them. Heat 2 tablespoons peanut or vegetable oil in a large skillet and sauté the slices over high heat until they are golden brown. Put them in a flame-proof casserole. Add 1/2 cup water or chicken stock, 2 tablespoons soy sauce, and salt and pepper to taste. Cook the squash, covered, over low heat for 10 minutes, or until it is tender. The sauce may be slightly thickened with cornstarch, or made sweet and sour by adding sugar and vinegar to taste. Serve in the casserole with chopped parsley sprinkled over the top.

Orange Hubbard Squash 🐾

COOK 6 cups peeled and cubed Hubbard squash in the top of a double boiler over boiling water for about 20 minutes, or until it is tender. Mash the squash with a fork or purée it in a blender. In a saucepan combine 2/3 cup orange juice, 4 tablespoons heavy cream, 3 tablespoons butter, 2 tablespoons honey, and 1 1/2 tablespoons grated orange rind. Bring the sauce to a boil and gradually beat it into the squash to obtain a light and fluffy mixture that will hold its shape. Pile the squash into a serving dish and sprinkle it with toasted slivered almonds.

Pumpkin Pancakes 🐾

COMBINE 1 1/2 cups pumpkin purée with 4 tablespoons flour, 2 tablespoons cottage cheese, 1 tablespoon chicken stock, and salt and pepper to taste. Beat the batter until it is well blended and drop it by spoonfuls onto a lightly buttered griddle. When the underside of each pancake is delicately browned, turn it and cook the other side. Sprinkle the pancakes with salt and pepper. Serve with ham.

Pumpkin Purée 🐾

WASH and cut into quarters a ripe pumpkin, discard the seeds and fibers, and put the pumpkin in a baking dish. Set the dish in a pan of hot water and bake the pumpkin in a moderate oven (350° F.) for about 45 minutes, or until it is tender. Scrape the pulp from the rind and rub it through a sieve or purée it in a blender.

If the purée is to be served as a vegetable, stir it over moderate heat until most of the moisture has evaporated and season it with butter, salt, pepper, and a pinch of ginger. Serve garnished with slivered toasted almonds.

Zucchini in Sour Cream 🐾

PEEL and shred coarsely 2 pounds zucchini. Cook the shreds in a little boiling salted water for 3 minutes and drain them well. Add to the zucchini 1 tablespoon melted butter, 1/4 cup finely chopped parsley, and salt and white pepper to taste. Fold in 1 cup sour cream. Heat the mixture slowly but do not let it boil. Serve sprinkled with paprika.

🦐 Sautéed Zucchini

CUT 2 pounds medium zucchini, unpeeled, into slices. Sauté the slices in a generous amount of butter for 10 minutes, or until they are transparent, but do not let them brown. Sprinkle the zucchini with salt and pepper.

🦐 Sautéed Zucchini and Tomatoes

CUT 2 pounds medium zucchini, unpeeled, into slices 1/4 inch thick. Heat 2 tablespoons oil in a heavy skillet and cook the zucchini slices with 1 crushed garlic glove, turning frequently, for about 5 minutes, until they are transparent. Add 2 tomatoes, peeled and diced, and cook the mixture until the tomatoes are soft. Add salt and pepper to taste. Arrange the vegetables in a serving dish. Cover with 12 black olives, pitted and cut in half, and sprinkle with finely chopped parsley.

🦐 Casserole Corsoise

PEEL 4 potatoes and cut them into thin slices. Peel a small eggplant and cut it into medium dice. Arrange the vegetables in a large, shallow, and well-buttered earthenware baking dish. Chop finely 4 tomatoes, 2 onions, 3 green peppers, 3 carrots, 3 garlic cloves, 4 sprigs of parsley, and a sprig of fresh basil. Combine the chopped vegetables, season them with salt and pepper to taste, and spread them over the potatoes and eggplant. Carefully add 2 cups water and bake the vegetables in a moderately hot oven (375° F.) for about 45 minutes, or until they are tender. Sprinkle the casserole with 6 tablespoons olive oil and bake it for 20 minutes longer. Serve cold, cut from the casserole in wedges.

🦐 Ratatouille

COMBINE the following vegetables in a large shallow pan: 2 small eggplants, peeled and cut into medium dice, 6 tomatoes, peeled and diced, 4 green peppers and 4 zucchini, all sliced, 2 onions, chopped, and 2 garlic cloves, crushed with a little salt. Sprinkle the vegetables with 5 tablespoons olive oil and a little salt and pepper. Add 1/2 cup water, cover the pan, and cook the *ratatouille* over very low heat for about 1 1/2 hours, or until all the vegetables are very tender. Serve hot or cold.

Vegetables with Aioli Sauce 🦪

COOK separately in boiling salted water until tender 1 cup each of sliced Italian green beans and whole snap beans, 1/2 cup each of green peas, chick-peas, flageolets, and sliced zucchini, and 6 artichoke hearts. Combine the vegetables gently and put them in a buttered baking dish. Heat them in a very slow oven (200° F.) for about 15 minutes. Carefully mix 1 cup aioli sauce into the hot vegetables.

Curried Vegetables 🦪

CUT into dice 2 pounds mixed vegetables—potatoes, cabbage, carrots, pumpkin, kohlrabi, and the like. In a large saucepan heat 1/4 cup clarified butter. Stir in 1 tablespoon each of curry powder and grated coconut and cook the mixture, stirring occasionally, for 5 minutes. Add 1 onion, coarsely chopped, and 2 garlic cloves, minced, and cook for 3 minutes. Add 3 tomatoes, peeled, seeded, and chopped, and cook, stirring, for 3 minutes. Add the diced vegetables and water to cover, cover the pan, and simmer the vegetables for 15 to 20 minutes, until they are tender.

Tian 🦪

SOAK 1 pound dried white beans in water to cover overnight. Drain the beans, cover them with 2 quarts fresh cold water, and simmer them, covered, until they are tender. Just before the beans are finished, add salt to taste. Drain the beans, sprinkle them with 2 tablespoons olive oil, and toss well.

In a deep skillet, in 4 tablespoons olive oil, cook 8 to 10 small summer squash and 7 or 8 zucchini, unpeeled but finely diced, and 3 garlic cloves, finely chopped, for about 6 minutes, or until the vegetables are almost tender. Transfer the vegetables to 2 large shallow earthenware casseroles, leaving the oil in the skillet. Wash thoroughly 4 pounds spinach, chop it finely, and cook it in the oil remaining in the skillet until it wilts. Drain the spinach, pressing out as much liquid as possible, and combine it with the vegetables in the casseroles. Add the cooked white beans and season with salt, pepper, and crumbled orégano to taste. Sprinkle the top with 1 cup freshly grated Parmesan mixed with 1 cup bread crumbs and 10 anchovy filets, finely minced. Bake the *tian* in a moderate oven (350° F.) until the topping is golden and the cheese is melted. Serve hot or cold. Makes 20 servings. This dish takes its name from the Provençal earthenware casserole in which it is baked.

Salads

☙ Chicory and Fennel Salad

IN a salad bowl put the tender leaves of a head of chicory, finely shredded, 1 bulb of fennel and 6 radishes, both finely sliced, and 2 anchovy filets, finely chopped. Toss the salad lightly with French dressing.

☙ Chicory and Mushroom Salad

SALADE DE CHICORÉE ET DE CHAMPIGNONS

COMBINE 1 cup thinly sliced mushrooms with 1/2 cup olive oil, 1/4 cup wine vinegar beaten with 2 teaspoons heavy cream, 1/2 teaspoon each of salt and sugar, and 1/4 teaspoon freshly ground black pepper, and marinate the mixture for 1 hour. Combine the mushrooms and marinade with 1 onion and 1 peeled and cored tart apple, both thinly sliced, and the shredded leaves from 1 head of chicory. Sprinkle the salad with 1 teaspoon each of chopped chervil and chives.

Dandelion Salad

THE dandelion greens used for salad are best when they are just sprouting, because they have white hearts and tips of delicate green. They are tender to eat and delicate in flavor. Clean the greens well, cut them into small pieces, and chill well. Just before serving, toss them with French dressing.

Endive Salad

CLEAN the endive, cut them into lengthwise slices, and arrange them on individual salad plates. Pour 1 tablespoon French dressing over each salad and sprinkle with chopped chervil.

Endive and Avocado Salad

CLEAN the endive and halve the stalks lengthwise. Arrange the endive halves on individual plates alternately with slices of avocado. Sprinkle with French dressing and a mixture of chopped chives and chervil.

Salad Elisabeth

CLEAN the endive and halve the stalks lengthwise. Arrange the endive on plates and cover them with thin slices of cooked beets mixed with French dressing. Sprinkle the salad with a mixture of chervil, tarragon, and chives, all finely chopped.

Endive and Watercress Salad

CLEAN 3 firm endive and cut them crosswise into 1/2-inch disks. Put the endive in a salad bowl rubbed with a cut garlic clove and add the leaves from a large bunch of watercress. Toss the salad lightly with French dressing.

⟨⟩ Field Salad Vinaigrette

CLEAN thoroughly 1 pound of field salad (also called corn salad and lamb's-lettuce), and drain the leaves well. Handle the greens carefully because they are fragile and bruise easily. Just before serving, toss the greens lightly with vinaigrette sauce.

⟨⟩ Hearts of Lettuce Salad

ARRANGE hearts of lettuce in a salad bowl. Discard the stems from 1 bunch of watercress, chop the leaves, and sprinkle them over the lettuce. Put the yolk and white of 1 hard-cooked egg through a fine sieve and sprinkle it over the watercress. Just before serving, toss the salad with French dressing.

⟨⟩ Romaine and Hearts of Palm Salad

CUT 6 hearts of palm into pieces 1 inch long and arrange them on individual salad plates on crisp leaves of romaine. Pour 2 tablespoons French dressing over each salad and sprinkle generously with paprika.

⟨⟩ Chiffonade Salad

COMBINE equal amounts of romaine, lettuce, and chicory torn in uniform pieces, watercress leaves, celery cut in julienne, peeled and quartered tomatoes, chopped hard-cooked eggs, and chopped beets. Sprinkle the salad with finely chopped chives and toss it lightly with vinaigrette sauce.

⟨⟩ Caesar Salad

TEAR 2 heads of romaine lettuce into medium pieces and put them into a salad bowl rubbed with garlic. Add 1/2 teaspoon salt, 1/4 teaspoon each of dry mustard and black pepper, and 1/2 cup grated Parmesan. Sprinkle the mixture with 6 tablespoons olive oil and the juice of 2 lemons, and add 4 or 5 anchovy filets, cut into small pieces.

Cook 2 eggs for 1 1/2 minutes in barely simmering water and break the coddled

Caesar Salad

eggs on the greens. Toss the salad gently but thoroughly, until no trace of egg is seen and the leaves are well coated. There should be no excess liquid in the bowl. Taste for seasoning. Just before serving, add 2 cups French bread croutons, browned lightly in garlic-flavored olive oil. Toss the salad briefly.

ᖶᕠ Spinach Salad

WASH and drain thoroughly 3 pounds spinach and chop it very finely. Moisten the spinach with French dressing made with lemon juice and sprinkle the salad with 2 hard-cooked eggs, sieved. Garnish with tomato wedges.

ᖶᕠ Spinach and Watercress Salad

WASH and pat dry 1 pound spinach, remove all the large stems, and tear the leaves into pieces. Wash and pat dry 1 bunch of watercress and remove all the stems. Chill the leaves until they are crisp and mix them together in a large bowl. Toss the greens lightly with Mediterranean dressing and crumble 6 slices cooked crisp bacon over the salad.

ᖶᕠ Watercress Salad   SALADE DE CRESSON

WASH 2 large bunches of watercress, discard the stems, and dry the leaves thoroughly. Put the cress in a salad bowl, sprinkle it lightly with salt, and chill it well. Just before serving, sprinkle 3 tablespoons olive oil, 2 tablespoons red-wine vinegar, and the juice of 1/2 lemon over the salad. Add 1/2 cup toasted bread crumbs and toss lightly.

ᖶᕠ Watercress and Scallion Salad

WASH 2 bunches of watercress, discard the stems, and dry the leaves. Wrap the leaves loosely in aluminum foil and chill them for 30 minutes. Wash and trim 24 scallions, slice them thinly into a salad bowl, and add the watercress. Toss the salad with French dressing.

SALADE AU CHAPON   ## Green Salad with Garlic Toast

SELECT an assortment of salad greens—lettuce, romaine, chicory, or escarole—in any desired combination. Separate the leaves, discarding any bruised or brown parts, and wash them thoroughly under running cold water. Drain the greens in a colander and break the leaves into fork-sized pieces. Put the greens in a wire salad basket or in a linen towel to remove as much water as possible. Handle the greens carefully so as not the bruise the leaves. Chill the greens thoroughly.

Prepare a *chapon* by rubbing both sides of a large piece of toasted French bread with the cut side of a garlic clove. Sprinkle the *chapon* with olive oil and put it in a salad bowl. Arrange the chilled greens on top. Sprinkle the salad with 2 teaspoons mixed finely chopped parsley and chives and 1 teaspoon each of chopped tarragon and chervil. Just before serving, add French dressing and toss the salad carefully but thoroughly, so that the garlic flavor of the *chapon* will coat the greens.

Mimosa Salad

COMBINE equal amounts of Boston lettuce, escarole, and romaine, torn in uniform pieces, in a salad bowl and toss the greens lightly with garlic French dressing. Sprinkle the top with 2 hard-cooked egg yolks, forced through a sieve.

Vegetable and Sour Cream Salad

COMBINE 1 cup each of cucumbers and tomatoes and 1/2 cup each of radishes and sweet onion, all sliced. Toss the vegetables lightly with sour cream horseradish dressing. Arrange the salad on a bed of crisp salad greens.

Vegetable Salad with Feta Cheese

WASH and dry 1 head of romaine lettuce and tear the leaves into medium pieces. Add 1 cucumber, peeled and sliced, 2 tomatoes, peeled, seeded, and cut into strips,

Swiss Cheese Salad

1/2 cup green onions, chopped, 5 radishes, sliced, 1 garlic clove, crushed, and 1/2 cup each of parsley, dill, and mint, all finely chopped. Grate 1/4 pound Feta cheese and mix it into the vegetables with 1/2 cup French dressing. Sprinkle the salad with 1/2 teaspoon lemon juice.

Salade Caroline

MIX together diced cucumbers, bits of sweet red pepper, slivers of Swiss cheese, and tiny croutons. Toss the salad with French dressing and arrange it in pyramids on individual salad plates lined with escarole. Sprinkle with finely chopped hazelnuts.

Musetta Salad

COMBINE in a salad bowl 1 celery heart and 1 fennel heart, both coarsely chopped, 1 head of chicory, finely shredded, 3 small cooked potatoes and 1/4 cup Swiss cheese, both diced, 6 artichoke hearts preserved in oil, 6 mushrooms, washed and trimmed, 1 teaspoon capers, and 2 hard-cooked eggs, sliced.

Combine 1/2 cup olive oil, 1 tablespoon each of wine vinegar and mayonnaise, and salt and pepper to taste. Toss the vegetables lightly with the dressing.

Swiss Cheese Salad

CUT 1/2 pound Swiss cheese into 1-inch sticks and toss the cheese sticks lightly with 6 hard-cooked eggs, finely chopped, and 1/2 cup thick sour cream mixed with 1 1/2 teaspoons dry mustard, 1 teaspoon grated horseradish, a pinch of ground cuminseed, and 1/2 teaspoon each of salt and pepper. Arrange the salad on a bed of crisp salad greens or green leaves.

Stuffed Tomatoes Idaho

PREPARE 6 tomatoes for stuffing. Combine 4 Idaho potatoes and 1/2 pound Swiss cheese, both finely diced, 1 onion, finely chopped, 1 tablespoon minced dill, and 1/2 cup French dressing. Stir the mixture gently until it is well coated with the dressing. Fill the tomato shells with the stuffing and cover the top of each with 2 teaspoons mayonnaise.

ʃ❧ Asparagus Salad

FOR each serving, arrange 6 cold cooked stalks of asparagus on a bed of lettuce. Mix 2 hard-cooked eggs, chopped, with 1 tablespoon chopped parsley and sprinkle the mixture over the asparagus. Pour 1 teaspoon French dressing over each salad.

ʃ❧ Jockey Club Salad

ARRANGE 6 stalks of cold cooked asparagus on each salad plate. Sprinkle the asparagus with finely chopped truffles and serve with mayonnaise.

ʃ❧ Asparagus Salad with Shrimp and Water Chestnuts

ARRANGE on a salad platter uniform groupings of cold cooked asparagus tips, cooked shrimp, shelled and deveined, and slices of water chestnuts. Sprinkle the salad with French dressing made with lemon juice and with parsley, chives, and chervil, all finely chopped.

ʃ❧ Avocado and Mushroom Salad

LINE a salad bowl with leaves of Boston lettuce. Cover the lettuce with thin slices of avocado and completely cover the avocado with thinly sliced raw mushrooms. Pour French dressing made with lemon juice over the salad.

ʃ❧ Avocado and Litchi Salad

TEAR the tender leaves of 2 heads of romaine into pieces and mix them with the leaves of 1 bunch of watercress. Toss the greens lightly with French dressing and heap the salad on individual salad plates. Arrange a thick ring of avocado slices on top and put several preserved litchi nuts, drained and chilled, in the center. Squeeze a little lemon juice over the avocado and sprinkle the litchi nuts with chopped parsley or shredded radishes.

Avocado and Spinach Salad

SAUTÉ 2 onions, sliced, in 2 tablespoons butter until they are golden. Blend them with 1/2 pound spinach, cooked and well drained. Chop the mixture coarsely, add 1 hard-cooked egg and 1 avocado, both sliced, and chop the salad finely. Season the salad with salt to taste and serve with vinaigrette sauce.

PURÉE D'AVOCAT À LA COQUE ## Avocado Purée Shells

CHILL 3 avocados, halve them lengthwise, and discard the stones. Scoop out the pulp, leaving the avocado shells intact. Mash the pulp with a silver fork and force it through a sieve. Add 1 tablespoon confectioners' sugar and beat the purée until it is smooth. Stir in 3 tablespoons lime juice, fold in 1/2 cup heavy cream, whipped, and pile the purée back into the avocado shells.

Green Bean Salad

COVER 1 pound cold cooked green beans with French dressing and let them marinate for 30 minutes. Mix the beans with 1 cup celery, cut in fine julienne. Garnish the salad with chopped chives and the sieved yolk and white of 1 hard-cooked egg. Add more French dressing, if necessary, and chill thoroughly.

Green Bean and Cucumber Salad

COMBINE 1/2 pound cold cooked green beans with 1 small unpeeled cucumber, diced, and 12 radishes, thinly sliced. Toss the salad lightly with French dressing and sprinkle it with chopped hard-cooked egg.

ೞ Spiced Beet Salad

CUT 18 young beets, cooked and peeled, into thin slices and arrange them on a platter. Combine in a saucepan 3/4 cup cider vinegar, 1/2 cup sugar, 1 teaspoon each of cinnamon and mustard seed, 1/4 teaspoon salt, and a pinch of cloves, and simmer the dressing for 5 minutes. Pour the hot dressing over the beets, let them cool, and chill thoroughly.

ೞ Brussels Sprouts Salad

COOK 2 pints washed and trimmed Brussels sprouts in boiling salted water to cover for about 15 minutes, or until they are tender, and drain them. Toss the sprouts with chervil French dressing, chill them well, and serve on chilled salad plates, garnished with slices of lemon.

ೞ Cauliflower Salad

BREAK a head of cauliflower into flowerets and cook it in boiling salted water for about 10 minutes, or until it is barely tender. Drain the cauliflower, rinse it in cold water, and put it in a salad bowl with 6 anchovy filets, cut into thin strips, 1 tablespoon each of capers and chopped shallots, and 12 olives, pitted and sliced. Sprinkle the salad with freshly ground pepper, pour over it 3 tablespoons olive oil and 1 tablespoon wine vinegar, and marinate it in the refrigerator for 30 minutes. Serve in lettuce cups.

ೞ Celery Salad

WASH 2 heads of celery, cut the stalks into slices, and chop the leaves. Put the celery in a salad bowl and toss it lightly with French dressing. Chill the salad thoroughly.

ೞ Celery and Black Olive Salad   SALADE D'ESTRÉES

ON salad plates arrange ripe black olives and celery, both cut into small even strips. Serve with mayonnaise seasoned with dry mustard and cayenne.

Celery and Radish Salad 🖎

WASH and slice 1 bunch red radishes. Combine the slices with 2 cups diced celery. Toss the salad with French dressing and sprinkle it with toasted bread crumbs and the sieved yolk of 1 hard-cooked egg.

Celeriac Salad 🖎

CUT cooked celeriac into julienne. Arrange the celeriac in a salad bowl lined with romaine and pour French dressing over it. Garnish with the chopped yolk and white of 1 hard-cooked egg.

Celeriac and Artichoke Salad 🖎

LINE a salad bowl with leaves of romaine and arrange on top cooked artichoke bottoms and raw celeriacs and pimiento, both cut into julienne. Chill the salad and serve with vinaigrette sauce.

Celeriac and Watercress Salad 🖎

BLANCH 1 large celeriac in boiling salted water to cover for 5 minutes and drain it. Cool the root and cut it into fine julienne. Toss the celeriac gently with herb French dressing and arrange the salad on a bed of watercress leaves.

Saint Alain Salad 🖎

ARRANGE cooked celeriac, cut into thick strips, in the center of a platter and surround it with mounds of raw mushrooms, finely chopped, truffles cut in thin julienne, and the grated whites of hard-cooked eggs. Surround the platter with a border of watercress and sprinkle the salad with the sieved yolks of hard-cooked eggs. Serve with French dressing.

ᔌ Chinese Cabbage Salad

SHRED finely Chinese cabbage and put it in a salad bowl. Toss the cabbage lightly with sour cream horseradish dressing blended with 1 tablespoon grated Swiss cheese.

ᔌ Cucumber Salad

SALADE DE CONCOMBRES

SCORE 4 unpeeled cucumbers lengthwise with a silver fork. Slice the cucumbers thinly, shake them in a small bowl with 1 teaspoon salt, and let them stand, uncovered, for 30 minutes. Bring to a boil 1/2 cup tarragon vinegar, 1/4 cup water, and 1 teaspoon sugar. Cool the dressing. Drain the cucumbers well, cover them with the dressing, and sprinkle generously with freshly ground black pepper. Chill the salad thoroughly.

ᔌ Danish Cucumber Salad

CUT 3 young cucumbers into paper-thin slices. Combine 1/2 cup each of water and vinegar, 1 teaspoon celery seed, a pinch of salt, and freshly ground pepper to taste. Pour the dressing over the cucumber slices and let them stand for 1 to 1 1/2 hours. Drain the cucumbers and serve the salad chilled, sprinkled with 1 tablespoon finely minced parsley.

ᔌ Lebanese Cucumber Salad

ON salad plates arrange thin slices of unpeeled cucumber on a bed of watercress. Top with whipped yoghurt and dust with finely chopped mint.

ᔌ Norwegian Cucumber Salad

BRING to a boil 1 cup vinegar, 3 tablespoons sugar, 2 tablespoons chopped fresh dill, 1/2 teaspoon pepper, and 1/4 teaspoon salt. Stir the mixture to dissolve the sugar and cool it. Scrub but do not peel 3 large cucumbers, slice them thinly, and cover them with the cooled dressing. Chill the salad for 20 minutes, sprinkle it with 1 tablespoon chopped dill, and serve as a relish.

Fennel Salad

WASH and drain 2 bulbs of fennel and cut them crosswise into pieces 1/2 inch thick. Arrange the fennel in a salad bowl. Sprinkle the greens with French dressing, add salt and freshly ground pepper, and toss the salad lightly.

Onion and Tomato Salad

CUT 1 large Spanish onion into thin slices and spread the rings on the bottom of a large bowl. Cover the onion rings with 6 large tomatoes, peeled and thickly sliced, and sprinkle with 2 tablespoons each of chives, basil, and dill, all chopped, 1 teaspoon celery seeds, 1/2 teaspoon sugar, 3/4 teaspoon salt, and a dash of freshly ground pepper. Chill the salad thoroughly.

Red Onion Salad

PEEL 4 red onions, cut them into paper-thin slices, and sprinkle the slices with 2 teaspoons salt. Cover the onions with ice water and a few ice cubes and let them rest for 30 minutes. Drain the slices and pat them dry. Arrange them in layers in a salad bowl and sprinkle with a mixture of 1/2 cup olive oil and 3 tablespoons wine vinegar. Garnish the salad with anchovy filets and pitted black olives.

COEURS DE PALMIER EN SALADE   ## Hearts of Palm Salad

ARRANGE 2 or 3 slices of hearts of palm lengthwise on individual salad plates. Serve with French dressing mixed with a little chopped watercress.

Radish Salad

BEAT 1 quart yoghurt with a wooden spoon until it is smooth. Stir in 4 garlic cloves, pounded to a paste with 2 tablespoons vinegar and a dash of salt. Add 2 bunches of radishes, sliced, and chill the salad thoroughly.

❧ Yellow and Red Tomato Salad

CUT 1 large Spanish onion into thin slices and spread the rings on a large flat serving dish. Cover the onion rings with 3 large yellow tomatoes and 3 large red tomatoes, all peeled and thickly sliced. Sprinkle the onions and the tomatoes with 3/4 teaspoon salt, 1/2 teaspoon sugar, a dash of pepper, 1 generous tablespoon of mixed chives, basil, and dill, all chopped, and 1 teaspoon celery seeds. Cover the bowl and chill the salad well.

❧ Tomato and Mushroom Salad

CHOP finely 1/2 pound mushrooms and sauté them with a crushed garlic clove in 3 tablespoons olive oil for 5 minutes, shaking the pan frequently. Discard the garlic and season the mushrooms with lemon juice and salt and pepper to taste and a little finely chopped orégano. Chill the mushrooms well. Arrange thick slices of peeled tomato on leaves of romaine on individual salad plates. Heap the mushrooms on the tomatoes and sprinkle the salads lightly with French dressing. Garnish with sprigs of parsley.

❧ Tomato and Onion Salad with Dill

SLICE thinly 6 peeled tomatoes and 2 onions and arrange the slices on overlapping layers on a platter. Sprinkle with 2 tablespoons lemon juice and with a mixture of 4 tablespoons chopped dill, 2 teaspoons sugar, 1 1/2 teaspoons salt, 1 teaspoon celery seed, and 1/2 teaspoon freshly ground black pepper. Chill the salad thoroughly.

❧ Zucchini Salad

COOK 6 scrubbed but unpeeled zucchini in boiling salted water for 6 minutes and drain them. Cut the squash into slices 1/8 inch thick and put them in a bowl with 1 onion and 2 garlic cloves, both sliced, and enough French dressing to cover. Marinate the zucchini overnight in the refrigerator. Drain off the dressing and discard the onion and garlic. Arrange the zucchini on thin overlapping slices of tomato on a platter. Sprinkle the squash with grated Parmesan and garnish the platter with lettuce leaves filled with mayonnaise.

Andalusian Salad

IN a large salad bowl mash 3 hard-cooked egg yolks with 4 tablespoons garlic olive oil to a smooth paste. Add 4 tomatoes and 2 cucumbers, peeled, seeded, and chopped, and 1/4 cup each of diced green pepper and diced onion. Pour the juice of 2 limes over the vegetables, mix them gently, and chill. Serve the salad in chilled bowls and sprinkle generously with chopped parsley.

Barcelona Salad

ON a bed of chicory arrange tomatoes, cut in dice, green pepper, cut in julienne, and quartered hard-cooked eggs. Serve with French dressing.

Garden Vegetable Salad

COMBINE equal amounts of sliced unpeeled cucumbers, cooked asparagus tips, green beans cooked until barely tender and cut into diagonal slices, and raw cauliflower buds. Toss the salad with French dressing seasoned with *fines herbes*.

SALADE DU LIBAN

Lebanese Salad

PEEL and dice 3 tomatoes and 1 cucumber and combine the dice with 3 scallions, sliced, and a bunch of parsley, chopped. Toss the salad with a dressing made of 1 part lemon juice and 2 parts olive oil, and sprinkle it with chopped black olives.

Niçoise Vegetable Salad

COMBINE equal amounts of diced potatoes and diced green beans, both cooked until barely tender, and chill the vegetables thoroughly. Mix them lightly with French dressing made with lemon juice. Mound the vegetables on a platter and cover them with pitted black olives and capers. Garnish the platter with quarters of peeled tomatoes and sprinkle generously with chopped basil.

ॐ Russian Salad

SCORE large unpeeled cucumbers with a silver fork, cut them into 2-inch lengths, and hollow out the centers. Put the cucumber rings on a lettuce leaf.

Mix together 1/2 cup each green peas, carrots, and green beans, all cooked until barely tender and finely diced. Marinate the vegetables in French dressing to cover for 1 hour. Drain off any excess dressing and add mayonnaise to taste. Fill the cucumber rings with the mixture.

ॐ Truffle Salad Gambetta   SALADE DE TRUFFES GAMBETTA

RUB a salad bowl lightly with a cut garlic clove. Press 4 hard-cooked egg yolks into the bowl and mash them with 2 tablespoons prepared mustard. Gradually blend in 1/2 cup each of olive oil and tarragon vinegar and add salt and very little pepper to taste. Combine 6 white truffles, finely chopped, with 6 cooked artichoke bottoms, cut into quarters, and mix them carefully with the dressing. Coat the salad with 1/2 cup green mayonnaise.

ॐ Flageolet Salad

MIX lightly 4 cups cold cooked flageolets with 1 large onion, chopped, 1/4 cup finely chopped parsley, and 3 tablespoons each of olive oil and vinegar or lemon juice. Add salt and pepper to taste. Marinate the beans for at least 1 hour and serve them on lettuce leaves, garnished with cucumber wedges and olives.

ॐ Garbanzo Salad

COVER 1 pound *garbanzos*, or chic-peas, with water and soak them overnight. Drain the *garbanzos*, cover them with fresh water, and cook them for about 30 minutes, or until they are tender. Drain and cool the *garbanzos*. Combine them with 1/2 cup each of cooked diced bacon and finely chopped onion, 2 garlic cloves, minced, and 1/2 cup French dressing. Serve the salad on crisp lettuce leaves and garnish with anchovy filets.

Kidney Bean Salad 𝄢

COMBINE in a kettle 6 cups water, 2 cups kidney beans, and 2 teaspoons salt, and let the beans soak overnight. Bring the beans to a boil in their liquid, simmer them for about 2 hours, or until they are tender, and drain them. Add 1 large onion, finely chopped, 1/2 cup chopped parsley, 1/4 cup each of salad oil and vinegar, 1/4 teaspoon pepper, and a sprinkling of paprika. Mix the salad lightly and chill it. Serve the beans on lettuce and sprinkle them generously with chopped parsley.

White Bean and Lentil Salad 𝄢

SOAK 1 cup each of dried white beans and lentils overnight in water to cover. Drain the beans, cover them with fresh salted water, and cook them for 45 minutes, or until they are tender but still slightly crisp. Drain the beans and chill them. Marinate the beans in 1/4 cup each of olive oil and tarragon vinegar, seasoned with salt and pepper and a pinch of dry mustard. Just before serving, sprinkle the beans with a mixture of hard-cooked egg and chives, both finely chopped.

Picnic Potato Salad 𝄢

IN a large bowl combine 1 cup finely chopped celery and a few celery leaves, 2 large onions and 1 large green pepper, both finely chopped, 4 pimientos, cut into small pieces, 3 tablespoons parsley, coarsely chopped, 3 tablespoons juice from sweet gherkin pickles, and 2 cups mayonnaise. Mix the ingredients thoroughly and chill them for several hours. Add 1/4 cup capers, 12 small stuffed olives, thinly sliced, 1 cup diced cucumber, 8 sweet gherkins, diced, and 2 pounds cooked potatoes, cut into cubes and cooled but not chilled. Add salt and pepper to taste and sprinkle generously with paprika.

Potato Salad Dumas 𝄢

COOK 6 peeled potatoes in chicken stock and slice them. While the potatoes are still hot sprinkle them with salt and pepper, a little olive oil, and a dash of wine vinegar. Pour over the salad 2 cups white wine and let it stand in a cool place for 2 hours. Just before serving, sprinkle the salad with 2 tablespoons *fines herbes*.

ૐ Potato Salad with Chestnuts

PEEL 24 small cooked potatoes and, while they are still warm, combine them with 1/4 cup scallions and 2 tablespoons parsley, both minced, 1/4 cup melted butter, 3/4 cup white wine mixed with 2 tablespoons white-wine vinegar and a scant 1/2 cup olive oil, 2 pimientos, cut in small pieces, and 3/4 cup whole cooked chestnuts. Add salt and pepper to taste and let the salad stand in a cool place for several hours before serving.

ૐ Red Radish Coleslaw

SHRED finely 1 head of cabbage and combine the shreds with 12 crisp radishes, cut into thin slices.

To 1 1/2 cups mayonnaise add 1 teaspoon prepared mustard and 1 teaspoon each of capers, tarragon, chives, parsley, gherkins, chervil, and shallots, all chopped. Pour this dressing over the cabbage and garnish the slaw with radish roses. Chill thoroughly.

ૐ Black Radish Coleslaw

GRATE coarsely 1 small head of cabbage, 1 black radish, peeled, and 1 carrot. Sprinkle the vegetables lightly with salt, let them stand for 1 hour, and drain off any liquid that accumulates. Combine the vegetables with 1 cup sour cream and 3/4 cup cottage cheese, and sprinkle the slaw with 1/4 cup chopped chives. Chill thoroughly.

ૐ Sesame Coleslaw

SHRED finely 1 small head of cabbage and combine the shreds with 1/2 cup sliced water chestnuts, 4 tablespoons each of shredded green pepper and celery, and 2 tablespoons shredded green onions.

Combine 1/3 cup sesame oil, 2 tablespoons soy sauce, 1 teaspoon prepared mustard, and the juice of 1 lemon. Mix this dressing with the vegetables and chill.

Potato Salad with Chestnuts

🦢 Sour Cream Coleslaw

SHRED finely 1 head of cabbage, arrange it in a heap on a chilled platter, and cover it with thin slices of peeled tomato.

To 1 1/2 cups mayonnaise add 1 tablespoon each of celery, pimiento, green onion, and chervil, all finely chopped. Stir in 2 scant teaspoons chili powder and 1/2 cup sour cream. Pour this dressing over the tomatoes and cabbage and chill the slaw thoroughly.

🦢 Grapefruit and Water Chestnut Salad

IN a salad bowl combine 2 heads of Bibb lettuce, shredded, the sections of 2 grapefruits, and 12 water chestnuts, thinly sliced. Toss the salad with French dressing and dot the surface with tiny croutons.

🦢 Alexander Salad

ARRANGE small center leaves of romaine and grapefruit sections like spokes of a wheel on individual salad plates. Between the spokes put celery cut into julienne, anchovy filets, and hard-cooked eggs, diced. Top with mayonnaise and with a circle of anchovy filled with caviar.

🦢 Chicory and Orange Salad

REMOVE the skin and pith from a large orange. Cut the orange into paper-thin slices and put the slices into a salad bowl half full of torn leaves of chicory. Toss the salad lightly with French dressing.

🦢 Orange and Olive Salad

REMOVE the skin and pith from 2 large oranges. Cut the oranges into paper-thin slices and cut the slices into quarters. Put them in a salad bowl half full of torn leaves of romaine. Add 6 thin slices of sweet Italian red onion, separated into rings, and 12 Greek black olives, pitted and sliced. Toss the salad with French dressing.

Beet and Orange Salad 🐏

PLACE alternate slices of orange and cold cooked beets on leaves of romaine lettuce. Chill the salad and serve with vinaigrette sauce.

Watercress and Orange Salad 🐏

FILL a salad bowl with alternate layers of thinly sliced oranges and crisp watercress leaves. Sprinkle the salad with French dressing to taste and chill it thoroughly.

Fruit and Tomato Salad 🐏

MIX together 2 cups nuts, chopped or grated, 6 dates and 3 figs, all quartered, 2 tablespoons raisins, 1 large apple, chopped, 1/4 cup fresh shredded coconut, and 1 tablespoon melted butter. Separate the leaves of 1 head of lettuce and arrange them on individual salad plates. Put 2 or 3 slices of tomato on each plate and cover them with French dressing. Mound the fruit and nut mixture in the center of each salad and garnish with a spray of watercress.

Romaine and Pineapple Salad 🐏

ON individual salad plates arrange crisp leaves of romaine and chunks of fresh pineapple. Garnish the salads with watercress and serve with mayonnaise.

Pineapple Fresh Fruit Salad 🐏

CUT the peeled sections of 1 grapefruit and 2 oranges into several pieces. Combine the fruits with 2 apples and 1 pear, both unpeeled and diced, 1 cup fresh pineapple, cut in large dice, and 1/2 cup red grapes, halved and seeded. Toss the salad with a dressing made of 1/2 cup each of olive oil and cider vinegar and the juice of 1 lime.

Tabbooli

Avocado Mousse 🐏

WITH a silver fork mash enough peeled and pitted avocados to make 2 cups pulp. Stir into the pulp 1 teaspoon salt, 1/2 teaspoon white pepper, and 1 tablespoon onion juice or lemon juice. Combine 3/4 cup heavy cream, whipped, with 1/2 cup mayonnaise. Add 1 tablespoon gelatin, softened in 1/4 cup cold water and dissolved over hot water. Fold this into the mashed avocado. Turn the mousse into a 1-quart mold rinsed in cold water. Chill the mousse for about 3 hours. Unmold it on a chilled platter and garnish it with leaves of Belgian endive and chopped parsley.

Avocado Ring

FOR the wedding reception, double the ingredients and pour the mixture into 2 ring molds. Serve on chilled platters garnished with watercress.

Cucumber Mousse 🐏

PEEL, seed, and grate enough cucumbers to make 1 cup pulp. Drain off the juice and in it soften 1 tablespoon gelatin for 5 minutes. Dissolve the gelatin thoroughly over hot water, cool it, and add it with 1 tablespoon chopped chives to the grated cucumber. Chill the mixture until it starts to thicken. Beat 1 1/2 cups cottage cheese until it is smooth and blend in the gelatin mixture, stirring well. Season with salt and white pepper to taste. Pour the mixture into a 3/4-quart mold rinsed in cold water and chill it thoroughly. Unmold the mousse on a chilled platter and garnish with cucumber slices and lettuce leaves.

LEBANESE CRACKED WHEAT SALAD   Tabbooli 🐏

SOAK 2 cups fine bulgur (cracked wheat) in water to cover for 2 hours. Drain the wheat well and squeeze out any excess moisture. Put the bulgur in a salad bowl with 1 1/2 cups finely chopped green onions and season with salt and pepper to taste. Add 2 cups finely chopped parsley, 3/4 cup peeled, seeded, and chopped tomatoes, and 1 cup each of olive oil and lemon juice. Toss the salad with two forks, to keep the grains separate. If desired, add more salt and lemon juice to taste. Serve the *tabbooli* garnished with sections of tomato and with fresh mint leaves. For the summer buffet, make 2 salads to serve 18.

Rice Salad

COMBINE 3 cups cold cooked rice with 1 cup green beans, cooked and diced, 3/4 cup ripe black olives, chopped, 1/2 cup pimiento, diced, and salt and pepper to taste. Using two forks, toss the salad lightly with French dressing and chill it. Pile the salad gently into a bowl and garnish with cherry tomatoes. For the formal buffet, double the recipe and make 2 salads to serve 16 to 20.

Rice and Green Pea Salad

PUT 3 cups cold cooked rice in a salad bowl rubbed with a split garlic clove and season with salt and pepper to taste. Stir in 1/4 cup French dressing and add 1 cup cold cooked peas, 6 scallions, finely chopped, and 3 tablespoons minced parsley. Arrange the salad in mounds on individual plates and garnish with radish roses and parsley bouquets.

Wild Rice Salad

TOSS 3 cups cool cooked wild rice lightly with French dressing and fold in 1/2 cup each of cooked artichoke hearts and pimiento, both diced. Serve without chilling.

Jellied Vegetable Salad

CHILL a 1-quart ring or decorative mold in a pan of cracked ice and line it with cool but still liquid aspic. Let the aspic set. Decorate the sides with cooked chicken or vegetables, cut into rounds or decorative shapes and dipped in aspic. Chill the mold in the cracked ice to fix the decorations, pour in aspic 1/4 to 1/2 inch deep, and chill again. Mix 1/2 cup each of cooked green beans, carrots, and peas, and raw celery and cucumbers, all diced or cut in small julienne, with 3/4 cup *mayonnaise collée*. Fill the mold nearly to the top with the vegetables, add liquid aspic to the brim, and chill well. Unmold the aspic on a chilled serving dish lined with lettuce leaves and garnish it with sliced hard-cooked eggs and cherry tomatoes.

Fisherman's Salad 🐟

LINE a salad bowl with a head of shredded lettuce and arrange on it 6 cold cooked potatoes, sliced. Remove the skin and bones from 1 1/2 pounds poached salmon and flake the fish. Arrange the fish flakes on the potatoes and sprinkle them with 2 tablespoons each of finely chopped onion and pickle. Add salt and pepper to taste and enough French dressing just to moisten the salad. Decorate the salad with the whites and yolks of 2 hard-cooked eggs, put separately through a fine-meshed sieve, and with 1 tablespoon finely chopped green pepper.

Lobster Salad 🐟

COMBINE 3 cups cooked lobster meat, cut in large dice, with 1 cup raw celeriac, shredded. Cover the mixture with 1/2 cup French dressing and marinate it for 3 hours. Blend the lobster mixture with enough mayonnaise to bind it, and arrange the salad on a bed of greens on a platter. Encircle the salad with a ring of sliced sautéed mushroom caps.

Lobster Salads with Caviar 🐟

REMOVE all the meat from the shells of 10 pounds cooked lobsters, keeping the claw meat as intact as possible and the tail meat in one piece. Cut the tail meat of the lobsters into 30 medallions 1/2 inch thick. Mix 1 cup each of string beans, carrots, and potatoes, all diced and cooked, with 1 cup Russian dressing. Mound some of this vegetable mixture on each lobster medallion to make individual portions. Top each salad with 1 teaspoon black caviar and garnish the platter with the reserved claw meat. Makes 30 servings.

Scallop and Potato Salad with Shallot Mayonnaise 🐟

PEEL 6 cooked potatoes and, while they are still warm, cut them into slices and cover them with a little white wine. Poach 1 pound scallops in equal parts of white wine and water for 10 minutes, or until they are firm, and drain and cool them. Arrange the potatoes and the cooked scallops in a salad bowl. Toss the salad lightly with a generous amount of shallot mayonnaise. Serve without chilling.

ᔰ Dilled Shrimp in Lettuce Cups

REMOVE the coarse outer leaves from small heads of lettuce, wash the lettuce well, and drain it thoroughly. Carefully remove the hearts, without disturbing the outside leaves. Fill the cavities with cold poached shrimp, coarsely chopped, bound with mayonnaise, and seasoned with finely chopped dill.

ᔰ Victorian Shrimp Salad

MARINATE 4 cups cooked shrimp, shelled and deveined, in vinaigrette sauce for 2 hours. Drain the shrimp and add 2 cups finely chopped celery, 4 tablespoons grated onion, and enough mayonnaise to bind the mixture. Heap the salad on a serving dish, sprinkle it lavishly with finely chopped dill, and surround it with cooked asparagus tips.

ᔰ Edwardian Chicken Salad

MARINATE 2 cups cooked diced white meat of chicken in 1/2 cup French dressing for 2 hours. Drain the chicken and add 1 cup finely diced celery, 1 teaspoon grated onion, and enough mayonnaise to bind the salad. Garnish the salad with quartered hard-cooked eggs and sprinkle it with capers.

ᔰ Baked Chicken Salad

COMBINE 2 cups each of diced cooked chicken or turkey and sliced celery, 1 cup mayonnaise, 3/4 cup coarsely chopped walnuts, 3 tablespoons lemon juice, 3 teaspoons minced onion, and salt and pepper to taste. Heap the mixture in individual shells or baking dishes and sprinkle with dry bread crumbs. Bake the chicken in a very hot oven (450° F.) for about 15 minutes, or until it is delicately browned.

ᔰ Chicken and Sweetbread Salad

PREPARE 2 pairs of sweetbreads and cool them. Dice the sweetbreads and combine them with 2 cups diced cooked chicken and 1/2 cup slivered sautéed almonds. Add

1 1/2 cups mayonnaise, or enough to bind the salad, and salt to taste. Chill the salad thoroughly. Serve it on a platter lined with watercress and sprinkle it with an additional 1/2 cup almonds.

Sweetbread and Pear Salad

PREPARE 3 pairs of sweetbreads and cool them. Dice the sweetbreads and combine them with 1 cup peeled and cubed ripe pears, 1/2 cup finely shredded celery, and 1/4 cup thinly sliced filberts or hazelnuts. Sprinkle the salad with salt and freshly ground pepper and moisten it lightly with mayonnaise.

Rock Cornish Salad

CHOP finely the meat of 2 or 3 poached or roasted Rock Cornish game hens. There should be about 4 cups. Combine the meat with 4 truffles, finely chopped, and enough French dressing to moisten, and chill the salad for 2 hours. Line a salad bowl with shredded lettuce and heap the salad on the greens. Sprinkle chopped chives over the salad and serve with a sauceboat of mayonnaise flavored with tarragon.

Duck and Orange Salad

COMBINE 2 1/2 cups poached duck meat, cut into rather large dice, with the sections of 4 small navel oranges, peeled and free of membranes, 12 ripe olives, pitted and sliced, and 1 small red onion, thinly sliced. Sprinkle the mixture lightly with salt and add a generous pinch of rosemary. Chill for 1 hour.

Line a large salad bowl with leaves of romaine and chicory and put the duck and orange mixture on top. Toss the salad lightly with French dressing made with lemon juice. Garnish the salad with blanched slivered toasted almonds. Serve cool but not chilled.

Roast Beef Salad

CUT into julienne 1 pound sliced cold cooked roast beef, free of fat and gristle. Put the meat in a salad bowl with 2 tablespoons each of minced onion and chopped gherkins, 2 cooked beets, 2 boiled and peeled potatoes, and 2 hard-cooked eggs, all sliced, a few sorrel leaves, and 4 sprigs of tarragon. Combine 1 cup each of Rhine wine and olive oil and 2 tablespoons tarragon vinegar. Beat the dressing with a wire whisk and pour it over the salad. Toss the salad and chill it for 4 hours. Before serving, drain off the excess dressing and surround the salad with romaine lettuce.

ৡ Ham and Green Salad

ARRANGE in a salad bowl 1 head of lettuce, chopped, and assorted chopped greens —watercress, dandelion leaves, field salad, or chicory. In the center of the salad put 1 cup diced cooked ham, 1/2 cup croutons, and the chopped whites of 3 hard-cooked eggs. Sprinkle with 1 tablespoon chopped chives and riced egg yolks. At the table, add 1/2 cup French dressing and toss the salad.

ৡ Mayonnaise

RINSE a mixing bowl with hot water and dry it well. In it beat 2 egg yolks with a rotary beater and blend in well 1 teaspoon vinegar, 1/2 teaspoon each of salt and dry mustard, and a little white pepper. Add 1 cup olive oil, drop by drop at first, beating continually until a little more than 1/4 cup has been added. Add 1/2 teaspoon vinegar, still beating, and pour in the rest of the oil in a thin steady stream. Beat continually and stop adding the oil from time to time make sure the mixture is well combined. When the oil has been added and the mayonnaise is thick, finish with 1/2 teaspoon vinegar or lemon or lime juice.

If the mayonnaise curdles, wash the beater, beat 1 egg yolk in another bowl, and very slowly add the curdled mayonnaise to the fresh egg yolk, beating constantly to form a new emulsion.

If an electric beater is used, set it at medium speed.

Makes about 1 1/4 cups.

Blender Mayonnaise 🍃

IN the container of a blender put 2 eggs, 1/2 cup olive oil, 4 tablespoons lemon juice or vinegar, 1/2 teaspoon each of salt and dry mustard, and 1/8 teaspoon white pepper. Cover the container and turn the motor on high. Immediately remove the cover and add in a thin steady steam 1 1/2 cups olive oil. As soon as all the oil is added turn off the motor. Makes about 2 1/2 cups.

Chive Mayonnaise 🍃

To 1 cup mayonnaise add 2 tablespoons chopped chives and 2 teaspoons lemon juice.

Cucumber Mayonnaise 🍃

To 1 cup mayonnaise add 1 cup finely chopped cucumber and, if desired, 1 teaspoon finely chopped fresh mint leaves.

Curry Mayonnaise 🍃

To 2 cups mayonnaise add 4 tablespoons or more curry powder and 2 tablespoons soy sauce. Chill the dressing well.

Green Mayonnaise 🍃

To 2 cups mayonnaise add 2 tablespoons parsley, 1 tablespoon each of chives and tarragon, and 1 teaspoon each of chervil and dill, all finely chopped. Chill the mayonnaise for 2 hours.

Blender Green Mayonnaise 🍃

IN the container of a blender put 1 egg, 1/4 cup olive oil, 2 tablespoons wine vinegar, 1 tablespoon each of dill and chives, both coarsely chopped, 1 teaspoon dry mustard, 1/2 teaspoon salt, and 1/2 garlic clove. Cover the container and turn the motor on low. Immediately remove the cover and add in a thin steady stream 3/4 cup olive oil. As soon as all the oil is added turn off the motor. Chill the dressing before using.

Horseradish Mayonnaise

To 2 cups mayonnaise add the grated rind of 1/2 lemon and salt to taste. Just before serving stir in 1/4 cup freshly grated horseradish.

Pink Mayonnaise

To 1 cup mayonnaise add 1/3 cup tomato purée, the juice of 1 lemon, 1 teaspoon grated lemon rind, and salt and pepper to taste.

Roquefort Mayonnaise

To 1 cup mayonnaise add 1 cup Roquefort cheese, pressed through a fine sieve, 1 cup sour cream, and a few drops of Tabasco sauce.

Russian Dressing I

To 2 cups mayonnaise add 5 tablespoons chili sauce, 2 teaspoons each of pimientos and chives, both chopped, and 1 tablespoon lime juice.

Russian Dressing II

To 1 cup mayonnaise add 2 tablespoons caviar, 1 tablespoon finely chopped onion, 1 1/2 teaspoons Worcestershire sauce, and 1/2 teaspoon dry mustard. Let the dressing stand for 2 hours before using.

Mayonnaise

ৡ৶ Shallot Mayonnaise

POUND 6 to 8 shallots, finely chopped, in a mortar with 1/4 teaspoon salt. Soak 4 tablespoons bread crumbs in a little warm water, press them to drain, and blend them thoroughly with the shallot paste. Blend the mixture with 1 cup mayonnaise.

ৡ৶ Tarragon Mayonnaise

TO 1 cup mayonnaise add 1 tablespoon tomato ketchup and 1 teaspoon each of chopped fresh tarragon and vinegar or lemon juice.

ৡ৶ Green Goddess Dressing

COMBINE well in a bowl 1 egg yolk, 2 tablespoons tarragon vinegar, 1 tablespoon anchovy paste, and 1/2 teaspoon salt. Beat in, 2 tablespoons at a time, 1 cup salad oil. Stir in 1/4 cup light cream, 1 tablespoon lemon juice, 1 teaspoon onion salt, a dash of garlic salt, and 2 tablespoons each of chopped chives and chopped parsley.

ৡ৶ Roquefort and Sour Cream Dressing

IN the container of a blender combine 1 cup sour cream and 1/2 teaspoon each of salt, dry mustard, and minced onion. Cover the container and blend the dressing for 15 seconds. Add 1/4 cup crumbled Roquefort and blend the dressing for 30 seconds, or until it is smooth. Chill before using.

ৡ৶ French Dressing

TO 1/2 cup vinegar—wine, cider, tarragon, or malt—add 3/4 teaspoon salt and 1/4 teaspoon freshly ground white or black pepper. Stir the mixture well with a fork and add 1 1/2 cups olive oil. Beat the dressing with a fork until it thickens. Lemon juice may be substituted for the vinegar. Makes about 2 cups.

Creamy French Dressing

FOR a creamier, thicker dressing, put an ice cube into the mixing bowl and stir the dressing for a minute or so longer. Or set the mixing bowl into another bowl filled with ice, while the dressing is being stirred. The dressing may be mixed and shaken in a bottle.

Garlic French Dressing

IF a garlic flavor is desired, make the dressing with garlic olive oil or with garlic vinegar.

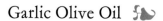

Garlic Olive Oil

HANG a peeled garlic clove by a thread in a bottle of olive oil for at least 4 days before making the dressing.

Garlic Vinegar

IN a bowl crush 3 large garlic cloves, add 1 quart vinegar, and mix well. Store the vinegar, covered, in the refrigerator for at least 2 days. Strain the vinegar through filter paper or a double layer of cheesecloth, pour it into hot sterilized bottles, and seal the bottles. Store in a cool dark place.

Herb Vinegar

PUT into a quart jar 6 tablespoons chopped chives, 1 tablespoon each of mint leaves and chervil, both chopped, 1 teaspoon each of chopped tarragon leaves and dried marjoram, 1 small bay leaf, and 1 whole clove. Fill the jar with vinegar and let it stand for a week. Strain the vinegar through filter paper or a double layer of cheese-cloth, pour it into hot sterilized bottles, and seal the bottles. Store in a cool dark place.

❧ Mint Vinegar

SHRED 2 cups firmly packed mint leaves, mix them well with 1 cup sugar, and let them stand for 5 minutes. Bring 1 quart cider vinegar to a boil, add the mint and sugar mixture, stirring constantly and crushing the leaves against the sides of the pan, and simmer the mixture for 3 minutes. Strain the vinegar through a flannel cloth, pour it into hot sterilized bottles, and store it in a cool dark place for several weeks before using.

❧ Mint Vinegar, Quick Method

BRUISE 2 dozen mint leaves with the fingers and soak them in 1/2 cup cider vinegar for 30 minutes. Crush the leaves with a wooden spoon, stir for 1 minute, and strain the vinegar through filter paper or cheesecloth before using.

❧ Shallot Vinegar

PUT into a large jar 1/4 pound shallots, peeled and finely chopped, and fill the jar with 1 quart vinegar. Cover the jar and let the vinegar stand for 10 days, shaking it once daily. Strain the vinegar through filter paper or a double layer of cheesecloth, pour it into hot sterilized bottles, and seal the bottles. Store in a cool dark place.

❧ Tarragon Vinegar

PACK a quart jar loosely with sprays of fresh tarragon and fill the jar with vinegar. Cover the jar and let it stand for 10 days in a dark place. Strain the vinegar through filter paper or a double layer of cheesecloth, pour it into hot sterilized bottles, and seal the bottles. Store in a cool dark place.

❧ Fines Herbes

EQUAL parts of chopped parsley, chives, tarragon, and chervil, which may be used in any combination, are the traditional components of this classic flavoring mixture. Use *fines herbes* to flavor salads, omelets, and vegetables.

Aniseed Dressing 🍃

To 1 cup French dressing add 1 small apple, chopped, 1 tablespoon heavy cream, and 1/4 teaspoon aniseed, crushed.

Avocado French Dressing 🍃

To 1 cup French dressing add 1 ripe avocado, mashed, 1 small onion, chopped, and 1/4 teaspoon nutmeg.

Bellevue Dressing 🍃

To 1 cup French dressing add 6 tablespoons sour cream and 1 tablespoon finely chopped chives.

Caper Dressing 🍃

To 1 cup French dressing add 2 tablespoons chopped hard-cooked egg yolk, 2 teaspoons chopped capers, a bit of anchovy paste the size of a pea, 1 large garlic clove, finely grated, and a few drops of Tabasco sauce.

Chervil French Dressing 🍃

To 1 cup French dressing made with lemon juice, add 1/4 cup chopped fresh chervil.

Chiffonnade Dressing 🍃

To 1 cup French dressing add 3 hard-cooked eggs, finely chopped, 2 tablespoons each of pickled beets and green olives, both finely chopped, and 1 tablespoon each of grated onion and finely chopped parsley or chervil.

Chutney Dressing

To 1 cup French dressing add 3 tablespoons each of finely chopped mango chutney and walnut ketchup and 1 teaspoon finely chopped parsley, chervil, or tarragon.

Cottage Cheese Dressing

To 1 cup French dressing add 3 tablespoons cottage cheese, 1 tablespoon each of chopped scallions and parsley, and 1/2 teaspoon dry mustard.

Curry French Dressing

To 1 cup French dressing add 1 teaspoon curry powder and 1 tablespoon finely chopped shallots.

Herb French Dressing

To 1 cup French dressing add 1 teaspoon Dijon-type mustard and 1 generous table-spoon *fines herbes*.

Horseradish French Dressing

To 1 cup French dressing add 3 tablespoons well-drained grated horseradish, 2 tea-spoons paprika, and a few drops of Tabasco sauce.

Lemon and Shallot Dressing   SAUCE ÉCHALOTE AU CITRON

To 1 cup French dressing made with lemon juice add 1 tablespoon finely chopped shallots, 1/2 teaspoon mustard, and a few drops of Worcestershire sauce.

Mustard French Dressing 🐚

To 1 cup French dressing add 1/4 cup prepared brown mustard. Blend well and add 1/2 teaspoon lemon juice.

Baked Onion Dressing 🐚

To 1 cup French dressing add 1/4 cup Spanish onion, baked until tender and finely chopped. Mix well and add 1/4 teaspoon coarse salt.

Radish Dressing 🐚

To 1 cup French dressing add 1 generous tablespoon chopped green celery leaves and 1 generous teaspoon each of prepared mustard and horseradish. Add 12 radishes, well trimmed and chopped, and blend well.

Tarragon French Dressing 🐚

To 1 cup French dressing made with tarragon vinegar add 2 teaspoons chopped fresh tarragon leaves.

Tomato French Dressing 🐚

To 1 cup French dressing add 3 tomatoes, peeled, seeded, and mashed, 1/8 teaspoon orégano, and a pinch of thyme. Stir well and add 1/4 cup grated Parmesan cheese.

Vinaigrette Sauce 🐚

To 1 cup French dressing add 1 teaspoon each of finely chopped green olives, capers, chives, parsley, and gherkins, and 1 hard-cooked egg yolk, finely chopped.

﹗ Avocado Dressing

WITH a silver fork mash the pulp of 1 large avocado, force it through a sieve, and add to the purée 2 tablespoons lime juice, 1 1/2 tablespoons finely chopped onion, 1 garlic clove, minced, and 1 teaspoon salt. Blend the ingredients well, add 1 large tomato, peeled, seeded, and chopped, and chill the dressing.

﹗ Red-Wine Dressing

To 1/2 cup dry red wine add 1 small onion, grated, 3/4 teaspoon salt, and 1/4 teaspoon freshly ground black pepper. Stir the mixture and let it stand for at least 30 minutes. Strain the dressing and add 1 1/2 cups garlic olive oil. Beat the dressing with a fork until it thickens.

﹗ Roquefort Salad Dressing

To 1/2 cup vinegar add 3/4 teaspoon salt and 1/4 teaspoon freshly ground pepper. Stir the mixture well with a fork, add 1 1/2 cups olive oil, and beat the dressing with the fork until it thickens. Add 1/2 cup crumbled Roquefort cheese and chill the dressing thoroughly.

﹗ Sour Cream Horseradish Dressing

BEAT 1 1/2 cups sour cream with a wooden spoon until it is slightly aerated. Add 1 teaspoon freshly grated horseradish soaked in 1 tablespoon white-wine vinegar, 1/2 teaspoon each of salt and dry mustard, and 1/4 teaspoon freshly ground black pepper.

﹗ Mediterranean Dressing

COMBINE 1 garlic clove, crushed, 1/2 teaspoon each of salt and grated lemon rind, 1/4 teaspoon each of paprika and pepper, and 2 tablespoons tarragon vinegar. Add gradually 1/2 cup olive oil, beating constantly, and beat in 2 tablespoons sour cream. Chill the dressing.

Sauces and Garnishes

Clarifying Stock 𝔰

BEAT 4 egg whites until they are stiff and turn them out of the bowl onto the stock. Do not fold them in. The egg-white mass will flatten out on the surface. Bring the mixture to a boil and, using a large wire whisk, move it constantly back and forth across the center of the pan. Do not use a circular motion or the stock will become cloudy. When the mixture reaches a rolling boil, remove the pan from the heat and let it stand for 10 minutes.

Line a large fine-meshed sieve with cheesecloth wrung out in cold water. Put the sieve over a deep bowl or saucepan and slowly pour in the stock and egg-white mixture. Let the mixture stand until it has completely dripped through and discard the egg whites. Do not press the stock through the strainer or it will be cloudy.

Clarifying Stock, Quick Method 𝔰

BEAT 1 egg white lightly with 2 teaspoons cold water and add it to the stock with 1 eggshell, broken in pieces. Bring the stock to a boil over low heat and boil it for 2 minutes. Let it stand in a warm place for 20 minutes and strain it through a sieve lined with cheesecloth wrung out in cold water.

ᕙ Mirepoix

SOME sauces begin with a mixture of vegetables and herbs cooked in butter. The stock and other ingredients are then added. The vegetables in the *mirepoix* are strained out of the sauce when it is completed. *Mirepoix* is also used in the bottom of a cooking vessel in which meat, poultry, or fish is cooked. The flavor of the dish is augmented by the *mirepoix* and the vegetables are used as the basis for the sauce served with the dish. The usual ingredients for a *mirepoix* are 1 carrot and 1 onion, both finely diced, 3 sprigs of parsley, a bay leaf, and a little thyme.

ᕙ Bouquet Garni

DRIED or powdered herbs should not be used to season a clear sauce for they will tend to cloud the stock. It is best to use a *bouquet garni*, an assortment of fresh herbs tied together with string or enclosed in a cheesecloth bag.

ᕙ Thickening Sauces

SAUCES are thickened primarily by reduction. The sauce is cooked slowly and occasionally stirred until it is reduced to the desired thickness. Sauces which are thickened by reduction should be salted only at the last moment.

Sauces may also be thickened at the start of cooking with a *roux*, or at the end of cooking with *beurre manié*.

Sauces such as hollandaise and *beurre blanc* are thickened by adding butter, bit by bit, over very low heat.

Egg yolk is the thickening agent in some sauces. A little of the hot sauce is added to the egg yolks to warm them, and the warmed egg yolks are then slowly stirred into the sauce.

Some sauces are based on purées and need no further thickening. Other sauces —Polonaise is one—are thickened by the addition of fine bread crumbs.

ᕙ Roux

MANY sauces begin with a *roux*, a thickening mixture of fat and flour. Melt the fat (usually butter) in a saucepan and, when it is hot but not sizzling, add the flour.

Cook the *roux* over low heat, stirring constantly. For brown sauces the *roux* is generally cooked until it attains a deep color. Add the hot liquid, stirring constantly. As the liquid and the *roux* blend and cook, the sauce thickens. For each cup of sauce, melt 1 or 2 tablespoons of butter and use an equal amount of flour, unless the specific recipe calls for different amounts.

Beurre Manié

THIS is a thickening agent for sauces rather than a true sauce or butter. Cream together butter and flour in proportions varying from 3 to 2 parts butter to 1 part flour, or about 1 tablespoon butter and 1 to 2 teaspoons flour. Add to the liquid, gravy, or sauce to be thickened and simmer the sauce without letting it boil.

Brown Stock

SPREAD 3 to 4 pounds beef bones and 2 pounds veal bones, both cut in rather small pieces, in a roasting pan and strew over them 1 large carrot and 1 large onion, both peeled and sliced. Put the pan in a hot oven (400° F.) for 30 to 40 minutes, or until the bones and vegetables are well browned. Transfer the bones and vegetables to a large soup kettle and add 4 quarts water.

Discard the fat from the pan in which the bones were browned, add some water, and bring it to a boil, scraping in the brown bits clinging to the pan. Turn the liquid into the soup kettle. Add a handful of celery stalks and tops, 1 or 2 leeks, 1 onion, 1 carrot, several sprigs of parsley, 1 tablespoon salt, and 6 peppercorns. Bring the liquid slowly to a boil, removing the scum as it accumulates on the surface. Simmer the stock for at least 3 hours.

Carefully remove the bones and vegetables from the kettle and discard them. Strain the stock through cheesecloth, working carefully to avoid stirring up the sediment in the bottom of the kettle. Pour the stock into jars and cool it as quickly as possible. Store it in the refrigerator for no longer than a week. As the stock cools, the fat will rise to the top; discard the fat before using the stock for sauces. A fine layer of sediment may settle in the jar. Be careful not to disturb this in removing the stock as it will cloud the liquid. Makes about 3 quarts.

ꕔ Glace de Viande   MEAT EXTRACT

HAVE enough beef and veal bones with some meat clinging to them, and any leftover poultry carcasses that may be available, to half fill a large heavy kettle. For each 10 pounds bones weigh out 2 pounds mixed celery stalks and leaves, carrots, and onions and chop them. Brown the bones lightly in a roasting pan in a very hot oven (450° F.) and put them in the kettle with the vegetables. Fill the kettle with un-salted water, cover it, and simmer the bones and vegetables, without adding more water, for 18 to 24 hours. Strain out the bones and vegetables. Return the broth to the kettle and, whatever the quantity, cook until it is reduced by more than half. Strain the broth through a muslin or flannel cloth, wrung out in cold water, into a large saucepan. Cook the broth, stirring frequently, until it is reduced to the thickness of a brown sauce. Put the *glace de viande* into jars, cool it, and store the jars in the refrigerator. *Glace de viande* will keep for about 1 week.

ꕔ Brown Sauce   SAUCE ESPAGNOLE

MELT 1/2 cup beef, veal, or pork drippings in a very heavy saucepan, add 2 onions and 1 small carrot, all coarsely chopped, and cook them until the onions start to turn golden, shaking the pan to ensure even cooking. Add 1/2 cup flour and cook the vegetables, stirring, until they are a rich brown. Add 3 cups hot brown stock, 3 sprigs of parsley, 1 stalk of celery, 1 small bay leaf, 1 garlic clove, crushed, and a pinch of thyme, and cook the mixture, stirring frequently, until it thickens. Add 3 more cups stock and simmer the sauce slowly, stirring occasionally, for at least 1 hour, or until it is reduced to about 3 cups. As it cooks, skim off the fat which accumulates on the surface. Add 1/4 cup tomato sauce or 1/2 cup tomato purée, cook the sauce for a few minutes longer, and strain it through a fine sieve. Add 2 more cups stock and continue to cook the sauce slowly for about 1 hour, skimming from time to time, until it is reduced to about 4 cups. Cool the sauce, stirring it occasionally, seal it with a layer of melted fat, and store it, covered, in the refrigerator. If it is not used within a week, discard the fat seal, bring the sauce to a boil, and cool and reseal it.

ꕔ Brown Sauce, Quick Method

IN a saucepan melt 1 1/2 tablespoons butter and add a generous 1 1/2 tablespoons flour. Cook the *roux* slowly over low heat, stirring occasionally, until it is thoroughly blended and about the color of brown wrapping paper. Add gradually 2 cups strong brown stock or beef stock, bring the sauce to a boil, and cook it for 5 minutes, stirring constantly. Lower the heat and simmer the sauce gently for 30 minutes, stirring occasionally. Skim off the fat and strain the sauce through a fine sieve.

Bordelaise Sauce

COOK 2 shallots, finely chopped, in 1/2 cup red wine until the wine is reduced by three fourths. Add 1 cup brown sauce and simmer the sauce gently for 10 minutes. Just before serving, add to the sauce 2 tablespoons poached beef marrow and 1/4 teaspoon chopped tarragon.

Lyonnaise Sauce

IN a saucepan brown 2 onions, finely chopped, in 2 tablespoons butter. Add 1/3 cup dry white wine and cook the sauce until it is reduced by about half. Add 1 cup brown sauce, cook the sauce slowly for 15 minutes, and add 1 teaspoon chopped parsley.

Périgourdine Sauce

COOK 2 ounces truffles, chopped, with 1/2 cup Madeira until the liquid is almost evaporated. Add 2 cups hot brown sauce and season the sauce with salt and cayenne to taste.

Uncooked Marinade

COMBINE 1 carrot and 1 onion, both sliced, 4 sprigs of parsley, 1 bay leaf, 1 small pinch of thyme, 1 teaspoon salt, 6 to 8 peppercorns, 1 tablespoon salad oil, and 3/4 cup white wine.

Put the meat to be tenderized and flavored into an enamel or earthenware bowl and pour the marinade over. Use uncooked marinade when the marinade is to become part of the sauce, as it does for less tender cuts of meat that require long slow cooking.

❦ Cooked Marinade

IN a saucepan combine 4 cups water, 1 1/2 cups vinegar, 2 onions, chopped, 1 carrot, sliced, 4 sprigs of parsley, 1 garlic clove, 1 teaspoon thyme, 2 bay leaves, 12 peppercorns, and 1 tablespoon salt. Bring the mixture to a boil and simmer it for 1 hour. Cool the marinade thoroughly before pouring it over the meat.

❦ Poivrade Sauce

PREPARE the following *mirepoix*: Sauté 1/2 cup each of chopped carrots and onions in 1/4 cup olive oil with a *bouquet garni* composed of 1 stalk of celery, 3 sprigs of parsley, 1/2 bay leaf, and a pinch of thyme until the vegetables begin to take on color, stirring frequently. Drain the oil, moisten the *mirepoix* with 1/4 cup tarragon vinegar and 1/2 cup cooked or uncooked marinade, strained, and cook the mixture, stirring constantly, until it is reduced by one third. Add 1 1/2 cups brown sauce and simmer the sauce gently for 30 minutes. Add 6 crushed peppercorns, simmer the sauce for 10 minutes more, and strain it through a fine sieve. Return the sauce to the heat, bring it to a boil, and add salt to taste. At serving time, stir in 1 1/2 tablespoons sweet butter.

❦ Sauce Diable

ADD 3 shallots, chopped, and 8 peppercorns, crushed, to 1/3 cup dry white wine or vinegar and cook the mixture until it is reduced to a thick paste. Add 1 cup brown sauce, 1 teaspoon Worcestershire sauce, and 1/2 teaspoon chopped parsley.

❦ Madeira Sauce

COOK 2 cups brown sauce until it is reduced to about 1 cup. Add 1/3 cup Madeira, bring the mixture just to the boiling point, and remove it from the heat immediately.

White Stock 𝔣𝔩

PARBOIL 1 pound veal or chicken bones or both for a few minutes, just long enough for the first scum to rise to the top. Drain the bones, cover them with 2 1/2 quarts cold water, and add 2 leeks, 2 onions, 1 carrot, 1 teaspoon salt, and a *bouquet garni* composed of 4 sprigs of parsley, 1 stalk of celery with the leaves, a sprig of thyme, and 1 bay leaf. Bring the water to a boil, skim off the fat, and simmer the stock for 3 hours. Remove the fat, strain the stock, and store it in the refrigerator for no longer than a week. Makes about 1 1/2 quarts.

White Sauce 𝔣𝔩

MELT 2 tablespoons butter and add gradually 2 tablespoons flour. Cook the *roux*, stirring constantly, over low heat for 3 to 5 minutes. Add gradually 1 cup scalded milk or cream, stirring constantly to blend well. Season the sauce with salt and white pepper to taste and cook it over hot but not boiling water until it is thick and smooth.

Thin White Sauce

FOLLOW the recipe for making white sauce, using 1 tablespoon each of butter and flour for each cup of milk or cream.

Thick White Sauce

FOLLOW the recipe for making white sauce, using 3 or 4 tablespoons each of butter and flour for each cup of milk or cream.

Rich White Sauce

TO 1 cup white sauce add 1 or 2 egg yolks, beating well after each addition. Heat the sauce but do not let it boil.

Mushroom Sauce I 𝔣𝔩

COOK 1/2 pound mushrooms and 2 shallots, finely chopped, in 3 tablespoons butter until the moisture is cooked away. Add to the pan 1/2 cup dry white wine and reduce it to 2 tablespoons. Melt 4 tablespoons butter, stir in 4 tablespoons flour, and cook the *roux*, stirring, for a minute or two. Gradually add 1 cup milk and simmer the sauce, stirring, until it is very thick. Blend the sauce with the mushrooms and season with salt and pepper to taste.

Mushroom Sauce II

MELT 2 tablespoons butter in a saucepan and in it sauté 1 pound trimmed mushrooms, cut in quarters, for 5 minutes. Sprinkle 1/2 tablespoon flour over the mushrooms and blend it in well. Add 1 cup light cream and cook the mushrooms, stirring frequently, for 10 to 15 minutes. Finish the sauce with 2 tablespoons heavy cream and 1 tablespoon Madeira and correct the seasoning with salt and pepper.

Velouté Sauce

MELT 1/3 cup butter, add 1/3 cup flour, and cook the *roux*, stirring, for a few minutes. Add gradually 3 cups white stock, chicken stock, or veal stock and cook the sauce, stirring constantly, until it thickens. Add 1/2 teaspoon salt and a little pepper and cook the sauce, stirring occasionally, until it is reduced to about 2 1/2 cups and is thick and creamy.

Sauce Suprême

COOK 2 cups chicken stock with 3 mushrooms, sliced, or some mushroom stems and peelings until the liquid is reduced by two thirds. Add 1 cup velouté sauce and cook the sauce until it is reduced to about 1 cup. Gradually stir in 1 cup heavy cream, correct the seasoning with salt and a little cayenne, and strain the sauce.

Fish Velouté

IN a saucepan melt 2 tablespoons butter, stir in 2 tablespoons flour, and cook the *roux*, stirring, until it is golden. Gradually stir in 2 cups fish stock and cook the sauce, stirring, until it is smooth and thickened. Cook the sauce for 15 to 20 minutes longer, correct the seasoning with salt, and strain it.

Velouté Base for Shellfish 🦐

PUT the bones and trimmings of 2 pounds white-fleshed fish in a pan with 2 quarts water, 1 cup white wine, 1 carrot and 1 onion, both sliced, 1/2 bay leaf, a pinch of thyme, 2 sprigs of parsley, and 8 peppercorns. Bring the liquid to a boil and simmer the stock for 30 minutes, skimming as necessary. Strain the stock.

In another pan combine 1/4 cup melted butter with 3/4 cup flour and cook the *roux*, stirring, until it is golden. Stir the fish stock into the *roux* and cook the *velouté*, stirring constantly, until it is thick and smooth. Cook it for 20 minutes longer, stirring occasionally and skimming as necessary, and strain it through a fine sieve.

Béchamel Sauce 🦐

SAUTÉ 1/2 onion, finely minced, in 4 tablespoons butter until it is golden. Stir in 1/2 cup flour and gradually add 4 cups milk, heated just to the boiling point. Cook the sauce, stirring constantly, until it is smooth.

Sauté 1/4 pound chopped veal in 2 tablespoons butter over very low heat. Season the veal with a sprig of thyme or a tiny pinch of thyme leaves—powdered thyme will discolor the sauce—and a pinch each of white pepper and freshly grated nutmeg. Cook the veal for 5 minutes, stirring it frequently to prevent it from browning, and stir it into the sauce.

Cook the sauce in the top of a double boiler over hot water for about 1 hour, stirring it from time to time. Strain the sauce through a fine sieve and dot it with tiny flecks of butter; they will melt and prevent a film from forming. Makes about 1 quart.

Rich Béchamel Sauce

To 2 cups béchamel sauce, add 1 or 2 beaten egg yolks. Heat the sauce, stirring constantly, but do not let it boil.

Caper Cream Sauce 🦐

To 1 cup béchamel sauce add 1/4 cup chopped capers, 1 tablespoon melted butter, and 1 1/2 teaspoons lemon juice.

Poulette Sauce

COOK 6 or 8 mushrooms, minced, in 1 tablespoon butter until they just start to brown. Add 2 shallots, finely chopped, and 1/2 cup light cream. Cook the cream until it is reduced by one half. Add 1/2 cup béchamel sauce. Bring the sauce to a boil and add salt to taste. Add 2 egg yolks, slightly beaten and mixed with a little hot cream, and bring the sauce to a boil, stirring constantly. Do not let it boil. Add the juice of 1/2 lemon and 1/2 teaspoon chopped parsley.

Mornay Sauce

MIX 3 egg yolks, lightly beaten, with a little hot cream and combine them with 2 cups hot béchamel sauce. Cook the sauce, stirring constantly, until it just comes to a boil. Add 2 tablespoons each of butter and grated Parmesan or Swiss cheese. Use the sauce with fish, poultry, poached eggs, macaroni mixtures, and other creamed foods that are to be browned in the oven. The top may be sprinkled with grated cheese just before browning.

If an even golden brown is desired, reserve a few tablespoons of the sauce, fold in 1 tablespoon whipped cream, and spread this sauce on the creamed mixture.

Soubise Sauce

COOK 2 cups finely chopped onions in 1/2 cup beef stock for 3 to 4 minutes and drain them. Melt 2 tablespoons butter in a saucepan, add the onions, and cook them over low heat until they are soft. Combine the onion purée with 1 cup hot Mornay sauce. For a thinner sauce, combine the onion purée with 2 cups Mornay sauce.

Anchovy Butter

CREAM 6 tablespoons butter with 2 tablespoons anchovy paste or a well-pounded anchovy filet. Press the butter through a sieve and chill it. Use with hot fish or as a canapé butter.

Garlic Butter ❧

SIMMER 6 garlic cloves in water to cover for a few minutes and drain them. Crush and pound the garlic well with 6 tablespoons butter and rub the mixture through a fine sieve. Or crush the garlic and mix it with creamed butter to taste.

Herb Butter ❧

BLEND 1 cup soft butter with 1 shallot, finely minced, 1 tablespoon each of parsley, chervil, and chives, all minced, and 1/4 teaspoon salt.

Lobster Butter ❧

COMBINE the shell from 1 pound cooked lobster, any of the creamy part of the lobster that clings to it, and the coral, if available, with 1/2 cup butter. Pound the mixture to a paste in a mortar. Melt it slowly in a saucepan, strain it through cheese-cloth, and cool it. Any small particles of shell that may have passed through the cloth will sink to the bottom and the creamy pink butter can be spooned off the top.

Lobster Roe Butter ❧

POUND 1 tablespoon lobster coral, or roe, and 2 tablespoons butter to a paste.

Maître d'Hôtel Butter ❧

CREAM 1/2 cup butter with 1 tablespoon chopped parsley, the juice of 1/2 lemon, and salt and pepper to taste.

Mustard Butter ❧

COMBINE 3 tablespoons prepared Dijon-type mustard and 1 1/2 teaspoons dry mustard with 1 teaspoon lemon juice. Blend the mixture with 1 cup creamed butter, season it with salt and pepper to taste, and chill it thoroughly.

Compound Butters

Anchovy Butter (p. 510), Mustard Butter (p. 511), Shrimp Butter (p. 513), Watercress Butter (p. 513).

Paprika Butter 🦆

COOK 3 tablespoons salted butter, 2 teaspoons finely chopped onion, and 1 1/2 teaspoons paprika over low heat for 5 minutes. Strain and cool the mixture and blend it well with 3 tablespoons salted butter.

Tarragon Butter 🦆

BLANCH 4 tablespoons fresh tarragon leaves and rinse them well with cold water. Pound the leaves to a pulp and cream them thoroughly with 1/2 cup soft butter and 1 tablespoon lemon juice. Force the butter through a very fine strainer.

Watercress Butter 🦆

BLEND together 1/2 cup each of sweet butter and finely chopped watercress leaves. Season the mixture with anchovy paste to taste.

Lemon Butter Balls 🦆

CREAM together 1/2 cup butter and 2 tablespoons lemon juice and chill the mixture. Shape the mixture into small balls, using about 2 teaspoons for each, and roll the balls in finely minced parsley.

Shrimp Butter 🦆

SHELL 1 pound shrimp, reserving the shrimp for another use. Dry the shells in a slow oven (300° F.) for a few minutes and pound them in a mortar until they are pulverized as finely as possible. In the top of a double boiler over hot water melt 1/4 pound butter with 2 tablespoons water and the pulverized shells. Cook the mixture for 10 to 12 minutes, but do not let the butter boil. Drain the mixture through a fine sieve, reserving the liquid. Return the shells to the pan, add a little boiling water, and drain the mixture again through a sieve. Reserve the liquid and discard the shells.

Combine the liquids and pour them through a cloth into a bowl of ice water. Set the bowl in the refrigerator until the butter hardens on the top. Skim off the butter and pack it into a jar. Cover it and store it in the refrigerator.

Beurre Blanc

IN a small saucepan combine 1/4 cup white-wine vinegar, 1 tablespoon each of finely chopped shallots and parsley, and a little salt and pepper. Simmer the mixture until the liquid is reduced by one half and gradually beat in 1/2 cup butter. Serve hot and foamy with fish, shellfish, or green vegetables.

Beurre Noisette BROWN BUTTER

MELT butter and cook it slowly until it is as brown as a hazelnut. Slow cooking will ensure a more even browning and a better flavor.

Beurre Meunière LEMON AND PARSLEY BUTTER

To brown butter add lemon juice and chopped parsley to taste.

Beurre Noir BLACK BUTTER

COOK brown butter until it is almost black.

Clarified Butter

MELT butter in a small saucepan and carefully pour the clear fat off the milky sediment that settles at the bottom. Clarified butter will not brown as it cooks.

Clarified Butter Sauce

IN a saucepan melt 1 cup butter. Pour the clear fat into a heated sauceboat and add the grated rind and juice of 1 lemon.

Drawn Butter

MELT 3 tablespoons butter in a saucepan, add 1 1/2 tablespoons flour, and slowly stir in 1 1/2 cups hot vegetable stock. Cook the sauce, stirring occasionally, until it is thick. Beat in 3 tablespoons butter, 1 1/2 tablespoons lemon juice, and salt to taste.

Almond Butter Sauce

TO 1/2 cup melted butter add a generous 1/2 cup sliced blanched almonds and cook the sauce over low heat, stirring constantly, until the almonds are slightly browned. Stir in 1 teaspoon each of onion juice, lemon juice, and finely chopped chives and heat the sauce, stirring gently, until it comes to a boil. Season it with a dash of nutmeg and salt and pepper to taste.

Anchovy Butter Sauce

RINSE and chop finely 10 to 12 anchovy filets. Add them to clarified butter sauce with 1 tablespoon each of chopped parsley and chives.

Butter Caper Sauce

MELT 1/2 cup butter over low heat and skim off the foam. Add 1 tablespoon lemon juice, 1/4 cup capers, and salt to taste.

Deviled Butter Sauce

MELT 6 tablespoons butter, add 3 tablespoons each of lemon juice and Worcestershire sauce, 2 tablespoons prepared mustard, and salt and pepper to taste. Heat the sauce, stirring, for a moment longer.

Polonaise Sauce

HEAT 6 tablespoons butter until it begins to brown slightly. Add 6 tablespoons fine bread crumbs and cook the sauce until the crumbs are brown and the butter has stopped bubbling. Add a few drops of lemon juice and finely minced parsley to taste. Serve with asparagus or cauliflower and garnish with chopped hard-cooked egg.

Shallot Sauce

SAUTÉ 12 shallots, peeled and finely chopped, in 1/2 cup butter over low heat until they are soft. Add 1/2 cup butter, bit by bit, stirring well with a whisk after each addition. Season the sauce with salt and tarragon vinegar to taste. Stir well and serve immediately.

Hollandaise Sauce

DIVIDE 1/2 cup butter into 3 parts. In the top of a double boiler over hot water, or in a bowl set in hot water, put 4 egg yolks and 1 part of the butter. Stir the mixture rapidly and constantly until the butter is melted. Add the second piece of butter. As the mixture thickens and the butter melts, add the third part, continuing to stir constantly from the bottom of the pan until the butter is thoroughly incorporated. Do not let the water over which the sauce is cooking come to a boil.

Remove the saucepan from the heat and beat the sauce for at least 2 minutes longer. Add 2 teaspoons lemon juice or vinegar and a pinch each of white pepper and salt. Replace the saucepan over hot but not boiling water and beat the sauce for 2 minutes longer.

Should the mixture curdle, immediately beat in 1 to 2 tablespoons boiling water to rebind the emulsion.

Blender Hollandaise Sauce

RUN warm water over the container of a blender until the container is warm. Combine in the container 3 egg yolks, 1 tablespoon lemon juice, and a pinch of salt.

Cover the container and put the blender on high speed for an instant, turning the machine on and off immediately. Put the switch on high, remove the cover, and immediately add 1/2 cup melted butter in a thin steady stream. When all the butter has been added turn off the switch. If the hollandaise sauce is not to be served at once, place the container in a pan of warm, not hot, water until serving time.

Maltaise Sauce

To 1 cup hollandaise sauce add 2 or 3 tablespoons orange juice and finely grated orange rind to taste. The sauce should be pink; if necessary, add a little pink food coloring.

Blender Maltaise Sauce

Put 4 egg yolks, 2 tablespoons lemon juice, and a pinch of cayenne in the container of a blender. Cover the container and turn the motor on low. Remove the cover and add slowly, in a thin steady stream, 1 cup bubbling hot, but not browned, melted butter. When all the butter has been added turn off the switch. Stir in 1 teaspoon grated orange rind and 1/2 cup orange juice.

Mousseline Sauce

In the top of a double boiler combine equal quantities of hollandaise sauce and stiffly whipped cream. Set the pan over boiling water and heat the sauce, stirring constantly.

Béarnaise Sauce

Combine 3 sprigs each of tarragon and chervil and 2 shallots, all finely chopped, 4 crushed peppercorns, and 1/4 cup each of tarragon vinegar and white wine in a heavy-bottomed saucepan. Cook the mixture over high heat until the volume is reduced by one third. Strain the mixture and set it aside to cool.

Put 3 egg yolks and 1 tablespoon water in a bowl set in a pan of hot water and gradually beat in the strained vinegar. Stir the mixture briskly over very low heat with a wire whisk until it is light and fluffy. Divide 1/2 pound butter at room temperature into 3 portions. Add the first portion of butter, stirring constantly until the sauce is thick and smooth. Stir in the second and third portions, stirring constantly after each addition, until the sauce is thick and glossy. Season with salt to taste and a pinch of cayenne and add 3 sprigs each of tarragon and chervil, both finely chopped. Finish the sauce with 1 teaspoon *glace de viande*, or meat extract.

ꙮ Blender Béarnaise Sauce

IN a saucepan combine 2 tablespoons white wine, 1 tablespoon tarragon vinegar, 2 teaspoons each of chopped shallots and chopped fresh tarragon (or 1 teaspoon dried tarragon), and 1/4 teaspoon freshly ground black pepper. Cook the mixture over high heat until almost all the liquid has evaporated. Pour the remaining purée into 3/4 cup hollandaise sauce and put the mixture in the container of a blender. Cover the container and blend the sauce at high speed for 4 seconds.

ꙮ Choron Sauce

TO 1 cup béarnaise sauce add 1/4 cup tomato purée.

ꙮ Pesto   BASIL SAUCE

WITH a mortar and pestle pound to a paste 1/2 cup grated Parmesan and a handful of lightly salted fresh basil leaves, or 2 tablespoons dried basil steeped in 2 tablespoons olive oil. Gradually add 1/4 cup pine nuts and continue to pound the mixture until it is a smooth paste. Blend in about 1/4 cup olive oil, or enough to moisten the paste, 1 tablespoon melted butter, 1/4 cup hot water, and salt to taste. The sauce should now be thick and creamy.

ꙮ Curry Sauce

COOK 1 cup chopped unpeeled apple, 3/4 cup finely chopped onion, and 1/4 cup chopped celery in 5 tablespoons butter, stirring frequently with a wooden spoon, until the apple is tender and the onion is soft. Remove the pan from the heat and sprinkle the mixture with 2 tablespoons curry powder, 1/2 teaspoon salt, and a few grains of cayenne. Blend the mixture well and return the pan to the heat. Gradually stir in 1 cup tomato juice. Bring the sauce to a boil and cook it, stirring constantly, until it thickens and bubbles. Reduce the heat and simmer the sauce for 5 minutes.

Spiced Cranberry Sauce

COMBINE 1 cup each of water and sugar with 1 piece green gingerroot. Boil the mixture for 5 minutes. Add 1 hard pear, peeled and diced, and simmer the mixture for 3 minutes. Add 2 cups raw cranberries and cook the sauce, without stirring, until the cranberries pop open. Cool the sauce. Just before serving, remove the gingerroot and stir in the grated rind and juice of 1 lemon.

Currant Jelly Sauce

SIMMER the slivered zest of 1 orange and 1 lemon in 1/4 cup water for 8 minutes. Drain the zest well and add it to the juice of 1 orange and 1 lemon. Stir in 2 cups red currant jelly and heat the sauce slowly, stirring occasionally, until the jelly is melted. Add 1/2 cup Port wine, 1 tablespoon shallot, blanched and finely chopped, 1/2 teaspoon Dijon-type mustard, a pinch of cayenne, and sugar and salt to taste. Simmer the sauce for 5 minutes. Serve hot.

Mint Sauce

COMBINE 3/4 cup hot vinegar with 4 tablespoons water and add 1/2 cup finely chopped fresh mint leaves and 3 tablespoons sugar. Stir the sauce until the sugar is dissolved. Serve warm or cold.

Mustard Sauce

IN a saucepan simmer 1/2 cup each of honey and strained orange juice until the liquid reduces slightly. Add 1/3 cup cider vinegar, 1 tablespoon each of dry mustard and turmeric, and 1 teaspoon ginger. Stir in 1 teaspoon arrowroot mixed to a paste with 2 tablespoons cold water and cook the sauce, stirring constantly, until it is thick and clear.

ᔓ᠊ Yoghurt Sauce

To 2 cups yoghurt add 1 onion and 1 tomato, both peeled and finely chopped, 1 teaspoon salt, 1/2 teaspoon cayenne, and 1/2 teaspoon caraway seeds browned in a small amount of butter. Blend the sauce well and chill it thoroughly.

ᔓ᠊ Peanut Dip

IN a saucepan combine 3 tablespoons peanut butter, 1 1/2 tablespoons soy sauce, 1 1/2 teaspoons each of butter and lemon juice, and 3/4 teaspoon minced garlic. Simmer the sauce over low heat for 10 minutes and blend in 1/3 cup light cream.

ᔓ᠊ Aspic

IN a large deep pan combine 7 cups cold fat-free chicken, veal, or beef stock, 1/4 cup white wine, and 1 tablespoon tomato paste. Sprinkle the stock with 5 tablespoons gelatin. It is not necessary to soften or dissolve the gelatin separately. Beat 4 egg whites until they are stiff and turn them out of the bowl onto the stock. Do not fold the egg whites into the stock. Bring the mixture to a boil, whisking it constantly with a back-and-forth motion across the center of the pan. The usual circular motion of whisking would cloud the aspic. As the stock heats, the whites attract any floating particles, expand, rise, and form a solid mass double the original bulk. When the mixture reaches a full boil, remove the pan from the heat and let it stand for at least 10 minutes.

Wring out a linen tea towel in cold water and use it to line a large fine-meshed sieve. Put the sieve over a deep bowl. Slowly pour the contents of the pan, egg whites and all, into the sieve. The whites contain a large part of the liquid and must be allowed to drip slowly for about 1 hour. Do not hurry the process by stirring, or the aspic will be cloudy. Discard the whites. There will be about 3 1/2 cups clear aspic.

Pour as much aspic as required into a small metal pan and set the pan in a bowl

Turkey in Aspic with Cherries

of ice. Stir the aspic with a metal spoon (metal retains the cold) until it is cool, thickens slightly, and pours from the spoon like a thick syrup. Stirring prevents the aspic around the edges from setting first, which would make the aspic lumpy. Aspic is ready to use when it is still liquid but just on the point of setting. If it begins to congeal, it may be liquefied by heating.

Aspic, Quick Method

SIMMER 2 1/2 cups chicken or veal stock, 1 onion, sliced, and the crushed shell and lightly beaten white of 1 egg for 10 minutes. Let the mixture stand for 20 minutes and strain it through cheesecloth to clarify. Soften 1 tablespoon gelatin in 1/2 cup cold stock and dissolve it in the clarified stock.

Wine Aspic

FOLLOW the recipe for aspic. When the aspic has been clarified, add 1/2 cup white Burgundy, Port, Sherry, or Madeira.

Tarragon Aspic

SIMMER 6 or 8 sprays of fresh tarragon in 1 cup clarified veal stock until the liquid is reduced by half. Strain the stock and dissolve in it 1 tablespoon gelatin softened in 1/2 cup white wine. Add 2 more cups veal stock.

Fish Aspic

PUT 2 pounds fish trimmings and bones in a saucepan with 1 cup white wine, the juice of 1 lemon, 2 onions, sliced, 4 sprays of tarragon, 4 sprigs of parsley, and 1 bay leaf. Bring the mixture to a boil, shaking the pan frequently to prevent scorching, and reduce the liquid over high heat by half. Add 2 quarts water and a little salt and pepper, bring the stock to a boil, and skim it carefully. Simmer the stock for 20 minutes. Strain it into a large saucepan, cool it, and skim again.

If fish trimmings are unavailable, 6 cups bottled clam juice and 2 cups white wine may be used as stock.

Sprinkle 6 tablespoons gelatin over the stock and add the stiffly beaten whites and crushed shells of 3 eggs. Do not fold them in. Bring the stock slowly to a full boil, whisking constantly back and forth across the pan. Remove the pan from the heat and let the stock stand for 30 minutes. Strain the aspic through a fine sieve lined with a cloth wrung out in cold water and cool it.

White-Wine Fish Aspic

FOLLOW the recipe for fish aspic. When the aspic is cool, flavor it with 1/2 cup Champagne or white Burgundy.

Red-Wine Fish Aspic

FOLLOW the recipe for fish aspic, using a good dry red wine, such as a Burgundy or Bordeaux, in place of the white wine. When the aspic is cool, flavor it with an additional 1/2 cup dry red wine. A few drops of red food coloring may be added to intensify the color, but the final shade should never be darker than pale rose.

Chaud-Froid Blanc

HEAT 3/4 cup vegetable oil in a saucepan and stir in 3/4 cup flour and 8 teaspoons gelatin. Gradually add 2 cups each of chicken stock and milk and cook the sauce over low heat, stirring constantly, until it just comes to a boil. Add 1 cup heavy cream. Put the saucepan in a bowl of cracked ice and stir the sauce with a metal spoon until it is very cold and on the point of setting. It is then ready for use.

Mayonnaise Collée

SOFTEN 2 tablespoons gelatin in 1/2 cup cold water for 5 minutes and dissolve it over hot water. Blend the gelatin into 2 cups mayonnaise. Use for binding salad mixtures that are to be molded, for coating cold shellfish, poultry, and meats, and for affixing decorations on the meat.

Vegetables with Aioli Sauce

GARLIC MAYONNAISE   Aioli Sauce ʃ⬥

CRUSH 6 to 8 garlic cloves thoroughly in a mortar and pound in 1/4 teaspoon salt. In a bowl blend the garlic with 2 egg yolks. Add a few drops of olive oil, beating vigorously with a whisk or rotary beater. Continue adding oil, a little at a time, until about 2 tablespoons have been added. Add the rest of the oil in a thin steady stream, beating constantly, until 1 cup in all has been incorporated. If the mixture seems too thick, beat in 1/2 teaspoon or more of water. Finish the sauce with the juice of 1 lemon. Season the sauce with salt and freshly ground pepper to taste and chill it thoroughly. If the sauce separates, rebind the emulsion by beating the sauce again while adding 1 egg yolk.

Green Sauce ʃ⬥

COMBINE 1/2 cup mixed fresh leaves of watercress, tarragon, chervil, parsley, and basil in a saucepan. Moisten the greens with 1/4 cup boiling water, mix well, and let them stand for 5 minutes. Force the softened greens through a sieve with 1/4 teaspoon crushed garlic. Add the purée to 1/2 cup each of sour cream and mayonnaise and season with a few drops of lemon juice and salt and mace to taste.

Rémoulade Sauce ʃ⬥

TO 2 cups mayonnaise add 1/2 cup finely chopped sour pickle and 2 tablespoons finely chopped capers, both thoroughly drained, 3 hard-cooked eggs, finely chopped, 1 tablespoon prepared mustard, and 1 tablespoon mixed chopped parsley, tarragon, and chervil.

Tartare Sauce ʃ⬥

TO 1 1/2 cups mayonnaise add 1 dill pickle, 4 shallots, and 2 anchovies, all finely chopped, 1 tablespoon each of capers, parsley, tarragon, and chervil, all chopped, and 1 teaspoon mustard. Thin the sauce with heavy cream and season it with 1/2 teaspoon each of lemon juice and sugar, and salt and pepper to taste.

࿊ Tomato Purée

PEEL, seed, and chop 4 ripe tomatoes and combine them in a heavy saucepan with 2 tablespoons butter. Cook the sauce, stirring frequently, until the tomatoes are reduced to a smooth purée. There will be less than a cup. (The amount will vary according to the liquid content of the tomatoes.) Season the sauce with salt to taste.

࿊ Fresh Tomato Sauce

IN a shallow pan cook 6 tomatoes, peeled, seeded, and chopped, in 1/4 cup olive oil until they are thoroughly cooked. Season the sauce with salt and freshly ground black pepper to taste.

࿊ Thick Tomato Sauce

IN a saucepan combine 4 large tomatoes, peeled, seeded, and chopped, 1/2 cup tomato paste, 2 tablespoons butter, 1 teaspoon brown sugar, 1/4 teaspoon each of tarragon and salt, and 1 bay leaf. Cook the mixture over medium heat for 10 minutes and discard the bay leaf. Continue cooking the tomatoes until they are mushy and the mixture is as thick as heavy cream. Strain the sauce and heat it.

࿊ Green Tomato Sauce

IN a saucepan heat 6 tablespoons oil and in it cook 2 onions, chopped, and 1 teaspoon minced garlic without letting the onion take on color. Add 1/2 cup *pepitas* (toasted pumpkin seeds) and 1/4 cup toasted sesame seeds and sauté the mixture for 3 to 4 minutes. Discard half the liquid from 3 eight-ounce cans of *tomatillos* (Mexican green tomatoes) and add the tomatoes to the saucepan with 1/2 cup chopped parsley and 8 canned green *chiles*, seeded. Bring the mixture to a boil and cook it over medium heat for 5 minutes. Put the sauce through a food chopper or purée it coarsely in a blender. Heat the tomato purée and thicken it, if necessary, by adding *beurre manié*, allowing 1 tablespoon of the mixture to 1 cup liquid. Cook the sauce for a few minutes after adding the *beurre manié*.

Tomato Sauce for Pasta

IN a large heavy saucepan heat 1/4 cup each of butter and olive oil and in it sauté 1 onion, 1 garlic clove, 1 carrot, and 1 stalk of celery, all minced, with a pinch of sweet basil until the vegetables are soft. Add 4 pounds fresh plum tomatoes, peeled and coarsely chopped (canned Italian plum tomatoes may be substituted; use 3 cans weighing 1 pound 12 ounces each), a generous pinch of sugar, and a little salt and freshly ground pepper. Bring the mixture to a boil. Put the pan on an asbestos pad over very low heat. Cover the pan and simmer the sauce very slowly, stirring occasionally to prevent sticking, for 2 to 3 hours. For a thicker sauce remove the cover during the last 1 1/2 hours of cooking. Adjust the seasoning if necessary. Use the sauce unstrained or rub it through a sieve. Makes enough for about 1 pound pasta.

Tomato Meat Sauce for Pasta

IN a large heavy saucepan heat 1/4 cup each of butter and olive oil and in it sauté 1 onion, 1 garlic clove, and 1 stalk of celery, all minced, until the vegetables are soft. Add 3/4 pound ground beef and 1/2 pound ground veal and brown the meat lightly. Stir in 2 pounds fresh plum tomatoes, peeled and coarsely chopped, and add salt and freshly ground pepper to taste. Bring the mixture to a boil. Put the pan on an asbestos pad over very low heat. Cover the pan and simmer the sauce very slowly, stirring occasionally, for 2 to 3 hours. For a thicker sauce remove the cover during the last hour of cooking. When the sauce is done, skim the fat from the surface. Makes enough for about 1 pound pasta.

Bolognese Meat Sauce

IN a large heavy saucepan heat 1/4 cup each of butter and olive oil and in it sauté 1 onion, 1 garlic clove, 1 carrot, and 1 stalk of celery, all minced, with a pinch of sweet basil until the vegetables are soft. Add 2 pounds ground beef and brown it lightly. Stir in 4 pounds fresh plum tomatoes, peeled and coarsely chopped, blend in thoroughly 1 can tomato paste, and add salt and freshly ground pepper to taste. Bring the mixture to a boil. Put the pan on an asbestos pad over very low heat. Cover the pan and simmer the sauce very slowly, stirring occasionally, for 2 to 3 hours. For a thicker sauce remove the cover during the last 1 1/2 hours of cooking. When the sauce is done, skim the fat from the surface. Makes enough for about 2 pounds pasta.

℘ Cocktail Sauce for Shellfish

MIX together thoroughly 1 cup tomato ketchup, 1/2 cup chili sauce, 1 tablespoon vinegar, 1 teaspoon each of Worcestershire sauce and grated horseradish, the juice of 1 lemon, 1/4 teaspoon celery salt, and 5 drops Tabasco.

℘ Blender Barbecue Sauce

COMBINE thoroughly 2 cups strained canned tomatoes, 1/3 cup A.1. Sauce, 2 garlic cloves, chopped, 1/4 cup each of lemon juice and chopped scallions, 2 teaspoons prepared mustard, 1 1/2 teaspoons salt, and 1 teaspoon each of pepper and dry mustard. Put the mixture in the container of a blender, cover the container, and blend the sauce thoroughly. If desired, add a dash of Tabasco to the blended sauce.

℘ Barbecue Sauce for Poultry

COMBINE thoroughly 1/2 cup each of peanut oil and lime juice, 2 tablespoons finely chopped onion, 2 teaspoons chopped tarragon, and 1/2 teaspoon Tabasco.

℘ Barbecue Sauce for Ham

COMBINE 1 cup brown sugar, 1/2 cup vinegar, 2 tablespoons prepared mustard, and 1 garlic clove, finely minced. Bring the sauce to a boil and simmer it for 3 minutes. Remove it from the heat and stir in 1 cup pineapple juice.

℘ Grilled Orange Slices   TRANCHES D'ORANGES GRILLÉES

DIP thick unpeeled slices of seedless oranges in melted butter and arrange them in a hinged broiler. Brown the fruit quickly on both sides and serve with duck or other game.

Sautéed Apples 🐦

PEEL firm apples, cut them into small thick pieces, olive shapes, or balls, and roll the pieces in flour. Heat enough clarified butter in a skillet to cover the bottom of the pan well and cook the apple pieces, turning them often, until they are golden brown and just tender. Sweeten, if desired. Serve as a garnish with meat or poultry.

Cranberry and Kumquat Relish 🐦

PUT 4 cups raw cranberries through a food chopper with 2 cups fresh kumquats. Blend in 2 1/2 cups sugar, or to taste, and chill the relish thoroughly.

Cranberry Apples 🐦

BOIL 1 cup each of cranberry juice and sugar for 3 minutes. Pare tart apples and cut the flesh into balls with a French ball cutter. Drop the apple balls, a few at a time, into the boiling syrup and cook them for about 6 minutes, or until they are just tender. Remove the fruit from the syrup with a perforated spoon and serve as a garnish for meat or poultry.

Glazed Crab Apples 🐦

COMBINE 1 cup each of sugar and water, the juice of 1 lemon, and the juice and grated zest of 1 orange. Bring the mixture to a boil and cook the syrup until it spins a light thread, or a candy thermometer registers 225° F. Add a few drops of red food coloring. Arrange 18 crab apples side by side in a baking dish, cover them with the syrup, and bake them in a moderate oven (350° F.), basting often, until the fruit is tender but not mushy. Serve hot or cold, as a garnish.

Spiced Crab Apples 🐦

WASH and dry 5 pounds crab apples and remove any stems. In an enamel kettle combine 5 cups sugar and 4 cups spiced malt vinegar. Or use ordinary malt vinegar and add to the kettle a cheesecloth bag holding cloves, cinnamon bark, and gingerroot to taste. Bring the liquid to a boil, add the apples, and simmer them until they are just tender. Do not overcook the fruit. Pack the apples in hot sterilized jars. Discard the spice bag and boil the syrup over high heat until it is reduced and thickened. Pour the syrup over the apples, filling the jars to overflowing. Seal the jars and store them in a cool dry place.

ᔆ Apple Chutney

PEEL 4 green apples and chop them in a wooden chopping bowl. Sprinkle them with salt and a little water and let them rest for 5 minutes. Drain the apples and combine them with 6 tablespoons grated coconut, 4 tablespoons chopped onion, and the juice of 1 lemon. Chop the ingredients until they are evenly and finely minced.

ᔆ Cucumber Chutney

PEEL and slice 1 pound cucumbers and sprinkle the slices with salt. Let them stand for 1 hour. Drain the cucumbers and chop them with 1 tablespoon chopped sweet pimiento, 1/2 tablespoon slivered heart of celery, 1 sprig of parsley, 1/2 garlic clove, a pinch of cayenne, and 1/4 teaspoon black pepper. Pound the ingredients, adding enough lemon juice to make a thick paste. This chutney may be made in a blender.

ᔆ Eggplant Chutney

BAKE a medium eggplant in a moderate oven (350° F.) for 1 hour. Cool and peel it. Sauté 1/2 cup chopped onion and 1/4 cup chopped green peppers in 1 tablespoon oil for 5 minutes. Combine the vegetables in a wooden chopping bowl with 1/4 cup grated coconut, 1/4 teaspoon dried ground chili peppers, and 1 1/2 teaspoons salt. Chop the ingredients, adding gradually 3 tablespoons cream and 2 tablespoons lemon juice, until they are evenly and finely minced. Serve chilled.

ᔆ Mint Chutney

IN a mortar combine the leaves from 25 sprigs of mint, 1 small onion, and 5 tablespoons parsley, all chopped. Add 3 tablespoons lemon juice, 2 tablespoons sugar,

3/4 teaspoon salt, and 1/4 teaspoon cayenne. Pound the mixture to a paste. This chutney may be made in a blender.

Pickled Mushrooms

TRIM small button mushrooms. Pack them in sterilized pint jars and to each jar add 1 teaspoon peppercorns, 1 bay leaf, 1 teaspoon salt, and 1 garlic clove. Bring to a boil 1 cup vinegar and 1 sprig of tarragon and pour it over the mushrooms, filling the jars to overflowing. Seal the jars immediately.

Dilled Beans

CUT off the stems of 6 quarts (about 8 pounds) uniform green beans. Plunge the beans into boiling water for 1 minute, drain them, and plunge them immediately into ice water. When the beans are thoroughly chilled, drain them and pack them upright in hot sterilized jars. Add 1 garlic clove and 2 sprigs of fresh dill to each jar. Combine 2 quarts white-wine or cider vinegar, 1 quart water, and 1/2 cup dill seed heads. Bring the mixture to a boil and pour it over the beans, filling the jars to overflowing. Seal the jars immediately. Makes about 6 quarts.

Red Pepper Relish

MIX 4 1/2 cups finely chopped sweet red peppers with 1 tablespoon salt and let them stand for 3 1/2 hours. Drain off the liquid, add 3 cups sugar and 2 cups cider vinegar, and boil the relish until it is very thick. Pour it into hot sterilized jars and seal at once.

Preserved Gingerroots

SOAK 1 pound peeled gingerroots in cold water for 1 hour. Drain the roots, cover them with fresh cold water, bring the water to a boil, and boil it for 5 minutes.

Drain the roots once more, cover with fresh cold water, and boil them for 5 minutes longer, or until they are tender.

Make a syrup of 2 cups sugar and 1 cup water and boil it for about 5 minutes, or until it is thick. Add the gingerroots and 1/2 teaspoon cream of tartar. Bring the mixture to a boil and cook it for 2 minutes. Pour the preserved ginger into hot sterilized jars, seal the jars, and store in a cool dark place.

ᔑᐤ Spiced Peaches

FOR each 2 pounds peaches, make a syrup of 3 cups sugar and 1 cup water. Bring the syrup to a boil, skim it, and reduce the heat so that the syrup just simmers. Add peeled whole fresh peaches, a few at a time, and cook them until they are tender but not mushy. Drain the peaches and reserve the syrup. Measure the syrup and pour it into a saucepan. Add half as much wine vinegar as there is syrup and flavor the mixture with 1 cinnamon stick, 1 teaspoon whole cloves, and mace and allspice to taste. Bring the spiced syrup to a boil and add the fruit. Remove the pan from the heat and let the fruit cool in the syrup.

ᔑᐤ Mango Preserve

PEEL mangoes that are just beginning to ripen and show color and cut the fruit into sections. For each pound of fruit make a syrup of 4 cups water and 2 cups sugar. Bring the syrup to a boil and boil it for 5 minutes. Add the fruit to the syrup, cook it rapidly until it is clear, and cool it. Return the pan to the heat, bring the syrup again to a boil, and cook the mixture until it is thick and a candy thermometer registers 220° F. Cool the fruit, pack it in hot sterilized jars, and cover it with the syrup. Seal the jars and process them in simmering water for 15 minutes.

$\mathcal{D}$esserts

Crêpes Sucrées

SIFT 1 cup sifted flour with 2 tablespoons sugar. With a wire whisk beat 4 eggs, add the dry ingredients, and beat the mixture until it is smooth. Add gradually 1 cup each of milk and water and stir the batter until it is smooth. It will have the consistency of heavy cream. Let the batter stand for at least 30 minutes before using. If it becomes too thick on standing, thin it with a spoonful of water or milk.

Heat a heavy 5-inch skillet or iron crêpe pan until it is smoking hot and coat it with soft butter. Remove the pan from the heat, tilt it away from you, and pour in a generous tablespoon of batter near the handle. Quickly tilt and rotate the pan so that the batter runs to the edges and coats the bottom thinly and evenly. Return the pan to the heat for a minute or two. When the top of the crêpe is just set and the bottom is golden brown, lift the edges with a spatula and carefully turn the crêpe over. If the crêpe is very fragile, use the fingers to ease it over. Brown the other side for about 30 seconds, or until the crêpe is cooked. Be careful not to over-cook. Slide the crêpe onto a wire rack. Cook the remaining crêpes and pile them on top of each other, to soften the edges before filling and folding. Crêpes may be kept warm in a slow oven (250° F.). Makes 24 to 30.

ꙮ Crêpes Flambées

MAKE dessert crêpes, fold them into quarters, and arrange them side by side in the buttered blazer of a chafing dish or on a heatproof platter. Heat together 1/2 cup prune-flavored liqueur, 4 tablespoons each of sugar, butter, and water, and 1 tea-spoon grated orange rind, and pour the sauce over the crêpes. Heat the crêpes for a few minutes. Sprinkle them with 1/4 cup heated Cognac and ignite the spirit. Spoon the flaming sauce over the crêpes until they are thoroughly saturated. Serve with the remaining sauce.

ꙮ Blueberry Crêpes

MAKE dessert crêpes and put a tablespoon of blueberries in the center of each crêpe. Roll up the crêpes and sprinkle them with crushed macaroons soaked in kirsch.

ꙮ Crêpes with Chocolate Cream   CRÊPES À LA CRÈME CHOCOLAT

MAKE dessert crêpes and keep them warm.

In a small mixing bowl combine 3 eggs, 1 1/4 cups sugar, and 4 ounces melted chocolate, and set the bowl in a larger bowl filled with cracked ice. Beat the mixture with a whisk until it is light. Add gradually 1 1/2 cups soft butter and beat the filling until it is thick and creamy. Put a generous tablespoon of the chocolate cream in the center of each crêpe. Roll up the crêpes and arrange them side by side in a shallow flameproof dish. Heat 1 cup thin orange marmalade and pour it over the crêpes. Sprinkle them generously with finely chopped walnuts and with heated brandy. Ignite the spirit and serve the crêpes flaming.

Crêpes with Chocolate Sauce 🐦

MAKE dessert crêpes about 7 inches in diameter. Put one of the pancakes on a heated dish and cover it with thin chocolate sauce. Continue to pile the crêpes, one on top of the other, covering each with sauce. Cover the top crêpe with more chocolate sauce and sprinkle with slivered blanched almonds. Heat the stacked crêpes in a moderate oven (350° F.). To serve, cut in wedges and pass sweetened whipped cream.

Crêpes with Currant Jelly 🐦

MAKE dessert crêpes and keep them warm.

Cream 1/2 cup soft butter with 2 tablespoons brandy and 2 teaspoons lemon juice, and stir in 4 tablespoons red currant jelly. Put a tablespoon of this mixture on each crêpe. Roll up the crêpes, arrange them side by side in a baking dish, and sprinkle them heavily with fine granulated sugar. Put the dish in a very hot oven (450° F.) or under the broiler until the sugar is caramelized.

Crêpes Simon 🐦

FOLLOW the recipe for dessert crêpes, flavoring the batter with cherry liqueur. Bake the crêpes and spread them with frangipane cream mixed with 2 tablespoons cherry jam. Fold the crêpes in quarters, sprinkle them with heated Cognac, and ignite the spirit.

Cream Beignets 🐦

IN a large saucepan sift together 1 cup sifted flour, 4 tablespoons sugar, and a pinch of salt. Add 1 egg and 2 egg yolks, mixing the batter thoroughly, and repeat the process twice, using 3 eggs and 6 egg yolks altogether. Stir the batter until it is very smooth. Scald 2 cups milk with a piece of vanilla bean, discard the bean, and pour the hot milk slowly into the egg batter, stirring briskly with a wire whisk. Add 2 tablespoons butter and cook the cream over moderate heat for about 2 minutes, stirring vigorously. Pour a layer of cream about 3/4 inch thick into a buttered shallow pan and chill it thoroughly.

Turn the pan upside down on a lightly floured board, turn out the thickened cream, and cut out 1 1/2-inch squares or decorative shapes. Dip the pieces of cream in blender fritter batter and fry them, a few at a time, in deep hot fat (375° F.) until they are golden brown. Drain the *beignets* on absorbent paper, arrange them in a buttered shallow pan, and sprinkle them with fine granulated sugar. Glaze them under the broiler.

Blender Fritter Batter

IN the container of a blender combine 1 cup plus 1 tablespoon sifted flour, 1 cup hot milk, 1/2 cup kirsch, Cognac, or rum, 1 tablespoon each of melted butter and sugar, 2 eggs, and a pinch of salt. Cover the container and blend the batter at high speed for 30 seconds, stopping the motor once during the process to scrape the batter down with a rubber spatula. Pour the batter into a bowl and let it stand for 2 hours before using.

❧ Beignets Soufflés

IN a small saucepan combine 1 cup water, 1/2 cup butter, 1 teaspoon sugar, and 1/4 teaspoon salt, and bring the mixture to a rapid boil. Remove the pan from the heat and add 1 cup plus 2 tablespoons sifted flour all at once, stirring vigorously. Cook the mixture over low heat, beating briskly, until the ingredients are thoroughly combined and the dough cleanly leaves the sides of the pan and forms a ball. Remove the pan from the heat. Add 4 eggs, one at a time, beating well after each addition, and beat the paste until it is smooth and glossy. If an electric mixer is used, set it at medium speed. Stir in 1 tablespoon orange-flower water or rum, or 1 teaspoon vanilla.

Drop the dough by a teaspoon into deep hot fat (365° F.) and fry the *beignets*, a few at a time, until they start to color. Raise the heat to 370° F. and fry the *beignets* until they are brown. Drain the *beignets* on absorbent paper and sprinkle them with confectioners' sugar. Serve hot, with raspberry sauce.

❧ Macaroon Beignets

SCOOP out a few of the crumbs from the bottoms of 12 macaroons, fill the hollows with thick raspberry jam, and sandwich the macaroons together in pairs. Sprinkle

Beignets Soufflés with Raspberry Sauce

them with a few drops of kirsch and let them stand for 5 minutes. Dip each pair in beaten egg and in fresh bread crumbs, finely ground. Fry the macaroons, a few at a time, in a wire basket in deep hot fat (370° F.) until they are lightly browned. Drain the *beignets* on absorbent paper and sprinkle them with confectioners' sugar. Serve hot, on a napkin.

❧ Golden Lemon Puffs

BEAT 4 egg yolks with 10 tablespoons sugar until the mixture is thick and fluffy. Stir in 1 1/2 cups sifted flour and the grated rind of 2 large lemons. Beat 4 egg whites until they are stiff but not dry and fold them into the batter. Drop the batter by a teaspoon into deep hot fat (370° F.) and fry the puffs, a few at a time, until they are golden brown. Drain the puffs on absorbent paper and sprinkle with confectioners' sugar. Serve hot, with red-wine sauce.

❧ Danish Rice Fritters

COMBINE and blend well 2 cups cold cooked rice, 2 eggs, lightly beaten, 1/3 cup seedless raisins, 1/4 cup chopped blanched almonds, 2 tablespoons flour, and 1 tablespoon grated lemon rind. Drop the batter by spoonfuls into 1/4 cup hot butter in a heavy skillet, and fry the fritters, turning them once, until they are golden and cooked through. Drain the fritters on absorbent paper, sprinkle with confectioners' sugar, and serve with apricot jam.

❧ Cream Cheese and Apricots

SOFTEN 1 pound cream cheese. Add 1/2 cup sugar and 1/4 cup Cognac and beat the mixture until it is smooth. Stir in 6 very ripe apricots, peeled, pitted, and lightly mashed. Chill before serving.

❧ Grapes Flambé

IN the blazer of a chafing dish combine the juice and finely grated rind of 1 orange with 1/4 cup sugar and cook the syrup for 5 minutes. Add 3 cups seedless grapes and cook them, stirring, for 1 minute. Pour in 1/2 cup heated brandy and set it aflame. Serve the flaming grapes over vanilla ice cream.

Snapdragon

MOUND a cluster of seeded Malaga raisins on a large silver platter and put it in the center of the table. Pour 1 cup heated Cognac over the raisins and ignite the spirit. Keep ladling the burning Cognac over the raisins to keep it aflame. The guests quickly put their fingers through the flame and pull out one raisin at a time.

Grapefruit Shells

REMOVE the core and pulp from halved grapefruits. Sprinkle the shells lightly with sugar and fill them with grapefruit and orange sections. Sprinkle the fruit with finely chopped crystallized ginger.

Grapefruit and Cantaloupe Juice

COMBINE in a blender 3 cups each of diced cantaloupe and grapefruit juice and 1 teaspoon grated lemon rind. It will be necessary to blend the fruits in 3 loads. Blend the mixture until it is smooth. Serve in chilled glasses set in cracked ice.

Cantaloupe and Blackberries

HALVE 3 cantaloupes and scoop out the seeds and filaments. Cut the pulp into small balls with a melon-ball cutter and combine the balls with blackberries, using 1 cup blackberries to each 2 cups melon balls. Sprinkle the fruit with a little lemon juice and pile it in the cantaloupe shells. Sprinkle lightly with sugar and chill thoroughly.

Stuffed Cantaloupe

CUT a 1/2-inch slice from the tops of 6 small cantaloupes and remove the seeds and filaments. Remove the pulp, leaving a 1/4-inch lining. Put the pulp through a sieve

Raspberry Fool

or purée it in a blender. Combine the purée with 1 1/2 pints blueberries, sugar to taste, and 1/2 cup kirsch. Divide the mixture among the 6 cantaloupes, replace the tops, and chill before serving.

Cantaloupes with Strawberries &

HALVE 3 small cantaloupes and remove the seeds and filaments. Fill the melon halves with strawberries sprinkled with a little kirsch. Sprinkle the strawberries with fine granulated sugar and chill the melons thoroughly.

Cantaloupe Frappé &

SELECT 2 large ripe cantaloupes. Peel and slice one of them, discard the seeds and filaments, and put the pulp through a fine sieve or purée it in a blender. There should be about 2 cups purée.

Combine 1 1/2 cups water with 3/4 cup sugar and boil the syrup rapidly for 5 minutes. Stir the syrup into the melon purée, let it cool, and freeze it in a refrigerator tray until it is mushy. Beat the ice well, return it to the freezer, and freeze it until it is solid.

Cut a circular plug from the stem end of the second melon, reserving the plug. Discard the seeds and filaments and remove the pulp with a small melon-ball cutter. Put the melon balls in a bowl, sprinkle them with 2 tablespoons fine granulated sugar, and cover them with 4 tablespoons Port, rum, Curaçao, or maraschino liqueur. Chill the melon balls and the melon shell thoroughly.

Lay the shell on a bed of cracked ice, fill it with alternate layers of the melon ice and the chilled fruit, and replace the cover. To serve, spoon the mixture from the shell onto chilled serving plates.

Raspberry Fool &

SWEETEN 1 1/2 pints raspberries with sugar to taste and let the fruit stand for about 1 hour. Force the fruit through a fine sieve or purée it in a blender and strain out the seeds. Chill the purée and add more sugar, if desired. In a large chilled bowl whip 2 cups heavy cream until it is stiff. Pile the cream into a chilled glass bowl and gently swirl in the raspberry purée. Serve at once.

Raspberries Romanoff

HULL 1 1/2 quarts ripe raspberries and reserve the most perfect ones as a garnish. Sweeten the remaining berries with fine granulated sugar to taste and cover them with 1/2 cup orange juice and 1/4 cup Curaçao. Chill the berries thoroughly. Turn them and the juice into a serving dish. Cover the berries with swirls of whipped cream and sprinkle the cream with a little sugar. Garnish with the reserved berries.

Raspberries and Chocolate

WHIP 2 1/2 cups heavy cream until it is stiff and fold in 1 cup grated semisweet chocolate and 1 quart raspberries. Chill the mixture thoroughly.

Raspberries Chantilly with Chocolate Sauce

HULL 2 quarts ripe raspberries and sprinkle them lightly with sugar. Whip 1 quart heavy cream until it almost holds its shape. Fold in 3 tablespoons sugar and raspberry liqueur to taste. Chill both mixtures well. To serve, combine the raspberries and whipped cream and spoon the mixture into sherbet glasses. Serve with thin chocolate sauce. Makes 12 servings.

Melon Filled with Raspberries

CUT a small slice from the bottom of a large honeydew melon so that it will stand firmly. Slice off the stem end 2 inches from the top, set it aside to use as a cover, and remove the seeds and filaments from the melon. Remove the pulp with a melon-ball cutter and reserve the shell. Combine the melon balls with 1 quart ripe raspberries, 1/2 cup sugar, and 1 tablespoon chopped fresh mint, and sprinkle the fruit with 2 tablespoons apricot liqueur. Let the fruit mellow for 20 minutes. Fill the melon shell with the fruit, replace the cover, and chill the filled melon thoroughly. Serve the melon on a platter surrounded by a ring of whole perfect raspberries.

Gingered Honeydew Melon 🐦

PEEL and slice a ripe honeydew melon. Discard the seeds and arrange the slices in an overlapping design on a chilled serving platter. Sprinkle them with a mixture of 1 tablespoon confectioners' sugar and 1/4 teaspoon ground ginger.

Honeydew Melon and Kirsch 🐦

CUT a circular plug from the stem end of a ripe honeydew melon, reserving the plug. With a long-handled spoon, scoop out the seeds and filaments. Pour into the cavity 1/2 cup kirsch. Replace the plug and chill the melon until serving time. Remove the plug and pour out the liqueur. Strain it and add grenadine syrup to taste. Cut the melon into wedges and pour a little of the kirsch and syrup mixture over each portion.

Melon Compote 🐦

PEEL any ripe melon and cut the pulp into cubes, discarding the seeds. For every 5 cups melon cubes make a syrup by simmering 1 1/2 cups water, 3/4 cup sugar, and 2 teaspoons rose water for 30 minutes. Pour the hot syrup over the melon cubes and chill the compote overnight.

Melon and Blackberry Compote 🐦

SPRINKLE 1 quart ripe blackberries with sugar to taste and 2 tablespoons kirsch and chill the fruit for several hours. Cut 1 ripe honeydew melon into small dice and combine with the blackberries.

Melon and Citrus Frappé 🐦

DICE enough honeydew melon and cantaloupe to make 1 cup, reserving the juices. Place the melon in a blender with the juice of 1 lime, 1 cup orange juice, and 1/2 cup finely cracked ice. Cover the container and blend the mixture until it is smooth. Pour it into glasses and decorate each glass with a sprig of mint.

❧ Watermelon with Rum

CUT a plug 2 1/2 inches square by 3 inches deep in a very ripe watermelon. Pour 1 pint rum into the melon and replace the plug. Chill the melon for 6 hours before serving.

❧ Orange Meringues

WITH a sharp knife slice the tops from 6 large navel oranges and remove the pulp, leaving the shells clean. Chill the orange shells and fill them almost to the top with orange ice. Cover the upper portions of the shells generously with a meringue made by beating 2 egg whites until stiff and gradually adding 4 tablespoons honey. Sprinkle the meringues with sugar and shredded coconut. Place the oranges on a wooden board and bake them in a very hot oven (450° F.) for 3 to 5 minutes, or until the meringue is delicately browned.

❧ Peaches and Grapes with Sour Cream

ARRANGE 6 large peaches, peeled and sliced, and 2 cups seedless grapes in a bowl. Sprinkle the fruit liberally with maple sugar and cover lavishly with sour cream.

❧ Stuffed Pineapple

HALVE lengthwise a large ripe pineapple and its tuft of leaves. Cut out the pulp, leaving a shell 1/2 inch thick. Discard the core and cut the pineapple into tiny dice. Fill the halves with thin overlapping slices of fresh peaches well soaked in kirsch, cover the peaches with a layer of the diced pineapple, and sprinkle with sugar. Cover the pineapple with a design of fresh strawberries. Sprinkle all with sugar and kirsch and chill well.

❧ Pineapple with Crème de Menthe

CUT a large ripe pineapple into 6 lengthwise wedges, leaving the leafy top on each segment. Separate the flesh from the shell, cut away the core, and score each piece evenly. Return the fruit to the shell, sprinkle with grated fresh coconut, and chill it. Just before serving, sprinkle each portion liberally with white crème de menthe.

Pineapple and Grapes in Kirsch

PEEL and core a ripe pineapple and cut it into small dice. Sprinkle the dice with 1/2 to 3/4 cup sugar and add 1 pound seedless green grapes. Sprinkle the fruit with kirsch and chill it for 3 hours.

COMPOTE ROUGE
Compote of Red Fruits

REMOVE the stems and stones from 1 1/2 pounds ripe cherries. Hull 1 1/2 quarts each of strawberries and raspberries and 1 pint each of red and white currants. Arrange the berries in a bowl and sprinkle them liberally with confectioners' sugar and 1/2 cup brandy. Let the fruit rest for 30 minutes before serving. Makes 20 servings.

Strawberries Isabelle

CRUSH 1 pint fresh strawberries and force them through a fine sieve or purée them in a blender. Sweeten the purée with sugar to taste and chill it thoroughly. Arrange 1 1/2 quarts vanilla ice cream in a crystal serving bowl. Dip 36 washed and hulled strawberries in the purée, coating them well, and arrange them on and around the ice cream. Pour any remaining purée over the ice cream. Serve at once.

Strawberry Orange Juice

COMBINE 3 cups each of strawberries and orange juice, both well chilled, with 3 tablespoons sugar. Force the mixture through a sieve or purée half of it at a time in a blender.

🐚 Frosted Fruit

WITH a sharp knife halve 3 small grapefruit and carefully remove the pulp, discarding the seeds and membranes. Reserve the shells. Combine the pulp with 9 or 10 nectarines, peeled and sliced. Boil together 2 cups water and 1 cup sugar for 5 minutes, cool the syrup, and pour it over the fruit. Let it stand for about 2 hours, drain it, and pile into the grapefruit shells. Sprinkle each shell with 2 tablespoons *crème de cassis* and freeze them for 20 minutes before serving.

🐚 Fresh Fruit Compote Chartreuse

IN a crystal serving bowl combine 1 pint raspberries, 1 small pineapple, diced, 3 peaches, peeled and sliced, 1/2 cup blueberries, and 1/4 cup blanched almonds. Boil together 1/2 cup each of water and sugar for 5 minutes. Cool the syrup, pour it over the fruit, and add 1/2 cup Chartreuse. Chill the compote thoroughly.

🐚 The Queen's Custard

IN a large bowl beat 8 egg yolks until they are light and beat in 3 cups milk and 3 tablespoons orange sugar. Strain the mixture into a buttered glass baking dish and bake the custard in a slow oven (300° F.) for about 1 hour, or until it is firm. Pour 2 tablespoons orange-flavored liqueur over the custard and let it stand in a cool place until the liqueur is absorbed into the custard. Beat 5 egg whites until they are stiff, gradually beating in 3 tablespoons orange sugar. Spread this meringue over the custard and bake it in a moderate oven (350° F.) for about 15 minutes, or until the meringue is brown. Decorate the custard with mint leaves dipped in confectioners' sugar.

🐚 Gooseberry Custard

WASH and trim 1 quart gooseberries, combine them with 2 cups sugar, and cook them slowly until the fruit is mushy. Press the fruit through a sieve, pour the purée into a glass bowl, and chill it. In the top of a double boiler beat 4 egg yolks lightly and stir in 1/4 cup sugar and a dash of salt. Stir in gradually 2 cups scalded milk. Set the pan over hot water and cook the custard, stirring constantly, until it coats the spoon. Chill the custard and flavor it with 1/2 teaspoon vanilla. Pour the custard over the gooseberries and chill the mixture. Decorate with swirls of sweetened whipped cream.

Maple Custard 🎿

COMBINE thoroughly 3 beaten eggs, 2 cups milk, 1/2 cup maple syrup, and a pinch of salt, and pour the mixture into 6 buttered custard cups. Set the cups in a pan of warm water and bake them in a moderate oven (350° F.) for about 40 minutes, or until the custard is set and a knife inserted near the center comes out clean.

Pumpkin Custard 🎿

COMBINE 1 1/2 cups milk, 2/3 cup cooked pumpkin, 2 tablespoons honey, and a dash each of nutmeg, cinnamon, and cloves. Beat the mixture well with a rotary beater or purée it in a blender. Beat in 2 eggs. Pour the custard into 6 buttered custard cups and put the cups in a pan of hot water. Bake them in a moderately slow oven (325° F.) for about 20 minutes, or until the custard is set and a knife inserted near the center comes out clean.

Macaroon Trifle 🎿

SOAK 24 dry almond macaroons in Sherry. Arrange half the macaroons in a glass bowl. Spread the macaroons with thick apricot purée, add the remaining macaroons, and top with a layer of the apricot purée. Sprinkle the whole with slivered toasted almonds and decorate with tufts of whipped cream.

Raspberry Trifle 🎿

SWEETEN 1 pint raspberries with sugar to taste and reserve them. Beat 6 egg yolks until they are light and lemon-colored, add 1/2 cup sugar, and gradually stir in 1 cup white wine. Put the egg-yolk mixture in the top of a double boiler and cook it over hot water, stirring constantly, until it coats the spoon. Let the custard cool. Arrange a layer of whole macaroons in an ovenproof glass bowl. Cover the macaroons with a layer of the raspberries and add a layer of custard. Continue to fill the dish with alternate layers of custard and raspberries.

Beat 6 egg whites with a pinch of salt until they are stiff, add 6 tablespoons sugar, and continue to beat the meringue until is is well blended. Spread the meringue over the trifle and decorate it with meringue rosettes piped through a pastry tube. Bake the trifle in a slow oven (300° F.) for 15 to 20 minutes, or until the meringue is delicately browned. Cool and chill the trifle before serving.

Edwardian Trifle

IN the top of a double boiler beat 4 egg yolks until they are light and stir in 1/2 cup sugar. Add gradually 1 cup each of milk and light cream, scalded with 1/2 vanilla bean. Set the pan over hot water and cook the custard, stirring constantly, until it coats the spoon. Strain and cool the custard, stirring occasionally.

Line the bottom and sides of a glass bowl with half-inch slices of jelly roll. Moisten the cake with Sherry or Madeira. Fill the bowl with the cooled custard. Using a pastry bag fitted with a fluted tube, pipe rosettes of whipped cream around the trifle and decorate with thinly sliced strawberries.

Highland Mist

WITH a rolling pin crush 18 stale macaroons into fine crumbs. Add 2 to 3 tablespoons light cream and stir the mixture to a paste. Spread a layer of the mixture in a crystal bowl and cover it with a layer of vanilla whipped cream. Repeat the layers until all the macaroon mixture is used, and finish with a layer of the whipped cream. Chill the mist and serve it with fresh blueberries.

Scotch Mist

BEAT 1 1/2 cups heavy cream until it is light and fluffy. Stir 1 1/2 tablespoons heavy cream into 3 tablespoons chestnut purée and fold the mixture into half of the whipped cream. Pile the mixture into a glass dish and top with the remaining whipped cream. Dip the ends of ladyfingers into Sherry and arrange them, dipped ends down, in the cream.

In a large saucepan combine 1 cup each of sugar and water and boil the syrup

Edwardian Trifle

for 5 minutes. Add 6 oranges, thickly sliced, and cook them for 5 minutes. Put the orange compote in a serving dish and chill it. Serve the compote with the chestnut and whipped-cream mixture.

❧ Apple Macaroon Soufflé

COMBINE 1 cup unsweetened applesauce with 1/2 cup macaroon crumbs soaked in 2 tablespoons brandy. Cream 6 tablespoons each of butter and sugar, stir in 3 egg yolks, lightly beaten, and add the apple and macaroon mixture. Fold in 3 egg whites, stiffly beaten. Pour the soufflé into a buttered and sugared 1-quart soufflé dish and bake it in a moderate oven (350° F.) for about 40 minutes, or until it is well puffed. Sprinkle the soufflé with confectioners' sugar and serve it with whipped cream flavored with brandy. Serve at once.

❧ Hazelnut and Prune Soufflé

MAKE a *roux* by blending together 3 tablespoons each of melted butter and flour. Gradually add 3/4 cup hot prune juice, stirring constantly. Stir in 1/4 cup sugar and a pinch of salt and continue to stir the sauce over low heat until it is smooth and thick. Remove the pan from the heat and stir in 4 beaten egg yolks, 1 cup chopped cooked prunes, 1/2 cup finely chopped hazelnuts, and 1 teaspoon vanilla. Fold in 5 egg whites, stiffly beaten. Pour the soufflé into a buttered and sugared 1 1/2-quart soufflé dish and bake it in a moderate oven (350° F.) for about 35 minutes, or until it is well puffed. Sprinkle with confectioners' sugar and serve with whipped cream sweetened to taste and flavored with Cognac. Serve at once.

❧ Honey Soufflé

BEAT 4 egg yolks until they are thick and light and beat in 1 tablespoon kirsch. Sift 1 cup sugar with 1 tablespoon flour and beat this gradually into the eggs. Gradually beat in 1 cup strained honey mixed with 1/2 cup clarified butter. Fold in 5 egg whites, stiffly beaten. Turn the batter into a buttered 1 1/2-quart soufflé dish, sprinkle it with 1 tablespoon ground pistachio nuts, and set the dish in a pan of hot water. Bake the soufflé in a moderately hot oven (375° F.) for 35 to 40 minutes, or until it is well puffed. Serve at once, with whipped cream or fruit sauce.

Molasses Soufflé

IN a saucepan melt 3 tablespoons butter, stir in 4 tablespoons flour, and cook the *roux*, stirring, for a minute or two. Add gradually 3/4 cup milk and cook the sauce, stirring, until it is thick and smooth. Add 1/2 cup molasses, 1/4 teaspoon each of ginger and cinnamon, and a pinch of salt, and cool the sauce. Beat 4 egg yolks with 2 tablespoons sugar until they are thick and add them to the batter. Fold in 4 egg whites, stiffly beaten. Pour the mixture into a buttered and sugared 1 1/2-quart soufflé dish and bake the soufflé in a moderately slow oven (325° F.) for about 50 minutes, or until it is well puffed and lightly browned. Serve with rum sauce.

Rum Sauce

BEAT 2 eggs with 1/2 cup sugar until the mixture is very light and fluffy. Fold in 1/2 cup heavy cream, stiffly beaten, and flavor with rum to taste. Chill the sauce and serve very cold with the hot soufflé.

Soufflé Rothschild

COMBINE 2 tablespoons melted butter with 1 1/2 tablespoons flour and cook the *roux*, stirring, until it starts to turn golden. Stir in gradually 1/2 cup scalded milk, add a 1-inch piece of vanilla bean, and cook the sauce, stirring constantly, for about 5 minutes. Remove the vanilla bean. Add to the sauce 5 egg yolks beaten with 3 tablespoons sugar. Beat 6 egg whites until they are stiff, adding 1 tablespoon sugar during the last minute of beating. Carefully fold one fourth of the egg whites into the batter. Fold in the remaining egg whites lightly but completely. Pour half the batter into a buttered and sugared 2-quart soufflé dish and sprinkle with 3 tablespoons finely chopped candied fruit soaked in 2 tablespoons Cognac. Add the remaining batter and bake the soufflé in a moderately hot oven (375° F.) for about 20 minutes, or until it is well puffed and lightly browned. Garnish with glacéed cherry halves and serve at once.

Cold Chocolate Soufflé

Chafing Dish Peach Soufflé 🦢

BEAT 5 egg yolks until they are light and foamy, add 1/3 cup sugar and a pinch of salt, and fold in 1/3 cup peach preserves and 2 tablespoons dark rum. Fold in 5 egg whites, stiffly beaten. Pour the mixture into the hot buttered blazer of a chafing dish, cover it, and set the pan over hot water. Cook the soufflé for about 25 minutes, or until it rises and is set. Remove the blazer from the hot-water pan and sprinkle the soufflé with 1/4 cup finely chopped toasted almonds. Cover the pan again and cook the soufflé for another 2 minutes over hot water. Heat a scant 1/4 cup warm rum, pour it over the soufflé, and ignite it. Serve at once.

Flaming Omelet Soufflé 🦢

BEAT 8 egg yolks with 1/2 cup sugar and 1 teaspoon vanilla until the mixture is very light. Beat 12 egg whites until they are stiff and fold them in lightly but completely. Butter an ovenproof platter, sprinkle it with sugar, and heap the egg mixture on it in an oval-shaped mound. Smooth the surface with a spatula and make a furrow about 2 inches deep the length of the oval. Bake the omelet in a hot oven (400° F.) for about 20 minutes, or until it is well puffed and browned. A few minutes before taking it from the oven, glaze the top with a light sprinkling of sugar. At the table, ignite 1/3 cup heated rum and pour it flaming over the omelet. Serve at once.

Cold Chocolate Soufflé 🦢

COMBINE in a bowl 4 eggs, 3 egg yolks, and 1/2 cup sugar. Beat the mixture with an electric beater for about 15 minutes, or until it is very thick and pale in color. Or put the bowl over hot water and beat vigorously with a rotary beater.

Soften 1 1/2 tablespoons gelatin in a mixture of 1/4 cup water and 2 teaspoons orange juice, dissolve it over hot water, and let it cool slightly. In a small heavy saucepan melt 5 ounces dark sweet chocolate and 1/2 ounce unsweetened chocolate in 3 tablespoons coffee and 2 tablespoons brandy. Add the cooled gelatin and chocolate mixtures to the beaten eggs and mix well. Whip 1/2 cup heavy cream until it forms soft peaks and fold it in.

Oil a 6-inch band of wax paper and tie it around a 1-quart soufflé dish to form a standing collar. Fill the dish with the soufflé mixture (it should extend 3 inches above the rim of the dish), and chill it until it is set. Carefully remove the paper collar and press shredded sweet chocolate around the exposed sides of the *soufflé froid*. Decorate the top with rosettes of whipped cream, pressed through a pastry bag fitted with a fluted tube.

❦ Cold Chestnut Soufflé

COMBINE in a bowl 4 eggs, 3 egg yolks, and 1/2 cup sugar. Beat the mixture with an electric beater for about 15 minutes, or until it is very thick and pale in color. Soften 2 tablespoons gelatin in 6 tablespoons rum and dissolve it over hot water. Beat the gelatin and rum mixture quickly into the beaten eggs, combine with 1 cup sweetened chestnut purée, and mix well. Fold in 1 cup heavy cream, stiffly beaten.

Oil a 6-inch band of wax paper and tie it around a 3/4-quart soufflé dish to form a standing collar. Fill the dish with the soufflé mixture and chill it until it is set. Carefully remove the paper collar and decorate the top of the *soufflé froid* with rosettes of whipped cream, pressed through a pastry bag fitted with a fluted tube, and with whole *marrons glacés*.

Serve with chocolate whipped cream sauce.

❦ Cold Lemon Soufflé

BEAT 4 eggs with 3 egg yolks and 1/4 cup sugar until the mixture is very thick. Use an electric mixer if possible. Beat in very gradually 2 tablespoons gelatin softened in 1/2 cup lemon juice and dissolved over hot water. Strain the mixture and fold in the grated rind of 1 large lemon and 1 cup heavy cream, whipped. Oil a 6-inch band of wax paper and tie it around a 3/4-quart soufflé dish to form a standing collar. Fill the dish with the soufflé mixture (it should extend 2 inches above the rim of the dish) and chill it until it is set. Carefully remove the paper collar and decorate the soufflé with rosettes of whipped cream, pressed through a pastry bag fitted with a fluted tube.

❦ Applesauce

CUT into quarters 12 large unpeeled tart apples (red-skinned fruit makes the most attractive sauce). Put the apples in a saucepan, add a little water, and cook the fruit, covered, for about 20 minutes, or until it is soft. Force the fruit through a sieve or a food mill and discard the skins. Add sugar and cinnamon, nutmeg, or mace to taste. Makes about 3 cups.

Almond Macaroon Applesauce

PUT a 2-inch layer of applesauce in a buttered baking dish and sprinkle it with ground blanched almonds and with macaroon crumbs. Dot with butter and bake the applesauce in a hot oven (400° F.) for 15 minutes. Serve warm.

Poached Apples

PEEL, core, and cut into thick wedges 2 pounds apples. Sauté the wedges in 2 table-spoons butter for 3 minutes and sprinkle them with 1/2 cup sugar. Add 1/2 cup each of water and white wine, 1 tablespoon lemon juice, and a small piece of lemon peel and cook the fruit, covered, over low heat for about 10 minutes, or until the wedges are tender but still whole.

Stewed Apples with Orange

COMBINE 3/4 cup each of orange juice and sugar, 2 tablespoons grated orange rind, and 1 teaspoon grated lemon rind. Bring the syrup to a boil, stirring constantly. Core and quarter 6 red cooking apples and add them to the syrup. Lower the heat and simmer the apples for about 15 minutes, or until they are just tender. Serve warm.

Chafing Dish Apples

PEEL, core, and slice 3 large tart apples and soak them in rum to cover for 3 hours. Drain the slices, dry them, and dust them lightly with flour. Melt 1/2 cup butter in the blazer of a chafing dish and in it brown the apple slices delicately on both sides, adding a little more butter as necessary. Sprinkle the apple slices with con-fectioners' sugar.

❧ Cointreau Apples

CORE 6 large baking apples and peel the upper half of each. Put the fruit in a baking dish and pour around it 3/4 cup water mixed with 1 1/2 tablespoons apple jelly. Bake the apples in a moderate oven (350° F.) for about 45 minutes, or until they are tender but still hold their shape. Carefully remove the apples to a platter. Fill the centers with 1/3 cup apricot jam mixed with 1 tablespoon lemon juice. Reduce the liquid in the baking dish by half and add to it 1/4 cup Cointreau. Pour this sauce over the apples and serve at room temperature.

❧ Minted Baked Apples

CORE 6 Rome Beauty apples and peel the upper quarter of each. Lay a few mint leaves in the bottom of a baking dish, arrange the apples on the leaves, and fill the cavity of each apple with a mixture of 2 tablespoons honey, 1 teaspoon water, 1/2 teaspoon butter, and 1 mint leaf.

Cover the pan and bake the apples in a moderately hot oven (375° F.) for 50 to 55 minutes, or until they are tender, basting frequently with the syrup in the pan.

❧ Rose Geranium Apples

CORE 6 large apples and peel the top third of each. Put the peelings with 1 cup each of sugar, water, and apple jack flavored with rose geranium in a large heavy skillet. Add 1 or 2 drops of red food coloring and boil the mixture for 10 minutes. Put a lightly buttered rose geranium leaf in each apple and stand the apples upright in the pan. Cover the pan and cook the apples over moderate heat, turning them repeatedly, for 15 to 20 minutes, or until they are just tender but still hold their shape. Pour the pan juices over the apples from time to time as they cool.

❧ Apple Crisp

CUT 5 apples into 1/4-inch slices. There should be about 4 cups slices. Arrange the slices in a buttered baking dish and sprinkle them with 1 teaspoon each of cinnamon and nutmeg and 1/2 cup apple juice. Mix 1/2 cup brown sugar, firmly packed, with

3/4 cup sifted flour and rub in 1/2 cup butter. Sprinkle the crumbs over the apple slices. Bake the apples in a moderately hot oven (375° F.) for about 35 minutes, or until they are tender. Serve the apple crisp hot with plain or whipped cream.

Apricots Cardinal

COVER 18 large firm apricots with boiling water, let them stand for 5 minutes, and drain them. Peel the apricots, reserving the peel, halve them, and remove the stones. Combine 2 cups sugar and 3 cups water, boil the syrup for 5 minutes, and add the apricots. Remove the saucepan from the heat and let the apricots cool. Chill them in the syrup for several hours. Drain the apricots, reserve the syrup, and arrange the fruit in a crystal bowl. Add to the syrup the reserved apricot peel and 1 pint raspberries and cook the mixture for 10 minutes. Strain the syrup through cheesecloth, discarding the raspberry seeds and apricot peel. Cook the syrup for 10 minutes longer, or until it is slightly reduced. Cool the syrup to lukewarm, add 2 tablespoons kirsch, and pour it over the apricots. Sprinkle the fruit with 1/2 cup almonds, blanched, toasted, and coarsely chopped.

Apricots in Honey

PEEL 18 ripe apricots, halve them, and remove the stones. Bring to a boil 1 cup honey, 1/4 cup lemon juice, and 1/4 cup water. Add the apricot halves, reduce the heat, and simmer the fruit very gently for 8 to 10 minutes, or until it is tender. Cool the fruit in the syrup, add 1/4 cup kirsch, and turn the compote into a large glass bowl. Chill it thoroughly and serve with heavy cream.

Apricots with Strawberry Purée

PLUNGE 18 ripe apricots into boiling water and slip off the skins. Halve the apricots and remove the stones. Arrange the halves in a glass bowl, sprinkle them with sugar, and cover them with the following sauce: Force 1 pint ripe strawberries through a fine sieve and add 1/2 cup Champagne and sugar to taste. Serve at once.

ꜰ Chafing Dish Bananas

MELT 1/2 cup butter in the blazer of a chafing dish and stir in 1/2 cup sugar, the juice and grated zest of 2 tangerines, 1 lemon, and 1 orange, and 1/2 cup Curaçao. Simmer the sauce for a minute and add 6 bananas, peeled and halved lengthwise. Cook the bananas slowly until they are heated through. Serve the fruit on heated dessert plates and pour a generous spoonful of the sauce on each.

ꜰ Blackberry Compote

BRING to a boil 1/2 cup sugar, 1 small cinnamon stick, and the rind of 1 lemon. Cook the syrup for 5 minutes and discard the lemon rind and cinnamon stick. Add 1 quart blackberries, washed and drained, bring the syrup to a boil, and simmer the fruit gently for 2 or 3 minutes. Add 2 tablespoons orange-flavored liqueur. Chill the compote well and serve it with ice cream or whipped cream.

ꜰ Cherries in Claret

STONE 2 pounds fresh black cherries, cover them with 2 cups claret, 1/4 cup sugar, and a pinch of cinnamon, and cook them gently for 8 to 10 minutes, or until they are soft. Remove the cherries with a perforated spoon to a bowl. Simmer the syrup in the pan until it is reduced by one third. Stir in 3 tablespoons currant jelly and, when is has melted, pour the sauce over the cherries. Cool the compote and chill it.

ꜰ Cherry Compote

STONE 2 pounds cherries, crack 2 dozen of the stones, and tie them in a cheesecloth bag. Put the bag of stones in a saucepan with 2 cups claret and 1 1/2 cups sugar, bring the syrup to a boil, and cook it for 5 minutes. Add the cherries, cover the pan, and simmer them for 8 to 10 minutes. Remove half the cherries with a perforated spoon to a glass bowl. Discard the bag of stones, rub the remaining cherries through a sieve, and stir the purée into the whole cherries in the bowl. Cool the compote.

Beat 5 egg whites with a pinch of salt until they are stiff but not dry. Beat in gradually 3/4 cup fine granulated sugar, a tablespoon at a time, and continue to beat the meringue until it is thick and smooth. Fold in gently 1/4 cup sugar, 1 teaspoon vanilla, and 3/4 cup grated almonds. Arrange the meringue in tufts over the cherries.

Currant Purée

COOK 1 pound (about 3 1/4 cups) red or black currants with 1/2 cup sugar over low heat, stirring occasionally, for about 10 minutes, or until the fruit is very soft. Force it through a sieve, return it to the saucepan, and add a dash of lemon juice. Heat the purée and serve it hot with cold heavy cream.

Broiled Grapefruit

HALVE 3 grapefruit, cut out the centers, and separate the sections from the membranes. Sprinkle each grapefruit half with 1 tablespoon brown sugar and a dash of mace and dot it with 1 tablespoon butter. Broil the grapefruit 4 inches from the heat for 5 minutes, or until the top is golden brown and the fruit is hot.

Spiced Oranges

IN a saucepan combine 1 1/2 cups water, 1/2 cup sugar, the peel of 3 oranges, 6 whole cloves, 5 cinnamon sticks, and 1 bay leaf. Bring the syrup to a boil and cook it for 10 minutes. Remove the peel from the syrup and discard it. Add the sections of 6 oranges to the pan and cook them for 2 minutes. Remove the pan from the heat. Add 3 tablespoons lemon juice and cool the fruit. Chill the oranges for at least 12 hours.

Persian Oranges

WITH a sharp knife cut a 1/2-inch slice from the tops of 18 oranges and remove the pulp, leaving the shells clean. Dice the orange sections and combine them with 3 cups small Persian melon balls and 8 teaspoons each of shredded orange rind and raisins soaked in brandy. Boil together 3 cups water and 2 cups sugar for 5 minutes, cool the syrup, and use it to cover the fruit. Let the fruit stand in a cool place for

2 hours, drain it, and arrange it in the orange shells. Pour 1 tablespoon Sherry into each shell. Serve the oranges on sprays of mint leaves. Makes 18 servings.

⟡ Rice and Oranges

COMBINE 2 cups milk, 1/2 cup sugar, and 1/4 cup orange-flavored liquor. Add 1 cup rice and cook the mixture slowly for 20 minutes. Stir in 1 cup light cream and 2 tablespoons butter and turn the rice into a serving dish. Boil together for 5 minutes 1 cup water and 1/2 cup sugar. Add to the syrup 1/4 cup orange-flavored liqueur and the peeled sections of 3 large oranges. Poach the fruit for 3 or 4 minutes. Decorate the rice with the orange sections and chill well before serving. Serve the syrup as a sauce.

⟡ Chestnut and Orange Compote

COMBINE 2 cups water with 3/4 cup sugar and a 1-inch piece of vanilla bean. Boil the syrup for 5 minutes, add 1 pound chestnuts, shelled and peeled, and simmer them for about 30 minutes, or until they are soft. Cool the chestnuts. Peel 3 large oranges, remove the pith, and slice the fruit thinly. Add the cooled chestnuts and chill the compote thoroughly.

⟡ Poached Peaches

IN a saucepan bring to a boil 1 cup sauterne and 1/2 cup each of water and sugar. Add 6 large peaches, peeled, pitted, and halved, two at a time, and poach them over low heat for about 5 minutes, or until they are tender. Remove the peaches to a bowl and pour the cooking syrup over them. Chill the peaches and, just before serving, add 1/4 cup rum.

⟡ Peach Compote

PLUNGE 15 large perfect freestone peaches in boiling water for a second or two and then into cold water. Slip off the skins. Split 3 of the peaches, extract the stones, break the stones with a hammer, and remove the kernels. Reserve the halved peaches for another use. With a sharp knife peel off the brown skins of the kernels.

Cook 2 cups each of sugar and water for 5 minutes, skimming the syrup carefully when it first comes to a boil. Poach the 12 whole peaches and the 3 kernels gently in the syrup for about 5 minutes. Discard the kernels. Cool and chill the peaches in the syrup. Turn the compote into a dish and sprinkle it generously with blanched, slivered, and toasted almonds.

Baked Pears

IN a saucepan combine 6 tablespoons brown sugar with 1/2 cup water and 1/4 cup butter. Bring the syrup to a boil and pour it over 6 large Bosc pears, placed upright in a baking dish. Add 6 strips of lemon peel and cover the dish with aluminum foil. Bake the pears in a moderately hot oven (375° F.) for about 1 hour, basting them frequently, or until they can easily be pierced with a fork. Serve hot, with a pitcher of heavy cream.

Caramel Pears

PEEL, halve, and core 6 firm pears. Arrange the pear halves close together in a shallow baking dish, sprinkle them lavishly with sugar, and put 2 teaspoons butter in the hollow of each half. Bake the pears, basting them frequently, in a very hot oven (500° F.) for about 20 minutes, or until the fruit is tender and the sugar is caramelized. Stir 3/4 cup heavy cream into the pan juices and serve warm or at room temperature.

Pear and Ginger Compote

BOIL together 1 cup each of water and sugar for 5 minutes and add 2 tablespoons ginger syrup or 1/2 teaspoon ground ginger. Add 6 pears, peeled, cored, and halved, two at a time, and simmer them, covered, for about 25 minutes, or until they are tender. Remove the pears from the syrup and arrange them in a dish. Pour the syrup over them and garnish with 1 tablespoon preserved ginger, cut in julienne. Serve with whipped cream.

✍ Pears in Red Wine

COMBINE and cook together for 5 minutes 1 cup each of dry red wine and sugar, one 2-inch cinnamon stick, and 3 whole cloves. Peel, halve, and core 6 pears and poach them in the syrup for about 25 minutes, or until they are tender. Cool the pears in the syrup, remove the cinnamon stick and cloves, and chill the fruit. Serve with sour cream flavored with ground cinnamon.

✍ Pears Zingara

COMBINE 1 cup each of sugar and water and boil the syrup for 5 minutes. Peel, core, and cut into thick slices 6 large ripe pears. Poach the pears in the syrup for about 15 minutes, or until they are tender, and transfer them with a perforated spoon to a platter. Cook the syrup until it is reduced by half and pour it over the pears to glaze them.

Combine 1 cup each of sugar and water and boil the syrup for 5 minutes. Peel and cut in thick slices 6 large oranges. Remove the syrup from the heat, add the orange slices, and let them steep for 1 hour. Remove the oranges and reserve the syrup. Arrange the orange and pear slices in alternate layers on the platter. Trim angelica in leaf shapes and garnish the pear slices with the leaves. Flavor the syrup in which the oranges were steeped with orange-flavored liqueur to taste and pour it over the compote.

✍ Chafing Dish Pineapple

IN the blazer of a chafing dish sauté 1 ripe pineapple, peeled and diced, in 1/2 cup butter until the dice are golden brown. Sprinkle the fruit with 3 tablespoons brown sugar and 1/3 cup rum and cook it until the liquid has been absorbed. Add 1 cup heavy cream and serve as soon as the cream is heated through.

✍ Grilled Pineapple

CUT whole unpeeled pineapples into 6 wedges, cut away the core, and sprinkle the wedges with a little dark rum. Place the wedges, skin side down, directly on a grill and cook them until they are heated through and begin to soften.

Pineapple Rice 🐾

BOIL together 1 cup each of sugar and water for 5 minutes. Cut the flesh of a ripe pineapple into sticks and poach the sticks in the syrup for 5 minutes. Drain the pineapple and reserve the syrup.

Line the bottom and sides of a baking dish with the pineapple sticks and cover with a layer of half the rice for desserts. Cover the rice with apricot jam and finish with the remaining rice. Bake the rice in a moderate oven (350° F.) for 10 minutes. Add 1 tablespoon rum to the pineapple syrup and in it poach 4 bananas, peeled and halved lengthwise. Arrange the bananas on the rice and pour the remaining syrup over them.

Rice for Desserts

WASH 1 cup rice, put it in a saucepan, and cover it generously with cold water. Bring the mixture to a boil, turn off the heat, and let it stand for 5 minutes. Drain the rice in a sieve and rinse it well under running cold water. Return the rice to the pan with 2 1/2 cups scalded milk, 6 tablespoons sugar, 1/2 teaspoon salt, and a piece of vanilla bean. Bring the milk to a boil and add 1 tablespoon butter. Cover the pan and simmer the rice very gently for about 30 minutes, or until it is tender. Toss it with a fork to separate the grains and, using the fork, stir in 3 egg yolks, mixed with 2 tablespoons heavy cream. Spread the mixture on a platter to cool.

Greengage Plums in Port 🐾

BRING to a boil 4 cups water and 1 cup sugar and add 3/4 cup white Port and 12 greengage plums, washed and unpeeled. Simmer the fruit for 5 minutes, or until it is tender, taking care that the skin does not break. Cool and chill the plums thoroughly.

Brandied Tangerines and Cheese 🐾

BOIL together 2 cups water, 1 cup sugar, 4 tablespoons brandy, and 1/4 teaspoon ground cloves for 5 minutes. Add the peeled sections of 6 tangerines and simmer them for about 5 minutes, or until they are tender. Drain the fruit and cool it. Force 1 pound cream cheese through a fine sieve, or purée it in a blender, and add gradually 1/2 cup each of sugar and white wine and the juice of 1 lemon. Top each serving with the brandied tangerines.

ᔥ Dried Fruit Compote

WASH and drain 3/4 pound mixed dried fruits and 1 cup raisins and put them in a baking dish with 3 cups water. Bake the fruits in a moderately slow oven (325° F.) for 1 hour. Add 1/3 cup sugar and the juice of 1 lemon, stir the fruits until the sugar is dissolved, and add 1 orange, peeled and thinly sliced. Cool the compote, chill it, and serve with sour cream.

ᔥ Fruit Compote Angleterre

BRING to a boil 2 cups water with 3/4 cup sugar and skim the syrup carefully. Add 1/4 cup orgeat syrup and cook for 5 minutes.

Plunge 8 small peaches and 6 to 8 apricots into boiling water for a second or two and then into cold water. Slip off the skins. Wash 6 greengage plums. Add the peaches, apricots, and plums to the syrup, cover the saucepan, and simmer the fruit very slowly for 5 to 10 minutes, or until it is tender. Cool and chill the fruit in the syrup. Combine 1/2 cup orange sections, free of pith and membranes, and 1/4 cup each of seedless grapes, sliced bananas, and melon balls, and add them to the chilled poached fruit. Turn the compote into a crystal dish and sprinkle it with shredded blanched orange rind. Serve very cold.

ᔥ Fruit Compote with Iced Champagne

COMPOTE DE FRUITS AU CHAMPAGNE FRAPPÉ

BOIL together 2 cups water and 1 cup sugar for 5 minutes. Peel, core, and quarter 2 apples and poach them in the syrup for about 15 minutes, or until they are tender. Remove the apples and reserve them. Poach 6 stoned greengage plums in the same syrup for about 5 minutes, or until they are tender. Remove them from the syrup and reserve them. To the syrup add 2 pears, peeled, cored, and quartered, and a drop or two of red food coloring, and poach the pears for about 15 minutes, or until they

Fruit Compote Angleterre

are tender. Remove the pears and reserve the syrup. Arrange all the poached fruit in a crystal compote dish, cool it, and chill it. Cool the syrup, add 1 1/2 cups Champagne and the juice of 1 lemon, and freeze it in a refrigerator tray until it is mushy. Pour the frozen Champagne over the fruit.

Macédoine of Fruit Flambé

MELT 4 tablespoons butter in the blazer of the chafing dish and in it sauté 2 pears, peeled, cored, and sliced, 1/2 cup pineapple, diced, 1/2 pint strawberries, and 1 banana, sliced, until the fruit is heated. Add 1 cup apricot purée and cook the fruit for 1 minute longer. Pour 1/2 cup heated rum over the fruit and set it aflame. Serve the macédoine over slices of poundcake.

Crème Brûlée à l'Orange

IN the top of a double boiler scald 3 cups heavy cream. Beat 6 egg yolks in a bowl, gradually beat in 6 tablespoons sugar, and beat the mixture until it is light and creamy. Slowly add the warm cream to the egg yolks and add 2 tablespoons orange-flavored liqueur and 1 tablespoon grated orange rind. Return the custard to the double boiler, set the pan over hot but not boiling water, and cook the custard, stirring constantly, until it thickens and coats the spoon. Pour the custard into a shallow glass baking dish and chill it thoroughly.

At serving time, cover the top of the custard completely with a 1/4-inch-thick layer of sieved light-brown sugar. Put the dish on a tray of crushed ice and put the tray under the heat of a broiler until the sugar melts and forms a thin caramel glaze. This procedure takes only a moment; watch carefully or the sugar may burn. To serve the *crème brûlée*, tap the glaze lightly with a spoon to crack the surface.

Frangipane Cream

IN a saucepan combine 1/2 cup flour, 3/4 cup sugar, and a pinch of salt. Stir in 2 eggs and 2 egg yolks and mix thoroughly to make a smooth paste. Scald 2 cups milk with a 1-inch piece of vanilla bean and stir the milk gradually into the paste. Cook the cream, stirring constantly, until it almost reaches the boiling point, and continue to cook it gently, still stirring, for 2 minutes. Remove the cream from the heat, discard the vanilla bean, and stir in 2 tablespoons butter and 4 macaroons, finely crushed. Cool the cream over cracked ice, stirring it from time to time.

Mocha Cream ঽঌ

IN the top of a double boiler combine 1 cup each of strong coffee and heavy cream, 1/4 cup sugar, and 1/8 teaspoon salt. Heat the mixture, stirring, until it almost comes to a boil, and cool it. Beat 10 egg yolks until they are light and foamy. Pour the cooled cream gradually over the egg yolks, stirring constantly. Melt 4 ounces sweet chocolate in the top of a double boiler over hot water, and stir it into the cream and egg mixture. Set the pan over hot water, stir the mixture until it is well blended and warm, and add 1 tablespoon dark rum. Strain the cream through a fine sieve and pour it into custard cups or *petits pots*. Serve cold, with whipped cream.

Prune Cream ঽঌ

HEAT 1 cup heavy cream with 1/2 cup sugar and add 1 tablespoon gelatin, soaked in 2 tablespoons cold water for 5 minutes. Stir the cream until the gelatin is dissolved. Add 1 1/2 cups prune purée, 1/2 cup chopped blanched almonds, and 1 tablespoon grated lemon rind. Cool the mixture and, when it begins to set, add 2/3 cup heavy cream, stiffly whipped with 1 teaspoon vanilla. Pour the prune cream into a buttered mold and chill it.

Danish Rum Cream ঽঌ

BEAT 5 egg yolks with 2/3 cup sifted confectioners' sugar and stir in 1/2 cup rum. Carefully fold in 2 cups heavy cream, whipped, 1 tablespoon gelatin softened in 4 tablespoons water and dissolved over hot water, and 5 egg whites, stiffly beaten. Pour the cream into a glass bowl and let it cool. Decorate the pudding with rosettes of whipped cream forced through a pastry tube and serve it with clear raspberry sauce.

Clear Raspberry Sauce

BRING to a boil 1 cup each of raspberry juice and water and 4 tablespoons sugar.

Marbled English Cream

Add 2 teaspoons cornstarch dissolved in enough water to make a thick paste, cook the sauce until it thickens, and cool it.

Marbled English Cream ෩

WITH a wire whip or a wooden spoon beat 4 egg yolks with 1/2 cup sugar and 3 tablespoons flour until the mixture is thick and pale in color. Gradually blend in 2 cups milk. Strain the cream through a fine sieve into a heavy saucepan. Cook the mixture very slowly, stirring constantly with a wooden spoon, until it almost comes to a boil. Do not let it boil. Remove the custard from the heat and stir in the grated rind of 1 lemon. Let the custard cool, stirring it from time to time to prevent a crust from forming, and strain it into a serving bowl.

In a heavy shallow pan melt 1 cup sugar over low heat, stirring constantly with a wooden spoon, until it is golden brown. Dip a fork into the caramel and quickly and lightly shake it off in a marbled pattern on the surface of the custard. Chill the cream. Serve the marbled cream within 3 or 4 hours or the caramel will melt into the custard.

Almond Pudding ෩

BEAT 8 egg yolks until they are thick and light, add 1 cup sifted confectioners' sugar, and beat the mixture for 2 minutes. Stir in 1/2 pound blanched almonds, finely ground, and fold in 8 egg whites, stiffly beaten. Turn the pudding into a buttered baking dish and bake it in a moderate oven (350° F.) for 30 minutes. Serve with white-wine sauce.

POUDING AUX MARRONS   ## Chestnut Pudding ෩

FOLLOWING the recipe for chestnuts for desserts, cook and purée 1 pound chestnuts. Add to the purée 1/4 cup rum, 1 teaspoon confectioners' sugar, and 1/2 teaspoon vanilla, and chill the mixture. Whip 1 cup heavy cream, gradually adding the juice of 1 orange and 1 tablespoon orange-flavored liqueur. Blend in the puréed chestnuts, beat all together well, and chill the pudding.

ᕽ Citron Pudding

BEAT 6 egg yolks until they are light and stir in 2 tablespoons flour. Add gradually 2 cups milk or light cream, 1/2 cup brandy, 4 ounces citron, finely chopped, and 2 tablespoons sugar. Pour the batter into 6 buttered custard cups and bake the pudding in a hot oven (400° F.) for about 20 minutes, or until it is firm.

ᕽ Graham Pudding

BEAT 1 egg well and stir in 1 cup each of molasses and milk. Sift together 1 cup each of white flour and graham flour and 1 teaspoon each of soda and salt. Gradually stir the dry ingredients into the molasses mixture. Stir in 1 cup chopped raisins and turn the batter into a buttered pudding mold. Steam the pudding for 2 1/2 to 3 hours. Serve with vanilla ice cream sauce.

ᕽ Honeycomb Pudding

COMBINE 3 tablespoons melted butter with 2 tablespoons milk. Add 1 cup molasses, 3 egg yolks, beaten, and 1 tablespoon lemon juice. Sift together 1 cup sifted flour, 1/2 teaspoon cinnamon, and a dash of salt, and add to the molasses mixture. Fold in 3 egg whites, stiffly beaten, and pour the pudding into a buttered baking dish. Bake the pudding in a slow oven (275° F.) for 1 hour. Serve with whipped cream.

ᕽ Orange Brioche

CUT stale brioche into slices 1 inch thick. Using a biscuit cutter, cut rounds from the slices. Dip each round into orange juice, beaten egg, and crushed macaroon or cookie crumbs. Brown the toast on both sides in clarified butter. Dust with confectioners' sugar and serve with orange marmalade.

ᕽ Queen of Puddings

SOAK 2 cups fine dry bread crumbs in 4 cups milk for 5 minutes. Cream 2 tablespoons butter with 1 cup sugar. Add 4 egg yolks, well beaten, and the grated rind of 1 lemon. Stir in the bread crumbs and pour the pudding into a well-buttered baking dish. Set the baking dish in a pan of hot water and bake the pudding in a moderate oven (350° F.) for about 1 hour, or until it is firm. Spread a layer of strawberry jam on the pudding. Beat 4 egg whites until they are stiff and gradually beat in 1/2 cup sugar. Spread the meringue over the pudding. Return the pudding to the oven and bake it until the meringue is delicately browned.

Raspberry Pudding

CRUSH 1 pint raspberries and a few red currants and force the fruit through a sieve. Beat 3 egg yolks with 6 tablespoons sugar until the mixture is thick and light, and stir it into the raspberry purée. Add 1/4 cup dry bread crumbs. Fold in 3 egg whites, stiffly beaten, and turn the batter into a buttered pudding mold. Set the mold in a pan of hot water and cook the pudding over direct heat for 35 minutes. Remove the mold from the water and finish cooking the pudding in a slow oven (300° F.) for about 10 minutes. Serve with heavy cream whipped to a light froth.

Summer Pudding

LINE a deep mold or bowl with overlapping slices of trimmed bread. Cut a round of bread for the bottom. The bread should completely cover the mold. In a saucepan combine 1 1/2 quarts raspberries, 1/2 pound (about 1 3/4 cups) red currants, and 3/4 cup sugar and cook the mixture for 4 minutes. Transfer the fruit to the bread-lined mold, pour in the juice, and cover with a layer of bread. Put a plate that fits the inside of the mold on the bread and on the plate a 2- or 3-pound weight. Chill the pudding overnight. Unmold it on a chilled platter, garnish with fresh berries in season, and serve with heavy cream. Other fruits, such as blueberries, blackberries, and loganberries, may be used.

White-Wine Pudding

IN the top of a double boiler beat 4 egg yolks with 1 cup sugar until they are light, stir in 1 cup orange juice, 3/4 cup sauterne or sweet Rhine wine, and 2 tablespoons lemon juice, and beat the mixture until is is well blended. Put the pan over hot water, and cook the custard, stirring constantly, until it is thickened. Stir in 2 tablespoons gelatin, softened in 1/4 cup cold water and dissolved over hot water. Pour the custard into a bowl, let it cool, and fold in 1 cup heavy cream, whipped, and 4 egg whites, stiffly beaten. Pour the pudding into a glass serving bowl and chill it for 2 to 3 hours, or until it is set.

Banana Cream Mold

SOFTEN 1 tablespoon gelatin in 1/4 cup cold water and dissolve it with 1/4 cup sugar in 1 1/2 cups hot water. Cool the liquid and add 3 ripe bananas, mashed or rubbed through a sieve. Fold in 1 cup heavy cream, whipped, pour the mixture into an oiled mold, and chill it until it is set. Turn the cream out on a chilled dish and garnish it with sliced bananas and fresh strawberries.

Banana Gelée Catawba

SOFTEN 2 tablespoons gelatin in 1/4 cup cold water for 5 minutes. Heat 2 1/4 cups Catawba grape juice just to the boiling point and add 1/2 cup sugar, 1/4 cup banana liqueur, 1 tablespoon lemon juice, and the gelatin. Stir the mixture until the sugar is dissolved. Pour it into a mold rinsed in cold water and chill it to the syrupy stage. Add 1 cup seeded white grapes and chill the mold until it is set. Dip the mold in warm water and turn it out upside down on a serving dish. Garnish with preserved kumquats or white grapes.

Crème de Cacao Chantilly

SOFTEN 2 tablespoons gelatin in 1/2 cup water and dissolve it in 2 cups strong hot coffee. Add 3/4 cup crème de cacao and 3 tablespoons sugar and stir the syrup until the sugar is dissolved. Pour the mixture into a mold rinsed in cold water and chill it until it is set. Dip the mold in warm water, turn the cream out on a chilled platter, and garnish it with wafers of mocha chocolate, whipped cream sweetened and flavored with crème de cacao, and a ring of finely grated chocolate.

Cordial Colettes 🐏

IN the top of a double boiler, over boiling water, heat 6 ounces dark sweet chocolate until it is almost melted. Remove the pan from the heat and stir the chocolate until it is smooth. With a teaspoon, swirl the chocolate around 6 paper baking cups, coating the entire inner surface of each. Put the cups in muffin pans and chill them until the chocolate coating is firm. Peel off the paper and chill the chocolate cups until ready to use.

Soften 1 teaspoon gelatin in 1 tablespoon cold water, dissolve it over hot water, and mix it into 1 pint soft vanilla ice cream. Half fill the chocolate cups with the gelatin cream. With the back of a teaspoon make a depression in the cream and fill it with 1 1/2 tablespoons cherry liqueur and a maraschino cherry. Fill the cups with more gelatin cream, mounding it as high as possible. Top each colette with a maraschino cherry and sprinkle with chopped pistachio nuts. Freeze the colettes until they are firm.

Green Curaçao Crown 🐏

SOFTEN 2 tablespoons gelatin in 1/2 cup cold water and dissolve it in 1/2 cup hot water. Combine it with 2/3 cup sugar, 1/2 cup lime juice, and a pinch of salt, and stir until the sugar is dissolved. Stir in 3/4 cup green Curaçao and 3 tablespoons lemon juice. Pour the mixture into a mold rinsed in cold water and chill it until it is set. Dip the mold in warm water, turn it out on a serving dish, and surround with balls of honeydew or Persian melon.

Lime Cream with Strawberries 🐏
CRÈME AU LIMON AVEC DES FRAISES

SOFTEN 1 tablespoon gelatin in 1/4 cup cold water. In a saucepan combine the gelatin, 1/3 cup sugar, and 1/4 cup each of lime juice, white wine, white crème de cacao, and green crème de menthe. Stir over low heat until the sugar and gelatin are dissolved. Set the pan in a bowl of crushed ice and stir the syrup until it is cold and beat it until it is foamy. Fold in 2 egg whites, stiffly beaten, and 1/2 cup heavy cream, whipped. Pour the mixture into a lightly oiled 6-inch mold. Chill the mold for 3 hours, or until the cream is set. Dip the mold in warm water and turn it out on a bed of fresh green leaves. Sprinkle lightly with chopped pistachio nuts. Dip fresh whole strawberries in whipped red currant jelly and arrange them in a wreath around the base of the mold. Chill thoroughly.

✺ Marsala Sponge

IN a saucepan soften 1 tablespoon gelatin in 1/4 cup cold water for 5 minutes and dissolve it in 1 cup boiling water. Add 1/2 cup sugar, 1/3 cup Marsala, and 1 teaspoon lemon juice and stir the syrup until the sugar is dissolved. Set the pan in a bowl of cracked ice to cool the mixture. When the sponge begins to thicken, beat it until it is light and foamy and fold in 3 egg whites, stiffly beaten. Turn the sponge into an oiled mold, chill it for 2 to 3 hours, or until it is set, and serve with whipped cream sweetened to taste.

✺ Melon in Sauterne Jelly

SOFTEN 4 tablespoons gelatin in 2 cups cold water and dissolve it over hot water. Add 4 tablespoons sugar, 2 tablespoons lime juice, and 2 cups sauterne and stir the mixture until it is thoroughly blended. Let the wine gelatin cool until it is thick and syrupy.

Cut thin slices of 1 cantaloupe and 1 honeydew melon into decorative shapes and chill them. Line a chilled mold with a thin layer of the still liquid wine gelatin, rolling it to coat the mold evenly, and chill it until the jelly is set. Arrange some of the melon cutouts in the mold in an attractive pattern, affixing them with a little of the liquid jelly. Cover them with another layer of jelly and chill. Fill the mold in this manner with alternate layers of melon and jelly. Chill the mold until the jelly is set. Unmold the jelly on a chilled serving platter and garnish it with rosettes of whipped cream, piped through a pastry tube.

✺ Mocha Cream Mold   CRÈME AU MOKA

MELT 4 ounces unsweetened chocolate with 1/3 cup sugar and 1/4 cup strong coffee over low heat, stirring to make a smooth mixture. Soften 2 tablespoons gelatin in 1/2 cup strong cold coffee and dissolve it over hot water. Add the gelatin to the chocolate mixture, blending well, and pour it into a large bowl.

In the top of a double boiler scald 1 cup milk, remove it from the heat, and stir in slowly 4 egg yolks beaten with 1/3 cup sugar. Set the pan over hot water and cook the custard, stirring constantly, until it thickens. Blend the custard with the chocolate mixture, and cool it over cracked ice, stirring occasionally. Fold in 2 cups heavy cream, whipped with 1/2 cup sugar and 2 teaspoons vanilla or 1 tablespoon dark rum. Pour the mixture into a chilled oiled mold and chill it for several hours, or until the cream is set. Unmold the cream on a chilled platter and garnish with chocolate curls.

Oranges Mandarin

ORANGES À LA MANDARINE

SOFTEN 1 1/2 tablespoons gelatin in 3 tablespoons cold water and dissolve it over hot water. Combine it in a saucepan with 1/4 cup sugar and 6 tablespoons each of apricot and lime juice and heat the syrup until the sugar is dissolved. Add 1/2 cup each of apricot-flavored brandy and orange-flavored liqueur and 4 tablespoons mandarin liqueur. Strain the mixture through a fine sieve. Slice the tops from 6 navel oranges and carefully scoop out the pulp. With a sharp knife, cut the edges of the oranges in a zigzag pattern. Pour the gelatin mixture into the orange shells and chill them for about 2 hours, or until the jelly is set. Serve chilled, on a bed of lemon leaves. Garnish with preserved mandarin orange sections, or with sections of glacéed oranges or tangerines and candied mint leaves.

Peach Cream Mold

SOFTEN 1 tablespoon gelatin in 1/4 cup cold water and dissolve it over hot water. Mix the gelatin with 1 heaping cup chopped fresh peaches, 1/2 cup confectioners' sugar, and 1 tablespoon dark rum. Combine 1 cup heavy cream, whipped, with 2 egg whites, stiffly beaten, and fold in the fruit. Pour the cream into a chilled oiled mold and chill it for several hours. Unmold the cream on a chilled platter and garnish it with fresh peach slices.

Raspberry Parfait

THAW and heat 1 cup frozen raspberries and put the fruit through a sieve. Soften 2 tablespoons gelatin in 1/3 cup cold water and add it to the raspberry pulp, stirring until the gelatin is dissolved. Add 1 cup Champagne, 3/4 cup sugar, and 1/2 cup *noyau* liqueur. Stir the mixture over cracked ice until it begins to thicken and fold in 2 cups heavy cream, whipped. Fill small parfait or stemmed glasses with the raspberry cream and chill them for several hours. Garnish the parfaits with whipped cream and candied violets.

Strawberry Cream

FORCE 1 1/2 quarts mashed strawberries through a sieve or purée them in a blender, add sugar to taste, and let the purée stand for 3 hours. Soften 2 tablespoons gelatin in 1/2 cup cold water for 5 minutes and dissolve it over hot water. Stir the gelatin into the purée and, when the mixture starts to thicken, fold in 2 cups heavy cream, whipped. Turn the strawberry cream into an oiled mold and chill it for several hours. Unmold the cream on a chilled serving platter and garnish it with whole straw-berries.

Apricot Mousse

SIMMER 1 pound dried apricots in water to cover for 25 minutes. Stir in 1/2 cup sugar or more to taste and cook the fruit for 5 more minutes. Put the apricots through a sieve or purée them in a blender. Stir in 1/4 cup slivered blanched almonds. Whip 3/4 cup heavy cream and sweeten it to taste with sugar and vanilla. Fold the whipped cream into the puréed apricots and pour the mousse into porcelain *petits pots* or other small dessert dishes. Sprinkle the mousse with grated chocolate and chill thoroughly.

Banana Rum Mousse

IN the top of a double boiler scald 1 cup each of milk and light cream. Beat 4 egg yolks with 1/2 cup sugar until they are light and lemon-colored, and carefully stir the mixture into the hot milk and cream. Set the pan over hot water and cook the custard, stirring constantly, until it coats the spoon. Strain the custard through a fine sieve and cool it. Fold in 2 cups each of cream, whipped, and banana purée, made by mashing bananas, and 2 tablespoons heavy dark rum. Freeze the mousse in a mold buried in 2 parts crushed ice to 1 part rock salt for 3 hours, or until it is set.

Blackberry Mousse 🦢

CRUSH 1 quart blackberries with a fork, sprinkle them with 1 cup fine granulated sugar, and let them stand for 1 hour. Force the fruit through a fine sieve to remove the seeds. Stir 1 teaspoon lemon juice into the purée and fold in 1 quart heavy cream, whipped. Turn the mixture into a 1 1/2-quart mold, seal the mold, and freeze the mousse, without stirring, in the home freezer or buried in ice and rock salt. Serve garnished with whole blackberries.

MOUSSE DU CHOCOLAT CARAÏBE Chocolate Mousse with Rum 🦢

IN the top of a double boiler over hot water melt 1/4 pound sweet chocolate. In a saucepan cook 1/2 cup sugar with 1/4 cup water until the mixture is a little syrupy. Pour the syrup slowly into the chocolate, stirring briskly. Add 4 egg yolks, one at a time, beating vigorously after each addition. Remove the pan from the heat and add 2 tablespoons rum. Carefully fold in 4 egg whites, stiffly beaten. Heap the mousse into a large bowl or into individual dessert dishes and chill overnight.

Sour Cream Chocolate Mousse 🦢

MIX thoroughly 2 cups sour cream, 1/2 cup each of sugar and coarsely crumbled macaroons, 6 tablespoons melted sweet chocolate, 1 tablespoon brandy, and 1 teaspoon vanilla. Turn the mousse into a refrigerator tray and freeze it for 3 hours, or until it is solid. Pile the mousse in sherbet glasses and garnish each serving with shaved sweet chocolate.

MOUSSE DE FROMAGE À LA CRÈME Cream Cheese Mold 🦢

SOFTEN 1 1/2 tablespoons gelatin in 6 tablespoons cold water and dissolve it in 1 1/2 cups hot milk. Slowly mix in 9 ounces soft cream cheese, well mashed, and

1/2 teaspoon salt. Cool the mixture and fold in 1 1/2 cups heavy cream, whipped. Pour the cream into a 1 1/2-quart mold or a large ring mold dipped in cold water. Chill well. Unmold the cream on a chilled platter and surround it with preserved figs.

℘ Hazelnut Praline Mousse   MOUSSE AU PRALIN DE NOISETTES

SOFTEN 2 tablespoons gelatin in the juice of 2 oranges for 5 minutes and dissolve it over hot water. In the top of a double boiler, over hot water, beat together 5 egg yolks with 5 tablespoons sugar until the mixture is very thick and pale in color. Stir in the dissolved gelatin. Fold in 1/2 cup each of hazelnut praline powder and heavy cream, whipped, and 2 tablespoons bourbon. Pour the mousse into a crystal dish and chill it until it is set. To serve, sprinkle the top with hazelnut praline powder and swirls of whipped cream.

Hazelnut Praline Powder

IN a heavy saucepan combine 3/4 cup sugar, 1/4 cup water, and 1/4 teaspoon cream of tartar and bring the mixture to a boil. Add 1/2 cup hazelnuts and cook the syrup without stirring until it turns a rich amber. Pour the syrup into a lightly buttered shallow pan to cool and set. Pulverize the praline in a mortar, put it through the medium blade of a food chopper, and press it through a sieve. Put any praline that remains in the sieve through the chopper and sieve again. When all the praline is reduced to a fine powder, put it into a jar with a tight-fitting cover and store in a cool dry place.

℘ Macaroon Mousse

LINE a pudding mold with 18 macaroons and pour 1/2 cup dark rum over them. In the top of a double boiler beat 5 egg yolks with 1 cup sugar until they are light and add 3 cups milk and 1/8 teaspoon salt. Set the pan over hot water and cook the custard, stirring constantly, until it is thick and creamy. Soften 2 tablespoons gelatin in 1/4 cup water and dissolve it in the hot custard. Fold in 5 egg whites, stiffly beaten, and add 1 teaspoon vanilla. Pour the custard over the macaroons in the mold and chill the mousse for 3 hours, or until it is firm. Unmold the mousse on a platter and serve it with rum-flavored whipped cream.

Mango Mousse 🥄

PEEL and mash enough mangoes to make 1 cup. Stir in 1 cup apple juice and sugar to taste. Freeze the mixture for 30 minutes. Beat it well and fold in 2 cups heavy cream, whipped, and a dash of nutmeg. Pour the mousse into porcelain *petits pots* and chill for several hours.

Pineapple Framboise Mousse 🥄

PUT enough ripe pineapple, peeled and cored, through the finest blade of a food chopper to make 1 cup pulp and juice. Combine the pineapple with 1 cup sugar, 3/4 cup water, and 1/4 teaspoon salt and simmer the mixture for 10 minutes.

Soak 1 teaspoon gelatin in 2 tablespoons cold water, dissolve it in the hot pineapple mixture, and chill the mousse thoroughly. Add 1/4 cup framboise and fold in 1 cup heavy cream, whipped. Freeze the mousse, without stirring, in a mold or in refrigerator trays for 4 hours.

Raspberry and Peach Mousse 🥄

MASH lightly 3/4 cup raspberries and enough diced peaches to make 1/2 cup. Add 3/4 cup sugar to the fruit and fold in 1 1/2 cups heavy cream, whipped. Turn the mixture into a refrigerator tray and freeze it for 3 to 4 hours, or until it is solid.

Strawberry Pernod Mousse 🥄

BEAT 4 egg yolks with 4 tablespoons sugar until the mixture is light and lemon-colored. Soften 1 tablespoon gelatin in 1/4 cup milk and dissolve it over hot water. Heat 1 1/4 cups milk, stir in the gelatin, and pour the mixture slowly over the egg yolks. Cook the custard over low heat, stirring constantly, until it starts to thicken. Remove the pan from the heat, put it in a bowl of cracked ice, and stir the custard until it is smooth and thick. Beat 4 egg whites until they are stiff, and whip 1 cup heavy cream. Fold the egg whites and 3 tablespoons of the whipped cream into the custard and reserve the remaining whipped cream for garnishing. Flavor the mousse with Pernod to taste, add 1 cup crushed strawberries, and pour the mousse into an oiled mold. Chill the mousse until it is firm, unmold it on a chilled platter, and decorate with the reserved whipped cream and whole strawberries.

﮼ Lemon Mousse

SOFTEN 1 tablespoon gelatin in 2 tablespoons water, add 6 tablespoons lemon juice, and stir the mixture over hot water until the gelatin dissolves. Beat 3 egg yolks until they are very light and add 1/3 cup sugar and the gelatin mixture. Beat 3 egg whites until they are stiff, gradually adding 1/3 cup sugar and grated rind of 1 1/2 lemons. Fold the meringue into the yolk mixture. Turn the mousse into a glass bowl and chill it until it is firm. Serve with raspberry and currant jelly sauce.

Raspberry and Currant Jelly Sauce

BRING to a boil 1/2 cup each of strained raspberry juice and currant jelly, and add 1 teaspoon cornstarch mixed to a paste with 2 teaspoons cold raspberry juice. Cook the sauce until it is clear and slightly thickened, and cool and chill it.

﮼ Italian Lemon Mousse

BEAT 4 egg yolks until they are thick and pale in color. Beat in 1/2 cup sugar, 3 tablespoons lemon juice, and 2 teaspoons grated lemon rind. Cook the mixture in the top of a double boiler over hot water, stirring constantly, until it is thick. Cool the mixture and fold in 4 egg whites, stiffly beaten, and 1 cup heavy cream, whipped. Pour the mixture into individual glass dishes and chill thoroughly.

﮼ Frozen Lemon Cream

STIR 1 cup milk, 1 cup heavy cream, and 1 cup sugar until the sugar is thoroughly dissolved. Pour the mixture into a refrigerator tray and freeze it until it is mushy. Add the grated rind and juice of 2 lemons, beat the mixture well with a rotary beater, and freeze it again for 2 hours. Beat the cream again thoroughly, return it to the freezer, and freeze it until it is solid.

Frozen Lemon Cream

Slice off the tops of 6 large perfect lemons and, with a grapefruit knife and spoon, remove all the pulp. Cut a thin slice from the bottom of each lemon shell so that it will stand upright. Fill the shells with the frozen lemon cream, piling it high. Serve on individual plates, garnished with a lemon leaf.

Ice Cream or Sherbet, Crank Freezer Method

CHILL the ice-cream mixture and fill the freezer can less than three fourths full. Pack the can in the freezer bucket with a mixture of 3 or 4 parts ice to 1 part rock salt. Churn until the paddles stop. Remove the paddles and pack the cream down in the can. Close the can, seal it, and wrap the bucket with blankets or layers of newspaper. Most ice creams and ices profit from a spell of mellowing, so allow 2 or 3 hours before serving.

Ice Cream or Sherbet, Refrigerator Tray Method

POUR the ice cream in refrigerator trays and freeze it in the freezing compartment of the refrigerator as quickly as possible for 1 hour, or until it is mushy but not solid. Turn the cream into a chilled bowl and quickly beat it with a rotary beater until it is smooth. Return the cream to the freezing compartment and, when it is almost solid, beat it until it is smooth. Return the tray to the freezer, cover it with aluminum foil or wax paper to prevent crystals from forming on the cream, and freeze the cream or ice until it is solid.

Lemon Ice

COMBINE 4 cups water and 2 cups sugar and boil the syrup for 5 minutes. Cool the syrup, add 1 cup lemon juice and 1 tablespoon grated lemon rind, and freeze the mixture in a crank freezer or in a refrigerator tray. Serve in chilled sherbet coupes.

Melon Sherbet

REMOVE the seeds from a large casaba melon or cantaloupe and scoop out enough pulp to make 2 cups. Cook the melon with 1 cup sugar and the grated rind of 1/2 lemon for 5 minutes. Add the juice of 3 lemons and 1/2 cup kirsch and cool the mixture. Strain the melon through a fine sieve into a refrigerator tray and freeze it. Stir the sherbet before serving and spoon it into chilled coupes.

Coffee Ice 🐾

IN a pitcher combine 3/4 cup finely ground coffee and 6 tablespoons sugar, and add 1 quart boiling water. Set the pitcher in a saucepan of hot water over low heat and let the coffee infuse for 30 minutes. Cool the infusion and strain it through a double layer of cheesecloth. Freeze the mixture in a refrigerator tray, without stirring, for 3 hours, or until it forms a granular mass. Serve the ice in sherbet glasses accompanied by a pitcher of heavy cream.

Black Currant Ice 🐾

COMBINE 2 cups water with 1 cup sugar and boil the syrup for 5 minutes. Add 2 cups black currants and 1 cup young black currant leaves and cook the syrup for a minute or two. Remove it from the heat and let it stand, covered, for 2 hours. Strain the syrup and stir in the juice of 6 lemons. Freeze the mixture in a crank freezer or in a refrigerator tray.

Red Currant Sherbet 🐾

COMBINE 2 cups ripe red currants and 1/2 cup water. Crush the fruit, bring it to a boil, and simmer it, covered, for 8 to 10 minutes. Strain the juice through a jelly bag. Cook 2 cups sugar in 1 1/2 cups water for 5 minutes. Add 1 3/4 cups of the currant juice. Soften 2 tablespoons gelatin in the remaining juice, dissolve it over hot water, and add it to the currant syrup mixture. Cool the mixture and freeze it in a refrigerator tray.

GLACE À L'ANANAS ## Pineapple Sherbet 🐾

COMBINE in a saucepan 1 cup each of grated fresh pineapple, pineapple juice, water, and sugar, and the grated rind of 1 lemon. Bring the mixture to a boil, cook it for

Plum Milk Sherbet

5 minutes, and strain it. Add the juice of 1 lemon. Freeze the mixture in a crank freezer or in a refrigerator tray. Just before serving, soften the sherbet slightly, beat it well, and fold in 1 cup heavy cream, whipped, and 3 tablespoons kirsch.

Plum Milk Sherbet

BEAT 2 egg whites until they are stiff and beat in gradually 1/4 cup sugar, 2 cups milk, 1 cup corn syrup, and 2/3 cup lemon juice. Beat in 2 cups puréed cooked plums. Freeze the mixture in a crank freezer. Or freeze all but the fruit in a refrigerator tray. When the sherbet reaches the mushy stage beat it until it is smooth and beat in the plums. Return it to the refrigerator and, when it is almost solid, beat it again until it is smooth. Cover the tray and freeze the sherbet for several hours, or until it is firm.

GLACE À LA FRAMBOISE   ## Raspberry Ice

BRING to a boil 1 cup sugar and 2 cups water and cook the syrup for 5 minutes. Cool it and add 2 cups raspberry purée, the juice of 1/2 lemon, and 1 to 2 tablespoons raspberry liqueur. Freeze the mixture in a crank freezer or refrigerator tray.

Rhubarb Sherbet

COOK 4 cups rhubarb, diced, in 1/2 cup water for 5 minutes, or until it is tender. Add 1 cup sugar, 1/2 cup each of light corn syrup and orange juice, 2 tablespoons lemon juice, and 1 teaspoon grated lemon rind, and bring the mixture to a boil. Cool the rhubarb, pour it into a refrigerator tray, and freeze it for about 1 hour, or until the mixture is mushy. Turn the sherbet into a chilled bowl, whip it, and fold in 2 egg whites, stiffly beaten with 2 teaspoons sugar and 1/4 teaspoon salt. Return the sherbet to the freezing tray and freeze it until it is solid, stirring occasionally.

Strawberry Ice

PUT 1 quart fresh strawberries through a sieve or purée them in a blender, and add to the purée the juice of 1/2 lemon and 1/2 orange. Boil 1 cup sugar and 1/2 cup water for 5 minutes. Cool the syrup and add it to the strawberry purée. Freeze the mixture in a crank freezer or in a refrigerator tray.

ᔯ Vanilla Ice Cream

ADD 1 1/2 cups sugar to 8 cups scalded heavy cream and stir the mixture until the sugar is dissolved. Stir in 1 tablespoon vanilla. Cool and chill the mixture and freeze it in a crank freezer.

ᔯ Chocolate Ice Cream

BEAT 4 egg yolks slightly, combine them with 2/3 cup sugar and a pinch of salt, and beat the mixture until it is thoroughly blended. Scald 2 cups light cream and blend in 2 ounces unsweetened chocolate, melted, and 2 tablespoons cocoa. Pour the cream over the eggs, continuing to stir briskly. Strain the mixture into the top of a double boiler and cook the custard over hot water, stirring constantly, until it coats the spoon. Strain the custard through a double thickness of cheesecloth and chill it. Mix 1 cup heavy cream with 1 teaspoon vanilla, stir it into the chilled custard, and freeze the ice cream in a crank freezer or in a refrigerator tray.

ᔯ Banana Ice Cream

STIR 1 cup sugar and 1/8 teaspoon salt into 1 cup warm light cream until the sugar is dissolved. Chill the mixture, stir in 3 cups light cream and 1 1/2 teaspoons vanilla, and turn it into a refrigerator tray. Freeze the ice cream until it reaches the mushy stage. Mash enough bananas to make 1 cup purée and beat it into the ice cream with 1/2 cup lemon juice. Return the ice cream to the refrigerator tray and beat it at half-hour intervals until the mixture is frozen solid.

ᔯ Peach Ice Cream

ADD 1 1/2 cups sugar to 8 cups scalded heavy cream and stir the mixture until the sugar is dissolved. Stir in 3 cups crushed fresh peaches and the strained juice of 2 lemons. Cool and chill the mixture and freeze it in a crank freezer.

Pineapple Ice Cream 🐾

COMBINE thoroughly 4 cups light cream, 2 cups fresh pineapple, crushed and sweetened to taste, 1 cup each of sugar and milk, and a pinch of salt. Chill the mixture. Freeze it in a crank freezer packed with 6 parts crushed ice to 1 part rock salt.

Pistachio Ice Cream 🐾

COMBINE in a saucepan 1/2 cup sugar, 1/4 cup water, 1/4 teaspoon cream of tartar, and a pinch of salt. Bring the syrup to a boil and cook it until it spins a light thread, or a candy thermometer registers 230° F. Beat 4 egg yolks until they are thick and lemon-colored and pour the syrup over the eggs in a thin steady stream, beating constantly until the mixture thickens. Add 1 cup ground pistachio nuts, 1 teaspoon almond extract, and a few drops of green food coloring. Stir in 3 1/2 cups heavy cream. Freeze the custard in a crank freezer or in a refrigerator tray.

Raspberry Ice Cream 🐾

MASH 1 quart raspberries, add 1 cup sugar, let the fruit mellow for several hours, and force it through a sieve. Bring to a boil 1 quart light cream and 1 cup sugar and cool the cream mixture. Beat 6 egg yolks until they are light and lemon-colored, stir them into the cream, and cool the mixture to room temperature. Add the raspberry purée to the cream with the juice of 1 lemon. Freeze the ice cream in a crank freezer or in a refrigerator tray.

Bombe Don Juan 🐾

LINE a *bombe* mold rinsed in cold water with a 1-inch layer of peach ice cream, adjust the lid, and store it in the freezer. Prepare a *pâte-à-bombe*: Boil together 1/2 cup each of water and sugar until a candy thermometer registers 217° F. Cool the syrup. Beat 4 egg yolks in the top of a double boiler until they are light. Set the pan over simmering water and add the sugar syrup in a thin stream, beating constantly. Cook the *pâte-à-bombe*, stirring slowly, for about 12 minutes, or until it is thick and has doubled in volume. Set the pan in a large pan of ice and beat the *pâte-à-bombe* until it is cold. It will be smooth, pale, and thick. Fold in 1 1/2 cups heavy cream, whipped, 1/2 cup praline powder, and 2 tablespoons kirsch. Pour this mixture into the hollow center of the *bombe* mold, cover the cream with wax paper or plastic wrap, and adjust the lid. Freeze the *bombe* for 6 hours in a mixture of 3 parts chopped ice to 1 part rock salt. Unmold the *bombe* and circle the base with candied cherries.

Bombe Saigon

LINE a chilled *bombe* mold with a 3/4-inch layer of chocolate ice cream. Add lemon ice by spoonfuls until the mold is filled to the top. Cover the mold with buttered wax paper and adjust the lid. A thin coat of butter will seal the seam and make the mold waterproof. Put the mold into the home freezer or pack it in a mixture of 3 or 4 parts ice to 1 part rock salt, allowing several hours for the *bombe* to freeze before serving. To unmold the *bombe*, dip the mold quickly in hot water, dry it, and invert it quickly on a chilled platter.

Skewered Caramel Apples

SKEWER large apples and roast them over hot coals until the skins can easily be removed. Peel the apples and roll them in brown sugar, coating them thoroughly. Return the sugared apples to the fire and continue to cook them, turning them slowly, until the sugar melts and browns lightly.

Skewered Peaches

DIP peeled halves of firm peaches in melted butter and roll them in a mixture of 1 cup brown sugar and 1 teaspoon finely chopped ginger. Thread the fruit on skewers and broil them under moderate heat, turning once, for 8 to 10 minutes.

Skewered Mixed Fruit

CUT into manageable chunks or sections peeled peaches, oranges, pineapple, grapefruit, apples, nectarines, or any combination of firm fresh fruits. Soak the fruit in a mixture of 2 parts kirsch to 1 part honey for 2 hours. Thread the fruit on skewers and broil them over hot coals, turning once, for 8 to 10 minutes. Sprinkle the fruits lightly with lemon juice.

Glacé Syrup

IN a heavy-bottomed 2-quart saucepan combine 2 cups sugar with 2/3 cup water., Cook the syrup slowly, stirring constantly with a wooden spoon, until the sugar is dissolved. Increase the heat and, when the syrup comes to a boil, add 1/4 teaspoon cream of tartar. Put in a candy thermometer. Boil the syrup, without stirring, until the thermometer registers 300° F. (During the cooking, remove any crystals that form on the sides of the pan with a fork or brush wrapped in muslin and moistened in hot water. Use an upward motion, to prevent the crystals from falling in the syrup.) Remove the pan from the heat and set it over boiling water to prevent the glaze from hardening.

While dipping nuts or fruits into the glaze, disturb the syrup no more than necessary or it may crystallize. Neither glacéed nuts nor glacéed fruits keep for a long time, and neither should be made in humid or rainy weather.

Glacéed Nuts

WALNUT or pecan halves, almonds, Brazil nuts, or preserved chestnuts drained of their syrup, may be coated with clear or tinted glacé syrup. Chill and dry the nuts thoroughly before dipping. Drop the nuts, a few at a time, into the hot glacé syrup. Remove them, one by one, with a fork, draining the excess syrup against the side of the pan, and put the nuts on an oiled platter to dry, spacing them so they do not touch one another.

Glacé Syrup for Fruit

MAKE glacé syrup, omitting the cream of tartar and blending 2 tablespoons corn syrup with the sugar and water before cooking.

⟡ Glacéed Grapes

WASH, dry, and chill Malaga or black grapes. Cut the grapes from the bunch, leaving about 1/2 inch of stem on each. Following the procedure for glacéed nuts, dip each grape by its stem into hot glacé syrup for fruit.

⟡ Stuffed Glacéed Prunes

STONE large, plump, and tender dried prunes, fill each with a piece of candied ginger, and chill them. Following the procedure for glacéed nuts, dip the prunes into hot glacé syrup for fruit. Sprinkle immediately with chopped pistachio nuts.

⟡ Glacéed Strawberries

BRUSH firm strawberries carefully with a soft brush and chill the fruit well. Following the procedure for glacéed nuts, dip each strawberry, up to the green hull only, into hot glacé syrup for fruit.

⟡ Glacéed Tangerines

PEEL 4 tangerines, separate them into sections without breaking the membranes, and remove the pith. Let the sections remain exposed to air in a cool place for 2 or 3 hours to dry. Following the procedure for glacéed nuts, dip the fruit into hot glacé syrup for fruit. Remove the fruit from the syrup without piercing the skin, let it dry, and arrange it on a plate. Glaze 1 or 2 peeled whole tangerines and use them to garnish the plate. A leaf of candied mint may be placed on the whole tangerines.

⟡ Chestnuts for Desserts

COOK 1 pound peeled shelled chestnuts in hot milk flavored with a piece of vanilla bean for 20 minutes, or until they are tender but not mushy.

If the nuts are to be used for chestnut purée, cook them for 10 minutes longer. Force them through a ricer or purée them in a blender. Moisten the purée with a few tablespoons of the milk in which the chestnuts were cooked.

Sweetened Chestnut Purée 🦢

FOLLOWING the recipe for chestnuts for desserts, cook and purée 1 pound chestnuts. Combine in a heavy saucepan 2/3 cup sugar, 1/4 cup water, and a 1-inch piece of vanilla bean. Cook the syrup until it forms a soft ball when a little is dropped into cold water, or until a candy thermometer registers 234° F. Discard the vanilla bean and blend the syrup with the chestnut purée, working the mixture vigorously until it forms a thick paste. Let it cool to lukewarm and stir in 1 tablespoon soft butter.

Sugared Brazil Nuts 🦢

COMBINE 1/2 cup sugar, 2 teaspoons cinnamon, and 1 teaspoon cloves. Stir 2 cups Brazil nuts in the unbeaten whites of 2 eggs and coat the nuts evenly. Roll the nuts in the sugar mixture and roast them in a moderate oven (350° F.) for 15 minutes.

Candied Mint Leaves 🦢

WASH and dry large perfect mint leaves and carefully brush each leaf with egg white, using a small camel's-hair brush. Dredge the leaves with fine granulated sugar and let them dry on wax paper in a cool place. Serve the leaves as a confection or use them as a garnish for ices, puddings, or cakes.

Chocolate Sauce 🦢

IN the top of a double boiler over hot water melt 4 ounces unsweetened chocolate with 1 tablespoon butter. Combine 1 cup each of sugar and light cream and add them to the melted chocolate. Put the saucepan over direct heat and cook the sauce, stirring, until it reaches the boiling point. Reduce the heat to very low and continue to cook the sauce until it thickens slightly. Stir in 1 teaspoon vanilla.

Thin Chocolate Sauce 🦢

IN the top of a double boiler combine 1 pound sweet chocolate, grated, and 1 cup each of water and coffee. Put the pan over hot water and cook the sauce, stirring constantly, until it is smooth. Put the sauce through a fine sieve and flavor it to taste with brandy or orange-flavored liqueur.

❧ Chocolate Whipped Cream Sauce

COMBINE 2 cups water with 1 pound grated sweet cooking chocolate. Bring the mixture to a boil and cook the sauce, stirring, until it is smooth. Rub the sauce through a fine sieve. Cool the sauce and fold in 3/4 cup heavy cream, whipped.

❧ Clear Lemon Sauce

IN a saucepan mix 1/2 cup sugar with 1 tablespoon cornstarch. Stir in 1 cup water and cook the sauce over low heat, stirring, for about 5 minutes, until it is thick and clear. Stir in 3 tablespoons each of butter and lemon juice, 1 tablespoon grated lemon rind, and 1/8 teaspoon salt.

❧ Pecan Sauce

IN a saucepan heat slowly 2 cups brown sugar, 2 tablespoons water, and a pinch of salt, stirring constantly with a wooden spoon until the sugar is melted. Add 1/2 cup each of heavy cream and chopped pecans and stir the sauce until it is smooth.

❧ Raspberry Sauce

DEFROST 1 box frozen raspberries and rub the fruit through a fine sieve or purée it in a blender. Stir in 1 teaspoon arrowroot mixed to a paste with 2 tablespoons cold water and cook the purée over low heat until it thickens slightly. Add the juice of 1/2 lemon or 2 tablespoons kirsch and serve the sauce hot.

❧ Raspberry Whipped Cream Sauce

COMBINE 1 pint raspberries, 1/4 cup sugar, and 3 tablespoons water in a saucepan. Cook the berries over very low heat, crushing them with a wooden spoon, until the

Cold Chestnut Soufflé with Chocolate Whipped Cream Sauce

mixture comes to a boil. Skim the surface. Rub the fruit through a fine sieve or purée it in a blender and strain out the seeds. Add the juice of 1/2 lemon and return the purée to the heat. Bring it to a boil and add 1 teaspoon cornstarch or arrowroot mixed with 2 tablespoons cold fruit juice. Cook the sauce until it is clear and thickened. Cool and chill it. Fold in 1/2 cup cream, stiffly whipped, just before serving.

ꙮ Vanilla Ice Cream Sauce

BEAT 2 cups soft vanilla ice cream until it is smooth. Fold in 1 cup heavy cream, whipped, and stir in 2 tablespoons rum.

ꙮ Red-Wine Sauce

IN a small saucepan combine 1 1/2 cups red wine, 1/2 cup brandy, and 3 tablespoons lemon juice. Stir in 1 teaspoon potato starch, mixed to a paste with 2 teaspoons water, and a pinch each of cinnamon and cloves. Bring the sauce to a boil and remove the pan from the heat. Add sugar to taste and serve the sauce hot.

ꙮ White-Wine Sauce

IN the top of a double boiler combine 1/4 cup sugar, 2 teaspoons cornstarch, and a dash of salt. Stir in 3/4 cup white wine and add 1/2 unpeeled lemon, sliced, and a 1-inch cinnamon stick. Put the pan over hot water, cook the sauce, stirring constantly, for 5 minutes, and drain it. Beat 2 egg yolks lightly with 1/4 cup water and gradually stir in the sauce. Return the mixture to a double boiler and cook it, stirring constantly, over hot water until it thickens and coats the spoon.

ꙮ Blueberry Syrup

CRUSH 6 quarts ripe blueberries, washed and stemmed, and put them in a kettle with 2 1/2 quarts water. Bring the liquid to a boil and boil the berries rapidly for 10 minutes. Lower the heat and simmer them for 5 minutes. Strain the juice through a jelly bag and measure it. To each 6 cups juice add 5 cups sugar. If there is less juice, reduce the amount of sugar proportionately. Boil the juice and sugar rapidly for 10 to 15 minutes, or until the syrup begins to thicken slightly. Do not overcook the syrup or it will begin to jell. Pour the syrup immediately into hot sterilized bottles, cork them, and seal with paraffin.

Blackberries may be substituted for blueberries.

Mock Devonshire Cream

BEAT 8 ounces soft cream cheese with 1/2 cup thick sour cream until the mixture is smooth and light, adding a little more cream if necessary. Serve with fresh strawberries, peaches, or any desired fruit.

Hard Sauce

CREAM 1/2 cup soft butter, gradually add 1 cup granulated sugar or brown sugar, and beat the mixture until it is light and fluffy. Flavor the sauce with rum, Sherry, or brandy to taste. If a fluffier sauce is desired, add 1 egg white, stiffly beaten. Serve with hot puddings and other hot desserts.

Brandy Hard Sauce

CREAM 1/2 cup sweet butter and gradually beat in 1 1/4 cups sifted confectioners' or brown sugar and 2 tablespoons or more brandy. Beat the sauce until it is very light and fluffy. Pack it in small decorative molds and put them in a cool place. Unmold the sauce on a small silver plate and dust it lightly with cinnamon.

Chocolate Cheesecake

Cakes and Pastry

Chocolate Cheesecake

WITH a rolling pin crush enough chocolate cookies to make 2 cups crumbs. Mix in 1/2 teaspoon cinnamon and blend in 1/2 cup melted butter. Press the crumbs firmly against the bottom and sides of a well-buttered 9-inch springform pan and chill the shell.

Beat 3/4 cup sugar with 3 eggs until the mixture is light and add gradually 1 1/2 pounds soft cream cheese. Stir in 8 ounces semisweet chocolate, melted, 2 tablespoons cocoa, and 1 teaspoon vanilla, and beat in thoroughly 3 cups sour cream. Fold in 1/4 cup melted butter and pour the batter into the chilled shell. Bake the cake in a moderate oven (350° F.) for 45 minutes. It will seem quite liquid when it is removed from the oven. Chill the cheesecake, remove the outer edge of the springform pan, and decorate the top rim with whipped cream and candied violets.

꒰ Cognac Cheesecake

WITH a rolling pin, crush enough zwieback to make 1 cup fine crumbs. Mix in 2 tablespoons each of melted butter and sugar and 1/2 teaspoon mixed cinnamon and nutmeg. Press the crumbs lightly against the bottom and sides of a well-buttered 8-inch pie plate and chill the shell.

Add gradually 1 1/4 cups heavy cream to 6 ounces soft cream cheese and beat the mixture thoroughly. Beat 3 eggs with 3/4 cup sugar until they are light, add 4 tablespoons Cognac, 1/2 teaspoon grated orange rind, and 1/4 teaspoon salt, and beat the mixture until it is smooth. Combine the egg and cheese mixtures and beat the filling until it is very smooth. Pour the filling into the prepared shell and bake the cheesecake in a slow oven (275° F.) for about 35 minutes, or until it is set. Turn off the heat, open the oven door, and let the cheesecake cool in the oven.

꒰ Honey Cheesecake

IN a large mixing bowl beat well, preferably with a mixer, 2 pounds cottage cheese, 1 cup sugar, and 1 pound honey. Beat in 8 eggs, well beaten. Butter a rectangular baking pan, line it with sweet tart pastry, and turn the filling into the shell. Bake the cake in a moderate oven (350° F.) for 30 to 35 minutes, or until the top is golden brown. Sprinkle the cake with 2 tablespoons cinnamon, cut it into diamond shapes, and serve it cool.

꒰ Country Cheesecake

COMBINE 1 1/2 cups zwieback crumbs with 1/2 cup melted butter, 6 tablespoons each of sugar and finely ground unblanched almonds, and 2 tablespoons heavy cream. Press the crumbs thickly against the bottom and sides of a well-buttered 9-inch springform pan. Bake the shell in a moderately hot oven (375° F.) for 15 minutes, let it cool, and chill it.

Beat together 12 ounces soft cream cheese, 2 eggs, well beaten, 1/2 cup sugar, 1 teaspoon lemon juice, and 1/2 teaspoon salt. Pour the filling into the prepared shell and bake the cake in a moderately hot oven (375° F.) for about 20 minutes, or until it is just set. Turn off the heat, open the oven door, and let the cheesecake cool in the oven. Dust the surface lightly with cinnamon.

Combine 1 1/2 cups sour cream, 2 tablespoons sugar, 1/2 teaspoon vanilla, and a dash of salt, pour the mixture over the cheesecake, and bake the cheesecake in a very hot oven (425° F.) for 5 minutes. Again, let the cheesecake cool in the oven and chill it. It is better to make this cheesecake a day before serving it.

Graham-Cracker Cheesecake 🦃

LINE a well-buttered 9-inch springform pan with graham-cracker piecrust and chill the shell.

Beat 3/4 cup sugar into 3 well-beaten eggs and add gradually 1 1/2 pounds cream cheese. Add 1 teaspoon vanilla, 1/2 teaspoon lemon juice, and the grated rind of 1 lemon, and beat in 3 cups sour cream. Blend the mixture well and fold in 1/4 cup melted butter. Pour the batter into the prepared shell and bake the cheesecake in a moderate oven (350° F.) for 45 minutes. Turn off the heat, open the oven door, and let the cheesecake cool in the oven. Chill the cheesecake thoroughly.

Mexican Cheesecake 🦃

BEAT 1 pound soft cream cheese until it is light and smooth. Beat 4 egg yolks with 1/2 cup sugar until they are light and stir in 2 tablespoons rum or tequila. Add the egg mixture gradually to the cream cheese, stirring until it is thick. Fill a buttered shallow glass dish with the mixture and cover the top with thin vanilla wafers. Chill the cheesecake for at least 4 hours before serving.

Palermo Cheesecake 🦃

COMBINE 1 1/2 pounds *ricotta* cheese, 1/3 cup each of sugar and milk, and 2 tablespoons rose water. Force the mixture through a sieve and beat it well. Stir in 1/2 cup each of diced candied fruit and chopped toasted almonds and 1/2 ounce unsweetened chocolate, chopped. Cover the mixture and chill it thoroughly.

Split a spongecake, 10 to 12 inches in diameter, into 3 layers and spread the filling between the layers. Pour 1/4 cup rum over the cake and chill it.

Beat 1 egg white until it is light and frothy and gradually beat in 2 cups sifted confectioners' sugar, 1 tablespoon lemon juice, 1 teaspoon almond extract, and 3 drops red food coloring. If the icing is too thick, thin it with a little warm water. Frost the cheesecake with the icing just before serving.

ᘓ Ricotta Pie

CREAM 1 pound *ricotta* cheese and add 1/4 cup sugar, 1 tablespoon each of grated orange rind and finely chopped citron, 1/2 teaspoon vanilla, and 3 egg whites, stiffly beaten. Pour the filling into a shallow rectangular pan lined with flaky pastry. Cover the pie with a latticework crust made from the pastry trimmings and bake it in a moderate oven (350° F.) for 35 to 45 minutes, or until the crust is golden brown.

ᘓ Rum Cheese Pie

WITH a rolling pin, crush enough zwieback to make 1 1/2 cups fine crumbs. Mix in 1/4 cup each of melted butter and sugar and 1/4 teaspoon cinnamon. Press the crumbs firmly against the bottom and sides of a well-buttered 9-inch glass pie plate, and chill the shell.

Blend 6 ounces cream cheese with 1 1/4 cups heavy cream until the mixture is completely smooth. In another bowl beat 3 eggs with 3/4 cup sugar until they are light and fluffy and add 1/4 teaspoon salt, 4 tablespoons rum, and 1/2 teaspoon grated lemon rind. Beat the mixture until it is thick and creamy. Combine the egg and cream-cheese mixtures and beat the filling with a rotary beater until it is absolutely smooth. Pour the filling into the crumbs crust. Bake the pie in a moderate oven (350° F.) for about 45 minutes, or until the filling is set. Chill the pie thoroughly.

ᘓ Lemon Pudding Cake

CREAM 1 1/2 tablespoons butter with 3/4 cup sugar until the mixture is light and fluffy and beat in 2 teaspoons grated lemon zest. Add 3 egg yolks and beat well. Stir in 3 tablespoons flour alternately with 1/4 cup lemon juice and 1 cup milk. Fold in 3 egg whites, stiffly beaten with a pinch of salt. Turn the batter into a buttered casserole, set the casserole in a pan of hot water, and bake the cake in a moderate oven (350° F.) for about 1 hour, until the cake tests done on top. The bottom of the casserole will contain a thick, lemony sauce.

New England Poundcake ✍

CREAM 1 pound butter, add gradually 2 cups sugar, and beat the mixture until it is light and fluffy. Add 9 large egg yolks, one at a time, beating well after each addition. Stir in 1 tablespoon vanilla and 2 teaspoons orange extract. Add gradually 4 cups sifted flour, beating only enough to blend the batter. Gently fold in 9 egg whites, stiffly beaten. Pour the batter into 2 loaf pans lined with buttered wax paper. Bake the cakes in a moderately slow oven (325° F.) for about 1 1/2 hours, or until they test done.

Maple Syrup Cake ✍

CREAM 1/2 cup butter with 1 cup sugar until the mixture is light and fluffy and stir in 4 egg yolks, lightly beaten. Sift 1 1/2 cups cake flour with 2 teaspoons baking powder and add it to the egg mixture alternately with 1/2 cup milk, stirring after each addition until the batter is smooth. Stir in 1 teaspoon vanilla and fold in 1 egg white, stiffly beaten. Line the bottoms of 2 buttered 8-inch layer-cake pans with wax paper and butter the paper. Turn the batter into the pans and bake the layers in a moderate oven (350° F.) for about 25 minutes, or until they test done. Turn them out on wire racks to cool. Fill and frost the cake with maple syrup icing. Using a pastry bag fitted with a fluted tube, decorate the top of the cake with more maple syrup icing and sprinkle it with finely chopped walnuts.

Pecan Cake ✍

CREAM together 1/2 cup butter and 1 cup sugar and beat in 2 egg yolks. Add 1/2 cup milk alternately with 2 cups sifted flour sifted with 2 teaspoons baking powder. Add 1 teaspoon vanilla extract and 1/2 cup chopped pecans and fold in 2 egg whites, well beaten. Pour the batter into a buttered loaf pan and bake the cake in a moderate oven (350° F.) for 1 hour, or until it tests done.

GREEK NUT CAKE

Karidopita ✍

IN a mixing bowl combine 1 1/2 cups each of finely grated walnuts and almonds, 8 zwieback, rolled into fine crumbs, and the grated rind of 1 orange. Beat 6 egg yolks with 3/4 cup sugar and 1/2 teaspoon vanilla until they are thick and light, and fold in 6 egg whites, stiffly beaten. Fold the egg mixture into the nut and crumb mixture. Pour the batter into a buttered baking pan, 9 by 13 inches, and bake the cake in a moderate oven (350° F.) for 45 minutes. Remove the cake from the oven and pour over it spiced rum syrup. Cool the cake in the pan and cut it into diamond shapes. Makes about 24 slices.

Spiced Rum Syrup

BRING to a boil 2 1/4 cups water, 1 cup sugar, a 1-inch cinnamon stick, and 1 slice of lemon. Simmer the syrup until the sugar is dissolved and add 1/4 cup light rum.

Seed Cake

CREAM 2 cups butter and gradually beat in 1 2/3 cups sugar. Work in 2 tablespoons caraway seeds, 1 teaspoon freshly grated nutmeg, and a pinch of ground mace. Beat in 6 egg yolks, well beaten, and gradually fold in 2 cups sifted flour. Fold in 6 egg whites, stiffly beaten. If the batter seems very heavy before the egg whites are added, thin it with a little milk. Put the batter in a buttered and floured pan at least 4 inches deep. Bake the cake in a moderate oven (350° F.) for 1 1/2 to 2 hours, or until it tests done. The cake will be browned and firm to the touch.

Spongecake   BISCUIT DE SAVOIE

BEAT 8 egg yolks, 1 1/2 cups sugar, and 1/2 teaspoon lemon, orange, or vanilla extract in a warm bowl with a hand whip or an electric beater until the mixture is thick and creamy. Add 1 whole egg and continue to beat until the sugar is dissolved and the mixture is very light and fluffy. Measure 1 3/4 cups sifted cake flour (or use 1 1/2 cups sifted flour and 1/4 cup cornstarch) and fold it into the mixture, a third at a time, with a metal spatula.

Beat 8 egg whites until they are stiff and cut and fold them into the batter. Butter a deep pan or fancy mold, sprinkle it with sugar, and fill it about two thirds full. Bake the spongecake in a slow oven (300° F.) for 45 to 50 minutes, or until the cake tests done.

Almond Carrot Torte

CHILL and grate 1 pound cooked carrots. Blanch 1 pound almonds and chop them finely. Beat 8 egg yolks until they are thick and light and gradually beat in 2 cups sugar. Add 1 tablespoon orange juice, the grated rind of 1 large orange, the carrots, and the almonds. Blend the ingredients thoroughly and fold in 8 egg whites, stiffly beaten. Pour the batter into a buttered springform pan and bake it in a moderately slow oven (325° F.) for 45 to 50 minutes, or until it tests done. Cool the cake, cover it with sweetened whipped cream, and chill it for several hours before serving.

GÂTEAU D'AMANDES AU CHOCOLAT   Almond Chocolate Torte

BEAT 10 egg yolks with 2 cups sugar until they are thick and lemon-colored and add 4 ounces unsweetened chocolate, grated, 1 tablespoon cinnamon, 1/4 teaspoon ground cloves, the juice and rind of 1 lemon, 2 cups ground blanched almonds, and 1/2 cup brandy. Fold in alternately 10 egg whites, stiffly beaten, and 1 cup sifted cracker meal. Turn the batter into a buttered springform pan and bake the *Torte* in a moderate oven (350° F.) for 50 minutes, or until it tests done. Frost the cake with rum icing.

Orange Madeira Cake

CREAM 1/2 cup butter with 1 cup sugar until the mixture is fluffy. Stir in 2 eggs, beaten, 1 cup seedless raisins, 1/2 cup chopped blanched almonds, the grated rind of 3 oranges, and 1 teaspoon vanilla. Sift together 2 cups sifted cake flour, 1 teaspoon baking soda, and 1/2 teaspoon salt. Stir the dry ingredients into the creamed mixture alternately with 1 cup sour milk. Turn the batter into a buttered and floured 9-inch-square cake pan and bake the cake in a moderate oven (350° F.) for 30 to 40 minutes, or until it tests done. Cool the cake on a wire rack.

Combine in a saucepan 3/4 cup water, 1/2 cup sugar, and 1/4 cup Madeira. Boil the syrup for 5 minutes. Add the peeled sections of 3 oranges, poach them for 5 minutes, and drain them, discarding the syrup. Frost the cooled cake with Madeira icing and decorate it with a radiating circle of the orange sections.

Orange Fruitcake

SIFT together 2 1/2 cups sifted cake flour, 1 teaspoon baking powder, and 1/2 teaspoon salt. Mix together 4 1/2 ounces each of pitted dates and pecans, all finely chopped, and 2 ounces candied orange peel, finely shredded. Stir 3 tablespoons of the sifted flour into the nut and date mixture and set aside.

Cream 1 cup butter until it is smooth and gradually add 1 cup sugar. Add 2 eggs, one at a time, beating well after each addition. Stir 1 teaspoon baking soda into 1 cup buttermilk and add it to the creamed mixture alternately with the remaining flour. Stir in the grated rind of 2 lemons and 1 teaspoon vanilla and fold in the dates and nuts.

Pour the batter into a buttered 10-inch tube pan and bake the cake in a slow oven (300° F.) for 1 hour and 20 minutes. Boil the juice of 2 oranges with 1 cup sugar for 5 minutes and pour the hot syrup over the cake. Cool the cake in the pan. It will keep for several weeks if it is wrapped in foil and stored in the refrigerator.

Brandied Fruitcake

MIX together 3/4 pound each of candied pineapple, shredded, and golden raisins, 1/2 pound each of candied red and green cherries, halved, seeded raisins, and currants, 5 ounces each of candied orange peel and candied lemon peel, coarsely chopped, and 2 ounces candied citron, finely chopped. Pour 1/2 cup Cognac over the fruits, cover the bowl, and let them stand for 1 to 2 days. Blend the soaked fruits thoroughly with 4 ounces almonds, blanched and finely shredded, 4 ounces pecans, coarsely chopped, and 1/2 cup sifted flour.

Cream 1/2 cup butter and beat in gradually 1 cup each of dark-brown sugar, firmly packed, and granulated sugar. Add 5 eggs, one at a time, beating well after each addition, and stir in 1 tablespoon milk mixed with 1 teaspoon almond extract. Sift 1 1/2 cups sifted flour with 1/2 teaspoon each of cinnamon and baking powder and 1/4 teaspoon each of cloves and mace. Add the sifted ingredients gradually to the creamed mixture, blending the batter thoroughly. Pour the batter over the fruits and nuts and, with the hands, blend the mixture thoroughly.

Butter 2 loaf pans, 9 by 5 by 3 inches, line them with wax paper, and butter the paper. Pour the batter into the pans, pressing it down firmly in the middle and at the corners. Bake the cakes in a slow oven (275° F.) for about 3 hours, or until they test done. Let the cakes cool in the pans for about 30 minutes. Turn them out on a wire rack and peel off the paper. Wrap the cooled cakes in cheesecloth soaked in

Cognac and store them, tightly covered, for at least 1 1/2 months. Sprinkle them with a shower of Cognac several times a week.

To serve the cakes, frost them with almond cream paste, let the paste dry, and coat it with confectioners' sugar glaze made with almond extract.

Génoise 🐦

MELT 1/2 cup sweet butter over low heat without letting it bubble and cool it to lukewarm.

In a warm metal mixing bowl combine 9 tablespoons sugar and 4 large eggs, warmed to room temperature. With an electric mixer beat the mixture at moderate speed for about 15 to 20 minutes, or until it is light and thick enough to form a "ribbon" when the beater is withdrawn. Add 1 cup minus 2 tablespoons sifted flour, sifting it lightly over the batter in three portions and folding it in gently with a metal spoon. Use as few strokes as possible. Tip the bowl and pour the clarified butter over the batter, being careful not to include the milky sediment on the bottom. If desired, stir 1 teaspoon vanilla extract into the butter. Quickly fold in the butter. Turn the batter into a deep 8-inch springform pan, buttered and sprinkled lightly with flour. If a trace of butter appears on the surface, press it into the batter with a single stroke of the spoon. Bake the *génoise* in a moderate oven (350° F.) for about 45 minutes, or until it is browned and shrinks from the sides of the pan. Remove the cake from the pan at once and cool it on a wire rack. As the cake cools it will sink slightly in the middle. Trim the upstanding crisp edge before icing.

Kirsch Butter Spongecake 🐦

BAKE *génoise* batter in a buttered 10-inch flan ring set on a prepared baking sheet, or in a shallow 10-inch cake tin, and cool the cake. Split it into 2 layers and cover the bottom layer with kirsch butter cream about 1/2 inch thick.

Tint 1/2 cup granulated sugar by rubbing it between the palms with 3 drops green food coloring. Sprinkle the cake generously with the green sugar. Sprinkle confectioners' sugar heavily over the green sugar, allowing the green coloring to show through slightly. With the dull side of a knife, press parallel marks on the top of the cake. The cake will resemble a whole Brie cheese.

Chocolate Cream Cake

BAKE *génoise* batter in a cake pan 9 inches in diameter and 2 inches deep and cool the cake. Split it into 3 layers and assemble the layers with cooled pastry cream flavored with rum. Using a knife dipped in hot water, spread chocolate frosting on the top and the sides of the cake. Garnish the top and sides with walnut halves and let the frosting set near an open window so that it will remain glossy and soft.

Mocha Cake

BAKE *génoise* batter in an 8-inch springform pan and cool the cake. Spread the cake thickly with mocha butter cream. Pack the remaining cream into a pastry bag fitted with a 3/4-inch rose tube. From an imaginary circle 2 inches in diameter in the center of the cake, pipe 4 strips 2 inches long and 90 degrees apart. Make the strips into X's by piping overlapping strips of equal length. Make a large rosette with the same tube in the center circle, and 4 more rosettes between the X's. With a 3/8-inch rose tube finish the outer ends of the X's with small shell shapes.

Bichettes

BAKE *génoise* batter in an 11-inch-square baking pan and cool the cake. Cut the cake into strips 1 inch wide. With a pastry bag fitted with a plain round 3/8-inch tube, pipe 2 rolls, side by side, the length of the strip, and a third in the top center. Chill the strips for 2 to 3 hours and coat them with chocolate fondant. When the fondant has set, cut the cake strips on the bias into 1/2-inch slices.

Chocolatines

BAKE *génoise* batter in a rectangular pan, 10 by 12 inches, and cut the cooled cake into small squares. Sandwich the squares with chocolate butter cream and spread the top and the sides of the *petits fours* with more cream. Roll the cakes in finely chopped sweet chocolate, or set thin squares of chocolate candy wafers around the sides, forming a box.

Gitanes 🐾

BAKE *génoise* batter in a rectangular pan, 10 by 12 inches, and cut the cooled cake into small circles. With a pastry bag fitted with a plain 1/2-inch tube, pipe a dome of strawberry butter cream on each circle. Chill the cakes for 2 or 3 hours and coat them with untinted fondant. When the fondant has set, cut a small cross in the top of each *petit four*, so that the strawberry butter cream will show through slightly.

Petits Fours with Candied Fruits 🐾

BAKE *génoise* batter in a rectangular pan, 10 by 12 inches, and cut the cooled cake into varied small shapes. Split the cakes in half, assemble the layers with jam or marmalade, and let the jam set. Ice the cakes with fondant tinted and flavored to taste, and decorate them with candied fruits or with nut meats.

Pineapple Petits Fours 🐾

BAKE *génoise* batter in a rectangular pan, 10 by 12 inches, and cut the cooled cake into small ovals. Sandwich the ovals with pineapple butter cream. Spread the cream high on the cakes, mounding it to make a rounded surface. Chill the cakes for 2 to 3 hours and coat them with fondant tinted and flavored to taste. Decorate the ovals with lengthwise rows of tiny dots of chocolate butter cream. At one end of each oval place a small piece of candied angelica, to make a stem for the "pineapple."

Jelly Roll 🐾

BRUSH a jelly-roll pan, 10 by 15 inches, with oil, line it with wax paper, allowing two inches extra at either end, and oil the paper.

Separate 5 eggs. Using a heavy whisk, beat the yolks with 4 tablespoons sugar until the mixture is pale in color and thick enough to "ribbon." Carefully fold in 3 tablespoons sifted cake flour, 1 teaspoon vanilla, and the 5 egg whites, stiffly beaten.

Spread the batter in the prepared pan. Bake the cake in a hot oven (400° F.) for about 12 minutes, or until it is golden and tests done. Sprinkle the cake with fine granulated sugar and turn it out on a board covered with two long overlapping sheets of wax paper. Lift the pan off the cake and gently strip off the paper from the bottom of the cake. Roll up the cake lengthwise in the paper and let it cool. Unroll the cake, spread it with 5 tablespoons red currant jelly, and roll it up again, using the paper as an aid. Slide the roll onto a flat serving platter.

﴾ Walnut Roll

BRUSH a jelly-roll pan, 10 by 15 inches, with oil, line it with wax paper, and oil the paper.

Separate 7 eggs. Using a heavy whisk, beat the yolks with 3/4 cup sugar until the mixture is pale in color and thick enough to "ribbon." Beat in 1 1/2 cups ground walnuts and 1 teaspoon baking powder. Fold in the egg whites, stiffly beaten. Spread the batter in the prepared pan and bake the cake in a moderate oven (350° F.) for 15 to 20 minutes, or until it is golden. Cool the cake in the pan, cover it with a damp towel, and chill it.

Dust the cold cake generously with sifted confectioners' sugar and turn it out on a board covered with two overlapping sheets of wax paper. Carefully strip the paper from the bottom of the cake. Spread the cake with 1 cup heavy cream, whipped and flavored with sugar and vanilla to taste. Roll up the cake, using the paper as an aid, and slide the roll onto a flat serving platter. Sprinkle the roll with more sifted confectioners' sugar.

﴾ Orange Butter Cream Roll

BRUSH a jelly-roll pan, 10 by 15 inches, with oil, line it with wax paper, and oil the paper.

Separate 3 eggs. Beat the yolks with a heavy whisk, or for about 10 minutes in a mixer, until they are pale in color and thick enough to "ribbon." In another bowl beat the whites until they are foamy, add 1 teaspoon cider vinegar, and beat the whites until they form soft peaks. Gradually beat in 1/2 cup fine granulated sugar and 1/2 teaspoon orange extract and beat the meringue until it is stiff. With a spatula, carefully fold the beaten yolks into the meringue. Sift 1/2 cup sifted flour with 1/8 teaspoon salt and sift the mixture over the top of the batter. Fold it in carefully but thoroughly.

Walnut Roll

Spread the batter smoothly in the prepared pan. Bake the cake in a hot oven (400° F.) for 12 to 15 minutes, or until it shrinks from the sides of the pan. Sprinkle the cake generously with sifted confectioners' sugar.

Turn the hot cake out on a board covered with two long overlapping sheets of wax paper. Gently strip off the paper from the bottom. Roll up the cake lengthwise in the wax paper and let it cool. Unroll the cake and spread the entire surface thickly with orange butter cream. Roll up the cake again, using the wax paper as an aid. Slide the roll onto a flat serving platter and chill it.

ᔓ Hazelnut Roll

BRUSH a jelly-roll pan, 10 by 15 inches, with oil, and sprinkle it with fine bread or cake crumbs.

Separate 3 eggs. Using a heavy whisk, beat the yolks with 1/2 cup sugar until the mixture is pale in color and thick enough to "ribbon." Beat the egg whites until they are stiff and fold them in, a little at a time, alternately with 1/2 cup ground hazelnuts. Spread the batter in the prepared pan and bake the cake in a moderate oven (350° F.) for about 15 minutes, or until it tests done.

Turn the cake out on a board covered with two long overlapping sheets of wax paper. Sprinkle it generously with sugar, roll it up in the paper, and let it cool. Unroll the cake and spread it with 1 1/2 cups heavy cream, whipped and mixed with a few strawberries and a dash of kirsch. Roll up the cake again, using the paper as an aid, and slide the roll onto a flat serving platter.

ᔓ Pâte à Chou

CREAM PUFF PASTE

SIFT 1 cup plus 2 tablespoons sifted flour onto a sheet of wax paper. In a heavy saucepan bring to a rapid boil 1 cup water, 1/2 cup butter, cut into small pieces, 1 teaspoon sugar, and 1/2 teaspoon salt. Using the wax paper as a funnel, pour the flour all at once into the boiling mixture and cook the paste over low heat, beating it rapidly and vigorously with a wooden spoon, until the ingredients are thoroughly combined and the mixture cleanly leaves the sides of the pan and forms a ball. Remove the pan from the heat and beat into it by hand or with a mixer

4 eggs, one at a time, beating well after each addition. Let the paste cool slightly before shaping it.

Mocha Éclairs 🐾

USING a pastry bag fitted with a plain round tube, press out cream puff paste on a lightly buttered baking sheet into strips 3 or 4 inches long. Hold the pastry bag at an oblique angle and finish each strip with a backward motion to cut off the end evenly. Brush the strips with *dorure* and bake them in a hot oven (400° F.) for 30 minutes. Reduce the temperature to slow (300° F.) and bake the strips for 10 minutes longer, or until all the beads of moisture have disappeared. Cool the shells on a wire rack and split them in half horizontally. Fill them with mocha pastry cream and frost them with mocha confectioners' icing.

CHOUX

Cream Puffs 🐾

FILL a pastry bag with cream puff paste. Hold it over a lightly buttered baking sheet and press the bag to force out the paste into a small high mound. Lift the bag and press again, until the mound is the desired size. Turn the bag to finish the mound with a twist. Brush the puffs with *dorure* and bake them in a moderately hot oven (375° F.) for 20 minutes, or until they are golden brown, light, and dry. If necessary, prick the puffs with the tip of a sharp knife and let them stand in a slack oven for 10 minutes, to make sure that the centers are quite dry. Cool the puffs on a wire rack, split them in half, and fill them with sweetened whipped cream, pastry cream, or Saint Honoré cream. Lightly replace the tops of the puffs and dust them heavily with sifted confectioners' sugar.

Profiteroles 🐾

To form *profiteroles*, or miniature cream puffs, fill a pastry bag with cream puff paste and press out small mounds on a lightly buttered baking sheet. Or drop the paste from the tip of a teaspoon. Brush the puffs with *dorure* and bake them in a hot oven (425° F.) for 15 to 18 minutes, or until they are puffed and lightly browned. Reduce the temperature to slow (300° F.) and bake the puffs for 5 minutes longer, or until they are well browned, dry, and light. Cool on a wire rack.

Triplet Cream Puffs

For hors-d'oeuvre, drop cherry-sized mounds on the baking sheet to form walnut-sized puffs.

Triplet Cream Puffs 𝕾

WITH a teaspoon or a pastry bag fitted with a plain round tube, shape cream puff paste into 3 small puffs together on a lightly buttered baking sheet. Brush the triplets with *dorure* and bake them in a hot oven (425° F.) for 20 to 30 minutes, or until they are well puffed and lightly browned. Reduce the temperature to slow (300° F.) and bake the puffs for 10 minutes longer, or until they are well browned, dry, and light. Cool the triplets on a wire rack. With a serrated knife cut the tops from the puffs and fill them with Saint Honoré cream, praline pastry cream, or sweetened whipped cream. Lightly replace the tops of the puffs and dust them heavily with sifted confectioners' sugar.

Pâte Feuilletée 𝕾

THE secrets of puff paste are two. First, the butter and the *détrempe*, or flour and water paste, must have exactly the same consistency. If the butter is too hard, it will break through the soft paste during the rolling. If the *détrempe* is too hard, the butter will ooze out the sides instead of being evenly distributed between the layers of dough. Second, the *détrempe* should weigh exactly twice as much as the butter. Since flours differ in their absorption qualities, it is impossible to measure the flour precisely, so accuracy and consistency in results are assured by weighing the butter and using twice its weight in *détrempe*.

Fill a large bowl half full with ice water. Put 1/2 pound sweet butter into the water and knead it, squeezing it through the fingers until it is smooth and waxy but firm and not soft. Shape the butter into a flat rectangular cake, pressing it gently to expel air and water. Dry the butter cake with a cloth, wrap it in plastic wrap, and chill it until it is firm but not hard.

Sift 1/2 pound (about 2 cups) flour and 1 teaspoon salt into a heap on a marble slab or pastry board. Make a slight depression in the flour and pour into it about 1 1/2 tablespoons ice water. Gather in enough of the surrounding flour to make a firm cone of dough, shaping the dough and turning it in the flour with the finger-tips and thumb of one hand. The dough should not be dry, stiff, or sticky. Put the cone aside. Add more ice water, 1 1/2 tablespoons at a time, and repeat the process, piling the cones firmly on top of each other and shaping them into one mass of dough. Bits of flour and water paste that remain when one cone is completed should be incorporated into the next, since they harden quickly on standing. When all the flour is taken up, weigh the *détrempe*, or dough. It should be exactly twice the weight of the creamed butter, and the texture of the two should be equally firm.

With the fist, flatten the ball of dough. Sprinkle the slab or board and the rolling pin very lightly with flour and roll out the dough, straight back and forth, in a rectangle. Turn the dough so that the long side faces you and roll it out in a rough square 1/4 to 1/2 inch thick, slightly thinner at the edges. Lay the chilled butter in the center of the square. Fold all four sides of the dough over the butter in the center and seal the package by pressing the edges firmly. Wrap the dough in plastic wrap and chill it for 15 minutes.

With the rolling pin, flatten the dough with uniform, successive impressions. With quick, light motions, roll the dough from the center away from you to within 1/2 inch of the end. Reverse the strip on the board and again roll away from you to make a rectangle. If a little butter breaks through the dough during this first rolling, dust the dough and pin lightly with flour and continue rolling with quick, light motions. Keep rolling the dough, being careful not to wrinkle it. Turn the dough, not the pin, to shape it, and always roll straight back and forth, to avoid stretching the dough and to distribute all the butter evenly. At the end, the rectangle should be about 12 inches long and 1/2 inch thick.

Fold the top third of the rectangle over the center and the bottom third over the top. Turn the folded dough on the board so that an open side faces you. With the rolling pin, flatten the dough with uniform impressions. Roll the dough from the center away from you to within 1/2 inch of the end. Reverse the strip on the board and again roll the dough away from you to make a rectangle about 12 inches long. Do not roll the pin over the ends, or the air and butter will be expelled. Fold the strip in three as before. This completes 2 "turns." Wrap the dough in plastic wrap and chill it for 15 minutes. Make 2 more turns and chill the dough again. Repeat, making 6 turns in all. Chill the puff paste before using.

❧ Puff-Paste Shell

DIVIDE puff paste in half and roll out each half about 3/8 inch thick into a rough square. Trim each piece to make two 7-inch squares. Lay one square, top side down, on a baking sheet moistened with water. Cut out a 5-inch square from the other 7-inch square of puff paste, leaving a 1-inch rim. Reserve the 5-inch square, as a lid.

Brush the edges of the square on the baking sheet with water and on it lay the cutout rim, top side down. Press the borders firmly together and lay the reserved 5-inch square inside the rim. Chill the pastry for at least 20 minutes. Brush the top of the shell with *dorure*. Do not let it drip down the sides as it will prevent the paste from rising. Bake the shell in a very hot oven (450° F.) for about 10 minutes, or until it is well puffed and lightly browned. Reduce the temperature to moderately hot (375° F.) and bake the shell for 25 to 30 minutes longer. With a sharp knife gently lift out the 5-inch square and reserve it as a lid for the filled shell.

To make individual shells of puff paste, or boat-shaped *barquettes*, follow the procedure above. Bake the tiny shells in a very hot oven (450° F.) for about 10 minutes, reduce the temperature to moderately hot (375° F.), and bake the shells for about 10 minutes more.

Dorure

BEAT 1 egg yolk with 1 tablespoon milk or water. For glazing breads and pastries.

Bouchées

ROLL out puff paste 1/4 inch thick on a lightly floured board and cut out small rounds. Cut the centers from half the rounds to make rings. Brush the edges of the remaining rounds with water and press a ring on top of each. Lay the shells on a baking sheet moistened with cold water and brush them with *dorure*. Lay the tiny cutouts in each ring. Chill the *bouchées* for 20 minutes. Bake them in a very hot oven (450° F.) for 10 minutes, or until they are well puffed. Reduce the temperature to moderately hot (375° F.) and bake the shells for about 10 minutes more, or until they are golden.

OX TONGUE PASTRIES ### Langues de Bœuf

ROLL out puff paste 1/8 inch thick on a lightly floured board and cut out 2-inch rounds. Shape the rounds into ovals with a rolling pin and lay them on a baking sheet moistened with cold water. Sprinkle the ovals with sugar and chill them for

20 minutes. Bake them in a moderately hot oven (375° F.) for 7 or 8 minutes, or until they are puffed and golden.

Mille-Feuille

ROLL out puff paste on a lightly floured board into a rectangle 1/4 inch thick, turning the dough to shape it. Cut the rectangle into 3 equal strips, 12 to 14 inches long and 4 to 5 inches wide. Trim the edges evenly and reserve the trimmings. Fold each strip loosely in half, transfer it carefully to a baking sheet moistened with cold water, and unfold. Separate the strips by about 1 inch. Lay the trimmings around the edges of the sheet and chill for 20 minutes. Brush the pastry with *dorure* and bake it in a very hot oven (450° F.) for 15 minutes. Reduce the temperature to moderate (350° F.) and bake the strips for 15 minutes longer, or until they are crisp and golden brown.

Cool the strips and flatten them lightly with the hand. Form a 3-layer cake, using vanilla whipped cream or almond cream paste between the layers. The top pastry layer should be bottom side up, to make a smooth surface. Sprinkle the top heavily with confectioners' sugar. Or spread it with a little of the cream and sprinkle it with the baked trimmings, coarsely crumbled. To serve the cake, cut it into 2-inch slices with a serrated knife.

Napoléons

ROLL out puff paste 1/8 inch thick on a lightly floured board and cut out 2-inch rounds. With a rolling pin shape the rounds into ovals. Put 1/2 teaspoon almond cream paste in the center of half the ovals, moisten the edges with water, and cover the filling with a second pastry oval. Press the edges to seal the pastries. Lay them on a baking sheet moistened with cold water. Brush the tops with a little almond cream paste thinned with egg white and sprinkle with confectioners' sugar. Chill for 20 minutes. Bake the *napoléons* in a hot oven (400° F.) for 15 minutes.

Palmiers

GIVE puff paste four turns and chill the dough for 20 minutes. Roll it out into a long strip on a board sprinkled with sugar. Give it two more turns and chill the dough for 20 minutes. (Trimmings of puff paste may be rerolled and used for *palmiers*.) Roll out the dough 1/8 inch thick into a 16-inch square and sprinkle with sugar. Double-fold each side of the square onto itself over to the middle of the strip. Fold the sides together as though closing a book, thus making 6 layers of paste. With a floured sharp knife cut the roll into 1/2-inch slices. Moisten baking sheets with cold water and put the slices on them, cut sides down, spreading the ends to make a small V. Chill for 20 minutes. Bake the *palmiers* in a hot oven (400° F.) for 12 to 15 minutes, turning them for the last 3 minutes of baking.

Small *palmiers* may be made by folding the ends of the strip of paste to the middle only once and closing them together, making 4 layers of paste. Cut small *palmiers* into 1/4-inch slices.

WELLS OF LOVE — Puits d'Amour

ROLL out puff paste 1/4 inch thick on a lightly floured board and cut out 1 1/2-inch rounds with a fluted cutter. Cut the centers from half the rounds to make rings. Brush the edges of the remaining rounds with water and press a ring on top of each. Lay the shells on a baking sheet moistened with cold water and brush them with *dorure*. Chill for 20 minutes. Bake the shells in a very hot oven (450° F.) for 15 minutes, or until they are well puffed. Reduce the temperature to moderate (350° F.) and bake the shells until they are golden. Cool the *puits d'amour* and fill the centers with red-currant jelly. Sprinkle the edges with confectioners' sugar.

Currant Tarts

LINE 6 tart shells with puff paste and brush each shell with 1 teaspoon raspberry jelly. Stir 1/4 cup sugar into 1 pint red currants and divide the currants among the tart shells. Sprinkle the currants with a little sugar and bake the tarts in a moderate oven (350° F.) for 15 minutes. Pour a little melted raspberry jelly over the currants and return the tarts to the oven for 5 minutes. Serve warm or cold.

ALMOND TWISTS — Sacristains

ROLL out puff paste or trimmings of puff paste on a lightly floured board into a long band 1/8 inch thick and 4 to 5 inches wide. Brush the surface with beaten egg and sprinkle it with very finely chopped blanched almonds and confectioners' sugar. Cut the band crosswise into 1/2-inch strips and twist each strip several times like a corkscrew. Put the almond twists 1 inch apart on a baking sheet moistened with cold water and chill for 20 minutes. Bake them in a very hot oven (450° F.) for 8 to 10 minutes, or until they are golden.

ᶚ Mango Turnovers

ROLL out puff paste 1/4 inch thick on a lightly floured board and cut out 4-inch circles. Put 3 or 4 slices peeled ripe mango on half of each round. Dot the fruit with butter and sprinkle it with sugar. Fold the other half of each round over the fruit, brush the edges with water, and crimp them to seal. Brush the turnovers with *dorure*, arrange them on a moistened baking sheet, and chill for 20 minutes. Bake the pastries in a hot oven (425° F.) for 10 minutes, reduce the temperature to moderately slow (325° F.), and bake them until the fruit is tender and the crust is golden brown. Sprinkle with confectioners' sugar and serve warm, with whipped cream.

ᶚ Flaky Cheese Roll

PUT 1 pound cottage or pot cheese and 3 ounces soft cream cheese through a sieve. Stir in 2 eggs, 3 tablespoons sour cream, 2 tablespoons grated Parmesan, and 1/2 teaspoon finely chopped garlic. Fold in 2 egg whites, stiffly beaten.

On a lightly floured board roll out half the recipe for puff paste into a very thin rectangle, 12 by 18 inches. Brush it lightly with melted butter and spread it with the cheese mixture. Roll up the dough as for jelly roll and slide it onto a moistened baking sheet. Brush the roll with *dorure* and chill it for 20 minutes. Bake the cheese roll in a moderately hot oven (375° F.) for 45 minutes, or until the crust is golden brown.

ᶚ Flaky Pastry

SIFT 2 cups sifted flour and 1 teaspoon salt into a chilled mixing bowl. With 2 knives or a pastry blender cut in 1/3 cup cold butter until the mixture resembles meal. Cut in another 1/3 cup cold butter, to make lumps the size of small peas.

Sprinkle 4 to 6 tablespoons ice water (using as little as possible), a tablespoon at a time, over the dough and stir it in very quickly until it can be gathered together with the fork and cleans the bowl. Form the dough into a ball, wrap it in wax paper, and chill it for 30 minutes.

Roll out the dough into a rectangle about 1/3 inch thick and cover it with 3 tablespoons hard butter, cut in thin shavings. Fold the upper third of the dough over the center and fold the lower third of dough over the upper flap, making 3 layers. Give the dough a quarter turn, roll it out thinly in a rectangle, and fold it again in thirds. Chill the dough for several hours or overnight. Makes enough for a 2-crust pie.

To shape and bake a flaky pastry shell before filling, roll out the chilled dough 1/4 inch thick on a lightly floured board. Press the dough against the bottom and sides of a 9-inch pie plate or flan ring. Prick the shell well, fill it with wax paper and rice, and bake it in a very hot oven (450° F.) for about 25 minutes, or until it is golden brown. Discard the paper and rice and cool the shell before filling.

To shape and bake flaky pastry *barquettes*, roll out the dough 1/8 inch thick and cut out boat-shaped pieces to fit *barquette* molds. Fill the shells with wax paper and rice and bake them in a very hot oven (450° F.) for about 15 minutes, or until they are golden brown. Cool the *barquettes* and carefully remove them from the molds before filling.

Grated Apple Pie

BEAT together thoroughly 4 egg yolks and 1 cup sifted confectioners' sugar. Stir in 6 green apples, peeled, seeded, and grated, 1/4 pound almonds, blanched and ground, and the grated rind of 1 lemon. Turn the filling into a 9-inch pie plate lined with flaky pastry. Bake the pie in a hot oven (400° F.) for 20 to 30 minutes.

Beat 4 egg whites with 4 tablespoons sugar until they are very stiff and shiny. Cover the pie completely with the meringue and bake it at the same temperature for 8 or 10 minutes, or until the meringue is brown.

Sour Cream Blackberry Pie

BLEND 1/2 cup brown sugar with 1 tablespoon flour and blend in thoroughly 1 cup sour cream. Line a 9-inch pie plate with flaky pastry, and brush the dough with lightly beaten egg white to keep it firm. Fill the pie shell with 3 cups blackberries, well washed and drained, and pour the sour cream mixture over them. Bake the pie in a very hot oven (450° F.) for 10 minutes, reduce the temperature to moderately slow (325° F.), and bake the pie for 30 minutes more.

Mincemeat Flan

LINE a 9-inch flan ring with flaky pastry. Fill the shell to the top with mincemeat and cover it with a latticework of pastry. Sprinkle into the pie 3 tablespoons melted butter. Bake the pie in a moderate oven (350° F.) for 40 minutes and serve warm.

Mincemeat

PUT 3/4 pound white beef suet through the finest blade of a food chopper twice. Combine the suet in a large baking dish with 3/4 pound each of raisins, currants, sultanas, and chopped apples, 1/2 pound mixed chopped citron, candied orange peel, and candied lemon peel, all finely chopped, 1/2 pound blanched almonds and 1 ounce blanched bitter almonds, both finely chopped, and 1/8 teaspoon each of cinnamon, mace, salt, and white pepper. Heat the mixture in a slow oven (300° F.) for 30 minutes. Stir in 3/4 cup brandy and the grated rind and juice of 2 lemons. Store the mincemeat, covered, in a cool place. Makes enough mincemeat for several pies or flans.

Mocha Chiffon Pie

LINE a 9-inch pie plate with flaky pastry and bake it. Soften 1 tablespoon gelatin in 1/4 cup cold water. In the top of a double boiler combine 1/3 cup cocoa, 1/2 cup sugar, and 1/2 teaspoon salt. Stir in 4 egg yolks, well beaten, and 1 cup strong black coffee. Set the pan over hot water and cook the custard, stirring constantly, until it coats the spoon. Dissolve the softened gelatin in the hot custard. Strain the mixture through a fine sieve into a cold bowl to cool, stirring from time to time to prevent a crust from forming. Beat 4 egg whites with 1/2 cup sugar until they are very stiff and glossy and fold the meringue into the mocha custard. Pour the filling into the baked shell and decorate the pie with tufts of whipped cream.

Dried Peach and Raisin Pie 🐾

COVER 1/4 pound dried peaches with 2 1/2 cups cold water and simmer them slowly, stirring occasionally, for 30 minutes. Add 3/4 cup black seedless raisins and cook the fruits for 15 minutes more. Add 6 tablespoons light-brown sugar, 2 tablespoons sugar, 1/2 teaspoon cinnamon, and a dash of nutmeg and cook the fruits for 5 minutes. Cool the mixture and stir in 2 tablespoons Cognac. Line a 9-inch pie plate with flaky pastry, fill the shell with the fruit mixture, and dot it with 2 tablespoons butter. Cover the pie with a top crust and bake it in a very hot oven (450° F.) for 30 minutes, or until the crust is golden. Cool the pie and serve it with hard sauce.

Jefferson Davis Pie 🐾

LINE a 9-inch pie plate with flaky pastry and bake it. Combine 1 cup sugar, 3 tablespoons flour, and 1 teaspoon each of cinnamon and ground cloves, and gradually add 1 cup milk, stirring the mixture until it is smooth. With a fork beat together 2 egg yolks and 1 whole egg, add 1 cup light cream, and mix well. Combine both mixtures in the top of a double boiler over hot water and cook the custard, stirring it constantly, until it thickens. Remove the custard from the heat, stir in 1 teaspoon vanilla, and pour the filling into the baked shell.

Beat 4 egg whites with 1/4 cup sugar, 1/4 teaspoon cream of tartar, and 1/8 teaspoon salt until the meringue is very stiff and glossy. Cover the pie completely with the meringue and bake it in a hot oven (400° F.) for 10 minutes.

SWEET TART PASTRY   ## Pâte Sucrée 🐾

MOUND 2 cups sifted flour on a marble slab or a pastry board, make a well in the center, and in it put 5 tablespoons sugar, 4 large egg yolks, and 1/2 cup soft butter, broken into pieces. With the fingers work the center ingredients to a smooth paste and quickly work in the flour, to form a smooth round ball. If the dough seems too dry, add a few drops of water. Knead the dough very lightly, wrap it in wax paper, and chill it for at least 1 hour, or overnight. Makes enough pastry for two 9-inch flan rings or pie plates or 12 small tarts.

To shape and bake a flan ring before filling, roll out the chilled dough 1/4 inch thick on a lightly floured board. Gently ease the dough into a 9-inch flan ring set on a baking sheet, pressing it against the sides. Pleat the rim and cut off the excess dough. Chill the ring for 30 minutes. Fill the shell with aluminum foil or wax paper, leaving a tall collar all around, and fill the shell with rice. Bake the flan in a moderate oven (350° F.) for about 10 minutes, or until the edges brown slightly. Lift out the paper and rice, return the flan to the oven, and bake it for 5 to 10 minutes longer, or until it is a light golden brown. Cool the shell on the baking sheet and lift the ring away from the sides. Slide the shell onto a serving dish and cool it before filling.

To shape and bake small tart shells, roll out the dough in a sheet 1/8 inch thick. Cut out rounds to fit tart pans and press the pastry firmly against the bottoms and sides of the pans. Fill the shells with wax paper and rice and bake them in a hot oven (400° F.) for about 5 minutes, or until the edges brown slightly. Discard the paper and rice and bake the shells for about 5 minutes more, or until they are a light golden brown. Cool the shells and carefully remove them from the pans before filling them.

Applesauce Tarts

LINE 6 tart pans with sweet tart pastry, bake them, and cool. Brush the bottoms and sides of the baked shells with apricot jam and fill the tarts with thick applesauce mixed with toasted shredded almonds and finely chopped candied orange peel.

Beat 4 egg whites with 4 tablespoons sugar until they are stiff and glossy. Cover the tarts with a swirl of the meringue pressed through a pastry tube. Sprinkle the meringue with fine granulated sugar and bake the tarts in a hot oven (400° F.) for about 8 to 10 minutes, or until the meringue is lightly browned and glazed. Chill before serving.

Apricot Tart

LINE a 9-inch flan ring with sweet tart pastry, bake it, and cool.

Boil 2 cups water with 3/4 cup sugar and 1/4 teaspoon vanilla for 5 minutes. In the syrup poach 12 fresh apricots, peeled, halved, and pitted, until they are tender, and cool them in the syrup. (Very ripe uncooked apricots may be used.) Spread the tart shell with 1/2 cup sieved apricot jam and arrange the apricots, cut sides down, on the jam. Coat the fruit with apricot glaze and let it set. Sprinkle the tart with chopped almonds and dust with confectioners' sugar.

Pear Cream Tart 🐾

LINE a shallow 9-inch pie plate with sweet tart pastry.

Peel, core, and quarter enough firm pears to make about 5 cups. Fill the pastry shell with the pears, sprinkle the fruit generously with sugar, and dot it well with sweet butter. Bake the tart in a hot oven (425° F.) for about 25 minutes, or until the pears are tender and the crust is golden. Just before serving pour 1/4 cup flaming rum over the fruit. Serve with equal amounts of whipped cream and sour cream, blended together.

Raspberry and Red-Currant Tart 🐾

LINE a 9-inch flan ring with sweet tart pastry, bake it, and cool.

In a saucepan combine 3 cups raspberries and 1 cup red currants with 3/4 cup sugar and cook the fruit over low heat for 2 or 3 minutes. Drain the fruit, reserving the juice. Fill the tart shell with the fruit and bake it in a moderate oven (350° F.) for 10 minutes. Add 1 tablespoon red-currant jelly to the fruit juice and cook the syrup over moderate heat until it is thick. Cool the tart and spoon the syrup over it.

Strawberry Cream Tart 🐾

LINE a 9-inch flan ring with sweet tart pastry, bake it, and cool. Fill the tart shell to the top with whipped cream sweetened to taste and flavored with kirsch or vanilla. Cover the cream with well-brushed (but not washed) strawberries, arranging them in even rings and keeping the fruit as close together as possible, so that very little of the cream shows. With a soft pastry brush glaze the berries and the cream between them with 5 tablespoons red-currant jelly, melted with 1 tablespoon water and cooled. Dust the rim of the tart with confectioners' sugar, or pipe small rosettes of whipped cream around the edge.

Favoris 🐾

ROLL out sweet tart pastry and cut small rounds with a plain cutter. Roll the rounds lightly into ovals and place them on a baking sheet. Using a pastry bag fitted with a small round tube, pipe a figure **8** of *pâte à chou* onto each oval. Bake the *favoris* in a hot oven (425° F.) for 10 to 12 minutes, or until they are brown. Cool the puffs and fill the loops of the figure 8's with *crème pâtissière*. Set half a candied cherry on the cream.

ᕟ Honey and Brazil Nut Turnovers

CREAM 1 cup butter, add 2 egg yolks, and beat the mixture until it is smooth. Stir alternately into the butter mixture 1 cup sour cream and 2 cups sifted flour sifted with a pinch of salt, adding more flour, if necessary, to make a firm dough. Wrap the dough in wax paper and chill it for at least 1 hour.

Roll out the dough 1/8 inch thick on a lightly floured board and cut it into 3-inch rounds. Put a teaspoon of honey and Brazil nut filling on half of the top of each round, fold the rounds in half, and crimp the edges with a fork. Place the turnovers on a buttered baking sheet and bake them in a moderate oven (350° F.) for about 8 minutes, or until they are brown.

Honey and Brazil Nut Filling

COMBINE 1 cup each of chopped Brazil nuts, sugar, and honey and 1 teaspoon cinnamon. Stir the mixture to make a paste.

ᕟ Pâte à Foncer   PLAIN TART PASTRY

SIFT 2 cups sifted flour onto a pastry board, make a well in the center, and into the well put 3/4 cup soft sweet butter, 1 1/2 tablespoons sugar, and 1/2 teaspoon salt. Work the center ingredients to a smooth paste and quickly work in the flour, adding gradually about 5 to 6 tablespoons water, or enough to make a firm dough that just cleans the board. Do not handle the dough unnecessarily. Mix the dough well but lightly, wrap it in wax paper, and chill it. Make enough dough for two 9-inch flan rings or 12 small tarts.

To shape and bake tart shells, roll out the dough 1/8 inch thick and cut out rounds to fit the tart pans. Press the dough into the pans and prick well with a fork. Fill the shells with wax paper and rice and bake them in a very hot oven (450° F.) for about 15 minutes. Cool before filling.

Gooseberry Tart 🦋

LINE a 9-inch flan ring with plain tart pastry and fill it with 1 quart gooseberries, washed and tailed. Sprinkle 1 cup sugar over the gooseberries and cover with a top crust. Bake the tart in a moderate oven (350° F.) for 45 minutes, or until the crust is golden brown. Serve with whipped cream.

Nectarine Tarts 🦋

LINE 6 tart shells with plain tart pastry, bake them, and cool. Fill the shells with nectarines, peeled, stoned, and thinly sliced. Glaze the fruit with apple jelly melted over hot water and stirred to a smooth thick syrup.

Sandtorte Pastry 🦋

WITH the fingers combine 1/2 cup soft butter, 1 1/2 cups sifted flour, 1 teaspoon baking powder, 1/4 cup vanilla sugar, and 2 egg yolks. Work the dough until it has the texture of clay. It will be very crumbly.

To bake tart shells, pat the pastry onto the bottom and sides of small tart pans. Bake the shells in a moderately hot oven (375° F.) for about 30 minutes, or until they are firm and golden. Cool before filling.

Banana Tarts 🦋

LINE 6 tart pans with *Sandtorte* pastry, bake them, and cool. Spread a layer of apricot jam in the baked shells. Fill each tart with thinly sliced bananas and pour 1 tablespoon Cognac over the fruit. Cover the fruit with jam and bake the tarts in a moderate oven (350° F.) for 10 minutes, or until the jam has melted. Sprinkle the tarts with finely chopped toasted almonds. Chill before serving.

Orange and Apple Tarts 🦋

LINE 6 tart pans with *Sandtorte* pastry, bake them, and cool.

Peel 2 oranges, reserving the juice, and simmer the orange peel in water to cover for 5 minutes, or until it is tender. Drain the peel and cut it into shreds. Peel, core, and quarter 10 or 12 apples and put them in a saucepan with just enough water to prevent them from scorching. Cook the apples, stirring, for about 15 minutes, or until they are barely tender. Add 1 cup sugar, the orange peel, and the reserved orange juice and cook the apples, stirring, until they are reduced to a thick paste. Cool the mixture and pour it into the baked shells. Pipe a rosette of whipped cream on each tart and sprinkle with chopped pistachio nuts.

ᔓ Green Grape Tarts

LINE 6 tart pans with *Sandtorte* pastry, bake them, and cool. Pour a layer of *crème pâtissière* into the shells. Arrange perfect very ripe green seedless grapes on the cream and glaze the grapes with melted crab-apple jelly.

ᔓ Unsweetened Tart Pastry

SIFT 2 cups sifted flour onto a pastry board, make a well in the center, and in it put 2/3 cup soft sweet butter, broken into pieces, 1/4 cup ice water, and 1/2 teaspoon salt. With the fingers work the center ingredients to a smooth paste and quickly work in the flour. Knead the dough lightly, wrap it in wax paper, and chill it for at least 1 hour before rolling.

To make small tart shells, roll out the pastry in a sheet 1/8 inch thick. Cut out rounds or boat-shaped pieces to fit tart pans or *barquette* molds. Press the pastry firmly against the bottom and sides of the pan.

To bake the tart shells before filling, prick the pastry well, fill the shells with wax paper and rice, and bake them in a very hot oven (450° F.) for 10 to 12 minutes, or until they are golden brown. Discard the paper and rice and carefully remove the shells from the pans or molds before filling them.

ᔓ Raised Kuchen Dough

SOFTEN 1 package of yeast in 1/4 cup lukewarm water and dissolve it in 3/4 cup milk, scalded and cooled to lukewarm.

Cream 1/2 cup butter with 1/2 cup sugar and add 2 eggs, beaten, and 1/2 teaspoon salt. Add the yeast mixture and 3 1/2 cups sifted flour, a little at a time, beginning and ending with the flour and beating well after each addition. Add a little more flour, if necessary, to make a soft dough easy to handle. Turn the dough out on a lightly floured board and knead it until it is smooth and elastic. Cover the dough lightly with a damp towel and let it rise in a warm place until it doubles in bulk. Roll the dough out 1/8 inch thick and use to line baking pans with narrow upright rims, according to the recipe.

Damson Kuchen

WASH 1 quart damson plums, make 4 lenghtwise incisions to within 1/4 inch of one end, and remove the pits. Place the plums upright and close together in a square pan lined with kuchen dough. Sprinkle the fruit with 1 1/2 cups brown sugar and 1 teaspoon cinnamon and dot it with butter. Let the kuchen rise in a warm place for 1 hour and bake it in a moderate oven (350° F.) for 15 minutes. Beat 2 egg yolks with 4 tablespoons heavy cream and drip this custard mixture over the fruit. Bake the kuchen for 25 to 30 minutes, or until the fruit is tender and the crust browned.

Peach Kuchen

LINE a rectangular pan with kuchen dough and fill the pan with peeled, stoned, and quartered peaches, arranging the fruit in parallel rows. Sprinkle the fruit with spiced maple sugar, allowing 1 cup sugar and 1/2 teaspoon ground cloves for each 4 cups fruit, and dot with butter. Bake the kuchen in a moderate oven (350° F.) for 15 minutes. Beat 1 egg yolk with 3 tablespoons heavy cream and drip this over the peaches. Bake the kuchen for about 20 minutes longer, or until the fruit is tender. Serve warm or cold.

PLAIN MERINGUE   ## Pâte à Meringue

SEPARATE 4 eggs while they are very cold, using a piece of eggshell to remove any bits of yolks from the whites, if necessary. Let the egg whites stand until they reach room temperature. Using a heavy whisk, a rotary beater, or a mixer, beat the egg whites with a pinch of salt until they are stiff and almost dry. This takes about

5 minutes by hand or 3 minutes in a mixer. Beat in 1/2 cup very fine granulated sugar, about 1 tablespoon at a time, beating constantly after each addition until the sugar is dissolved. Continue beating the meringue until it is thick and glossy and forms a stiff peak when the whisk or beater is withdrawn. Add 1 teaspoon vanilla. Sprinkle another 1/2 cup sugar over the entire surface of the meringue and fold it in without further beating.

℥ Meringues Mont Blanc

DROP 6 rounds of plain meringue from the end of a round soup spoon onto an oiled and floured baking sheet, spacing the meringues about 1 inch apart. Bake the meringues in a very slow oven (200° F.) for about 1 hour. Do not let them color. Remove the meringues to a flat surface to cool and crisp.

Put a meringue on each of 6 dessert plates. Fill a pastry bag fitted with a large star tube with sweetened chestnut purée. Press out a ring around the base of each meringue and continue to encircle the meringues with purée until the rings are high enough to form nests. Fill the center of the nests with swirls of sweetened whipped cream. Serve the meringues at once.

℥ Pâte à Meringue aux Amandes   ALMOND MERINGUE

BEAT 5 egg whites with a pinch of salt until they are stiff but not dry. Beat in gradually 3/4 cup very fine granulated sugar, about 1 tablespoon at a time, and continue to beat the meringue until it is thick and smooth. Fold in gently 1/4 cup sugar, 1 teaspoon vanilla, and 3/4 cup grated almonds.

℥ Strawberry Meringue Cake   GÂTEAU AUX FRAISES

BRUSH 2 baking sheets with vegetable oil and dust them lightly with flour. Using an 8-inch cake pan as a guide, trace 2 circles on each baking sheet and spread them evenly with almond meringue. Bake the meringues in a slow oven (250° F.) for about 1 hour, or until they are set. With a heavy spatula remove them to a flat surface to cool and dry.

Whip 2 cups heavy cream until it is stiff and reserve 1 cup for decorating the cake. Into the remaining cream fold 2 cups fresh strawberries, sweetened and slightly

Strawberry Meringue Cake

crushed. Assemble the 4 layers of meringue with the strawberries and cream. Spread the top and sides of the cake with the reserved whipped cream and decorate the top with ribbons of whipped cream and whole strawberries. The sides of the cake may be further decorated with thin ribbons of cream and candied mint leaves. Serve at once.

Almond Rolla Cake   GÂTEAU ROLLA AMANDINE

BRUSH 2 baking sheets with vegetable oil and dust them lightly with flour. Using a 9-inch cake pan as a guide, trace 2 circles on each baking sheet and spread them evenly with almond meringue. Bake the meringues in a slow oven (250° F.) for about 30 minutes, or until they are set. With a heavy spatula remove the meringues to a flat surface to cool and dry.

Beat 4 egg whites in the top of a double boiler until they are foamy. Set the pan over hot but not boiling water and beat in gradually 1 cup sugar, 2 cups soft sweet butter, 8 ounces sweet chocolate, melted, and 3 teaspoons cocoa. Beat the filling until it is thick and smooth, remove it from the heat, and let it cool until it is firm enough to spread.

Assemble the 4 layers of meringue with the chocolate cream and cover the top and sides of the cake with the icing. Sprinkle the top with shredded toasted almonds and sprinkle the almonds with confectioners' sugar. Let the cake ripen for 24 hours before serving. Makes 16 to 20 servings.

Meringue Shells

BRUSH a baking sheet with vegetable oil and dust it lightly with flour. With an oval spoon scoop out ovals of plain meringue about the size of an egg. Using the forefinger, push the ovals off the spoon onto the baking sheet, spacing them about 1 inch apart. Or fit a pastry bag with a large round tube and fill the bag with the meringue. Press out ovals 1 inch apart onto the baking sheet, pushing the bag gently backward several times while the meringue is being forced out, to give the shells a wavy surface.

Sprinkle the meringues with very fine granulated sugar and bake them in a very slow oven (250° F.) for about 30 minutes. Do not let them color. If they are very thick, bake them for 1 hour. During the baking, leave the oven door ajar, wedged with a piece of paper. If the meringues start to take on color, lower the oven temperature. Or turn off the oven heat completely and leave the meringues in the oven for 4 to 5 hours, or overnight.

While the meringues are still warm, hold each in the palm of the hand and press the undersurface with the end of an eggshell or thumb, to make a shell. Put the shells upside down on the baking sheet, and let them dry in the still warm oven with the heat off.

Whipped Cream Meringues

MAKE 12 meringue shells and pair them. (Make the shells small for *petits fours* on a pastry tray, or large for dessert meringues.) Press one shell on each side of a scoop of whipped cream, sweetened and flavored to taste, or vanilla whipped cream. If desired, tint the cream pale green with food coloring.

The whipped cream may be flavored with any liqueur and enriched by chopped almonds or pistachios.

Or whip red currant jelly with a fork and fold it into the whipped cream before joining the meringue shells. Decorate further with rosettes of whipped cream and fresh currants, raspberries, or strawberries.

OMELETTE NORVÉGIENNE AUX CERISES ## Cherry Alaska

PIT and cut in half 1 pound sweet black cherries. Sprinkle them lightly with sugar to taste, add 1/2 cup kirsch, and chill the fruit.

Beat 4 egg whites until they are stiff enough to form peaks and gradually fold in 3/4 cup sifted confectioners' sugar. Set the meringue aside.

Cover a bread board with white paper and place a thin round layer of spongecake on the paper. Cover the cake base with a layer of the cherries, reserving about half the quantity for the decoration. Arrange 1 quart raspberry ice in brick or melon form on the cake, leaving a 1/2- to 1-inch border of cake. Trim the cake border to the shape of the ice. Cover the entire surface of the ice and the rim of the cake as quickly as possible with a thick coating of the meringue. Dust the meringue well with sifted confectioners' sugar and set the Alaska in a very hot oven (450° F.) for 3 to 5 min-

Coffee Rum Pie

utes, or just until the meringue is delicately browned. The board, paper, cake, and meringue are poor conductors of heat and will help prevent the ice from melting, but be sure the ice is as cold as possible.

Slip the baked Alaska quickly onto a chilled platter and surround it with the rest of the cherries. Sprinkle the fruit with heated kirsch or brandy, ignite the spirit, and serve at once.

Coffee Rum Pie

BEAT 4 egg whites with a pinch of salt until they are foamy and add 1/8 teaspoon cream of tartar. Beat in 1 cup very fine granulated sugar, a tablespoon at a time, and beat the meringue until it is stiff and glossy. Spread some of the meringue on the bottom of a buttered 9-inch pie plate. Using a pastry bag fitted with a decorative tube, pipe the remaining meringue in a border around the pie plate, to make a shell. Pipe small rosettes of meringue on a buttered baking sheet. Bake the shell and rosettes in a slow oven (275° F.) for about 50 minutes, or until the meringue is golden and firm, and cool the shell.

In the top of a double boiler combine 1 cup heavy cream with 1/2 cup each of strong coffee and light rum, 6 tablespoons sugar, 3 tablespoons flour, and 1/2 tablespoon cornstarch. Bring the mixture to a boil, stirring constantly, and set the pan over boiling water. Cook the mixture for a few minutes until it thickens. Beat 5 egg yolks until they are light and lemon-colored. Blend a little of the cream mixture with the egg yolks and stir the eggs slowly into the pan. Cook the custard, stirring constantly, for 2 or 3 minutes longer. Add 2 tablespoons dark rum and stir the custard over cracked ice until it is cool. Pour the filling into the shell and decorate it with the meringue rosettes.

Graham-Cracker Piecrust

WITH a rolling pin crush enough graham crackers to make 1 1/2 cups fine crumbs. Add 1/4 cup sugar and 1/2 cup melted butter and mix thoroughly. Line a buttered 9-inch pie plate with the mixture, pressing it firmly with the back of a spoon against the bottom and sides. Before filling the crust, chill it for 20 minutes, or bake it in a moderately slow oven (325° F.) for 10 minutes and cool it.

⤳ Lime Pie

LINE a buttered 9-inch pie plate with graham-cracker piecrust. In the top of a double boiler combine 4 egg yolks, 1/2 cup sugar, 6 tablespoons lime juice, 1 tablespoon butter, and 1 teaspoon grated lime rind. Cook the custard over simmering water, stirring constantly, until it is as thick as heavy cream. Remove the pan from the heat. Stir in 2 teaspoons gelatin, softened in 1/4 cup cold water and thoroughly dissolved over hot water, and cool the custard. Fold in 4 egg whites, stiffly beaten with 1/3 cup sugar and 1/2 teaspoon vanilla. Pour the filling into the prepared shell and chill the pie for several hours.

⤳ Mango Chiffon Pie

LINE a buttered 9-inch pie plate with graham-cracker piecrust. Press enough mango sauce through a sieve to make 2/3 cup purée. Add the purée to 4 egg yolks, lightly beaten, stir in 1/4 cup sugar, and cook the custard in the top of a double boiler over hot water, stirring constantly, until it thickens. Stir in 1 tablespoon gelatin, softened in 1/4 cup cold water, and cook the custard, stirring, until the gelatin is dissolved. Remove the pan from the heat and add 1 teaspoon lemon juice. Cool the custard and fold in 4 egg whites, stiffly beaten with 1/4 cup sugar. Pour the filling into the prepared shell, chill the pie, and spread it with whipped cream.

Mango Sauce

WASH, peel, and slice enough half-ripe mangoes to make 6 cups. Add 1 1/2 cups water and cook the fruit until it is soft. Add 1 1/2 to 2 cups sugar and cook the sauce for 5 minutes longer.

⤳ Grasshopper Pie

WITH a rolling pin crush enough chocolate wafers to make 1 1/2 cups fine crumbs. Mix the crumbs with 1/4 cup each of sugar and melted sweet butter. Press the crumbs firmly against the bottom and sides of a well-buttered 9-inch pie plate. Bake the crust in a very hot oven (450° F.) for 5 minutes and cool it.

Soften 1 1/2 teaspoons gelatin in 1/3 cup heavy cream and dissolve it over hot water. Beat 1/4 cup sugar into 4 beaten egg yolks. Stir in 1/4 cup each of crème de cacao and green crème de menthe, and the dissolved gelatin. Chill the mixture until it is slightly thickened. Fold in 1 cup heavy cream, whipped. Pour the filling into the prepared shell and chill the pie until it is firm. Sprinkle the pie with crushed mint-flavored chocolate.

Walnut Pastry

SIFT 1 1/2 cups sifted flour with a pinch of salt and add 1/2 cup ground walnuts. With a pastry blender or 2 knives cut in 1/2 cup butter. Add gradually 3 tablespoons ice water, or enough to hold the particles together. Chill the dough thoroughly. Makes enough for two 9-inch flan rings or 12 small tart shells.

Prune Tart with Walnut Pastry

SOAK large sweet prunes in water to cover for 1 hour, simmer them for 10 minutes, and drain them. Measure 2 cups prunes, pit them, and cut them into quarters. Line a 9-inch flan ring with walnut tart pastry and sprinkle it lightly with a little flour. Add the prunes and sprinkle them with the juice of 1 orange. Cover the prunes with 1/2 cup sugar sifted with 1 tablespoon flour and dot them with butter. If the filling seems too dry, add 3 or 4 tablespoons prune juice. Bake the tart in a hot oven (400° F.) for 10 minutes, reduce the heat to moderately slow (325° F.), and bake the tart for 15 minutes more, or until the pastry is firm and golden.

SAVARIN DOUGH

Pâte à Savarin

SPRINKLE 1 package of yeast into 2/3 cup lukewarm milk and stir until the yeast is dissolved. Sift 2 cups sifted flour into a warm bowl, make a well in the center, and add the dissolved yeast, 2 teaspoons sugar, and 1/4 teaspoon salt. Break 4 eggs, warmed to room temperature, into the well and blend the center ingredients together thoroughly. With the fingers mix the flour into the center ingredients. Beat the dough thoroughly, raising it up high with the fingers and letting it fall back again into the bowl with each motion. Cover the bowl lightly with a damp towel and let the dough stand in a warm place for about 45 minutes, or until it doubles in bulk. Stir the dough down, spread it with 1/2 cup soft sweet butter, and beat it again by hand for about 10 minutes, or with the bread-hook attachment of a mixer for 5 minutes. The dough should be soft, but it should not stick to the sides of the bowl or to the hand. The *pâte à Savarin* is now ready to be transferred by hand to well-buttered molds.

Manon

BUTTER a deep charlotte or timbale mold and fill it half full with Savarin dough. Cover the mold with a damp towel and let the dough stand in a warm place until it rises almost to the top. Bake the cake in a hot oven (400° F.) for 40 to 45 minutes, or until it tests done. Unmold the cake and cut it crosswise into 5 layers. Sprinkle the layers lightly with kirsch and assemble the cake, spreading each layer thickly with pastry cream. Spread the top and sides with hot sieved apricot jam and cover the jam thickly with blanched almonds, slivered and toasted. Sprinkle with confectioners' sugar.

Savarins with Strawberries

BUTTER small Savarin molds and fill them half full with Savarin dough. Cover the molds with damp towels and let them stand in a warm place until the dough rises to the top. Bake the cakes in a hot oven (400° F.) for about 25 minutes, or until they test done. Wrap the molds in towels and invert them on a wire rack. After 5 to 10 minutes, loosen the edge of each cake with a sharp knife and unmold.

While the cakes are still warm saturate them with sugar syrup II flavored with Madeira or Grand Marnier to taste. Fill the centers of the cakes with lightly sugared fresh strawberries sprinkled, if desired, with a few drops of vanilla. A large Savarin may be finished and served in the same way.

Almond Refrigerator Cookies

CREAM 1 cup butter with 1/2 cup each of white and brown sugar until the mixture is light and fluffy. Add 2 beaten eggs, 1 cup coarsely chopped blanched almonds, and 2 tablespoons vanilla, and blend the mixture thoroughly. Sift 2 3/4 cups sifted flour with 1/2 teaspoon each of baking soda and salt, and gradually blend the dry ingredients into the creamed mixture. Form the dough into a long roll about 2 1/2 inches in diameter. Wrap the roll in wax paper and chill it for several hours. Cut the cookies into 1/8-inch slices, place them on a buttered baking sheet, and bake them in a hot oven (400° F.) for 6 minutes. Makes about 6 dozen cookies. Store in an airtight tin.

Almond Wafers 🐾

CREAM together thoroughly 1/2 pound soft butter and 1 heaping cup sifted confectioners' sugar. Work in 3 cups finely ground blanched almonds. Drop the mixture by teaspoons onto a buttered baking sheet, spacing the cookies well apart, and bake them in a moderately slow oven (325° F.) until they are golden brown.

LANGUES DE CHAT

Cats' Tongues 🐾

CREAM 1/4 cup butter, add 1/4 cup sugar and 1/2 teaspoon vanilla, and beat the mixture until it is light and fluffy. Add 2 egg whites, one at a time, mixing well after each addition. Sift 1/4 cup flour, a little at a time, over the surface of the mixture and carefully fold it in. Pack the batter in a pastry bag fitted with a small plain tube and pipe tiny strips, about 2 inches long and as thick as a pencil, onto a buttered and floured baking sheet. Bake the cats' tongues in a very hot oven (450° F.) for about 4 minutes, or until the edges become golden. Remove them from the baking sheet and cool on unglazed paper.

Chocolate Sablés 🐾

MOUND 2 cups sifted flour on a marble slab or pastry board. Make a well in the center and add 1 cup sugar. Add the sieved yolks of 4 hard-cooked eggs, 4 raw egg yolks, 2 ounces dark sweet chocolate, melted and cooled, and 1/2 cup soft butter. Blend the center ingredients together thoroughly, work in the flour, and knead the dough very lightly until it forms a smooth round ball. Chill the dough, roll it out 1/4 inch thick on a lightly floured board, and cut it into rounds. Put the rounds on a buttered baking sheet and bake them in a moderate oven (350° F.) for about 15 minutes, or until they are browned and firm to the touch. Cool the rounds and sandwich them together with a thick layer of chocolate butter cream.

❦ Hazelnut Cookies

BEAT 3 egg yolks with 2/3 cup sugar and 2 tablespoons lemon juice until the mixture is light and creamy. Add the grated rind of 1 lemon, 1 1/2 cups hazelnuts, ground, 2 tablespoons flour, and 1/2 teaspoon baking powder. Roll out the dough 1/4 inch thick on a board sprinkled with sugar. Cut it into diamond shapes, dipping the cutter in sugar after each cookie is cut. Arrange the cookies on buttered and floured baking sheets and bake them in a moderately slow oven (325° F.) for 12 to 15 minutes, or until they are puffed. Remove them from the sheets and cool them. Beat together 1 cup confectioners' sugar and 2 tablespoons lemon juice and coat the cookies with the glaze.

❦ Honey Cookies

CREAM 1/2 cup butter and gradually beat in 1/2 cup sugar and 1 cup honey. Beat in 2 egg yolks, well beaten, and 1 teaspoon vanilla. Sift 3 cups sifted flour with 3 teaspoons baking powder and 1/4 teaspoon each of salt and cinnamon. Stir in 1/4 cup chopped blanched almonds and 1/2 cup chopped citron. Gradually blend the dry ingredients into the creamed mixture. Drop the batter by teaspoons onto a buttered baking sheet and bake the cookies in a moderate oven (350° F.) for 12 minutes.

Some honey is thinner than others; if a sample cookie spreads too much, add a little more flour to the batter.

❦ Ladyfingers

BEAT 3 egg whites until they are stiff but not dry and beat in, a little at a time, 1/3 cup sugar. Beat 3 egg yolks until they are thick and pale in color and fold them into the egg whites with 1 tablespoon vanilla, a pinch of salt, and 1 tablespoon hot water. Fold in carefully 1/2 cup sifted flour.

Spoon the batter into a pastry bag fitted with a plain round tube and press out strips, about 2 1/2 inches long and 3/4 inch wide, onto a baking sheet covered with heavy paper. Sprinkle the strips lightly with fine granulated sugar and bake them in a moderate oven (350° F.) for about 12 minutes, or until they are a delicate golden brown. Let the ladyfingers cool on the paper and store them in a tightly closed container in a cool dry place.

Meringue Ladyfingers

IN a heavy saucepan boil 1 cup sugar and 1/3 cup water until the syrup forms a soft ball when a little is dropped into cold water, or until a candy thermometer registers 250° F. Beat the syrup very gradually into 4 egg whites, stiffly beaten, and beat the mixture until it holds its shape when the beater is withdrawn. Stir in 1/4 teaspoon almond extract and fold in 1 1/4 cups sifted confectioners' sugar. Pack the batter into a pastry bag fitted with a small round tube and press out strips approximately 3 inches long and 3/4 inch wide onto a buttered and floured baking sheet. Bake the ladyfingers in a very slow oven (275° F.) for 20 to 30 minutes without letting them color. Remove them from the baking sheet while they are still warm and dry them on a wire rack.

Lace Cookies

CREAM 3 tablespoons butter with 1 cup brown sugar and beat in 4 tablespoons flour, 1 beaten egg, 1 cup ground blanched almonds, 1 teaspoon vanilla extract, and 1/2 teaspoon almond extract. Drop the dough by teaspoons onto a buttered baking sheet, spacing the cookies 3 inches apart. Bake the cookies in a moderately hot oven (375° F.) for about 8 to 10 minutes, or until they are crisp. Remove the cookies from the sheet immediately and cool them on a wire rack.

Rolled Lace Cookies

COMBINE 1 cup each of sifted flour and finely chopped nuts. Combine in a saucepan 1/2 cup light or dark corn syrup, 1/4 cup each of butter and shortening, and 2/3 cup firmly packed brown sugar, and bring the mixture just to the boiling point. Remove it immediately from the heat and gradually blend in the flour and nut mixture. Drop the dough by rounded teaspoons onto a buttered baking sheet, spacing the cookies 3 inches apart. Bake them in a moderately slow oven (325° F.) for 8 to 10 minutes, or until they are delicately browned. Let them cool for a minute and remove them carefully from the baking sheet with a spatula. Roll the cookies into cone shapes while they are still warm and cool them on a wire rack. Makes about 5 dozen.

ᔐ Macaroons

BLEND 1 cup (1/2 pound) almond paste with 1 cup sugar. Work the mixture with the hands until it is well blended and work in 3 egg whites, one at a time, mixing well after each addition. The mixture should be soft enough to go easily through a pastry tube yet firm enough to hold its shape on the baking sheet, and the amount of egg white must be judged accordingly.

Pack the dough in a pastry bag fitted with a plain round tube and press it out into small mounds, spaced well apart, onto a baking sheet covered with unglazed paper. Or drop the dough from the tip of a teaspoon. Sprinkle the macaroons with a little fine granulated sugar and bake them in a slow oven (300° F.) for 25 to 30 minutes. Transfer the baking paper to a damp cloth and carefully loosen and remove the macaroons. Cool the cookies on a wire rack.

ᔐ Christmas Spice Cookie Birds

IN a heavy saucepan cook 2 cups brown sugar and 1/2 cup honey over low heat, stirring, until the sugar is dissolved. Stir in 1/4 cup butter and cool the mixture. Sift together 3 cups sifted flour, 1 tablespoon baking powder, 1 teaspoon cinnamon, and 1/4 teaspoon each of ground cloves and nutmeg. Stir the dry ingredients into the sugar mixture alternately with 1 egg beaten with 2 tablespoons milk. Add 1/4 cup finely ground citron, the grated rind and juice of 1 lemon, and more flour, if necessary, to make a light dough that is easy to work. Roll out the dough 1/8 inch thick on a lightly floured board and cut it in the shape of birds. Place the cookies on a buttered baking sheet and bake them in a moderate oven (350° F.) for 6 minutes. Decorate the birds in any desired pattern with decorator's icing.

ᔐ Swiss Bowknots

SIFT 4 cups sifted flour and 14 tablespoons sugar into a mixing bowl and add the grated rind of 1 lemon. Make a well in the center and in it put 4 eggs and 1 cup heavy cream. Mix the center ingredients together and gradually work in the flour mixture, making a paste stiff enough to roll out. Cover the dough and let it stand for 1 hour.

Roll out the dough thinly on a lightly floured board and cut it into strips 6 inches long and 1 1/2 inches wide. Make a slit 2 inches long in the middle of each strip and draw the ends of the strip through the slit to form a knot. Fry the knots, a few at a time, in deep hot fat (370° F.), until they are golden. Drain the knots on absorbent paper and sprinkle them with confectioners' sugar.

Almond Paste 🐎

GRIND 1 cup almonds, blanched and thoroughly dried, and pound them to a smooth paste in a mortar. Add 1/4 cup each of sifted confectioners' sugar and granulated sugar and blend the paste thoroughly. Store in a tightly covered container.

Almond Cream Paste 🐎

MIX together 1/2 cup each of ground blanched almonds and sifted confectioners' sugar. Add 1 egg yolk and pound the mixture until it is smooth. Gradually work in 1/4 cup each of soft butter and rum or brandy and 1 beaten egg yolk.

Apricot Purée 🐎

SOAK 1 pound dried apricots overnight in water barely to cover. Cook the fruit in the same water until it is very tender. Force the apricots through a sieve or purée them in a blender and chill the purée well.

Apricot Glaze 🐎

ADD 1/2 cup sugar to half the recipe for apricot purée and cook the purée until the sugar is dissolved, stirring it constantly to prevent scorching. Pour the glaze into a jar, cover it, and cool. To use, thin the glaze with a little hot water.

Prune Purée 🐎

SOAK 1 1/2 pounds dried prunes overnight in water barely to cover. Cook the fruit in the same water until it is very tender. Cool the fruit and remove the pits. Force the prunes through a sieve or purée them in a blender and chill the purée well.

❧ Coconut Milk

CRACK a coconut by holding the end with the eyes in it firmly in the hand, and giving the other end a series of glancing blows all around with a hammer. Grate the meat of the coconut, add to it 1 quart hot milk, and let it stand for 1 hour. Strain the liquid through a double layer of cheesecloth and squeeze the coconut meat until it is dry. The liquid thus obtained is coconut milk.

❧ Lemon or Orange Zest

SELECT firm lemons or oranges. Using a sharp knife or a lemon stripper, pare off a layer of rind, or zest, so thin that none of the white part is included. Cut the zest into julienne, simmer the strips in water to cover for 2 minutes, and drain them. The parboiling will make the zest tender and keep the flavor from overpowering the dish.

❧ Orange Sugar

REMOVE the zest of 6 oranges, taking care not to include any of the pith. Place the strips of rind in a warm dry place for 1 or 2 days, or until most of the moisture has evaporated. Pound them in a mortar with 2 cups sugar. Sift the orange sugar into a pint jar and cover it tightly.

❧ Vanilla Sugar

BURY a 1-inch piece of vanilla bean in a jar of granulated sugar and cover the jar tightly. The sugar will have absorbed the flavor of the bean in a few days.

Or split a piece of vanilla bean and scrape out the little seeds. Combine the seeds with sifted confectioners' sugar and crush together thoroughly.

❧ Crème Chantilly   VANILLA WHIPPED CREAM

WHIP heavy cream slowly in a chilled bowl until it begins to thicken. The cream should not be too stiff or heavy. Into each cup whipped cream stir 1 to 1 1/2 tablespoons vanilla sugar, or 1 to 1 1/2 tablespoons sugar and 1/2 teaspoon vanilla extract. Continue beating the cream until it is thick enough to hold its shape.

Crème au Beurre

IN a heavy saucepan combine 9 tablespoons sugar with 1/3 cup water and 1/4 teaspoon cream of tartar. Cook the syrup slowly, stirring with a wooden spoon, until the sugar is dissolved. Increase the heat and boil the syrup rapidly, without stirring, until a candy thermometer registers 238° F., or a drop pressed between thumb and forefinger forms a thin thread when the fingers are separated about 1/2 inch. Remove the pan from the heat.

Beat 5 egg yolks, preferably with an electric beater, until they are light and fluffy, and gradually beat in the syrup in a thin steady stream. Continue to beat the mixture until it is thick and cool. Still beating add, bit by bit, 1/2 pound sweet butter, slightly soft but still firm. In warm weather the cream may be too soft to hold its shape; chill it for a few minutes until it is firm enough to spread on the cake.

Chocolate Butter Cream

MELT 3 ounces dark sweet chocolate or 2 ounces unsweetened chocolate over hot water and cool it. Add the chocolate to the finished butter cream and flavor with rum or brandy to taste.

Kirsch Butter Cream

FOLLOW the recipe for butter cream, adding 1 or 2 tablespoons kirsch to the sugar syrup. Or stir the kirsch carefully and thoroughly into the finished cream.

Lemon or Orange Butter Cream

STIR 1 tablespoon grated lemon or orange rind and 1 tablespoon lemon or orange juice into the finished butter cream and tint with a few drops of yellow or orange food coloring. Flavor with orange-flavored liqueur to taste.

Mocha Butter Cream

FOLLOW the recipe for butter cream, substituting very strong coffee for water in making the sugar syrup. Flavor the finished cream with 1 tablespoon coffee essence and with rum, if desired.

Pineapple Butter Cream

STIR 1/2 cup crushed and drained ripe pineapple into the finished butter cream and flavor it with a few drops of kirsch to taste.

ꙅ Crème Pâtissière   PASTRY CREAM

SCALD 1 1/2 cups milk with a large piece of vanilla bean. If vanilla extract or liqueur flavorings are used, add them when the cream is cooked.

In a heavy saucepan beat 1/2 cup sugar and 4 egg yolks with a wire whisk until the mixture is thick and creamy enough to form a "ribbon" when the whisk is withdrawn. Sift into the mixture 1/4 cup flour, mixing just enough to blend. Stir in the scalded milk very gradually until the batter is smooth. Cook the mixture over low heat, stirring it vigorously with a whisk, until it reaches the boiling point. Remove the vanilla bean (and add a few drops of any desired flavoring) and strain the cream through a fine sieve. Stir the cream as it cools.

Chocolate Pastry Cream

MELT 2 ounces unsweetened baking chocolate over hot water. Follow the recipe for pastry cream, adding the chocolate to the scalded milk before combining it with the egg and sugar mixture.

Mocha Pastry Cream

FOLLOW the recipe for pastry cream. Scald the milk with 1/3 cup ground coffee. Cover the pan tightly and let the milk infuse for 15 minutes.

Praline Pastry Cream

To 1 cup pastry cream flavored with coffee, chocolate, or vanilla, add 4 tablespoons praline powder.

Praline Powder

IN a heavy saucepan combine 1 cup each of sugar and unblanched almonds or hazelnuts. Cook the mixture over medium heat, stirring constantly, until the syrup turns a rich amber. Pour the syrup and nuts into a lightly buttered shallow pan to cool. Pulverize the praline in a mortar and store the powder in the refrigerator.

SAINT HONORÉ CREAM   ## Crème Saint-Honoré 𝕱🐾

SOFTEN 1 tablespoon gelatin in 2 tablespoons cold water and dissolve it in 1 1/2 cups hot pastry cream. Beat 6 egg whites until they are stiff but not dry and beat in 1/3 cup sugar. Fold this meringue into the cream.

Fondant 𝕱🐾

IN a heavy-bottomed 2-quart saucepan combine 2 cups sugar with 3/4 cup boiling water. Cook the syrup slowly, stirring constantly with a wooden spoon, until the sugar is dissolved. Still stirring, bring the mixture to a boil and blend in 1/8 teaspoon cream of tartar. Cover the pan and boil the syrup for 3 minutes: the steam will wash down and melt any crystals that may have formed on the sides. Remove the cover and put in a candy thermometer. Increase the heat and boil the syrup, without stirring, until the thermometer registers 238° F. (During the cooking, remove any crystals that form on the sides of the pan with a fork or brush wrapped in muslin and moistened in hot water. Use an upward motion, to prevent the crystals from falling in the syrup.) Remove the syrup from the heat without jarring the pan and let it stand until bubbles no longer rise to the surface.

Pour the syrup onto a moistened and chilled marble slab or large flat platter to cool, pouring only that which leaves the pan easily. Do not shake the pan or scrape the sides to remove the remaining syrup. When the center of the mass of fondant feels slightly warm, about 110° F., work the fondant vigorously with a wooden paddle or spatula, scraping and folding it over and over until it becomes white and opaque. When it forms a crumbly white mass and can no longer be worked with a paddle, let it rest for a few minutes and knead it with the hands until it becomes soft and creamy. Cover the fondant with a damp cloth and put it in a tightly covered jar. Let it ripen at room temperature for at least 2 days before using it. Add coloring and flavoring after the fondant has ripened.

To use the fondant as icing: warm it over hot water, thin it to the desired consistency with boiling water, and flavor it to taste with vanilla or almond extract or with any liqueur.

Flavorings for Fondant

FONDANT may be flavored with a variety of liqueurs, fruit juices, syrups, or extracts. For each cup of fondant, use 1 tablespoon rum, kirsch, brandy, Curaçao, or anisette, or 1/2 teaspoon almond or vanilla extract.

Coffee Fondant

ADD 1/2 teaspoon instant coffee dissolved in 1 teaspoon hot water to 1 cup warmed fondant. Or add 1/2 teaspoon coffee extract to 1 cup warmed fondant.

Chocolate Fondant

ADD 2 squares unsweetened baking chocolate, melted and cooled to lukewarm, to 1 cup warmed fondant.

Sugar Syrup I

IN a heavy saucepan combine 2 1/2 cups sugar, 1 1/4 cups water, and 3/4 cup white corn syrup. Cook the syrup over low heat, stirring constantly, until the sugar is completely dissolved. Wash down the crystals that form on the sides of the saucepan with a spoon wrapped in a damp cloth. Cover the pan tightly and let the syrup stand for 5 minutes, so that the steam will dissolve any remaining crystals on the sides of the pan. Remove the lid and boil the syrup for 5 minutes without stirring. Cool the syrup and store it at room temperature in a tightly covered container.

Special Acknowledgments

We wish to express our appreciation to the many firms who made available the beautiful accessories that appear in the color photographs of this book.

17, *pewter platter, butter plate, honey pitcher, knife and fork*—Julia E. Kuttner; *background print*—New York Graphic Society; *printed fabric*—Brunschwig & Fils, Inc.

20, *serving spoon and fork*—Royal Worcester Porcelain Co., Inc.; *salt shaker and pepper mill*—Bloomingdale's; *blue glass*—Ginori Fifth Avenue; *screen*—Molla, Inc.; *tablecloth and napkins*—The Irish Linen Guild.

25, *chop plate, serving spoon and fork, glasses, vermeil flowers*—Tiffany & Co.; *table*—Mills-Denmark, Inc.; *linen mat and napkins*—Leron, Inc.

28, *cream soup dish, dinner plate, wooden salt shaker, napkin*—Bloomingdale's; *silver flatware*—Towle Silversmiths; *background print*—New York Graphic Society.

37, *antique chafing dish*—S. Wyler, Inc.; *antique bronze busts*—Past and Present; *background fabric*—Henrose Co., Inc.

40, *antique platter, fish servers*—S. Wyler, Inc.; *pottery handkerchief bowl*—Leigh Hammond, Inc.; *dinner bell*—Past and Present; *background fabric*—Brunschwig & Fils, Inc.

45, *silver platter and carving set*—Plummer and McCutcheon; *flower holder, hurricane candlesticks*—Bergdorf Goodman Co.; *background fabric*—Brunschwig & Fils, Inc.

48, *platter*—Lenox China Co.; *glasses*—Baccarat; *silver bowl, serving spoon and fork*—Reed & Barton.

57, *casserole, ladle, raffia mat*—Bonniers, Inc.; *screen*—Chequer.

60, *plate, bowl*—Tiffany & Co.; *tablecloth*—Brunschwig & Fils, Inc.

69, *china leaf platter*—Bonwit Teller; *bird cage*—Stuart Gifts; *glass pig*—Soupçon Food & Gift Shop; *background fabric*—Brunschwig & Fils, Inc.

72, *marble trivets*—Bergdorf Goodman Co.; *antique wire baskets*—Stark Valla Emporium.

81, *compote dish, china figurines*—Lord & Taylor; *metal ribbon bow*—Soupçon Food & Gift Shop; *background fabric*—Jofa, Inc.

84, *brass pot, wooden spoon, wooden dove*—Bloomingdale's; *wine rack*—Sherry Wine & Spirits Co., Inc.

93, *tureen, plate, bowl*—La Cuisinière, Inc.

96, *silver platter, serving spoon and fork*—Reed & Barton; *glasses, flower holder, porcelain figurine*—Bonwit Teller; *tablecloth*—Mosse Linens.

105, *salad bowl, salad servers, cruets*—Bloomingdale's; *duck*—Bergdorf Goodman Co.

108, *fish platter*—Laurent Restaurant; *spice box*—Liebholden-Wallach, Inc.; *napkins*—Plummer and McCutcheon; *metal wreath*—Stuart Gifts.

117, *gold-plated silver platter and carving set*—International Silver Co.; *gold attelet*—Cartier, Inc.; *music box*—Sponholz; *background fabric*—Crompton-Richmond Co., Inc.

120, *platter*—Plummer and McCutcheon; *owl salt and pepper shakers*—Soupçon Food & Gift Shop; *background fabric*—F. Schumacher & Co.

129, *plate*—Soupçon Food & Gift Shop.

132, no special acknowledgments.

141, *teak trays*—Jon's Scandinavian Shop.

144, *papier-mâché tray*—Azuma:

153, *plate, antique candelabra, shell flower holder*—Past and Present; *silver salt and pepper shakers, fork*—Tiffany & Co.; *background fabric*—Brunschwig & Fils, Inc.

156, no special acknowledgments.

173, *background fabric*—Jofa, Inc.

176, *Italian celery dishes*—Stark Valla Emporium; *background fabric*—F. Schumacher & Co.

185, *bowl, ladle, forks*—Bloomingdale's; *mosaic marble table*—Niccolini, Inc.

188, *Creuset pot, Swiss strainer, cutlet bat*—Bazar Français; *antique wrought iron*—Liebholden Wallach, Inc.; *linen cloth*—Jofa, Inc.

197, *red birds, owl salt and pepper shakers, butter plate, dinner plate, soup plate and dish, tureen, vermeil flatware, glasses*—Bonwit Teller; *tablecloth and napkin*—The Irish Linen Guild.

200, *ironstone tureen, dinner plate, soup plate*—Bloomingdale's; *glass candy jar, wooden canister*—A. Sajet; *wooden map panels*—Interiors' Import Co., Inc.

209, *sauce bowl, spoon*—Reed & Barton; *plate, soup plate*—Fostoria Glass Co.; *tablecloth*—Motta, Inc.; *carnations*—Colorado Carnations.

212, *dinner plate, soup plate*—Lenox China Co.; *soup spoon*—International Silver Co.; *temple, silk sari*—Government of India Tourist Office; *brass lion*—Sojani & Co., Inc.

229, *antique French café au lait set*—Soupçon Food & Gift Shop; *cups and saucers, sugar bowl*—The Mediterranean Shop; *basket*—

Bloomingdale's; *background fabric*—F. Schumacher & Co.

232, *antique plate and salad bowl, bird salt and pepper shakers*—Soupçon Food & Gift Shop.

241, *scales, glass jar, spice rack*—Bloomingdale's *background wallpaper*—F. Schumacher & Co.

244, *iron pot*—Bloomingdale's; *soldiers*—Lord & Taylor; *antique wooden scoop*—Liebholden Wallach, Inc.; *linen cloth*—Jofa, Inc.

253, *omelet plate, caviar holder, toast rack*—La Cuisinière, Inc.; *silver flatware*—Towle Silversmiths.

256, *egg holder, warmer*—Soupçon Food & Gift Shop; *spoon, pewter salt dish and pepper shaker*—La Cuisinière, Inc.; *background fabric*—Jofa, Inc.

261, *serving spoon and fork, straw mats, crystal fish*—Lord & Taylor.

264, *platter*—Henri Bendel, Inc.; *antique glass inkwell*—Stuart Gifts; *wire basket*—Soupçon Food & Gift Shop; *carnations*—Colorado Carnations.

273, *chop plate*—Lenox China Co.; *serving spoon and fork*—Towle Silversmiths; *table, chair*—Molla, Inc.; *napkins*—Bloomingdale's.

276, *platter*—Bonwit Teller; *china flower basket*—Henri Bendel, Inc.; *background fabric*—F. Schumacher & Co.

281, *antique pot*—Mary Muller; *background wallpaper*—F. Schumacher & Co.

284, *scale*—Bazar Français; *platter*—Plummer and McCutcheon; *background fabric*—Brunschwig & Fils, Inc.

293, *meat platter, vegetable bowl, carving set*—International Silver Co.; *tablecloth*—Belgian Linen Association; *salt shaker, pepper mill*—Bloomingdale's.

296, *wire basket, glasses*—Bloomingdale's; *tablecloth*—The Irish Linen Guild.

305, *platter*—Lord & Taylor; *carving set*—Plummer and McCutcheon; *flower box*—Bonwit Teller; *background fabric*—Jofa, Inc.

308, *copper chafing dish, luncheon plates*—Ginori Fifth Avenue; *marble table*—Niccolini, Inc.; *napkins*—The Irish Linen Guild.

313, *platter, wood carving, pottery roses, grape flower holder*—Leigh Hammond, Inc.; *background fabric*—Jofa, Inc.

316, *china stand, plates*—Bonwit Teller; *background fabric*—Henrose Co., Inc.

325, *silver platter*—S. Wyler, Inc.; *birds*—Plummer and McCutcheon; *background fabric*—Brunschwig & Fils, Inc.

328, *silver tray*—James Robinson, Inc.; *background fabric*—F. Schumacher & Co.

333, *platter*—The Mediterranean Shop; *carving set*—Tiffany & Co.; *background wallpaper*—F. Schumacher & Co.

336, *terrine*—Bazar Français; *cruet*—La Cuisinière, Inc.

345, *platter, carving set, sauceboat*—Reed & Barton; *decanter*—Fostoria Glass Co.; *wall flower holder*—Soupçon Food & Gift Shop; *tablecloth*—The Irish Linen Guild; *background fabric*—Brunschwig & Fils, Inc.

348, *silver platter, serving spoon and fork*—Black Starr & Frost, Ltd.; *crystal swans and glasses*—Georg Jensen, Inc.

357, *copper au gratin dish, basket strainer, antique glass box*—La Cuisinière, Inc.

360, *casseroles*—La Cuisinière, Inc.

369, *basket grill*—Hammacher Schlemmer; *bowl, sauce pail, pepper mill, cutlery board, glass jar*—Bonniers, Inc.; *background wallpaper*—Brunschwig & Fils, Inc.

372, *silver platter*—Black Starr & Frost, Ltd.; *silver attelet*—Bazar Français; *background fabric*—Jofa, Inc.

389, *brass tray, tole bracket*—Bloomingdale's; *cheese shaker, ramekins for sauces*—La Cuisinière, Inc.

392, *pewter casserole, serving spoon*—La Cuisinière, Inc.; *pewter pitcher, salt and pepper shakers*—Bloomingdale's; *tablecloth*—Belgian Linen Association.

401, *copper paella*—Bazar Français.

404, *plate, flower holder, candle holder*—Bloomingdale's.

413, *silver vegetable dish, vinegar rack*—S. Wyler, Inc.; *tablecloth*—Jofa, Inc.; *background wallpaper*—Jackson Ellis Co., Inc.

416, *glass platter*—Bergdorf Goodman Co.; *serving spoon and fork*—International Silver Co.; *baby chickens salt and pepper shakers*—Mayhew.

425, *pewter pitcher*—Richard Ginori.

428, *plates, flower holders*—Bonwit Teller; *background fabric*—Jofa, Inc.

437, *fluted baking dish*—Bazar Français; *background fabric*—F. Schumacher & Co.

440, *soufflé dishes*—Bazar Français; *plates*—Bloomingdale's; *antique miniature desk*—Bergdorf Goodman Co.; *background fabric*—F. Schumacher & Co.

453, *brass platter, planter, screen*—Lord & Taylor; *bell*—La Cuisinière, Inc.

456, *stainless steel platter*—Bloomingdale's; *bowl*—The Mediterranean Shop; *salad basket*—La Cuisinière, Inc.; *background fabric*—Jofa, Inc.

465, *bowl, decanter*—Bonwit Teller.

468, *wooden bowl and spoon*—Bonniers, Inc.

481, *cruet set*—Bonwit Teller; *serving fork*—Bonniers, Inc.; *background wallpaper*—Brunschwig & Fils, Inc.

484, *salad bowl, salad servers*—Lord & Taylor; *table*—Mills-Denmark, Inc.; *background brick composition*—Katzenbach & Warren, Inc.

493, *mixing bowl, white bowl*—La Cuisinière, Inc.; *hanging plate, pitcher, sand timer, pewter plate, pewter salt shaker, pewter mug*—Bloomingdale's; *flask*—Bonniers, Inc.; *background wallpaper*—F. Schumacher & Co.

512, *butter tubs*—Henrietta Tischler; *china mortar and pestle, butter paddle*—Bazar Français; *wooden bowl, salt shaker, pewter dishes*—Bloomingdale's.

521, *platter, flower holders*—Ginori Fifth Avenue; *stone flowers*—Piazza Sixty Fifth St.; *serving spoon and fork*—Plummer and McCutcheon; *background fabric*—F. Schumacher & Co.

524, *pottery basket dish*—Judith Garden; *pewter sauceboat and serving spoon*—Mayhew; *salt shaker and pepper mill*—Bonniers, Inc.

537, *sandwich tray, bowl, ladle, spoon, fork, muffineer*—Towle Silversmiths; *flower bowl, glasses*—Baccarat; *tablecloth*—Thaibok Fabrics, Ltd.

540, *dessert bowl, candle holders*—Fostoria Glass Co.; *serving spoon*—Towle Silversmiths; *tablecloth*—The Irish Linen Guild; *carnations*—Colorado Carnations.

549, *dessert bowl*—Tiffany & Co.; *tablecloth,* Lord & Taylor; *figurine, glass*—Lillian Nassau.

552, *hot plate, serving spoon and fork, baking dish, gallery tray, glasses, box, decanter, picture*—Bonwit Teller; *tablecloth*—The Irish Linen Guild.

565, *vermeil flowers*—Tiffany & Co.; *background fabric*—Dazian's, Inc.

568, *crystal compote, china cachepot*—Bonwit Teller; *background fabric*—Jofa, Inc.

581, *dessert plates, flower dish*—Soupçon Food & Gift Shop; *spoons*—Mayhew; *tablecloth*—The Irish Linen Guild; *background brass wire*—William Hunrath Co., Inc.

584, *sherbet cup, dessert plate, spoon*—Carole Stupell Salon; *tablecloth, napkins*—Belgian Linen Association; *fruit bowl, louvered wooden screen*—Mayhew.

593, *baking dish*—Charles Martine Imports, Inc.; *pottery quail*—Carbone, Inc.; *sauceboat, ladle*—Mayhew.

596, *cake dish, antique scales, spice jars*—Bloomingdale's; *background fabric*—Jofa, Inc.

609, *coffee pot, cake plate, cake server*—Mayhew; *tablecloth, napkins*—The Irish Linen Guild; *sconce*—Niccolini, Inc.

612, *plates, forks*—S. Wyler, Inc.; *antique castle*—Bloomingdale's; *flower holder*—Lord & Taylor; *background fabric*—Brunschwig & Fils, Inc.

629, *cake stand*—Tiffany & Co.; *antique candelabra*—Bergdorf Goodman Co.; *background fabric*—Jofa, Inc.

632, *carved relief*—David Weiss; *pie holder*—International Silver Co.; *carnations*—Colorado Carnations.

INDEX

In order to make this index as useful as possible, certain types of page entries have been specially marked. Numbers given in *italic* type refer to the *menu* pages on which the dishes are listed. Roman figures followed by the abbreviation "ill." refer to photographs in which dishes appear. All other references, whether to recipes or to mentions in the text, are simply set in roman type. All recipes, unless otherwise noted, are for six persons.